MANAGEMENT

MANAGEMENT
A Problem-Solving Process

ROBERT KREITNER
Arizona State University

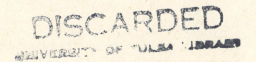
HOUGHTON MIFFLIN COMPANY   BOSTON
Dallas   Geneva, Illinois   Hopewell, New Jersey
Palo Alto   London

With love to
Margaret, Mom,
and Falling Rock

Study guide for this text:
Understanding Management, by Robert Kreitner and Margaret A.
Sova

Cover Helioptix by Henry Ries.

Printed in the U.S.A.
Library of Congress Catalog Card Number: 79-88719

ISBN: 0-395-28490-2

Contents

Preface

The management of productive organizations is the focus of this book. The principles and concepts discussed here apply equally well to large and small organizations, whether profit or nonprofit, manufacturing or service, public or private. Despite differing structures, purposes, and sources of funds, today's productive organizations face the same overriding problem: *How can we best use our limited human, financial, and material resources to accomplish our objectives in a constantly changing environment?* The quality of life for ourselves, our children, and our children's children hinges to a great extent on how well today's and tomorrow's managers go about solving this problem.

As the world's growing population further strains our planet's resources, dramatic new demands are being placed on our economic, social, and political institutions. In response, many are calling for a return to fundamental principles and tested solutions. Unfortunately, yesterday's solutions are likely to be inappropriate for tomorrow's problems. What we need is an updated set of fundamentals that will help us *create* solutions for tomorrow's problems.

In response to that need, this book examines contemporary fundamentals of management from a problem-solving perspective. As a general introduction to management theory and practice for college students, the book is as clear and concise as possible. It is informative, interesting, and complete in coverage without the clutter of unnecessary detail.

Management theory and practice go hand in hand. As the practice of management has become increasingly complex in recent years, management theory has also grown in complexity. In fact, management theory has divided and subdivided into specialized perspectives with dizzying speed. Amid all this change, one aspect of management has remained constant. Management was, is, and always will be *a problem-solving process.* By adopting a problem-solving perspective, this book integrates diverse management theories and practices in a useful and valid manner.

An effective introductory text satisfies the principal needs of both the student and the instructor. Although it is impossible for a single text to be everything to everyone, special care has been taken during the research and writing of this book to fulfill the needs of those who will use it. For example, students and instructors alike should find the problem-solving process a useful integrating theme that binds the textual matter together. Those who are new to management theory, as well as experienced managers and teachers, will appreciate the realistic breadth of coverage. No single approach to management has been emphasized to the exclusion of other recognized approaches. Every approach to management discussed here, whether old or new, conventional or radical, provides something of value for today's and tomorrow's managers.

What do management students want in a textbook? Research of student opinion indicates a desire for relevant and contemporary material presented in an interesting manner that makes learning easier. Furthermore, students prefer texts of manageable proportions written in understandable language, rather than voluminous and intimidating treatments. Finally, they like texts that are enlivened with real-life examples, contemporary cartoons, and visual impact.

In addition to satisfying these expressed needs, this text contains a number of helpful learning aids. Among them are specific learning objectives preceding each chapter, concise definitions of key terms throughout the text, comprehensive chapter summaries for review purposes, a list of key terms, thought-provoking discussion questions, and stimulating case studies following each chapter.

What do management instructors want from an introductory management text? Experience and research suggest that they want a book that is comprehensive in coverage yet flexible enough in format to adapt to their own special teaching styles. The problem-solving theme in this book is carried out through coverage of management history, organizational behavior, planning and controlling, organization design and development, operations management, decision theory, social responsibility, and international management. Although the book is organized along traditional functional lines, it can be adapted readily to systems, contingency, or a variety of other specialized approaches.

Instructors also like real-life examples that help capture the essence of contemporary management. Understanding the social, political, economic, and technological pressures on the organization is a necessity in today's fast-paced world. A unique feature of this book is the comprehensive treatment of the external environment of management in Part VI. The thirty-six end-of-chapter cases are also designed to stimulate discussion of key concepts against a realistic backdrop.

A study guide, *Understanding Management*, is available for use with the text. Written by Robert Kreitner and Margaret A. Sova, the Study Guide is designed to give students structured practice in working with the terms and concepts presented in the text. In addition, it helps students evaluate their own knowledge and understanding. For each chapter in the text, the Study Guide provides an opportunity for review of the learning objectives and chapter summary, an extended self-test consisting of fifty objective questions, and five discussion questions. Answers to the objective questions are provided at the end of the Study Guide. An instructor's manual is also available for those teaching the course.

Comments, questions, or criticisms from readers of this text are earnestly sought (see the last two pages of the book). Through their comments it will be possible to provide future materials to enhance the teaching and learning of management principles and concepts.

Friends and colleagues at Arizona State University and elsewhere have given generously of their time, talent, and enthusiasm during the development of this project. My warm thanks go especially to Professors Louis Grossman, William Ruch, and Frank Shipper. Others who have helped in very special ways are Richard Esposito and Joyce Vesper. To the following, who reviewed the manuscript in various stages and offered constructive criticisms, suggestions, and comments, I owe a great deal: Professor Kenneth M. Bond, Creighton University; Professor David Jack Cherrington, Brigham Young University; Professor Robert A. Comerford, University of Rhode Island; Professors Curtis W. Cook and Edward J. Harrick, Southern Illinois University at Edwardsville; Professor Kamal Fatehi, Western Illinois University; Professor David A. Gray, University of Texas at Arlington; Professor Jack A. Hill, University of Nebraska at Omaha; Professor Marie R. Hodge, Bowling Green State University; Professor Michael Jay Jedel, Georgia State University; Professor Robert F. Lawrence, Jr., Monmouth College; Professor Robert C. Maddox, University of Tennessee; Professor Douglas M. McCabe, Georgetown University; Professor M. J. Riley, Kansas State University; Professor Richard W. Scholl, San Diego State University; Professor Richard H. Schoning, California Polytechnic University at Pomona; Professor Larry E. Short, Drake University; Professor Dwight Smith, University of Arizona; Professor Glen L. Tischer, Bergen Community College; Professor Richard S. Walbaum, Purdue University; Professor David D. Van Fleet, Texas A & M University; Professor Edward P. Zilewicz, Parkland College.

The section on mentorship in Chapter 14 is dedicated with respect and appreciation to Coach Don Watchorn and Professor Fred Luthans, two mentors who were there when I needed them.

For their wise counsel, I want to extend a special note of appreciation to two colleagues and good friends, Professor Keith Davis and Professor William Reif. To my wife and closest friend, Margaret, go my warmest thanks for valuable editorial assistance, emotional support, patience, and, most of all, for being herself. Finally, I would like to thank the hundreds of introductory management students I have had the pleasure of working with over the years for teaching me a great deal about tomorrow's managers. To them and all other students of management, best wishes for a happy and productive life in their chosen field.

R. K.

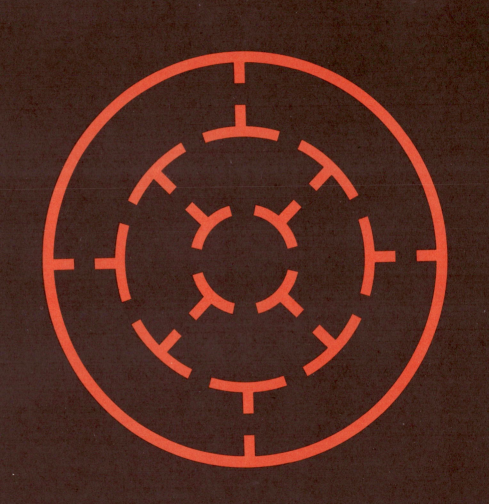

I

The Problem-Solving
Management Process

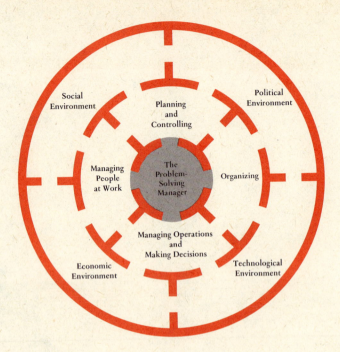

PART I IS A DEFINITIONAL, HISTORICAL, AND CONCEPTUAL DEPARTURE point for the rest of this book. In Chapter 1, we formally define the term *management* and examine it from a number of different perspectives. Chapter 2 amounts to a brief history of management thought. Historians tell us that it is difficult for us to appreciate where we are and where we appear to be headed if we do not know where we have been. In Chapter 3, the problem-solving process that lies at the heart of the practice of management is introduced and discussed. Those who fully appreciate the central role this problem-solving process plays in the practice of management will be better prepared to face a constantly changing administrative world where questions typically outnumber answers. Skillful problem solving is required to derive the answers to new and different questions.

Chapter 1

Management: Definition and Perspectives

The only choice for an institution is between management and mismanagement. . . . Whether it is being done right or not will determine largely whether the enterprise will survive and prosper or decline and ultimately fail.

Peter F. Drucker

LEARNING OBJECTIVES

When you finish reading this chapter, you should be able to

- Define the term management.
- Draw a distinction between effectiveness and efficiency and tell how each is important to successful management.
- Trace the evolution of the modern manager.
- Discuss the status of management as a profession.
- Describe the compromise view of management as both a science and an art.

People change as the world changes. Less than four decades ago large and small nations alike began healing the wounds of World War II. In Europe, Russia, and Japan the huge task of rebuilding war-torn cities and factories was the top national priority. Meanwhile, in the United States, Canada, and Australia the shift from a wartime to peacetime economy moved into high gear. The future looked promising, especially for the United States, which enjoyed an abundance of optimism, natural resources, and space in which to grow and prosper.

But as the sixties dawned, things began to go sour. The botched Bay of Pigs invasion in Cuba embarrassed the nation; periodic economic recessions continued to plague the economy; a young and popular president was assassinated. Since then we have been almost overwhelmed by a discouraging chain of events, including the growth of the drug culture, a demoralizing defeat in Vietnam, the Watergate scandal, the energy crisis, and stubborn inflation coupled with high unemployment. As a result, pessimism and doubt have replaced wide-eyed optimism as we approach the end of the century. But there is much more to the future than gloom and doom.

Putting things in perspective, an attitude of cautious optimism seems appropriate for what lies ahead. A pair of earth-shaping events that occurred in recent years help to justify this attitude. The two events, apparently unrelated, symbolically represent the ultimate in successful management and in mismanagement.

On July 20, 1969, Neil Armstrong became the first human being to set foot on the moon. The largest television audience ever assembled held its breath as the Apollo 11 commander spoke unforgettable words, "One small step for man, one giant leap for mankind," from a quarter of a million miles out in space. An event that many considered a total impossibility just a few years earlier had become reality. Human imagination swelled with visions of how wonderful the world could become through the application of space-age technology.

Less than one year later, on April 22, 1970, a second significant but less heralded event took place. The first Earth Day was observed. Noisy but relatively peaceful demonstrations took place around the world to protest the careless destruction of our natural environment. Human imagination was haunted by visions of a polluted, ugly, and unlivable earth.

According to some observers, the single most important product of the space age is the photographs of earth taken from far out in space. These photos, along with the growing threat of pollution and environmental decay, are tangible evidence that the huge and seemingly limitless planet we call earth is in fact a small, delicate, and vulnerable blue marble circling the sun. As a result, more and more people have adopted a "spaceship earth" perspective. According to this twentieth-century outlook, planet earth is a tiny dot racing through space with a passenger list of more than five billion people.

The view of earth as a spaceship is useful because it encourages us to step back and see the world as an integrated system that needs to be properly managed rather than a collection of unrelated and self-sufficient parts. We are all in this together: all races, all nationalities, all religions, all political ideologies. From a spaceship earth perspective, Earth Day and our presence on the moon represent a bold constrast for those interested in management.

Neil Armstrong's walk on the moon was a glowing testimony to effective management. It dramatically demonstrated that systematically managed technology and resources could extend our reach to unbelievable limits. For example, the 500,000-mile round trip of Apollo 11 involved eighty-eight major steps. The failure of any one of these could have destroyed the mission or cost the lives of the crew, yet the mission was successful. As the largest peacetime program ever undertaken, it amounted to an incredible investment of talent and money. Construction of the Apollo rockets, spacecrafts, and support equipment required the efforts of 20,000 industrial contractors and a total of 400,000 people. The final price tag for the Mercury, Gemini, and Apollo programs was over $25 billion.[1] While reviewing the efforts of his Apollo executive group, made up of the chief executive officers of the U.S. industrial giants that contributed to America's moon landing effort, Dr. George Mueller saw "no black magic in what they did—only determined management."[2]

If Apollo 11 was a testimony to effective management, then Earth Day was a recognition of mismanagement. Earth Day protesters pointed to smog-filled skies, sewage-choked rivers and streams, and vegetation-stripped land as evidence of unplanned and haphazard mismanagement of our natural resources. Many people suddenly realized on Earth Day that all earthly resources are scarce. Even once-abundant and traditionally free resources like fresh air and clear water have proven to be scarce. According to editorialist Dael Wolfle, "Earth Day was a day of excitement, indignation, and dedication. That was a start, but the problems Man has given Earth require more than a day; they need permanent attention."[3] That permanent attention must come in the form of careful management.

Earth Day presented the field of management with its greatest

---

[1] References appear at the end of the chapter.

challenge. Apollo 11 showed that management is capable of meeting that challenge. Without a doubt, good management is the key to our future on spaceship earth. Management requires us to look ahead through systematic planning. It also requires us to make the best of difficult situations through problem solving and wise decision making. Proper management of resources, technology, and people will allow modern civilization to grow and prosper without wasting scarce resources or destroying the planet in the process.

MANAGEMENT DEFINED

At this point, a formal definition of management is like the foundation of a house; it provides a firm base for further development. Offering a quick but static textbook definition is not enough, however. Instead, we will build our definitional foundation in two phases. First, the definition itself will be presented. Second, and importantly, the key terms of the definition will be examined. Both phases are necessary for an adequate understanding of the term *management* as it is used throughout this book. Also, by considering the meanings contained in a formal definition of management, the importance, relevance, and necessity of studying management become apparent.

Management is a problem-solving process of effectively achieving organizational objectives through the efficient use of scarce resources in a changing environment.

Like an alarm clock taken apart by an inquisitive youngster who wants to know what makes it tick, this definition of management needs to be broken down into its key terms to reveal what makes it tick. The terms examined here include (1) problem-solving process, (2) organizational objectives, (3) effectiveness versus efficiency, (4) scarce resources, and (5) changing environment.

PROBLEM-SOLVING PROCESS

In general terms, day-to-day management amounts to identifying and attempting to solve an endless stream of problems. Managers face problems at every turn. Some of those problems can be anticipated with tried and tested solutions readily available. For example, when a production supervisor notes that product quality has slipped below standard, a maintenance trouble-shooter is called in to readjust a faulty machine and the problem is solved. On the other hand, managers often are called upon to address unique problems for which no handy solutions exist. A contemporary example is the high rate of absenteeism among routine-task personnel, which is causing managers great concern today. For this type of new and unique problem, new and unique solutions must be found.

Problem solving is a learned skill. Within the ranks of management, problem solving often is awkwardly handled, principally because managers have not taken the time to study problem solving as a logical process with identifiable steps. To leave out a step is to risk not solving the problem at all.

Managers who are good problem solvers are careful not to get caught in the "same old rut." They are not afraid to try new and different things, and they are capable of learning from their experience. Because problem solving is discussed in detail in Chapter 3, it is sufficient to say at this point that managers who do not understand and aggressively pursue their role as problem solvers are likely to be trapped in a quicksand of irrelevant detail. For instance, a personnel director who fails to see an inequitable pay plan as the true cause of an increase in employee grievances about everything from working conditions to the company cafeteria may run down innumerable blind alleys, always looking for the right answers to the wrong problems.

ORGANIZATIONAL OBJECTIVES

Every successful organization has objectives. An objective is a target, a goal to be worked toward and attained.

There are personal objectives, too, as well as organizational ones. Systematic planning for one's life becomes possible only when one has carefully formulated personal objectives. For example, only after setting an objective to graduate from college at a certain time can a student proceed to plan exactly what courses to take when.

While personal objectives are typically within the reach of individual effort, organizational objectives require collective or group action. For example, a nationwide fast food chain may strive to achieve the objective of serving customers in sixty seconds or less. A great deal must be done by many people throughout the organization to accomplish this objective. The complexity of collective action necessitates systematic management. Organizational objectives give the management process purpose and direction. Without organizational objectives the management process is like a trip without a specific destination, aimless and wasteful.

EFFECTIVENESS VERSUS EFFICIENCY

Drawing a distinction between effectiveness and efficiency amounts to much more than a semantic exercise. The relationship between these two terms is important, and it presents managers with a never-ending challenge. *Effectiveness* is accomplished by achieving a stated objective. Swinging a sledgehammer against the wall may be an effective way of killing a bothersome fly. In addition, one demonstrates *efficiency* if that objective is achieved without wasting scarce resources such as time, talent, or money. Efficiency thus has to do with the relationship between inputs and outputs. Although a sledgehammer is an effective way of killing flies, it is not very efficient when one takes into consideration the wasted effort and smashed walls. A fly swatter is both effective and efficient.

Let us look at the distinction between effectiveness and efficiency from another angle. Suppose, for example, that a four-cylinder compact car averaging thirty-two miles per gallon and an eight-cylinder luxury car averaging eleven miles per gallon arrive in Chicago at the same time. Both cars started from St. Louis at the same time, stopped for gas together, carried one passenger each, and cruised at the legal speed limit. What occurred in terms of effectiveness and efficiency? Both cars were equally effective; that is, each reached its destination or objective at the planned time. However, the smaller car was much more efficient because it used less resources (gasoline, steel, glass, rubber, road space, and so on) to achieve the same objective as the larger car.

Managers are responsible for creating a balance between effectiveness and efficiency. On the one hand, they must be effective by getting the job done. On the other, they must be efficient by reducing costs as much as possible and conserving scarce resources. Too much emphasis in either direction leads to mismanagement. A manager who is too stingy with resources will not get the job done. A manager who wastes resources may get the job done but go bankrupt in the process.

SCARCE RESOURCES We live in a world of scarcity. There is only so much of any given resource to go around. Economics, as a formal discipline, derives from the fundamental assumption of scarcity. In brief, economics is the study of how scarce resources are distributed among alternative users. In productive organizations, managers are the trustees of scarce resources. It is their job to see that the basic factors of production—land, labor, and capital—are used efficiently and effectively. The relationship between economics and management is very close.

CHANGING ENVIRONMENT Increasingly, the world is characterized by rapid change. Social standards change, styles change, resource availability changes, technology changes, and laws change. Unemployment, for example, is not as great a personal threat today as it was during the 1920s because today we can fall back on various forms of government-sponsored unemployment assistance. During the 1920s, however, those who could not turn to their family or church for help went begging. Needless to say, our grandfathers worked long and hard to protect their jobs. Because of this change in the laws, today's managers find it difficult to motivate people to work harder by threatening them with the loss of their jobs. Motivating people is therefore more difficult today than it was formerly. Because of the importance and complexity of management's changing environment, an entire section (Part VI) of this book is devoted to it.

Now that we have discussed the key terms of our definition of management, it is important to see how each part relates to the whole picture. You may find it helpful at this point to go back and reread the definition of management to make sure you understand the relationship of the various terms. Then we will go on to consider three common perspectives of management.

THE THREE FACES OF MANAGEMENT

When asked what management is, the average individual will probably respond, "It's the people in charge, the people who run the place." Perhaps early conditioning by jobs in one's teens, when the primary contact with management is in being "bossed around," is responsible for this perception. Granted, management is the group that oversees the work of others, but over the years people have developed other views of management as well. In fact, the term *management* can be interpreted to mean at least three different things. As illustrated in Figure 1.1, one view of management has to do with a *group* enjoying superior position in the organization hierarchy, a second view considers management as an area of *academic study*, and a third serves to identify the *process* of management, as we defined it in the previous section.

MANAGEMENT AS A GROUP

A distinction people generally make in an organization is between management and nonmanagement. A milling-machine operator who is promoted to supervisor, for example, is very much aware of this distinction. The work area may be the same and the pay not much higher, but the new supervisor has taken a big jump in status and relative importance in the organization. Increased rights, privileges, and responsibilities go along with the new status as a member of management.

In reference to this group at the top of the organizational pyramid, management expert Peter Drucker noted in 1954:

Management, its competence, its integrity and its performance will be decisive both to the United States and to the free world in the decades ahead. At the same time the demands on management will be rising steadily and steeply.[4]

Another general distinction is between management and organized labor. Hardly a day goes by without newspaper accounts of

FIGURE 1.1
The three faces of
management

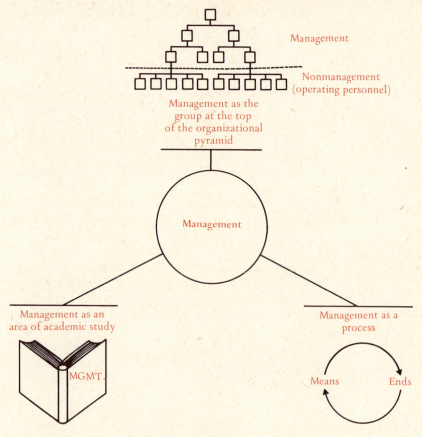

important union-management negotiations. Many are familiar with the term *management* in this context. Here it refers to the representatives of the organization in its bargaining with organized labor unions such as the United Auto Workers, the Teamsters, or the International Brotherhood of Electrical Workers.

MANAGEMENT AS AN
AREA OF STUDY

This book is physical evidence of the second general view of management, that of a body of knowledge. Although some scholars may argue that the systematic study of management is an end in itself, most agree that the purpose of studying it is to refine its practical application. At the present time in the United States, hundreds of thousands of people are studying management in one form or another in university and college classrooms, executive development sessions, and company training programs. The results of sophisticated laboratory and field research are reported, along with a great deal of theoretical material, in over sixty-four management journals.[5] The study of management today is very active and growing.

MANAGEMENT AS A PROCESS

True, management is both a group and a recognizable area of academic study. But the term *management* also identifies a process or way of behaving. This third view has to do with the *what* and *how* of day-to-day managerial performance. As we have seen, "The management process is a necessary feature of all organized activity."[6] It may be carried out knowingly with favorable results or haphazardly with dismal results. One can enhance his or her chances of being a successful manager by carefully studying specific functions within the management process, such as planning, organizing, decision making, leadership, and control.

THE EVOLUTION OF THE MODERN MANAGER

Managers as we know them today have emerged from a unique set of historical circumstances. To begin with, the private business sector of the late nineteenth century provided fertile ground from which the modern manager could develop. At that time virtually all businesses had two things in common. They were relatively small, and they were managed directly by their owners. One individual, a single family, or a select partnership of individuals provided the necessary money, technical know-how, and managerial expertise. While the rewards of early business ventures were sometimes great, the risks were *always* great.

Eli Whitney is an excellent case in point. He's the man who became rich and famous by inventing the cotton gin, right? Well, almost right. While he indeed became famous as the inventor of the machine that cleaned the seeds from raw cotton, he certainly did not become rich in the process. In attempting to turn the idea for a cotton gin into a profitable enterprise, Whitney and his colorful partner, Phineas Miller, were constantly frustrated by problems with ill-trained workers, poor tools, inadequate supplies, insufficient working capital, a weak monetary system, and inadequate patent protection. With his partner dead, his patent rights compromised, and his money gone, Whitney eventually turned to manufacturing guns for the military. One historian remarked about Whitney's experience as an early owner-manager, "Like other inventors of the young Republic, Whitney paid a high price in emotion for whatever he gained."[7]

No corporate veil of limited owner-liability protected the early owner-managers from losing personal and family resources along with their original investment. Managerial success in precorporate days meant personal profits and high social position. Managerial failure, on the other hand, often led to personal financial ruin and social disgrace. The early owner-managers indeed put everything on the line.

Toward the end of the nineteenth century things began to change. Robert Presthus, a political scientist, reflects:

> The period in which the typical enterprise was operated in a competitive milieu by a single entrepreneur or family existed only briefly. The succeeding corporation era encouraged the development of huge organizations by making capital accumulation easier, by permitting risk sharing, and by divorcing ownership from management.[8]
>
> Owner-operators were often replaced by professional executives whose behavior reflected their scientific management, hired hand role. Stockholders, the absentee landlords of the twentieth century, were remote and uninterested, playing the only role that atomized ownership permitted—the calculation of dividends. Power shifted to those who could operate large-scale enterprises rationally and with proper regard for the new arts of human and public relations.[9]

As business corporations grew in number and size, a new social class emerged, that of the managerial specialist. According to one historian:

> The immediate social effect of the big company in finance, canals, local public utilities, and railroads was to produce a small but new social strata of well-paid, and generally well-educated careerists. They were not usually rich, but were influential in the business community because of the power of their corporations.[10]

Thus the modern manager, the hired supplier of specialized managerial talent, came into being.

Although small, owner-managed businesses still exist today, the vast majority of productive assets are controlled by large, diversified, multinational corporations. The scale of these organizations boggles the imagination. For example, in 1969 the annual sales of General Motors exceeded the combined gross national product of Norway, New Zealand, and Israel. In 1975, the five hundred largest industrial corporations in the United States had a net worth of over $600 billion and employed 14 million people, more than 15 percent of the entire U.S. labor force. General Motors alone employs over three quarters of a million people today. These giants, as well as smaller corporations, require hundreds of thousands of highly skilled managers who work for a salary rather than an owner's share of the profits.

CONVERSATION WITH . . .

Paul F. Oreffice
President and Chief Executive
   Officer
The Dow Chemical Company
Midland, Michigan

Courtesy of Dow Chemical Company.

**PERSONAL
BACKGROUND**

As far as managerial positions in industry are concerned, Paul Oreffice is on the top rung of the ladder. Ranked twenty-seventh among the 1979 *Fortune* 500, Dow Chemical has over 53,000 employees and annual sales approaching $7 billion. Paul's international background has prepared him well to head a giant multinational corporation. Born in Venice, Italy, Paul and his family emigrated to the United States to escape Fascist persecution when he was twelve. He joined Dow as a sales trainee in 1953 after receiving a B.S. in chemical engineering from Purdue University and serving two years as a private in the U.S. Army. After assuming a managerial position in 1956, Paul moved up through the ranks swiftly. Steps in his career progression have included managerial posts in Brazil and Spain, the presidency of Dow Chemical Latin America, financial vice president, president, and now chief executive officer of Dow Chemical. Today, Paul Oreffice is an outspoken critic of what he calls "the ever increasing encroachment of the government in business."

QUOTABLE QUOTES

Do you have any guiding principles regarding the practice of management?
Mr. Oreffice: One brain is never as good as several. A good manager is one who delegates and motivates others to do the job.

You must lead by example. A manager's personal conduct, honesty, standing in the community, and so on, will influence how the whole organization works and acts.

What advice would you give an aspiring manager?

Mr. Oreffice: 1. Get the best people you can, and then delegate, delegate, delegate.
2. Always stand up for what you think is right, but be graceful if you lose.
3. Communicate well, up and down. Be short, but clear.
4. Motivate your people by making them look good. Push their ideas and give them recognition.
5. Be optimistic. Behind every problem there is an opportunity.

ENTER: BIG GOVERNMENT AND NONPROFIT ORGANIZATIONS

Private business is not the only employer of managerial talent today. Rapidly expanding demands for national defense, education, transportation, and public welfare since World War I have made the federal government the largest single employer in the United States. Approximately three million people are on the federal payroll at the present time, with about one-third of them concentrated in the Department of Defense. More recently, the growth of state and local governments has been dramatic. For instance, California paid its 484,000 civil servants $600 million *each month* in 1975. In the same year, New York City's monthly bill for its 375,000 employees was $386 million![11]

Accompanying the growth of government has been the proliferation and growth of nonprofit organizations such as private schools and hospitals. Of course, churches, another form of nonprofit organization, have been around for a long time. When one stops to think about it, an administrator in a federal, state, or local agency or in a nonprofit hospital or church is just as much a manager as a division head at General Motors. Today managers practice their trade in all kinds of organizations: large and small, public and private, profit and nonprofit.

MANAGERS AS PROFESSIONALS

A natural by-product of the evolution of the modern manager has been the lively debate in management circles over whether or not management is a profession. Some say yes, managers are professionals, just like doctors and lawyers. Others disagree and present evidence to the contrary.

At first glance many of our more visible top-level managers do present the outward appearance of professionals. They have approximately the same prestige as doctors or lawyers, and they wield a great deal of power. However, the most visible people in the biggest organizations are not necessarily representative of all managers; the owner-operator of the local pornographic bookstore is a manager, too! A closer look is needed. The purpose here is not to finally resolve the issue but rather to frame the issue to permit identification of patterns and trends.

The logical starting point involves coming up with a more precise meaning of the term *profession*. Although there is no universally accepted list of criteria for *professional status*, a number of general characteristics have been suggested. Typically mentioned are: (1) formal education in a specialized body of knowledge, (2) unselfish service motive, (3) controlled entry, (4) a universal ethical code, and (5) a sanctioning organization.[12] Arguments for and against management as a profession, based on these five characteristics, are listed in Table 1.1.

After allowing for varying interpretations of the arguments presented in Table 1.1, the balance seems to tip *against* interpreting management strictly as a profession. Granted, managers, particularly those at higher levels and in larger organizations, appear to be moving toward professional status. But taken as a diverse group with representatives in organizations of all sizes and purposes, management has considerable ground to cover before qualifying as a full-fledged profession.

The drive for greater professionalism among managers should not be taken too lightly, or abandoned because management is not now a full-fledged profession. Positive steps can be taken. Hardly anyone would object to promoting an unselfish service motive among managers, for example. In general, managers with a sense of broad responsibility can do much to improve the professional image of management in today's highly organized world.

Along the same lines, increased management professionalism through widely accepted ethical codes is also desirable. As a possible indication of things to come in this area, model nationwide professional codes for managers are being tried out in three European countries: Britain, Germany, and Greece. The 45,000-member British Institute of Management, for example, hopes to become large enough to put some teeth, or sanctions, in its guidelines. But as one writer has cautioned:

> To have sanctions and to have the power to enforce them requires a broad membership in a strongly organized body with high standards of admission. For this reason, in the United States and in many other countries it would be impossible to impose

TABLE 1.1
Management as a profession

THE CASE FOR	PROFESSIONAL CHARACTERISTIC	THE CASE AGAINST
A growing number of today's managers have degrees from uniformly accredited colleges of business.[a]	1. Formal education in a specialized body of knowledge	The ranks of management include those with no formal higher education and those with nonbusiness degrees.
Socially responsible managers have become trustees of the public welfare.	2. An unselfish service motive	Occasional convictions for price fixing, collusion, and antitrust violations have eroded the public's confidence in management's unselfish service motive.
A college degree is usually required for a position in management today.	3. Controlled entry	Managers are not licensed to practice like doctors, lawyers, dentists, and other professionals. Entry into management ordinarily depends on the right combination of ability and opportunity.[b]
Many professional and trade organizations have formally written codes of ethics and conduct for managers.	4. Universal ethical code	Unlike the traditional professions of law and medicine, not all managers have or adhere to a common code of ethics.
Trade organizations (such as the National Association of Manufacturers and the U.S. Chamber of Commerce), professional and academic organizations (such as the Academy of Management), and educational organizations (such as the American Management Association) guide, direct, and encourage responsible and ethical management.	5. A sanctioning organization	There is no equivalent of the American Medical Association or the American Bar Association in the field of management. Today's managers are not subject to censure by a single professional organization.

[a]Originally formed in 1916, the American Assembly of Collegiate Schools of Business imposes strict curricular standards on its member institutions.

[b]It is interesting to note that at least one well-known management writer has taken a firm stand against the licensing of managers. Peter Drucker has stated in *The Practice of Management* (p. 10) that "no greater damage could be done to our economy or to our society than to attempt to 'professionalize' management by 'licensing' managers, for instance, or by limiting access to management to people with a special academic degree." Drucker feels that performance and achievement are the only valid criteria for determining who stays or goes in the field of management.

sanctions at the present time. The effective organization does not exist.[13]

Still, we can expect the battle for greater professionalism among managers through ethical codes to continue. There is no doubt that all of society benefits when its public and private organizations are managed by qualified and professionally ethical and responsible men and women.

IS MANAGEMENT A SCIENCE OR AN ART?

As the college student is likely to hear repeatedly, science is marked by theoretical frameworks, operational definitions, controlled and systematic data gathering, objective analysis, and concise reporting. Scientists attempt to leave a clear record of their progress and methods so that others can "climb on their shoulders" to reach still farther into the unknown. Art, on the other hand, is more subjective than science; it relies more on impulse and emotion. Personal feelings legitimately play a greater role in artistic endeavor. Give six scientists an identical research protocol and each will replicate its findings in a uniformly predictable manner. But give six artists the same figure to paint, and each will turn out a different but equally valid interpretation. There appears to be more room for the personal touch in art than in science. The question we need to ask here is: Does the practice of management demand objective scientific rationality or the subjective flair of the artist? Like the question of professionalism, this question is a source of considerable controversy in management circles.

MANAGEMENT AS A SCIENCE

There are many who firmly believe that management is a science. In fact, the word *science* has been in the management vocabulary for a long time. The reader will encounter such terms as *scientific management* and *management science* later in this book. Briefly, scientific management was an early twentieth-century school of management thought based in part on systematic time study and work measurement. Management science is a more modern approach based on sophisticated quantitative decision-making models. Both approaches share a common assumption: subjectivity and intuition should be replaced by objectivity and scientific methodology. Proponents of the scientific approach have severely criticized seat-of-the-pants management. In defense of the scientific position, one writer has said: "Management is already a field of knowledge, and is becoming a science because the interrelationships involved are being explained systematically and the emerging theories are being tested and improved by logic and the facts of life."[14]

MANAGEMENT AS AN ART

Management practitioners—that is, managers in the workaday world—often claim that management is an art. Advocates of this approach contend that practical experience must be translated into "horse sense" or intuitive feeling. One practitioner has argued:

> Without that clear vision that underlies all good art, the manager's components are merely isolated bits and pieces. As with the other arts, there are no objective criteria by which the manager can judge whether one arrangement is superior to another. The criteria he uses to select a configuration are subjective. Each criterion is weighted by his personal prejudice, belief, tradition, and temperament. He builds and destroys every time he makes rearrangements of his possibilities, much as any artist does in composing, painting, or sculpting.[15]

Both sides present convincing arguments. A good case can be made for viewing management as a science, and an equally good case can be made for viewing it as an art. Here we suggest a compromise view that suggests how a manager can make use of the best of both worlds. In Figure 1.2 at the extreme left we find management being practiced strictly as an art. Here the visionary relies on hunch and intuition to the total exclusion of precise techniques. On the extreme right we find the technician practicing management strictly as a science.

Each extreme has its shortcomings. The visionary may lose touch with reality, but the technician may fail to see the forest because the trees get in the way. Recognizing that the practice of management is both an art *and* a science, the successful manager strikes a balance

FIGURE 1.2
Management as an art *and* a science

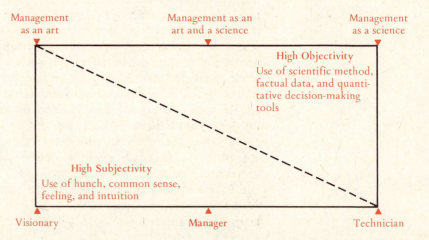

Management as an art   Management as an art and a science   Management as a science

High Objectivity
Use of scientific method, factual data, and quantitative decision-making tools

High Subjectivity
Use of hunch, common sense, feeling, and intuition

Visionary   Manager   Technician

by relying on subjective feelings or on objective scientific techniques as the situation warrants. For example, all the scientific techniques available to the modern manager may not be of any use at all when a personality conflict arises. The effective manager learns when to use scientific objectivity and when to go with his or her "gut feelings."

MANAGEMENT: MEETING A UNIVERSAL NEED

If we adopt the spaceship earth perspective, it is readily apparent that the limited resources of our planet need to be carefully and imaginatively managed. Even now, almost every aspect of our lives is enhanced by organized endeavor, touched by the product or service of some organization. While we are sleeping, we enjoy the service of around-the-clock fire and police protection. During our waking hours we benefit from organizations that harvest, process, store, ship, package, sell, manufacture, investigate, collect, pay out, finance, underwrite, communicate, advertise, govern, educate, and publish. In all these organizations, resources must be obtained; people hired, trained, paid, and promoted; plans made; technology applied; and public demands measured and satisfied. Who is responsible for all this activity? The modern manager.

The task of learning more about modern management, about what "makes the world go 'round," is a tremendous challenge. The key is to look beyond specific individuals, goals, or organizations to discern common patterns and trends. In a sense, that is the purpose of this book: to look for the patterns and trends that most management situations have in common. Moreover, it is the purpose of this book to show how the manager can use these trends and patterns to solve everyday problems.

To ensure covering the ground thoroughly, we need a kind of roadmap, or guiding strategy. Figure 1.3 outlines the territory we will cover and shows how the different parts of our search are related to each other. This strategy is designed to help the student and practitioner of management take advantage of all existing approaches to management, both traditional and modern, and tie them in with what has been learned through personal experience.

Figure 1.3, in a way, illustrates the title of this book: *Management: A Problem-Solving Process*. At the very center of this management process is the problem-solving manager. The various management functions, through which the manager influences the organization, are treated in different sections of the book. Part I (Chapters 1 through 3) defines and examines management from a number of different perspectives. It also surveys management theory through the years and shows how the problem-solving process serves as an integrating link between different kinds of management

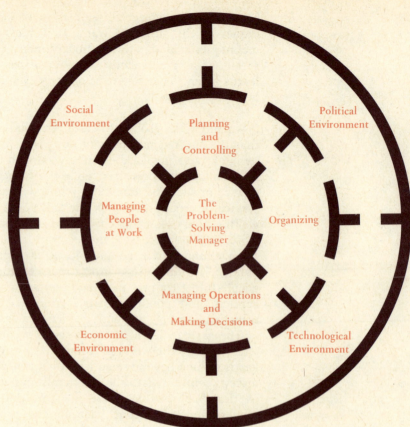

theory. Chapter 3 develops a working concept of the problem-solving process. Part II (Chapters 4 and 5) describes the planning and controlling functions. Together they encompass the beginning and end of all management, and the relationship between them is clearly delineated. Part III (Chapters 6 through 8) is about organizing. This section not only analyzes what an organization is but tells how to design effective organizations. A chapter on Organization Development rounds out this section. Part IV (Chapters 9 and 10) takes up operations management and decision making. Part V (Chapters 11 through 15) explores the human side of management: organizational behavior, staffing, group dynamics, communicating, leading, and improving job performance. The final part of the book (Chapters 16 through 19) is represented in Figure 1.3 by the outermost circle. This section surveys the social, political, economic, and technological environments of management. Because the world is changing so rapidly and unpredictably today, managers must be aware of what is going on outside their organizations.

All organizations, regardless of their purpose, have one thing in common. They must be *managed*. Although a barbershop owner-manager, a university dean, an insurance executive, and a NASA administrator go about their managerial chores in different ways, they have more in common than meets the eye. Each must solve an endless string of problems while attempting to achieve organizational objectives efficiently in an environment marked by constant change. To the extent that this book addresses the needs of managers in large and small, public and private, and profit and nonprofit organizations, it is more than simply a business management book. It is an *organization* management book. It focuses on a problem-solving approach to the management of all kinds of modern organizations, whatever their purpose.

SUMMARY   Management is an exciting, interesting, and relevant field of study. It involves the entire range of organized activity on our "spaceship earth." Students of management are in a good position to understand and influence a world characterized by limited resources and rapid change. Management, as defined in this opening chapter, is a problem-solving process of effectively achieving organizational objectives through the efficient use of scarce resources in a changing environment.

The term *management* can be interpreted from a number of different views. Included among them are management as a group, management as an area of study, and management as a process. This book represents an academic study of the management process.

Today's managers are hired specialists. They can be found in public agencies, private nonprofit institutions, and profit-making businesses. While some view managers as full-fledged professionals, they have yet to achieve a professional status equal to that of doctors and lawyers.

Is management a science or an art? After considering the arguments on both sides of this issue, we are encouraged to adopt a compromise view. The practice of management appears to require both scientific precision and artistic intuition. Management meets a universal need, since so much of our lives is influenced by organizations. Figure 1.3, which serves as a roadmap for this book, shows the problem-solving manager at the center of the management process. The manager reaches out through the various management functions but is influenced, at the same time, by many environmental forces. All organizations, whether public or private, profit or nonprofit, need good management.

TERMS TO UNDERSTAND

Management	Efficiency
Effectiveness	Professional status

QUESTIONS FOR DISCUSSION

1. What is the value of a spaceship earth perspective?
2. Why is management important in today's world?
3. How is management affected by scarce resources and rapid change?
4. In what ways is management a problem-solving process?
5. Which is most important in your opinion: management as a high-status group, as a field of study, or as a process? Support your answer.
6. How have the corporation and big government influenced the development of the modern manager?
7. On the basis of what you have read and your own opinion, is the typical manager a professional?
8. Do you think that managers should work for more professional status? Give reasons for your answer.
9. What would be an appropriate managerial balance between scientific thinking and artistic intuition?
10. Think of someone you know who is a manager. Does he or she approach management as a science or an art?

CASE 1.1
TOM'S SECRET OF SUCCESS

Sam Hernandez is a painting contractor. At the present time he has twelve full-time crews doing both interior and exterior work. Recently, Sam's accountant informed him that his quarterly profits had decreased by 15 percent. That information puzzled and troubled Sam, because he had completed a record number of jobs in recent months. After giving it some thought, Sam decided to visit a couple of job sites to see if he could pinpoint the problem. First, he decided he would visit his most productive crew. Perhaps by studying the work habits of this crew he could find out why his less productive crews were eating up the profit margin.

Sam felt good as he arrived at Tom Stevenson's job site. Since Tom had joined the organization six months before, he had consistently accounted for more finished jobs than his fellow crew managers. Sam hoped that he could discover Tom's secret of success, so he could pass it along to the other crew managers. However, after observing Tom's crew for only ten minutes, Sam's good feelings about Tom turned to doubt. While it was true that Tom's crew was fast, their work habits were a disaster. They completely ignored safety regulations when it came to anchoring ladders and securing scaffolds. It was a miracle that one of Tom's crew hadn't suffered a dangerous fall yet. In addition, paint was spilled all over the work site, and a number of expensive brushes had been thrown aside hopelessly crusted with half-dried paint. Expensive drop cloths were torn and dirty, and at least two ladders had broken rungs. The drop cloths and ladders would have to be replaced right away.

After passing the time of day with Tom, Sam jumped back into his pickup and drove off. His mind was filled with questions, especially about Tom. For example, was Tom really his best crew manager?

FOR DISCUSSION
1. How does the relationship between effectiveness and efficiency enter this case?
2. Can you think of any other information Sam needs before taking action in this matter?
3. Do you think Sam is a good manager, being caught by surprise as he was?

**CASE 1.2
A COURSE IN
MANAGEMENT?**

Jean and Janis, twin sisters, are in the process of preregistering for next fall's classes at Central University. The two are reminiscing about how much fun they had taking courses together before declaring their majors last year. Jean is an ecological sciences major while Janis is working toward a degree in criminology. Both think it would be fun to take at least one more class together before graduating. However, they have had little luck finding a single elective relevant to both of their specialized areas of study. While discussing the problem with some friends, a business major that they know recommends an introductory management course. Noting that they don't know a thing about either business or management, Jean asks their friend, "How can a course in management help someone who isn't a business major?"

FOR DISCUSSION
1. Put yourself in their friend's place and answer Jean's question.
2. What do you expect to learn from a course in management?

REFERENCES

Opening quotation

Peter F. Drucker, *People and Performance: The Best of Peter Drucker on Management* (New York: Harper & Row, 1977), p. 8.

1. John Noble Wilford, *We Reach the Moon* (New York: Norton, 1971), p. 19.
2. Evert Clark, "The Moon Program's Business Brain Trust," *Nation's Business* 58 (May 1970): 36.

3. Dael Wolfle, "After Earth Day," *Science* 168 (May 8, 1970): 657.

4. Peter F. Drucker, *The Practice of Management* (New York: Harper, 1954), pp. 4–5.

5. Charles N. Weaver, "Evaluations of Sixty-four Journals Which Publish Articles on Management," Working Paper for the Management Education and Development Division of the Academy of Management, 1975, table 1.

6. Henry H. Albers, *Principles of Management: A Modern Approach*, 3rd ed. (New York: Wiley, 1969), p. 94.

7. Constance Mcl. Green, *Eli Whitney and the Birth of American Technology* (Boston: Little, Brown, 1956), p. 94.

8. Robert Presthus, *The Organizational Society*, rev. ed. (New York: St. Martin's Press, 1978), p. 48.

9. Ibid., pp. 49–50.

10. Thomas C. Cochran, *Business in American Life: A History* (New York: McGraw-Hill, 1972), p. 85.

11. Presthus, *The Organizational Society*, p. 63.

12. This list has been synthesized from the following sources: Paul Donham, "Is Management a Profession?" *Harvard Business Review* 40 (September-October 1962): 60–68; Ernest Greenwood, "Attributes of a Profession," *Social Work* 2 (July 1957): 44–55; and Wilbert E. Moore, *The Professions: Roles and Rules* (New York: Russell Sage Foundation, 1970), pp. 3–22.

13. Nancy G. McNulty, "And Now, Professional Codes for the Practice of Management: But Not in the U.S.," *The Conference Board Record* 12 (April 1975): 23.

14. Luther Gulick, "Management Is a Science," *Academy of Management Journal* 8 (March 1965): 11.

15. Henry M. Boettinger, "Is Management Really an Art?" *Harvard Business Review* 53 (January–February 1975): 59.

Chapter 2

The Evolution of Management Thought

From an almost unrecognized position in 1900, management has risen today to be the central activity of our age and economy—a powerful and innovative force on which our society depends for material support and national well-being.

Claude S. George, Jr.

In the renewing society the historian consults the past in the service of the present and the future.

John W. Gardner

LEARNING OBJECTIVES

When you finish reading this chapter, you should be able to

○ Identify Henri Fayol's five management functions and discuss why they can be considered universally applicable.

○ Explain how experimentation played a role in F. W. Taylor's scientific management.

○ Discuss the circumstances from which the human relations movement emerged.

○ Explain how systems theorists differentiate between closed and open systems.

Identify three characteristics of the contingency approach.

Through the years, the study of management has grown and subdivided. One important subdivision of management is management history. Management historians firmly believe that a better knowledge of the past will lead to a more productive future. They contend that students of management who fail to pause and reflect on the development of management thought are likely to repeat past mistakes.

Management history, like any other historical perspective, is part fact and part interpretation. A brief management history is presented in this chapter by selecting and interpreting important facts from the evolution of management thought. The word *evolution* is appropriate here because management has developed in bits and pieces through the years. A historical perspective puts the pieces together to form a meaningful whole.

THE PRACTICE AND STUDY OF MANAGEMENT

Although the practice of management may be traced to earliest recorded history, the systematic study of management is relatively new. Management, as an area of academic study, is basically a product of the twentieth century. Only three universities—Pennsylvania, Chicago, and California—offered business management courses before 1900.[1]

Combined effort requiring some sort of management has been around for a long time. The great pyramids of Egypt, for example, stand as tangible evidence of the ability to manage in the ancient world. It took over one hundred thousand individuals twenty years to construct the great Egyptian pyramid of Cheops. This tremendous effort did not come about by luck or accident; it had to be managed. Although the Egyptians approached and carried out their jobs differently than modern managers do, they had to face many of the same fundamental problems. For example, they needed to make plans, obtain human and material resources, coordinate individual and group efforts, keep records, and make adjustments to ensure that the job was completed.

AN INFORMATION EXPLOSION

Since the building of the great pyramids, the world has seen entire civilizations rise and fall. In one form or another, management was practiced in each. Unfortunately, one modern element was missing during those thousands of years of management experience. The missing element was a *systematically recorded body of management knowledge.* In early cultures, management was something one learned and did by trial and error, not something one studied, theorized about, experimented with, and wrote about.

Modern information technology has allowed us to compress the collective genius of countless thousands of management theorists and practitioners into a mountain of textbooks, periodical journals, monographs, microfilms, movies, audio tapes, and computer tapes and disks. A walk to the nearest library gives us access to much of this information. The bigger the library, the greater the amount of information available. Never before have managers had such a vast array of experience at their fingertips. In fact, so much information on management exists today that it is difficult to keep abreast of it all. The field of management is experiencing an information explosion. The problem-solving manager must learn to draw selectively on the growing body of management knowledge, and not be overwhelmed by it.

THE MANAGEMENT THEORY JUNGLE

The major cause of the information explosion in management is the interdisciplinary nature of the field. Individuals from many different academic and professional areas have contributed to management's body of knowledge. Academic scholars from several fields—including psychology, sociology, cultural anthropology, mathematics, philosophy, statistics, political science, logistics, information science, and history—have, at one time or another, shown an interest in management. In addition, administrators in business, government, health care, and education have all drawn from and contributed to the study of management. Each group of scholars and practitioners has interpreted and reformulated management according to its own unique perspective. With each new perspective have come new assumptions, new research techniques, different technical jargon, and new conceptual frameworks. The net result has been what one management writer has labeled "the management theory jungle."[2]

It can be safely stated that there is no single theory of management that enjoys universal acceptance today. Management theory *does* resemble a jungle. But the situation is not hopeless. As the various management theories have evolved during the present century, some distinct patterns or approaches have become evident. By identifying and following the signposts of these general approaches we can find our way through the management theory jungle. The major approaches to management presented in this chapter include (1) the universal process approach, (2) the operational approach, (3) the behavioral approach, (4) the systems approach, and (5) the contingency approach. A general understanding of these approaches places the student of management in a position to appreciate how management thought has evolved, where it is today, and where it appears to be headed.

THE UNIVERSAL PROCESS APPROACH

The universal process approach is the oldest and one of the most popular streams of management thought. This approach is also known as the universalist or functional approach. The primary underlying assumption of the *universal process approach* is that the administration of all organizations, public or private, large or small, involves the same basic process. It also assumes that this universal process can be reduced to a set of principles or fundamental administrative truths. Organizational success supposedly depends on the extent to which these common denominators of organized endeavor are followed. The literature of the early universal process writers emphasizes structure (that is, who reports to whom, who does what, and who is responsible for it all).

HENRI FAYOL'S UNIVERSAL MANAGEMENT PROCESS

In 1916, at the age of seventy-five, Frenchman Henri Fayol published his now classic book, *Administration Industrielle et Generale*. Fayol's work did not become widely known in England and America until an English translation became available in 1949.[3] However, despite its delayed exposure to the English-speaking world, and despite having to compete with an enthusiastic scientific management movement, Fayol's work has left a permanent mark on twentieth-century management thinking. Today Fayol is considered the father of the universal process approach.

Initially as an engineer and later as a very successful top-level administrator in a large French mining and metallurgical concern, Fayol did not resort to abstract theory in his writing. He was a practitioner of management who attempted to formulate a comprehensive theory of management in practical terms. His universal management process was applicable to all organizations.

According to Fayol, all managers must carry out five *universal functions*, or areas of managerial activity. Fayol viewed these five functions—planning, organizing, command, coordination, and control—as essential for managerial success. In contemporary terms, *planning* relates to the necessity of looking ahead. *Organizing* takes place as human and material resources are acquired and arranged into productive form. *Command* involves the use of authority to get individuals to perform their jobs as intended. A harmonizing of all organizational activities is achieved through the *coordination* function. Finally, through the *control* function the manager checks to see if everything is proceeding according to plan. Fayol's management functions have withstood the test of time because of their general applicability; often they are viewed as fundamental truths. In spite of years of reformulation, rewording, expansion, and revision, evidence of Fayol's original management functions can be found in most modern management textbooks (including this one).

A COMMENT ON THE UNIVERSAL PROCESS APPROACH

Fayol's list of management functions has a great deal of practical value, but we need to keep in mind that it constitutes a good beginning rather than an adequate end. For the problem-solving manager, management functions are a useful conceptual framework for what managers do. Newer approaches to management help bring these basic functions to life by introducing other useful concepts and techniques.

THE OPERATIONAL APPROACH

The term *operational approach* is a convenient descriptive label for a specialized area of management that has worn a number of labels since the turn of the century. It has been labeled scientific management, management science, operations research, and operations management. Underlying this somewhat confusing evolution of terms has been a single purpose: to make man-machine systems work as efficiently as possible. Throughout its historical development, the operational approach has been more technical, more quantitatively oriented, and more scientific than the universal process approach.

FREDERICK W. TAYLOR'S SCIENTIFIC MANAGEMENT

Born the son of a Philadelphia lawyer in 1856, Frederick W. Taylor became in all respects a self-made man. After a temporary failure in eyesight kept him from attending Harvard, Taylor went to work as a common laborer in a small Philadelphia machine shop. In just four years he picked up the trades of the patternmaker and machinist.[4] After learning his trades, Taylor went to work at Midvale Steel Works. During his twelve years at Midvale his growth and accomplishments were nothing short of amazing. Taylor rose rapidly from a common laborer and odd-job man to machine shop foreman and, eventually, to chief engineer. At the same time, he obtained a mechanical engineering degree by going to night school, teamed up with a friend to win the U.S. tennis doubles championship, and gained a reputation as a manager who marched to the beat of a different drummer.

As a manager at Midvale, Taylor was appalled at what went on in industry. He observed little if any cooperation between managers and workers. Inefficiency and waste were everywhere. Output restriction among workers, called systematic soldiering by Taylor, was widespread. Ill-equipped and inadequately trained workers were typically left on their own to determine how their jobs should be

The Bettman Archive.

accomplished. Taylor's frustrations as a practicing manager provided fertile ground from which scientific management was to grow.

Scientific management techniques were unique for early
twentieth-century management because they were based on systematically derived standards rather than traditional rules of thumb.
An early definition of scientific management tells how these
standards were derived. *Scientific management* is "that kind of
management which *conducts* a business or affairs by *standards*
established by facts or truths gained through *systematic* observation, experiment, or reasoning."[5] The word *experiment* deserves
special emphasis, because it was Taylor's trademark. Through
experimentation he reduced waste and increased efficiency.

Taylor's career amounted to a constant search for better ways of
doing things. When better ways were discovered through careful
study and experimentation, standards were developed to guide and
assess future performance. For example, by closely studying metal-
cutting machine operations at Midvale and later at Bethlehem Steel,
Taylor collected a mountain of data on the optimum speed and
efficiency for each job. The resulting standards were posted for
convenient reference by the machine operators. Additional efficiencies were achieved by systematically cataloging and storing the

cutting tools. Operators could go to the carefully arranged tool room and check out the right tool for each job. Taylor's metal-cutting standards caused productivity to jump and costs to fall.

The shoveling experiments carried out by Taylor represent an excellent example of his efforts to achieve a degree of standardization in the way workers carried out routine tasks. According to the traditional rule-of-thumb approach, there was no "science of shoveling." Any fool could swing a shovel. But Taylor looked at things differently. After thousands of observations and stopwatch recordings, he detected a serious flaw in the way various materials were being shoveled. To begin with, each laborer brought his *own* shovel to work. Taylor knew the company was actually losing rather than saving money when a laborer attempted to shovel both heavy and light material with his own shovel. A shovel-load of iron ore weighed about thirty pounds, whereas a shovel-load of rice coal weighed only four pounds. Systematic experimentation revealed that a shovel-load of twenty-one pounds was optimum (permitted the greatest movement of material in a day).

Taylor's solution was fairly simple. The laborers were instructed to leave their shovels at home. They checked out company shovels appropriate for each job. Large shovels were used for light materials; smaller shovels were used for heavier materials such as iron ore. Even the shapes of the shovels were determined through experimentation. As a result of Taylor's scientific study of shoveling, a greater amount of material was moved by fewer laborers at lower cost to the company.[6]

OPERATIONS MANAGEMENT

Although portions of operations management are traceable to Frederick W. Taylor's scientific management, it is essentially a product of the post–World War II era. Operations management is like scientific management in that it is intended to objectively determine the most efficient way of doing things. On the other hand, operations management differs from scientific management because of its broader scope. Whereas scientific management was limited to hand labor and machine shop situations, operations management specialists apply their technical expertise to all types of productive operations. They are concerned with the purchase and storage of materials, product design, the flow of work, quality control, and data processing. According to one expert in the field, *operations management* "encompasses the design, implementation, operation, and control of systems made up of men, materials, capital equipment, information, and money to accomplish some set of objectives.[7] Operations management specialists attempt to put all the pieces of the productivity puzzle together by using sophisticated models and quantitative techniques. Chapter 9 in this book is devoted entirely to operations management.

A COMMENT ON THE OPERATIONAL APPROACH

Scientific management often appears rather unscientific to those who have been exposed to a world of miracle drugs, manned moon landings, and nuclear power. By strictly scientific standards, much of what is labeled scientific management appears relatively crude and primitive. However, when placed in proper historical context, scientific management stands out in sharp contrast to the haphazard rule-of-thumb methods it replaced. Few management historians have failed to acknowledge the dramatic impact of scientific management on modern industrial management.

Operations management theorists and practitioners take credit for major contributions to the practice of management. For example, computerized inventory control programs that tell management when to order raw materials can reduce inventory expense significantly. It is difficult to argue with their claim. But some critics oppose the manner in which operations management specialists tend to reduce everything to numbers. Behaviorists, who tend to be less quantitatively oriented, feel that operations management is useful to a point—and that point is human behavior. They argue that people are too unpredictable to have their behavior reduced to abstract models and mathematical formulas. Although operations management has its limits, those who study and practice management can expect many exciting and productive ideas from this area.

THE BEHAVIORAL APPROACH

Like the other approaches to management, the behavioral approach has evolved step by step over many years. Advocates of the behavioral approach to management point out that *people* are the common denominator of all organized activity. A successful manager must be able to understand and work with people. The evolution of this people-oriented approach from the human relations movement to organizational behavior has greatly influenced management thinking.

THE HUMAN RELATIONS MOVEMENT

The *human relations movement* was a concerted effort among practitioners and theorists to make managers more sensitive to the needs of employees. It emerged from a unique set of circumstances during the second, third, and fourth decades of this century. As illustrated in Figure 2.1, the human relations movement may be likened to the top of a pyramid. Just as the top of a pyramid requires support, the human relations movement is supported by three very

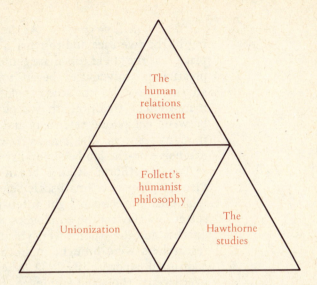

FIGURE 2.1
The human relations
pyramid

The human relations movement

Follett's humanist philosophy

Unionization

The Hawthorne studies

different historic influences: (1) unionization, (2) the Hawthorne studies, and (3) the work of a pioneering human relations philosopher: Mary Parker Follett.

Unionization   To understand why the human relations movement evolved, we need first to appreciate its sociopolitical background. From the late 1800s on into the Roaring Twenties, American industry pretty much had its own way as it attempted to satisfy the many demands of a rapidly growing population. Cheap labor was readily available, and a seller's market prevailed for finished goods. Management was primarily concerned with how to produce more goods at a faster pace. Influential people were too busy enjoying the finer things of life, made possible by the world's first mass production economy, to give much thought to the working man and woman.

Then came the Great Depression. Hundreds of thousands stood in bread lines rather than pay lines. Many believed that business was responsible for the Great Depression. Public sympathy shifted from management to labor. Congress consequently began to pass prolabor legislation. When the Wagner Act was passed in 1935 legalizing union-management collective bargaining, management began looking around for ways to counter all-out unionization. According to management thinking at the time, satisfied employees would be less inclined to join unions. Human relations was adopted as a partial answer because of its emphasis on employee morale.

The Hawthorne studies   As the sociopolitical setting was changing in the twenties and thirties, a second development was taking place in the field of management. Behavioral scientists from prestigious universities began to conduct on-the-job behavioral studies. They did not study tools and techniques in the scientific management tradition; they studied *people*. Face-to-face contact between behavioral scientists and managers changed management in many respects. The famous Hawthorne studies paved the way for extensive on-the-job behavioral research.

The Hawthorne studies began in 1924 in a Chicago Western Electric plant as a small-scale scientific management study of the relationship between light intensity and productivity. Initially a select few Hawthorne employees were involved. One finding led to another and the studies were steadily expanded. Behavioral science researchers were brought in from Harvard University to provide additional expertise. By 1932, when the Hawthorne studies ended, over twenty thousand employees had participated in the studies in one way or another. The Hawthorne studies fired a human relations shot heard around the world.

Three significant lessons in human relations were learned during the Hawthorne studies:

o People have higher morale and work harder under supportive supervision. A supportive supervisor is one who shows sincere concern for subordinates.
o Indirect interviewing is superior to traditional direct-question techniques. Indirect questions (those that require more than simply a yes or no answer) make interviewees feel comfortable and more willing to share personal thoughts and opinions.
o Workers operating under traditional nonsupportive supervision tend to restrict output systematically by establishing and enforcing their own standards.[8]

These conclusions from the Hawthorne studies inspired a great deal of discussion within the management field on the best way to manage people. The result has been greater appreciation of the importance of the human side of organized endeavor.

Mary Parker Follett's philosophy   Unionization gave the human relations movement an opportunity to emerge, and on-the-job behavioral research gave the movement substance. But the movement still lacked philosophical direction. Only a philosophy of human relations could answer such questions as: "Why should all managers be interested in human relations?" Philosophical direc-

Radcliffe College Archives.

tion finally was found in the work of a remarkable woman who talked and wrote about modern human relations concepts long before it became fashionable to do so.

Although Mary Parker Follett was a management consultant rather than a manager, prior to her death in 1933, her background in law, political science, and philosophy produced in her a strong conviction that managers should be sensitive to the fact that each employee is a complex collection of emotions, beliefs, attitudes, and habit patterns. In order to change employees (get them to work harder), she felt managers had to consider the psychological state of the individual. Accordingly, managers should *motivate* performance rather than simply demand it. Cooperation, a spirit of togetherness, and coordination of effort were seen by Miss Follett as the keys to productivity.[9]

Mary Parker Follett's philosophy that a healthy, productive society is built on the satisfaction of individual and group motivational needs served as an inspiration for early human relationists. For the human relations movement, Mary Parker Follett's writings were a candle in the dark.

ORGANIZATIONAL BEHAVIOR

Organizational behavior is a modern approach to management that attempts to determine the causes of human work behavior. As such, it is a research-oriented field. Organizational behaviorists have borrowed various theories and research techniques from psychology, sociology, and anthropology and applied them to the management of modern organizations. The net result has been a somewhat difficult-to-define interdisciplinary field of study. Organizational behaviorist Joe Kelly has tagged the field as "a fledgling, schizophrenic, fragmented subject."[10] Nevertheless, in spite of its new and relatively immature state, organizational behavior has had a significant impact on modern management thought.

Definitions of organizational behavior are numerous. While there are no universally accepted definitions of organizational behavior, a few, like this one, are general enough to be fairly well accepted.

> Organizational behavior is an academic discipline concerned with understanding and describing human behavior in an organizational environment. It seeks to shed light on the whole, complex human factor in organizations by identifying causes and effects of that behavior.[11]

This definition indicates that organizational behavior actually amounts to a scientific extension of the human relations approach. Organizational behaviorists rely more on theory and research than did the early human relationists. The results of their work are covered in detail in Chapter 11. Because organizational behavior is an evolutionary by-product of human relations, people are still the center of attention. But it has improved the ways in which human work activity is studied.

A COMMENT ON THE BEHAVIORAL APPROACH

Human relationists saw people as the key to productivity. They felt that the morale of workers had to be considered first, not last. Technology and management principles, according to the human relationists, could not in themselves guarantee high productivity. Only a sincere sensitivity to people on the part of the manager could foster the cooperation necessary for high productivity.

The human relations approach has had its critics, those who feel the human relations approach is vague and simplistic. According to these critics, relatively primitive on-the-job behavioral research does not justify the sweeping conclusions drawn by the human relationists. The critics do not believe that supportive supervision and good human relations will lead automatically to higher morale and hence to higher productivity. Fortunately, organizational behavior, as a scientific extension of human relations, promises to fill in some of the gaps left by the human relationists while, at the same time, retaining the emphasis on people. Organizational behaviorists are attempting to determine the multiple causes of effective performance.

THE SYSTEMS APPROACH

In recent years there has been a growing trend toward viewing organizations as complex systems of interrelated variables. This trend is in direct opposition to the traditional practice of examining organizational variables separately out of context. Systems thinking appeals to managers because it permits them to consider all relevant organizational variables at once (the big picture). Arguing that earlier approaches to management tell only part of the story (such as functions, tasks, and interpersonal relationships), systems theorists have attempted to interrelate all organizational factors in a realistic fashion.

In general, a *system* is a collection of parts that operate interdependently to achieve a common purpose. Viewing organizations as systems has presented the field of management with an immense challenge: to identify the parts of the organization and to discover how those parts operate interdependently. The scope of this challenge will become more apparent as we briefly trace the development of systems thinking in management.

CHESTER I. BARNARD'S EARLY SYSTEMS PERSPECTIVE

In one sense, Chester I. Barnard followed in the footsteps of Henri Fayol. Like Fayol, Barnard wrote about management on the basis of a lifetime of experience as a practicing manager. However, the former president of New Jersey Bell Telephone took a different approach than Fayol. Rather than defining universal management functions, Barnard adopted a more abstract systems approach. In his 1938 classic, *The Functions of the Executive*, Barnard characterized all organizations as *cooperative systems*:

A cooperative system is a complex of physical, biological, personal, and social components which are in a specific systematic relationship by reason of the cooperation of two or more persons for at least one definite end.[12]

As illustrated in Figure 2.2, Barnard identified willingness to serve, common purpose, and communication as the principal elements in an organization (or cooperative system).[13] He felt that an organization did not exist if these elements were not present and working interdependently.

Willingness to serve According to Barnard's view, the mere presence of people does not automatically create an organization.

**FIGURE 2.2
Barnard's cooperative
system**

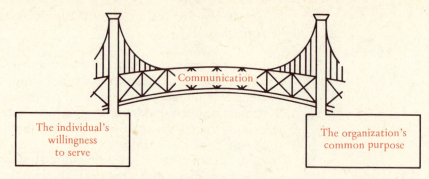

Those people must be willing to work actively for the goals of the organization. They must be *willing to serve*.

The Egyptian slaves who helped construct the great pyramids lacked willingness to serve. They served to avoid the sting of the slave master's whip. In modern organizations, according to Barnard's thesis, an individual's willingness to serve depends to a large extent on the satisfaction experienced. If the individual gains

**Chester I. Barnard (right)
1886–1961**

Historical Pictures Services, Inc.

greater satisfaction from contributing to the organization's goals than from engaging in alternative activities, then he or she will be a willing participant in the organization.

Barnard viewed willingness to serve as the result of a combination of personal and organizational factors. *Motives* come from within the person, and potentially satisfying *rewards* are offered by the organization. A proper combination of motives and rewards creates a willingness to serve.

Common purpose   The second element of Barnard's cooperative system is fairly self-explanatory. Individuals who are willing to serve must have a common objective that is beyond the reach of a single individual. Otherwise, each individual would pursue selfish objectives, and there would be no need for cooperative effort.

Communication   Evidently influenced by his career in a communications-oriented industry (the telephone company), Barnard viewed communication as the energizing and dynamic element of organizations. Communication acts as a bridge between the individual's willingness to serve and the organization's common purpose. According to Barnard, "Obviously a common purpose must be commonly known, and to be known must be in some way communicated."[14]

THE SIGNIFICANCE OF BARNARD'S CONTRIBUTION

The overriding message of Barnard's work is that when two or more people willingly join together to achieve a common purpose, a complex cooperative system emerges. Paraphrasing the Greek philosopher Aristotle, the whole is greater than the sum of its parts. The whole in this case is the organization, and the parts are its members.

This systems view of organizations has had a great impact on those who study the management of modern organizations. Barnard's early systems perspective has encouraged management and organization theorists to study organizations in the whole rather than piece by piece. Barnard opened a very interesting and promising door for management.

GENERAL SYSTEMS THEORY

Inspired by the work of Barnard, a number of management scholars began searching the literature of other fields for better ways of viewing organizations as systems. Their search proved fruitful when they came across *general systems theory*. *General systems theory* is the belief that everything is part of a larger interdependent arrangement.

Ludwig von Bertalanffy
1901–1972

Ludwig von Bertalanffy The father of general systems theory was Ludwig von Bertalanffy, a biologist. Professor von Bertalanffy was a man who excited people with his belief that our seemingly disordered world is made up of orderly systems. Significantly, von Bertalanffy's key to understanding the world of systems was to reverse the traditional scientific practice of analytically breaking everything down to easily examined units. Instead, he suggested that systems should be studied *synthetically* as collections of interrelated and interdependent parts. According to von Bertalanffy, "In order to understand an organized whole we must know both the parts and the relations between them."[15]

Levels of systems Envisioning the world as a collection of systems is only the first step for general systems theorists. One of the more important recent steps has been the identification of *hierarchies* of systems, running from very specific systems to general ones. As one writer has observed, "The universe contains a hierarchy of systems, each higher *level* of system being composed of systems of lower levels."[16] This approach has helped in translating highly abstract general systems theory into more concrete terms. It is easier for the average person to identify with specific levels of

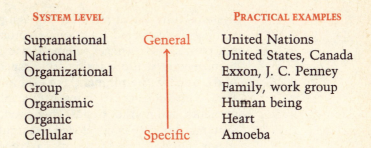

FIGURE 2.3
Levels of living systems

SYSTEM LEVEL		PRACTICAL EXAMPLES
Supranational	General	United Nations
National		United States, Canada
Organizational		Exxon, J. C. Penney
Group		Family, work group
Organismic		Human being
Organic		Heart
Cellular	Specific	Amoeba

systems. One example of this approach is the seven-level scheme of living systems listed in Figure 2.3.

Of course, this hierarchy of living systems represents only one specialized view of general systems. Another view would include mechanical systems, such as clocks and machinery, or physical systems, such as the solar system. However, a hierarchy of living systems is particularly relevant for students of management because management revolves around people, whether in groups, organizations, or nations. The more a problem-solving manager knows about group, organizational, and societal systems and how those systems interrelate, the more effective that manager will be.

Closed versus open systems   In addition to identifying hierarchies of systems, general systems theorists have drawn a distinction between closed and open systems. A *closed system* is one that is self-sufficient, whereas an *open system* is one that must depend on the surrounding environment for survival. Actually, these two kinds of systems cannot be neatly divided into two distinctly different types. The key to classifying a system as *relatively* closed or *relatively* open is the amount of interaction between the system and its environment. A battery-powered digital watch, for example, is a relatively closed system because, once the battery is in place, it runs without help from the outside environment. In contrast, a solar-powered clock is a relatively open system because it cannot operate without an outside source of energy. The human body is a highly open system because life depends on the body's ability to regularly import energy and export waste.

Along the same lines, general systems theorists have told us that all organizations tend to be open systems because organizational survival depends on interaction with the surrounding environment. Just as "no man is an island," no organization is an island, according to systems theorists.

**A COMMENT ON THE
SYSTEMS APPROACH**

Systems thinking in management is a promising alternative to the somewhat restricted traditional approaches. A systems view does not permit the manager to emphasize one aspect of organizational management while ignoring other aspects, whether internal or part of the outside environment. For example, a business manager needs to take into consideration resource availability, technological developments, and market trends when producing a product. If and when systems thinking is developed to its full capabilities, it will play a major unifying role in the management theory jungle. Moreover, systems thinking provides "a basis for understanding organizations and their problems which may one day produce a revolution in organizations comparable to the one brought about by Taylor with scientific management."[17]

There are critics, of course. Some management scholars see systems thinking as high on basic appeal and catchy terminology and low on verifiable fact and practical benefit. Even two staunch advocates of a systems perspective have advised caution: "Recognizing that the social organization is a contrived system cautions us against making an exact analogy between it and physical and biological systems."[18] While hurrying to jump on the systems bandwagon, some management and organization theorists apparently have overlooked or have chosen to ignore this good advice. At the present time, systems thinking is useful as a way of thinking rather than as a final answer describing complex phenomena.

After balancing the pros and cons, it becomes clear that the systems perspective will play a significant role in future management theory and practice. To a large extent, it is the problem-solving manager who will determine the exact nature of that role.

**THE CONTINGENCY
APPROACH**

A new line of thinking among management theorists has been labeled the *contingency approach*. Contingency management theorists have attempted to take a step away from universal concepts of management and toward situational reality. According to one management writer, "The traditional approaches to management were not necessarily wrong, but today they are no longer adequate. The needed breakthrough for management theory and practice can be found in a contingency approach."[19] Here the *contingency approach* is defined as an attempt to determine through research which managerial practices and techniques are appropriate in specific situations.

Generally, the term *contingency* relates to the exercise of alternative courses of action. For example, a hostess may plan to move her patio party indoors if it rains. Her plans are said to be *contingent* (or dependent) on the weather. Within a management context, the term *contingency* has become a synonym of *situational management*. As one contingency theorist writes, "The effectiveness of a given management pattern is contingent upon multitudinous factors and their interrelationship in a particular situation."[20] This means that the management tool or technique must be appropriate to the particular situation, because each situation presents the manager with unique problems. In real-life management the success of any given technique is dictated by the situation. For example, it has been found that highly structured organizations with many layers of management function best when environmental conditions are relatively stable. Unstable surroundings dictate a more flexible and streamlined organization that can adapt to change quickly. Consequently, a growing number of management teachers and practitioners have begun to question the idea of universally applicable concepts and principles of management. They find the contingency perspective appealing because it promises to help them understand the relationship between the situation and the probable success of various management practices and techniques.

CONTINGENCY CHARACTERISTICS

Some management scholars are attracted to contingency thinking because it represents a workable compromise between the systems approach and what can be called a pure situational perspective. Figure 2.4 demonstrates the relationship. The systems approach is often criticized for being too general and abstract. On the other hand, a purely situational view, which assumes that every real-life situation requires a distinctly unique approach, has been called hopelessly specific. Contingency advocates have attempted to

FIGURE 2.4
The contingency view of management as a compromise

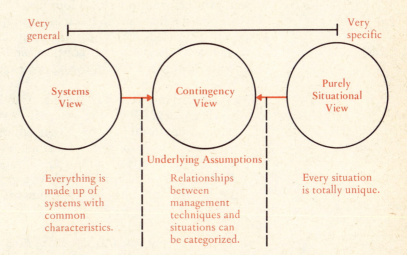

include the best of both extremes in their models. This compromise view is evident in the following description of the contingency view of management:

> The contingency view of organizations and their management suggests that an organization is a system composed of subsystems and delineated by identifiable boundaries from its environmental suprasystem. The contingency view seeks to understand the interrelationships within and among subsystems as well as between the organization and its environment and to define patterns of relationships or configurations of variables. It emphasizes the multivariate nature of organizations and attempts to understand how organizations operate under varying conditions and in specific circumstances. Contingency views are ultimately directed toward suggesting organizational designs and managerial systems most appropriate for specific situations.[21]

Stop! If this description of the contingency approach seems too complex and not entirely clear, then slowly reread it with emphasis on the three following characteristics:

1. An open-system perspective
2. A practical research orientation
3. A multivariate approach

Each of these contingency characteristics deserves a closer look.

An open-system perspective   Open-system thinking is a major part of the contingency view. Contingency theorists are not satisfied with focusing just on the internal workings of organizations; they see a need to understand how organization subsystems combine to interact with larger social, political, and economic systems. Fred Luthans has offered the following open-system perspective:

> In the past, most effort in the theory and practice of management has been devoted to the internal environmental factors. The external environment was either ignored or treated as a given. Only recently with open-system analysis has the external environment been given attention in management literature. . . . Contingency management must of course give attention to both the external and internal environments.[22]

A practical research orientation   Practical research is that which ultimately leads to more effective on-the-job management.

According to a pair of contingency thinkers, "The area of management is based on a body of knowledge generated by practical experience *and* eclectic scientific research concerning organizations."[23] Contingency advocates demand practical, down-to-earth research inputs.

A multivariate approach   Traditional closed-system thinking has led management theorists and practitioners to search for simple one-to-one causal relationships. This is called bivariate analysis. For example, the traditional human relations assumption that higher morale leads to higher productivity was the result of a bivariate analysis. Only one variable, morale, was seen as responsible for a second variable, productivity. Subsequent *multi*variate analysis has shown that a large number of variables including nature of the work, rewards, and job and life satisfaction collectively contribute to higher productivity. *Multivariate analysis* attempts to determine how a combination of variables interacts to cause a particular outcome. Contingency management theorists appear to be firmly committed to carrying out practical and relevant multivariate analyses.

A COMMENT ON THE CONTINGENCY APPROACH   Contingency theorists pick up where systems theorists leave off. The systems approach is a unifying, synthetic force in management theory. Contingency management appears to be giving that unifying force purpose and direction. Stated another way, contingency management is a practical expression of systems thinking.

Like any other perspective of management, the contingency approach has its critics. Some criticism, as can be expected with anything new, is based on plain, old-fashioned resistance to change. Other critics see limitations in the contingency approach:

> The findings of contingency investigations do not constitute a new school of thought in organization and management; they simply indicate a willingness among theorists to begin to approach their discipline on a more systematic level. . . . Present aggregative treatments of contingency views strive to move the contingency appreciation too far and too fast.[24]

The point is, contingency theory to date remains more theory than demonstrated fact.

Whether the contingency management theorists have bitten off more than they can chew remains to be seen. At present they appear to be headed in a productive direction, but keep in mind that the contingency approach is a promising beginning rather than the ultimate end in management theory.

SUMMARY   Although the practice of management is very old, the systematic study of management is a product of the twentieth century. The development of modern management thought has been an evolutionary process. In recent years an information explosion has created what one writer has called a management theory jungle. Although there is no universally accepted theory of management, five major approaches can be identified. These five approaches to management are the universal process approach, the operational approach, the behavioral approach, the systems approach, and the contingency approach.

Although it dates back many years, the universal process approach is still popular today. Henri Fayol, the father of this approach, identified five functions of management that he believed were universally applicable. They are planning, organizing, command, coordination, and control.

The operational approach to management is based on the premise that man-machine systems can be made more efficient if they are studied scientifically. Frederick W. Taylor is considered the father of scientific management. Taylor was primarily interested in increasing efficiency and cutting waste in workshop operations. Scientific management was based on experimentation. It evolved into operations management. Operations management specialists rely on mathematical models and quantitative techniques to help solve management problems.

Like the other approaches to management, the behavioral approach has evolved from a number of different areas. The major contributions to the behavioral approach have come from the traditional human relations movement and the modern area called organizational behavior. The human relations movement can in turn be traced to three sources: unionization, the Hawthorne studies, and the humanist philosophy of Mary Parker Follett. Organizational behavior is a scientific extension of human relations. Modern organizational behaviorists attempt to identify the various causes of job behavior by studying both organizations and the individuals who make up those organizations.

A fourth major approach to management is the systems approach. Systems thinking stresses the importance of studying the organization as a whole rather than as a collection of unrelated parts. Chester I. Barnard, an early management writer, saw organizations as cooperative systems. The systems approach to management has also drawn heavily on the work of Ludwig von Bertalanffy, a general systems theorist. According to systems thinking, all organizations should be viewed as open systems.

A promising new trend in management thinking is called the contingency approach. Contingency theorists point out that situations govern the effectiveness of managerial action. According to contingency theory, every situation encountered by a manager has some unique aspects; therefore, managers must learn to select the right management technique for that situation.

TERMS TO UNDERSTAND

Universal process approach
Universal functions
Scientific management
Operations management
Human relations movement
Organizational behavior
System

Cooperative system
General systems theory
Closed system
Open system
Contingency approach
Multivariate analysis

QUESTIONS FOR DISCUSSION

1. Why is it important to recognize that the study of management has been an evolutionary process?
2. Why have Henri Fayol's management functions remained popular to this day?
3. What was unique about F. W. Taylor's approach to shop management?
4. Would the human relations movement have come about if its sociopolitical setting had been different?
5. Why were the Hawthorne studies important to the human relations movement?
6. What is the role of communication in Chester I. Barnard's cooperative system concept?
7. Why do systems theorists feel that it is productive to view organizations in open-system terms?
8. Can you think of a relatively open system? Why do you believe it is an open system?
9. What is the value of the contingency approach to management?
10. Taking all five approaches to management into consideration, which do you find the most appealing? Why?

**CASE 2.1
WHAT'S HAPPENING
TO QUALITY?**

Kim Tang is the quality control (QC) manager at an automobile assembly plant. It has taken Kim twelve years to move up from stock handler to his present position. Over the last couple of years, Kim's QC inspectors have observed a steady decline in product quality. Today it is not uncommon to find cars coming off the assembly line with missing or broken parts, cracked windows, dirty upholstery, or tools left in the passenger or engine compartments.

FOR DISCUSSION

1. Imagine that you are F. W. Taylor. What would you advise Kim Tang to do?
2. Imagine that you are Mary Parker Follett. What would you advise Kim Tang to do?
3. Imagine that you are Chester I. Barnard. What would you advise Kim Tang to do?
4. What kind of solution would you yourself recommend?

CASE 2.2
TUNNEL VISION

As Rick Jones settles his car into the thick stream of freeway traffic leading out to the suburbs, his mind shifts to his day at the office. It has been a rough one. As assistant commercial loan officer at Keystone State Bank, Rick is responsible for screening loan applications from individuals intending to start their own businesses. He sees his job as an important one and is proud of what he has accomplished since assuming the position a year and a half ago. Naturally, his boss's criticism in front of everyone at today's meeting was quite disturbing.

After pointing out that the default rate on small business loans had doubled from 5 percent to 10 percent during the past year, his boss proceeded to cut Rick's arguments to shreds. According to his boss, the bank directors wouldn't stand for a default rate above 6 percent in *any* of the loan operations. Neither the board nor his boss seems to feel, as Rick does, that small business start-up loans are riskier than loans to established clients. As his boss said, "Start-up loans aren't risky if the money is used *right*!" When Rick responded, "I make sure that all my clients have the technical ability to produce a good product," his boss fired back, "Having a good product or service does not make a business. If that's all you think it is, you've got tunnel vision! A business is a *system* and it must be run like a system."

FOR DISCUSSION

1. Using the systems approach to management as a reference point, explain what Rick's boss meant.
2. If Rick is to determine whether his loan applicants know how to run a business as a system, what internal and external factors must he ask them about? List as many as you can.

REFERENCES

Opening quotations

Claude S. George, Jr., *The History of Management Thought*, 2nd ed. (Englewood Cliffs, N.J.: Prentice-Hall, 1972), p. 1.
John W. Gardner, *Self-Renewal: The Individual and the Innovative Society* (New York: Harper & Row, 1964), chap. 11.

1. For a discussion in this area, see: "How Business Schools Began," *Business Week* (October 19, 1963): 114–116.
2. See: Harold Koontz, "The Management Theory Jungle," *Academy of Management Journal* 4 (December 1961): 174–188.
3. See: Henri Fayol, *General and Industrial Management*, trans. Constance Storrs (London: Isaac Pitman & Sons, 1949), p. 19.
4. Frank B. Copely, *Frederick W. Taylor: Father of Scientific Management* (New York: Harper & Brothers, 1923), I:3.
5. George D. Babcock, *The Taylor System in Franklin Management*, 2nd ed. (New York: The Engineering Magazine Company, 1927), p. 31.
6. For an expanded treatment, see: Frederick W. Taylor, *The Principles of Scientific Management* (New York: Harper & Brothers, 1911), pp. 64–71.
7. Thomas E. Vollmann, *Operations Management: A Systems/Model-Building Approach* (Reading, Mass.: Addison-Wesley, 1973), p. 5.
8. The Hawthorne studies are discussed in detail in: F. J. Roethlisberger and William J. Dickson, *Management and the Worker* (Cambridge: Harvard University Press, 1939).
9. See: Mary Parker Follett, *Freedom and Coordination* (London: Management Publications Trust, 1949).
10. Joe Kelly, *Organizational Behaviour: An Existential-Systems Approach*, rev. ed. (Homewood, Ill.: Irwin, 1974), p. vii.
11. Keith Davis, *Human Behavior at Work: Human Relations and Organizational Behavior*, 4th ed. (New York: McGraw-Hill, 1972), p. 5.
12. Chester I. Barnard, *The Functions of the Executive* (Cambridge: Harvard University Press, 1938), p. 65.
13. Ibid., p. 82.
14. Ibid., p. 89.
15. Ludwig von Bertalanffy, "The History and Status of General Systems Theory," *Academy of Management Journal* 15 (December 1972): 411.
16. James G. Miller, "Living Systems: Basic Concepts," *Behavioral Science* 10 (July 1965): 212.
17. Charles J. Coleman and David D. Palmer, "Organizational Application of Systems Theory," *Business Horizons* 16 (December 1973): 77.
18. Fremont E. Kast and James E. Rosenzweig, *Organization and Management: A Systems Approach*, 2nd ed. (New York: McGraw-Hill, 1974), p. 113.
19. Fred Luthans, *Introduction to Management: A Contingency Approach* (New York: McGraw-Hill, 1976), p. 28.

20. Y. K. Shetty, "Contingency Management: Current Perspective for Managing Organizations," *Management International Review* 14, no. 6 (1974): 27.
21. Fremont E. Kast and James E. Rosenzweig, "General Systems Theory: Applications for Organization and Management," *Academy of Management Journal* 15 (December 1972): 460.
22. Luthans, *Introduction to Management*, p. 30.
23. Fremont E. Kast and James E. Rosenzweig, *Contingency Views of Organization and Management* (Chicago: Science Research Associates, 1973), p. 321.
24. Dennis J. Moberg and James L. Koch, "A Critical Appraisal of Integrated Treatments of Contingency Findings," *Academy of Management Journal* 18 (March 1975): 122.

Chapter 3

An Integrative Problem-Solving Approach

In the future, we will tend to have fewer and fewer answers at our disposal, and new solutions to the emerging problems will have to be developed.

Charles E. Watson

LEARNING OBJECTIVES

When you finish reading this chapter, you should be able to

o Discuss problem solving as the missing link in management theory.
o Identify the four basic steps in the problem-solving process.
o Explain what the manager must do when "problem finding."
o Discuss the selection criteria in managerial problem solving.
o Draw a distinction between systematic and intuitive thinking.
o Discuss the four kinds of barriers to managerial creativity.

After exploring the various approaches to management discussed in Chapter 2, the student is likely to feel justified in regarding management theory as a kind of jungle. Certainly the field is highly fragmented and subject to a variety of theoretical interpretations. An unfortunate by-product of this situation is confusion about the day-to-day practice of management. This confusion is hardly surprising. Not only is management theory itself divided, but management theorists and practicing managers tend to see things differently. Of primary concern to the theorist is the question: "Is this concept or technique consistent with a particular theoretical orientation?" Theoretical purity, however, is of secondary concern to managers who face a challenging combination of problems, uncertainties, competing demands, and time constraints. They are more likely to ask: "Will this concept or technique help me get the job done?" Managers need an integrative approach that draws existing management theories together and strikes a balance between theoretical consistency and practical relevance.

This chapter introduces an *integrative problem-solving approach* to enhance the day-to-day relevance of management theory. Problem-solving managers cannot afford to get trapped into narrow devotion to a particular theoretical approach when every approach offers a wealth of resources. With the integrative problem-solving approach, they can draw on all management theories by practicing a special way of thinking. We begin our discussion by describing and contrasting three basic mental processes.

DIFFERENT WAYS OF THINKING

Thinking is one of those key life processes we engage in constantly but seldom stop to examine. However, it is useful to reflect on how we think, because specific patterns of thinking can be learned and developed. In this section we consider three complementary modes of thinking: analysis, synthesis, and problem solving.

ANALYSIS

Those who think analytically approach the task of learning more about the world by taking things apart. Then, if they are skilled in analysis, they study the parts and see how they work together as a whole.

> Analysis consists, first, of taking what is to be explained apart—disassembling it, if possible, down to the independent and indivisible parts of which it is composed; secondly, of explaining the behavior of these parts; and, finally, aggregating these partial explanations into an explanation of the whole.[1]

Analysts assume that the whole is equal to the sum of its parts and that the whole can be explained in terms of its parts. An example of analytical thinking in management theory is Henri Fayol's division of management practice into the universal functions of planning, organizing, command, coordination, and control. Fayol felt, in typical analytical fashion, that these functions were what management was all about.

Investigation of the unknown through analysis has been a common practice for centuries. Modern chemistry and modern medicine are based at least in part on facts learned through early analysis. Medieval alchemists, for example, isolated many chemicals while analyzing compounds for the secret of making gold. Similarly, dissection of cadavers by early physicians supplied a great deal of our present knowledge of anatomy. In fact, analysis lies at the very heart of most modern scientific research. There is no doubt that *Homo sapiens* has learned a lot by taking things apart.

Can everything be learned through analysis? Many experts say no. They believe analysis leads to only partial understanding. Furthermore, analysis has a tendency to reduce all complex phenomena to isolated bits and pieces. The end result of this reductionism, as the saying goes, is that one "can't see the forest for the trees." Taking all factors into consideration, analysis has weaknesses as well as many strengths.

SYNTHESIS Synthesis is essentially the opposite of analysis. Whereas something is taken apart through analysis, things are combined to form a complex whole through synthesis. For example, the synthetic fabric nylon is a synthesis or combination of chemical compounds. *Synthesis*, then, can be defined as putting parts together to form a meaningful whole.

Synthetic thinking amounts to systems thinking. Russell Ackoff, an early proponent of systems thinking applied to management, observed, "In synthetic thinking, something to be explained is viewed as part of a larger system and is explained in terms of its role in the larger system."[2] He continues:

> Analytic thinking is, so to speak, outside-in thinking; synthetic thinking is inside-out. Neither negates the value of the other, but by synthetic thinking we can gain understanding that we cannot obtain through analysis, particularly of collective phenomena.[3]

The "collective phenomena" of primary concern to modern managers are their organizations and the general environments in which they operate. Synthetic thinking helps managers get the big picture, but it does not supply detailed understanding.

PROBLEM SOLVING Partial understanding can be achieved by taking the unknown apart through analysis or by viewing it in its complex wholeness through synthesis. But in management, as in all sophisticated endeavors, partial understanding is not enough. Both the student and the practitioner of management need to bring their creative abilities into play to arrive at the best course of action. In a sense, problem solving acts as the creative bridge between analysis and synthesis. It allows us to rearrange knowledge gained through analysis and synthesis to come up with new ways of doing the job at hand.

"A question for which there is at the moment no answer is a

"You can be glad you're having problems, Harkness. A man without problems is usually dead."

Drawing by Drucker: © 1975 The New Yorker Magazine, Inc.

problem."[4] This is how B. F. Skinner, the noted Harvard psychologist, defines a problem. *Problem solving* can be defined very generally as the process of finding answers to questions, an essentially creative process.

This creative activity, however, cannot take place without prior analysis and synthesis. It is through analysis and synthesis that questions emerge. Peter Drucker has pointed out that managers need to ask the right questions as well as find the best answers: "The most common source of mistakes in management decisions is emphasis on finding the right answers rather than the right questions."[5] Analysis, synthesis, and problem solving complement each other; analysis and synthesis provide *questions*, and problem solving provides *answers*.

The need for problem solving in management has been voiced many times. For example, Fred C. Foy, a corporate president, put practical problem-solving ability at the top of the list of skills that business schools should teach future managers. According to this practicing manager:

> I mean by practical problem-solving ability the ability to take a problem, large or small; to size it up and sort out the major considerations involved; to recognize the additional information needed and to get it as far as this is feasible; and to come to an operational decision or recommendation, after weighing the major alternative courses of action. . . . Good business school training, I would think, would strive to develop this kind of practical problem-solving ability. . . . It is clear that such problem-solving can be developed—we do it in business all the time.[6]

This statement represents a great challenge for both students and teachers of management. *Problem solving can be learned.* Robert M. Gagné, a noted learning theorist, sees problem solving as the highest and most sophisticated level of human learning.[7] It is our uniquely human ability to solve complex problems that sets us apart from all other animals.

Analysis, synthesis, and problem solving are complementary. In *complementary thinking*, each mode of thinking reinforces or strengthens the others. Consider Julie Juarez, for example, as she approaches the task of registering for her final semester of classes. First she consults the catalog and lists the courses she needs in order to graduate (analysis). Next she compares her list with next semester's schedule of classes (synthesis) and discovers that one class she needs to graduate is not being offered. Naturally upset with the prospect of not graduating on time, Julie goes to see her adviser and learns that she can file an appeal to have the course requirement waived (problem solving). Both analysis (the little details) and synthesis (the big picture) were needed to let Julie know that she had a problem requiring solution. Similarly, managers need to develop a balanced approach by using all three of these complementary forms of thinking.

Figure 3.1 shows how the various approaches to management discussed in the last chapter tend to be primarily analytic or synthetic in orientation. While both perspectives raise valid questions and suggest workable answers, an important element is missing: the manager's day-to-day role as a problem solver. Problem solving, the creative bridge between analysis and synthesis, must be brought into play to help managers make the most of existing management theory. Today's managers will find something of value in each of the various approaches to management. But it is the managers themselves who must turn theory into action through problem solving.

No book can provide the answers to all the problems modern managers face. Paraphrasing a time-honored axiom: "Give managers the answers and they'll manage for a day; teach managers how to get

FIGURE 3.1
Managerial problem solving as the bridge in management theory

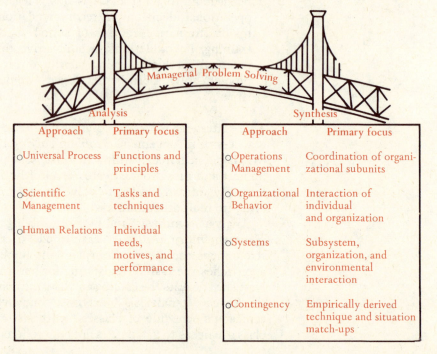

their own answers and they'll manage for a lifetime." This book, in describing many of the options open to managers, does not pretend to be a collection of final answers; it is, in a sense, a collection of questions. The reader's willingness and ability to solve organizational problems will determine whether or not those questions are satisfactorily answered.

THE PROBLEM-SOLVING PROCESS

We are all problem solvers. However, this does not mean that all of us are good problem solvers or, for that matter, that we even know how to go about solving problems. Most day-to-day problem solving occurs on a rather haphazard, intuitive basis. Some difficulty arises, we quickly look around for an answer, jump at the first workable solution to come along, and move on to other things. In a primitive sense, this sequence qualifies as a problem-solving process. It works quite well for impromtu social activities. But managers, those who are charged with effective and efficient organizational goal accomplishment, cannot afford to take such a haphazard approach to problem solving. The problem-solving steps they follow need to be clear, precise, and properly sequenced. The process presented here consists of four basic steps: (1) identifying the problem, (2) generating alternatives, (3) selecting a solution, and (4) evaluating the results. As indicated in Figure 3.2 these steps occur in a fixed sequence.

IDENTIFYING THE PROBLEM

As strange as it may seem, the most common problem-solving difficulty centers around inadequate problem identification. Managers have a tendency to rush into the problem solution stage without first pinpointing the problem to be solved. As one management expert put it, "The manager's job is not only to solve well-defined problems. He must also identify the problems to be solved."[8] In short, managers must be problem *finders*.

What is a problem? This is a deceptively simple question. Ask three people how they identify problems and you will probably get three different answers. In management, a *problem* is the difference between an actual state of affairs and a desired state of affairs. Normally, an organization's goals and objectives help define "the desired state of affairs."

For example, an insurance salesperson who has achieved only 60 percent of his or her yearly sales quota after nine months has a problem. However, contrary to what one might initially suspect, the problem is not the 60 percent figure. Instead, the problem is the 15 percent shortfall. (The 15 percent amounts to the difference between the actual situation, 60 percent of quota after nine months, and the

FIGURE 3.2
The problem-solving
process

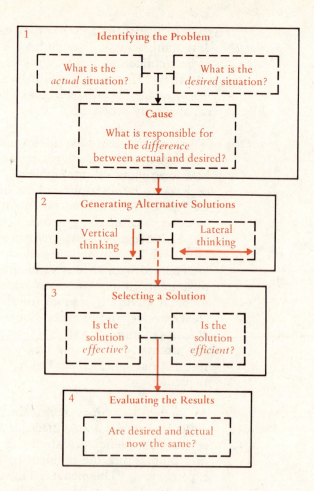

desired state, which is 75 percent of quota after nine months.) This is much more than simply an academic distinction. By focusing on the *difference*, attention is directed to a deficiency requiring corrective action.

Preoccupation with the 60 percent figure points the problem solver in the wrong direction. After all, the 60 percent is what is *right* with the situation. It is not a problem. By focusing on the deficient 15 percent, the salesperson is led to consider two important facts: (1) the actual sales, and (2) the desired sales. The difference, once again, is the problem.

This problem identification procedure places special demands on managers. They must be able to monitor performance accurately so that "hard" data or information is available when needed (analytical thinking). Furthermore, they must know where they are headed (synthetic thinking). Then, as Figure 3.3 indicates, problem-finding managers concern themselves with the relationship between "actual" and "desired."

Causes rather than culprits   In discovering problems, some managers fall into a common trap. "All too often problem solvers look for who is to blame when a problem arises instead of trying to determine what went wrong and why."[9] It is a mistake for managers to be overly concerned with whose head they have to chop off when something goes wrong; they have narrowed their sights only to the personalities involved.

Managers who begin by comparing "actual" with "desired" are in a much better position to track down causes rather than culprits. But what exactly is a cause? Very simply, the *cause* of an organizational problem is the situation that is ultimately responsible for a

FIGURE 3.3
Problem finding

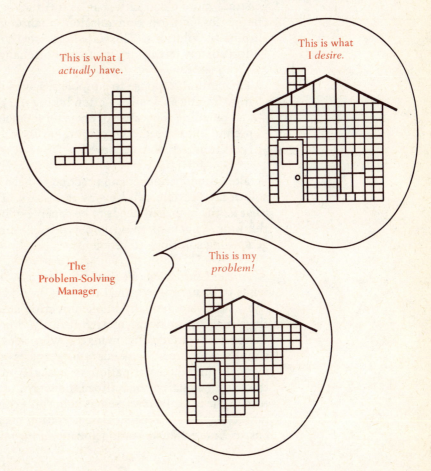

discrepancy between actual and desired conditions. Causes are not always readily apparent. When engaged in problem identification, the manager must do analytical and synthetic detective work to first identify the problem, then determine the probable cause. There is a simple two-way test for finding out whether one has the right cause. It goes as follows: "If I introduce this variable, will the problem disappear?" or "If I remove this variable, will the problem disappear?" Causes, then, are variables that, through their absence or their presence, are responsible for the difference between actual and desired conditions.

GENERATING ALTERNATIVE SOLUTIONS Once a problem and its most probable cause have been properly identified, attention must turn to generating alternative solutions. The greater the number of potential solutions, the more likely that a workable solution will be found. Just as public utilities need to generate more electricity than is ultimately consumed, because of energy loss during transmission, managers need to generate a surplus of solutions. This is where creativity plays a major role. Unfortunately, creativity is often shortchanged.

> The natural response to a problem seems to be to try to get rid of it by finding an answer—often taking the first answer that occurs and pursuing it because of one's reluctance to spend the time and mental effort needed to conjure up a rich storehouse of alternatives from which to choose.[10]

It takes time, patience, and practice to become a good generator of solutions. Flexible thinking is necessary. The solution generator (that is, the manager) needs to be capable of both vertical and lateral thinking.[11] Each of these two types of thinking has its place in generating solutions to problems.

Vertical thinking Vertical, or "straight up-and-down" thinking tends to be narrow. Vertical thinkers are likely to start at one point and work systematically in one direction at a time. For this reason, they may be unaware of significantly different alternatives. For example, a purchasing manager who sees sales representatives simply as sources of goods and services and not as sources of valuable market information is the victim of restricted vertical thinking. Similarly, the railroad industry in the United States at the turn of the century saw itself as being purely in the railroad business rather than in the broader transportation business. To the early rail bosses, more transportation meant more rails, more locomotives, more freight and passenger cars. Their thinking was too narrow to consider nonrail modes of transportation.

Vertical thinkers are often accused of walking around with blinders on and of being uncreative. However, we need to make a distinction between habitually narrow thinkers and the kind of vertical thinking that can help managers find and solve problems. Thomas Edison persisted in vertical thinking in his search for an incandescent lamp filament. He tried dozens of different materials before hitting on a high-resistance tungsten filament in a vacuum-filled glass globe. Without this kind of single-minded persistence in a direction he felt to be promising, he might well have given up on incandescent lighting. Similarly, a salesperson who refuses to abandon a new pitch in spite of early setbacks owes later success to appropriate vertical thinking.

The critical factor is being able to discern which lines of approach are worth this kind of intensive exploration. For the manager who can judge between a promising line of inquiry and a dead end, vertical thinking can be very rewarding.

Lateral thinking   Lateral thinkers start at one point—or several—and move sideways in a number of different directions. They are broad thinkers. While a vertically-thinking oil well driller would tend to keep drilling deeper and deeper to find oil, a laterally-thinking driller would drill to moderate depth in a number of different locations. The lateral thinker does not put all of his or her problem-solving eggs in one basket. Since more than one potential solution should be thought up for each problem, every manager should be capable of shifting from vertical thinking to creative lateral thinking. And he or she should take the time to do so, even though lateral thinking may be somewhat difficult for managers who have been conditioned to steadfastly pursue objectives. (How is your lateral thinking? Try the exercise in Figure 3.4.)

SELECTING A SOLUTION   To solve problems so they stay solved, or at least have a good chance of staying solved, managers need to screen alternative solutions carefully to determine the best solution. But what does "best" mean? Is the best solution the easiest to implement? The cheapest? The one most popular among the people affected? A productive way of sorting out all these considerations is to recall the definition of management in Chapter 1. There management was defined as a problem-solving process of *effectively* achieving organizational objectives through the *efficient* use of scarce resources in a changing environment. *Effectively* and *efficient* have been emphasized here

FIGURE 3.4
A test of lateral thinking

Exercise: Assume that a steel pipe is imbedded in the concrete floor of a bare room as shown at left. The inside diameter is .06″ larger than the diameter of a ping-pong ball (1.50″) which is resting gently at the bottom of the pipe. You are one of a group of six people in the room, along with the following objects:

100′ of clothesline	A file
A carpenter's hammer	A wire coat hanger
A chisel	A monkey wrench
A box of Wheaties	A light bulb

List as many ways you can think of (in five minutes) to get the ball out of the pipe without damaging the ball, tube, or floor.

Reprinted with permission of The Portable Stanford from *Conceptual Blockbusting*, by James L. Adams, Copyright © 1974, 1976 by James L. Adams (New York: Norton, 1978).

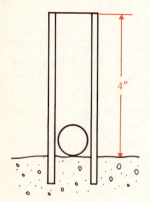

4″

because they are the two main criteria of solution selection; the final solution must be both effective and efficient. A particular solution is effective if it eliminates the difference between the actual state of affairs and the one desired. The same solution may or may not be efficient, depending on whether or not it represents a favorable cost/benefit relationship. The manager needs to weigh effectiveness against efficiency to find a workable balance.

Suppose, for example that the packaging department in a pharmaceutical company is two weeks behind. Unpackaged stock from the processing department has created an unwieldy backlog. Furthermore, a growing number of complaints about back orders have been coming in from customers. The new packaging department manager, Jim Koritsky, is tempted to just leave the situation alone, hoping it will work itself out during a slack season later on. But he realizes that with the introduction next month of a new line of vitamin supplements, there may not be a slack season. He decides he really has only two alternatives. He can have all his people work overtime to catch up on the backlog, or he can bring in temporary workers who are unfamiliar with the department's operations. Either approach would eliminate the backlog, but he feels that his own people could do the work more quickly. Accordingly, he decides to solve his problem by having his people work two hours overtime every day for three weeks.

At first glance, this solution appears to be effective; it should at least partially close the gap between actual (a backlog) and desired (no backlog). However, the efficiency of the solution is questionable. Overtime requires time-and-a-half wages, and experience has shown that performance tends to drop during overtime. Although effective, at least in the short run, the packaging department manager's solution is not very efficient. Scarce resources are being wasted.

EVALUATING THE RESULTS   Time is the true test of any solution. Until a particular solution has had time to prove its worth the manager can rely only on his or her judgment concerning its anticipated effectiveness and efficiency. Ideally, the solution selected will completely eliminate the difference between actual and desired in an efficient manner. However, the only way a manager can tell for certain whether this will happen is to go ahead and implement the solution, then evaluate the results.

Surprising lessons can sometimes be learned during the evaluation phase. For instance, it may turn out that the wrong problem was isolated in the first place. The manager may have uncovered a symptom, rather than the basic problem. Usually the first hint that this has happened is the reappearance of the supposed problem.

Consider once again the packaging department of the pharmaceutical company. The manager has selected overtime as the solution to the department's problem. After three weeks of expensive overtime 80 percent of the backlog has been erased. Unfortunately, a week's backlog builds up only two weeks later. Has any true problem solving occurred? Not really. The packaging department manager has merely isolated and treated a symptom of an underlying problem. The next step in the evaluation process is to go back and carefully retrace the packaging process to find the actual cause of the backlog. Analytical detective work may pinpoint packaging machine breakdowns as the true cause. Alternative solutions can then be generated. One obvious alternative would be to buy new packaging machines. Or maybe leasing would be better. Perhaps new machines would not be necessary if an additional maintenance specialist were hired. After vertical and lateral thinking have produced a good list of workable alternatives, the manager needs to select and implement the one that seems most likely to be effective and efficient. If the backlogs do not reoccur, then and only then will the problem actually have been solved.

One other benefit of the evaluation phase requires brief mention. The experience of implementing and evaluating a variety of different solutions helps the manager build a personally relevant collection of workable solutions. These solutions can then be selectively mixed and matched when new and different problems arise. Of course, the possibility of new alternatives should not be ignored;

new problems sometimes demand new and radically different solutions. Nonetheless, a little actual problem-solving experience goes a long way.

DIMENSIONS OF INDIVIDUAL PROBLEM SOLVING

There is much more to problem solving than following a fixed sequence of steps. This is not to say that managers do not need a general problem-solving model. They do. However, individual problem solving has several important dimensions. The purpose of this section is to examine three of these: problem-solving styles, managerial creativity, and barriers to creativity.

PROBLEM-SOLVING STYLES

People do not all think alike, nor should they. As it is used here, the term *thinking* refers to the mental problem-solving that permits us to process information from our environment and in turn manipulate that environment. The human mind is amazingly varied when it comes to analyzing, synthesizing, and problem solving. Although these basic mental processes are common to all healthy people, a great many individual differences exist. Two common styles of thinking are those exhibited by *systematic thinkers* and *intuitive thinkers*.[12] See if you can identify your style from Table 3.1 and the following descriptions. Keep in mind that one style is not better than the other.

TABLE 3.1 Systematic versus intuitive thinkers

SYSTEMATIC THINKERS TEND TO	INTUITIVE THINKERS TEND TO
o Look for a method and make a plan for solving a problem.	o Keep the overall problem continuously in mind.
o Be very conscious of their approach.	o Redefine the problem frequently as they proceed.
o Defend the quality of a solution largely in terms of the method.	o Rely on unverbalized cues, even hunches.
o Define the specific constraints of the problem early in the process.	o Defend the solution in terms of fit.
o Discard alternatives only after careful analysis.	o Consider a number of alternatives and options simultaneously
o Move through a process of increasing refinement of analysis	o Jump from one step in analysis or search to another and back again.
o Conduct an ordered search for additional information.	o Explore and abandon alternatives very quickly.
o Complete any discrete step in analysis that they begin.	

Systematic thinkers   Managers who rely primarily on systematic thinking prefer to attack a problem in a logical manner. The problem-solving model in Figure 3.2 appeals to the systematic thinker because it consists of a logical sequence of steps. According to this type of thinking, a logical sequence is the only way that one can efficiently come up with the best solution. Systematic thinkers shake their heads in dismay at the comparatively unsystematic way in which intuitive thinkers attack problems. Managers with a systematic style like to grab hold of a problem and not let go until it is solved. They may even ignore their health, finances, family, and other interests in the process.[13] Positions in auditing, logistics, production, finance and accounting, computer programming, and research attract systematic thinkers.

Intuitive thinkers   These thinkers tend to see the systematic thinker as an unemotional and coldly rational individual who isn't particularly interested in people's feelings. Fixed problem-solving sequences typically do not appeal to intuitive thinkers, because they like to jump around from technique to technique and from idea to idea. They prefer to come up with a solution and test it through trial-and-error. Often intuitives have a hard time verbalizing exactly how they solve problems. They just *do*! Managers with an intuitive style may seem to jump to conclusions, possess little patience for detail, and prefer new and different problems. "The intuitive manager is suffocated by stable conditions and constantly seeks out and creates new possibilities."[14] Positions in sales, advertising, personnel, and public relations appeal to intuitive thinkers.

Taking both styles into consideration, it is important to remember that one is not superior to the other. Many creative and valuable solutions have come from both systematic and intuitive thinkers. Actually, many people combine aspects of the two styles of thinking, but they still have a tendency one way or the other. Productive organizations need both types. Systematics are great at working out the details, while intuitives are needed to help fit everything into proper perspective. The organization stands to gain if the demands of the job and the problem-solving style of the individual are carefully matched rather than haphazardly mismatched.

MANAGERIAL CREATIVITY

The creative dimension makes the practice of management endlessly exciting. Nearly all problem solving requires a healthy measure of creativity as managers mentally take things apart, rearrange the pieces, and look outside the normal framework to discover new solutions. This process is like turning the kaleidoscope of one's mind. Thomas Edison used to retire to an old couch in his laboratory to do it. Henry Ford did it while staring at a blank wall in his shop. Although the average manager's attempts at creativity may not be as dramatically fruitful as Edison's or Ford's, managerial creativity should be encouraged and nurtured. The purpose in this section is to define creativity, discuss the management of creative individuals, and consider the learning of creativity.

What is creativity?   Since creativity is a rather mysterious process, known chiefly by its results, it is difficult to define. About as close as we can come is to say that *creativity* is the reorganization of experience.[15] When we stop to think about it, a creative painting is simply a unique combination of otherwise familiar canvas, pigments, and brush strokes. Similarly, the rearrangement of the information on an old form by a financial management trainee may turn out to be quite creative. Creativity is often subtle and not readily apparent to the untrained eye. But seemingly insignificant, day-to-day breakthroughs make up a good deal of management progress.

Identifying general types of creativity is easier than defining the basic process. One pioneering writer on the subject isolated three overlapping domains of creativity: art, discovery, and humor.[16] These have been called the "ah!" reaction, the "aha!" reaction, and the "haha!" reaction, respectively.[17]

The discovery, or "aha!" variation is the one most relevant to management. Staff and patients alike benefited when a hospital administrator said, "Aha! Why don't we realize a savings by sharing our purchasing, laundry, and housekeeping functions with other hospitals?" Similarly, television network profits went up when a network executive said, "Aha! Why don't we start basing our evening programs on the plots of successful movies?" "Aha! Do you know that microwaves will cook better than heating elements do?" "Aha! Do you know that an internal combustion engine doesn't need pistons?" "Aha! Do you know that typewriters do not need movable carriages?" "Aha! Do you know that we can raise our productivity by setting a fair standard and letting our people go home early when they reach standard?" "Aha! Do you know that computers can communicate with one another over the telephone?" The list of significant "aha's" goes on and on. Each has made life a little better, thanks to effective managerial problem solving.

A word on managing the creative individual   The relatively few truly creative people one encounters on the job present managers with a dilemma. On the one hand, creatives tend to be nonconformists in behavior, dress, and grooming. On the other hand, attempts to get creatives to conform to rules and regulations may serve to stifle their creativity. Creative individuals often like to get lost in interesting aspects of the job and resent managerial attempts to get them back on the track. The following account of a highly creative engineer employed at a U.S. naval shipyard, where employees are expected to dress as neatly as the military personnel, demonstrates how creatives sometimes require special consideration.

> In appearance we see a skinny frame whose shoulders under his cape look like a wire coat hanger. Yes, cape. It formerly belonged to a Salvation Army lieutenant colonel. Blue jeans, an Aloha shirt, and tennis shoes—no socks—complete his attire. Charlie drives to and from work in a yellow dump truck whose previous owner was the State Highway Department. He lives in a 1952-model house trailer pulled aboard a barge. . . . Yes, Admiral Miles winces every time he sees the dump truck come snuffling into the parking lot. Admiral Miles and Charlie don't share too much in the way of a common life style, but Admiral Miles has strong positive feelings toward [Charlie], as well he should. Charlie is one of the yard's most valuable assets.[18]

If organizations are to grow and prosper because of creative ideas, then managers need to be flexible in their handling of creative subordinates. Many creative people dislike close supervision, so the manager may need to be primarily a resource person who provides help when it is requested. If creative employees like to work at night or on Sunday, perhaps they can be given a key or special pass to get into the building. If they spend a lot of time staring out the window, it might make sense to measure their productivity by the week or even longer, instead of by the hour. They may be working out their best ideas while apparently daydreaming. If they never get around to writing reports or filling out forms, the manager can find out what they are doing and direct their efforts through informal discussions. A heavy hand seldom works well. With creative individuals, especially, the manager needs to cultivate a style that is easygoing about everything except important organization objectives. Unfortunately, some managers become unduly preoccupied with superficial aspects of personality and performance and end up with a conforming but uncreative employee.

Learning to be more creative   Some people seem to be more creative than others. But that does not mean that those who feel the need cannot develop their creative capacity. Although we don't know all there is to know about creativity, it does seem clear that creative ability can be learned, in the sense that our creative energies can be released from the bonds of convention and narrow thinking. We can all learn to be more creative. The best place to begin is by looking at things differently. We tend to get in perceptual and thinking ruts just as we get in behavioral ruts. It is unfortunate that much of the creative imagination we display as children is conditioned out of us by adulthood. However, it is possible to relearn the mental freedom of our earlier years. The exercises in Figure 3.5 are intended to help get the creative wheels turning once again.

If the exercises in Figure 3.5 seem silly, then you are letting inhibitions stifle your creativity. Everyone has the potential to be creative. Some people are just more bound by their inhibitions than others. We all need to learn how to shed inappropriate inhibitions when pursuing a creative endeavor.

OVERCOMING BARRIERS TO MANAGERIAL CREATIVITY   All too often managers try the same old solutions over and over again. They have fallen into perceptual ruts. This unfortunate situation does not occur by accident; it is caused when managers run into *barriers* to creativity.[20] In this section we examine four common barriers to creativity and ways to overcome them.

Perceptual barriers   Through perception we select, organize, and interpret the world we live in. It is one of the most important behavioral processes. Within an organization, managers need to perceive problems accurately, discern causes, and find workable solutions. But perceptual barriers often block the way. *Perceptual defense* may unduly influence a manager's view of a situation, causing the wrong problem to be identified or the right problem to be inaccurately interpreted. For example, a sales manager plagued by customer complaints may fall into the trap of thinking that public dissatisfaction with the company is the problem, when the real problem is an inferior product. Rigid *perceptual set* may also block managerial creativity as far as problems, causes, and solutions are concerned. A commonly encountered example of this second type of perceptual barrier is the manager who insists on blaming low morale for every difficulty that comes along. It doesn't take much imagination to blame everything on one problem time after time. Managers need to perceive situations clearly and accurately, without prejudice, if they are to be effective problem finders and solvers.

The question is, How do we overcome perceptual barriers? Simply being aware of them is the first step, of course, so that we can recognize them in ourselves and try consciously to go outside

FIGURE 3.5
Developing your creativity

EXERCISE 1

ABSTRACT THINKING

Instructions: Draw abstract figures to fit each of the following nonsense terms.

Sample: Floop

Zunk	Nurt
Elow	Biss
Clat	Prot
Thackitty	Ohlot
Gof	Splurp

EXERCISE 2

VOCABULARY STRETCHING

Instructions: Think of as many words as you can in one minute that begin with the letter "W". (Test your creativity with other letters, too.)

EXERCISE 3

CONCENTRATION

Instructions: See how fast you can identify the famous management personality whose name is spelled out by the missing letters. Each grid contains only 25 of the 26 letters of the alphabet. Find the missing letters. (Answer at end of chapter in reference #19.)

1 ____

L	O	H	R	D
B	C	J	P	I
M	E	Y	A	W
N	T	S	G	U
K	X	V	Q	Z

2 ____

P	M	W	H	L
A	G	D	K	Y
X	C	V	O	I
B	F	E	S	Z
U	N	J	R	Q

3 ____

J	K	M	N	E
P	T	D	O	L
B	F	V	G	I
H	X	C	W	Q
S	Z	U	R	Y

4 ____

G	D	A	W	F
P	J	O	M	Q
L	V	K	R	N
I	H	B	U	C
Z	X	E	T	S

5 ____

U	N	B	M	V
W	A	F	P	I
Q	K	X	O	T
R	C	Z	S	D
J	G	E	Y	H

6 ____

S	Z	T	M	I
F	B	C	P	V
W	R	N	D	Y
L	J	U	X	G
K	H	E	Q	A

7 ____

D	Y	F	N	Q
U	C	L	X	W
S	G	Z	I	V
O	T	K	J	M
E	A	B	H	P

EXERCISE 4

FUTURE PERSPECTIVE

Instructions: Describe each of the following.

Your clothes in 1992. The most popular T.V. show in 1989. Mass transit in 2021. The 1997 Chevrolet. Halloween, 3124.

our usual frame of reference. Happily, the activities that train us to make these mental leaps are a great deal of fun.

A lifestyle that takes advantage of all the variety life has to offer predisposes the mind to new and different solutions to management problems. Meeting new people, traveling, taking up a new sport—all help us keep our minds alert to new possibilities. Creative exercises like laughing at jokes, reading science fiction or magazines like *The Futurist*, working puzzles, painting pictures, writing poetry, planning a new house—all help the mind discover new patterns in familiar things. Techniques like noncritical brainstorming also help break down perceptual barriers.

Keeping the mind stocked with a steady stream of new management ideas is also important. There are dozens of management journals and hundreds of seminars, workshops, and trade journals. Talking with other managers, especially those in other companies, can be very stimulating. Volunteering to help run a community organization can broaden one's practical experience.

The mind continues to grow and develop as long as it is aware of new experiences. All the activities mentioned here—and thousands of others—will keep the mind alive to new ideas and will help suggest specific problem solutions to the creative manager.

Cultural barriers   In today's global business community managers often encounter cultural barriers. For someone who has lived strictly within the safe behavioral boundaries of a single culture, it frequently comes as a shock that people from other cultures do things *differently*. For example, Americans sometimes unwittingly offend Saudi Arabian, Mexican, or Japanese business clients by pushing to close a business deal. For the American, who received a wristwatch at the age of ten, time is a precious commodity not to be wasted on long negotiations. In contrast, a Japanese may savor every moment of a big business deal in which all verbal and nonverbal communications fit into a complex negotiating pattern. Time is only a secondary consideration in the Japanese cultural context. Those who cross cultural boundaries in the process of managerial problem solving are advised to tread carefully. Importantly, these boundaries are not necesarily international. Black, Spanish-speaking, Asian, and American Indian subcultures within the United States contain potential cultural barriers to which managers should be sensitive.

Fortunately, dealing with the differences between two cultures in a business situation is not particularly difficult once they are recognized and accepted. If the manager can study the other culture and achieve some understanding of it ahead of time, his or her negotiations will certainly be more effective than if this understanding were lacking.

More important is the manager's willingness to accept the fact that people in other cultures have a right to do things differently. Their effectiveness and efficiency in specific areas may be greater or less than one's own. Their goals, motives, values, and methods may be different from one's own—and still be valid. Managers can learn from those in other cultures, just as they learn from those in other companies and organizations. Above all, they need to keep in mind that an attitude of acceptance and willingness to work with people despite cultural differences is the most important part of overcoming cultural barriers.

Emotional barriers Human beings are thinking and feeling animals. We can be rational and logical; yet at the same time we are charged with strong emotions. Love and joy fill us with delight; they are no problem. But strongly negative states like hate, fear, and anger can choke us so much that we can hardly function. Hate and fear can be huge emotional barriers to creativity. A design engineer who hates his or her job probably cannot generate good alternative solutions to on-the-job problems. Similarly, a manager who refuses to assume any risk because of a strong fear of failure is handicapped in creative problem-solving.

We cannot rid our lives of negative emotions; they are a part of being human. But we can learn to recognize them and deal with them in an effective way. Take Syd Cohen, for example, who is traffic manager for a local delivery firm. It's the last Tuesday in November, and all the stores want immediate delivery of their orders. But by ten o'clock in the morning, three out of ten drivers have called in sick, two drivers have phoned in from the next county to report mechanical breakdowns, and the company's biggest customer just called to chew Syd out for not making delivery last Friday. Obviously, he's got problems. When his assistant tells him the president of the firm wants to see him immediately, Syd flies off the handle. He yells at everyone in the vicinity and angrily stamps off to see the president. Obviously, he's in no shape to help either himself or the organization.

Syd's predicament, though difficult, is not uncommon, and there are ways he could have dealt with it. The first step would have been to recognize and admit his negative emotions. He needed to realize that he was angry, however unreasonably, at the men who had called in sick. He was angry at the garage that was supposed to maintain the trucks, and he was angry at himself for overlooking earlier signs of careless maintenance. He was afraid he wouldn't be able to solve the situation very quickly, and he was afraid of what the president might say to him. All these emotions overwhelmed him and he went to pieces. Anger and fear were interfering with problem solving. Instead, Syd might have been honest enough to say to himself, "I'm in a bad spot. And I'm so mad about it, and so scared that things will get worse, I can't even think straight."

The next step would be for Syd to deal with his emotions before trying to deal with any of his other problems. He might say, "If I don't take a few minutes right now to cool off and get things in perspective, anything I do will make matters worse." The key to cooling the situation off is to figure out an appropriate way of expressing the negative emotions. Here Syd has several choices, and he can use the rational part of his brain to help him select the appropriate alternative.

Practically speaking, there are three possibilities. The first is to defuse the negative emotions, perhaps by discussing them with someone else—a trusted coworker, a friend, a boss, or a spouse. Humor can help defuse a situation, too ("laughter is the best medicine"). And sometimes, not often, an instant solution appears and the strong emotions melt away. If defusing isn't possible (and unless Syd can talk his feelings out with someone in the next few minutes, it isn't), then Syd can consider the second possibility: postponement. Maybe he can make a deliberate decision to put off expressing his feelings until he can talk to his wife that night or take out his anger on the squash court. He can at least postpone seeing the president for five minutes and use that time to sort out his feelings, put the problems in perspective, and try to come up with one or two alternative solutions. The third way of handling strong emotions is to use them to provide energy for positive actions. (This alternative seems to work better for hate and anger than for fear.) Syd might say, for example, "If I'm this charged up, I might as well use some of this energy to brainstorm new ideas for dealing with the situation." Or he might decide to phone the garage and use his anger to insist on immediate repairs to the broken-down trucks.

In brief, strong negative emotions can block creative endeavor. It is important to recognize them, to admit them to oneself, and to select appropriate ways to handle and express them. Three ways of dealing with negative emotions are defusement, postponement, and channeling them into positive action. If negative emotions are recognized and dealt with in an appropriate way, they need not be barriers to creative management.

Expressive barriers   The prevailing culture in America places great emphasis on verbal communication. We often fail to realize just how dependent we are on language. The game of charades with its crazy sign language and awkward bodily gyrations helps drive home the point that we are lost without words. To complicate matters, in today's highly specialized world, technical languages have developed. Sometimes communication between two specialists becomes a game of charades. Many a computer programmer has been frustrated by an expressive barrier while trying to describe a situation or outline a problem to a general manager. They simply speak two different languages.

It takes time, patience, and the ability to understand others' special abilities and limitations to overcome expressive barriers. This statement implies that listening is as important as talking and writing to the creative manager. Being willing to listen includes taking the time to consider not only another's words, but also the factual background and the feelings that prompt the words. In this way, listening itself becomes creative. Also, as we noted above, managers need to understand the special language and vocabulary of those they are dealing with.

As for speaking and writing, practice helps. Courses in public speaking and report writing are readily available, as are workshops in group dynamics, salesmanship, and so on. Most managers will attest to the fact that the more they take advantage of opportunities to use the written and spoken language, the more powerful and persuasive their messages become.

Considering the many barriers, it is a wonder that any creative problem solving can take place at all. But that is part of the challenge of management. Just as each manager must build a storehouse of alternative solutions to problems, he or she also needs experience in recognizing and overcoming various barriers to creativity in order to deal flexibly and creatively with new problems. Simply being aware of the danger of perceptual, cultural, emotional, and expressive barriers is the first and most important step.

SUMMARY   Management, as a field of study, is highly fragmented. Theorists devoted to the various specialized approaches have created a degree of confusion as to how management should be practiced on a day-to-day basis. A problem-solving approach that attempts to balance analytic, synthetic, and problem-solving ways of thinking integrates existing management theory. The problem-solving manager can learn many valuable lessons from each of the analytic and synthetic approaches to management, but one particular approach should not be emphasized to the exclusion of others. Problem-solving managers mix and match management concepts and techniques to fit the problem at hand.

Problem solving itself is a well-defined process consisting of four basic steps: (1) *identifying the problem* and its causes, (2) *generating alternative solutions* through flexible vertical and lateral thinking, (3) *selecting the solution* that is most effective and efficient, and (4) *evaluating the results* to see if the problem has actually been solved. Like anything that is learned, one's problem-solving ability improves with practice.

People tend to think in habitual ways and to develop definite problem-solving styles. Systematic thinkers and intuitive thinkers display two common styles. Systematic thinkers place a great deal of emphasis on how they go about solving a problem. Intuitive thinkers, in contrast, prefer to free-wheel while quickly coming up with a solution. From an organizational standpoint, neither style is preferable to the other; inputs are needed from both types of problem solvers.

Managers need to be concerned with creativity because management itself is a creative endeavor. Also, creative employees often present managers with a dilemma because their creativity can be stifled by the organization's rules and standard procedures. Although some people just seem to be more creative than others, managers can increase their personal creativity through the use of mind-expanding exercises and by recognizing and removing barriers to creativity, whether perceptual, cultural, emotional, or expressive.

TERMS TO UNDERSTAND

Analysis	Vertical thinker
Synthesis	Lateral thinker
Problem solving	Thinking
Complementary thinking	Systematic thinker
Problem	Intuitive thinker
Cause	Creativity

QUESTIONS FOR DISCUSSION

1. In what ways are analysis, synthesis, and problem solving complementary modes of thinking?
2. Why is the problem-solving approach called an "integrative" approach to management?
3. Why does problem solving follow a fixed sequence of steps?
4. What are the most important factors in identifying a problem?
5. How can vertical thinking and lateral thinking both help in generating solutions to problems?

6. What factors need to be considered in selecting a solution to a problem?
7. What are the benefits of evaluating the results after a solution has been implemented?
8. Who is likely to come up with better solutions to problems, the intuitive thinker or the systematic thinker? Support your answer.
9. Do you know a truly creative person? If so, do you think it would be a problem getting that person to pursue organizational objectives?
10. What kind of barrier to creativity poses the most difficulty for managers today? Why do you feel this problem is more important than others? Describe the problem in detail and suggest solutions.

CASE 3.1
I'VE USED THEM ALL

Lincoln Cogswell bowed his head graciously as he was being applauded by Professor Winkler's introductory management class. Mr. Cogswell, the owner of a very successful drugstore chain in New England, had just finished speaking about the importance of studying management. The students were obviously impressed by the fact that he had started out as the fifth child of a poor tenant farmer in Alabama fifty-five years before. Now Lincoln Cogswell owned forty drugstores and was well on his way to his second million. He was a self-made man in every way.

Later, during an informal question and answer session, Deborah Francis asked Mr. Cogswell the following question:

Mr. Cogswell, you mentioned that you sent yourself through business school at night, so you know something about both management theory and management practice. Well, we just finished reading about a number of different traditional and modern approaches to management. Could you tell us what your favorite approach has been?

After thinking for a moment, Mr. Cogswell answered by saying, "I don't have a favorite approach to management. I'm sure I've used them all."

FOR DISCUSSION

1. Give your own interpretation of what Mr. Cogswell meant.
2. Is it possible that Mr. Cogswell was referring to a problem-solving approach without actually using the term?

CASE 3.2
I'LL KNOW, I'LL KNOW

A week has passed since Fred Dirks, the marketing manager for a large laundry products company, assigned Maryann Morris and Sean Wilson to a special market research project. This project is one of a series intended to expose management trainees to the major functions of the business, such as production, finance, personnel, and marketing. Every six weeks the trainees are assigned new partners and rotated to a new function. Top management considers the firm's management trainee program a model for the industry. The trainees not only get to know and work with each other, but they learn a great deal about the operation of the company as a whole.

Maryann, who holds an engineering degree, and Sean, a former liberal arts major, are meeting today to compare notes on their market research project. Each has spent the last week researching and pinpointing alternative courses of action. At first, things go smoothly. They exchange general comments, then Sean takes about twenty minutes to outline his recommendations. In response to Maryann's question about how he developed his recommendations, he replies, "Oh, they just kind of came together for me after looking at some figures and talking to some people."

An hour and a half later, after listening to Maryann's detailed explanation of her research methodology and statistical interpretation of several population trends, Sean loses patience and snaps, "Do me a favor, Maryann. Cut the methodological garbage and get to your recommendations!" Obviously angered by this rude interruption, Maryann shoots back, "What kind of sloppy thinking is that? How on earth can you hope to understand my recommendations if you haven't the faintest notion of where they came from?" "I'll know," replies Sean, "I'll know."

FOR DISCUSSION

1. Who is the systematic thinker and who the intuitive thinker in this case?
2. What lessons can each of these two different kinds of thinkers learn from one another?
3. Do you suppose the marketing manager purposely teamed up a systematic thinker and an intuitive thinker on the same project?
4. Relative to the firm's management training program, how do analysis and synthesis enter the picture?

REFERENCES

Opening quotation

Charles E. Watson, "The Problems of Problem Solving," *Business Horizons* 19 (August 1976): 94.

1. Russell L. Ackoff, "Science in the Systems Age: Beyond IE, OR, and MS," *Operations Research* 21 (May–June 1973): 661.
2. Ibid., p. 664.
3. Ibid.
4. B. F. Skinner, "An Operant Analysis of Problem Solving," in Benjamin Kleinmuntz, ed., *Problem Solving: Research, Method, and Theory* (New York: Wiley, 1966), p. 225.
5. Peter F. Drucker, *The Practice of Management* (New York: Harper & Row, 1954), p. 531.
6. Fred C. Foy, "A Businessman Looks at Business Education," in American Association of Collegiate Schools of Business, *Views on Business Education* (Chapel Hill, N.C.: University of North Carolina, 1960), p. 15.
7. Robert M. Gagné, *The Conditions of Learning*, 2nd ed. (New York: Holt, Rinehart & Winston, 1970), pp. 246–251.
8. William F. Pounds, "The Process of Problem Finding," *Industrial Management Review* 11 (Fall 1969): 1.
9. Watson, "The Problems of Problem Solving," p. 90.
10. James L. Adams, *Conceptual Blockbusting* (San Francisco: Freeman, 1974), p. 7.
11. For an interesting discussion, see: Edward de Bono, *New Think* (New York: Basic Books, 1968), chap. 1.
12. This distinction comes from: James L. McKenney and Peter G. W. Keen, "How Managers' Minds Work," *Harvard Business Review*, 52 (May–June 1974): 79–90.
13. See: Don Hellriegel and John W. Slocum, Jr., "Managerial Problem-solving Styles," *Business Horizons* 18 (December 1975): 29–37.
14. Ibid., p. 33.
15. Drawn from: N. R. F. Maier, Mara Julius, and James Thurber, "Studies in Creativity: Individual Differences in the Storing and Utilization of Information," *The American Journal of Psychology* 80 (December 1967): 492–519.
16. Arthur Koestler, *The Act of Creation*, (London: Hutchinson, 1969), p. 27.
17. Adams, *Conceptual Blockbusting*, p. 35.
18. John Senger, "Organizational Problem Solving and Creativity," *Public Personnel Management* 3 (November–December 1974): 541.
19. The answer is F. Taylor.
20. Discussion of these four barriers to creativity has been adapted from Adams, *Conceptual Blockbusting*, chaps. 2–5.

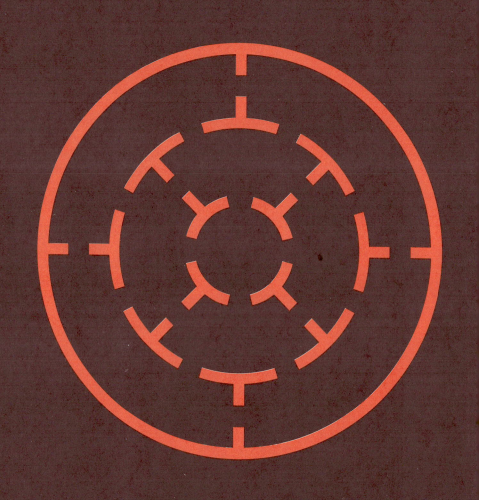

II

Planning and Controlling

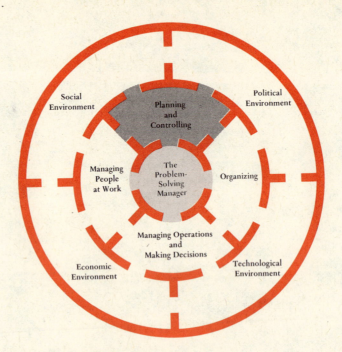

PART II TAKES UP PLANNING AND CONTROLLING, FUNDAMENTAL MAN-
agement functions that complement one another. Planning helps
managers determine where they want to go, and controlling helps
them make sure they get there. The distinction between planning
and controlling is really a matter of theoretical convenience,
because it is difficult to establish exactly where one leaves off and
the other picks up. Relative to planning, the overriding problem to
be solved is to determine the organization's purpose and direction in
spite of an uncertain environment and limited resources. A comprehensive planning system with strategic, intermediate, and operational components helps ensure an appropriate balance between
organizational effectiveness and efficiency. The problem to be
solved in controlling is to monitor organizational performance so
that corrective action can be taken.

Chapter 4

Planning

Despite the fact that planning is considered the foundation of management, it is still too often the poorest performed task of the managerial job.

Harold Koontz

LEARNING OBJECTIVES

When you finish reading this chapter, you should be able to

- Explain why planning is important.
- Identify the 5 P's of planning and briefly explain the significance of each.
- Describe what top management does when engaged in strategic planning.
- Tell why the following statement does not qualify as an objective: "Increase new product sales."
- Compare and contrast flow charts, Gantt charts, and PERT networks.

The only thing certain about the future of any organization today is change. AT&T, the government of Mexico, the New York Mets, and Smilin' Ed's Used Cars are all sure to change along with everything else as they move into the future. Managers everywhere face a highly fluid social, political, economic, and technological environment. Ignoring or stubbornly resisting change practically guarantees organizational failure. Effective managers keep informed as to what is going on around them, actively anticipate change, and plan for the future.

Planning is defined as the process of preparing for change and coping with uncertainty by formulating future courses of action. Because planning is the bridge between the present and the future, it has been called the primary management function. The purpose of this chapter is to examine the planning function as it relates to the problem-solving management process.

Basically, there are two reasons why planning is particularly important today. Those reasons are scarce resources and an uncertain environment. Let us examine each for a moment.

Resource scarcity is an especially grave problem because it looks as if it will be a permanent feature of life on our planet from now on. At the very least, as two scientific observers noted, "dwindling supplies of energy and materials resources pose what may be the most significant problem for the United States in the last quarter of the twentieth century."[1] As surprising as it may sound, in view of the worldwide population explosion, even human resources are limited. This is true because an uneducated or untrained person, or one who lives too far from the work place, can contribute little to a productive organization. There would be little need for planning if material, financial, and human resources were unlimited. Waste and inefficiency could prevail as in the past if fresh resources were endlessly available. Unfortunately, as the smog alerts, water shortages, and energy crunches of the 1970s demonstrated, even seemingly limitless resources such as air, water, and petroleum are exhaustible. Modern planners need to base their plans on the intelligent use of limited resources. Otherwise, wasteful inefficiencies will drive up prices, delay deliveries, and help create outright shortages.

In general, the environment in which we live and work is uncertain. It is often remarked that the only sure things in life are death and taxes. This is a gloomy prospect, but it captures a key theme of modern life. We are faced with a great deal of uncertainty. But this does not mean that we should throw up our hands in dismay and stop trying to get things accomplished. We need to understand that uncertainty is relative. Some aspects of the future are fairly certain—say, the continuance of a peacetime economy in the United States for the next five years. Others are highly uncertain, such as the price of gas three months from now. And there are degrees of uncertainty in between.

Management's challenge is to determine degrees of uncertainty and act accordingly. Concrete plans can be made for areas of high certainty. Areas marked by low certainty require flexible plans that can be adjusted to suit changing conditions. Planning is always needed. But the higher the degree of environmental uncertainty, the greater the need for flexibility in planning.

The organization derives several benefits from the planning process. As we will see later in this chapter, planning gives managers and the organizations they oversee purpose and direction. If we liken the organization to a ship, plans can ensure that the ship has enough supplies for the voyage, sails in the right direction, and reaches the right port at the right time. Besides providing purpose and direction, plans help motivate managers and other employees. Everyone likes to feel that he or she is part of an important enterprise. If plans are communicated to all levels of the organization, then everyone can feel involved in carrying them out. Remember that old story of two laborers digging with their shovels? One, when asked what he was doing, replied, "I am digging a ditch." The other said, "I am building a cathedral." Clearly, the latter was motivated by a long-range plan. A third benefit of the planning process is that it provides standards for measuring the organization's progress. We will explore this aspect of planning in the next chapter, on control.

THE 5 P'S OF PLANNING

We can best analyze the basic components of planning by discussing the 5 P's of planning: purpose, philosophy, premises, policies, and plans. These 5 P's represent a logical sequence, starting with the most general considerations and funneling down to the most specific. Figure 4.1 illustrates the relationships among the 5 P's.

Each of the five P's forms part of the overall, ongoing planning process. The first P, *purpose*, is a statement of the reason for the organization's continued existence. *Philosophy* consists of fundamental beliefs about the way in which the organization's purpose is to be achieved. The third P, *premises*, is an organization's assumptions about the environment and about its own strengths and weaknesses. *Policies* are general guidelines, or constraints, for managerial thinking and action. Finally, specific *plans* translate general purpose, philosophy, premises, and policies into specific objectives and action statements. We will explore each of these components of planning in the following sections.

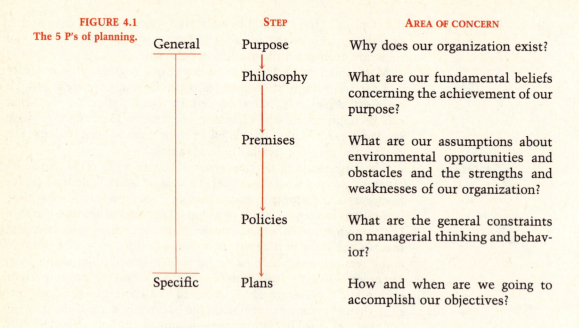

FIGURE 4.1
The 5 P's of planning.

	STEP	AREA OF CONCERN
General	Purpose	Why does our organization exist?
	Philosophy	What are our fundamental beliefs concerning the achievement of our purpose?
	Premises	What are our assumptions about environmental opportunities and obstacles and the strengths and weaknesses of our organization?
	Policies	What are the general constraints on managerial thinking and behavior?
Specific	Plans	How and when are we going to accomplish our objectives?

PURPOSE   To some people, concern about defining an organization's purpose is a waste of time. According to their line of thinking, an organization would not exist if it did not have a purpose. But this is not true. Some organizations never have a clear purpose, while others lose sight of theirs. Also, an organization may achieve its purpose and, by doing so, lose its reason for being. A prime example is the March of Dimes organization, which had to shift its purpose from fighting polio to fighting birth defects when a polio vaccine was developed. General Motors, Ford, Chrysler, and American Motors have broadened their purpose from producing cars to providing transportation. Similarly, petroleum companies now see themselves in the energy business rather than simply the oil and gas business.

A clear, formally written, and publicized statement of organization purpose is a necessary foundation for an effective planning system. It does more than just express generalities such as "to make money." Instead it helps define the organization's special niche in the economy or culture, spelling out the organization's areas of endeavor that differentiate it from other organizations. An example of such a statement is displayed in Table 4.1. United Technologies' purpose statement gives managers, stockholders, customers, and other interested parties an idea of why the company is in business. An organization's planning efforts will probably achieve limited

TABLE 4.1
A sample statement of
organizational purpose

United Technologies Corporation is a diversified, multi-market industrial organization which designs, develops, manufactures and markets a wide variety of technological products to serve commercial and government needs worldwide.

Its products are applied in areas such as air, surface, and sea transportation, power, energy, communications, construction, national defense and space exploration. They include aircraft engines, elevators and escalators, electrical-electromechanical conductors and controls, helicopters, flight systems, industrial equipment and space and rocket propulsion systems.

Through its various established flight products, such as engines, helicopters and propellers, United long has been involved in technologies related to the efficient use of energy. These technologies now also have been applied by the Corporation to numerous other fields—automotive and appliance manufacture, construction, industrial processes, and power generation.

Source: United Technologies Corporation, *Facts and Figures*, July 1977, p. 11. Courtesy United Technologies Corporation.

success or even fail unless top management develops a clear statement of purpose.

PHILOSOPHY

Organizations may take any number of different paths to achieve a given end. To accomplish the purpose of the organization, management can operate honestly and straightforwardly, or it can fall back on deception and fraudulent dealing. Both paths may get the job done. However, if the organization is to assure its long-term survival, then it needs to adopt a philosophy that is ethical and meets the expectations of the culture in which it operates. A version of General Motors' company philosophy is displayed in Table 4.2. Philosophies of this kind, expressed in formal statements, lend further direction and precision to the planning process. In a sense,

TABLE 4.2
A sample statement of
organizational philosophy

We are determined to continue to offer our customers the quality products and service they require; to provide our employes with the compensation, the opportunities, and working conditions to which they are entitled; to deal with everyone involved in our business in accordance with the highest ethical standards; and to work to earn a deserved return for our stockholders.

Source: *General Motors Corporation Annual Report for 1976*, p. 3, Courtesy General Motors Corporation.

they outline top management's beliefs about how the company intends to pursue its stated purpose. General Motors' philosophy is based on profitability through quality, service, and ethical behavior. Notice how the General Motors philosophy could fit virtually all profit-making organizations. Only minor adjustments would be necessary for nonprofit-making organizations and government agencies.

PREMISES In planning, especially in top-level strategic planning, management adopts certain premises, or assumptions. One cluster of assumptions involves environmental uncertainties. Another involves organizational capabilities. By taking advantage of all available information, including forecast data, management can make reasonable assumptions about opportunities and obstacles presented by the outside environment. Similarly, by turning an analytical eye inward, management can make reasonable assumptions about the organization's strengths and weaknesses.

Texas Instruments (TI), the giant Dallas-based electronics firm, is a prime example of an organization that owes much of its success to accurate premises. For instance, back in the early 1970s, when its competitors were plowing huge sums of research and development money into computer memories and microprocessors, TI formulated a plan to focus on consumer products such as calculators and watches. Unlike its competitors, TI assumed that the Japanese could be undersold in the consumer electronics business. TI's management was confident that its proven ability as an innovator in product design, production technology, and marketing techniques was the key to competitive pricing. As things worked out, TI's assumptions about its opportunity in consumer electronics and its strength as a cost-cutting innovator proved valid. The firm drove prices down dramatically and quickly established itself as the number-one producer worldwide of hand calculators and digital watches.[2]

As it exists today, premising ranges from highly subjective "guesstimates" to extremely sophisticated computer-assisted modeling. The importance of premising must not be overlooked, because plans are only as valid as the underlying premises. One respected management expert has concluded: "Perhaps the most important cause of failure in planning is neglecting or underestimating the importance of planning premises or assumptions."[3]

POLICIES Policies are still another step toward specificity in planning. Organizational policies may be defined as general guidelines, or constraints, for managerial thinking and action. A policy is more specific than a philosophy, but not as specific as a rule. The following breakdown illustrates this distinction.

o *Philosophy*   This organization will provide a safe working environment for all employees.
o *Policy*   All flammable substances will be stored and handled in accordance with existing federal, state, and local regulations.
o *Rule*   No smoking within fifty feet of gasoline storage tanks.

Policies such as the foregoing help top management make sure all managers adhere to the organizational philosophy when engaged in lower-level planning. Policies can and usually do affect all aspects of performance. In the typical business organization there are production policies, financial policies, marketing policies, and accounting, personnel, and purchasing policies.

PLANS   Plans represent the translation of general purpose, philosophy, premises, and policies into specific objectives and action statements. Objectives are the ends; action statements are the means. Stated differently, an objective gives management a target to shoot at, and an action statement provides the appropriate arrow for hitting the target. Every good plan has both an objective and an action statement.

Consider the following example. Suppose that loss from punch press scrap is costing XYZ Manufacturing Company $200,000 per year. Analysis of the situation by the production department staff has uncovered clogged and dirty machines as the cause of the excess scrap problem. It seems that the machines get clogged and dirty because maintenance personnel get around to checking and cleaning each machine only once a week on the average. Experimentation with two operators has demonstrated that scrap loss can be cut in half if the operators are trained to check and clean their own presses twice a day. Consequently, the production manager has formulated the following plan:

Cut punch press scrap loss by $100,000 over the next year by teaching punch press operators how to check and clean their machines twice a day.

Remember: Every plan should specify an objective and include an action statement. Let's go back and check the production manager's plan to see if it meets the requirements of an adequate plan. What is the objective? It is to "cut punch press loss by $100,000 over the next year . . ." Is there an action statement? Yes, the objective is to be achieved. ". . . by teaching punch press operators how to check and clean their machines twice a day." Both elements of an adequate plan are present. Anything less would not be a plan. Plans specify *how* something is to be accomplished as well as *what* and *when*.

The plan for reducing punch press scrap loss was expressed in a fairly simple statement. Other plans may take the form of budgets, projects of all sorts, long-term programs such as putting a human being on Mars, standing procedures, and so on. All can be stated as objectives and action statements. A large project or program would have broad objectives and action statements defined by ever more specific ones.

Though most plans are written, some need to be expressed only orally, as in "Let's forget the Idex campaign for today and concentrate on getting those promotion pieces in the mail." Written plans may take nearly any form, including memos, budgets, and formal proposals running to a hundred pages or more.

To be effective, planning must begin at the top of the organizational pyramid and filter down to lower levels. After all, four of the five P's of planning are largely top management's responsibility. Only top-level managers can specify the overall purpose of the organization and frame a suitable philosophy. Otherwise there would be little coordination among subunits. Premises and policies, too, are the responsibility of top management. Only after the first four P's have been identified can specific plans be formulated.

Planning takes place at all levels of the organization. Figure 4.2 outlines the three major levels: top management, middle management, and lower management. Top management engages in strategic planning, middle management is given the job of intermediate planning, and operational planning is done by lower management. *Strategic planning* is the process of determining what direction the overall organization should take. *Intermediate planning* is the process of determining the proper allocation of resources needed to achieve strategic plans. Finally, *operational planning* is the process of determining how specific jobs will be accomplished with the resources available. Each level of planning is important to organizational success and cannot effectively stand alone without the support of the other two levels.

Time is the key variable when it comes to drawing a distinction between strategic, intermediate, and operational planning. As shown in Figure 4.2, planning horizons vary from one level to another. That is, each level of planning goes farther into the future than the one below it in the pyramid. A longer time elapses between the formulation and the execution of the planned activity. As the

FIGURE 4.2
Levels of planning

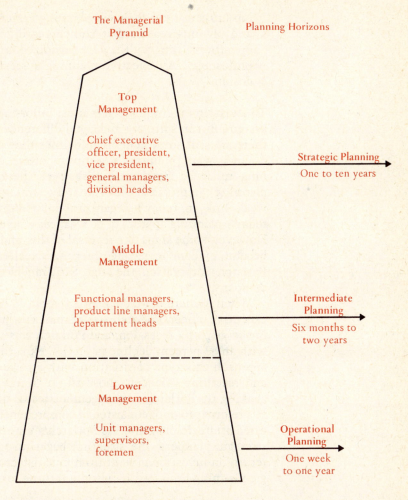

The Managerial
Pyramid

Planning Horizons

Top
Management

Chief executive
officer, president,
vice president,
general managers,
division heads

Strategic Planning
One to ten years

Middle
Management

Functional managers,
product line managers,
department heads

Intermediate
Planning

Six months to
two years

Lower
Management

Unit managers,
supervisors,
foremen

Operational
Planning

One week
to one year

planning process filters down the organization pyramid, planning horizons become shorter and plans become more specific. Naturally, we can be more confident and hence more specific about the near future than about the far distant future. Notice, however, how the three planning horizons overlap; they do not have rigid boundaries. Top and lower management both engage at times in intermediate planning. In the next section we examine strategic planning in some detail, because this is how the planning process begins.

STRATEGIC PLANNING   Planning should be approached systematically, not on a hit-or-miss basis. However, when managers begin thinking about building a planning system for their organization, they should keep the following qualification in mind:

No universal, off-the-shelf planning system exists for the simple and obvious reason that companies differ in size, diversity of operations, the way they are organized, and managers' style and philosophy. An effective planning system requires "situational design."[4]

To a certain extent, managers must tailor-make their own planning system. But in spite of situational differences among organizations, there are still some general guidelines they can all follow.

Once again, planning is a top-to-bottom process. Strategic planning must be firmly established at the top before lower-level planning can proceed. Unfortunately, strategic planning is often the weak link in today's organizational planning programs. In fact, today's planning appears to be weakest where it should be strongest. However, some signs of a reversal of this undesirable situation have become evident in recent years. An excellent case in point is the Potlatch Corporation, the large, San Francisco–based forest products company.[5]

When Richard B. Madden took over in 1970 as president and chief executive officer, Potlatch was floundering badly. The economy was in the grip of a recession, and Potlatch was trailing its competitors with an 83 percent decline in profits. New top managers commonly approach this type of situation with an eye toward reorganization and restaffing. Madden chose to do things differently. Instead of shaking up Potlatch's management team, he decided to reform it. His reform program consisted of comprehensive training in sophisticated strategic planning. As Potlatch's top managers became better strategic planners, the situation began to improve and the firm's return on investment went from unsatisfactory to excellent. Strategic planning produced handsome returns for Potlatch.

WHAT IS A STRATEGY? In the words of one respected management scholar, "Strategies are general programs of action with an implied commitment of emphasis and resources to achieve a basic mission."[6] As indicated in Figure 4.2, strategic planning typically has a horizon of from one to ten years. The more stable the environment, the longer the horizon. Continental Can Company, which produces a strictly standardized line of products, can plan farther into the future than Texas Instruments, a firm that responds to rapid technological change. But whatever the necessary planning horizon, strategy cannot be ignored. As one expert has emphasized, "Strategy is the conceptual glue that binds the diverse activities of a complex organization together."[7]

IDENTIFYING OPPORTUNITIES AND OBSTACLES

The first place to look when engaged in strategic planning is outside the organization, to the surrounding social, political, economic, and technological environment. What opportunities are present? Where are the obstacles? The search for answers to these important questions has been referred to as "environmental scanning."[8] There are many ways to scan the environment for opportunities and obstacles. Top management can study telltale shifts in the economy, recent innovations, growth and direction among competitors, market trends, and demographic redistributions. Not least among factors to be considered are the tax rates. Favorable tax rates in the "sun belt" states have given many northern companies the opportunity to relocate and grow in recent years.

Since planning involves an assessment of the future as well as of current conditions, it requires a degree of crystal-ball gazing. Planners must attempt to forecast the future. *Forecasts* may be defined as predictions, projections, or estimates of future events or conditions in the environment in which the organization operates.[9] Forecasts may be little more than educated guesses, or they may be the result of highly sophisticated statistical analysis. They may be relatively short run (six months to one year) or long run (five or more years). The sophistication and time horizon of a particular forecast depend on several factors. Among these factors are the type of forecast data required, management's knowledge of forecasting techniques, and the time and money management is willing to invest.

Broadly speaking, there are two kinds of forecasts. *General forecasts* try to outline the social, political, economic, and technological future. These environmental factors are so broad in scope that usually only government agencies—such as the Departments of Commerce, Labor, or Energy or the Department of Health, Education, and Welfare—can afford to make forecasts of them. Fortunately, the results of government forecasts are available for little if any expense from the various agencies.

In contrast to general forecasts are *specific forecasts* of factors that immediately impact the organization. Primary among these factors are demand for the organization's goods or services, available labor supply, and raw materials supply. If a luggage manufacturing company, for example, can accurately forecast demand for its products, then it can calculate a projected sales revenue figure that in turn becomes a premise for production, finance, and marketing plans. Similarly, labor and raw materials supply forecasts also serve as planning premises. Unexpected shortages of skilled labor and vital raw materials can bring even the largest corporation to a halt.

CONVERSATION WITH . . .

Gerard A. Fulham
Chairman of the Board and Chief
  Executive Officer
Pneumo Corporation
Boston, Massachusetts

Bachrach Studios.

PERSONAL BACKGROUND

Gerard Fulham was born in Winthrop, Massachusetts, a small town outside Boston. While attending Roxbury Latin School, young Gerard spent his summers working in his father's wholesale fish business in Boston. He was graduated from Harvard College in 1942. Upon returning from World War II, he initially worked in the fish business and later joined an investment banking firm. During this period Gerard studied accounting in night school. After his father's death, he joined his two brothers in managing the family fish business, which branched into real estate and the operation of a fleet of fishing boats. In 1958, Gerard Fulham went to work for the predecessor company of Pneumo as chief financial officer. Eleven years later he assumed his present position. Today, Pneumo is a diversified company that manufactures landing gear for commercial and military aircraft, operates the chain of P&C Food Markets in New York and New England, and produces a host of industrial products such as insulated thermocouple wire and cable. Its annual sales exceed $600 million.

QUOTABLE QUOTES

What is your most significant achievement as a manager?

Mr. Fulham: In the late 1960s Pneumo was in aerospace and machine tool markets that have severely coincident cycles. Capital requirements and sales both have wide swings that precipitate cash shortages. By divesting the machine tool business and acquiring a retail and wholesale food business, a desirable cash diversity has been achieved.

What do you think it takes to be a successful manager today?

Mr. Fulham: The key to successful management is to have a clear view of corporate strategy and the resources required by the strategy chosen. Many companies continue to go aground through their failure to plan and monitor their cash flow. Managers at all levels within the company have to be aware of and control their cash resources.

Forecasting helps management anticipate and adjust to threatened shortages.

Modern managers often turn to one of three techniques for specific forecasts. Those techniques are informed judgment, surveys, and trend analysis.

Informed judgment   Occasionally, time and money constraints force managers to rely on their own best judgment when attempting to anticipate the future. While this approach to forecasting is highly subjective and intuitive, its potential value should not be underestimated. Judgmental forecasts are both fast and inexpensive. However, the accuracy of a manager's judgmental forecasts depends a great deal upon how well informed he or she is. A well-informed manager stays in close touch with members of the organization, like those in sales, purchasing, and public relations, who regularly interact with outside sources of information. Furthermore, faithful reading of a large metropolitan daily newspaper, *The Wall Street Journal*, *Business Week*, *Fortune*, *Nation's Business*, and selected trade publications helps keep the manager informed. Attending executive development seminars also is beneficial.

To a great extent, today's managers can be likened to data processing machines; the better the information and data they receive, the better equipped they are to make judgmental forecasts. Like any other skill, judgmental forecasting tends to improve with practice.

A prime example is that of Donald Frey, the chief executive officer of Bell & Howell Company. *Fortune* magazine reports that Frey subscribes to twenty different magazines that cover a broad range of topics from foreign affairs to the arts. In addition he reads one to two books a week. "Frey's intellectual range extends well beyond his own company or industry, and well beyond business in general."[10] Consequently, Frey has become very good at making valid judgmental forecasts. For instance, while a product-planning manager at Ford Motor Company, Frey fought to introduce the Mustang in spite of gloomy market forecasts of only 86,000 units. Frey won out, Mustang sales skyrocketed to 418,000 units in 1964, and he was promoted to division head.

Surveys   Valuable forecast information concerning demand as well as labor and raw materials supply may be obtained via face-to-face interviews, telephone surveys, or mailed question-naires. Whatever the mode of communication, all surveys are structured in basically the same way. Clearly stated, easily under-stood questions are presented to a random sample of some popula-tion of individuals or representatives of organizations. Surveys have the advantage of yielding comprehensive and valuable information. They suffer the disadvantages of being somewhat difficult to construct, time consuming, and expensive. Fortunately, there are research organizations such as A. C. Nielsen that will construct custom surveys on an economical contract basis. The long lists of research organizations found under the heading "market research" in the yellow pages of metropolitan telephone books attest to the resources available in this area.

Trend analysis   Basically, a *trend analysis* is the hypothetical extension of a past pattern of events into the future. The underlying assumption or hypothesis, is that the future will be a continuation of the past. Provided that sufficient historical data are readily available, trend analysis can be carried out rather quickly and inexpensively. If the data need to be collected, however, this kind of analysis may be prohibitively expensive.

In any trend analysis, caution should be exercised to avoid misinterpretation of short-term trends. Figure 4.3 illustrates how trend analysis can be rather misleading. Trend A is overly optimistic because it is based on three unusually good years. Trend B forecasts an unduly pessimistic picture of future sales because it is based solely on a four-year downturn. Trend C represents a more realistic forecast because it is based on ten years of fluctuating sales.

The major drawback of trend analysis is the premise that all relevant variables will remain relatively constant in the future. For this reason, trend analysis has a poor track record when it comes up against sudden changes in environmental variables. But if sufficient historical data are available and relevant environmental variables are considered, trend analysis can be a handy forecasting tool for the manager.

FIGURE 4.3
Trend analysis—helpful or
misleading?

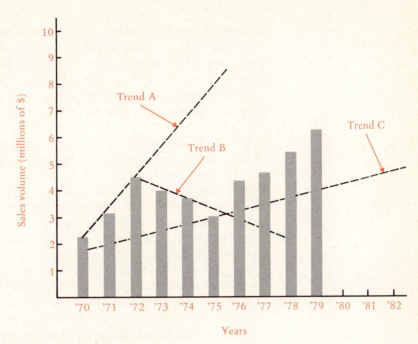

Years

OBSTACLE OR OPPORTUNITY?

A perceived obstacle may turn out to be an opportunity, and vice versa. In the late 1970s a number of cement manufacturers saw the natural gas shortage as a serious obstacle because the cement production process requires extremely high temperatures for proper chemical conversion. As it turned out, they switched to coal and ended up saving money with a cheaper and more readily available source of energy.

On the other hand, an apparent opportunity may turn out to be a major obstacle. One organization that fell into this strategic trap was W. T. Grant Company.[11] Top managers at Grant saw the trend toward credit-card buying as an excellent opportunity to increase sales. They responded by formulating liberal credit policies to put Grant credit cards into as many hands as possible. Unfortunately, Grant discovered that half of its $500 million in credit-card receivables was uncollectable. The once giant seventy-year-old chain of 1,100 stores was liquidated by a bankruptcy court in 1976. Opportunities and obstacles need to be read very carefully.

IDENTIFYING STRENGTHS AND WEAKNESSES

After scanning the outside environment for opportunities and obstacles, top management needs to direct its attention inward to discover the organization's strengths and weaknesses. This process is sometimes referred to as a "resource evaluation program" or a "capability profile."[12] When it comes to tackling a job this big the usual question is, "Where should we begin?" The list of organizational attributes presented in Table 4.3 represents an excellent starting point. By generating such a list of variables and carefully considering the strengths or weaknesses of each one, top management is taking a major step in the strategic planning process.

FINDING THE RIGHT NICHE

Webster's defines *niche* as "a place, employment, or activity for which a person is best fitted."[13] By stretching this definition just a bit, the term can just as well be applied to organizations. Every organization conceivably can identify a purpose for which it is best suited. Management should use strategic planning to match outside opportunities with inside strengths. Texas Instruments' move into consumer electronics, discussed earlier, is a good case in point. This matching process is much more difficult than it appears at first glance. Rather than dealing with snapshots of the environment and the organization, management is faced with a "movie" of rapidly changing events. One researcher has described the changing nature of the matching process in these words: "The task is to find a match between opportunities that are still unfolding and resources that are still being acquired."[14] Constant reevaluation to determine whether the organization is doing the right thing, in the right place, and at the right time is one of management's most important concerns.

ESTABLISHING PRIORITIES

Once the organization has found the right niche for itself, management must turn to establishing *priorities*, which can be defined as activities or objectives ranked in order of importance. Since material, financial, and human resources are limited, organizational objectives have to be arranged in order of importance. Many top-level managers have said that this is the toughest part of their job, because there are no hard and fast guidelines.

The fact is, priority establishment is largely subjective and judgmental. And subjective judgments are difficult to render when the organization is subject to competing and conflicting demands. For example, imagine how difficult it is for the president and board of a large hospital to establish priorities when the demands of the medical staff conflict with patient demands. Does the medical staff get the newest, most sophisticated, and expensive equipment, which they say they must have, or do the patients get the low-cost treatment they demand? Something has to give; both groups cannot possibly be completely satisfied. Priorities have to be established in ordering new equipment, so that costs and thus patient billing can be kept in line. Unavoidably, someone's feelings will get hurt when management begins arranging objectives in order of importance.

TABLE 4.3
Identifying organizational strengths and weaknesses

GENERAL CATEGORY	ATTRIBUTES
Organization	Structure
	Degree of decentralization
	Policies and procedures
	The planning system
	The control system
	The communication network
Personnel	Number of employees
	Employee attitude profile
	Employee age and skill profiles
	Union/nonunion status
	Absenteeism and turnover rates
	Grievance rate
Marketing	Size of sales force
	Sales force turnover
	Knowledge of customers' needs
	Market share
	Breadth of product line
	Channels of distribution
	Product quality
	Credit and refund policies
	Customer service
	Reputation
Technical	Production facilities
	Condition of machinery
	Production techniques
	Quality control program
	New product innovation
	Research program
	Purchasing system
	Inventory system
Finance	Financial size
	Liquidity
	Return on investment
	Price-earnings ratio
	Credit rating
	Lines of credit
	Growth record

Based on: Howard H. Stevenson, "Defining Corporate Strengths and Weaknesses," *Sloan Management Review* 17 (Spring 1976): 51–68.

And some important activities may need to be curtailed. But in a world of limited resources, these results are inevitable. Managers find management by objectives (MBO), which is discussed in detail in the next chapter, useful in this area.

TYING IN INTERMEDIATE AND OPERATIONAL PLANS

Although strategic planning requires a great deal of top management's time and effort, it is only the beginning. The planning process, largely through the use of well-defined and clearly communicated objectives, must filter down through the managerial pyramid. Middle management inherits the task of refining top management's strategic plans. It is the middle managers who must determine the most effective and efficient mix of human, material, and financial resources. They must establish priorities, too, but their plans are more specific and cover a shorter time horizon than top management's strategic plans. In a manner of speaking, middle management gets the wheels rolling in turning broad strategic plans into reality.

Lower management has the task of getting specific jobs done in the best way possible with the resources available. Operational plans may cover a day or two, a couple of weeks, a month, or a year. In general, the lowest management level formulates the most specific plans within the shortest time horizons.

DEFINING OBJECTIVES

After the first four P's—purpose, philosophy, premises, and policies—have been clearly identified, the organization is ready to formulate specific plans: strategic, intermediate, and operational. As we have seen, plans consist of two parts: objectives (the what and when) and action statements (the how).

Objectives are sometimes viewed as the single most important feature of the planning process. Without objectives managers at all three levels of the organization have a difficult time making decisions in a purposeful and coordinated fashion. According to a team of management consultants: "It is very difficult to see how an organization or an individual can even begin to plan until concrete objectives are clearly defined."[15] Objectives are targets. And managers *must* have targets if they are to accomplish anything. In this section, we define the term *objective*, discuss the value of objectives in organizations, and examine objectives in terms of ends-means chains.

WHAT IS AN OBJECTIVE?

An *objective* is a statement of intention concerning the accomplishment of an intended result. One authority recommends: "As far as possible, objectives are expressed in quantitative, measurable, concrete terms, in the form of a written statement of desired results to be achieved within a given time period."[16] In other words, objectives reflect specific rather than general vague intentions. They must specify *what* is to be accomplished and *when* it is to be accomplished. In the following objectives, note how the desired results are expressed in quantitative terms such as units, dollars, or percentages.

○ To increase subcompact car production by 240,000 units during the next production year.
○ To reduce bad-debt loss by $50,000 during the next six months.
○ To achieve an 18 percent increase in Brand X sales by December 31 of the current year.

To test objectives like these for appropriate specificity, managers should ask themselves the following three questions:

○ *Test 1* Does this objective tell me exactly *what* the intended result is?
○ *Test 2* Does this objective specify *when* the intended result should be accomplished?
○ *Test 3* Can the intended result be *measured*?

Statements of intention that fail one or more of these three tests do not qualify as objectives and will hinder rather than help managers. All three tests must be passed.

WHY SET OBJECTIVES?   Some critics contend that defining objectives is nothing more than a bureaucratic hassle. In fact, it may become just that if improperly handled. But an organization with a clear purpose, a widely accepted philosophy, and a set of valid premises and policies can achieve a great deal when managers at all levels set specific objectives as part of the planning process. The benefits of setting objectives are twofold. First, the effort put into careful definition of objectives increases the manager's perceptual grasp of what needs to be done. Second, objectives are motivational. They serve as goals for performance, just as the end zone serves as the goal for a football team. Goals offer a challenge, something to be reached for, something to be attained. After examining dozens of research studies on goal setting, a pair of organizational behaviorists concluded that

○ Specific goals tend to increase performance.
○ Difficult goals, if accepted, stimulate greater performance than do easy goals.
○ Goal setting is effective at both the managerial and operative levels.

○ Both assigned and participatively set goals are effective at improving performance.[17]

THE ENDS-MEANS CHAIN

As we have seen, the five P's of planning proceed in a logical flow from general to specific. Purpose identification leads to a statement of philosophy. Premises and policies pave the way for plans. In a similar fashion, general strategic objectives pave the way for more specific intermediate objectives which in turn pave the way for highly specific operational objectives. Using different terminology, the downward flow of objectives creates an ends-means chain. As illustrated in Figure 4.4, high-level objectives (ends) are supported

FIGURE 4.4
A typical ends-means chain.

POSITION IN ORGANIZATION	LEVEL OF PLANNING	OBJECTIVE
Corporate president	Strategic	"To increase corporate sales by 15% during the next two years."
		End ↑ Means
Laundry Products Division marketing manager	Intermediate	"To increase market share of 'Soapy Suds' detergent by 5% during the next year."
		End ↑ Means
Regional advertising manager (Atlanta region)	Operational	"To increase 'Soapy Suds' radio advertising spots by 50% during the next three months."

by middle-level objectives (means). These middle-level objectives in turn become ends that require the support of lower-level objectives.

The organizational hierarchy in Figure 4.4 has been telescoped for illustrative purposes. Typically there would be two or three layers of management between the president and the division marketing manager. Three or four more layers would separate the division manager from the regional advertising manager. But the telescoping helps point up the fact that higher-level objectives cannot be achieved unless lower-level objectives provide the necessary means. For example, in Figure 4.4, there are many ways to achieve the president's objective of a 15 percent increase in sales. The Laundry Products Division marketing manager, who is just one of several division managers, has decided that the best way to help contribute to the president's objective, or end, is to sell more Soapy Suds detergent. The division manager's objective provides the necessary *means* to accomplish the president's *end*. And so it goes, down the managerial pyramid, from one level of management to the next. The net result is a hierarchy of objectives that, with appropriate action plans, can be translated into a hierarchy of organizational plans.

ADDING ACTION STATEMENTS

Writing clear, measurable objectives is the most difficult part of formulating specific plans. But this does not diminish the importance of *action statements*, which explain *how* objectives are to be accomplished. Recalling from earlier discussion, a plan consists of both an objective *and* an action statement. When writing action statements, the following questions need to be kept in mind:

1. Can this action be completed with the resources available?
2. Will this action permit the effective, efficient, and timely accomplishment of the objective?

Properly written action statements should leave little doubt about how one intends to accomplish a particular objective. As with any other learned skill, steady practice is the key to writing good action statements.

PLANNING AIDS

Since the turn of the century, a number of planning aids have been developed. These aids have helped many successful managers anticipate and prepare for the future. Three specific planning aids are presented and discussed in this section: (1) flow charts, (2) Gantt charts, and (3) PERT networks. Planners should make sure these aids are in their "tool kits."

SEQUENCING WITH FLOW CHARTS

Although flow charts have achieved their greatest popularity among computer programmers,[18] they should not be overlooked by general planners. Basically, a *flow chart* is a visual device to help sequence significant events. Sequencing simply involves arranging events in the order of desired occurrence. For instance, this book had to be purchased before it could be read. Thus the event "purchase book" would come before the event "read book" in a flow chart sequence.

A sample flow chart is displayed in Figure 4.5. Notice how the chart consists of boxes and diamonds in addition to the start and stop ovals. Each box contains a major event. Each diamond contains a yes or no *decision.*

Planners at all levels of management can identify and properly sequence important events and decisions with flow charts of this kind. In doing so, they are forced to consider all relevant links in a particular endeavor as well as their proper sequence. This is a major advantage because it encourages analytical thinking. On the other hand, flow charts have two disadvantages. First, they do not indicate the time dimension, that is, the varying amounts of time that may be required to complete each step and make each decision. Second, flow charts are not practical for showing details of extremely complex operations. In flowcharting a complex sequence, only major events and decisions should be considered.

SCHEDULING WITH GANTT CHARTS

Gantt charts are named for Henry L. Gantt, who first developed this basic technique.[19] Gantt worked with Frederick W. Taylor at Midvale Steel beginning in 1887 and was a proponent of scientific management. According to a management historian:

> The [Gantt] chart shows output on one axis with units of time on the other. Nothing could be simpler, yet at the time nothing could have been more revolutionary in the area of production control.[20]

Things have changed since the early 1900s, and so have the applications of the Gantt chart. Updated versions of Gantt charts like the one displayed in Figure 4.6 (page 104) are used as a planning aid by managers in many areas.

Figure 4.6 also shows how a Gantt chart can be used for more than simply scheduling the important steps of a job. By filling in the time lines, *actual* progress can be compared easily with *planned* progress. Like flow charts, Gantt charts have the advantage of forcing managers to be analytical, since jobs or projects must be reduced to separate steps. Moreover, Gantt charts improve on flow charts by allowing the planner to specify the *time* to be spent on

**FIGURE 4.5
Planning an evening on
the town**

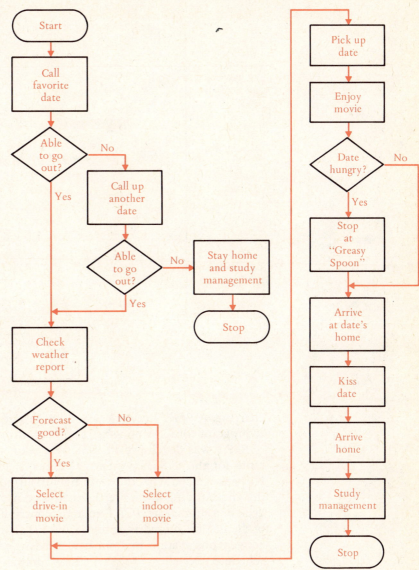

each activity. A disadvantage that Gantt charts share with flow
charts is that overly complex situations are difficult to chart.

**PROGRAMMING WITH
PERT NETWORKS**

Programming amounts to simultaneous sequencing and scheduling.
One of the most popular programming techniques is called PERT,
which is short for Program Evaluation and Review Technique. In a
sense, PERT is a sophisticated synthesis of flow charting and Gantt

FIGURE 4.6
Sample Gantt chart

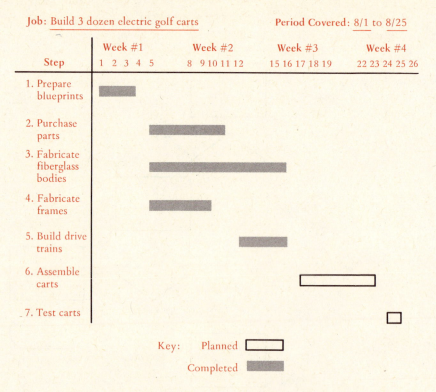

Job: Build 3 dozen electric golf carts   Period Covered: 8/1 to 8/25

charting. A *PERT network* is a visual device that permits managers to program complex projects in spite of uncertainties about timing.

PERT was developed in 1958 by a team of management consultants for the U.S. Navy Special Projects Office. At that time the Navy was faced with the seemingly insurmountable task of designing and building a missile that could be fired underwater from the deck of a submarine. PERT not only contributed to the development of the Polaris submarine project, but it helped bring the sophisticated weapons system to combat readiness nearly two years ahead of schedule. Needless to say, these dramatic results caught the attention of managers around the world. However, as one user of PERT has reflected: "No management technique has ever caused so much enthusiasm, controversy, and disappointment as PERT."[21] Realizing that PERT is not a cure-all but rather a tool with appropriate and inappropriate applications, let us examine it more closely.

In order to understand PERT, we first need to define four key terms relating to it.

○ *Event*   A PERT event is a performance milestone. It represents the start or finish of some activity. An A grade on a management exam is an *event*.

○ *Activity*   A PERT activity represents work in process. Activities are time-consuming. Studying for a management exam is an *activity*.

○ *PERT time*   PERT times are estimated times for the completion of PERT activities. PERT times are weighted averages of three separate time estimates: (1) *optimistic time* (T_o)—the time an activity should take under the best of conditions, (2) *most likely time* (T_m)—the time an activity should take under normal conditions, and (3) *pessimistic time* (T_p)—the time an activity should take under the worst possible conditions. The formula for calculating *estimated* PERT time (T_e) is

$$T_e = \frac{T_o + 4T_m + T_p}{6}$$

○ *Critical path*   A critical path is the chain of activities and events in a PERT network that will take the longest time to complete.[22]

The sample PERT network in Figure 4.7 puts these definitions into a working context. The job is to build three dozen electric golf carts, the same job as that shown in the Gantt chart in Figure 4.6. PERT events are coded by circled letters. PERT activities, shown by lines connecting the PERT events, are coded by number. A PERT time (T_e) has been calculated and recorded for each PERT activity. Study the PERT network in Figure 4.7 to see if you can pick out the critical path. By calculating which path will take the most time from beginning to end, the *critical path* turns out to be A-B-C-F-G-H-I. That path will require an estimated 21¾ workdays to complete. If the project is delayed, it will probably be along this critical path.

It is obvious that PERT networks are much more complex than flow charts or Gantt charts. This complexity leads to both advantages and disadvantages.

On the plus side, PERT is excellent for one-time-only projects such as constructing a new plant or moving from one office building to another. PERT forces managers to do some analytical planning and gives them a tool for predicting the impact of schedule changes. If an activity runs over or under the estimated time, the impact of lost or gained time can be calculated for the entire project. Computerized PERT networks update time estimates very quickly and efficiently. Importantly, PERT also gives managers an opportu-

FIGURE 4.7
Sample PERT network.

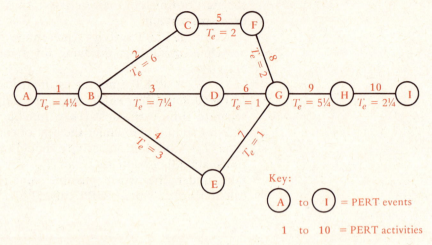

FIGURE 4.7
Sample PERT network.

BUILDING THREE DOZEN ELECTRIC GOLF CARTS

Key:

(A) to (I) = PERT events

1 to 10 = PERT activities

PERT EVENTS

A. Receive contract
B. Begin construction
C. Receive parts
D. Bodies ready for testing
E. Frames ready for testing

F. Drive trains ready for testing
G. Components ready for assembly
H. Carts assembled
I. Carts ready for shipment

PERT ACTIVITIES AND TIMES

ACTIVITIES	T_o	T_m	T_p	T_e*
1. Prepare final blueprints	3	4	6	4¼
2. Purchase parts	4	5	12	6
3. Fabricate bodies	5	7½	9	7¼
4. Fabricate frames	2½	3	4	3
5. Build drive trains	1½	2	3	2
6. Test bodies	½	1	1½	1
7. Test frames	½	1	1½	1
8. Test drive trains	1	1½	5	2
9. Assemble carts	3	5	9	5¼
10. Test carts	1	2	5	2¼

*Rounded to nearest ¼ workday

nity, through the calculation of PERT times, to factor in uncertainty about planning horizons.

On the minus side, PERT networks share with other planning aids the disadvantage of being only as good as the underlying assumptions about events, activities, and estimated times. False assumptions and miscalculations render PERT ineffective. Also, PERT is not appropriate for fixed-sequence jobs such as assembly line work because everything follows a fixed pace dictated by machines. Less costly alternatives, such as flow charts and Gantt charts, are more suitable for relatively simple, repetitive processes. On balance, PERT has great potential for helping managers plan complex, costly, and one-time-only projects.

SUMMARY   Planning appropriately is called the primary management function. It is only through planning that today's managers can prepare to act in an uncertain environment marked by scarce resources.

The five P's of planning represent the basic components of all effective planning systems. They are purpose, philosophy, premises, policies, and plans. Top management, as it engages in strategic planning, is primarily responsible for the first four. Purpose, philosophy, premises, and policies give organization members a general idea of what the organization is supposed to be doing and how it is to be accomplished. Plans translate this general information into specific objectives and action statements. Plans pinpoint *how* a result is to be accomplished as well as *what* and *when*.

Effective planning begins at the top of the organization and works its way downward. The three levels of management engage in three different types of planning. Top management takes care of strategic planning, middle management is responsible for intermediate planning, and lower management is given the job of formulating specific operational plans. Each successively lower level of planning is more specific and covers a shorter time horizon.

Strategic planning is important but often inadequately carried out. It includes identification of environmental opportunities and obstacles, both present and future. While informed judgment is relatively inexpensive and expedient, more precise environmental forecasts are available through surveys and trend analyses. The latter two methods, however, tend to be quite costly and time-consuming. Strategic planning also includes identification of the organization's strengths and weaknesses, finding the right economic and/or social niche, and establishing priorities. The final result of strategic planning should be a firm conviction that the organization is doing the right thing, in the right place, and at the right time.

After strategic planning comes the formulation of a planning system, which begins with a hierarchy of objectives. Objectives at all three levels of planning must specify *what* the intended outcome is, *when* it is to be achieved, and how it can be *measured*. The net result of proper planning is an ends-means chain from the top of the managerial pyramid to the bottom. The planning process is completed by action statements that spell out *how* each objective is to be achieved.

A number of specific techniques have been developed to aid managers in the planning process. Three of them are flow charts, Gantt charts, and PERT networks. Flow charts are useful when it comes to sequencing fairly simple operations. Gantt charts should be brought into play when it becomes necessary to add the time dimension to schedule a number of activities. More complex projects can be programmed with PERT networks. PERT allows managers to take into account uncertainty about planning horizons.

TERMS TO UNDERSTAND

Planning	Niche
Purpose	Priorities
Philosophy	Objective
Premises	Action statement
Policies	Flow chart
Plans	Gantt chart
Strategic planning	PERT network
Intermediate planning	PERT event
Operational planning	PERT activity
Forecast	PERT time
Trend analysis	Critical path

QUESTIONS FOR DISCUSSION

1. Why do an uncertain environment and scarce resources increase the need for planning?
2. What does an organization stand to gain from the planning process? Are there any disadvantages?
3. Can you formulate purpose and philosophy statements for your college or university and/or your place of employment?
4. How do premises and policies influence the planning process?
5. What makes strategic planning so important?
6. Write at least six objectives for projects you are involved in at the present time. Does each one pass all three tests of a good objective?
7. What are suitable action statements for these objectives? Combine your objectives and action statements to form complete plans.

8. Would flow charts help you better plan some of your present activities? Chart one out for practice.

9. What advantage do Gantt charts have over flow charts?

10. How do PERT networks allow managers to cope with uncertain timing?

CASE 4.1
YOU CAN'T PLEASE
ALL THE PEOPLE
ALL THE TIME

As general manager of a southern Arizona copper smelting firm, Fred Briggs reports directly to headquarters in New York. Because strategic planning is centralized at headquarters, Fred has been asked to forward a "situational assessment." Headquarters will use this information for the annual update of strategic plans.

Fred shakes his head in dismay as he signs the final version of his report. The "obstacles and weaknesses" section of the report points to a rocky road ahead. Some of the major items included in this section of the report are:

o Smelting costs are rising because the quality of the local ore is diminishing. Although company geologists estimated a fifty-year reserve of low-grade ore ten years ago, a new geological survey using the latest equipment is needed. The estimated cost is around $2 million.

o The 45-year-old smelter facility is literally falling apart. Approximately $6 million in annual capital improvements and maintenance could stretch the life of the facility to ten more years.

o Copper prices on the world market remain low due to foreign competition.

o A strike is threatened at this time next year if the union's demand for a 9 percent wage hike is not met. This translates to an annual payroll increase of $17 million. Headquarters is holding firm at 5 percent.

o The federal Environmental Protection Agency (EPA) is demanding an 85 percent decrease in sulfur dioxide emissions from the smelter's smokestacks by the end of four years. Given this standard and timetable, the cost could range as high as $135 million, or approximately one-third of the smelter's present book value.

o A petition signed by nearly 4,000 of the town's 7,800 residents was received last month requesting the smelter to rebuild rather than relocate. Relocation of the smelter in another area would skyrocket the town's unemployment rate to 80 percent.

FOR DISCUSSION

1. Summarize this case from the standpoint of planning in an uncertain environment.

2. In your opinion, what should the firm's top priority be? How

would you arrange the other considerations in order of priority?
Defend your position.
3. Which of these obstacles/weaknesses could actually turn out to
be opportunities/strengths?

CASE 4.2
YOU CALL THESE
OBJECTIVES?

Martha Roseman works full time for the United Way, the umbrella
fund-raising organization. Because the United Way distributes the
funds it collects among dozens of private nonprofit agencies serving
the needy and handicapped, a great deal of money must be collected
each year. In her capacity as a regional coordinator of corporate
campaigns, Martha plays an important part in this massive fund-
raising effort. Each year it is her job to gather together a task force of
volunteers from companies in her region to spearhead the annual
corporate campaign drives.

In recent years, Martha's job has gotten tougher and tougher.
There are several contributing factors. Among them are stiff
competition from sophisticated "telethon" campaigns, a scarcity of
capable volunteer managerial talent, and a growing reluctance to
donate due to inflationary pressure on the dollar. Consequently,
Martha's managerial abilities have been pushed to the limit. In fact,
during a preliminary planning meeting of this year's corporate task
force, her managerial ability was bluntly questioned. It seems that
one volunteer campaign manager, on loan from a major airline,
flatly told Martha that her "campaign objectives" weren't objectives
at all. Among the objectives that came into question were the
following:

o Increase average donation per person.
o Increase average donation total per company.
o Increase the number of participating companies.
o Increase volunteer corporate campaign staff.

FOR DISCUSSION

1. Was the volunteer campaign manager's criticism of Martha's
objectives justified?
2. How would you rewrite these objectives to make them technically correct? Feel free to use your imagination to insert realistic
details.
3. How will better objectives help Martha deal with the many
pressures of her job?

REFERENCES   *Opening quotation*

Harold Koontz, "Making Strategic Planning Work," *Business Horizons* 19 (April 1976): 38.

1. Bill Christiansen and Theodore H. Clark, Jr., "A Western Perspective on Energy: A Plea for Rational Energy Planning," *Science* 194 (November 5, 1976): 578.
2. "Texas Instruments Shows U.S. Business How to Survive in the 1980s," *Business Week* #2552 (September 18, 1978): 66–92.
3. Koontz, "Making Strategic Planning Work," p. 38.
4. Peter Lorange and Richard F. Vancil, "How to Design a Strategic Planning System," *Harvard Business Review* 54 (September-October 1976): 75.
5. "At Potlatch, Nothing Happens Without a Plan," *Business Week* #2406 (November 10, 1975): 129–133.
6. Koontz, "Making Strategic Planning Work," p. 37.
7. Richard F. Vancil, "Strategy Formulation in Complex Organizations," *Sloan Management Review* 17 (Winter 1976): 18.
8. See: Lorange and Vancil, "How to Design a Strategic Planning System," p. 78.
9. George A. Steiner, *Top Management Planning* (New York: Macmillan, 1969), p. 17.
10. Arthur M. Louis, "Donald Frey Had a Hunger for the Whole Thing," *Fortune* 94 (September 1976): 141.
11. Rush Loving, Jr., "W. T. Grant's Last Days—As Seen from Store 1192," *Fortune* 93 (April 1976): 108–112, 114.
12. For example, see Howard H. Stevenson, "Defining Corporate Strengths and Weaknesses," *Sloan Management Review* 17 (Spring 1976): 51–68.
13. *Webster's Seventh New Collegiate Dictionary* (Springfield, Mass.: G. & C. Merriam, 1963), pp. 569–570.
14. Vancil, "Strategy Formulation in Complex Organizations," p. 6.
15. Charles D. Flory, ed., *Managers for Tomorrow* (New York: New American Library, 1965), p. 98.
16. Anthony P. Raia, *Managing by Objectives* (Glenview, Ill.: Scott, Foresman, 1974), p. 24.
17. Based on discussion and conclusions found in: Gary P. Latham and Gary A. Yukl, "A Review of Research on the Application of Goal Setting in Organizations," *Academy of Management Journal* 18 (December 1975): 824–845.
18. Marilyn Bohl, *Flowcharting Techniques* (Chicago: Science Research Associates, 1971).

19. For a look at some early Gantt charts, see: H. L. Gantt, *Organizing for Work* (New York: Harcourt, Brace and Howe, 1919), chap. 8.
20. Claude S. George, Jr., *The History of Management Thought*, 2nd ed. (Englewood Cliffs, N.J.: Prentice-Hall, 1972), p. 104.
21. Ivars Avots, "The Management Side of PERT," *California Management Review* 4 (Winter 1962): 16–27.
22. These PERT definitions have been adapted from: John Fertakis and John Moss, "An Introduction to PERT and PERT/Cost systems," *Managerial Planning* 19 (January/February 1971): 24–31.

Chapter 5

Controlling

When the objectives of [an organization] are reasonably coherent and consistent, it is feasible to develop a control system that will reinforce the objectives by measuring the level of accomplishment and its cost.

William H. Sihler

LEARNING OBJECTIVES

When you finish reading this chapter, you should be able to

o Explain how the criteria for organizational effectiveness vary in the near, intermediate, and distant future.
o Explain the difference between feedforward and feedback control.
o Describe at least three kinds of control program.
o Explain why delegation is a challenging control problem.
o Describe how management by objectives integrates the planning and control functions.
o Explain why budget variances are a useful control tool.
o Outline what a good management information system should do.

The separation of planning and control is more a conceptual convenience than a reflection of actual managerial practice. As cornerstones of management, planning and control are basic parts of the management process. Managers plot their future course through planning. But even the most carefully prepared plan is no guarantee of success, since unanticipated events can and do cause plans to go astray. According to the so-called Murphy's Law, "If anything can go wrong, it will!" Perhaps Murphy's Law is a bit too pessimistic. But it does drive home the point that things don't always go according to plan. Managers need to take definite steps to keep things headed in a productive direction. This is where the control function enters the picture. Control complements planning by introducing corrective action as the future becomes the present, as plans become reality. Because control is a key determinant of overall organizational effectiveness, let us explore the concept of organizational effectiveness before defining and discussing control.

ORGANIZATIONAL EFFECTIVENESS

The term *management*, as defined in Chapter 1, highlighted the point that managers must strive to be both effective and efficient. Effectiveness relates to whether or not organizational objectives are accomplished. Efficiency, on the other hand, involves the relationship between inputs and outputs. Theoretically, wasteful organizations may be effective but not efficient. In an era of rapidly diminishing resources and increasing concern about civil rights, however, society has become reluctant to grant the label "effective" to any organization that wastes scarce resources or shortchanges civil rights. Consequently, management's definition of organizational effectiveness requires refinement.

According to one management scholar: "There is no ultimate criterion of effectiveness. Complex organizations pursue multiple goals. Real effectiveness can only be measured relative to a particular set of derived or prescribed goals."[1] More and more, those goals are being prescribed by society in the form of regulations and laws. In the private sector, profitability is no longer the sole criterion of effectiveness. Managers today are caught in a whole cobweb of regulations and laws covering employment practices, working conditions, job safety, pensions, product safety, pollution, and competitive practices. To be truly effective, today's organization must not only achieve its own goals, but it must also satisfy the requirements imposed by society.

Any refinement of the concept of organizational effectiveness would be incomplete if we were to leave out the time dimension. As indicated in Figure 5.1, the organization needs to be effective in the near future, the intermediate future, and the distant future. Consequently, *organizational effectiveness* can be defined as meeting organizational objectives and societal expectations in the near, intermediate, and distant future. Most people think only of the near future. It is in the near future that the organization has to produce goods and services, use resources efficiently, and satisfy those both inside and outside the organization with its progress. But things do not abruptly end there. If the organization fails to adapt to new environmental demands and does not develop in the intermediate future, its effectiveness will decline. If it does adapt and develop, it will probably grow. Above all, in a long-run perspective, the truly effective organization survives. Without survival there can be no subsequent near or intermediate future. An organization needs to be effective through all time dimensions if it is to survive. This can only happen when carefully conceived plans are followed up by judicious control.

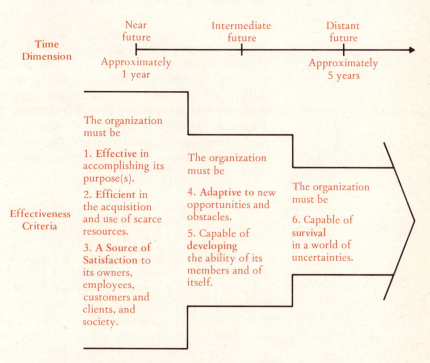

FIGURE 5.1
The time dimension of organization effectiveness

Adapted with permission from James L. Gibson, John M. Ivancevich, and James H. Donnelly, Jr., *Organizations: Behavior, Structure, Processes*, rev. ed. (Dallas: Business Publications, Inc., © 1976), p. 65.

CONTROL DEFINED   Mere mention of the word *control* brings to mind actions involving the checking, testing, regulation, or verification of something. As a management function, *control* can be defined as the process of making sure that organizational objectives are accomplished effectively and efficiently as planned. Objectives are yardsticks against which actual performance can be measured. If actual performance is consistent with the appropriate objective, then things should proceed as planned. If not, then changes need to be made. Just as a driver controls a car by detecting potential hazards and steering around them, a manager needs to detect deviations from desirable standards and make appropriate adjustments. Those adjustments can range from ordering more raw materials to overhauling a production line; from discarding an unnecessary procedure to hiring additional personnel. While the possible adjustments exercised during the control function are countless, the purpose of the control function is always the same: *objectives are to be achieved as efficiently as possible in spite of environmental, organizational, and behavioral obstacles and uncertainties.*

TYPES OF CONTROL   Some managers find it productive to view organizations in open-system terms. As discussed in Chapter 2, every open system processes inputs from the surrounding environment to produce a unique set of outputs. Natural open systems such as the human body are self-controlled through automatic feedback mechanisms. Man-made open systems such as work organizations, in contrast, are lacking in automatic controls. They require constant monitoring and adjustment to control for deviations from standard. Figure 5.2

FIGURE 5.2
Feedforward and feedback
control

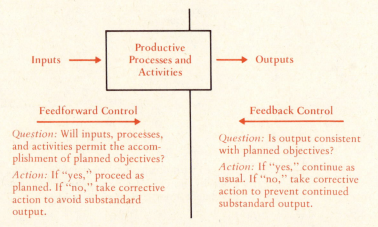

Inputs ⟶   **Productive Processes and Activities**   ⟶ Outputs

Feedforward Control ⟶

Question: Will inputs, processes, and activities permit the accomplishment of planned objectives?

Action: If "yes," proceed as planned. If "no," take corrective action to avoid substandard output.

⟵ Feedback Control

Question: Is output consistent with planned objectives?

Action: If "yes," continue as usual. If "no," take corrective action to prevent continued substandard output.

illustrates the control function. Notice that there are two types of control, feed*forward* control and feed*back* control.

According to two early proponents of feedforward control, "the only way [managers] can exercise control effectively is to see the problems coming in time to do something about them."[2] *Feedforward control* is the active anticipation of problems and their timely solution, rather than passive reaction. Naturally, anticipation can be effective only if management has a clear idea of how things ought to proceed. At this point planning and control link together. When an operation has been thoroughly planned out, perhaps through the use of flow charts, Gantt charts, or PERT networks, deviations from standard can be spotted while the work is still in process. For instance, if the purchasing manager in a home appliance manufacturing company alerts the production and marketing managers to a delay in the receipt of an important subcomponent, corrective steps can be taken to avoid costly delays. The production manager can reschedule the workload, and the marketing manager can negotiate a new delivery date for the final product. This type of feedforward control helps managers adjust to unexpected changes *before* rather than after it is too late.

Feedback control is beneficial because it permits managers to use information on past performance to bring future performance into line with planned objectives and acceptable standards. Basically, *feedback control* consists of information about a completed activity, evaluation of that information, and steps to improve similar activities in the future. For example, by monitoring the complaints from discharged patients about billing errors, a hospital's comptroller learns that the performance of billing clerks requires attention. Some critics, however, say that the effectiveness of feedback control is limited because it takes place *after* mistakes have been made. Since corrective action takes time, costly problems and deviations from standard tend to persist.

A second benefit of feedback control is that it tests the quality and validity of objectives and standards. Objectives that prove impossible to attain need to be made more reasonable. Those that prove too lenient need to be bolstered. For example, a bank loan officer may discover that too much potentially profitable business is being turned away because the credit-granting criteria are too strict. By exercising feedback control in the form of loosening the credit standards that loan applicants must meet, the bank's lending operation can be made more profitable. Of course, if this adjustment leads to a default rate that eats up the additional profits, then the credit criteria will have to be tightened up again through feedback control.

In summary, it is important for managers of complex organizational systems to rely on both feedforward and feedback control. Feedforward control helps managers avoid mistakes in the first place; feedback control keeps them from repeating past mistakes. A combination of feedforward and feedback control is necessary to strike an appropriate balance between effectiveness and efficiency.

CONTROL IN ACTION

Typically, like the planning and control functions, feedforward and feedback control are not neatly separated in day-in, day-out activity. The two types of control are blended together in most ongoing control programs. There are at least three different control programs in most productive organizations: inventory, quality, and financial performance. Each focuses on a special area of organizational activity, yet all three are needed for organizational effectiveness.

CONTROLLING INVENTORY

Organizations that produce goods and services tend to have a great deal of working capital tied up in inventory. There are raw material and subcomponent inventories, unfinished goods inventories, and finished goods inventories. No matter what type of inventory is involved, management faces a two-edged cost problem. On the one hand, costly delays, emergency orders, and unmet commitments result from inventory shortages. On the other, excessive storage and carrying costs, and possible loss due to spoilage and obsolescence, result from inventory surpluses. Consequently, a sophisticated science of inventory control has evolved to optimize inventory levels and costs.

The experience of Devro, Inc., for example, shows how systematic inventory control can cut costs.[3] The Lubbock, Texas, firm manufactures edible protein sausage casings for both domestic and foreign use in sausage making. Because the firm's production operation is highly mechanized, a stock of more than one thousand different kinds of spare machine parts must be kept on hand for preventive maintenance and repairs.

For years, the firm's inventory procedure called for periodic review of the spare parts inventory and reordering as needed. Inventory excesses and shortages were common. Frequently, a machine would break down, it would be discovered that the needed part was not in stock, and an emergency order would have to go out. Because emergency orders often did not go to suppliers offering the lowest prices and because air freight rather than cheaper ground transportation was used, Devro's inventory costs mushroomed.

Then the company took the situation in hand. By taking time to

"WITHIN THESE GIVEN PARAMETERS IT'S ADVISABLE TO STRENGTHEN OUR CASH FLOW WHILE MAXIMIZING THE VIABLE COST-PRICE RATIO. ORDER MORE JELLYBEANS."

identify the relatively few parts that accounted for most of the inventory expense (feedback) and by streamlining the ordering procedure for these priority parts (feedforward), the firm cut its annual air freight charges alone by 45.8 percent. Part of the streamlining involved printing all specifications for the priority parts directly on the requisition forms. This procedure eliminated the time-consuming search for specifications every time an order went out. The overhaul in the inventory control program saved money and enhanced Devro's organizational effectiveness in a number of other ways as well.

CONTROLLING QUALITY

Quality has always been a concern of productive organizations. It is well known that if a product fails to work properly, customer dissatisfaction will grow, sales will drop, and profits will decline. The relationship between product quality and profitability may be indirect, but it is critical. Recent events have underscored the importance of quality control. Here *product liability* enters the picture, the concept that companies are legally responsible for the safety of their products. Increasingly, customers who are injured or have their property damaged by a faulty product are turning to the courts. Not only have product liability lawsuits increased in number but the average settlement has increased as well. According to the U.S. Department of Commerce, the average product liability settlement rose from $11,644 in 1965 to $79,943 in 1973. Settlements topping $1 million are not uncommon today. In response to the dramatic rise in product liability insurance premiums, "many big corporations are spending vast sums on rigorous programs of product inspection and quality control in order to lessen their risks of being sued."[4]

Quality control expert Edward M. Schrock firmly believes that "it is always cheaper to make it right the first time" because of the burdensome costs of scrap, rework, customer complaints, and product recalls. He advises managers to keep an eye on the following quality control "hot spots":

1. *Raw materials*   What is the quality of incoming raw material?
2. *Receiving and stores*   Are raw materials and purchased subcomponents subject to damage during shipment or deterioration during storage?
3. *Manufacturing*   Will existing machines consistently produce goods of desired quality?
4. *Assembly*   Can parts be put together wrong or damaged during assembly?
5. *Inspecting and testing*   Are existing quality control equipment and procedures capable of producing accurate results?
6. *Packaging and shipping*   What is the danger of finished goods being damaged during packaging or shipment?
7. *Field experience*   What are the problems encountered by consumers?[5]

With a few changes in wording here and there, these quality considerations can be translated to fit service industries and nonprofit organizations as well. Hospital patients, government agency clients, restaurant patrons, and students demand quality, too. Like the need for management, the need for quality control is universal.

CONTROLLING FINANCIAL PERFORMANCE

Medical doctors would not think of recommending further tests or offering a diagnosis without first monitoring the patient's vital signs. By comparing the patient's pulse, temperature, and blood pressure with accepted standards, the doctor is in a much better position to recommend further tests or corrective action. Similarly, managers require a convenient way to check the vital signs of their organizations. *Financial ratios*, measures that compare the financial performance of an organization with industry standards, often fill this need. Financial ratios can be classified into four basic types.

1. *Liquidity ratios*, which measure the firm's ability to meet its maturing short-term obligations.
2. *Leverage ratios*, which measure the extent to which the firm has been financed by debt.
3. *Activity ratios*, which measure how effectively the firm is using its resources.
4. *Profitability ratios*, which measure management's overall effectiveness as shown by the returns generated on sales and investment.[6]

By calculating the various ratios in each area, as described in Table 5.1, and then comparing them with industry standards compiled and published by such firms as Dun & Bradstreet, Inc., managers can generate the financial guidelines they need to exercise feedforward and feedback control.

As with quality control, financial ratios are not restricted to use by profit-making businesses. They may be used quite effectively to assess the financial health of nonprofit organizations as well.[7]

DELEGATION: A UNIQUE CONTROL PROBLEM

Former President Harry S Truman is said to have had a little sign on his White House desk that read, "The Buck Stops Here!" Just as President Truman had his ultimate responsibilities, which he could not pass along to others, managers also have key responsibilities they cannot pass along. However, managers can and should involve subordinates in the process of meeting their key responsibilities.

The process of assigning to subordinates the authority to carry out specified duties is called *delegation*. For example, a personnel manager may delegate to an assistant the job of recruiting minorities. By delegating certain clearly defined jobs to subordinates the

TABLE 5.1
Using ratios for financial
control

RATIO	FORMULA FOR CALCULATION
Liquidity	
Current	$\dfrac{\text{current assets}}{\text{current liabilities}}$
Quick, or Acid, Test	$\dfrac{\text{current assets} - \text{inventory}}{\text{current liabilities}}$
Leverage	
Debt to Total Assets	$\dfrac{\text{total debt}}{\text{total assets}}$
Times Interest Earned	$\dfrac{\text{profit before taxes plus interest charges}}{\text{interest charges}}$
Fixed Charge Coverage	$\dfrac{\text{income available for meeting fixed charges}}{\text{fixed charges}}$
Activity	
Inventory Turnover	$\dfrac{\text{sales}}{\text{inventory}}$
Average Collection Period	$\dfrac{\text{receivables}}{\text{sales per day}}$
Fixed Assets Turnover	$\dfrac{\text{sales}}{\text{fixed assets}}$
Total Assets Turnover	$\dfrac{\text{sales}}{\text{total assets}}$
Profitability	
Profit Margin on Sales	$\dfrac{\text{net profit after taxes}}{\text{sales}}$
Return on Total Assets	$\dfrac{\text{net profit after taxes}}{\text{total assets}}$
Return on Net Worth	$\dfrac{\text{net profit after taxes}}{\text{net worth}}$

TABLE 5.1 *(cont.)*

CALCULATION	INDUSTRY AVERAGE	EVALUATION
$\dfrac{\$\ 700,000}{\$\ 300,000} = 2.3$ times	2.5 times	Satisfactory
$\dfrac{\$\ 400,000}{\$\ 300,000} = 1.3$ times	1.0 times	Good
$\dfrac{\$1,000,000}{\$2,000,000} = 50$ percent	33 percent	Poor
$\dfrac{\$\ 270,000}{\$\ 70,000} = 3.9$ times	8.0 times	Poor
$\dfrac{\$\ 298,000}{\$\ 98,000} = 3.04$ times	5.5 times	Poor
$\dfrac{\$3,000,000}{\$\ 300,000} = 10.0$ times	9.0 times	Satisfactory
$\dfrac{\$\ 200,000}{\$\ 8,333} = 24$ days	20 days	Satisfactory
$\dfrac{\$3,000,000}{\$1,300,000} = 2.3$ times	5.0 times	Poor
$\dfrac{\$3,000,000}{\$2,000,000} = 1.5$ times	2.0 times	Poor
$\dfrac{\$\ 120,000}{\$3,000,000} = 4$ percent	5 percent	Fair
$\dfrac{\$\ 120,000}{\$2,000,000} = 6.0$ percent	10 percent	Poor
$\dfrac{\$\ 120,000}{\$1,000,000} = 12.0$ percent	15 percent	Fair

personnel manager, like any other manager, can avoid becoming swamped in endless details. One of the most common causes of managerial failure is reluctance to delegate authority to others. Managers who try to attend to every little detail themselves are headed for trouble.

Suppose for the moment that the personnel manager willingly delegates important duties to subordinates. This situation then gives rise to a special control problem, since managers can delegate authority but not responsibility. The ultimate responsibility for successfully recruiting minorities is still the personnel manager's. The manager must assess subordinate performance periodically to make sure the work is completed in a timely and effective manner. This kind of assessment requires standards against which subordinate performance can be measured. As discussed in Chapter 4, the most appropriate standard is a plan based on a clear, challenging, yet attainable objective.

Delegation can be a tricky business. Managers have to trust subordinates to get jobs done according to plan rather than simply do the jobs themselves. This kind of trust involves a degree of risk that some managers are unwilling to accept, and so they avoid delegating. The whole issue of delegation forces managers to live with one of two risks. On the one hand, the risk of personal failure is great if they do not delegate. On the other hand, managers who delegate run the risk of having their trust betrayed. The best way to deal with this dilemma is to surround oneself with skilled and motivated subordinates who respond favorably to challenging objectives. In this manner, managerial time can be used efficiently, and trust is rewarded when subordinates perform satisfactorily.

Whatever the degree of delegation or the specific control program, managers can control the organization much more effectively if they are familiar with three specific control techniques. They are (1) management by objectives, (2) budgets, and (3) management information systems. All three are in wide use today.

CONTROL THROUGH MANAGEMENT BY OBJECTIVES

Management by objectives (MBO) is a comprehensive management system based on measurable and participatively set objectives. MBO has come a long way since it was first suggested by Peter Drucker in 1954 as a way of promoting managerial self-control.[8] In one form or another, and under one label or another, MBO has been adopted by a great many organizations around the world. Most large and many small organizations in both the public and private sectors have tried MBO. This activity is not surprising when one realizes that, as George Odiorne, a leading spokesman for MBO, has pointed out, there are over 700 books, articles, and technical papers on MBO.[9]

MBO currently is the closest thing there is to a universal management technique. The common denominator that has made MBO-type programs so popular is an emphasis on objectives that are *measurable* and *participatively set.* As might be expected with such a widely known and widely used technique, MBO has been both praised and criticized.

A MANAGEMENT SYSTEM

From a relatively simple performance appraisal technique, MBO has evolved to a complex planning and control tool and finally to a comprehensive management system. According to one MBO expert:

> Within the past few years MBO has emerged as a system designed to integrate key management processes and activities in a logical and consistent manner. These include the development of overall organizational goals and strategic plans, problem solving and decision making, performance appraisal, executive compensation, manpower planning, and management training and development.[10]

When MBO is applied as a comprehensive management system, it is not something added on to the manager's job; instead it is a way of doing the manager's job.

THE MBO CYCLE

At the heart of MBO is the four-step cycle illustrated in Figure 5.3. Steps 1 and 2 make up the planning phase, while steps 3 and 4 comprise the control phase. MBO effectively integrates the planning and control functions of management, as we can see when we examine the MBO cycle step by step.

Step 1 is to set objectives. This is obviously important, since the success of all subsequent steps depends on establishing clear and internally consistent objectives. Objective setting must begin at the top of the managerial pyramid and filter down, as discussed in Chapter 4. MBO's primary contribution to the objective-setting process is an emphasis on the participation and involvement of subordinates.

> The underlying assumption is that involvement leads to commitment, and if an employee is committed he will be motivated to perform in a manner that directly contributes to the achievement of organizational objectives.[11]

Step 2, the development of plans, completes the planning phase of the MBO cycle. Managers at each level develop plans that incorporate the objectives established in step 1. Higher managers see to it

**FIGURE 5.3
The MBO cycle**

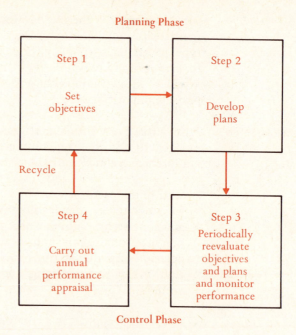

Adapted from a general MBO model found in William E. Reif and Gerald Bassford, "What MBO Really Is," *Business Horizons* 16 (June 1973): 23–30.

that their subordinates' plans complement one another and do not work at cross-purposes.

The control phase begins during step 3, the periodic monitoring of performance. MBO experts typically recommend superior-subordinate meetings at three-, six-, and nine-month intervals. These periodic checkups permit those who are responsible for a particular objective to determine if it is still valid. If it is not, an adjustment is made. Otherwise, progress toward its successful achievement is assessed. Periodic checkups also give managers an excellent opportunity to provide subordinates with much-needed and appreciated feedback.

During step 4 annual performance is matched with previously agreed-to objectives. Emphasis is on results, not personalities or excuses. The control cycle is completed as success is rewarded with promotion, merit pay, or other benefits, and failure is flagged for future corrective action. When appraising performance during steps 3 and 4, managers should keep the following behavioral principles in mind:

○ *Principle of participation*   Motivation tends to increase as participation in decision making and objective setting increases.

- *Principle of feedback* Motivation tends to increase when employees know where they stand.
- *Principle of reciprocated interest* Motivation tends to increase when the pursuit of organizational objectives is accompanied by the achievement of personal objectives.
- *Principle of recognition* Motivation to achieve organizational objectives tends to increase when employees are recognized for their contributions.[12]

After one round of MBO the cycle repeats itself, with each cycle contributing to the learning process. Higher productivity through more realistic objectives and more comprehensive control is the natural by-product of a well-developed MBO system.

BARRIERS TO SUCCESSFUL MBO

A number of valuable lessons have been learned from the widespread application of MBO. Among them are the reasons why MBO does *not* work.[13] Any one of the following three barriers can deal a fatal blow to an otherwise well-designed and well-intentioned MBO program.

Lack of top-management commitment Like the planning process, MBO must start at the top and filter down one level at a time. If top management gives only lip service to the importance of implementing a workable MBO program, then the chances of success will be greatly diminished. It stands to reason that subordinate managers cannot be expected to value something their bosses obviously do not value. As visible role models, top managers can best reinforce the importance of the MBO program by performing in accordance with it. They must carefully set their own objectives and patiently cooperate with the subordinates who bring the next layer of objectives into line.

Lack of trust and participation As mentioned earlier, delegation is a troublesome control problem. This is particularly true when higher managers do not trust lower managers enough to let them participate in the objective-setting process. An absence of subordinate participation can lead to alienation among those who feel that objectives are being forced on them. Subordinates who actively take part in setting objectives tend to see those objectives as "ours." Imposed objectives, in contrast, tend to be viewed as "theirs." The probability of personal commitment is much higher when one has a personal stake in the objectives one is expected to achieve.

Unrealistic expectations   When it comes to expectations, managers are just like everyone else. We all tend to be disappointed when actual experience does not live up to our lofty expectations. Unfortunately, overzealous accounts of successful MBO programs have fostered some unrealistic expectations among potential adopters. Many managers expect prompt and dramatic results from the implementation of MBO. In fact, it typically takes five or more years for even a moderate-sized organization to evolve a full-blown MBO system that ties together such areas as planning, control, performance appraisal, and the reward/punishment system. It takes time for each layer of management to be introduced to the steps in the MBO cycle, try them out, and learn through trial and error to carry them out effectively.

CONTROL THROUGH BUDGETING   Many experts feel that budgets are an excellent control device because they keep track of the flow of money into, through, and out of the organization. The importance of money in measuring organizational effectiveness, of course, is that it serves as a common language for describing and comparing unlike goods, services, processes, and activities. It is a convenient common denominator. Profit-making businesses acquire revenue through the sale of goods or services. Nonprofit-making organizations acquire money through fees, appropriations, grants, or voluntary contributions. Both profit-making and nonprofit-making organizations try (1) to acquire enough revenue to meet their objectives and (2) to stretch their dollars farther by keeping costs in line. *Budgets*, which may be defined as formally prepared projections of revenues and costs over a specified time period, serve as a measuring stick for both these purposes. (Technically, a projection of revenues and costs is an operating budget. There are also capital budgets, which keep track of capital sources and uses, and financial budgets, which keep track of cash flow and balance sheet items.) Because all budgets are projections, or plans, of future events, they provide managers with standards for control.

BUDGET VARIANCE AS A CONTROL TOOL   Like MBO, budgets have a planning phase and a control phase. Planning takes place when the budget figures are projected for a given period of time. Control occurs when actual figures are compared with budgeted figures. The difference between the actual figures and the budget is called a *budget variance*. Obviously, if variances occur, managers would like to see favorable variances. A look at the operating budget displayed in Table 5.2 shows that things do not always work out this way. Whether variances are favorable or not, a great deal can be learned by studying them. For instance, the $11,000 unfavorable variance in direct labor expense in Table 5.2 should prompt management to search for the cause. Perhaps too much was spent on costly overtime. Favorable variances should trigger control action in the form of tightening future budget figures. Following up on variances is vital for feedback control.

MAKING BUDGETS FLEXIBLE

One shortcoming of the standard type of budget illustrated in Table 5.2 is that it limits managers to feed*back* control. It lets managers assess financial performance only after the fact. A *flexible budget* is a technique involving the use of standardized costs that allows managers to exercise feed*forward* control over the expenditure of funds. In a flexible budget, standard costs are calculated from past records or on the basis of informed judgment. These standard costs are tied to revenue. For example, assume that the standard cost for direct labor is $1 for every $2 of revenue, or a ratio of 1 to 2. After three months, $95,000 has been spent for direct labor while $142,500 has been received in revenue. Since the ratio of direct labor cost to revenue is now 1.33 to 2, management knows that something needs to be done to limit spending on direct labor. Flexible budgets based on standard costs allow managers to keep a running tab on financial performance, so that they can take corrective action immediately instead of waiting until the entire budget period has elapsed.[14]

BUDGETS HAVE MOTIVATIONAL IMPACT

Realistic budgets established with the full participation of responsible managers can motivate high performance. Once again, commitment is the key. Participation encourages commitment, but performance appraisal and rewards enter the picture as well. "When managers realize that their level of compensation and their upward

TABLE 5.2
Budget variances

			Variance	
	Budget	*Actual*	*Favorable*	*Unfavorable*
XYZ COMPANY				
Operating Budget for the Year ____				
Revenue	$325,000	$329,350	$4,350	
Expenses				
Direct Labor	195,000	206,000		$11,000
Materials	70,000	67,200	2,800	
Overhead	35,000	33,700	1,300	
	300,000	306,900		
Pretax Profit	$ 25,000	$ 22,450		2,550

mobility depend to a large degree on their performance, their commitment to budgeted objectives may be enhanced."[15] However, if budgets are arbitrarily imposed by top management, loosely tied to performance appraisal, and associated with punishment rather than reward, then they will hamper rather than motivate performance.

ELIMINATING BUDGET GAMES WITH ZERO-BASE BUDGETING

Although budgets have done much through the years to improve managerial planning and control, they have also prompted some cat-and-mouse games between those who request funds and those who distribute them. These *budget games* might be defined as tactics motivated by distrust between superiors and subordinates that result in unreasonably high budgets and expenditures. In some organizations, it is common practice to pad the budget by following two unwritten rules. The first is to "ask for more than you need." This tactic makes a lot of sense to managers who have consistently received less than they requested in the past. The second unwritten rule of budget games is to "spend everything you get." The rationale for this second tactic is that higher management typically sees a year-end budget surplus as a sign that the budget was too big to begin with. Consequently, to avoid suffering budget cuts the following year, managers tend to spend their entire budget, even if it means a wasteful spending binge at the year's end. For instance, one government official used up his budget surplus at the end of the fiscal year by purchasing filing cabinets that none of his staff needed or wanted. Although the psychology of budget games makes sense, they are responsible for chronic waste and inefficiency.

Among the many solutions recommended, zero-base budgeting is one of the most promising. Under traditional budgeting schemes managers create their new budgets by adding to, subtracting from, or otherwise modifying their present budgets. This is fine, if the present budget is realistic. Unfortunately, this practice often creates worse budgets out of already bad budgets and encourages the budget games just discussed. A practical alternative is *zero-base budgeting*, a technique for building budgets from the ground level up without consideration of past budgets. Managers using zero-base budgeting start from scratch by identifying separate activities in their areas of responsibility along with associated costs and benefits. The manager arranges the activities in order of priority in accordance with organizational objectives. This process is repeated at each higher level of management, integrating ever wider areas of the organization, until the priorities for the entire organization are clearly understood. Finally, available funds are allocated down the list of priorities until the funds are exhausted. This approach forces each organizational activity to stand on its own merit. The claim ''but we've always done it this way'' becomes irrelevant.

Zero-base budgeting is not a panacea; it does not work equally well in all situations. It appears to be more appropriate for areas with a great many discretionary expenditures, such as marketing or research and development. Areas such as production, where many costs are clearly tied to the level of output, may benefit little from zero-base budgeting. Complaints about existing zero-base budgeting programs stem from the increased effort, paperwork, and expense of pinpointing cost-benefit activities year after year. Large organizations may have tens of thousands of such activities. Identifying valid measures for support functions such as personnel and finance is also a stumbling block. It takes on-the-spot judgment to determine whether zero-base budgeting is appropriate for a given situation.

> There is good and bad in zero-base budgeting. Only you know the budgeting problems of your organization; whether you need to really dig into program costs; whether you have the talent to meaningfully review the budget; and whether the operating environment of the organization would be receptive to a zero-base program.[16]

CONTROL THROUGH MANAGEMENT INFORMATION SYSTEMS

If managers are to carry out their control responsibilites in an efficient manner, they require ready access to current information concerning what, when, and how things have happened in their spheres of influence. Managers who don't anticipate, read, and react to changes in the organization's vital signs cannot do their jobs well, if at all. Information is the lifeblood of problem-solving management. Full-fledged, computerized *management information systems* (MIS) have been developed to integrate the collection, handling, and transmission of information so that the right manager gets the right information at the right time. Management information systems can be a tremendous boon to the control function.

WHAT SHOULD A GOOD MIS DO?

Management information systems may vary in sophistication all the way from traditional pencil-and-paper voucher systems to modern electronic computer systems with remote input-output terminals. Nevertheless, the basic purpose remains the same.

> The purpose of an MIS is to raise the process of managing from the level of piecemeal spotty information, intuitive guesswork, and isolated problem solving to the level of systems insights, systems information, sophisticated data processing, and systems problem solving.[17]

In short, the movement of information into, through, and out of complex organizations cannot be left to chance. It must be managed systematically. When managers evaluate the management information systems they have created and are using, they should ask themselves the following five questions:

1. Does the system support the objectives of the organization and its subunits?
2. Does the system enhance rather than violate formal authority?
3. Are managers provided with information they can and *do* use?
4. Is information sent to those who can do something about it?
5. Do managers receive the information they need in time to act?[18]

Information systems that fail to satisfy one or more of these criteria are probably a waste of time and money. Even a mountain of information becomes useless if it goes to the wrong person or to the right person at the wrong time.

FITTING THE SYSTEM TO THE PEOPLE   Time and time again, computer and information specialists create technically sound management information systems that fail miserably. According to these specialists, managers who are supposed to use the MIS don't know what they are doing and are resistant to change. Although the specialists may be partly correct, they are probably overlooking the fact that they tend to be systematic thinkers, whereas line managers tend to be intuitive thinkers. Intuitive thinkers like to grab a few facts and run. Consequently, a major MIS problem from their viewpoint is that it produces a flood of too much information rather than too little. "Many efforts at 'scientific management' have foundered because managers have been unable to make sense of the mass of information that was provided, often in relatively undigested form and in bulky computer printout format."[19]

The key appears to be tailor-made management information systems. One leading critic of unrealistic management information systems has made the following recommendations:

> To build an MIS relevant for managers, the designer might begin by finding out what information a particular manager really needs by studying what he seeks, what he receives, and what he uses.
> The MIS designer can then piece together a carefully designed information system that not only covers more channels but also does much of the manager's scanning and filtering for him.[20]

Management information systems with an individual orientation are a bright spot on the control horizon.

SUMMARY   Planning and control are complementary functions that enable managers to be effective in the near, intermediate, and distant future. Unfortunately, after plans are made, events do not always go accordingly. Control is therefore needed as a complement to planning. Managers exercise control when they make adjustments, either during or after the implementation of a plan, to make sure that organizational objectives are met as effectively and efficiently as possible. Monitoring organizational inputs, processes, and outputs should result in a combination of feedforward and feedback control. Key organizational areas requiring control are inventory, quality, and financial performance. Delegation, which involves giving subordinates the authority to carry out specified duties, allows managers to devote their attention to nonroutine and important matters. At the same time, delegation increases the need for reliable control, since the manager is still responsible for seeing that objectives are met.

Three practical and tested control tools are management by objectives (MBO), budgets, and management information systems (MIS). The key to successful MBO is an effective integration of the planning and control functions by using objectives developed through the active participation of all involved as a measuring stick for performance. Budgets are helpful because they translate organizational objectives into monetary terms, thus providing a common language for widely varying activities. With care, managers can enhance the flexibility and motivational potential of budgets. Zero-base budgets, though criticized for being time-consuming, serve to eliminate costly budget games by forcing managers to justify specific activities on a cost-benefit basis. They also help top management evaluate all the organization's activities and allocate resources to those with the highest priorities. Management information systems enhance managerial control by providing the right managers with the right information at the right time. It is important to fit an MIS to the individual manager rather than vice versa.

TERMS TO UNDERSTAND

Organizational effectiveness
Control
Feedforward control
Feedback control
Product liability
Financial ratios
Delegation
Management by objectives (MBO)

Budgets
Budget variance
Flexible budget
Budget games
Zero-base budgeting
Management information systems (MIS)

1. How does control complement planning?
2. Why are both feedforward and feedback control necessary in today's organizations?
3. Can you suggest an inventory control program for a fast food restaurant?
4. Can you outline a quality control program for skate boards?
5. In what ways do basic behavioral principles contribute to the success of management by objectives?
6. What makes MBO fail?
7. How do budgets influence managerial performance?
8. What is the psychology of budget games and how can they be neutralized?
9. What are some of the advantages and disadvantages of zero-base budgeting?
10. If you were the owner of an auto repair shop, what elements would you want to integrate into your management information system?

CASE 5.1
A RECIPE FOR
RUBBER?

Reliable Rubber Company manufactures hydraulic hoses for use in heavy construction equipment and vehicles. Because the hoses must hold up under severe pressure and physical abuse, only the highest quality raw materials are used, and wire mesh is bonded right into the hose during the sophisticated fabrication process. The rubber mixing operation is especially important because it is the first major step in the costly production process. Mistakes or delays at that point ripple through the entire fabrication process.

When the raw chemicals used in making synthetic rubber arrive at the plant, an inspector checks each barrel for purity and evidence of water damage in shipment. Next, the bulk lots are broken down into conveniently handled and lábeled packets ranging in weight from one to twenty pounds. From then on everything is in the hands of the Banbury machine operators. Looking something like huge, front-loading, automatic washing machines, the Banbury machines make rubber out of an assortment of chemical compounds. Since each type of rubber is produced from a different combination of chemicals, the Banbury operators follow "recipes." These recipes must be followed exactly. After loading the Banbury according to a particular recipe, the operator mixes the product for a specified period of time at the appropriate pressure and temperature. At the conclusion of the mixing operation, a lever is tripped and the batch of hot rubber drops one floor onto rollers for kneading and further processing.

During the rolling operation another worker cuts off a small piece of rubber and sends it to the quality control office through a pneumatic tube. If the sample does not pass all the various quality control tests, then the quality control inspector calls the Banbury area. The Banbury operator responsible for the bad batch is told what the deficiency is, and the two individuals try to figure out what went wrong. Typically, careless deviation from the recipe is the problem. Sometimes, due to a backlog in the quality control room, the Banbury operators may turn out as many as a half dozen bad batches before being notified that something is wrong. Bad batches cannot be recovered and must be thrown away. The accounting department has calculated that Reliable Rubber loses approximately $350 for each batch rejected.

FOR DISCUSSION

1. What evidence of feedforward and feedback control can you find in this situation?
2. In this case, why is feedforward control superior to feedback control?
3. What changes would you recommned in Reliable's quality control program?

CASE 5.2
CARRY A
BIG STICK

Ann Romano is the dairy products manager for American Agriproducts, Inc. She is responsible for the work of 350 people and oversees an annual budget of over $17 million. Since coming to American a year ago after leaving a lower-paying government post with the Department of Agriculture, Ann has been a vigorous promoter of management by objectives (MBO). Ann learned to appreciate the value of a sound MBO program when she worked for the government under a division head who had built a model MBO system through the years. She was particularly impressed with the way her former division head got the best out of his managers without "breathing down their necks."

Ann's efforts to get American to start the wheels rolling on an MBO program recently paid off when a team of outside consultants was brought in to conduct an introductory MBO seminar. In spite of the fact that the president and two of American's four vice presidents were unable to attend the kickoff seminar, Ann remained enthusiastic about the firm's adoption of MBO. Just yesterday, however, Ann's enthusiasm was dampened considerably by a memo from the president's office. The president, whose favorite saying is "Walk softly and carry a big stick," sent the following memo to all of American's managers.

MEMO

TO: All Managers
FROM: President, American Agriproducts, Inc.
SUBJECT: The New Management by Objectives (MBO) Program

I understand that the MBO kickoff seminar went very well last month. Unfortunately, I was unable to attend because of important trade negotiations in New York City with the French government. I am confident that my vice presidents represented me satisfactorily during this critical step toward greater productivity at American Agriproducts.

As you all know, there is a big difference between words and action. Thus I expect each of you to have a final copy of your objectives for the next calendar year in your superior's hands by two weeks from today. There will be no excuses! We are all busy. Furthermore, to make sure that MBO works at American, your performance for each quarter next year will be measured by those objectives. Those of you who do not measure up will be dealt with accordingly.

Thank you for your continued enthusiastic support of our new MBO program. I am sure you all share my belief that we can have a comprehensive, top-to-bottom MBO system in force at American Agriproducts by this time next year.

FOR DISCUSSION

1. Why does Ann now feel less enthusiastic about the prospects for MBO at American?
2. What barriers to successful MBO are evident in this case?
3. How would you rewrite the president's memo?

REFERENCES

Opening quotation

William H. Sihler, "Toward Better Management Control Systems," *California Management Review* 14 (Winter 1971): 34.

1. Bruce A. Kirchoff, "Organization Effectiveness Measurement and Policy Research," *Academy of Management Review* 2 (July 1977): 352.
2. Harold Koontz and Robert W. Bradspies, "Managing Through Feedforward Control," *Business Horizons* 15 (June 1972): 27.
3. Drawn from: A. Dale Flowers and James B. O'Neill, II, "An Application of Classical Inventory Analysis to a Spare Parts Inventory," *Interfaces* 8 (February 1978): 76–78.
4. "The Dilemma in Product Liability," *Dun's Review* 109 (January 1977): 48.

5. Adapted from: Edward M. Schrock, "Why Management Must Act to Improve Quality," *Iron Age* 220 (August 1, 1977): 155.

6. J. Fred Weston and Eugene F. Brigham, *Managerial Finance*, 6th ed. (Hinsdale, Ill.: Dryden Press, 1978), p. 27.

7. For an interesting discussion of financial ratios applied to hospital administration, see: Fred Fitschen, "Look to Ratios to Measure Financial Health," *Hospital Financial Management* 6 (November 1976): 44–50.

8. See: Peter F. Drucker, *The Practice of Management* (New York; Harper & Row, 1954).

9. For a brief history of MBO, see: George S. Odiorne, "MBO: A Backward Glance," *Business Horizons* 21 (October 1978): 14–24.

10. Anthony P. Raia, *Managing by Objectives* (Glenview, Ill.: Scott, Foresman, 1974), p. 15.

11. William E. Reif and Gerald Bassford, "What MBO Really Is," *Business Horizons* 16 (June 1973): 26.

12. Adapted from: William E. Reif and John W. Newstrom, "Integrating MBO and OBM—A New Perspective," *Management by Objectives* 5, no. 2 (1975): 34–42.

13. For an extensive list of reasons why MBO programs tend to fail, see: Dale D. McConkey, "20 Ways to Kill Management by Objectives," *Management Review* (October 1972): 4–13.

14. For detailed discussion of flexible budgeting, see: Lawrence M. Matthews, *Practical Operating Budgeting* (New York: McGraw-Hill, 1977): pp. 30–34.

15. M. Edgar Barrett and LeRoy B. Fraser, III, "Conflicting Roles in Budgeting for Operations," *Harvard Business Review* 55 (July-August 1977): 138.

16. James D. Suver and Ray L. Brown, "Where Does Zero-base Budgeting Work?" *Harvard Business Review* 55 (November-December 1977): 84.

17. Robert G. Murdick and Joel E. Ross, *Introduction to Management Information Systems* (Englewood Cliffs, N.J.: Prentice-Hall, 1977), p. 8.

18. This is an expanded version of a shorter list found in: Sihler, "Toward Better Management Control Systems," p. 33.

19. Ibid., p. 37.

20. Henry Mintzberg, "The Myths of MIS," *California Management Review* 15 (Fall 1972): 96.

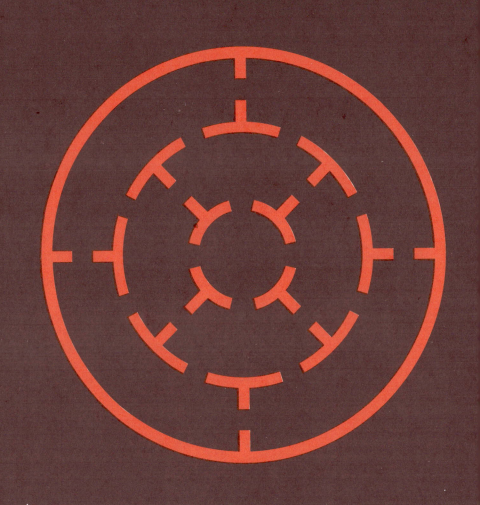

III

Organizing

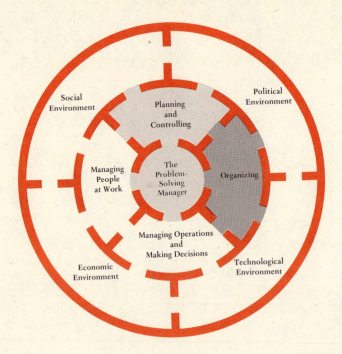

PART III DEALS WITH THE ORGANIZATION OF HUMAN ACTIVITY. WE LIVE in a world of countless organizations. Those organizations need to be managed effectively and efficiently regardless of whether they are large or small, profit-making or nonprofit-making. A working knowledge of organization theory, organization design alternatives, and organization development techniques helps the problem-solving manager combine individuals and work groups into productive units. The overriding problem here is to design and maintain an organization structure that is capable of survival in spite of new personnel, revised organizational objectives, and changing environmental demands. Skilled problem solving is especially important when organizing because research tells us that there is no single best organization design. Organization design and development techniques need to be mixed and matched as the situation warrants.

Chapter 6

Organization Theory

Organizations are social inventions or tools developed by men to accomplish things otherwise not possible.

Joseph A. Litterer

LEARNING OBJECTIVES

When you finish reading this chapter, you should be able to

- Identify and describe four characteristics common to all organizations.
- Classify organizations by purpose.
- Explain the nature of long-linked, mediating, and intensive technologies.
- In general terms, contrast traditional and modern organization theory.
- Describe Max Weber's bureaucracy.
- Explain the nature of the bureaucratic paradox.
- Identify and describe the four characteristics of open systems.

Organizations are an ever-present feature of modern industrial society. We look to organizations for food, clothing, education, employment, entertainment, transportation, and protection of our basic rights. Virtually every aspect of modern life is touched in one way or another by organizations, and the need for good managers continues to grow.

In Chapter 1 we saw that the purpose of the management process is the achievement of *organizational* objectives. Basically, organizations are social entities that enable people to work together to achieve objectives that they cannot achieve as individuals. This chapter introduces some basic theoretical concepts of organization.

WHAT IS AN ORGANIZATION?

In spite of the prevalence of organizations, the term *organization* is not easy to define. The difficulty is pointed up by the fact that several different definitions have been suggested by sociologists, psychologists, and organization and management theorists. Chester I. Barnard's definition, however, though formulated over forty years ago, is still popular among organization and management theorists. He viewed the *organization* as "a system of consciously coordinated activities or forces of two or more persons."[1] In other words, when people gather together and formally agree to combine their efforts for a common purpose, an organization is the result.

There are exceptions, of course, as when two individuals agree to push a car out of a ditch. In this case the task is a one-time affair. But if the same two individuals decide to combine their efforts to push cars out of ditches for a living, an organization would be created. The conscious coordination that Barnard referred to, which implies a degree of formal planning and division of labor, is present in the second instance but not the first.

Barnard's statement is a good general definition. However, it is helpful to identify some specific characteristics of organizations. According to Edgar Schein, a prominent organizational psychologist, there are four characteristics common to all organizations. They are (1) coordination of effort; (2) common goal or purpose; (3) division of labor; and (4) hierarchy of authority.[2]

COORDINATION OF EFFORT

As the old saying goes, "Two heads are better than one." When individuals join together and coordinate their mental and/or physical efforts, great and exciting things can be accomplished. The great pyramids, the conquering of polio, manned flights to the moon—all of these far exceed the talents and abilities of any single individual. Coordination of effort is responsible for multiplying individual contributions.

COMMON GOAL OR PURPOSE

Coordination of effort cannot take place unless those who have joined together want to accomplish something of mutual interest. A common goal or purpose gives organization members a rallying point. For example, during World War II, the management of an aircraft factory would announce, with great fanfare over the public address system, the completion of each new airplane. These announcements were greeted by loud cheering and applause from the employees. Even though each employee played only a small role in completing an airplane, the announcements reminded them that they all shared a common purpose.

DIVISION OF LABOR

Every individual possesses a unique combination of aptitudes and skills. By systematically breaking general tasks down into specialized jobs, an organization can make efficient use of each individual's potential. Moreover, through division of labor, each organization member can become highly proficient at doing a specialized task over and over again.

The advantages of division of labor have been known for a long time. One of its early proponents was the pioneering economist Adam Smith. While touring an eighteenth-century pin manufacturing plant, Smith observed that a group of specialized laborers could produce 48,000 pins a day. This was an astounding figure, considering that each laborer could produce only 20 pins a day when working alone.[3]

HIERARCHY OF AUTHORITY

If anything is to be accomplished through collective effort, certain individuals must be vested with the authority to see that the overall purpose is accomplished. Organization theorists have defined *authority* as the right to direct the work of others. Without a recognized hierarchy of authority, coordination of effort is difficult, if not impossible, to achieve. Some refer to this hierarchy of authority as the chain of command. For example, a grocery store manager has authority over the assistant manager who has authority over the produce department head who, in turn, has authority over the produce department employees. Without such a chain of command, the store manager would have the impossible task of directly overseeing the work of every employee in the store.

PUTTING ALL THE PIECES TOGETHER

All four of the foregoing characteristics are necessary if an organization is to be said to exist. Through the years, many well-intentioned attempts to create organizations have failed because something was missing. For instance, in 1896 a boyhood friend of Henry Ford named Frederick Strauss helped Ford set up a machine shop to produce gasoline-powered engines. But while Strauss was busy carrying out his end of the bargain by machining needed parts, Ford was secretly building an automobile in a workshop behind his home. Needless to say, their "organization" never got off the ground.[4] Although Henry Ford eventually went on to become an automobile-industry giant, his first attempt at organization failed because all the "pieces" of an organization were not present. His and his partner's efforts were not coordinated, they worked at cross-purposes, their labor was vaguely divided, and they had no hierarchy of authority. In short, they had an idea but not an organization.

CLASSIFYING ORGANIZATIONS

Classifications are natural to any systematic study. For example, zoologists have spent decades carefully identifying and classifying the many species of animals found on our planet. Similarly, epidemiologists have made great contributions to world health by systematically isolating and classifying contagious diseases. Organization theorists are no exception. Like zoologists and epidemiologists, they feel that classification systems provide convenient labels for systematic analysis, study, and discussion. However, as one organization theorist has pointed out, a universally accepted classification of organizations is not at hand: "The study of organizational classification is at such a primitive stage that there is not even agreement about terms, let alone agreement about a theory of classification."[5]

Since there is no single classification scheme for today's organizations, we will examine two alternative classifications. They are derived from two important dimensions of organizations, purpose and technology.

CLASSIFYING ORGANIZATIONS BY PURPOSE

One of the major characteristics of an organization is a common purpose. It must have a reason for being, and that reason is considered its purpose. By carrying out a wide range of purposes, organizations enable society as a whole to function.

The four-way classification discussed here includes business organizations, nonprofit service organizations, mutual benefit organizations, and commonweal organizations.[6] Although some organizations could be assigned to more than one category, it is useful for students of management to be able to classify organizations by these general purposes (see Table 6.1). Organizations with similar purposes typically experience similar kinds of management problems.

Business organizations   The fundamental purpose of business organizations like General Motors or the *Washington Post* is to make a profit in an ethical and nondestructive manner. Businesses

TABLE 6.1
Classifying organizations
by purpose

PURPOSE	PRIMARY BENEFICIARY	COMMON EXAMPLES	OVERRIDING MANAGEMENT PROBLEM
Business	Owners	Automobile manufacturers Newspaper publishers Railroads Fast-food restaurant chains	Must make a profit
Nonprofit service	Clients	Universities Welfare agencies Church schools Hospitals	Must selectively screen large numbers of potential clients
Mutual benefit	Members	Unions Clubs Political parties Trade associations	Must satisfy members' needs
Commonweal	Public at large	U.S. Post Office Police departments Fire departments Public schools	Must provide standardized services to large groups of people

cannot survive, let alone grow, without earning a profit. Of course, profits are earned by satisfying demands for products and services while, at the same time, operating the business in an efficient way. The economic production function is so important to society that many think primarily of businesses when the term *organization* is mentioned.

Nonprofit service organizations Many organizations survive, and even grow, without making any profits at all. They need to be solvent, of course, but they measure their successes not in dollars and cents but by how well they provide a specific service to some segment of society. Oberlin College, the YMCA, and the Massachusetts General Hospital are examples of nonprofit service organizations. Since their services are usually in great demand, one of their major problems is screening large numbers of applicants. Another major problem, for many nonprofit service organizations, is securing adequate funds for continued operation. These organizations need to be well designed and properly managed to meet their objectives.

Mutual benefit organizations   Often, as in the case of labor unions or political parties, individuals join together strictly to pursue their own self-interest. Occasionally, as in the case of the National Association of Manufacturers, *organizations* feel a need to join together in a blanket organization. Like all other types of organizations, mutual benefit organizations must be effectively and efficiently managed if they are to survive. Survival, in this instance, depends on satisfying the needs of the members.

Commonweal organizations   Like nonprofit service organizations, commonweal organizations provide public services. However, unlike nonprofit service organizations, a commonweal organization provides standardized service to *all* members of a given population. The U.S. Army, for example, protects all Americans, not just a select few. The same goes for the police and fire departments on a local level. Commonweal organizations generally are extremely large. Their size makes them somewhat unwieldy and difficult to manage.

CLASSIFYING ORGANIZATIONS BY TECHNOLOGY

Although the classification of organizations by purpose is useful, it does not reveal how the various purposes are carried out. It only indicates the kind of objective an organization is supposed to accomplish. Therefore, a second classification by technology can also be useful for certain organizations. Organization theorist James D. Thompson, in his often-cited text *Organizations in Action*, has suggested a three-way classification of organizations by technology. The three technologies are called long-linked, mediating, and intensive.[7]

Long-linked technology   This type of technology involves serial interdependence. In other words, person B's contribution can come only after person A's, C's only after B's, and so on. The classic example of long-linked technology is the assembly line. In an automobile assembly line every job fits into a carefully planned sequence of jobs. Each individual on an assembly line performs a highly specialized task over and over again.

The major strength of long-linked technology is speed. Some multiline automobile plants today are capable of turning out one hundred vehicles per hour. The major weakness of long-linked technology is its inflexibility. For example, an assembly line cannot produce one single unit unless replacement employees can be found for those who are absent from work.

Mediating technology   Many organizations today provide a standard service to large numbers of individuals who wish to be interdependent. These organizations rely on mediating technologies that link otherwise unassociated individuals together in some beneficial fashion. Commercial banks, insurance companies, and telephone companies mediate on behalf of their clients or customers. The word *mediate*, as used here, also refers to the broker's role of go-between for potential buyers and sellers of real estate.

Standardization plays a major role in organizations using mediating technologies. "Standardization makes possible the operation of the mediating technology over time and through space by assuring each segment of the organization that other segments are operating in compatible ways."[8] Imagine how difficult it would be to process claims in the U.S. Social Security Administration if each regional office used a different form. Standardization permits the organization to handle large numbers of clients efficiently. The other side of the coin is that mediating technology organizations tend to be highly bureaucratic with many rigid standards and procedures.

Intensive technology Intensive technology has been called a custom technology. Organizations based on intensive technology can, in a manner of speaking, custom build their product or service to fit each customer's unique set of needs. To accomplish this, the organization must have a number of technologies on hand to mix and match as the situation demands.

Consider, for example, the case of a general hospital. Not every patient admitted needs an appendectomy. Hospitals must rely on a wide variety of specialists to diagnose each patient's problem so that the right combination of technologies (x-ray, nutrition, surgery, and so on) can be applied. In effect, hospitals provide a customized service. While the major strength of intensive technology is flexibility, its major weakness is lack of cost effectiveness. Intensive technologies are not very cost effective because expensive equipment often sits idle between specialized applications.

In summary, classifying organizations according to purpose or technology is helpful because it encourages people to think analytically about organizations. For example, by drawing a distinction between business organizations and commonweal organizations, the advantages and disadvantages of each become more apparent. At this point we turn to more encompassing theories of organization, both traditional and modern.

CONTRASTING THEORIES OF ORGANIZATION It is impossible to tell exactly when organizations became an object of study. The Bible, to name only one early source, includes hundreds of references to the structure and management of organizations. For the most part, however, the study of organization theory is a twentieth-century development, although one organization theorist has philosophically observed, "The study of organizations has a history but not a pedigree."[9] His remark points up the fact that the history of organization theory is marked by disagreement rather than uniformity of thinking. The best way to approach the study of organization theory is to examine two very different ways of thinking about organizations, the traditional view and a modern view.

In the traditional view the organization is characterized by closed-system thinking. It assumes that the surrounding environment is fairly predictable and that uncertainty within the organization can be eliminated through proper planning and control. Its primary goal is economic efficiency. A dominant modern view, on the other hand, views the organization as an open system that interacts continuously with an uncertain environment. In this view, both the organization and its surrounding environment are filled with variables that are difficult to predict or control. The primary goal of the organization thus becomes survival in an environment of uncertainty and surprise. These contrasting approaches are summarized in Table 6.2.

THE TRADITIONAL VIEW

Traditional organization theory is the product of a diverse background. Practicing managers and theorists from both sides of the Atlantic made significant contributions. Typical were those by the early management writers and Max Weber.

TABLE 6.2
Contrasting Theories of Organization

	TRADITIONAL VIEW	MODERN VIEW
General Perspective	Closed system thinking	Open system thinking
Primary Goal of Organization	Economic efficiency	Survival in an environment of uncertainty and surprise
Assumption About Surrounding Environment	Predictable	Generally uncertain
Assumptions About Organization	All causal, goal-directed variables are known and controllable. Uncertainty can be eliminated through planning and controlling.	The organizational system has more varibles than can be comprehended at one time. Variables often are subject to influences that cannot be controlled or predicted.

Adapted from James D. Thompson, *Organizations in Action* (New York: McGraw-Hill, 1967), pp. 4–7.

**THE EARLY
MANAGEMENT
WRITERS**

Early contributors to the management literature such as Henri Fayol and Frederick W. Taylor treated organizing as a subfield of management. Fayol included it in his five universal functions of management. Taylor's narrow task definitions and strict work rules implied a tightly structured approach to organization design.

In general, Fayol and the other pioneering management writers who followed in his footsteps endorsed tightly controlled authoritarian organizations. For instance, managers were advised to have no more than six immediate subordinates. Close supervision and obedience were the order of the day. Emphasis in these organizations was on the systematic downward flow of authority in the form of orders and rules. Four traditional principles of organization that emerged were (1) a well-defined hierarchy of authority, (2) unity of command, (3) authority equal to responsibility, and (4) downward delegation of authority, but not of responsibility. These four concepts are developed in Table 6.3.

**MAX WEBER'S
BUREAUCRACY**

Writing around the turn of the century, a German sociologist named Max Weber described what he considered to be the most rational and efficient form of organization. He called this highly structured and rationally efficient form of organization a *bureaucracy*. It is important to realize that Weber's ideas about organizations were

**TABLE 6.3
Traditional principles of
organization**

1. *A well-defined hierarchy of authority*
   This principle was intended to ensure the coordinated pursuit of organizational goals by contributing individuals.

2. *Unity of command*
   It was believed that the possibility of conflicting orders, a serious threat to the smooth flow of authority, could be avoided by making sure that each individual answered to only one superior.

3. *Equal authority and responsibility*
   Authority was defined as the right to get subordinates to accomplish something. *Responsibility* was defined as the obligation to accomplish something. The traditionalists cautioned against holding individuals ultimately accountable for getting something done unless they were given formal authority to get it done.

4. *Downward delegation of authority, but not of responsibility*
   Although a superior with equal authority and responsibility can pass the *right* to get something accomplished along to subordinates, the *obligation* for getting it done remains with the superior. This arrangement was intended to eliminate the practice of "passing the buck."

shaped by the world in which he lived and worked. Before the turn of the century Germany was a semifeudal state struggling to meet the pressures of the Industrial Revolution. Weber was appalled at the way public administrators relied on subjective judgment, emotion, fear tactics, and nepotism (the prejudicial hiring and promoting of one's relatives) rather than on sound management practices.[10] He used the widely respected and highly efficient Prussian army as a model for his bureaucratic form of organization.

Weber's bureaucracy, in theory, was the perfect picture of efficiency. The organization, as Weber saw it, had a specific purpose, and all members of the organization were both aware of and identified with that purpose. Each member performed in a rational and predictable manner to contribute to the achievement of the organization's purpose. James D. Thompson has offered the following perspective:

> The rational model of an organization results in everything being functional—making a positive, indeed an optimum, contribution to the overall result. All resources are appropriate resources, and their allocation fits a master plan. All action is appropriate action, and its outcomes are predictable.[11]

Weberian bureaucracies were intended to run like well-oiled machines.

Among the several characteristics of bureaucracy mentioned by Weber, four stand out as significant.[12] These four characteristics are (1) division of labor, (2) hierarchy of authority, (3) a framework of rules, and (4) impersonality.

Division of labor   Weber felt that organizations can most efficiently achieve their purposes if individuals perform the same specialized task over and over. In this manner, every individual can become an expert.

Hierarchy of authority   According to Weber, there should be no doubt about who gives orders and who takes orders. He saw authority as flowing down the organizational pyramid, with the greatest amount of authority being retained at the top. In the words of two contemporary organization theorists:

> Each supervisory office is under the control of a higher one. Each official is accountable to his superior for his and his subordinates' job-related actions and decisions. All are accountable to the highest official at the top of the pyramidal hierarchy. Thus the

entire operation is organized into an unbroken, ordered, and clearly defined hierarchy.[13]

A framework of rules   Generally speaking, rules are nothing more than behavioral guidelines. When one follows a rule, one is behaving in a manner prescribed by the organization. Weber maintained that if organizational members are to behave in predictable ways, the organization must carefully conceive and enforce a framework of rules. Members of Weberian bureaucracies know how to behave because clearly specified rules tell them how to behave.

Impersonality   Weber was firmly committed to the idea that people should be hired and promoted on the basis of *what* they know, not *who* they know. Rational bureaucrats are supposed to be impersonal when deciding who should be hired for a particular position or who should be promoted or not. Weber felt that greater impersonality would help eliminate the rampant favoritism he observed in the organizations he studied. If Weber were alive today, he would probably label bureaucrats as professionals. Professionals, according to one modern definition, are impersonal because they focus strictly on the technical task at hand and avoid emotional involvement.[14]

THE BUREAUCRATIC PARADOX   A paradox is said to exist when something has apparently contradictory qualities. Bureaucracy qualifies as a paradox because of the contradiction between the basic concept and actual experience. As we have seen, Weber characterized bureaucracies as the most rationally efficient form of organization. But experience with bureaucracies has shown that they often get tangled up in red tape. In fact, the very term *bureaucracy* has become a synonym for inefficiency. What are bureaucracies? Are they the ultimate in efficiency or the ultimate in inefficiency? In support of the latter view, consider the case of poor Joe.

A case of bureaucracy in action   Rather than going right from high school to college as many of his friends did, Joe took a full-time job in a local factory. After six months on the night shift and a year on the day shift, Joe decided that he could do better if he got a college degree. So Joe quit his job and headed for the local university.

Joe's friends had told him that he had to go first to the admissions office to be accepted by the university. Aside from having to ask a couple of passersby how to find the admissions office, Joe's first visit to the campus went smoothly. He was admitted only on a probationary status because the university had not yet received an official transcript of his high school work—but he was admitted, and that was all that mattered to Joe.

A month later Joe received notice that his admittance to the university was official and that he should report the following week to register for classes. Joe's second trip to the campus started out on the wrong foot when it took him thirty-five minutes to find a parking space. Finally he settled for a spot in a section reserved for handicapped students. By this time he was already fifteen minutes late for his appointment, so Joe ran haphazardly across campus. Imagine his surprise, upon arrival at the registrar's office, to find about two hundred students in line ahead of him. The wait turned out to be all right, though, because he made a date with a girl friend from high school days.

After that everything took a turn for the worse. It seemed that Joe had to see an adviser. But the clerk in the registrar's office wasn't sure who the adviser would be, since Joe was an unclassified student. When Joe mentioned that he would probably become a business major, the clerk sent him to the Business College. After a ten-minute trip to the Business College Joe was informed that he should go to the central advising office clear across campus.

Joe was soaked with perspiration by the time he got to central advising. It couldn't have taken the adviser more than thirty seconds to look over Joe's registration form and sign it. While racing back across campus for registration, Joe felt resentful that he had had to wait forty-five minutes at the central advising office for such a short process. But now everything was okay, because he was finally on his way to register.

Later, as Joe sat in his car staring blankly at the $10 parking ticket he found on his windshield, he wondered what he should do now, since three of the four classes he wanted to sign up for were closed. At that point his old factory job didn't look so bad. "Darned bureaucracy," he muttered dejectedly.

Joe's plight is familiar to all of us. At one time or another each of us has been frustrated by bureaucratic red tape. But how can the most rationally efficient type of organization become the symbol of inefficiency?

Bureaucratic strengths can become weaknesses   Bureaucracy is a matter of degree. Once we recognize this, it is easier to appreciate how the factors that make bureaucracies efficient may, at some point, make them inefficient. Take rules, for example. While some rules help make organizational activity orderly and predictable, too many rules can inhibit organizational success. The term *red tape* refers to the tendency of organization members to forget the overall purpose of the organization and focus exclusively on following the rules. Too many rules can paralyze an organization. Similarly, extreme division of labor, highly centralized authority, and aloof impersonality can separately or together render an organization ineffective.

Poor Joe was the victim of a number of bureaucratic weaknesses. He kept running into administrative dead ends because he was dealing with a large, highly specialized organization. During peak load periods, such as registration time at a university, highly specialized bureaucracies may be too inflexible to adjust. The endless lines Joe had to stand in were a result of bureaucratic inflexibility.

However, from the standpoint of large nonprofit service organizations such as universities, a certain degree of bureaucracy is necessary to permit the efficient screening of potential clients from large populations. Exactly how much bureaucracy is desirable is problematical from a managerial standpoint. Although Joe was disgusted with the bureaucratic red tape, the university could not have carried out its mission without some degree of bureaucracy. Bureaucracy is a two-sided coin, and it is difficult to see both sides at once.

CHALLENGES TO THE TRADITIONAL VIEW

Because the traditionalists attempted to pinpoint the one best way to organize and manage, their somewhat cut-and-dried recommendations eventually began to be challenged. Prescriptions for machinelike efficiency that looked good on paper often failed to work out in real life. It turned out that Fayol's universal functions were no guarantee of success. Similarly, experience proved that there was more to organizing and managing than scientifically breaking down tasks as Taylor recommended. Even Weber's rationally efficient organizational formula, bureaucracy, sometimes in practice became the epitome of inefficiency. In addition to these rude awakenings, major challenges to traditional thinking about organizations came from two other sources.

BOTTOM-UP AUTHORITY

Traditionalists left no doubt about the origin of authority in their organizational models. They believed that authority was inextricably tied to property ownership, and so it flowed from the top of an organization to the bottom. In businesses, those farthest removed from the ownership of stock were entitled to the least amount of authority. This notion had a basic and rational appeal. However, when Chester I. Barnard wrote about organizations as cooperative systems in 1938, he challenged the traditional assumption about authority flowing from top to bottom. Instead, he proposed an *acceptance theory of authority*, which stated that a leader's authority is determined by his or her subordinates' willingness to comply. According to Barnard, a subordinate recognizes a communication from above as being authoritative and decides to comply with it only when the following four conditions are met:

1. He can and does understand the communication.
2. At the time of his decision he believes that it is not inconsistent with the purpose of the organization.
3. At the time of his decision he believes it to be compatible with his personal interest as a whole.
4. He is able mentally and physically to comply with it.[15]

Barnard's acceptance theory of authority opened the door wide for a whole host of ideas such as upward communication and the informal organization that is based on good will rather than rules. Prior to Barnard's contribution, these concepts had been talked about only among human relationists.

ENVIRONMENTAL COMPLEXITY AND UNCERTAINTY

Although twentieth-century managers tend to agree with the traditionalists that rationally structured and managed organizations should be effective and efficient, they experience difficulty because of outside complexity and uncertainty. As Charles Perrow said, in writing about the history of organization theory, "The increasing complexity of markets, variability of products, increasing number of branch plants, and changes in technology all required more adaptive organizations."[16] Plans typically have to be made on the basis of incomplete information. Consequently, things do not always work out according to plan. Similarly, many of the traditional principles of organization, such as how many people a manager can effectively manage, have proved naive.

The net result of these and other challenges to traditional thinking is an openness to new ways of looking at organizations. When open-system thinking appeared on the management horizon, it was greeted warmly because it promised to allow for flexibility and adaptability in organization structure.

A MODERN VIEW: ORGANIZATIONS AS OPEN SYSTEMS

Proponents of the systems approach to management have suggested that it is useful to study organizations as open systems. In spite of its complexity, this view is popular because it is realistic. Traditional closed-system perspectives such as bureaucracy and scientific management virtually ignore important organization-environment interactions. They are easy to understand but simplistic to the point of being unrealistic. For example, it is scarcely realistic to assume that the plans of a computer manufacturing firm will eliminate uncertainty, because technological breakthroughs are a regular occurrence in the computer industry.

Organizations are systems made up of interacting subsystems. Organizations are also themselves subsystems that interact with larger social, political, and economic systems. Those who take an open-system perspective realize that system-to-system interactions are often as important as the systems themselves. For example, we study movements of people in and out of the labor force (unemployment), movements of capital (stock exchanges and long-term borrowing), and movements of goods and services (transportation and trade). A highly organized and highly interactive world needs realistic models; that is why the open-system perspective of organizations is important.

SOME OPEN-SYSTEM CHARACTERISTICS Regardless of the open system under study—the human body, an organization, a society, or the solar system—all share certain common characteristics. By focusing on processes that take place rather than on static patterns or structures, we can identify four major characteristics of all open systems: (1) interaction with the environment, (2) synergy, (3) dynamic equilibrium, and (4) equifinality.

Interaction with the environment Open systems are not totally self-sufficient entities. The human body, an excellent example of an open system, must import air, food, water, and so on from the surrounding environment and then must export waste in order to survive. Similarly, in business organizations, materials, energy, and ideas move into, through, and out of the organization.

Synergy A system of parts working together behaves differently from its parts operating separately.[17] This is a simple statement, but it has substantial implications. What it means is that a whole (an organization, for example) is greater than the sum of its parts. One can study the structure, purpose, size, people, problems, and so on of an organization and still not get the whole picture. All these "parts" simply do not add up to the "whole" when they are examined out of context. For example, a football team is more than players, coaches, play books, and equipment. A team comes to life and works as a well-integrated unit only when all the parts are in place and cooperating with each other.

CONVERSATION WITH . . .

Janice C. Shields
District Accounting Manager
Pacific Telephone Company
El Segundo, California

Photo courtesy of Ms. Shields.

PERSONAL BACKGROUND

Janice Shields went to work as an elementary school teacher rather than a manager after earning a degree in sociology from the University of Illinois. The native Chicagoan broke into the business world in 1968 as a personnel specialist for General Electric Company in Schenectady, New York. After moving to the West Coast to take a position with Pacific Telephone in 1970, Janice started her career path in accounting. Prior to assuming her present position, she served as a unit supervisor, a section supervisor, a systems analyst, an auditor, and an accounting supervisor. In her capacity as district accounting manager, Janice is in charge of administering the twice-monthly payroll for 50,000 Pacific Telephone employees, a payroll that totals $90 million per month. In addition, Janice Shields and her staff of nearly 200 handle the data processing for personnel records, generate required reports, and phase in new computer hardware as needed.

QUOTABLE QUOTES

What is the most challenging aspect of your job as a manager and how are you addressing that challenge?

Ms. Shields: The most challenging aspect of this assignment is dealing with people. In my position, you must rely on being able to get the job done through others. In order to accomplish this, you must strive to keep the employees' interests, attitudes and opinions in mind, to treat them fairly and make them feel important as individuals in the organization.

Do you have any guiding principles regarding the practice of management?

Ms. Shields: Never be afraid to tackle a problem head on, even if it means having to take an unpopular position. Weigh all the facts and alternatives before acting, listen carefully, have a clear understanding of the consequences and then proceed on a course of action that is in the best interest of all parties involved.

Dynamic equilibrium   "When opposing variables in a system are in balance, that system is in equilibrium with regard to them. The equilibrium may be static and unchanging or it may be maintained in the midst of dynamic change."[18] An elementary example of dynamic equilibrium at work is the trampoline. The springs and frame of a trampoline hold the canvas surface in dynamic equilibrium whether someone is bouncing on it or not. Damage to the frame or a few missing springs will destroy the dynamic equilibrium of the surface. In a similar fashion, an organization may be thrown out of dynamic equilibrium by the unexpected absence of a key executive or by a shortage of working capital.

Equifinality   Open systems are made up of more than simple cause-and-effect relationships. *Equifinality* means that a number of different causes can produce the same effect in an open system. In organizations, "the concept of equifinality suggests that the manager can utilize a varying bundle of inputs into the organization, can transform these in a variety of ways, and can achieve satisfactory output."[19] To borrow a time-honored expression, equifinality means that "there is more than one way to skin a cat." For example, in the short run at least, a firm can enhance its profits by cutting back on quality while its competitors observe strict quality constraints. Of course, shabby quality eventually eats into sales. There are many ways of getting the job done.

DEVELOPING AN OPEN-SYSTEM MODEL   An understanding of the basic open-system characteristics is helpful because it forces us to break away from traditional closed-system thinking. Going back to Chapter 3, we can see that developing an open-system model involves synthetic thinking. It is rather naive to view organizations as closed systems, because organizations are shaped and molded by the surrounding environment. An excellent example of the shaping influence of environmental factors is the situation in which the *New York Times* found itself in the mid-1970s. Managers of the *Times* found themselves in a classic profit squeeze, with costs rising and revenues declining. *Business Week* described what was taking place at the time:

Some of the problems at the *Times* are the same ones worrying virtually all big-city newspapers. Costs of production, paper, and distribution are skyrocketing at the same time that television and other competing media are grabbing a growing chunk of advertising budgets. As an added worry, suburban newspapers are stealing a growing number of readers and advertisers from big-city dailies.[20]

As a direct consequence of these environmental influences, a massive reorganization effort was launched to streamline the *Times* organization so that it could more effectively adapt to its changing environment. This action was necessary for one reason: survival. If the *Times* management had continued to think in closed-system terms, the giant newspaper would have had to close its doors and go out of business.

An open-system model helps present and future managers of organizations appreciate the highly interactive nature of organizational activity. The model developed here relates primarily to profit-making businesses, but there is a great deal of carryover to all other types of organizations as well.

The organization as a black box   The most fundamental form of open-system model is the "black box." As depicted in Figure 6.1, the black-box model reveals nothing of what goes on inside the organization. It only identifies inputs and outputs. A business must acquire various inputs: capital, either through selling stock or borrowing; labor, by hiring people; raw materials, through purchases; and market information, through research. These are the basic inputs that enable a business to operate. Meanwhile, on the output side of the black box, goods and services are distributed throughout the market, profits (or losses) are realized, and waste materials are discarded or recycled.

Although the black-box model tells nothing of the internal workings of the organization, it clearly demonstrates the ongoing interaction between the organization and the surrounding environment. Now let's look at what goes on inside the black box.

FIGURE 6.1
The organization as a black box

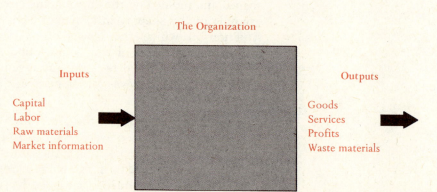

The Organization

Inputs

Capital
Labor
Raw materials
Market information

Outputs

Goods
Services
Profits
Waste materials

Organizational subsystems By relying on the open-system premise that systems are made up of interacting subsystems, we can identify three prominent subsystems in any organization. There are other subsystems that might be singled out, but these three, viewed together, provide a useful model of the entire organization as a subsystem. The three to be discussed here are the technical, boundary-spanning, and managerial subsystems. Figure 6.2 shows how these three subsystems fill the black box.

The technical subsystem, sometimes referred to as the productive subsystem, enables the organization to transform raw materials into finished goods and services. In a meat packing plant, for instance, steers become hindquarters, loins, ribs, lard, hides, hair, and blood. This transformation takes place through long-linked technology in an assembly-line manner. Specially trained and skilled personnel in combination with special equipment work within the technical subsystem of a meat packing plant to achieve the organization's purpose. The technical subsystem is responsible for turning people, ideas, and machines into a productive entity. But the ability to produce a good or service will not by itself enable the organization to survive. The technical or productive subsystem must rely on other subsystems.

Whereas technical subsystems may be viewed as being at the very core of organizations, boundary-spanning subsystems are directed outward toward the general environment. Most boundary-spanning jobs, or interface functions, as they are sometimes called, are easily identified by their titles. Purchasing managers are responsible for making sure that the organization has a steady and reliable flow of raw materials and subcomponents. Public relationists are in charge of developing and maintaining a favorable public image of the organization. Long-range planners have the responsibility of surveying the general environment for actual or potential opportunities

FIGURE 6.2
Looking inside the organizational black box

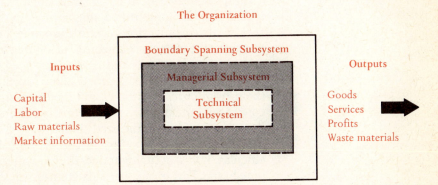

and obstacles. Sales personnel probe the environment for buyers for the organization's output. Purchasing managers, public relationists, long-range planners, and sales personnel all have one thing in common; they all work to make the organization's interaction with the general environment as effective as possible.

Although the technical and boundary-spanning subsystems are important and necessary, one additional subsystem must be brought into play to tie the whole organization together. As indicated in Figure 6.2, the managerial subsystem serves as a go-between for the technical and boundary-spanning subsystems. Managerial subsystems "comprise the organized activities for controlling, coordinating, and directing the many subsystems of the structure."[21] Thinking back to Chapter 1, we see that it is within the managerial subsystem that management is practiced as both a science and an art. This very book represents an operational definition of what takes place within the managerial subsystem.

None of the organizational subsystems can function properly alone. Each depends on the other two for necessary support. Some people find it rather artificial to view organizational subsystems out of context, but this analysis is intended to help point up the dynamic nature of organizations. It is not enough to view organizations as simple black boxes with inputs and outputs. An important part of open-system thinking is to examine the processes that take place inside the black box as well.

SUMMARY   Organizations are social entities that help people work together to achieve objectives that they cannot accomplish alone. All organizations, whatever their purpose or reason for being, are characterized by coordination of effort, a common goal or purpose, division of labor, and a hierarchy of authority. It is often useful to classify organizations by purpose or technology. The basic purpose of an organization may be business, nonprofit service, mutual benefit, or a commonweal function. Organizations may also be classified by technology as long-linked, mediating, or intensive. In some respects, all organizations share the same properties, but in other respects, the various categories of organization present managers with unique problems and challenges.

A good deal can be learned about organizations by examining them from both traditional and modern perspectives. Max Weber's concept of bureaucracy as a rationally efficient form of organization is representative of the traditional view. However, bureaucracies present us with a paradox. In theory, bureaucracies are extremely efficient. But in actual practice, they are often inefficient and snarled in red tape. Part of this paradox stems from the fact that bureaucratic strengths may become weaknesses when carried to extremes. It is important to realize that there are different degrees of bureaucracy; one organization may be more bureaucratic than another.

Modern organization theorists are showing a preference for open-system models when analyzing organizations. They contend that open-system thinking helps us appreciate the constant interaction between the organization and its environment; this interaction was typically ignored in traditional thinking. Furthermore, they feel that the open-system perspective more realistically represents the dynamic interaction among organizational subsystems.

TERMS TO UNDERSTAND

Organization	Responsibility
Authority	Bureaucracy
Commonweal organization	Acceptance theory of authority
Long-linked technology	Synergy
Mediating technology	Dynamic equilibrium
Intensive technology	Equifinality

QUESTIONS FOR DISCUSSION

1. What are the characteristics common to all organizations and why must they all be present?
2. Think of a commonweal organization that affects your life. Why do you think it would be somewhat difficult to manage?
3. Classify the local college bookstore according to purpose and technology. How might these perspectives help in analyzing some of the problems faced by the store?
4. Why is intensive technology called a custom technology?
5. Why did the traditional theorists stress the need for unity of command?
6. Why is it appropriate to say that bureaucracy is a matter of degree? Support your answer with examples.
7. What are your personal recommendations for reducing bureaucratic red tape?
8. How did Barnard's acceptance theory of authority challenge traditional organization theory?
9. In what ways is the open-system perspective of organizations realistic?
10. In what ways does your college or university exhibit the four characteristics of open systems?

CASE 6.1 DON'T ROCK THE BOAT!

Tom Simms, an administrator in charge of emergency admissions at a large county hospital, has held his present position for twenty years. He often boasts about how he whipped what used to be the hospital's worst-run department into a tight unit. Tom's boss, the director of the hospital, generally is pleased with Tom's work, although some complaints have come in from time to time about delays in the admission process.

Carla Reuter is a recent university graduate who has been with the hospital for eight months. Now that she is familiar with emergency admission procedures, Carla has discovered that the paperwork Tom requires for patient admission could be streamlined from five duplicate forms to two. She has even designed the new forms and calculated considerable time and cost savings by using them. When Carla shared her idea with Tom, he replied, "The present forms have worked fine since I designed them ten years ago. I don't see any reason to mess the system up now."

FOR DISCUSSION

1. What role does bureaucratic inflexibility play in this case?
2. Put yourself in Carla's shoes and explain what you would do next.

**CASE 6.2
TOP DOWN OR
BOTTOM UP?**

Grace Younger and Helen Pappas exchanged waves as they hurried out of the company cafeteria and headed back to their work areas. As Grace waited for her elevator, she reflected on how much she enjoyed her lunchtime discussions with Helen. They never were at a loss for anything to discuss. Their conversations ranged from national politics to science fiction.

Grace particularly enjoyed their somewhat philosophical discussions about management. Each had been a supervisor for roughly three years. These discussions usually raised some very important questions about what it takes to be a good manager. Today's discussion on authority was a good example. Today's "debate" centered around the source of managerial authority. Helen's words echoed in Grace's memory: "You have authority because you're a manager. Your superior position in the company hierarchy gives you authority over those below you." Of course, Grace had vigorously disagreed. As she told Helen, "My authority as a manager is based on my subordinates' willingness to do what I tell them."

FOR DISCUSSION

1. With whom do you agree? Why?
2. Is it possible that both positions have merit? Explain.

REFERENCES

Opening quotation

Joseph A. Litterer, *The Analysis of Organizations*, 2nd ed. (New York: Wiley, 1973), p. 5.

1. Chester I. Barnard, *The Functions of the Executive* (Cambridge, Mass.: Harvard University Press, 1938), p. 73.

2. Drawn from: Edgar H. Schein, *Organizational Psychology*, 2nd ed. (Englewood Cliffs, N.J.: Prentice-Hall, 1970), pp. 8–9.

3. See: Adam Smith, *The Wealth of Nations* (New York: The Modern Library, 1937), p. 7.

4. For an interesting biography of Henry Ford, see: Ann Jardim, *The First Henry Ford: A Study in Personality and Business Leadership* (Cambridge, Mass.: MIT Press, 1970), p. 40.

5. Bill McKelvey, "Guidelines for the Empirical Classification of Organizations," *Administrative Science Quarterly* 20 (December 1975): 509.

6. This classification scheme adapted from: Peter M. Blau and William R. Scott, *Formal Organizations* (San Francisco: Chandler, 1962).

7. For an expanded treatment, see: James D. Thompson, *Organizations in Action* (New York: McGraw-Hill, 1967), pp. 15–18.

8. Ibid., p. 17.

9. James G. March, *Handbook of Organizations* (Chicago: Rand McNally, 1965), p. ix.

10. For more detailed discussion, consult: Warren G. Bennis, *Changing Organizations* (New York: McGraw-Hill, 1966), pp. 4–5.

11. Thompson, *Organizations in Action*, p. 6.

12. Drawn from: Max Weber, *The Theory of Social and Economic Organization*, trans. A. M. Henderson and Talcott Parsons (New York: Oxford University Press, 1947).

13. Herbert Hicks and C. Ray Gullett, *Organizations: Theory and Behavior* (New York: McGraw-Hill, 1975), p. 129.

14. See: Harold L. Wilensky, "The Professionalization of Everyone?" *The American Journal of Sociology* 70 (September 1964): 137–158.

15. Barnard, *The Functions of the Executive*, p. 165.

16. Charles Perrow, "The Short and Glorious History of Organizational Theory," *Organizational Dynamics* 2 (Summer 1973): 4.

17. For an extensive discussion of this concept, see: R. Buckminster Fuller, *Synergetics* (New York: Macmillan, 1975), p. 3.

18. James G. Miller, "Living Systems: Basic Concepts," *Behavioral Science* 10 (July 1965): 224.

19. Fremont E. Kast and James E. Rosenzweig, *Organization and Management: A Systems Approach*, 2nd ed. (New York: McGraw-Hill, 1974), p. 119.

20. "Behind the Profit Squeeze at the New York Times," *Business Week* #2447 (August 30, 1976): 42.

21. Daniel Katz and Robert L. Kahn, *The Social Psychology of Organizations* (New York: Wiley, 1966), p. 42.

Chapter 7

Designing Organizations

With the environmental instabilities of today, we see that it is human versatility and the capacity for discretion, qualities once planned out of the system, that now constitute the best hope for the survival of any organization.

Albert B. Cherns

There is no one way of doing things.

Anant R. Negandhi

LEARNING OBJECTIVES

When you finish reading this chapter, you should be able to

- Describe the two main dimensions of organization charts.
- Explain the relationship between environmental uncertainty and organization design from a contingency perspective.
- Explain the difference between functional departments and product-service departments.
- Present the argument against an ideal span of control.
- Explain the role of functional authority in line and staff organizations.
- Summarize the arguments for and against decentralization.
- Highlight the advantages and disadvantages of committees.
- Explain why teams and matrix organizations tend to be organic design alternatives.

Traditional closed-system prescriptions for designing organizations often prove inadequate in today's ever-changing world. On the other hand, the modern open-system view is not the final answer either. Although the modern perspective helps promote awareness of organization-environment interaction, it tends to be rather vague as to precisely how organization subsystems should be designed. Clearly, a bridge must be built between the structurally oriented traditional view and the environmentally oriented modern view. Such a bridge may be found in the contingency approach introduced in Chapter 2. In designing organizations, the contingency approach means custom tailoring the organization to meet the unique demands of the situation.

The purpose of this chapter is to discuss design alternatives available to the manager who wants to enhance situational appropriateness and thus organizational effectiveness. First, however, the fundamental process of constructing an organization chart must be introduced, since organization charts serve as the primary visual aid in designing organizations.

ORGANIZATION CHARTS

An *organization chart* is a diagram of official positions and formal lines of authority in an organization. In effect, an organization chart is a visual display of an organization's structural skeleton. These displays, with their familiar pattern of boxes and connecting lines, are a useful management tool. They are a common sight in management offices.

Every organization chart has two basic dimensions, one representing vertical differentiation and one representing horizontal specialization. *Vertical differentiation* establishes the chain of command, or hierarchy. *Horizontal specialization* establishes a systematic division of labor. To highlight the nature and significance of these two dimensions, let's consider a short case study.

For years, George Terrell was an avid trout fisherman. The sight of George loading up his old sedan with expensive fly-casting gear and heading out to the nearest trout stream was all too familiar to his family and neighbors. About six years ago, George tried his hand at the difficult task of tying his own trout flies. Being a creative individual and a bit of a handyman, George soon created a fly that trout seemingly fought over to bite. Word about what came to be known as George's Super Fly spread rapidly among local and regional fishing enthusiasts. Within weeks he was swamped with orders. Three dollars turned out to be a reasonable price for his newly patented Super Flies. What had started out as a casual hobby turned into a lucrative business bringing in roughly $300 per week. George no longer found any time to fish; all his time was taken up tying and selling Super Flies. An organization chart at that point would have looked like the one in Figure 7.1. Since George was the entire operation, an organization did not really exist. There was no vertical differentiation or horizontal specialization at that early stage.

George soon found it impossible to tie more than a hundred flies a week and still get out to visit fishing tackle retailers who might carry his Super Flies. To free some of his time, George hired and trained a family friend named Amy to help him run the operation in a small building he had leased. Although George still did not have an organization chart, one would have been appropriate because an organization came into existence once an assistant was hired. A chart at that point would have resembled the one in Figure 7.2. Vertical differentiation had been introduced, since Amy was George's subordinate. However, horizontal specialization was still absent, because Amy did a lot of different things to help out.

As business picked up in the following months, George had to hire and train four full-time employees to work under Amy tying flies. He also hired Fred, a sharp salesman and old fishing buddy, to head up the marketing operation and recruit and train two regional sales representatives. Shortly afterward, an accountant was brought into the organization to set up and keep the books. Today Super Fly, Inc., is recording annual sales in excess of $450,000. George finally has gotten around to organizing the company he built in patchwork fashion through the years. His organization chart is displayed in Figure 7.3.

Notice that the company now has three layers of vertical differentiation and three distinct forms of horizontal specialization. The three specialized directors now do separately what George used

FIGURE 7.1
A one-person operation with no differentiation or specialization

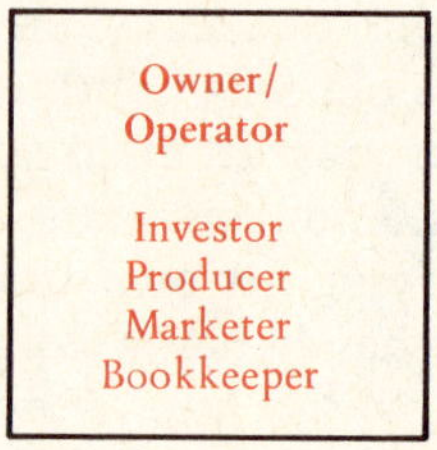

Owner/ Operator

Investor
Producer
Marketer
Bookkeeper

FIGURE 7.2
A two-person organization with vertical differentiation but no horizontal specialization

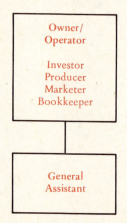

Owner/ Operator

Investor
Producer
Marketer
Bookkeeper

General Assistant

FIGURE 7.3
A mature organization
with both vertical
differentiation and
horizontal specialization

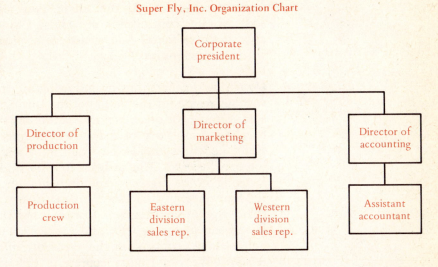

Super Fly, Inc. Organization Chart

to do all by himself. Imagine how George's job of general management will become progressively more difficult as additional vertical layers and horizontal specialists are added. Coordination is essential; the "right hand" must operate in concert with the "left hand." Generally, specialization is achieved at the expense of coordination. Problem-solving managers need to balance specialization and coordination when designing organizations. They can achieve this and other forms of organizational balance through contingency design.

INTRODUCTION TO CONTINGENCY DESIGN

As discussed in Chapter 2, contingency thinking amounts to situational thinking. Along this line, the contingency approach to organization design involves taking special steps to make sure that the organization fits the demands of the situation. In direct contrast to traditional bureaucratic thinking, contingency design is based squarely on the assumption that there is no single best way to design an organization. *Contingency design* involves a process of diagnosing the degree of environmental uncertainty and adapting the organization and its subunits to that environment. This does not mean that the organizations created by contingency designers are all different from each other. Instead, it means that managers who choose a contingency approach select from a number of design alternatives to create the most effective organization possible. Contingency managers often start with the same basic collection of design alternatives but end up with unique combinations of them. Contigency organization design requires problem solving in the truest sense of the word, as it involves both open-system and synthetic thinking. At the outset, two basic questions must be addressed by contingency designers: How much environmental uncertainty is there? And what type of organization can best deal with that uncertainty?

HOW MUCH ENVIRONMENTAL UNCERTAINTY?   Designing organizations by following arbitrary rules or principles without regard for the nature of the surrounding environment is a sure formula for organizational failure. But considering the mind-boggling complexity of today's environment, how can managers study the world outside the organization and come to any meaningful conclusions? The answer to this difficult question lies in focusing on the *degree* of environmental uncertainty. By answering the four questions in Table 7.1, managers can determine whether the degree of environmental uncertainty they must cope with is low, moderate, or high. Of course, since environmental uncertainty ranges along a continuum, the terms *low, moderate,* and *high* are all relative. We can readily appreciate this fact by examining the circumstances facing three contemporary organizations.

No competition for the IRS   The U.S. Internal Revenue Service (IRS) needs no introduction. Among other things, it is the agency responsible for collecting the federal tax ($400 billion in fiscal year 1978) on all individual and corporate income earned in the United States. The IRS is a huge bureaucracy with over four thousand employees in its Washington, D.C., headquarters and approximately seventy-seven thousand more in its seven hundred regional, district, and local offices across the United States.

The environment in which the IRS operates is characterized by a relatively low degree of uncertainty for a number of reasons.

TABLE 7.1
Organizational environments vary in uncertainty

| | DEGREE OF ENVIRONMENTAL UNCERTAINTY | | |
	Low	Moderate	High
1. How strong are social, political, and economic pressures on the organization?	Minimal	Moderate	Intense
2. How frequent are technological breakthroughs in the industry?	Infrequent	Occasional	Frequent
3. How reliable are resources and supplies?	Reliable	Occasional predictable shortages	Unreliable
4. How stable is the demand for the organization's product or service?	Highly stable	Moderately stable	Unstable

Primary among them is the fact that the IRS is shielded from direct social, political, and economic pressures by Congress, which is responsible for passing the tax laws. Except for occasional changes due to sporadic waves of tax reform legislation, the IRS carries out the same basic function year after year. Since the federal income tax appears to be here to stay, the demand for the IRS's service is stable and secure. Furthermore, as a legal monopoly, it has no competition to threaten its position. Even planning and staffing for the busy season can take place in an orderly fashion, because April 15, the annual filing deadline, is fixed by law rather than unpredictable market forces. Bureaucratic structure is appropriate for commonweal organizations such as the IRS that operate under conditions of low uncertainty. Stability and predictability are more important than flexibility and adaptability.

The Pentagon—a big customer   McDonnell Douglas Corporation, the $4 billion-a-year aircraft manufacturer headquartered in St. Louis, faces a moderate degree of uncertainty.[1] This situation is due partly to the company's huge size and large market share. It is the leading defense contractor in the United States, and it occupies the number-two position in commercial aircraft manufacturing. Among its more famous products are the A-4 Skyhawk and the F-4 Phantom, both fighter planes, and the DC-9 and DC-10, a pair of commercial airliners. Organizations the size of McDonnell Douglas usually enjoy a competitive advantage in the marketplace for raw materials because vendors tend to assign a high priority to customers who place dependably large orders. Since jet-age aircraft technology tends to be evolutionary rather than revolutionary, McDonnell Douglas is not threatened by technological obsolescence as long as it keeps pace with evolutionary changes.

In regard to demand for its products, the firm has been the Pentagon's chief contractor in recent years. But a degree of demand insecurity is introduced because Congress sometimes cuts military spending unpredictably. With its relatively long production runs (the Skyhawk and Phantom were introduced over twenty years ago), a moderately stable organization structure is appropriate for McDonnell Douglas.

David and Goliath   In 1970, Gene Amdahl left IBM, where he had been a principal architect of IBM's highly successful Series 360 computer. Since IBM was not interested in producing large-scale, general-purpose computers, Amdahl decided to go into business on his own and compete with IBM in a corporate David-and-Goliath fashion. The resulting company, Amdahl Corporation, located on the outskirts of San Jose, California, has faced a highly uncertain environment ever since. According to *Fortune*, things got off to a shaky start.

> Amdahl's first computer had to be scrapped on the eve of its planned introduction because I.B.M.'s new entries had rendered it obsolete. A public offering failed, and the company went deeply into debt with its backers. The development program fell behind schedule. There was a nearly complete turnover of the management team.[2]

In spite of having to cope with an uncertain environment characterized by severe competition, rapid technological change, and funding shortages, Amdahl Corporation has survived to become a profitable company with an admired reputation for quality. It has done so by creating a streamlined, highly fluid, and adaptive organization rather than a cumbersome bureaucracy.

Having looked at these examples of how environmental uncertainty can vary, we now turn to a second major question that contingency designers need to ask: What type of organization should be designed?

ORGANIZATION DESIGN: MECHANISTIC OR ORGANIC?

Tom Burns and G. M. Stalker, British behavioral scientists, have proposed a useful typology for categorizing organizations by design.[3] They have drawn a distinction between mechanistic and organic organizations. *Mechanistic organizations* tend to be rigid in design and possess strong bureaucratic qualities. In contrast, *organic organizations* tend to be quite fluid and flexible in design. Actually, these two types of organization are the extreme ends of a single continuum. Pure types are difficult to find, but it is fairly easy to check off the characteristics listed in Table 7.2 to determine whether a particular organization is relatively mechanistic or relatively organic.

However, the following excerpts from interviews by Studs Terkel, the Chicago radio personality, come very close to describing pure examples of mechanistic and organic organizations.

A long-distance telephone operator   You're in a room about the size of a gymnasium, talking to people thousands of miles away. You come in contact with at least thirty-five an hour. . . .

You have a number—mine's 407. They put your number on your tickets, so if you made a mistake they'll know who did it. You're just an instrument. You're there to dial a number. It would be just as good for them to punch out the number.

TABLE 7.2
The mechanistic and organic models of organization

CHARACTERISTIC	MECHANISTIC ORGANIZATIONS	ORGANIC ORGANIZATIONS
1. Task Definition for Individual Contributors	Narrow and precise	Broad and general
2. Relationship Between Individual Contribution and Organization Purpose	Vague	Clear
3. Task Flexibility	Low	High
4. Definition of Rights, Obligations, and Techniques	Clear	Vague
5. Reliance on Hierarchical Control	High	Low (reliance on self-control)
6. Primary Direction of Communication	Vertical (top to bottom)	Lateral (between peers)
7. Reliance on Instructions and Decisions from Superior	High	Low (superior offers information and advice)
8. Emphasis on Loyalty and Obedience	High	Low
9. Type of Knowledge Required	Narrow, technical, and task-specific	Broad and professional

Adapted from Tom Burns and G. M. Stalker, *The Management of Innovation* (London: Tavistock, 1961), pp. 119–125. Copyright © Tom Burns and G.M.Stalker 1961.

You've got a clock next to you that times every second. When the light goes off, you see the party has answered, you have to write down the hour, the minute, and the second. Okay, you put that in a special slot right next to the cord light. You're ready for another one. Still you've got to watch the first one. When the light goes on, they disconnect and you've got to take the card out again and time down the hour, the minute, and the second—plus keeping on taking other calls. It's hectic.[4]

A director of a bakery cooperative   I'm the director. It has no owner. Originally I owned it. We're a nonprofit corporation 'cause we give our leftover bread away, give it to anyone who would be hungry.

We have men and women, we all do the same kind of work. Everyone does everything. It's not as chaotic as it sounds. Different people take responsibility for different jobs. . . .

We try to have a compromise between doing things efficiently and doing things in a human way. Our bread has to taste the same way every day, but you don't have to be machines.[5]

It is important to interpret these examples properly. Employees are not necessarily unhappy in mechanistic organizations and happy in organic ones. Furthermore, profit-making as well as nonprofit organizations may be organic in design. Spotting the difference between the two types depends on identifying key characteristics such as task definition and flexibility, hierarchical control, and knowledge requirements.

Knowing the difference between mechanistic and organic organizations takes on added significance when we appreciate the organization-environment patterns uncovered in Burns and Stalker's research. They discovered that successful organizations in relatively stable and certain environments tend to be mechanistic. Conversely, they discovered that relatively organic organizations tend to be the successful ones when the environment is unstable and uncertain.

Given these tools for diagnosing the degree of environmental uncertainty and the mechanistic-organic distinction, managers are in a better position to engage in contingency design. If an environment is diagnosed as low in uncertainty, then mechanistic design alternatives are in order. But if the environment is characterized by high uncertainty, then organic design alternatives are appropriate. What the manager needs next is a collection of design alternatives that can be mixed and matched as the situation dictates. The balance of this chapter is taken up with a collection of alternatives suitable for designing relatively mechanistic or relatively organic organizations (and subunits) as the situation warrants.

ORGANIZATION DESIGN ALTERNATIVES

The contingency approach to organization design requires managers to select from a number of alternatives rather than follow fixed principles. Managers who face a relatively certain environment can promote effectiveness by designing a relatively mechanistic organization. Managers who must deal with high uncertainty will want to select design alternatives that lead to a relatively organic organization.

DEPARTMENTALIZATION

As discussed earlier, horizontal specialization involves division of labor. When labor is divided, complex jobs are broken down into distinct and less complex tasks. But specialization always needs to be balanced by some form of coordination. Aside from the hierarchical chain of command, one of the most popular forms of coordination is departmentalization. It is through *departmentalization* that jobs involving similar processes are grouped. For example, all jobs involving the recruitment, hiring, and training of organization members typically are grouped into a personnel department. The

CONVERSATION WITH . . .

Carol Fox
Founder and General Manager
Lyric Opera of Chicago
Chicago, Illinois

Washington Post.

PERSONAL BACKGROUND

Carol Fox is living proof that managers come from all walks of life. Originally from Chicago, she attended the Girls' Latin School of Chicago and studied music in Chicago, New York, and Italy. Since founding the Lyric Opera of Chicago in 1952 and serving as its general manager ever since, Carol's achievements have become legendary. Annually, her productions reach a quarter of a million people in the Chicago region. Her lifelong devotion to lyric opera has helped bring the arts to tens of thousands of students who have participated in her educational programs. Among her managerial credits is the transporting of an entire production, cast and chorus, to Italy where the work was presented at the Vatican before a special audience of Pope John Paul II. Carol Fox has been the recipient of numerous local and national honors and foreign decorations, including five honorary doctorates. She has enriched the lives of millions by being an effective and innovative manager.

QUOTABLE QUOTES

What is the most challenging aspect of your job as a manager and how are you addressing that challenge?

Ms. Fox: Keeping in balance the growing financial needs of the opera company with the company's income from ticket sales, donations, and other sources of funds in spite of the inflationary spiral, union contracts, rising audience expectations, and personal aspirations for ever higher artistic excellence. I hope I am keeping that balance by inspiring volunteers—our auxiliary arms, including the Board of Directors, Women's Board, Lyric Chapters, and Lyric Guild—to achieve new miracles in fund raising and by my personal participation and leadership in those efforts.

What advice would you give an aspiring manager in your organization?

Ms. Fox: Surround yourself with a top-flight staff and with volunteer strength from the community—and never forget that the standard of the art that is presented is of the essence. It is only on that foundation that we can achieve consistent success in building large, committed audiences and in providing the rationale for people giving us contributions.

---

grouping of jobs through the formation of departments, according to James D. Thompson, "permits coordination to be handled in the least costly manner."[6] Departmentalization works because all those in a separate department work on interrelated tasks, obey the same department rules, and report ultimately to the same department head.

Two popular types of departmentalization are functional departments and product-service departments.

Functional departments   Every organization can be broken down into a number of functions that contribute to the overall purpose of the organization. These functions are made up of related jobs that must be carried out if the organization is to be successful. For example, in a profit-making business, there must be a production function, a finance function, and a marketing function. Many businesses and other organizations are conveniently departmentalized along functional lines (see Figure 7.4). For example, functional departments in a nonprofit service organization such as a hospital might be as follows: administration, nursing, housekeeping, food service, laboratory and x-ray, admission and records, and accounting and billing.

Product-service departments   Functional departmentalization is often found in large, somewhat mechanistic organizations. Although it is a very rational approach to grouping jobs, critics contend that functional departments artificially fragment the organization. They feel that functional departmentalization increases specialization more than it improves coordination.

FIGURE 7.4
Two approaches to
departmentalization

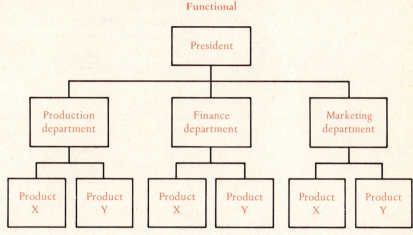

Functional

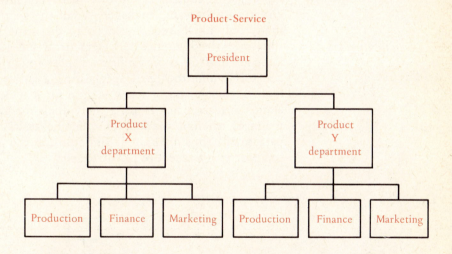

Product-Service

An alternative, relatively organic, form of departmentalization has therefore evolved. It is called the product-service type. As illustrated in Figure 7.4, the product-service approach permits each of, say, two products to be managed almost as an autonomous business. (Notice, however, that functional minidepartments may be found within each product organization.) In effect, the product managers in Figure 7.4 are responsible for managing their own minibusinesses. Coordination is enhanced, and the product managers will be better prepared to assume the duties of top management later on because of firsthand experience with all functions.

This approach has been used successfully by General Motors for years. The head of the Pontiac Motor Division at General Motors competes for resources and sales with other GM divisions such as Chevrolet in addition to traditional competitors such as Ford and Chrysler. The idea is that if Pontiac can stand on its own two feet it will make a greater contribution to the overall objectives of General Motors.

Not all organizations produce and sell a physical product; some, therefore, organize according to the services they provide. For example, a rug-cleaning company could have an industrial service department and a home service department. The process of creating miniorganizations within the service organization would be the same as organizing by physical products.

SPAN OF CONTROL   A second organization design alternative is to specify the number of individuals who report directly to a single manager. This part of organization design is called the manager's *span of control*. When the span of control is narrow, relatively few individuals report directly to the same manager. When the span of control is wide, many individuals report directly to the same manager. Figure 7.5 illustrates the difference between narrow and wide spans of control.

Specialization and coordination play important roles in span of control. In a narrow span, specialization is low and coordination is high. Precisely the opposite is true for a wide span of control. It stands to reason that if many individuals report directly to a single manager, then a number of different tasks probably are being performed, thus making it difficult for the manager to closely monitor every aspect of performance.

FIGURE 7.5
Spans of control vary

A Narrow Span of Control

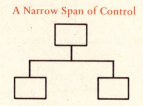

A Wide Span of Control

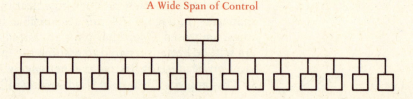

Is there an ideal span of control?   The concept of span of control has received a lot of attention through the years. It is too bad that all this attention has fostered more confusion than understanding and agreement. As a pair of management historians have observed:

> Development of a clear understanding of [span of control] has been complicated by the two-stage evolution of the concept. The first stage was marked by suggested numerical limitations and recommendations; the second by general statements of varying applicability.[7]

During the first stage referred to above, early management theorists confidently specified exactly how many individuals there should be in a manager's span of control. In the words of one pioneering management scholar, "No superior can supervise directly the work of more than five or, at the most, six subordinates whose work interlocks."[8]

As time went by and research results began to push aside strictly theoretical judgments, evidence emerged that wide spans of control could be effective. For instance, James C. Worthy, a vice president of Sears, Roebuck, reported that his company had gotten good results with spans of control far greater than six individuals. Specifically, Worthy found morale and effectiveness to be higher in one department store where thirty-six department managers reported to a single manager than in a second store where the span of control averaged only five.[9]

The gap between theory and actual practice led to revised thinking about spans of control. Rather than continuing to recommend specific numbers, management experts began to suggest that appropriate spans of control should depend on a number of situational factors. Among them are the nature of the task, technology, and leadership as well as the need for work group cohesiveness.[10]

The contingency approach to spans of control   The general feeling among management authorities today is that the span of control should be as wide as the situation will allow. A wider span helps create a relatively organic organization that gives subordinates more freedom of action because close supervision is difficult. However, there are some big "ifs" behind this push for wider spans. The span of control can be relatively wide *if* the subordinates are very knowledgeable about their jobs, *if* they are capable of exercising independent judgment, and *if* the task and technology permit the exercise of independent judgment. In a wide span of control, the erosion of coordination must be compensated for by employee self-control and commitment to organization objectives. When these factors are not present, then coordination must be achieved through hierarchical control via narrow spans of control. Narrow spans of control also become necessary when the job requires the manager to communicate frequently and extensively with each immediate subordinate.

LINE AND STAFF Through the years managers of large mechanistic bureaucracies have struggled to balance two structural needs. On one side of the equation has been the need for specialization; on the other has been the need for unity of command, which is the traditional principle that each member of the organization should report to one and only one boss. The design strategy that was developed to balance specialization and unity of command is called line and staff organization.

Briefly, *line and staff organization* combines line positions, which are in the formal chain of command, and staff positions, which are not. A line manager has the authority to make decisions and give orders to his or her subordinates. In contrast, those who occupy staff positions merely advise and support line managers. Typical staff positions include legal counsel, long-range planning, labor relations, and research and development. In mechanistic organizations, staff personnel must routinely work through a line manager. For example, on the advice of a specialized staff assistant, a financial manager might tell first-line supervisors that expensive overtime must be limited. The staff assistant would not have the authority to give the message directly to the first-line supervisors.

This strict division between line and staff tends to disappear in more organic organizations. *Functional authority* is an organic design alternative that involves giving staff personnel temporary, limited line authority for specific tasks. For example, the financial manager just mentioned may choose to give the staff assistant direct authority over supervisors in the area of controlling overtime expense. When used properly, functional authority can cut out bureaucratic redundancy.

A source of conflict On paper, the line and staff concept represents an excellent way to take advantage of specialized knowledge without diluting unity of command. In actual practice, however, much of the interpersonal conflict in today's large organizations can be traced to line and staff problems. Because staff personnel study problems in depth, they often are more qualified than line managers to make decisions. Nevertheless, the line and staff format requires line managers to take the work of staff assistants and translate it into workable decisions. In short, the staff advises and the line decides. As a result, the staff often feels powerless.

Staff specialists tend to become impatient at the slow and seemingly primitive manner in which line bosses respond to problems and situations. It should come as no surprise, then, that the traditional line and staff format has come under severe criticism in recent years. According to one critique, "The line and staff notion is arbitrary, artificial and obsolete. It needs to be replaced, *not* merely reformulated or redesigned."[11]

Organic alternatives Talk of getting rid of line and staff organizations is somewhat like the talk we hear today about getting rid of the automobile as our principal source of transportation. Both may be good ideas, but there is a disturbing lack of second bests. Regarding the search for alternatives to the traditional line and staff approach, two organization theorists have recommended the following approach:

> Fundamental changes are necessary in the relations between groups formerly categorized as line and staff. These changes should create interaction patterns of mutual problem-solving and collaborative influence between co-equal organization partners. The application of the contingency framework to line and staff relations would avoid the potentially resultant topdog/underdog syndrome. The contingency framework would not use line-staff distinctions, but instead would foster a balancing of decision-making, power and status, without labels of organizational inferiority implied to staff units.[12]

Although this recommendation may sound a bit idealistic, design alternatives such as functional authority, ad hoc committees, teams, and project management, as presented and discussed in this chapter, are workable alternatives. As increasingly complex and uncertain environments demand more organic organizations, alternatives to the relatively mechanistic line and staff format will have to be adopted.

DECENTRALIZATION Where are the important decisions made? Are they made strictly by top management or by middle and lower-level managers as well? These questions are at the very heart of the decentralization design alternative. Decentralization actually is at one end of a continuum;

at the other end is centralization. Centralization is evident if top management closely guards its right to make all important decisions. With *decentralization*, top management delegates a great deal of decision-making authority to middle and lower management. Mechanistic organizations tend to be centralized, and organic organizations tend to be decentralized.

Two types of decentralization   To fully understand the concept of decentralization we first need to know the difference between federal decentralization and simulated decentralization.[13] *Federal decentralization* is named for the relationship between the U.S. federal government and the fifty American states. In constitutional concept each state is an autonomous unit responsible for its own affairs. The role of the federal government is to act as a go-between among (and protector of) the various states. In a few instances this pure type of decentralization has been used successfully by private business.

For example, when plastic bottles came into use after World War II, Owens-Illinois a major manufacturer of glass bottles, adopted federal decentralization. It created two independent, competing businesses, under the general guidance of the home office. One produced and sold glass bottles; the other produced and sold plastic bottles. They competed for customers in the same market. For all practical purposes, these two subunits were two separate companies.[14] Federal decentralization is appropriate only in situations like this one where a subunit can be set up as a separate "business" (a self-contained, self-sufficient, profit-making entity).

The somewhat limited applicability of federal decentralization has led to the development of a modified version called *simulated decentralization*. According to Peter Drucker, the leading proponent of this design alternative:

> Simulated decentralization forms structural units which are not businesses but which are still set up as if they were businesses, with maximum possible autonomy, with their own management, and with at least a "simulation" of profit and loss responsibility.[15]

Simulated decentralization has great potential for involving middle and lower-level managers in the organization's important decisions. In today's giant conglomerate organizations, involvement is one of the most important weapons against feelings of alienation and powerlessness.

The case for decentralization   As the following statement by James C. Worthy, an early advocate of the concept, points out, decentralization is very appealing in a democratic society:

> Flatter, less complex structures, with a maximum of administrative decentralization, tend to create a potential for improved attitudes, more effective supervision, and greater individual responsibility and initiative among employees. Moreover, arrangements of this type encourage the development of individual self-expression and creativity, which are so necessary to the personal satisfaction of employees and which are an essential ingredient of the democratic way of life.[16]

Proponents of decentralization assume that middle and lower-level managers are both willing and able to shoulder the responsibility of making important decisions. In some cases this assumption is justified; in others it is not. Organization designers must respond accordingly.

The case against decentralization   One word sums up the major argument against decentralization. That word is *control.* For example, *Business Week* reported one proponent of tightly centralized management as saying, "One way to know the company is to have the problems on our hands all the time. We were not sitting in an ivory tower waiting for all the results to come in every month."[17] It is this desire to know exactly what is going on at all times that makes centralization attractive to many top managers. Otherwise, the argument goes, things will get out of control because managers at lower levels will make conflicting decisions and top management won't find out until it is too late.

Centralization is popular for another reason as well. It supposedly streamlines the organization by eliminating duplication of effort. For example, Studebaker-Worthington abandoned its decentralized design when it discovered that several of its subsidiaries were selling similar products to the same customers.[18] By centralizing, the firm was able to market its products more efficiently.

After reviewing the arguments pro and con, we walk away with the impression that decentralization is not a cure-all, but it has its appropriate and inappropriate applications. The challenge is to strike a workable balance between decentralized decision making among lower managers and control by top management. In other words, the head needs to know where the feet are going.

COMMITTEES Through the years committees have been both highly praised and severely criticized. Committees have borne the brunt of many jokes such as, "A camel is a horse designed by a committee." By way of formal definition, a *committee* is a group of organization members charged with a specific task. Most often, committees serve as fact-finding and problem-solving bodies, with the resulting decision made and/or implemented by a responsible line manager. It is important to note that committees are superimposed on the existing organization structure. Typically, they are not shown on organization charts. They are intended to add a degree of flexibility to an otherwise fixed structure.

There are two major types of committee. The first is the standing committee. *Standing committees*, although staffed by different individuals at different times, are charged with carrying out the same duty over and over again. For example, a company may have a standing committee to review hiring decisions to see that there is no systematic discrimination against women and minorities. The second type is called the ad hoc committee (from the Latin words meaning "to this" end). *Ad hoc committees* are charged with one-time tasks; they are dissolved as soon as the task is completed. For example, a committee may be formed to consider the best location for a new office building. Once the site is selected, the committee is disbanded. Organic organizations tend to rely more on ad hoc committees because they enhance flexibility. Committees, in general, have both advantages and disadvantages.

Advantages One of the major advantages of committees is that, if properly conceived, staffed, and run,[19] they can capitalize on the strengths of group problem solving, as presented in Table 7.3. Next, committees serve as a coordinating force in highly differentiated and specialized organizations. For example, a management committee made up of the production, finance, marketing, and personnel managers ensures that each functional specialist is aware of the others' needs and unique problems. A third and final advantage is that committees serve as a training ground for lower-level organization members.[20] Committee work develops needed skills in relating to people, leadership, and problem solving.

Disadvantages Committee action also may fall victim to the weaknesses of group problem solving, as highlighted in Table 7.3. Another frequently mentioned disadvantage is that committees are time-consuming (some say time-wasting) and costly. Assuming that the time of a $40,000-a-year executive is worth about $20 per hour, a three-hour committee meeting with five such executives uses up

TABLE 7.3
Major strengths and weaknesses of group problem solving

STRENGTHS	WEAKNESSES
1. *Greater pool of knowledge.* A group can bring a great deal more information and experience to bear on a problem than can an individual acting alone.	1. *Social pressure.* Unwillingness to "rock the boat" and pressure to conform may combine to stifle the creativity of individual contributions.
2. *Different perspectives.* Individuals with varied experience and interests help the group see problems from different angles.	2. *Minority domination.* Sometimes the quality of group action is reduced when the group gives in to those who talk the loudest and longest.
3. *Greater comprehension.* Those who personally experience the give-and-take of group discussion and problem solving tend to more fully understand the rationale behind the final recommendation.	3. *Logrolling.* Political wheeling and dealing can displace sound thinking when an individual's pet project is at stake.
4. *Increased acceptance.* Those who play an active role in the group problem-solving process tend to view resulting solutions or recommendations as "ours" rather than "theirs."	4. *Goal displacement.* Sometimes secondary considerations such as winning the argument, making a point, or getting back at someone displace the primary task of solving the problem at hand.

$300 worth of executive time. By holding several meetings in succession and by adding in travel, preparation, administrative support, and follow-up expenses, the cost of committee meetings piles up rapidly. A final disadvantage is that committee effectiveness is often neutralized by excessive compromise. While compromises may be democratic, they may serve only to balance the personal preferences of the members and not to achieve results that are best for the organization.

On balance, the advantages of committees seem to outweigh the disadvantages. If committee membership is kept down to between three to seven individuals (an odd number avoids voting deadlocks), committees can be an excellent problem-solving arena for management. However, line managers are advised not to turn over their decision-making authority to committees. Personal accountability is virtually impossible when a group makes a decision. If bad decisions are made, it is easier to "pass the buck" in a group.

THE TEAM APPROACH   At first glance, the team approach may appear to be little more than a fancy term for committees. However, there is an important difference between the two. Both standing and ad hoc committees are superimposed on existing organization structure. *Teams*, in contrast, involve permanent modifications in the organization structure to form problem-solving groups; these changes are reflected on the organization chart. In other words, committees are added onto the existing structure, whereas teams are incorporated into the structure. Teams are becoming popular because they greatly improve coordination.

Two very different approaches to designing teams are explored in this section. The first is at the top of the managerial pyramid; the second is at the blue-collar level. Both have helped relatively mechanistic organizations become more organic and adaptive. Both promise a bright future for teams as a design alternative.

Aetna's corporate office   Aetna Life and Casualty Company is one of the largest multiline insurance companies in the United States. Until 1973, Aetna had the reputation of being a very conservative organization, with the chairman of the board running a one-man show. But Aetna's adoption of the corporate office concept in 1973 represented a significant break with the past.[21] Instead of having the traditional single individual at the top, Aetna's organization structure was modified to accommodate a team of four at the top. This team consists of the chairman of the board, the president, the vice president in charge of insurance and mutual funds, and the vice president in charge of finance.

The team meets twice a week to engage in long-range planning, problem finding, and strategic discussion. It is important to note that Aetna's corporate office team does not make decisions. It simply serves as a forum for discussing the pros and cons of various decision alternatives. Each team member is still responsible for making the key decisions in his or her area. Aetna's team approach has not suffered from excessive compromise and indecision, as some originally feared. What it has done is to bring more voices into the decision-making process. The net results have been better decisions, an improved profit picture, and a greater feeling of unity among top management.

Volvo's auto assembly teams   In becoming one of the world's major automobile producers, Volvo has contributed greatly to Sweden's position as an exporting nation. Consequently, the Swedish government points with pride to Volvo's recent revolutionary shift to team assembly of automobiles. It all started in the late 1960s when Volvo, like its highly mechanized competitors around the world, began experiencing high rates of absenteeism and turnover among assembly line workers. Something had to be done. Volvo management studied the problem and decided to redesign its auto assembly operation from the ground level up. Many traditional practices, including the assembly line itself, came into question. One tangible result was a new, six-hundred–worker plant in Kalmar designed to permit car assembly by teams of about twenty people.

Compared with the traditional assembly line, in which workers are restricted to a small area while the work comes to them, Volvo's team approach allows the workers to move around while the work stands still. What has made this dramatic turnabout possible is the use of movable carts on which the partially completed automobiles rest. Each assembly team, made up of both men and women, has a great deal of latitude in deciding exactly who works on what. Consequently, the assembly teams are highly sociable. Individual incentives have been replaced by group bonuses. Volvo's organic team approach to assembling automobiles is evidently working, because the company reports that production costs have remained competitive while absenteeism and turnover have dropped.[22]

Are these results due to Sweden's unique socialistic system? Some observers think so. Nevertheless, problem-solving managers in the United States and other countries can learn from Volvo's team approach when searching for workable organization design alternatives. Although Volvo's entire team approach may not work in other cultures, perhaps various parts of it will.

MATRIX   This last design alternative is sometimes referred to as *project management*.[23] The term *matrix* refers to a combination of vertical and horizontal lines of authority in the same organization. Just as a checkerboard has both vertical and horizontal rows of squares, a matrix organization has both vertical and horizontal lines of authority.

Matrix design has become quite popular among construction and aerospace companies. To appreciate why this rather novel design alternative evolved, consider how difficult it is for a construction firm to complete a hydroelectric dam efficiently and on time. Because of unique demands imposed by physical topography, complex and exacting specifications, and heavy reliance on numerous subcontractors, mechanistic bureaucracies have not worked well for the prime contractors of dams and other large projects. A more organic alternative had to be found. Likewise, aerospace giants such as Lockheed, Grumman, and General Dynamics have had to turn to a more organic organization design strategy in order to build complex weapons systems and space vehicles for the U.S. government. The resulting design has been the matrix format.

Take a moment to study the matrix organization chart in Figure

FIGURE 7.6
A simplified matrix
organization chart

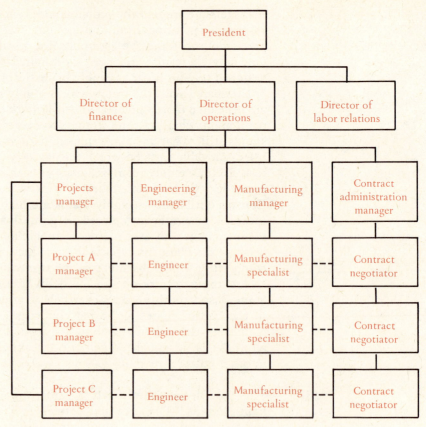

7.6. Notice the checkerboard configuration. In effect, the project managers borrow specialists from the line managers in charge of engineering, manufacturing, and contract administration. However, the project managers have only temporary and limited authority over the specialists who normally report to their line managers. This approach has both strengths and weaknesses.

Strengths The primary strength of matrix design is increased coordination. As discussed earlier, every organization requires a degree of coordination to balance specialization. This is particularly true for organizations whose success or failure depends on huge contracts representing millions of dollars. The matrix format places a project manager in a good position to coordinate the many interrelated aspects of a particular project, both inside and outside the organization. Normally, in mechanistic organizations, the various aspects of a project would be handled in a somewhat fragmented fashion by functional units such as production and marketing. A second strength, control, stems from the first. It stands to reason that greater coordination leads to greater control over both personnel and costs. Increased flexibility is a third strength. A project manager may need five engineers one month and sixteen the next. A typical mechanistic organization would have difficulty absorbing the surplus personnel during slack periods, but a matrix organization with several major projects can move specialists from one project to another as the situation warrants. This kind of organization reduces the need for short-term layoffs and the problem of costly idle talent.

Weaknesses   Matrix design, like the other design alternatives discussed in this chapter, is not a cure-all. It has some distinct limitations. First and foremost, matrix design flagrantly violates the traditional unity-of-command principle. A glance at Figure 7.6 reveals that an engineer, for example, actually has two bosses rather than the traditional one. This violation can and sometimes does cause conflicts of interest. Only frequent and comprehensive communication between functional and project managers can minimize unity-of-command problems. A second weakness has been called the "authority gap." This problem is due largely to the fact that project managers are responsible for getting things accomplished in spite of their lack of formal line authority. Research has shown that project managers tend to fall back on negotiation, persuasive ability, technical competence, and the exchange of favors to compensate for the authority gap.[24] A third weakness centers on the delicate balance the project manager must achieve between the technical and administrative aspects of a project.[25] It is not always easy to get highly technical engineers and scientists to realize that costs must be kept within reasonable bounds. Once again, the project manager must rely on interpersonal skills.

In general, matrix design is appropriate in situations that can take full advantage of the strengths while minimizing the weaknesses. To date, very large, one-time projects that threaten to overload the traditional functional organization have been the best bet.

SUMMARY   Organization charts are useful visual aids for organization designers. They have two basic dimensions, vertical differentiation and horizontal specialization.

Fixed principles of organization design without regard for the demands of the particular situation are no longer appropriate. A modern contingency approach to designing effective organizations has therefore evolved. According to contingency thinking, there is no single best way to design organizations and organization sub-units today.

The contingency approach requires managers to diagnose the degree of environmental uncertainty that an organization faces, and then to select design alternatives that will enable the organization to cope with its environment. The distinction between mechanistic (rigid) and organic (flexible) organizations is especially helpful when it comes to matching design alternatives to environmental demands. Research has demonstrated that mechanistic organizations tend to excel when key environmental variables are relatively stable and certain. In direct contrast are organic organizations, which are flexible enough to be effective in relatively unstable and uncertain situations. The contingency approach requires managers to diagnose the situation, select from a number of design alternatives, and design appropriately mechanistic or organic structures.

Seven different design alternatives are presented and discussed in this chapter. They are departmentalization, span of control, line and staff, decentralization, committees, teams, and matrix. Appropriately structured organizations can be designed by problem-solving managers who carefully mix and match these alternatives. Relatively mechanistic organizations can be created by combining functional departmentalization with limited spans of control, clear line and staff distinctions, centralized decision making, and standing committees. Going in the opposite direction, managers can build relatively organic organizations by combining product-service departmentalization with wide spans of control, functional authority for staff personnel, decentralized decision making, ad hoc committees, and teams. A radical approach to creating a highly organic structure is the matrix organization, which relies on project managers for necessary coordination in complex situations. Organization design requires a high degree of problem-solving skill.

TERMS TO UNDERSTAND

Organization chart	Functional authority
Vertical differentiation	Decentralization
Horizontal specialization	Federal decentralization
Contingency design	Simulated decentralization
Mechanistic organization	Committee
Organic organization	Standing committee
Departmentalization	Ad hoc committee
Span of control	Teams
Line and staff organization	Matrix

QUESTIONS FOR DISCUSSION

1. Why does an organization need both vertical differentiation and horizontal specialization?
2. Why is it important to design organizations to fit the situations they face?
3. How can a manager diagnose the degree of environmental uncertainty?
4. How do mechanistic and organic organizations differ? Why would a creative individual probably feel more at home in an organic organization?
5. Why would a product-service department manager be better qualified to assume the top position in an organization than a functional department manager?
6. How does a wide span of control affect coordination?
7. How does the introduction of functional authority make a line and staff organization more organic?
8. Why would a manager want to encourage decentralization?
9. What is the basic difference between committees and teams? Which do you personally see as more promising?
10. How can a project manager deal with the authority gap in a matrix organization?

CASE 7.1 WELCOME TO THE BIG TIME

In just five years Dwight Hawkins, originally a carpenter by trade, has built his construction firm into the second largest home-building firm in the Jacksonville, Florida, area. Last year alone, Hawkins Home, Inc., constructed over five hundred homes. The firm specializes in relatively small twenty- to thirty-unit custom home subdivisions. Hawkins Home stands out among local suburban land developers because it does an effective job of maintaining high quality while keeping construction costs well below average.

Hawkins attributes the firm's effectiveness to what he calls his flexible organization. Each of his six field construction managers has broad decision-making authority. In his words, "I encourage each field manager to run his construction project as if it were his own business. I'm a jack-of-all-trades, and I expect my managers to be, too. There isn't a thing they can't do." He adds, "They don't come running to me to wipe their noses for them on every little detail. They know what needs to be done, so I stay out of their way and let them get on with it." Hawkins has often been heard telling visitors proudly that they won't find any red tape with Hawkins Home.

During the past year, as commercial building in Jacksonville has begun to catch up with the residential boom, Hawkins has been thinking seriously about getting into commercial construction. Unfortunately, Hawkins Home lacks sufficient capital to purchase or lease the heavy equipment required to build schools, banks, stores, and small office buildings. At this point, the most promising alternative appears to be a merger with Interstate Builders, Inc., a large, Chicago-based commercial builder that specializes in large federal projects such as office buildings, post offices, and courthouses. Interstate's legal staff has worked out a very tempting stock-trade arrangement. Much of Hawkins's time in recent weeks has been taken up by frequent trips to Chicago to discuss details of the proposed merger. From a financial standpoint, the merger proposal looks good. But Hawkins is having second thoughts about how well he and his firm would fit into Interstate's huge operation.

In the first place, Hawkins is concerned because it takes such a long time to get something through the bureaucratic machinery at Interstate. For example, by the time a bid has passed through the engineering, finance, planning, and legal departments in Chicago, eight to ten months have gone by. In the local commercial construction that Hawkins is familiar with, the bid cycle rarely takes more than three to four months. With Interstate, a lag of three to four *years* between the time the government calls for bids and the actual start of construction is not uncommon.

Furthermore, Hawkins has serious doubts about Interstate's ability to adapt to small-scale commercial jobs. As far as he can tell, decision making is highly centralized at Interstate. For example, all purchases of materials exceeding $500 must be routed through the home office purchasing department. At Hawkins Home, the field managers regularly make purchases exceeding $5,000 on their own authority.

Finally, Hawkins is not enthusiastic about the prospect of reporting indirectly to the president of Interstate through three layers including a regional manager, a commercial construction department head, and a vice president of construction. During the recent merger talks it took Hawkins three trips to Chicago and half a dozen assorted meetings before he could even meet the president of Interstate Builders.

FOR DISCUSSION

1. Diagnose these two organizations in terms of the mechanistic-organic distinction.
2. Putting yourself in Hawkins's shoes, what organizational concessions would you demand from Interstate before agreeing to a merger?

**CASE 7.2
WHO'S IN CHARGE
HERE?**

Lisa Harrigan, a junior majoring in business administration at Midstates University, was spending the day at Computer Applications International as the guest of Sara Ronsen, a project manager. It had been an interesting but fairly routine morning as Lisa shadowed

Mrs. Ronsen during the course of her normal duties. After lunch, however, things warmed up considerably.

Lisa could not help her wide-eyed expression as she listened intently to the exchange between Mrs. Ronsen and Jim Wiseman, a sharp young computer programmer.

Mrs. Ronsen: Hi, Jim. Sorry to interrupt, but I've got a *hot* one! We're scheduled to run a final demonstration test on United Petroleum's refinery control computer tomorrow, and we've run into a couple of bugs. Think you could help us with a quick debugging search?

Jim Wiseman (obviously angered):   Who are you kidding? What kind of circus are we running around here? Jensen told me yesterday that I'd be on his project here for two weeks. Now you come along and try to steal me away. How the hell is anybody supposed to get anything done around here when management can't make up its mind who I'm working for?

FOR DISCUSSION
1. Why has this conflict situation developed?
2. Putting yourself in Mrs. Ronsen's role as a project manager, how would you have handled this particular situation? (Assume that crack computer programmers like Jim are hard to come by.)

REFERENCES   *Opening quotations*

Albert B. Cherns, "Can Behavioral Science Help Design Organizations?" *Organizational Dynamics* 5 (Spring 1977): 45.
Anant R. Negandhi, "Comparative Management and Organization Theory: A Marriage Needed," *Academy of Management Journal* 18 (June 1975): 334.

1. This case is drawn from: "Where Management Style Sets the Strategy," *Business Week* #2557 (October 23, 1978): 88–99.
2. Bro Uttal, "Gene Amdahl Takes Aim at I.B.M.," *Fortune* 96 (September 1977): 107.
3. See: Tom Burns and G. M. Stalker, *The Management of Innovation* (London: Tavistock, 1961), chap. 5.
4. Studs Terkel, *Working* (New York: Random House, 1974), pp. 36–37.
5. Ibid., p. 467, 470.
6. James D. Thompson, *Organizations in Action* (New York: McGraw-Hill, 1967), p. 59.
7. David D. Van Fleet and Arthur G. Bedeian, "A History of the Span of Management," *Academy of Management Review* 2 (July 1977): 356.

8. L. Urwick, *The Elements of Administration* (New York: Harper & Row, 1944), pp. 52–53.

9. See: James C. Worthy, "Organizational Structure and Employee Morale," *American Sociological Review* 15 (April 1950): 169–179.

10. For a complete discussion, see: Robert J. House and John B. Miner, "Merging Management and Behavioral Theory: The Interaction Between Span of Control and Group Size," *Administrative Science Quarterly* 14 (September 1969): 451–464.

11. Philip J. Browne and Chester C. Cotton, "The Topdog/Underdog Syndrome in Line-Staff Relations," *Personnel Journal* 54 (August 1975): 444.

12. Ibid.

13. For a complete discussion of this distinction, see: Peter F. Drucker, *Management: Tasks, Responsibilities, Practices* (New York: Harper & Row, 1974), pp. 585–591.

14. This case is drawn from: Ibid., pp. 589–590.

15. Ibid., p. 585.

16. Worthy, "Organizational Structure and Employee Morale," p. 179.

17. "General Dynamics: Winning in the Aerospace Game," *Business Week* #2430 (May 3, 1976): 88.

18. See: "If 'Satellization' Fails, Try Centralization," *Business Week* #2443 (August 2, 1976): 20–21.

19. For advice on running a committee meeting, see: Antony Jay, "How to Run a Meeting," *Harvard Business Review* 54 (March/April 1976): 43–57.

20. See: Angelos A. Tasklanganos, "The Committee in Business: Asset or Liability?" *Personnel Journal* 54 (February 1975): 90–92.

21. This discussion is drawn from: "Making Aetna's 'Corporate Office' Work," *Business Week* #2288 (July 14, 1973): 84–85.

22. For a complete discussion, see: Pehr G Gyllenhammar, "How Volvo Adapts Work to People," *Harvard Business Review* 55 (July-August 1977): 102–113.

23. See: David I. Cleland, "Why Project Management?" *Business Horizons* 7 (Winter 1964): 81–88.

24. Drawn from: Richard M. Hodgetts, "Leadership Techniques in the Project Organization," *Academy of Management Journal* 11 (June 1968): 211–219.

25. For an extensive discussion of problems in this area, see: David L. Wilemon and John P. Cicero, "The Project Manager—Anomalies and Ambiguities," *Academy of Management Journal* 13 (September 1970): 269–282.

Chapter 8

Organization Development

The one predictable thing about OD is its unpredictable consequences.

William J. Reddin

Successful intervention in large systems is becoming more of a science than an art, but it is still not a cookbook process, nor is it ever likely to be. However, the utilization of systematic procedures and technologies in the planning and management of large systems change can only help.

Richard Beckhard and
Reuben T. Harris

LEARNING OBJECTIVES

When you finish reading this chapter, you should be able to

o Define, in your own words, the term *organization development* (OD).
o Discuss the techniques that helped OD evolve into a diagnosis-prescription cycle.
o Identify and discuss the four underlying OD assumptions about people at work.
o Compare the basic OD process to an unfreezing-change-refreezing sequence.
o Identify a strength and a weakness of each of the four major diagnostic techniques.
o Explain how OD interventions can be aimed at the level of the individual, the group, or the organization.
o Identify and discuss two objectives that should be accomplished during the follow-up phase of OD.

According to Richard Beckhard, the behavioral scientist who originated the term *organization development* (OD) in the mid-1950s, managers continually face the dilemma of having to achieve, at the same time, organizational productivity and satisfaction of individual needs. Beckhard describes this problem as follows:

> If we are talking about the basic dilemma of managing work, the management problem has two horns. One horn is how do you take all that human energy and channel it towards the organization's mission? The other horn is how do you organize the work, the communications patterns, the decision making, the norms and values, the ground rules, so that people's individual needs for self worth, achievement, satisfaction and so on, are significantly met at the workplace?
>
> A great deal of attention has been pushed on to the second horn of the dilemma. But that alone doesn't solve the problem any more than the other way round. So the dilemma is how do you manage the dilemma, not how do you manage one horn of it. OD tries to work out, and organize, the interaction between the two.[1]

Organization development helps managers achieve a degree of organizational synthesis. It helps them put the many pieces of a complex system together into the best possible configuration. This complex system, the total organization, needs to be put together in a manner that encourages the subsystems to work together as effectively and efficiently as possible.

OD is helpful to managers because it forces them to view their organizations as dynamic open systems that actively interact with the surrounding environment. Furthermore, OD encourages managers to look not only at what individuals and groups are doing but also at how they are doing it. For instance, a manager taking an OD perspective is as concerned with how a committee reaches a decision as with what the final decision is.

Because OD involves synthesis, this chapter draws from a number of concepts, including organization theory, behavioral processes, group dynamics, organization design, problem solving, planning, and control. While it is still far from an exact science, OD represents a serious attempt to put all the pieces of the organizational puzzle together. In this chapter we define OD; examine its development, objectives, and underlying assumptions; and explore it as a systematic process that can help managers improve their organizations.

WHAT IS OD? It is difficult to reduce organization development to a quick and easy definition. Although relatively new, OD has become a convenient label for a whole host of techniques and processes aimed at making sick organizations healthy and healthy organizations healthier. As one proponent has noted, "It is a synthesis of many different disciplines which have never been brought together in any integrated way. There is a little bit of this and a little bit of that. It is sort of like goulash without much seasoning."[2]

A more serious definition comes from a researcher who sees *organization development* as "a planned, managed, systematic process to change the culture, systems, and behavior of an organization, in order to improve the organization's effectiveness in solving its problems and achieving its objectives."[3] In short, OD centers on planned change, as opposed to the haphazard change that organizations usually experience. This change is designed for the entire organization and its major subunits, and only limited attention is given to the individual. While planned change can conceivably involve technical, administrative, or behavioral subsystems, in practice it is the behavioral subsystem that gets the most attention from OD specialists. This emphasis is the natural result of the fact that most OD specialists have been trained in the behavioral sciences. They tend to be people-oriented.

THE DEVELOPMENT OF OD Like other approaches to management, OD has evolved over a period of years. Since the 1960s it has developed into an amalgam of many different behavioral science techniques. Two techniques influenced OD significantly in its early years, though they are no longer the only techniques used.[4] The first, laboratory training, is popularly referred to as sensitivity training, or T-group (T stands for "training"). The second technique is survey research and feedback. By examining each of these in some detail, we can more easily understand OD's origins and appreciate its development.

LABORATORY TRAINING In brief, *laboratory training* aims at emotional rather than intellectual learning by exposing a group of individuals to an unfamiliar situation that is ambiguous and anxiety-producing. The result, often enough, is that the participants develop sensitivity to others' opinions, acquire a more realistic self-image, and are better able to deal openly and effectively with others.

Outside consultants are typically brought into the organization to set up the sessions and to provide trained leadership. Group members may or may not know each other (if they do not, they are called a stranger group). The training sessions may last from only a day to as long as two weeks. Very often there is no agenda, no structured activity, and sometimes no visible leader. In the unstructured situation that results, members tend to confront each other with their opinions and feelings. They often find that their favorite defense mechanisms and long-held assumptions about others do not stand up. The trainer's role is primarily to focus attention on here-and-now emotional processes, rather than back-home problems, and to encourage a supportive and caring atmosphere.

After a prolonged period in the free give-and-take of the training session, participants' attitudes tend to change in the direction of greater self-awareness and greater sensitivity to the feelings and opinions of others. They learn that these attitudes actually facilitate group interaction. However, when they return to their normal work environments, especially after experience in a stranger group, they often discover that their coworkers are not responsive to the new attitudes of openness, and they are unable to interact with them unless they go back to their old behavior patterns. The two results that typified most early laboratory training were (1) frequent success in developing greater awareness and openness in individuals, and (2) relatively poor carryover to organizations, especially from stranger groups.

OD specialists today are split over the issue of laboratory training. Some use it with reportedly good results, both for individuals and for the organization. Others, because of its potential for ego-shattering confrontation among participants in the training sessions, question its overall value. Proponents maintain, however, that frank and open interaction can lead to a clearer self-image and greater sensitivity to interpersonal differences. With careful screening and orientation of participants, the option to withdraw at any time, a qualified group leader-facilitator, and supportive follow-up in the work environment, laboratory training can be a powerful technique for changing behavior.[5]

Regardless of the various arguments for and against laboratory training, it has taught OD specialists a great deal about how people act, react, and interact. It has also helped clarify the differences between effective and ineffective group interaction. In an effective group, socially mature individuals communicate well by exchanging relevant information, constructive feedback, sincere feelings, and trust. Members of an ineffective group, on the other hand, withhold needed information and feedback, guard their feelings, and withhold or betray trust. From an OD standpoint, the processes of group interaction are as important as what the group accomplishes.

SURVEY RESEARCH AND FEEDBACK

While one group of behavioral scientists was experimenting with laboratory training during the 1940s and 1950s, another was discovering the practical benefits of gathering and analyzing information, then feeding it back to the people who originally provided it. This process was called *survey research and feedback*. Attitude surveys proved to be particularly useful.

For example, outside consultants might develop a written questionnaire to allow employees to indicate their attitudes about their jobs, the company, their supervisors, their coworkers, the atmosphere in the organization, and so on. This information, once it is properly organized, tells top management a great deal about employee attitudes and values while, at the same time, preserving the privacy of individual employees. The attitudes of one department can be compared with another's, or the attitudes of shop foremen can be compared with those of clerical workers.

A more important function of the survey approach, however, occurs when the information is fed back to the employees who have filled out the questionnaire. The main idea behind the feedback is to let employees know where they stand without threatening their egos in the process. This purpose is usually accomplished by having employees compare their own attitude and opinion survey results (fed back privately) with those for the entire department or organization (fed back publicly).

This kind of comparison enables the individual to confront his or her personal shortcomings without social embarrassment. Moreover, the individual is likely to respond to appeals to change, develop, and improve. The most valuable lesson learned from experience with survey research and feedback is that many people welcome feedback and will make a good-faith effort to change once they are able to compare themselves objectively with other people.

OD AS A DIAGNOSIS-PRESCRIPTION CYCLE

As the field of OD began to evolve during the 1960s, it became evident to observers that both laboratory training and survey research and feedback could make valuable contributions. A marriage between the two techniques was possible once OD came to be viewed as a cycle involving diagnosis of an organization's ills and prescription for their cure.

The first step, diagnosis, helps an organization define its present situation. Two OD specialists emphasize the importance of good diagnosis by saying, "Just as a good physician will diagnose the patient's particular symptoms before determining which remedy to prescribe, so the manager must diagnose the organization's symptoms before prescribing the appropriate corrective techniques."[6]

Survey research in the form of attitude and opinion questionnaires is a convenient and effective diagnostic tool.

Once specific problem areas have been diagnosed, then survey feedback and group development exercises can be prescribed as the situation warrants. By interpreting the results of the diagnosis and, later, by evaluating the effects of the prescription, OD can be viewed as a complete *diagnosis-prescription cycle*, as shown in Figure 8.1. Note that *diagnosis* serves two purposes. First, it provides a clear picture of how things actually are. Second, it provides a measuring stick for evaluating the success of the prescribed techniques. A more detailed view of these processes is explored later in the chapter.

THE OBJECTIVES OF OD

OD programs vary because they are based, at least in part, on diagnosis of the situation. What is appropriate for one organization may be inappropriate for another. In spite of this, however, certain objectives are common to most OD-type programs. In general, OD programs involve the development of social processes such as trust, problem solving, communication, and cooperation to enhance personal and organizational effectiveness. More specifically, the typical OD program tries to achieve the five following objectives:

1. Enhance interpersonal trust, communication, cooperation, and support.
2. Encourage a problem-solving rather than problem-avoiding approach to organizational problems.

**FIGURE 8.1
OD as a
diagnosis-prescription
cycle**

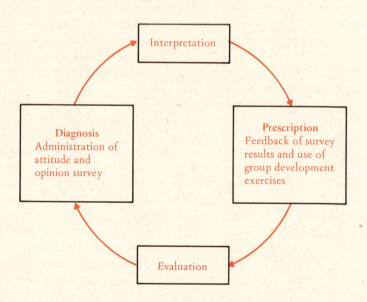

3. Develop a satisfying work experience capable of building enthusiasm.
4. Supplement formal authority with authority based on personal knowledge and skill.
5. Increase personal responsibility for planning and implementing.[7]

Critics of OD are quick to point out that there is nothing really new in this list of objectives. Directly or indirectly, each of these objectives is addressed in nearly all studies of general management. OD proponents respond to such criticism by noting that general management lacks a *systematic* approach. They feel that the usual practice of teaching managers how to plan, organize, solve problems, make decisions, motivate, lead, and control leads to a haphazard, bits-and-pieces management style. According to OD thinking, organization development provides managers with a vehicle for systematically applying a broad selection of management techniques as a unified and consistent package. This, they claim, leads to greater personal, group, and organizational effectiveness.

BASIC OD ASSUMPTIONS

In addition to several primary objectives, OD also has a number of underlying assumptions. By examining these assumptions, we can begin to see how OD programs go about accomplishing the objectives just reviewed.

A good deal of our individual behavior stems from our assumptions about people and things. For example, if we assume that a subordinate cannot be trusted to do a good job, we will be reluctant to give that individual anything difficult to do. When that person finally does get to work on a difficult project, chances are that it will be done poorly. Our negative assumption is confirmed, thus completing a vicious circle between our negative assumption and our subsequent behavior toward the individual. Unfortunately, many managers are victimized by their negative assumptions about organization members. OD therefore tries to translate managerial assumptions about people at work into *positive* terms. Basically, there are four OD assumptions about people at work.

COLLABORATION MORE EFFECTIVE THAN INDIVIDUAL ACTION

A number of people working together on one problem at a time is better than a number of individuals working alone on different problems. This assumption stems from the strengths of group problem solving. Few would deny that collaboration among coworkers is both desirable and possible. However, collaboration between superior and subordinate is another matter. In the words of one expert, "Authenticity in a relationship which depends on 'leveling' and honesty is a prime requisite for collaboration. Authenticity and authority seem almost antithetical to each other."[8] In other words, the cat-and-mouse game playing that often characterizes superior-subordinate interaction can be a major barrier to OD programs that are trying to promote vertical collaboration.

COOPERATION MORE EFFECTIVE THAN CONFLICT

Frequently, in the hustle and bustle of daily activity, organization members find themselves on different sides of issues, protecting their own vested interests. For example, a marketing manager may want to extend liberal credit terms to customers because it will help increase sales. Strong dissent comes from the financial manager, because liberal credit terms mean an increase in costly unpaid accounts. Conflict between both individuals and groups tends to erode trust, prohibit collaboration, and eventually limit the effectiveness of the organization. But in a healthy organization, as Richard Beckhard has observed, "There is a minimum amount of inappropriate win/lose activities between individuals and groups. Constant effort exists at all levels to treat conflict and conflict-situations as problems subject to problem-solving methods."[9] Again, we see the importance of viewing management as a *problem-solving process*. Group problem solving is an alternative to conflict; group problem solving requires cooperation.

PLANNED CHANGE MORE EFFECTIVE THAN HAPHAZARD CHANGE

We are living in an age of transience, an age of accelerating change. Conditions are going to change whether we like it or not, whether we are prepared or not. From a managerial perspective, there is an important choice between planned change and haphazard change. Planned change helps managers anticipate and avoid problems. Haphazard change leaves things to chance and puts the manager in the awkward position of running into unanticipated problems totally unprepared. Two OD advocates have detailed the following strategy for planned change:

> For an effective change strategy to be developed, it is first essential to adequately diagnose the need for change. A second prerequisite for developing a change strategy is to set clear and explicit descriptions of the desired state of affairs after the change. A third necessity is to have a clear picture of the present state of affairs as related to the change goals.[10]

If this strategy sounds slightly familiar, it should. It closely parallels the problem-solving and planning processes that were discussed in earlier chapters.

ORGANIC ORGANIZATIONS MORE EFFECTIVE THAN MECHANISTIC ORGANIZATIONS

In Chapter 7, we explored the differences between organic and mechanistic organizations. The organic variety tends to be flexible, adapting quickly to environmental changes and pressures. Mechanistic organizations, in contrast, tend to be bureaucratic and rigid. Organization theorists recommend organic organizations for fluid and changing environments and mechanistic organizations for stable and relatively unchanging environments. As the organization theorist sees it, both organic and mechanistic organizations have value; the choice depends on the nature of the surrounding environment.

OD theorists tend to disagree. They argue that today's external environment is highly turbulent and constantly changing. Because there is no such thing as a stable environment, the organic organization, with its limited number of hierarchical levels, wide spans of control, decentralized decision making, and reliance on teams, is the best organization for today's situation. It comes as no surprise, then, that OD programs typically place a great deal of emphasis on team building.

THE OD PROCESS

In spite of the fact that OD programs are often tailor-made and thus vary from situation to situation, it is possible to outline a general model. The best way to introduce the three major components of the model is to draw a simple analogy.

Suppose someone hands you a coffee cup filled with clear, solid ice. You look down through the ice and see a penny lying tails up on the bottom of the cup. Now, suppose that for some reason you want the penny to be frozen in place heads up rather than tails up. What can you do? There really is only one practical solution. You let the ice in the cup thaw, reach in and flip the penny over, then refreeze the cup of water. This is precisely how pioneering social psychologist Kurt Lewin recommended that change be handled in social systems. Specifically, Lewin suggested that change agents unfreeze, change, and refreeze social systems. Unfreezing prepares members of a social system for the change they are about to experience. Sudden, unannounced change, according to Lewin, is socially destructive. Similarly, once the change has been introduced, the change agent (or manager) must *refreeze* the situation by following up on problems, complaints, and unanticipated side effects. This seemingly simple approach to change has had a tremendous influence on the direction of modern organization development. OD specialists generally agree that change must be introduced carefully and systematically rather than haphazardly.

The OD model introduced here is based on Lewin's approach to change (see Figure 8.2). In some ways it is similar to the diagnosis-prescription cycle depicted in Figure 8.1, but it is expanded to include new concepts. Diagnosis is carried out during the unfreezing stage. Change is carefully introduced through a tailor-made intervention. Finally, systematic follow-up refreezes the situation. Each step is critical in successful organizational change and development. However, it takes continual recycling through this three-step sequence to make OD an ongoing system of planned change.

DIAGNOSIS   When approaching the diagnostic phase of OD, an organization's top management team has two important decisions to make. First, it must decide if it is capable of conducting its own diagnosis. If it does not have the time or talent to conduct an adequate diagnosis of the situation, then it will have to turn to an outside consultant. Great care should be exercised when hiring the services of any outside consultant. Management must be prepared to shop around for

FIGURE 8.2
A general OD model

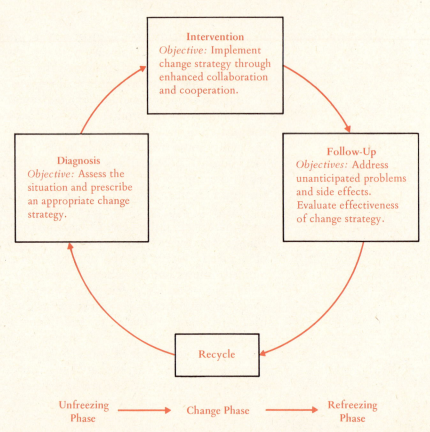

someone willing to do a thorough diagnosis. As one writer has observed: "There is always the temptation to respond favorably to slickly packaged programs and effective sales presentations. In most cases these are solutions looking for a problem to solve. . . ."[11] Outside consultants who insist they have all the answers to an organization's problems the minute they walk through the door should be politely dismissed.

The second important decision management must make before getting into the diagnostic phase centers on precisely what areas to probe. Because of the expense of conducting a diagnosis, management must try to pinpoint specific problem areas or organizational subunits that deserve close examination. Diagnoses that are overly comprehensive or carelessly directed are a waste of time and money.

Once it has made the foregoing decisions, management (or the outside consultants) can turn to three important aspects of the diagnostic phase: (1) unfreezing the situation, (2) designing the diagnostic strategy, and (3) interpreting the diagnostic data.

Unfreezing the situation   Although most of us like surprises when it comes to gifts and parties, we tend to fear surprises that affect our work. An organization development program should not come as a surprise. Management should pave the way for an OD program by first unfreezing the situation. Typically this is done by making announcements, holding meetings, and launching a promotional campaign in the organization's newsletter and on bulletin boards. All this activity should state the following message in clear and simple terms: "We can improve the effectiveness of our organization while increasing our personal satisfaction if we all cooperate in a comprehensive program of finding out *where we are*, *where we want to go*, and *how we can get there*." A message of this type prepares people for interviewers, questionnaires, unfamiliar consultants, and group activities that could be very threatening if they came as surprises. One word of caution is in order, however. While unfreezing the organization, management must be careful not to create unrealistic expectations on the part of organization members. Organization development is designed to introduce change, not miracles! Employees who are encouraged to expect miracles, are bound to come away disheartened. Realistic expectations, on the other hand, can enhance an OD program.

Designing the diagnostic strategy   Those about to tackle an OD diagnosis will find it helpful to view the typical organization as an iceberg. Figure 8.3 shows that just as most of an iceberg lies beneath the surface of the water, a great proportion of an organization's

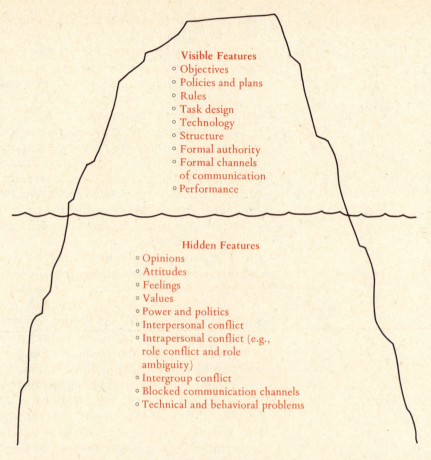

FIGURE 8.3
The organization as an iceberg. Different organizations have different configurations of visible and hidden features.

Visible Features
- Objectives
- Policies and plans
- Rules
- Task design
- Technology
- Structure
- Formal authority
- Formal channels of communication
- Performance

Hidden Features
- Opinions
- Attitudes
- Feelings
- Values
- Power and politics
- Interpersonal conflict
- Intrapersonal conflict (e.g., role conflict and role ambiguity)
- Intergroup conflict
- Blocked communication channels
- Technical and behavioral problems

activities and information is hidden from view. OD diagnosis is difficult because it must get at the hidden as well as the visible information. Of course, a complete diagnosis of every feature listed in Figure 8.3 would be prohibitively expensive and time consuming. It is important to select the right diagnostic strategy for the information sought. Four widely used approaches are described briefly below.

1. *Review of records*   Largely in response to the government's increased demand for reports, today's organizations possess a wealth of recorded information. When the change agents have the time and patience to carry out a records search, they are often rewarded with valuable information about the relative health or sickness of the organization. Much can be learned by reviewing personnel records for signs of excessive absenteeism and turnover

or for patterns of grievances. Similarly, a study of financial records can yield telling signs of cost overruns and other financial problems.

2. *Interviews* By using a carefully compiled list of specific questions (requiring yes or no answers) and general, open-ended questions (requiring detailed explanations), a skilled interviewer can discover a great deal about the individual in particular and the organization in general.

3. *Survey questionnaires* This alternative is probably the most widely used diagnostic strategy today. Questionnaires may be administered to people assembled in groups, or they may be mailed out separately. They may be constructed in-house or purchased.[12] Some of the more sophisticated published survey questionnaires include scoring and statistical analysis in the purchase price.

4. *Direct observation* It is well known that people tend to say one thing and do another. When this kind of discrepancy is likely to be a problem, then management may choose to have a neutral third party (usually an outside consultant) directly observe organizational members at work.

Each of these strategies has its appropriate place in OD diagnosis. By balancing the respective strengths and weaknesses of each approach (see Table 8.1), it is possible to develop a diagnostic strategy based on two or more approaches. For example, a carefully structured interview could be used to supplement the results of a records review or to fill in the gaps left by a prepackaged survey questionnaire. The overall objective, of course, is to get as much useful information as possible at a reasonable cost.

Interpreting diagnostic data Careful interpretation of the data collected during diagnosis paves the way for effective OD intervention. However, an extremely important point must be made here. Management should never wait until the diagnosis has been completed before giving thought to the interpretation phase. Diagnostic strategies should be selected with ease of interpretation in mind. Furthermore, as one OD expert has pointed out, "Data should be collected for a reason, not just 'because it's there,' and analysis should be done with direction and purpose, not as a fishing expedition to 'see what we come up with.'"[13]

Comparisons are helpful. If a similar diagnosis has been conducted in the past, then comparing past results with present results can show how things have changed. Comparisons between departments

TABLE 8.1
Strengths and weaknesses of various diagnostic approaches

DIAGNOSTIC APPROACH	Major Strengths	Major Weaknesses
Review of Records	Provides historical perspective over extended period	Time consuming
	Facts and figures confirm or refute employees' intentions and/or perceptions	Faulty record keeping can be disruptive
Interviews	Face-to-face contact is revealing (e.g., body language)	Respondents often try to look good in the interviewer's eyes
	Questions can be inserted on-the-spot to probe promising areas	Time consuming and costly if a large sample is required
Survey Questionnaires	Appropriate for large samples	Prepackaged questionnaires may ask the wrong questions
	Administration is time and cost-efficient	Preparation and interpretation of in-house questionnaires can be time-consuming and costly
Direct Observation	Behavior speaks for itself ("actions speak louder than words")	Presence of observer often causes people to behave abnormally
	Previously unrecognized problems may be spotted by trained outside observer	Time consuming and costly if a large sample is required

and other organizational subunits also can be revealing. For instance, a comparatively strong negative attitude toward supervision in one department may signal the need to train or replace a particular supervisor.

Careful interpretation of diagnostic data is, of course, the key to selecting an appropriate change or intervention strategy. Inaccurate or sloppy diagnosis will doom even the best-designed and best-intentioned OD intervention.

INTERVENTION   Once the organization or target group has been unfrozen and diagnosis is complete, the wheels of change can be set in motion. An *intervention*, in OD terms, is a systematic attempt to correct an organizational deficiency uncovered during diagnosis. Management teams, working either alone or in collaboration with an outside consultant, must select OD interventions carefully. The situation can become very confusing at this point if top management fails to keep itself adequately informed of the available intervention alternatives. Every year new OD techniques emerge. Some have great potential, while others promise more than they deliver.

In this section we review six popular OD interventions designed to enhance effectiveness at three different organizational levels (see Figure 8.4). *Life and career planning* and *skill development* are aimed at the individual. *Role analysis* and *team building* are aimed at the group. Finally, *survey feedback* and *Grid® OD* are aimed at the entire organization. These particular interventions have been chosen for review because they complement one another. Conceivably, all six interventions could play a role in a single, comprehensive OD program.

Life and career planning   Most employees today have no clear plans for their life and their career. Things just sort of happen. But individuals can be challenged to take greater responsibility for the direction of their lives. Just as challenging objectives can stimulate organizational productivity, life and career objectives can enhance personal effectiveness and satisfaction. Life and career planning, as an OD technique, gives the individual an opportunity to sit down and do a thorough self-analysis. Part of this self-analysis involves listing personal strengths and weaknesses. Discussion follows, with an eye toward taking greater advantage of the strengths while eliminating or neutralizing the weaknesses. If lack of formal education is a barrier, then a plan is formulated for going back to school. Perhaps a long-lost dream to master a second language, or learn a musical instrument, or get into computer programming can be rekindled.

The overall objective of life and career planning is to get

FIGURE 8.4
OD interventions for different organizational levels

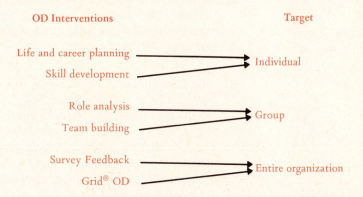

OD Interventions	Target
Life and career planning	Individual
Skill development	
Role analysis	Group
Team building	
Survey Feedback	Entire organization
Grid® OD	

individuals to define their personal goals for growth and development and to plan ways to achieve them. Underlying all this is the assumption that the personal growth of its members is an important part of an organization's growth and development.

Skill development This second kind of intervention also focuses primarily on the individual. When carried out alone (rather than as part of a comprehensive OD program), it is generally considered part of management training and development. Unlike most OD interventions, skill development involves content rather than process. For example, when an OD diagnosis uncovers the inability of a group of engineers in the research and development division of XYZ Company to write objectives and formulate plans, the deficiency is corrected through appropriate training. Similarly, managers and nonmanagers at all levels can be trained to polish their skills in problem solving, human relations, communication, decision making, and control. Emphasis in skill development clearly is on learning "how to."

Role analysis A role is a prescribed way of behaving. In an unhealthy organization, many people do not know what their roles are, and, if they do, their roles typically are in direct conflict with the roles of coworkers. In a healthy organization, behavioral scientists tell us, everyone knows his or her role, and the roles are interrelated in a manner that encourages cooperation and reduces conflict. For this reason many OD programs call for some sort of *role analysis*, which is the systematic clarification of interdependent modes of behavior.

The Diamond Shamrock Corporation, a large chemical and petroleum firm, once called on a team of OD consultants to deal with the rivalry, suspicion, and conflict that stemmed from a recent merger. Everyone seemed to be headed in a different direction. One part of the OD program involved role negotiation. A neutral observer from *Fortune* magazine explained the nature of this technique.

In the course of role negotiation, managers frankly discuss what they want from each other and explain why. Then they bargain. Nobody gets anything without promising something in return. For example, the head of a department might say to his plant manager, "If you give me production reports daily instead of weekly, I'll agree to review the salaries of your staff on a regular, annual basis." If they agree, they sign a contract and usually

CONVERSATION WITH . . .

Larry Pond
Executive Vice President—
  Distribution Group
Wyle Laboratories
Santa Clara, California

Photo courtesy of Wyle Laboratories.

PERSONAL BACKGROUND

Originally from Youngstown, New York, Larry Pond earned a bachelor's degree in electrical engineering from Clarkson College of Technology in 1960 and a master of business administration degree in 1967. His professional career was launched by spending ten years with Union Carbide Corporation in various engineering, marketing, and management positions. Next, he struck out on his own by becoming cofounder and marketing manager of Sperry Information Displays, a producer and distributor of electronic displays for clocks, calculators, and cash registers. Larry eventually joined Wyle when Sperry was sold. His present position calls for overseeing the distribution of electronic components from seven facilities in four western states that employ a total of 1,000 people. Larry Pond's distribution group records annual sales of $150 million by purchasing semiconductors and other electronic components from manufacturers such as Motorola, Intel, and Fairchild and marketing them to firms that produce computers, televisions, test instruments, TV games, and calculators.

QUOTABLE QUOTES

What is the most challenging aspect of your job as a manager?

Mr. Pond: The most challenging aspect is the management of growth. Our company is growing at an annual rate in excess of 20 percent. This puts great strains on the development of facilities, people, organization structure, and management systems.

What do you think it takes to be a successful manager today?

Mr. Pond: Three things: (1) An educated and dynamic thought process. (2) An understanding of people with knowledge of management processes that motivate. (3) A broad view of the business, economic, and social environment within which we live.

Do you have any guiding principles regarding the practice of management?

Mr. Pond: The principles of management are transferable across company and industry lines. The priorities and implementation may be different, but the principles are universal.

---

specify a penalty to be imposed if either party breaches the agreement.[14]

Although role negotiation alone did not turn Diamond Shamrock around overnight, it was instrumental in helping managers appreciate the benefits of cooperation rather than conflict.

Team building   As a process for developing group effectiveness, *team building* has become very popular in recent years. It takes many forms, from intensive laboratory training (T-group and sensitivity training) to structured exercises (such as formulation of strategic plans by a team of top managers). Team building is viewed by many as "pure" OD because it emphasizes interactive processes, the "how" of behavior within the task group. A noted OD specialist has ranked the purposes of team building as follows:

1. To set goals and/or priorities.
2. To analyze or allocate the way work is performed.
3. To examine the way a group is working, its processes (such as norms, decision making, communications).
4. To examine relationships among the people doing the work.[15]

It is important for the group itself to achieve these purposes by relying on its own leadership to solve real-life problems. The consultant-facilitator merely gets things headed in the right direction, quietly coaches as necessary along the way, periodically summarizes what has taken place, and selectively points out the impact of group processes such as communicating, problem solving, conflict resolution, and decision making. Ideally, managers should come away from a team-building session with a greater appreciation of how individuals can contribute effectively to group activity.

Survey feedback   The general nature of survey feedback is discussed earlier in this chapter. Information gathered through personal interviews and/or survey questionnaires is analyzed, boiled down into understandable forms, and shared with those who supplied the original information. Once again, the main purpose of survey feedback is to let people know where they stand relative to others on important organizational issues. Eight criteria for effective feedback, according to one authority, are as follows:

1. *Relevant*   Only information that is meaningful to the recipients should be fed back.
2. *Understandable*   To ensure clear communication, language and symbols should be familiar to the recipients.
3. *Descriptive*   Data should be in the form of real-life examples with which the recipients can identify.
4. *Verifiable*   Form of presentation should allow recipients to test the validity and accuracy of data fed back to them.
5. *Limited*   Too much feedback causes information overload; only significant highlights should be presented.
6. *Impactable*   Recipients should be given information on situations they can directly control.
7. *Comparative*   Comparative data let recipients know where they stand relative to others.
8. *Unfinalized*   Recipients must see feedback information as a beginning and a stimulus for action rather than as a final statement.[16]

Feedback that meets these criteria should be fed back to organizational subgroups as the situation allows until all employees have had a chance to see where and how they fit. At that point various OD interventions such as life and career planning, skill development, team building, and role analysis can be introduced as needed.

In a sense, as Figure 8.5 indicates, feedback is only the beginning. It can have either positive or negative consequences. Careful follow-up ensures that positive results such as personal growth outweigh negative aspects such as emotional conflict.

Grid OD   The Grid® approach is a trademarked, neatly packaged, and aggressively marketed OD program. Since the mid-1960s it has consistently ranked among the most popular OD approaches, and tens of thousands of managers have received Grid training. Grid

FIGURE 8.5
Possible effects of feedback

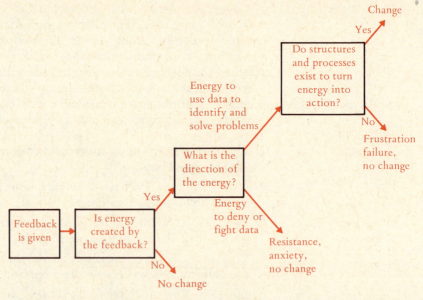

Adapted with permission from David A. Nadler, *Feedback and Organization Development: Using Data-Based Methods*, p. 146, Fig. 8.1, © 1977, Addison-Wesley, Reading, Massachusetts. Reprinted with permission.

proponents are quick to point out that it is a comprehensive kind of OD intervention because its six major phases unfold over a period of four, five, or more years. Briefly, the six phases are as follows:

○ *Phase 1* During a week-long seminar, participants have their management style diagnosed and discuss how they can improve their style.

○ *Phase 2* Participants learn how to be more effective contributors by going through a team-building workshop.

○ *Phase 3* Working from the skills developed in phases 1 and 2, managers work on developing intergroup problem-solving ability.

○ *Phase 4* Management teams (starting at the top and filtering down) work together to develop an organizational blueprint. This blueprint details where the organization ought to be headed.

○ *Phase 5* This action phase typically takes years to complete as the organizational blueprint conceived in phase 4 is put into practice.

○ *Phase 6* In this stabilization period newly acquired ways of solving problems, resolving conflict, and making decisions are refined for continued use.[17]

Clearly, Grid® OD is a combination of several OD techniques, arranged in an orderly fashion. No wonder it has been so popular in recent years.

FOLLOW-UP Effective OD programs do not end abruptly when the intervention phase is completed. They require a carefully monitored *refreezing* period to ensure lasting change. This follow-up phase has two objectives. First, management should attempt to evaluate the impact and effectiveness of the OD program. Second, it should take steps to maintain the changes that have been introduced. Let's examine each of these objectives in greater detail.

Evaluating the OD program Evaluation of changes in any complex social system is never easy.[18] Nevertheless, those in charge of an OD program owe it to themselves and to the target group or organization to determine whether they have done any good. Until now, evaluation has been one of the weak links in OD practice.

Two researchers who studied 160 assessments of OD-type programs carried out over a period of fifteen years concluded that organization development "has produced relatively little systematic evidence about its efficacy."[19] If any evaluation is made at all, it usually takes the form of subjective appraisal (see Boxes 1 and 2 in Figure 8.6). Needless to say, there is a tendency for participants to tell change agents what they want to hear and for change agents to selectively perceive only positive aspects. Subjective evaluations, although easy and inexpensive to obtain, offer change agents little hard evidence about the success or failure of their programs.

At the very least, a moderately objective evaluation can be carried out by comparing the actual accomplishments of the program with predetermined objectives. Not only should the objectives be defined at the beginning of the OD program, but they should be spelled out in workable, operational terms as well. For example, the somewhat

FIGURE 8.6
Measuring the success of OD interventions

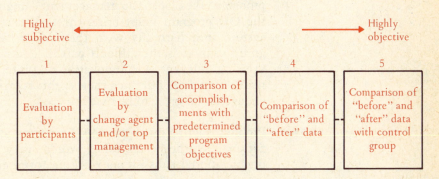

vague objective "to get engineering and production to work together" could be rewritten as "to establish weekly problem-solving meetings between engineering and production." Of course, a second operational objective would then be required to help evaluate the quality of the problem solving occurring at these meetings. As we have noted many times in this book, measurable objectives are at the very heart of effective management.

Ideally, users of OD techniques attempt to evaluate their programs in hard, factual terms. (Boxes 4 and 5 in Figure 8.6, for example, suggest comparing "before" data with "after" data, and comparing both of these with sets of data from a control group.) Attitude questionnaire results along with absentee, turnover, grievance, and financial data can be gathered before the OD program to serve as a baseline against which parallel data can be compared later. The use of a control group strengthens the evaluation by helping to rule out coincidental changes that might otherwise be attributed to the OD program. From a strictly scientific perspective, objective evaluations should be a part of every OD program, even though they are difficult, time consuming, expensive, and hence unappealing from an administrative standpoint. Meaningful improvement in an OD program is virtually impossible without an objective evaluation of the results.

Maintaining positive changes   The fundamental purpose of any OD program is to induce organization members to behave differently. Conflicting people should cooperate. Noncontributors should begin contributing. People working at cross-purposes should begin to collaborate.

While the various OD interventions are designed to get individuals to experiment with new modes of behavior, permanent behavior change is another matter. The key is a supportive climate for change back on the job. When the formal reward and punishment system and peer group pressure are supportive of change, then it will probably take place. Top management's unqualified commitment to the OD program helps bring the formal reward and punishment system into harmony with the desired behavioral change. Peer group support is the difficult part. It takes skillful unfreezing and exciting, relevant, and innovative OD interventions to get people really turned on. But once their enthusiasm builds up, no barrier to change is too great to be overcome.

SUMMARY   Problem-solving managers need a systematic way to achieve organizational synthesis. In other words, they must be able to get organizational subsystems working together in the most effective and efficient manner possible. Organization development (OD), a comprehensive approach to planned organizational change, answers this need for synthesis. From early work in the areas of laboratory training and survey research and feedback, OD has evolved into a diagnosis-prescription cycle.

Primary among the objectives of any OD program are increased trust, improved problem solving, more effective communication, and better cooperation. OD gets its positive orientation from four basic assumptions about people at work. These assumptions emphasize the organizational benefits of collaboration rather than individual action, cooperation rather than conflict, planned rather than haphazard change, and organic versus mechanistic structure.

The typical OD program is a three-phase process that recycles over and over again. During the unfreezing phase a diagnosis is completed. During the change phase interventions are carried out to enhance personal, group, and organizational effectiveness. Finally, during the refreezing phase the OD program is evaluated and steps are taken to maintain changes that have been introduced. The process then repeats itself as an ongoing commitment to planned change.

After deciding if the services of an outside consultant are required and identifying the probable target problem or area, management turns to unfreezing the situation, carrying out a diagnosis, and interpreting the diagnostic data. A great deal of valuable diagnostic information can be obtained by balancing the strengths and weaknesses of various techniques. Among them are record reviews, interviews, survey questionnaires, and direct observation. Careful interpretation of diagnostic data is needed to select the proper OD interventions.

OD interventions can be designed to bring about systematic change at the individual, group, or organizational level. Life and career planning and skill development enhance individual potential. Group performance affects all aspects of an organization. Consequently, role analysis and team building are very popular OD techniques for improving the problem-solving ability of work groups. Survey feedback and Grid® OD are recommended for improving overall organizational effectiveness. Since these interventions are designed to complement one another, they are often used in various combinations.

The third and final phase of OD, follow-up, involves evaluation of program effectiveness and maintenance of newly introduced changes. Altogether, the purpose of OD is to get people to behave in more productive and supportive ways with benefits accruing to both the individual and the organization.

TERMS TO UNDERSTAND

Organization development
Laboratory training
Survey research and feedback
Diagnosis-prescription cycle
Unfreezing

Intervention
Role analysis
Team building
Grid® OD
Refreezing

QUESTIONS FOR DISCUSSION

1. In what way is organization development (OD), synthetic in nature?
2. How did the field of OD develop?
3. What is the value of a diagnosis-prescription perspective in OD?
4. From your own experience, can you give examples of effective and ineffective organizations? Pinpoint the differences between them.
5. Why does an OD intervention without proper "unfreezing" have only a limited chance of success?
6. How do OD assumptions about human behavior contribute to the effectiveness of an organization? Do you agree with the four basic assumptions?
7. Drawing from your personal experience, what factors tend to erode the quality of superior-subordinate collaboration?
8. Which elements of effective feedback do you believe are most important? Support your answer.
9. What happens during the refreezing stage, and why is it important for the organization?
10. In what ways is evaluation the weak link in OD?

**CASE 8.1
VELVET TOUCH**

Roger Beaumont was visibly shaken as he hurried into his finely appointed executive suite. Thoughts of the afternoon's executive meeting made his thin face gaunt with worry as he dropped into his favorite leather chair. In twenty-three years of management, he had never witnessed such an intense and angry meeting. At one point, the discussion had erupted into a shouting match. It was unbelievable that such a great idea could create such a mess. Things were very different three weeks ago.

Roger's firm, Velvet Touch Cosmetics, Inc., had proudly announced a 15 percent jump in quarterly earnings. But as everyone in the highly competitive cosmetics industry knew, Velvet Touch owed it all to Stylex. Just six months earlier Velvet Touch had acquired Stylex, Inc., a medium-sized, highly profitable hair products firm. Velvet Touch's management was extremely pleased that the lengthy merger process had gone off without any major problems. The merger's chief effect was financial, as one condition of the merger was that Stylex would be allowed to retain its management team and run its own operations.

At the successful conclusion of the merger, Roger's superiors were naturally very receptive to his suggestion that an in-house OD program be launched to facilitate the postmerger process. Until today's meeting, Roger was happy with the way things were going. He was especially proud of how quickly his OD specialists had worked up and distributed the diagnostic survey. He had reviewed the survey instrument personally to make sure it was thorough. Even the interviews with Stylex's top management had gotten under way earlier this week. But that was before this afternoon's executive meeting.

As he sorted out the events of the day, Roger began to see things in perspective. First, one of the Stylex vice presidents angrily objected to what he called "Velvet Touch's heavy-handed snooping." And after that the discussion soured quickly. As it turned out, every single one of the Stylex executives had ill feelings about the "sneaky" way in which the OD survey and interviews were being handled. As they saw it, Velvet Touch was checking up on them for no apparent reason. "After all," they argued, "wasn't Stylex responsible for the recent upswing in profits?"

The Stylex executive team—young, aggressive, and extremely confident that they knew their business better than anyone else— could see no reason at all for the survey and the interviews. Throughout the merger process, the Stylex executives had been assured that they would be allowed to run their own show. Now they were angry.

FOR DISCUSSION
1. Do you believe the Stylex executives have a right to be angry? Support your answer.
2. How would you have "unfrozen" this situation?
3. What do you propose should be done now?

CASE 8.2
THAT WORRIES ME

Wanda Lacey has been in her present position as assistant director of organization development for five weeks. She joined Electrotech, a computer hardware manufacturer, as a management trainee just a year ago, shortly after earning her Master of Business Administration degree. She is not yet certain how well she is doing in her new position, but she is determined to work very hard and feels that the assignment given to her two weeks ago is a make or break situation from a career standpoint. Briefly, Wanda's new assignment involves screening the proposals of several OD consulting firms to see which one best suits the needs of the problem-ridden manufacturing operation in Rochester.

So far, Wanda has reviewed the written proposals of sixteen consulting firms and has selected three as exceptionally promising.

She has just heard presentations from representatives of each of the three finalists. Weighed against each other, the presentation by Jack Novak of Worldwide OD Consultants, Inc., appears to have been the best. Unfortunately, a disturbing question lingers in her mind. When she asked about Worldwide's plans for following up on their program, Novak casually replied, "That's a minor point. We'll simply send around our standard questionnaire to the program participants for their general impressions and comments."

FOR DISCUSSION

1. Why is Wanda concerned about Novak's answer?
2. If she makes a counterproposal, what should she ask for in the way of follow-up?

REFERENCES

Opening quotations

W. J. Reddin, "Confessions of an Organizational Change Agent," *Training and Development Journal* 31 (October 1977): 55.

Richard Beckhard and Reuben T. Harris, *Organizational Transitions*: *Managing Complex Change* (Reading, Mass.: Addison-Wesley, 1977), p. 110.

1. "Beckhard: An Agent of Change," *International Management* 30 (August 1975): 48.
2. "Bennis: Practice Versus Theory," *International Management* 30 (October 1975): 42.
3. Harold M. F. Rush, *Organization Development*: *A Reconnaissance*, Report No. 605 (New York: The Conference Board, 1973), p. 2.
4. The following historical interpretation is based in part on that found in: Wendell L. French and Cecil H. Bell, *Organization Development* (Englewood Cliffs, N.J.: Prentice-Hall, 1973), chap. 3.
5. For a more extensive discussion see: Robert J. House, "T-Group Training: Good or Bad?" *Business Horizons* 12 (December 1969): 69–77.
6. H. Kent Baker and Ronald H. Gorman, "Diagnosis: Key to O.D. Effectiveness," *Personnel Journal* 55 (October 1976): 506.
7. This list is adapted from a longer one found in: Wendell French, "Organization Development Objectives, Assumptions, and Strategies," *California Management Review* 12 (Winter 1969): 23–34.
8. Warren Bennis, *Changing Organizations* (New York: McGraw-Hill, 1966), p. 77.

9. Richard Beckhard, *Organization Development*: *Strategies and Models* (Reading, Mass.: Addison-Wesley, 1969), pp. 10–11.
10. Beckhard and Harris, *Organizational Transitions*, p. 27.
11. James Ross Warren, "Diagnosis of the Potential for Organizational Improvement," *Personnel Journal* 56 (June 1977): 302–304.
12. One useful collection of ninety-two instruments, many with diagnostic potential, is: J. William Pfeiffer, Richard Heslin, and John E. Jones, *Instrumentation in Human Relations Training*, 2nd ed. (1976). This book is published by University Associates, Inc., 8517 Production Ave., San Diego, CA 92121.
13. David Nadler, *Feedback and Organization Development*: *Using Data-Based Methods* (Reading, Mass.: Addison-Wesley, 1977), p. 143.
14. Arthur M. Louis, "They're Striking Some Strange Bargains at Diamond Shamrock," *Fortune* 93 (January 1976): 143.
15. Richard Beckhard, "Optimizing Team-Building Efforts," *Journal of Contemporary Business* 1 (Summer 1972): 24. *Note:* The entire summer 1972 issue of the *Journal of Contemporary Business* is devoted to an informative overview of organization development.
16. This list is adapted from: Nadler, *Feedback and Organization Development*, pp. 147–148.
17. For more extensive discussion see: Robert R. Blake and Jane Srygley Mouton, "An Overview of the Grid®," *Training and Development Journal* 29 (May 1975): 29–37.
18. For an interesting and thought-provoking discussion of evaluation see: Henry W. Reicken, "Memorandum on Program Evaluation," in *Organization Development: Theory, Practice, and Research*, ed. Wendell L. French, Cecil H. Bell, Jr., and Robert A. Zawacki (Dallas: Business Publications, 1978), pp. 413–423.
19. Jerry I. Porras and P. O. Berg, "The Impact of Organization Development," *Academy of Management Review* 3 (April 1978): 263.

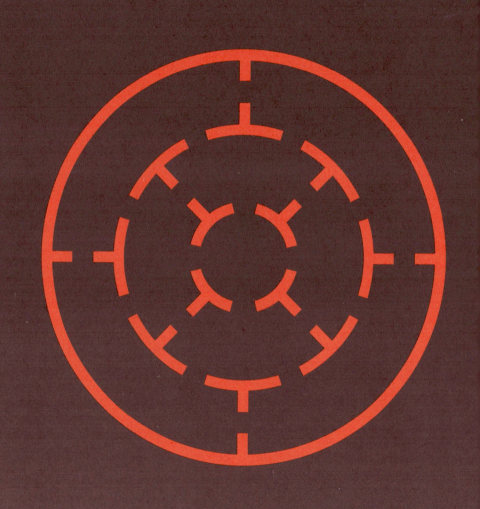

IV

Managing Operations and Making Decisions

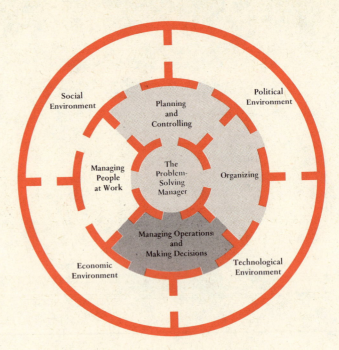

PART IV CONSIDERS OPERATIONS MANAGEMENT AND DECISION MAK-
ing. Formal organizations are created for the express purpose of
producing goods and/or services. The field of operations management has evolved in response to the problem of managing organizations as productive systems rather than patchworks of vaguely
related fragments. Relying heavily on the scientific method, open-
system thinking, and models, today's operations managers attempt
to find the most effective and efficient way of transforming raw
materials into useful end products and services. Operations management helps managers make better decisions. Operations management and decision making go hand in hand when decision making is
approached as a systematic and rational process. The overriding
problem facing decision makers is how to make prompt and
intelligent decisions in spite of imperfect information.

Chapter 9

Operations Management

*In the years to come . . . the theory of productive systems will be
pervasive and will embrace integrated systems as a whole, not just
segments of a system.*

Elwood S. Buffa

LEARNING OBJECTIVES

When you finish reading this chapter, you should be able to

o Describe the distinguishing characteristics of operations management.
o Explain how societal demands affect product design.
o Identify the six criteria for selecting vendors.
o Outline the factors favoring small inventories.
o Differentiate between product and process layouts.
o Explain why productive systems need both feedforward and
feedback quality control.

Through the years, our conceptual treatment of complex organizations has resembled the old story about the three blind men and the elephant. It seems that each man came up with an entirely different version of what an elephant resembled. One, clutching the trunk, said an elephant was like a vine. Another, feeling only a leg, confidently stated that elephants were like tree trunks. The third, touching the elephant's stomach, argued that elephants were round like boulders. So, too, the study of organizations has suffered from selective perception. Some experts have focused on administration, others on human behavior, and still others on structure. Although something has been learned from each of these restricted views, the big picture has all too often been ignored.

Thanks to modern systems thinking, however, strictly analytical treatments of organizations are beginning to be supplemented by more encompassing synthetic approaches. Organization development, for example, deals with organizations as complex *social* systems. But even OD, with its preoccupation with behavioral phenomena, cannot solve all organizational problems. Fortunately, a second synthetic view has evolved within the field of management. Operations management, which attempts to deal with organizations as complex *productive* systems, is a unique and promising perspective. The purpose of this chapter is to introduce operations management.

WHAT IS OPERATIONS MANAGEMENT?

As defined in Chapter 2, *operations management* "encompasses the design, implementation, operation, and control of systems made up of men, materials, capital equipment, information, and money to accomplish some set of objectives."[1] If we stop to think about it, this definition sounds much like the general management process itself. In effect, operations management amounts to a specialized version of the basic management process. Its specialization derives from an emphasis on logic, scientific methodology, and quantitative analysis.

This emphasis, unfortunately, has led those who tend to rely on less precise management techniques to discount operations management as being "up in the clouds," "too esoteric," or "impractical." Critics within the field constantly urge operations management specialists to stay in touch with practical reality. For example, after launching an attack on his quantitatively oriented colleagues for being impractical, one critic suggested an updated definition: operations management is "the application of logic and mathematics to a real-world problem, in such a way that the method used does not get in the way of common sense."[2] This could be regarded as good advice for virtually every aspect of management.

Every discipline has its unique set of distinguishing characteristics and its special point of view. Operations management is no exception. Operations management is (1) interdisciplinary, (2) scientific, (3) holistic, and (4) model-based. After we discuss these characteristics, we will take a look at operations management's special point of view.

INTERDISCIPLINARY APPROACH

Pursuit of practical solutions often leads those in operations management to cross disciplinary lines. This habit may not appeal to the academic or theoretical purist, but it often opens doors to exciting new ways of doing things. At various times, in order to solve a particular problem, operations management draws from general management, mathematics, statistics, logistics, computer science, numerous branches of engineering, and other fields. For example, an operations manager employed by a coal mining company needs to know something about geology, mining technology, mine safety legislation, human physiology, and a host of other factors. This kind of interdisciplinary perspective involves a great deal of lateral thinking when solving problems.

SCIENTIFIC METHOD

Those in management who emphasize logic and quantitative techniques see themselves as management scientists. That is, they make extensive use of the scientific method while studying ways to improve productive organizations. The scientific method involves establishing a hypothesis that may or may not prove true in actual practice. The manager needs to test the hypothesis in a carefully controlled situation while trying a different process in a similarly controlled situation. By comparing the two sets of data, the manager can learn the true effect of the original hypothesis. Conclusions can then be translated to actual practice to achieve efficiencies of operation.

HOLISTIC PERSPECTIVE

A holistic perspective means that complex phenomena are studied as whole systems rather than as isolated variables. We can discover important facts by studying the functional relationships among the parts that combine to form an integrated system. For example, in a profit-making manufacturing operation the production process is not studied in isolation. It is studied as one variable interdependently tied to others such as resource procurement, materials flow, quality control, and marketing. Operations managers believe that the only way to get the data needed to make good decisions is to look at the whole system.

USE OF MODELS   Operations managers typically rely on models to help make extremely complex real-life problems more readily subject to analysis and solution. *Models* are simplified representations of the real world created for the purposes of understanding, prediction, or control. They have been classified in the following manner:

1. An *iconic model* pictorially or visually represents certain aspects of a system (as does a photograph or model airplane).
2. An *analogue model* employs one set of properties to represent some other set of properties which the system being studied possesses (e.g., for certain purposes, the flow of water through pipes may be taken as an analogue of the "flow" of electricity in wires).
3. A *symbolic model* is one which employs symbols to designate properties of the system under study (by means of a mathematical equation or set of such equations).[3]

Computerized mathematical models are particularly popular today in the field of operations management because they combine the calculative speed of the computer with the logical precision of mathematics.

A SPECIAL POINT OF VIEW   Sometimes *what* you look at is less important than *how* you look at it. For example, an optimist sees a gallon jug containing a half gallon of water as being half full rather than half empty. Similarly, operations managers have their own special point of view. It has two dimensions.

First, they see organizations as *productive systems* with inputs, a transformation process, and outputs. As illustrated in Figure 9.1, we are dealing with an open-system perspective. The whole productive process consists of interrelated parts. Among the important parts of productive systems are six activities: product design; production

FIGURE 9.1
Viewing organizations as productive transformation systems

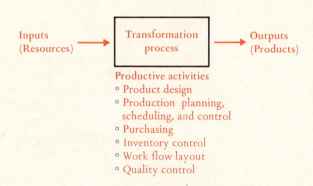

Inputs (Resources) → Transformation process → Outputs (Products)

Productive activities
° Product design
° Production planning, scheduling, and control
° Purchasing
° Inventory control
° Work flow layout
° Quality control

planning, scheduling, and control; purchasing; inventory control; work flow layout; and quality control. Together, these activities enable the organization to transform resources into products effectively and efficiently.

A second dimension of the operations manager's special point of view involves using the term *product* as a generic label. A product does not necessarily have to be a physical object such as a drill press, a typewriter, or a tape cassette. A product may be anything from a healthy patient leaving a hospital to a satisfied patron leaving a restaurant (see Table 9.1). Dealing with a generic "product" label means that operations management does not have to be restricted to factory operations. Today, operations management techniques are being applied in hospitals, restaurants, stores, government offices, schools and universities, military operations, and a host of other nonfactory organizations.

Much of the following discussion on productive activities refers to tangible products as a matter of convenience. However, the reader should feel free to translate the underlying concepts to nonfactory service organizations.

PRODUCT DESIGN   The product itself is the logical starting point when considering the creation and management of a productive system. Generally, a good product increases the probability of organizational success. A poorly designed product can come back to haunt the organization in the

TABLE 9.1
Productive systems come in many sizes and shapes

TYPICAL PRODUCTIVE ORGANIZATIONS	PRIMARY INPUTS	GENERAL TRANSFORMATION ACTIVITY	PRIMARY OUTPUT
American Motors	Steel, glass, rubber, and so on	Fabrication and assembly	Automobiles
California State University, Fresno	High school graduates	Academic instruction	Employable graduates
U.S. Federal Reserve	Information about state of the economy	Economic strategy formulation	Adjustments in the money supply
Clarkson Hospital, Omaha, Nebraska	Ill patients	Diagnostic and remedial medical care	Normally functioning individuals
Mama Leone's restaurant, New York City	Hungry tourists	Commercial food preparation and service	Satisfied patrons who will recommend restaurant

form of costly material and equipment changes and even product recalls. A case in point is Ford Motor Company's discovery in 1978 that 2.7 million of its four- and six-cylinder engines had a "small" design flaw. According to *Business Week*, the engines in question "were more susceptible to wearing out in cold climates because of a cost-savings move that eliminated two oil holes that normally would have been drilled into the piston connecting rods."[4] The estimated cost of *correcting* this design flaw in 56,000 recalls was approximately $250 per car, a total of $14 million. Needless to say, it would have been considerably less expensive to drill the holes in the first place. Seemingly insignificant product design decisions can have enormous long-term consequences.

Product design may be defined as the process of creating a set of product specifications appropriate to the demands of the situation. At first glance, the translation of demand into design specifications appears to be a fundamental marketing problem. This is true, but only from the standpoint of striving to satisfy *consumer* demand. For example, market researchers in the electric appliance industry routinely ask homemakers about their pet peeves and problems in the kitchen. Armed with this "grass roots" consumer information, design engineers then build a product to fill the demand. Electric knives, automatic ice cube makers, and eye-level ovens all resulted from this form of demand translation. But in today's complex world, products must do much more than satisfy consumers' demands for certain functions.

Modern products need to be designed to satisfy a rainbow of *societal* demands in addition to individual demands. Society's demands for safer products, a cleaner environment, and safer working conditions have fostered the establishment of federal watchdog agencies such as the Consumer Product Safety Commission, the Environmental Protection Agency, and the Occupational Safety and Health Administration.

Meeting the demands of these agencies necessarily begins at the product design stage. For example, toy makers can no longer use lead-base paint because of the possibility of lead poisoning among children, who commonly put toys in their mouths. Automobile engines have been redesigned, at great expense, to burn lead-free gasoline. Many building products have been redesigned to eliminate the use of asbestos, a proven lung cancer hazard for workers.

The translation of demand into product design specifications requires a great deal of open-system thinking because of the complex combination of individual and societal demands on today's organizations. The cost-quality trade off that trapped Ford in the case cited earlier is an example of the difficult decisions that need to be made in product design. Production costs have to be kept as low as possible without threatening the quality needed to satisfy individual and societal demands.

All products begin as ideas. Some turn out to be good ideas and some bad. Nevertheless, the path from idea to finished product is often long and difficult. The sequence of activities in Figure 9.2 points out the many hurdles an idea must clear before it becomes a physical reality. Problem solving must take place at each step.

PRODUCTION PLANNING, SCHEDULING, and CONTROL   This second phase of the productive transformation process combines all the other phases into a coordinated whole. Because a number of practical and widely used planning, scheduling, and control techniques were introduced and explained in Chapters 4 and

FIGURE 9.2
The product design process

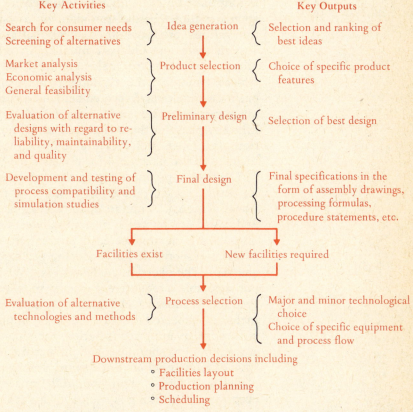

Key Activities

Key Outputs

Search for consumer needs
Screening of alternatives
} Idea generation {
Selection and ranking of best ideas

Market analysis
Economic analysis
General feasibility
} Product selection {
Choice of specific product features

Evaluation of alternative designs with regard to reliability, maintainability, and quality
} Preliminary design {
Selection of best design

Development and testing of process compatibility and simulation studies
} Final design {
Final specifications in the form of assembly drawings, processing formulas, procedure statements, etc.

Facilities exist   New facilities required

Evaluation of alternative technologies and methods
} Process selection {
Major and minor technological choice
Choice of specific equipment and process flow

Downstream production decisions including
° Facilities layout
° Production planning
° Scheduling

Used with permission from Richard B. Chase and Nicholas J. Aquilano, *Production and Operations Management: A Life Cycle Approach,* rev. ed. (Homewood, Ill.: Richard D. Irwin, 1977), p. 85. © 1977 by Richard D. Irwin, Inc.

5 on planning and controlling, only a brief overview relative to operations management is provided here. Nonetheless, the basic functions of planning and control are as important as ever when the focus narrows to the production of goods and services.

Production planning is defined as the process of allocating productive resources such as facilities and space, equipment, skilled and unskilled employees, and raw materials to ensure that demand for the organization's products is met in an efficient manner. Relative to the distinction between strategic, intermediate, and operational planning in Chapter 4, production planning occurs primarily at the intermediate and operational levels. Of course, top-level strategic planners must have done their homework on demand forecasts, competition, innovation, and resource availability.

Typically, a master production plan based on forecasted demand is formulated for the organization's entire range of products. This approach allows production planners to establish priorities among the various products so that productive capacity is used in a cost-effective and efficient manner. In profit-making businesses, products expected to make greater contributions to profits are allocated more of the available production capacity than are less profitable products. Expected demand dictates production priorities for managers in nonprofit service and government organizations. Like any phase of the overall planning process, the master production plan consists of measurable objectives and clear action statements (refer to Chapter 4 for review).

The master production plan then serves as the guiding document for more specific product-by-product or facility-by-facility operational planning. A hierarchy of objectives and plans is constructed as detailed in Chapter 4. It eventually gets right down to how many units of which product each production supervisor (and subordinates) is responsible for producing per day, week, month, quarter, and year. The overriding question is: "What is the best way to use our available productive capacity to effectively meet demand?" Productive capacity changes over time because of many factors including expected absenteeism and tardiness, vacations, holidays, strikes, wage and price inflation, inclement weather, raw material and equipment shortages, and projected equipment failure rates. In spite of relatively high uncertainty among these factors, production plans must reflect their potential impact. A healthy measure of open-system thinking is useful in this area.

Interwoven with the production planning process is production scheduling. Flow charts and Gantt charts (see Chapter 4) help ensure that productive capacity is employed efficiently without wasteful idleness due to work flow bottlenecks.

As discussed in Chapter 5 on controlling, even the best laid plans can go astray. Consequently, both feedforward and feedback production control are required to prevent and correct deviations from plan. We will direct our attention to inventory and quality control later in this chapter.

PURCHASING It is not uncommon today for purchased materials to account for more than 50 percent of a product's wholesale price. Automobiles, for example, are rolling off assembly lines at this very moment with tires, mirrors, windows, electrical wire, headlights, spark plugs, nuts and bolts, and even entire engines purchased from other firms. When an organization decides to buy rather than make a portion of its product(s), purchasing becomes an important link in the productive system. As the term is used here, *purchasing* refers to the procurement of raw materials, subcomponents, and equipment required in the productive process. A purchasing manager in a furniture manufacturing firm procures wood, metal fittings, and wood-working machinery, whereas a purchasing manager in a hotel chain deals with linen, cleaning equipment, and food and beverages. Given the huge sums of money that pass through purchasing managers' hands, intelligent buying is a must. Purchasing entails much more than simply spending money.

VENDOR SELECTION Purchasing managers typically agree that *who* you buy from is just as important as *what* you buy from them. The process of selecting vendors should be characterized by systematic analysis, not haphazard guesswork. It is helpful to screen each potential vendor on the basis of the six following criteria.

Price Shopping around for the lowest price possible is nearly always an essential step in deciding on a vendor. Even seemingly insignificant differences in price deserve careful consideration. For example, a large manufacturing firm that purchases five tons of copper wire quarterly can save $1,200 per year by taking advantage of a small three cent per pound price difference. Also, quantity discounts afford great potential for savings.

Quality In accordance with the well-known computer principle, "garbage in—garbage out," substandard and shoddy raw materials and subcomponents mean a substandard finished product. Purchasing specialists are constantly challenged to find the best possible product at the lowest possible price. Here is where product design and purchasing are married. Product design specifications can be used as a pattern for purchasing specifications. Naturally, all incoming orders need to be checked for quality against purchasing specifications.

Reliability   A favorable balance between price and quality means little if the vendor cannot reliably serve the buyer's needs. Taking time to check out a particular vendor's track record with other organizations can pay off handsomely in the long run. Vendors may fail to meet their obligations for a number of reasons. Among them are inadequate financing, raw material shortages, strikes and other labor problems, unreliable transportation, and overcommitment.

Service   Vendor follow-up becomes an important criterion when the purchase of complex capital equipment is involved. For example, typewriter and photocopy machine breakdowns can paralyze the flow of work in an office. Similarly, a construction company loses money when heavy equipment stands idle owing to lack of prompt repair. Those in charge of purchasing are advised to investigate the vendor's reputation for service and follow-up.

Credit   Does the vendor demand immediate payment or are liberal credit terms available? By working in concert with financial managers, purchasing personnel can effect measurable savings by negotiating favorable credit terms. Furthermore, it is possible to save money by taking advantage of cash discounts. For example, if a vendor's contract calls for terms of 2/10 net 30, it means that the buyer will receive a 2 percent discount if the account is paid within ten days. Otherwise, the entire amount is due in thirty days.

Shipping costs   Although it often receives insufficient attention, the cost of getting the purchased good from the point of manufacture or storage to the point of use is an important consideration in vendor selection. Otherwise favorable price and credit economies can be wiped out by shipping costs. When the buyer has to pay shipping costs, it sometimes makes sense to purchase from a higher-priced yet geographically closer vendor. Also, shipping costs can be kept in line by placing large orders well enough in advance of use to allow shipment by relatively less expensive forms of transportation (for example, by rail rather than air freight).

A PRODUCT LIFE CYCLE APPROACH It is evident from the foregoing discussion that purchasing necessarily includes a healthy measure of planning. Inflation combined with the growing threat of resource shortages make it all the more important for purchasing managers to plan ahead. The product life cycle concept has been suggested as a useful way of anticipating purchasing needs.[5] A *product life cycle* is a graphic representation of fluctuations in sales volume and profit over time. As illustrated in Figure 9.3, the typical product life cycle has six stages. They are introduction, growth, maturity, saturation, decline, and abandonment. Purchasing requirements vary with each stage. This is true regardless of whether the product life cycle is relatively short, as in the case of hula hoops, or extremely long, as in the case of Rolls Royce automobiles.

Introduction New products come in two basic varieties. Some are related to products already being produced by the firm, whereas others are totally new and different. Purchasing materials for the first variety is relatively easy, since there is parallel prior experience. Purchasing for the second variety, however, is much more difficult, because new, significantly different products tend to be turned out in relatively small lots by people with limited experience using unfamiliar technologies. All this means that purchasing managers need to find suppliers who are flexible enough to cover

FIGURE 9.3 The product life cycle

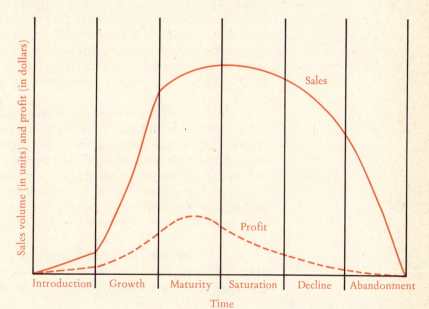

spotty demand. The introductory period is a good time to experiment with alternative vendors. But with low sales and almost nonexistent profits, expenses must be kept low. Quality of purchased items deserves extra attention during this introductory stage because the organization is attempting to establish a good reputation for the final product.

Growth   Sales often rise rapidly during this second stage. Profits tend to increase measurably because of competitive advantage. Simply being aware that this dramatic jump in output is likely to take place helps purchasing managers complete the necessary groundwork. A number of alternative suppliers capable of honoring frequent and rush orders must be lined up. Rapid growth also necessitates larger inventories or raw materials and subcomponents to reduce the chances of being caught short. Quantity discounts enter the picture as a cost-saving device during the growth stage.

Maturity   During the maturity stage, sales and profits reach record highs. Due to the high level of output, purchasers have an opportunity to commit the organization to long-term contracts. Other opportunities open up as well. For example, Mars Inc., the maker of such familiar candy bars as Snickers, M&M's, and 3 Musketeers, uses so much cocoa, sugar, and dried milk that it profitably invests in the futures markets for these commodities. Mars accomplishes this by having sophisticated operations research specialists project future prices and invest appropriately.[6] Weak or marginally reliable vendors can be weeded out during the maturity stage. High volume during this stage also opens up the possibility of making rather than buying important subcomponents.

Saturation   In almost all cases increased competition eventually leads to a downward turn in demand and profits. By the time this occurs, production facilities may be showing signs of wear or obsolescence. New equipment purchases should be resisted in favor of stopgap maintenance. Reductions in raw materials inventories are advisable to avoid being saddled with unusable surplus. All purchasing costs must be kept to a minimum because of the sharp decline in profits during the saturation stage.

Decline   As sales and profits continue to slide rapidly, purchasers need to stay away from long-term commitments. Purchasing costs and inventories should be pruned as much as possible.

Abandonment All good things must come to an end. There comes a time to drop old products to make way for new ones. Vendors should be notified of intentions to drop the product. Any leftover materials or supplies that cannot be shifted to use in new products should be disposed of as surplus.

INVENTORY CONTROL

As far as raw materials, subcomponents, and supplies are concerned, purchasing and inventory control go hand in hand. Because these inputs are not used the minute they arrive, they must be kept on hand for varying periods of time. But inventory control encompasses more than stockpiling purchased items. Partially completed products and finished goods waiting to be sold enlarge the task of inventory control. Considering all types of inventory as a whole,

Drawing by Chas. Addams; © 1978 The New Yorker Magazine, Inc.

manufacturing firms like General Electric typically tie up one-fourth of their invested capital in inventories.

During 1975 General Electric sold $13.5 billion worth of products and at the end of the year owned $2.1 billion worth of inventories—stocks of materials and products. General Foods sold $3.7 billion worth of products and ended the year owning $580 million of inventories. RCA sold $4.6 billion worth of products and services and finished the year owning an inventory of $600 million.[7]

Because inventories quickly add up to staggering investments, they are a major contributor to an organization's success or failure. At General Electric, for instance, a seemingly insignificant 5 percent increase in inventories would tie up an additional $105 million in working capital. A financial burden of this magnitude can spell disaster for a firm, even one as large as General Electric, because funds locked up in inventory cannot be used elsewhere. Consequently, *inventory control*, the process of establishing and maintaining reserve stocks of goods, is an important managerial concern.

TYPES OF INVENTORY   There are four basic categories of inventory: (1) raw materials and purchased subcomponents, (2) work in process, (3) supplies, and (4) finished goods. The first category, raw materials and subcomponents, feeds the productive system. Ideally, it is a steady and reliable source of input. Work-in-process inventories are necessary because the transformation process usually consists of a number of consecutive subprocesses requiring different lengths of time to complete. For example, automobile seats are made and stockpiled for eventual use in the general assembly process. Supplies such as paper, typewriter ribbons, lubricating oil, and cleansing agents, which are consumed during the transformation process, also require stockpiling for use as needed. Finally, a finished products inventory is necessitated by fluctuating demand.

In spite of subtle differences in the management of these various categories of inventory, all are subject to conflicting demands. On the one hand are demands to maintain large inventories; on the other are demands to keep inventories as low as possible. These competing demands are outlined in Table 9.2.

The factors favoring large inventories generally are the product of conservatism and fear of the unknown. Demands for small inventories are based primarily on cost considerations. Neither side is altogether right or wrong. Both sets of factors have merit. Managers

TABLE 9.2
Conflicting demands
concerning the size of
inventories

FACTORS FAVORING LARGE INVENTORIES	FACTORS FAVORING SMALL INVENTORIES
○ Fear of running out of stock ○ Anticipation of unexpected jumps in demand ○ Desire to keep ordering, shipping, and production costs low ○ Desire to take advantage of favorable prices and quantity discounts ○ Desire to have a hedge against inflation ○ Fear of unexpected events such as strikes, embargoes, and natural disasters	○ Desire to minimize working capital tied up in inventory ○ Desire to minimize storage costs ○ Limitations on storage capacity ○ Desire to keep insurance and tax expenses down ○ Fear of obsolescence ○ Danger of spoilage

are challenged to balance both sides of the equation so that inventoried items are available when needed without incurring unreasonable expense in the process.

MANAGING THE
INVENTORY CYCLE

Part of the answer to the challenge of determining the best inventory size lies in viewing inventory management as a cyclical process (see Figure 9.4). The heart of this cyclical process amounts to deciding how much to order and when. Assuming that demand for inventoried goods is relatively predictable, these two decisions are carried out on a regular, cyclical basis.

Before exploring the details of the inventory cycle in Figure 9.4, a qualification must be inserted. The cycle in Figure 9.4 is somewhat idealistic because demand for inventoried items tends to fluctuate. For example, approximately 60 to 70 percent of each year's toy sales occur during the six weeks before Christmas. Consequently, vigorous toy production early in the year requires large raw materials inventories that gradually taper as Christmas nears and production slows. This type of seasonal fluctuation also affects finished goods inventories. Nevertheless, even though seasonal fluctuations do occur, the basic points in Figure 9.4 remain valid.

The inventory cycle in Figure 9.4 has two dimensions, quantity and time. Inventory on hand in this example ranges from 0 to 200 units. A safety stock of 40 units has been created to reduce the chances of running out. Safety stock levels are based on prior experience and usage patterns. They amount to insurance against

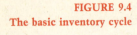

FIGURE 9.4
The basic inventory cycle

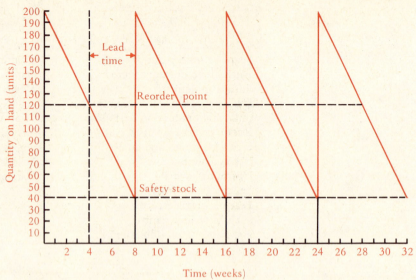

running out and being unable to meet demand. Exhaustion of raw materials inventory can bring the entire production process to a halt. For example, automobiles cannot leave the factory until the tires have been mounted. Running out of finished goods can be equally disruptive. "Selling from an empty wagon" means that time-consuming back orders must be processed later or, worse, that dissatisfied customers may be lost to competitors.

Once safety stock levels have been determined, attention then turns to ordering the right amount at the right time. Referring once again to Figure 9.4, assume that experience has shown that 160 units are used every eight weeks, or 20 units a week on the average. The order quantity would then be fixed at 160 units. Next, timing of the order needs to be determined. Suppose that experience has proven that it takes about four weeks from the time the order goes out to the time the goods are received. This means that orders have to be placed at least four weeks prior to the inventory level reaching the safety threshold of 40 units. This four-week period is referred to as the lead time. Consequently, when the inventory level reaches the reorder point of 120 units, which is 40 units plus 80 units (four times the weekly average), management knows it is time to reorder. Four weeks later, when the inventory stands at 40 units, 160 units are received, thus taking the inventory level up to 200. The inventory cycle repeats itself over and over again this way in sawtooth fashion.

CALCULATING ECONOMICAL ORDER QUANTITIES (EOQ)

Since World War II, precise statistical inventory control techniques have been developed to replace crude rules of thumb. One such technique is the economical order quantity (*EOQ*) model. This useful tool was developed to help managers achieve an economical balance between two important inventory control variables: (1) acquisition costs, and (2) carrying costs. It costs money not only to acquire inventory but also to keep it on hand. The EOQ model provides managers with a rational way of determining how much to order each time an order is placed.

The basic EOQ formula is

$$EOQ = \sqrt{\frac{2FU}{CP}}$$

with the variables defined as follows:

EOQ = the most economical quantity to order each time an order is placed

F = fixed costs incurred in placing and receiving a single order (acquisition costs)

U = units of the item used per year

C = carrying costs (storage, insurance, taxes, spoilage, and so on) expressed as a percentage of inventory value

P = purchase price per unit of inventory.[8]

To demonstrate the use of this model, assume that a manager calculates the following values:

F = $10
U = 100 units
C = 20%
P = $1

These values can then be worked into the model as follows:

$$EOQ = \sqrt{\frac{2FU}{CP}}$$

$$EOQ = \sqrt{\frac{2 \times 10 \times 100}{0.2 \times 1}} = \sqrt{\frac{2,000}{0.2}} = \sqrt{10,000} = 100 \text{ units}$$

Considering the acquisition and carrying costs involved, an order of 100 units is the most economical quantity for this item.

COMPUTERIZED INVENTORY CONTROL

Although this discussion of inventory control may seem a bit complicated, it really is only the tip of a huge, complex iceberg. Just imagine how complicated inventory control could become if an inventory of spare parts, for example, contained 10,000 or more items, each subject to fluctuating demand and price. But this is precisely the case today with many of our larger public and private organizations. For example, the Air Force Logistics Command carries a 250,000-item expendable spares inventory.[9] Consequently, sophisticated inventory classification and control techniques have been developed that take advantage of the calculative speed of electronic computers.[10] Thanks to the development of widely applicable "canned" computer inventory control programs and fairly inexpensive computer time-sharing services, small organizations that cannot afford a computer can still enjoy the benefits of computerized inventory control. Nevertheless, it is important for managers to know how inventory control fits into the overall process of productive transformation.

MATERIAL REQUIREMENTS PLANNING

The need to combat costly inefficiencies due to piecemeal handling of the various production functions (such as scheduling, purchasing, and inventory control) is being met in a growing number of organizations by a promising new technique. It is called material requirements planning or simply MRP. *Material requirements planning* is a systematic and comprehensive planning and control technique designed to increase the efficiency of material, labor, and facility use. MRP systems normally are computerized because of the massive data processing involved. In fact, a variety of MRP packages are now available from computer hardware and software vendors. Like management by objectives and management information systems, discussed in Chapter 5, MRP requires careful implementation and should not be considered an automatic cure-all.

To date, MRP systems have been implemented in relatively few organizations. But initial successes give promise of broader application of this technique in the future. Although a bit of situational tailoring is usually necessary to accommodate unique circumstances, there is an underlying logic to MRP systems that includes the following steps:

1. From forecasts of end products (finished items to be sold to customers) a master production plan is formulated to tell what products are to be completed and when. For example, the master

production plan may call for 200 toy wagons and 100 tricycles to be shipped August 1.

2. The bill of materials for each product is reviewed to determine the parts needed to manufacture it. For example, wagons require four wheels each and tricycles need three, so a total of 1100 wheels are needed. Determining all needed parts, components, and subassemblies for an end product by multiplying the quantity needed by the list of parts in the bill of materials is called "exploding" the product.

3. Time phasing is the next step. Wheels must be manufactured or purchased ahead of time so they will be ready when the final assembly of the end product begins. The wagons and tricycles must be shipped August 1 and one week is required for assembly, so the wheels should be available July 25. If it takes two weeks to order and receive wheels, they should be ordered no later than July 11.

4. It will not be necessary to order all 1100 wheels, because inventory records indicate that 500 wheels are already in the warehouse. Using all the foregoing information, the MRP system instructs management to place an order for 600 wheels on July 11.

This fairly simple procedure of working backward from sales forecasts to determine what materials are needed when becomes very complicated in a shop producing dozens of items each made up of hundreds of parts. The computerized MRP system performs millions of calculations and keeps track of material and scheduling requirements to help the manager make decisions based on facts rather than hunch and guesswork.

Managers both directly and indirectly involved with operations management can look forward to many exciting breakthroughs in organizational effectiveness and efficiency as MRP comes of age.

WORK FLOW LAYOUT   Because the transformation process is a system, every part of it is important, including the physical movement of work through the production cycle. This part of production is called *work flow layout*, the process of determining the physical arrangement of the productive system. People and machines can be scattered about haphazardly, or they can be arranged in a logical, orderly, and cost-effective manner. Experts in the field suggest that a good layout for a production operation will accomplish the following:

1. Minimize investment in equipment.
2. Minimize overall production time.

3. Utilize existing space most effectively.
4. Provide for employee convenience, safety, and comfort.
5. Maintain flexibility of arrangement and operation.
6. Minimize material-handling cost.
7. Minimize variation in types of material-handling equipment.
8. Facilitate the manufacturing process.
9. Facilitate the organizational structure.[11]

Balancing these often conflicting considerations is an immensely challenging task. An understanding of basic layout formats and process flow charting helps.

LAYOUT FORMATS

Although a manager can go out and find innumerable production layout configurations, there are three basic formats. Others are simply variations or combinations of these three. The three basic layout formats include product layout, process layout, and fixed-position layout. Operations management specialists Richard Chase and Nicholas Aquilano have defined these three layout formats as follows:

> A *product layout* is one in which the components are arranged according to the progressive steps by which the product is made. Conceptually, the flow is an unbroken line from raw material input to finished goods. This type of layout is exemplified in automobile assembly, food processing, and furniture manufacture.
>
> A *process layout* is one in which the processing components are grouped according to the general function they perform, without regard to any particular product. Custom job shops, department stores, and hospitals are generally arranged in this manner.
>
> A *fixed-position layout* is one in which the product, by virtue of its bulk or weight, remains at one location. The equipment required for product manufacture is moved to the product, rather than vice versa. Sound stages on a movie lot, aircraft assembly shops, and shipyards typify this mode of layout.[12]

Product layout   If a high volume of standardized products needs to be produced, the product layout format illustrated in Figure 9.5 may prove appropriate. This type of setup was referred to as long-linked technology in Chapter 6. Typically, some sort of conveyor arrangement is used to carry work in process past fixed work stations.

Product layouts have both advantages and disadvantages. On the

FIGURE 9.5
Basic production layout formats

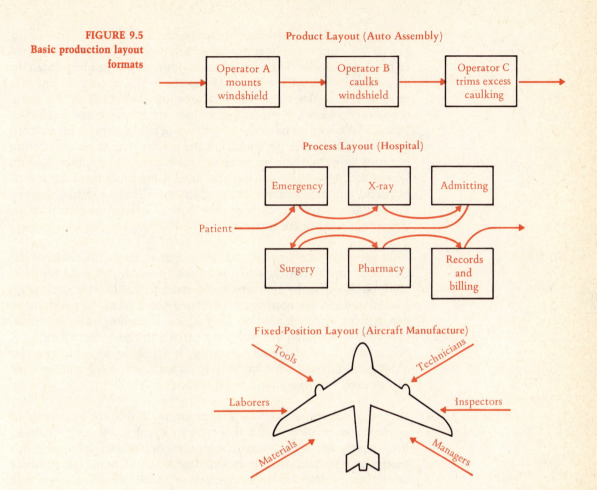

Product Layout (Auto Assembly)

| Operator A mounts windshield | Operator B caulks windshield | Operator C trims excess caulking |

Process Layout (Hospital)

Emergency   X-ray   Admitting

Patient

Surgery   Pharmacy   Records and billing

Fixed-Position Layout (Aircraft Manufacture)

Tools   Technicians

Laborers   Inspectors

Materials   Managers

plus side, relatively unskilled employees are able to perform clearly defined tasks, and a single supervisor can easily oversee the work of many people. The major disadvantage is inflexibility. For example, a major design change may trigger a costly restructuring of the entire line. Auto manufacturers normally shut down completely for such changes. Continuous assembly line operations also tend to be vulnerable to stoppages because they are only as strong as their weakest link. For instance, if operator A in Figure 9.5 runs out of windshields, operators B and C will have nothing to do, and the entire operation will grind to a halt. In recent years, large numbers of better educated employees have begun to rebel against the monotony and boredom of doing the same highly fragmented job over and over.

Process layout   Although process layouts such as the one in Figure 9.5 cannot duplicate the speed of product layouts, they tend to be more flexible. For example, a welding machine breakdown on an assembly line will probably tie up the whole operation. But in a process layout where all welding jobs are conducted in the same department, back-up welding machines are conveniently available. Process layouts also have the advantage of being suitable for custom processing of diverse products. On the minus side, work scheduling is much more difficult in process layouts than in product layouts where the production sequence is fixed. Care must be taken not to overload one department while others sit idle. In addition, expensively large work-in-process inventories tend to accumulate in custom process operations.

Fixed-position layout   Normally, operations managers have little choice in the matter when it comes to relying on fixed-position layouts. Huge ships that are three football fields long cannot be moved around on conveyors or transported from department to department with lift trucks. Everything, including raw materials, supplies, and equipment, must be carried to the construction site. While this type of layout is costly, it tends to be quite popular among employees, who are able to move about freely rather than being restricted to a single work station.

PROCESS FLOW CHARTING   Formally defined, a *process flow chart* is "a tool for recording an operation or process in the sequence in which it occurs."[13] Process flow charts are a convenient iconic model whose value depends partly on the fact that they employ a set of standard symbols developed by the American Society of Mechanical Engineers (see Figure 9.6). Creating a process flow chart of either proposed or existing production processes offers the following advantages:

1. It breaks complex processes down into key steps.
2. It provides a handy visual aid of the production process.
3. It helps determine equipment and manpower needs.
4. It helps pinpoint bottlenecks.
5. It helps identify overlooked or missing steps.
6. It helps pinpoint redundant or unnecessary steps.
7. It helps isolate unsafe arrangements.

If necessary, the value of process flow charts can be enhanced by recording the time required for each step and the distance traveled during each transportation step. The shorter the time required and distance to be traveled, the more cost-effective the operation.

FIGURE 9.6
Process flow charting in action

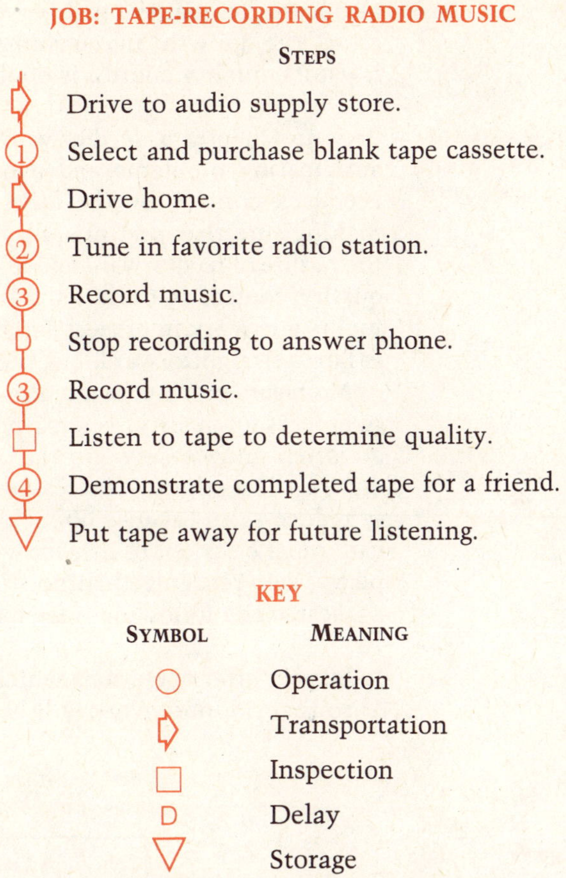

JOB: TAPE-RECORDING RADIO MUSIC

STEPS

⬦   Drive to audio supply store.

①   Select and purchase blank tape cassette.

⬦   Drive home.

②   Tune in favorite radio station.

③   Record music.

D   Stop recording to answer phone.

③   Record music.

□   Listen to tape to determine quality.

④   Demonstrate completed tape for a friend.

▽   Put tape away for future listening.

KEY

SYMBOL	MEANING
○	Operation
⬦	Transportation
□	Inspection
D	Delay
▽	Storage

A somewhat exotic variation of the basic process flow chart theme is the three-dimensional model. Here, scale model pieces of wood or plastic representing machinery and equipment are arranged on a floor plan of the production facility. This approach to layout is popular among people who prefer their models to be as lifelike as possible. By attaching small magnets to the pieces and using a metal floor plan, the analysis of layouts can resemble a productive and interesting game of chess.[14]

QUALITY CONTROL   Is the transformation system producing what it is supposed to? This deceptively simple question can be answered only through a comprehensive quality control program. *Quality control* is the process of ensuring that goods and services conform to design specifications. If products and services are designed to satisfy consumer demands for function, appeal, durability, and safety, then a concern for quality must pervade the productive process. Considering the growth in consumer activism and product liability lawsuits, quality control is doubly important today.

FEEDFORWARD AND FEEDBACK QUALITY CONTROL

Back in Chapter 5, feedforward control was discussed in terms of anticipating problems and avoiding mistakes before they occur. Feedback control, on the other hand, was seen as the process of making sure that past mistakes are not repeated. Figure 9.7 shows the nature of feedforward and feedback *quality* control. Feedforward quality control is exercised by making sure that both productive inputs and work in process satisfy acceptable standards. The former is fairly straightforward, but the latter can cause problems.

Managers face a cost dilemma when it comes to inspecting work in process for quality. Too many inspections can eat into profits and are often unnecessary. On the other hand, too few inspections can drive up costs through increased scrap and rework and can ultimately reduce sales because of customer dissatisfaction. Consequently, care must be taken to inspect work in process at the right time and place. Two recognized authorities in operations management have suggested the following rules for inspecting work in process:

1. Inspect *after* operations which are likely to produce faulty items so that no more work will be done on bad items.

FIGURE 9.7
Feedforward and feedback quality control

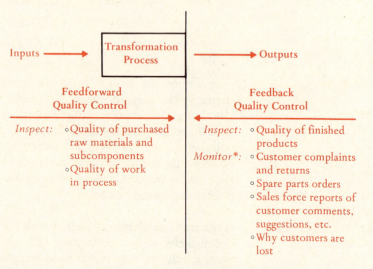

*This list is drawn from J. M. Juran and Frank M. Gryna, Jr., *Quality Planning and Analysis* (New York: McGraw-Hill, 1970), p. 559.

2. Inspect *before* costly operations so that these operations will not be performed on items which are already defective.
3. Inspect before operations where faulty products might break or jam the machines.
4. Inspect before operations which cover up defects (such as electroplating, painting, or assembly).
5. Inspect before assembly operations which can't be undone (such as welding parts or mixing paint).
6. On automatic and semiautomatic machines, inspect first and last pieces, but only occasional in-between pieces.
7. Inspect before storage (including purchased items).[15]

Adhering to these practical rules will help management deal effectively with the cost dilemma of feedforward quality control.

Feedback quality control occurs when finished goods are inspected and tested to see if they satisfy original design specifications. Items that fail must be reworked, if possible, or scrapped. At this point, the prudent manager remembers that the organization's reputation is shipped with every product. A bad product means a dissatisfied customer, and a dissatisfied customer means bad publicity. In addition to checking finished goods, attentive monitoring of feedback from the field is necessary. For example, orders of spare parts for the company's products, normally viewed only as a source of additional revenue, may pinpoint problems in product design or quality control.

STATISTICAL QUALITY CONTROL

Several conventional statistical techniques have been adapted to quality control in recent years. The result has been a great saving of time, effort, and expense. Imagine how costly it would be to inspect every nut, every ballpoint pen, every razor blade, or every golf ball prior to shipment. Fortunately, inferential statistics allow quality control specialists to sample relatively small numbers of items to make a judgment about the quality of the entire batch or "population." For example, if 100 golf balls have been randomly selected from a similarly processed batch of 1,000 and 5 turn out to be substandard, it is reasonable to assume that there are approximately 45 bad balls in the remaining 900. Of course, there is a degree of risk in this assumption. Accepting or rejecting an entire batch on the basis of inference means that bad products may pass unnoticed or that good products may be rejected. The trick is to identify and work within an acceptable degree of risk.

**OPERATIONS
MANAGEMENT AND
DECISION MAKING**

Operations management theorists contend that the primary purpose of their work is to help managers make better decisions. They claim that operations management can translate into precise decisions about designing a product, purchasing materials, building a new facility or remodeling an old one, scheduling work, controlling inventory and quality, or assessing risk. It stands to reason that if decisions are based more on objective fact and less on hunch and subjective intuition, decision quality will be enhanced.

It is worth noting, however, that the theoretical work behind this precise approach to decision making has been criticized. As one writer observed:

> Undoubtedly, much of the work published in the periodical literature nowadays has a very impressive facade. There is a great display of technical virtuosity to delight the mathematician. But the practical value of such work in the solution of managerial problems in many cases is marginal.[16]

Criticism of this theory-practice gap is healthy, but practicing managers should be careful not to throw the baby out with the bath water. In other words, operations management theory, although at times abstract and complicated, possesses great practical value if one approaches it properly.

The discussion in this chapter and the next represents a nontechnical introduction to operations management and decision theory for those who are not well versed in higher mathematics, statistical techniques, or computer science. It is hoped that this general introduction will encourage further study of organizations as productive systems.

SUMMARY   Like OD, operations management is a synthetic approach to management. Unlike OD, however, operations management involves viewing organizations as complex *productive* systems. Operations management is interdisciplinary, scientific, holistic, and model-based. Logic and quantitative precision are at the heart of this unique approach. Operations managers see productive organizations as open systems consisting of inputs, a transformation process, and outputs. Key activities in the transformation process are product design; production planning, scheduling, and control; purchasing; inventory control; work flow layout; and quality control.

Products need to be designed to satisfy both individual and societal demands. Product safety, environmental quality, and employee safety cannot be ignored when designing products and services.

Once a product has been designed and production plans and schedules have been formulated, the decision to make or buy key subcomponents must be made. Vendor selection is an important part of purchasing both raw materials and subcomponents. Six criteria for screening prospective vendors include price, quality, reliability, service, credit, and shipping costs. The planning of future purchasing needs is aided considerably by adopting a product life cycle approach.

Inventories typically represent huge commitments of working capital. Thus they need to be created and maintained with precision, not haphazardly. Keeping stocks of raw materials, subcomponents, and finished goods on hand involves balancing a set of conflicting demands. On the one hand is a demand for large inventories to meet unexpected circumstances; a conflicting demand calls for small inventories in order to minimize investment and carrying costs. Purchasing managers can balance these conflicting demands by managing the inventory cycle systematically and calculating economical order quantities. Computerized inventory control and comprehensive material requirements planning systems can promote production efficiencies.

Logical and orderly work flow layouts greatly improve cost effectiveness. Three basic work flow formats are product layout, process layout, and fixed-position layout. Each has inherent advantages and disadvantages. Process flow charting is a standardized tool for planning future layouts and assessing existing ones.

A transformation system is only as good as its output. Both feedforward and feedback quality control are necessary to ensure that goods and services conform to design specifications.

TERMS TO UNDERSTAND		
Operations management	Material requirements planning (MRP)
Model	Work flow layout
Productive system	Product layout
Product design	Process layout
Production planning	Fixed-position layout
Purchasing	Process flow chart
Product life cycle	Quality control
Inventory control	

QUESTIONS FOR DISCUSSION

1. In what ways is operations management a unique approach to management?
2. What is the significance of using the term *product* as a generic label in operations management?
3. How do product design and quality control complement each other?

4. Why are the six criteria for vendor selection useful for personal as well as organizational affairs?

5. How does the product life cycle concept affect purchasing?

6. What functional group within the typical business organization would argue for large inventories? Why?

7. Why would management go to the time and expense to calculate economical order quantities?

8. Why do custom operations tend to use process layouts? Give examples.

9. What would a process flow chart of your preparing a meal look like?

10. What is involved in feedback quality control?

CASE 9.1
OH, MY ACHING
INVENTORY!

Although he didn't know precisely why he had been called to the division manager's office, Bill O'Donnell looked forward to the meeting with confidence. On the way up in the elevator, his mind flashed back over recent events. Almost a year had passed since Bill had been promoted and transferred to the Denver office. Although he really enjoyed his work in the finance department at headquarters in Los Angeles, Bill had jumped at the chance to become a division financial manager. True, the Denver division was a modest manufacturing and sales operation, but it felt good to be running his own show. It had been a good year. His family had adapted well to the new surroundings and, after some initial shake-outs, things had fallen into place at work. As the elevator door opened, Bill's mind centered on the meeting at hand.

After an exchange of greetings and small talk, the division manager began to discuss Bill's handling of the inventory situation. He expressed pleasure over the way Bill had avoided what had become an annual embarrassment with raw materials inventory. The year before, for example, over $45,000 worth of raw materials had had to be declared a loss because of spoilage. Two years ago, nearly $100,000 dollars of purchased subcomponents and spare parts had had to be written off as obsolete. One thing the division manager had made very clear to Bill when he first arrived was that the firm's inventory mess had to be cleaned up. Now he complimented him for giving the inventory problem the attention it deserved.

Then, after a thoughtful pause, the division manager reached into his "pending" basket and pulled out a memo from the manufacturing manager. He asked Bill to read it. The tone of the memo quickly became clear to Bill. In short, the manufacturing manager was angrily protesting Bill's handling of the past year's purchasing budget. He claimed it was far too restrictive and offered the following points in support of his position:

- Ordering costs had risen 25 percent during the past year as a result of an increase in emergency spare parts orders that had to be shipped by air freight rather than rail or truck.
- Disruption of production due to materials shortages had become a weekly occurrence during the past year.
- In order to conform to the purchasing budget, raw materials had to be purchased in smaller and more frequent lots. Thousands of dollars of quantity discount opportunities had been missed as a result.
- Unexpectedly high last-quarter demand promised to totally exhaust raw materials inventories within the next month. Bigger inventories were needed to keep from being caught by surprise.

The division manager looked at Bill when he had finished reading the memo and said, "What do you think, Bill?"

FOR DISCUSSION

1. If you were Bill, how would you answer the division manager?
2. What recommendations would you make to Bill?
3. From a general management standpoint, what do you think about the division manager's handling of this situation?

**CASE 9.2
WHAT A MESS!**

Tom Bighorn's enthusiasm and pride in craft are evident as he describes to his guest how authentic Navajo silver and turquoise jewelry is handcrafted. He and the seven people who work for him learned the trade from their fathers as children on the reservation. Several years ago, when American Indian jewelry grew in popularity, Tom decided to turn his craft into a commercial venture. In spite of problems such as the rapid rise in the price of silver, Tom feels that his store-front jewelry operation is a healthy business.

Tom's guest, Esther Wilson, is the production manager of a local electronics firm. As a collector of Native American art, Esther is very interested in how Navajo jewelry is made. But, as she follows Tom through his production facilities, she can only wonder how anything ever gets done. The place is a mess.

Although the room itself seems spacious enough, there is no logical layout. The employees constantly interrupt each other as they reach for tools that seem to be scattered everywhere. As Esther looks on, two workers trip over packing boxes piled carelessly between two work benches. The two cabinets the employees seem to go to the most, one containing the silver and the other containing turquoise, are at opposite ends of the long room. A work bench halfway between the two cabinets effectively blocks any smooth flow of traffic.

On the way out to the sales area, Tom asks Esther, "Well, what do you think of my little production operation?" She replies that Tom seems to have a work flow layout problem and goes on to explain what she means. After a moment's pause, Tom asks, "What would the advantages of a better layout be?"

FOR DISCUSSION

1. What should Esther tell Tom?
2. Assuming that each piece of jewelry produced in Tom's shop is handcrafted by a single individual, which basic layout format would be most appropriate? Why?

REFERENCES   *Opening quotation*

Elwood S. Buffa, *Modern Production Management*: *Managing the Operations Function*, 5th ed. (New York: Wiley, 1977), pp. 14–15.

1. Thomas E. Vollmann, *Operations Management*: *A Systems/Model-Building Approach* (Reading, Mass.: Addison-Wesley, 1973), p. 5.
2. R. E. D. Woolsey, "Operations Research and Management Science Today, or Does an Education in Checkers Really Prepare One for a Life of Chess?" *Operations Research* 20 (May–June 1972): 737.
3. C. West Churchman, Russell L. Ackoff, and E. Leonard Arnoff, *Introduction to Operations Research* (New York: Wiley, 1957), p. 158.
4. "What Clouds Ford's Future," *Business Week* #2545 (July 31, 1978): 73.
5. For example, see: Conrad Berenson, "The Purchasing Executive's Adaptation to the Product Life Cycle," *Journal of Purchasing* 3 (May 1967): 62–68; G. E. Kiser and David Rink, "Use of the Product Life Cycle Concept in Development of Purchasing Strategies," *Journal of Purchasing and Materials Management* 12 (Winter 1976): 19–24; and Harold W. Fox and David R. Rink, "Purchasing's Role Across the Product Life Cycle," *Industrial Marketing Management* 7 (June 1978): 186–192.
6. See: "Mars: Behind Its Chocolate Curtain Is a Sweet Performer," *Business Week* #2547 (August 14, 1978): 52–57.
7. Franklin G. Moore and Thomas E. Hendrick, *Production/Operations Management*, 7th ed. (Homewood, Ill.: Irwin, 1977), p. 424.

8. Example drawn from: J. Fred Weston and Eugene F. Brigham, *Managerial Finance*, 6th ed. (Hinsdale, Ill.: Dryden Press, 1978), pp. 190–195.

9. See: Larry M. Austin, "Project EOQ: A Success Story in Implementing Academic Research," *Interfaces* 7 (August 1977): 1–12.

10. For instructive examples, see: Vincent G. Reuter, "ABC Method to Inventory Control," *Journal of Systems Management* 27 (November 1976): 26–33; and John M. Brennan, "Up Your Inventory Control," *Journal of Systems Management* 28 (January 1977): 39–45.

11. Richard L. Francis and John A. White, *Facility Layout and Location: An Analytical Approach* (Englewood Cliffs, N.J.: Prentice-Hall, 1974), pp. 33–34.

12. Richard B. Chase and Nicholas J. Aquilano, *Production and Operations Management: A Life Cycle Approach*, rev. ed. (Homewood, Ill.: Irwin, 1977), pp. 157–158.

13. Guy C. Close, Jr., *Work Improvement* (New York: Wiley, 1960), p. 117.

14. For an interesting discussion of *office* layout, see: Richard Muther and Lee Hales, "Six Steps to Making an Office Layout," *The Office* 85 (March 1977): 28–36.

15. This is a condensed version of a list found in: Moore and Hendrick, *Production/Operations Management*, p. 676.

16. Bjorn Larsen, "Theory and Application in Management Science," *Journal of Systems Management* 23 (September 1972): 15.

Chapter 10

Decision Making

Raising a manager's batting average on decisions by a few percentage points can mean all the difference between the major leagues and the minors.

Charles H. Kepner and
Benjamin B. Tregoe

LEARNING OBJECTIVES

When you finish reading this chapter, you should be able to

- ○ Explain how decision making is related to problem solving.
- ○ Identify and explain the nature of the three categories of environmental certainty.
- ○ Distinguish between programmed and nonprogrammed decisions.
- ○ Summarize the advantages and disadvantages of computer-assisted decision making.
- ○ Explain the difference between conditional payoff tables and expected payoff tables.
- ○ Outline how decision trees and histograms can contribute to the decision-making process.
- ○ Explain the roles of instrumental and terminal values in decision making.

Years ago, so the story goes, a jack-of-all-trades who had a difficult time staying employed finally landed the perfect job. He excitedly told his best friend that he had found a job sorting potatoes and that he was sure he would never quit. A couple of weeks passed before the two saw each other again. "How's the new job going?" asked the friend. "It was terrible," replied the jack-of-all-trades, "I quit last week." "Why?" asked the friend, "I thought it was easy and, besides, you loved it." "It was okay for a while because all I had to do was put the big potatoes in one bag, the medium in another, and the small in a third," replied the jack-of-all-trades, "but eventually all that decision making drove me crazy!"

As this story points out, decision making may be far from easy. Nevertheless, managers at all levels and in all types of organizations are continually called on to make decisions. The quality of their decisions on organizational inputs, transformation activities, and outputs affects not only their personal success but the ultimate survival of the organization as well. The purpose of this chapter is to examine the decision-making process and discuss some specific decision-making tools that apply not only to operations management but to management in general.

DECISION MAKING AND PROBLEM SOLVING

Decision making has been defined formally as the process of choosing an alternative course of action in an efficient manner appropriate to the situation.[1] The key word here is *choice*. A choice is made when one individual is hired instead of another. Similarly, a college instructor who uses an objective exam rather than an essay test is exercising choice. But, as we saw in Chapter 3, problem solving also involves choice. What exactly is the difference between decision making and problem solving?

Russell Ackoff, a recognized authority on decision making and problem solving, observes that "not every choice situation is a problem situation, but every problem involves a choice."[2] As this statement suggests, problem solving can be used to make a choice, but it is not always necessary. Many choices can be made without going through the four-step problem-solving process introduced in Chapter 3. Most of our daily decisions do not involve problem solving. Deciding what to wear, what route to take to work, or which movie to see involves a simple choice of alternative courses of action, not problem solving. Problem solving is much more rigorous. It requires the individual to identify a problem, creatively generate new solutions, choose the best one, and apply it to see if it works.

As shown in Figure 10.1, problem solving is a specialized form of decision making. Consequently, there are two types of decision

FIGURE 10.1
The relationship between
decision making and
problem solving

If decision making and problem solving were *unrelated*, the relationship would be:

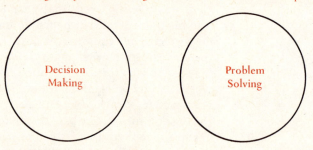

If decision making and problem solving were *identical*, the relationship would be:

However, because problem solving is a *specialized* form of decision making, the relationship is:

making; one involves problem solving and one does not. Both have their appropriate and inappropriate uses when it comes to making choices. Neither is better than the other. A simple comparison highlights this point. Suppose we think of problem solving as a jumbo jet, and decision making that does not involve problem solving as an automobile. The automobile is appropriate for getting across town, but the jet is the best way of getting across the country. Just as it is inefficient to take a jumbo jet across town, it is inefficient to use problem solving when a simple choice between familiar alternatives is all that is needed. Problem solving is best suited for identifying and carefully weighing new and different alternatives.

Translating this example into management terms, consider the task of quality control. For finished products, the overall problem involves keeping substandard items from reaching the marketplace. Identifying the most effective and efficient procedure for screening out bad units requires comprehensive problem solving. Completely new techniques or perhaps new combinations of familiar techniques need to be considered in order to decide what procedure to use. However, once the quality control procedure has been selected, decisions to accept or reject specific items become part of a familiar routine. After we have gone through the problem-solving procedure, decision making *without* problem solving becomes possible. One type of decision making dovetails with the other. Imagine how wasteful it would be if a quality control inspector had to develop a new procedure every time an item came up for inspection. Problem solving is reserved for the unique decisions that must be made under unfamiliar circumstances.

THE DECISION-MAKING PROCESS

In general, managers need to understand the decision-making process for two reasons. First, managers who understand how decisions are made tend to make better decisions. Second, they are in a good position to pass their decision-making skills along to others.

TWO KEY DECISION-MAKING VARIABLES

Decisions are never made in a vacuum; they are made within a context of situational variables. In this respect, decision making has something in common with the contingency approach to organization design discussed in Chapter 7. Just as the manager must consider the nature of the environment before selecting a design alternative, so too the manager must match the decision strategy to environmental demands, as well as to the situation inside the organization. The two variables discussed in this section are (1) environmental certainty and (2) decision strategy. Any realistic discussion of decision strategy needs to include an evaluation of the surrounding environment.

Environmental certainty One of the most valuable contributions made by decision theorists is the way they classify environmental certainty. Intuitively, we all are aware of gross differences in environmental certainty. Experience tells us that the sun will come up tomorrow, that our neighborhood grocery store will be there when we drive by, and that our favorite TV comedian will make us laugh. These are situations marked by relatively high certainty. But our confidence drops when the situation becomes less certain. Events such as getting a loan, receiving an A on a final exam, landing a high-paying job, and meeting the "perfect" friend are plagued by doubt and apprehension. Unfortunately, life is filled with such uncertainties, and uncertainty is an ever-present feature of the managerial experience. Managers, therefore, need to learn how to make the best decisions possible in spite of an uncertain environment.

As highlighted in Figure 10.2, environmental certainty falls along a range, or continuum, from low to high. A working appreciation of this range takes the manager a step closer to becoming an effective decision maker. Note also the relationship in Figure 10.2 between the degree of certainty and the manager's confidence in decision making. Confidence is high when conditions are certain, but it drops off significantly as certainty gives way to risk and finally to uncertainty. Each of these three categories of environmental certainty—certainty, risk, and uncertainty—deserves a closer look.

A *condition of certainty* exists when there is no doubt about the factual basis of a particular decision and the outcome of the decision can be predicted accurately.[3] The decision to order more rivets for the fabrication department of a manufacturing company is affected primarily by one important certainty—namely, the current rate of

**FIGURE 10.2
The impact of
environmental certainty
on confidence**

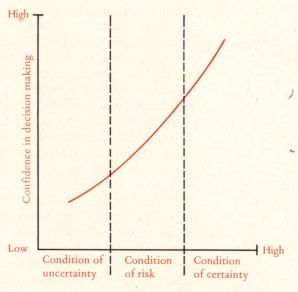

use will exhaust the supply of rivets on a specific date. Therefore, assuming that the vendor is reliable, the decision to order must be made early enough to allow for delivery before that date. Relatively few decisions are made under conditions of complete certainty. Even in the rivet example a degree of uncertainty creeps in because of possible supplier shortages and delays in delivery.

Conditions of risk are more common. A *condition of risk* exists when a decision must be made on the basis of incomplete but reliable factual information about environmental conditions. In this case, the risk taker assumes, on the basis of experience in similar situations, that a particular decision will yield approximate results. Experience allows the decision maker to calculate the probability that key environmental conditions will occur.

In decimal form, probabilities range from a low of 0.00 to a high of 1.00. Probabilities often are expressed in terms of percentages. When someone flips a two-sided coin, there is a 0.5, or 50 percent, chance that it will come up heads. The higher the probability, the more certain the outcome. There are two major types of probabilities, *objective* and *subjective*. Objective probabilities are derived mathematically from historical data, whereas subjective probabilities are estimated from past experience or judgment.

By way of practical application, suppose that the production manager in a bottling plant must decide whether to continue the filling operation or shut down the line because a number of bottles contain less than the required twelve ounces. First, the production manager decides that a 10 percent quality-control failure rate is acceptable. Next, a sample of one hundred bottles is randomly selected from the bottles coming off the filling line and examined to determine how many contain less than twelve ounces. A failure rate of ten or less will prompt the decision to continue production. On the other hand, more than ten failures will tell the production manager to shut down the filling line to permit adjustment of the filling machine. Because the manager cannot be 100 percent sure that the sample is perfectly representative of the entire batch, a degree of risk affects the final decision.

A great many managerial decisions are made under conditions of uncertainty. A *condition of uncertainty* exists when little or no reliable factual information is available about environmental conditions. Problem solving is a must when uncertain conditions prevail. Although there is no data base on which to calculate objective probabilities, judgmental or subjective probabilities can still be estimated. For example, experience and a general feel for the market would allow a retail manager to estimate the probable demand for a new line of dresses. The decision to carry the new line would be

CONVERSATION WITH...

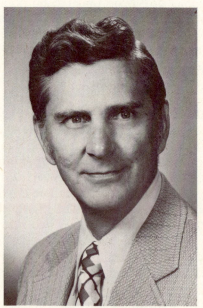

Dick Kasuba
Purchasing Manager and Associate
 Director of University Services
Michigan State University
East Lansing, Michigan

Michigan State University Photo.

PERSONAL BACKGROUND

Dick Kasuba is originally from Pittsfield, Massachusetts. After being graduated from Michigan State University with a B.A., he worked in both the private and public sectors. Among his early employers were Eaton Paper Company, Berkshire Woolen Company, General Electric Company, and the city of Lansing, Michigan. During his twenty-five years with Michigan State University, Dick has served in a number of capacities including buyer, assistant purchasing manager, associate purchasing manager, and purchasing manager. As head of the university's purchasing function, Dick Kasuba sets policies and procedures, works up statistical reports for upper management, generates forecasts of material availability and cost, develops an operating budget, and negotiates contracts for the statewide consortium of universities and colleges.

QUOTABLE QUOTES

What is your most significant achievement as a manager?

Mr. Kasuba: Building a team of dedicated purchasing personnel that provides efficient, fast, economical response and results for campus requisitioners.

What do you think it takes to be a successful manager today?

Mr. Kasuba: The same as it always did—interest in and a like for work, coupled to dedication in achieving desired results.

What advice would you give an aspiring manager?

Mr. Kasuba: Give it all you have, dress presentably, conduct yourself and your activities so that your actions are beyond reproach. Bring ideas and/or problems to the boss. Don't plow ahead if not positive, operate within policy and procedural guidelines. Recognition will take place, but don't be in a hurry to get to the top. Acquire the experience and expertise necessary to handle a manager's position once you get there.

---

accepted if the probability of high demand was reasonably great (that is, better than a 75 percent chance). With anything less than a 75 percent chance of high demand, the retailer would decide not to add the new line of dresses.

Decision strategy It stands to reason that if environmental conditions vary, then managers cannot rely on the same decision-making strategy all the time. Strategy must vary as conditions vary. As we have seen, one variable in the environment is the degree of certainty. A second important variable is the number of times a particular decision is made. Some decisions must be made frequently, perhaps several times a day. Others must be made only rarely or just once. Consequently, decision theorists have drawn a distinction between programmed and nonprogrammed decisions.[4]

Programmed decisions are those that are repetitive and routine. Managers tend to develop fixed procedures for handling these everyday decisions. Typical examples would include hiring decisions in a personnel office, billing decisions in a hospital, supply reorder decisions in a purchasing department, consumer loan decisions in a bank, and pricing decisions in a university bookstore. A majority of the decisions made by the typical manager tend to be programmed. The heart of a programmed decision procedure is a decision rule. A *decision rule* is a statement that identifies a situation in which a decision is required and specifies how the decision will be made. Problem solving is required only for the development of decision rules. Decision rules permit busy managers to make routine decisions quickly without having to go through the entire problem-solving process time and time again. Generally, decision rules should be stated in "if-then" terms. A decision rule for a consumer loan officer in a bank might be, "*If* the applicant is employed, has no record of loan default, and can put up 30 percent collateral, *then* a loan not to exceed $2,000 can be authorized." Properly conceived decision rules help managers streamline the decision-making process.

Nonprogrammed decisions are those made in complex, important, and nonroutine situations; often the situation is unique. These decisions are made much less frequently than programmed decisions. Examples of nonprogrammed decisions include deciding whether or not to merge with another company, deciding whether to open a branch office in a foreign country, and deciding how to design an entirely new product. Decision theorist Herbert Simon has this to say about nonprogrammed decisions:

> There is no cut-and-dried method for handling the problem because it hasn't arisen before, or because its precise nature and structure are elusive or complex, or because it is so important that it deserves a custom-tailored treatment.[5]

Nonprogrammed decision making involves exactly the same process as problem solving. The problem-solving model presented in Chapter 3 is therefore appropriate for nonprogrammed decisions. The four steps discussed there were (1) identifying the problem, (2) generating alternative solutions, (3) selecting a solution, and (4) evaluating the results.

A GENERAL DECISION-MAKING MODEL

Although different decision strategies are required in different situations, it is possible to develop a general decision-making model. Figure 10.3 shows the logical sequence of steps managers should follow when decision making. Each step contributes to the quality of the final decision.

The first step, a scan of the situation, is often underemphasized or ignored in discussions of managerial decision making, but it is nevertheless important. The scanning process answers the question; How do I know a decision should be made? One of the best approaches to answering this question was suggested over forty years ago by Chester I. Barnard:

> The occasions for decision originate in three distinct fields: (a) from authoritative communications from superiors; (b) from cases referred for decision by subordinates; (c) from cases originating in the initiative of the [manager] concerned.[6]

FIGURE 10.3
A general decision-making
model

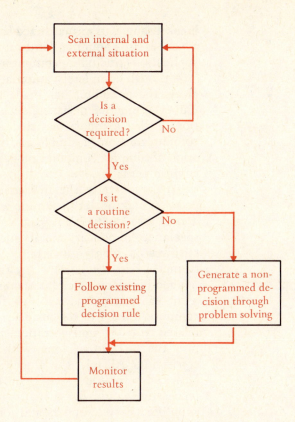

This three-pronged approach helps make scanning an orderly rather than haphazard process. In addition to helping determine whether a decision is required, scanning reveals the degree of environmental certainty.

Once the need for a decision has been established, the manager needs to decide whether the situation is routine. If it is, and an appropriate decision rule exists, then the rule is applied. However, if a unique situation demands a nonprogrammed decision, then comprehensive problem solving must begin. In either case, the results of the final decision must be evaluated to see if any further action is necessary.

COMPUTER-
ASSISTED
DECISION MAKING

The sophistication of computer hardware has increased at a phenomenal rate during the past twenty-five years. Computing speeds have skyrocketed, while the physical size of computers and auxiliary equipment has shrunk dramatically. Hardware that once took up an entire room has been reduced to suitcase size because of breakthroughs in miniaturized solid-state circuitry. Along with the advances in computer hardware have come a host of practical applications, including computer-assisted decision making.

Although completely automated decision making is a long way away, the computer has made significant inroads into the once universal practice of basing decisions strictly on hunch and intuition. Today computer-assisted decision making ranges from the computerization of simple and repetitive calculations to the creation of complex computer models of the entire organization and its environment.

To demonstrate the immense potential for computer-assisted decision making, let's examine what one company has done in this area. Cerro do Pasco is part of a large multinational firm that specializes in primary metals such as zinc. The mining and metals business is highly uncertain. Wide price swings and political turmoil in the countries where the ore is mined are serious threats to effective planning and decision making. Cerro do Pasco management has responded to the challenge by building a sophisticated computer model of its business. Data on metals prices and costs related to labor, transportation, raw materials, and capital are fed into the computer along with resource limitations and other constraints. All told, the model contains approximately 370 variables and relies on more than 150 algebraic equations. Manual processing would be virtually impossible. The final result is a simplified, easy-to-understand computer printout that recommends certain decisions. As new situations and problems arise, they are worked into the computer model to test their impact. Hypothetical decisions are handled in a like manner. The firm's profit picture has improved through computer-assisted decision making. However, as the users of this approach told *Business Week*, "It is no automatic system, but rather a management tool that must be used in connection with a hefty dose of human judgment."[7]

Computers offer decision makers both advantages and disadvantages. Among the advantages are speed, accuracy, and the ability to handle large numbers of variables and the complex interactions among them. On the minus side are costliness, delays while decisions are being analyzed, and the reality that computers are new and different and thus perceived as a threat by some traditionalists.

As computer technology continues to improve, the scale eventually will tip in favor of the advantages. Even the smallest organizations can take advantage of time-sharing computer services, and remote terminals now permit conversational interaction between individual managers and a central computer. Finally, confusing computer jargon is being replaced by easily understood printout terminology and language. Organizations stand to benefit greatly from computer-assisted decision making in the years ahead.

DECISION-MAKING AIDS

Many specific techniques have been developed to aid the decision maker. The aids discussed in this section are payoff tables, decision trees, histograms, linear programming, queuing theory, simulation, and gaming. The first three are explained in detail and accompanied by working examples, whereas the last four are introduced and discussed only briefly, to broaden the reader's familiarity with such techniques. Payoff tables, decision trees, and histograms have been selected for detailed examination because each is a relatively simple, straightforward, and above all *practical* aid to decision making. Furthermore, the use of these three techniques does not presuppose any knowledge of advanced mathematics or access to sophisticated computer facilities. They can be used by managers in large and small organizations alike.

PAYOFF TABLES

Even under the most predictable and stable conditions, selecting from among a number of alternative courses of action can be a difficult task. Conditions of risk and uncertainty further complicate decision making. More often than not, managers find themselves faced with two or more decision alternatives and a number of different environmental possibilities. This is where payoff tables can help sort things out. A *payoff table* lists decision alternatives and environmental conditions, and it gives the potential monetary payoff for each possible combination of variables.

The first thing we need to remember when working with payoff tables is that they deal in *net* amounts. For instance net profit for a particular product is the result of subtracting all related expenses from the sales revenue for that product. In these terms, it is evident that net profit will be higher if expenses are kept as low as possible and/or sales revenue is as high as possible.

Two types of payoff tables are displayed in Table 10.1, one for conditional payoff and the other for expected payoff. Assume that the payoff tables have been generated by managers in an automobile manufacturing company. They are trying to decide how many electric minicars the firm should produce for the coming year. Demand could vary, because these cars are a radically new form of family transportation. The conditional payoff for each combination of environmental condition and decision alternative is listed in Table A. This is where the conditional payoff table gets its name; it simply amounts to an "if-then" table. If management is certain that demand will be high, then production should be set at 6 percent because that would provide the highest payoff ($14,000,000) for that

TABLE 10.1
Payoff tables in action

TABLE A		
Conditional Profits from Electric Minicar Sales		

ENVIRONMENTAL CONDITIONS (Demand for Electric Minicars)	DECISION ALTERNATIVES (Production Capacity Devoted to Electric Minicars)		
	2%	4%	6%
High	$8,500,000	$11,000,000	$14,000,000
Moderate	8,000,000	8,000,000	7,000,000*
Low	7,000,000	5,500,000*	1,500,000*

*Reflects the added expense of unsold car inventory.

TABLE B			
Expected Profits from Electric Minicar Sales			

ENVIRONMENTAL CONDITIONS (Demand for Minicars)	Probability of Occurrence	DECISION ALTERNATIVES (Production Capacity Devoted to Electric Minicars)		
		2%	4%	6%
High	0.25	$2,125,000	$2,750,000	$3,500,000
Moderate	0.55	4,400,000	4,400,000	3,850,000
Low	0.20	1,400,000	1,100,000	300,000
		$7,925,000	$8,250,000	$7,650,000

particular environmental condition. Accordingly, either 2 percent or 4 percent of capacity is appropriate for moderate demand, because they have equally high payoffs ($8,000,000). Finally, if management is certain that demand will be low, then production should be set at 2 percent to achieve the highest payoff possible ($7,000,000) under that condition.

But what if management is not certain about demand? This is where *expected* payoff tables become useful decision-making aids. Notice in Table B that probabilities have been introduced to reflect management's uncertainty about demand. The chance of high demand is estimated to be 0.25 (or 25 percent). Moderate demand is given a 0.55 chance of occurring, and low demand is assigned a 0.20 probability. The expected payoff for each set of variables in Table B is calculated by multiplying each conditional payoff in Table A by the probability assigned to each of the various environmental conditions. For example, the $8,500,000 figure in the upper left corner of Table A yields, when multiplied by 0.25, the expected payoff of $2,125,00 found in the upper left corner of Table B.

Expected payoff tables also vary from conditional tables in the way the decision alternative is selected. Instead of selecting the highest payoff for each condition, as we did in Table A, we select a decision alternative based on the highest *total* payoff. In Table B, 4 percent production is recommended because it is associated with the highest total payoff ($8,250,000). This means that the *combination* of payoffs associated with 4 percent production is the best available, given uncertain demand and the relative probabilities assigned. In other words, the law of averages favors 4 percent production in this case.

In summary, payoff tables have two principal advantages. First, they force managers to define decision alternatives and possible environmental conditions. Second, payoff tables require decision makers to balance expenses against revenue. In addition, *expected* payoff tables are realistic in that they define probabilities of occurrence. These probabilities may be objective if reliable historical data are available. But even in the absence of hard data, judgmental or subjective probabilities can be estimated.

On the negative side, the main disadvantage of payoff tables is that they may encourage unwarranted confidence because they involve the calculation of exact values. People tend to place a great deal of faith in precise-sounding numbers, but they often fail to consider how the numbers were derived. Payoff tables are simply an aid to decision making. As such, they should supplement rather than replace sound managerial judgment.

DECISION TREES   Payoff tables are convenient when a single decision needs to be made. But what tool can the decision maker use when a *series* of decisions must be made? Decision trees satisfy this more complex need. A *decision tree* is "a network representation of sequences of action-event combinations that are available to the decision maker. Each possible sequence of decisions and consequences is shown by a different path through the tree."[8] To a limited extent, decision trees have something in common with PERT (as discussed in Chapter 4). Both techniques force managers to define future courses of action. Unlike PERT, however, decision trees contain sequences or branches that will be abandoned once key decisions are made. All branches in a PERT network represent desired action.

A sample decision tree is illustrated in Figure 10.4. The working example behind this particular illustration involves a pair of decisions facing the management team of ABC Company. The company has designed two promising products, X and Y, but

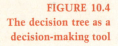

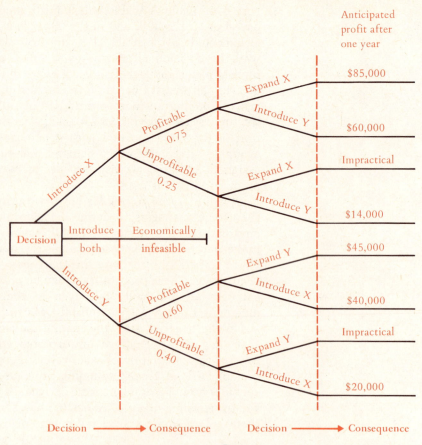

unfortunately it cannot afford to introduce both at once. Ideally, if one is introduced successfully, it will provide the funds needed to either (1) expand the production and marketing efforts for that product or (2) permit the introduction of the second product. The alternative sequences for these two decisions are traced out in Figure 10.4.

According to our decision tree, the most profitable sequence of decisions would be to introduce product X and later expand the production and marketing of that same product. The next best sequence would involve introducing X and then introducing Y. Notice how probabilities have been introduced to enhance the precision of the decision-making process. A decision tree provides a visual layout of the possible choices involved in making a sequence of decisions, and their results.

While the decision tree in Figure 10.4 is relatively simple, the technique is suitable for more complex situations. The most important key to using decision trees is to isolate all relevant decisions and assign realistic probabilities. Actual construction of the tree is then relatively simple.

HISTOGRAMS Decision makers faced with conditions of risk or uncertainty may find histograms useful. Although histograms have been around for a long time, their application to managerial decision making is relatively new. The main value of histograms is that they encourage managers to identify the various possible outcomes of a contemplated decision and attach a subjective probability to each. As a visual aid to decision making under conditions of risk or uncertainty, a *histogram* graphically profiles the probability of each outcome.

As an example, assume that the home office of a large insurance company is considering the purchase of a new, automated typing system. Due to a large number of mass mailings each year the company needs a fast, efficient way of producing handsome and accurate letters. The particular system being considered costs $25,000. One of the key decision points is the *payback period*. In other words, in how many years will the new system pay for itself? Generally, the shorter the payback period the better. As a first step toward pinning down the payback period three managers in the finance department have constructed the three histograms illustrated in Figure 10.5.

What do these three histograms tell us? First, as one proponent of histograms has pointed out, "From observing the width of the range of outcomes and the chance associated with each, a reader of the histogram is able to assess how confident the histogram maker feels about his judgments."[9] It seems that manager B is the *most* confident because the range of B's histogram includes only two years and each has a high probability. Manager C is the *least* confident because of the wide range of years and relatively low probabilities assigned to each. Manager A falls in between B and C in terms of confidence. As a technical point, notice how the probabilities in each histogram add up to 100 percent.

Next, the three histograms narrow the expected payback period to a range of two to seven years. Moreover, by calculating an average probability for each expected payback year, a *group* opinion can be obtained. For example, the average of the three estimates for a three-year payback is 33.3 percent (50 percent plus 45 percent plus 5 percent divided by 3). But 33.3 percent is not as high as the 36.6 percent for the four-year payback (30 percent plus 55 percent plus 25

FIGURE 10.5
Histograms as a
decision-making aid

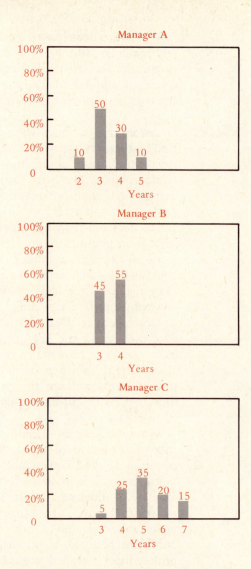

percent divided by 3). The group choice, therefore, is four years. If a four-year payback is acceptable to management, then the decision will be to purchase the new typing system.

Histograms are suitable for any decision in which conditions of risk or uncertainty prevail and a range of identifiable outcomes can be described. They may be used in either profit-making or nonprofit organizations, large or small. They can be used by a single manager or by groups of managers. However, since each manager develops only one histogram for a particular decision, two or more heads generally are better than one; multiple histograms permit useful comparisons. In general, histograms are extremely versatile.

LINEAR PROGRAMMING

Managers often are called upon to be both maximizers and minimizers. Business managers want to maximize profit as the situation will allow, and managers of government agencies and other nonprofit organizations want to maximize their budget allocation or operating funds. Meanwhile, regardless of the type of organization, expense minimization is a continuing concern. Resource allocation is the overriding problem. Prior to the development of linear programming managers had to rely on subjective, hit-or-miss judgment when allocating scarce resources. Now with the power of linear programming and the speed of the computer this aspect of decision making has become much more precise.

Linear programming is a process of identifying variables that compete for the same resources and of working them into either a graphical representation or a set of algebraic formulas. Linear programming techniques allow the manager to identify the best possible combination of resources. Here the term *best* means "maximum profit or minimum expense." For example, the management of a brewery that uses the same facilities to produce both a popular-priced brand of beer and a premium-priced brand is faced with the dilemma of deciding exactly how much of each brand to produce. Since only one brand can be brewed at a given time, the two brands are competing for the same resource (the brewing facilities). By taking the profit margins and the brewing times of the two brands into consideration, a linear programming model will give management an idea of the most profitable production mix.

Other applications of linear programming include the minimization of warehousing, transportation, raw material, energy, and personnel costs. Naturally, as with all other quantitative decision-making aids, solutions produced through linear programming are only as good as the underlying assumptions. Linear programming supplements rather than replaces sound judgment.

QUEUING THEORY

Waiting lines are a source of frustration to the average consumer. To the decision theorist, however, a waiting line is a *queue* to be managed systematically. There are obvious and not so obvious queues that affect our lives. Among the obvious ones are waiting lines in supermarkets, gas stations, class registration centers, airline ticket counters, and concert and theater box offices. Not so obvious but nonetheless important queues can be found in assembly line operations, truck depots, supply and toolroom check-out counters, and airport runways. The common denominator of all queues is the time and money it costs to wait in line. Thus the purpose of queuing theory is to minimize costs by identifying the relevant costs of waiting and balancing them against the costs of expanding facilities that would cut down on waiting.

Queuing theory enables the manager to achieve favorable trade-offs among relevant costs. For example, if a supermarket manager kept every check-out counter staffed all the time, few customers would have to wait in line. Staffing only one check-out counter no matter how many customers were waiting, would represent the other extreme. Both options are unworkable because labor costs would erode the profit margin in the first instance and lost customers would reduce sales revenue in the second. Queuing theory can help supermarket management determine the most profitable staffing schedule for the check-out counters. In spite of the fact that many managers still do not rely on formal queuing theory techniques, queuing theory has great potential because of its broad applicability.

SIMULATION AND GAMING

Exciting new decision aids have emerged since the development of high-speed computers. Complex calculations that would take weeks, months, or even years to complete by hand can be processed by computer in a matter of minutes. Greater accuracy of calculation is a second by-product of computer technology. Two of the most promising new developments in this area are simulation and gaming.

A computer simulation consists of a mathematical model of the key aspects of a system under study. Obviously, when the system under study is a large company or a huge government agency, it would be virtually impossible to include all conceivably relevant variables in the mathematical model. Therefore, a simulation represents, in a manner of speaking, the system's skeleton. It is a simplified representation of reality. Suppose, for example, that an aluminum manufacturer's operations management specialists have developed a computer simulation of the primary aluminum market. Important information about supply, demand, and price becomes available when various assumptions about the industry are worked through the simulation. For instance, management can gain valuable information beforehand about the impact of new competition from abroad, competition from substitute materials such as plastics, double-digit inflation, a housing slump or boom, and many other relevant circumstances. Computer simulation technology is still very much in the infant stage, but it promises to be a great help to decision makers.

Computerized gaming is useful when a win-lose or competitive situation is encountered. In competitive situations, any assumption that relevant variables will remain the same is false. When one competitor makes a move, a price cut, for example, then the adversary makes a countermove, typically a larger price reduction. Price cutting, in turn, affects profit margins. Competitive relationships are dynamic and constantly fluctuating. A change in one variable sets off a chain reaction of changes in other variables. Every action has one or more reactions.

Only a computer can keep track of all the variables and interactions among them. Hand calculation would be difficult and time consuming, if not impossible. Like simulation, gaming is still in the developmental stage. As the state of the art improves, gaming certainly will play an increasingly important role in competitive decision making.

A WORD ON PERSONAL VALUES

Decision-making models generally ignore the decision maker's personal value system. This is a serious oversight, because personal values unavoidably affect a manager's choices. Defined broadly, *values* are abstract ideals that shape an individual's patterns of thinking and behaving.[10] Contemporary social observers contend that too many managers have turned their backs on socially desirable values such as honesty, responsibility, and integrity. They point to mounting evidence of illegal campaign contributions, overseas payoffs, deceptive advertising, and other corrupt practices to support their case. Even if these questionable practices are the exception rather then the rule, they are widespread enough to justify a new look at personal values and their effect on decision making.

INSTRUMENTAL AND TERMINAL VALUES

Each manager, indeed each living person, values various means and ends in life. Recognizing this means-ends distinction, behavioral scientists have described two basic types of values: instrumental and terminal. An *instrumental value* is an enduring belief that a certain way of behaving is appropriate in all situations. For example, the time-honored saying "Honesty is the best policy" represents an instrumental value. An honest person behaves in an honest manner. A *terminal value*, on the other hand, is an enduring belief that a certain end-state of existence is worth striving for.[11] For example, one person may strive for eternal salvation while another strives for social recognition and admiration. Instrumental values (modes of behavior) help achieve terminal values (desired end-states).

Since a person may hold a number of different instrumental and terminal values in various combinations, it is easy to appreciate that individual value systems are somewhat like fingerprints. Every individual has a unique set.

GETTING IN TOUCH WITH YOUR OWN VALUES

By this point you are probably wondering, "What do I value? What are my own instrumental and terminal values?" To help you get in touch with your personal value system, refer to the Rokeach value survey in Table 10.2. (Take a few moments now to complete this survey.)

How did you come out? Surprised? If you are, it probably is because most of us take our basic values pretty much for granted. Seldom do we consciously arrange them according to priority.

The principal benefit of getting in touch with our values is to see if there are any serious conflicts among the values in each category or between the values in the two different categories. For instance, some people experience a serious conflict between the instrumental values relating to ambition and honesty. Honesty has been known to take a back seat for the hard-driving, extremely ambitious person.[12] Likewise, many have experienced a terminal value dilemma between accomplishment and pleasure. Someone who works hard to make a lasting contribution at the office may find little time for family, friends, or recreation. Finally, some managers find that their high-priority instrumental values will *not* help them achieve the terminal values they seek. For instance, imagine the frustration of a manager who values obedience (an instrumental value) while yearning for freedom and independence (terminal values).

There is another type of value conflict of which managers ought to be aware. It involves a conflict between the individual's values and the values of the organization. The classic conflict here is the one between the individual's desire for independence and the organization's insistence on obedience. A case in point involves IBM, known for years as the "white shirt company," an organization that demands selfless commitment and strict observance of rules. In a *Newsweek* interview, a former IBM employee complained of an atmosphere of blind obedience. He observed, "The guys who don't salute don't climb."[13]

THE EROSION OF PERSONAL VALUES

Under the pressures of modern life, many turn their backs on their personal values and engage in questionable conduct on the job. The sale of defective and dangerous products, the misuse of public funds, flagrant pollution of the natural environment, deceptive advertising, payoffs, and age, race, and sex discrimination in employment would not be as prevalent as they are today if decision makers at all levels did not compromise their personal values somewhere along the line. We are all familiar with the stock figure of the business tycoon who, say, is kind to his dog but allows sharp edges on the toys he manufactures.

Giving in to pressure from above seems to account for at least

TABLE 10.2
The Rokeach value survey

Instructions: Study the two lists of values presented below. Then rank the instrumental values in order of importance to you (1= most important, 18 = least important). Do the same with the list of terminal values.

INSTRUMENTAL VALUES	TERMINAL VALUES
Rank	Rank
_____ Ambitious (hard-working, aspiring)	_____ A comfortable life (a prosperous life)
_____ Broadminded (open-minded)	_____ An exciting life (a stimulating, active life)
_____ Capable (competent, effective)	_____ A sense of accomplishment (lasting contribution)
_____ Cheerful (lighthearted, joyful)	_____ A world at peace (free of war and conflict)
_____ Clean (neat, tidy)	_____ A world of beauty (beauty of nature and the arts)
_____ Courageous (standing up for your beliefs)	_____ Equality (brotherhood, equal opportunity for all)
_____ Forgiving (willing to pardon others)	_____ Family security (taking care of loved ones)
_____ Helpful (working for the welfare of others)	_____ Freedom (independence, free choice)
_____ Honest (sincere, truthful)	_____ Happiness (contentedness)
_____ Imaginative (daring, creative)	_____ Inner harmony (freedom from inner conflict)
_____ Independent (self-sufficient)	_____ Mature love (sexual and spiritual intimacy)
_____ Intellectual (intelligent, reflective)	_____ National security (protection from attack)
_____ Logical (consistent, rational)	_____ Pleasure (an enjoyable, leisurely life)
_____ Loving (affectionate, tender)	_____ Salvation (saved, eternal life)
_____ Obedient (dutiful, respectful)	_____ Self-respect (self-esteem)
_____ Polite (courteous, well-mannered)	_____ Social recognition (respect, admiration)
_____ Responsible (dependable, reliable)	_____ True friendship (close companionship)
_____ Self-controlled (restrained, self-disciplined)	_____ Wisdom (a mature understanding of life)

Source: Milton Rokeach, *The Nature of Human Values* (New York: Free Press, 1973), p. 28.

some of the erosion of personal values. For example, after surveying 238 managers from around the United States, Archie Carroll concluded

> Managers, particularly those below the top level, feel pressures to conform to what they perceive to be their superior's expectations of them, even though it may require the managers to compromise their personal values and standards.[14]

Compounding the problem of pressure from above is the problem of "creeping erosion." As the list of questionable employee behaviors in Table 10.3 indicates, the erosion of personal values begins in small ways. Unfortunately, seemingly minor indiscretions tend to pave the way for steadily greater abuses. It is easier to compromise the traditional values of honesty, responsibility, courage, and self-control when one is comforted by the notion that "everyone does it." If the practice of management is to achieve recognition as a profession, then individual managers need to stand by their socially responsible personal values and look for ways to use these values in achieving the organization's objectives.

TABLE 10.3
The erosion of personal values

1. Passing blame for errors to an innocent co-worker.
2. Divulging confidential information.
3. Falsifying time/quality/quantity reports.
4. Claiming credit for someone else's work.
5. Padding an expense account over 10 percent.
6. Pilfering company materials and supplies.
7. Accepting gifts/favors in exchange for preferential treatment.
8. Giving gifts/favors in exchange for preferential treatment.
9. Padding an expense account up to 10 percent.
10. Authorizing a subordinate to violate company rules.
11. Calling in sick to take a day off.
12. Concealing one's errors.
13. Taking longer than necessary to do a job.
14. Using company services for personal use.
15. Doing personal business on company time.
16. Taking extra personal time (lunch hour, breaks, early departure, and so forth).
17. Not reporting other's violations of company policies and rules.

Source: John W. Newstrom and William A. Ruch, "The Ethics of Management and the Treatment of Ethics," pp. 29–37, *MSU Business Topics* 23 (Winter 1975). Reprinted by permission of the publisher, Division of Reasearch, Graduate School of Business Administration, Michigan State University.

SUMMARY   Decision making is a universal managerial activity. In the broadest sense, decision making amounts to choosing among alternative courses of action. Problem solving also involves choice, but it is a specialized form of decision making. Most day-to-day decisions do not require full-fledged problem solving. Problem solving is necessary only when new and different alternatives need to be identified and systematically weighed.

Decision making does not take place in a vacuum. Consequently, managers must consider prevailing environmental conditions and their decision strategy, as well as the specific situation they face in the organization. The degree of certainty—certainty, risk, or uncertainty—is one key environmental variable. Confidence in the final decision decreases as the environment becomes progressively more uncertain. There are two fundamental decision strategies. The first involves programmed, or routine, decisions, and the second involves nonprogrammed decisions. Established "if-then" decision rules are appropriate for the more common, programmed variety. Comprehensive problem solving is necessary for nonprogrammed decisions, because the solutions need to be tailor made.

According to the general decision-making model presented in this chapter, managers first must scan the internal and external situation to determine whether a decision is required at all. If it is, the next step is to decide whether the situation demands a programmed or nonprogrammed decision. For a routine or programmed situation, an existing decision rule should be applied. For a nonprogrammed situation, a new decision must be created through problem solving. Managers must evaluate and follow up on both types of decision.

Modern computers, with their advantage of speed and accuracy, have become an increasingly valuable decision-making tool. As computers become less expensive and easier to use, computer-assisted decision making will become commonplace.

Three practical decision-making aids that do not require a knowledge of advanced mathematics or access to a computer are payoff tables, decision trees, and histograms. Payoff tables are helpful because they project the dollar outcome of various decision alternatives. When a series or sequence of decisions must be made, decision trees help clarify decision-consequence combinations. Histograms are a convenient visual aid when making decisions under conditions of risk or uncertainty, or when probabilities come into play. Linear programming, queuing theory, simulation, and gaming add sophistication to decision making by combining the precision of higher mathematics with the speed and accuracy of the computer.

The importance of personal values cannot be overlooked in managerial decision making. It is important for managers to be consciously aware of the relationship between their own values and organizational objectives.

TERMS TO UNDERSTAND

Decision making	Nonprogrammed decision
Condition of certainty	Payoff table
Condition of risk	Decision tree
Condition of uncertainty	Histogram
Programmed decision	Instrumental value
Decision rule	Terminal value

QUESTIONS FOR DISCUSSION

1. What is the relationship between decision making and problem solving?
2. How does environmental certainty affect decision making?
3. What is the practical value of a decision rule?
4. What is the significance of each step in the general decision-making model?
5. What role can the computer play in decision making?
6. How does an expected payoff table vary from a conditional payoff table?
7. What is a decision tree? Can you construct one for a series of decisions you are contemplating at this time?
8. How do histograms help managers make use of subjective probabilities?
9. How do the purposes of linear programming and queuing theory vary?
10. What is the difference between an instrumental value and a terminal value? Why is it important for decision makers to be in touch with their personal values?

**CASE 10.1
THEY DIDN'T DO IT THIS WAY IN THE ARMY!**

Pete Logan joined Fail-Safe Auto Insurance Company as an appraiser eight years ago, after he retired from the army. He has worked in that capacity ever since, and his extensive experience as an appraiser in the army has been a definite advantage. Pete has a reputation for thoroughness and dependability among his fellow appraisers at the regional claim center where he works. Recently, however, Pete's boss has become concerned about his performance. It's not that Pete hasn't been doing a good job. Technically, Pete is still one of the best appraisers in the business. His appraisals are usually right on the money, and he gets very few client complaints. It is the *manner* in which Pete is doing his job that concerns his boss at this point.

Three months ago the home office installed a remote terminal in

Pete's claim office so the appraisers could use a computerized appraisal routine. This sophisticated appraisal aid was developed by the home office over a three-year period at a cost of over $800,000. Now that the bugs have been worked out, management is looking forward to considerable savings in the firm's appraisal process. In fact, Pete's boss has already noted a significant improvement. For example, the average time required to process a claim has been cut by thirty-five minutes. This will eventually mean that fewer appraisers can handle more clients in less time. The only problem so far with the computerized appraisal system, as far as his boss can tell, is *Pete*.

Living up to his reputation for being outspoken, Pete has been totally against the new system right from the very beginning. Although he apparently understood the week-long training program that accompanied the new terminal, Pete has continued to use the old appraisal method of looking up all his data in the specification manuals and figuring out his estimates with a hand calculator. Although the quality of his appraisals has remained high, he typically takes a half hour longer to complete an appraisal than his coworkers. It is clear to Pete's boss that something must be done.

FOR DISCUSSION   1. In effect, the new appraisal program is a complex but consistent set of decision rules. Why would Pete resist using the new program?
2. How should Pete's boss handle this problem?

CASE 10.2 DOUBLE BIND   After seventeen years of marriage, Rose Rivera has learned to gauge her husband Al's moods accurately. Tonight he seemed uninterested in dinner and remained aloof from the table conversation. Later, after their two teenagers had left the room, Rose asked Al what was bothering him. "Nothing really," Al answered, "just a little problem at work." Rose immediately knew that it was more than a *little* problem, but she decided to drop the matter.

It wasn't until they were about to settle in for the night that Al finally opened up to his wife. What it all boiled down to was that Al, the supply room manager, had discovered a dusty old box of custom-made carbon steel cutting tools while rummaging through a bin of scrap steel. A little detective work with the purchasing records turned up a three-year-old purchase order for the box of tools. The order, totaling $2,400, carried the initials J.K. The pieces seemed to fit together as Al recalled that Jim Klien had been machine shop manager three years earlier. Later that same year Jim had been promoted to manufacturing manager. Ever since Al had assumed his present position as supply room manager, he had reported directly to Jim Klien. They enjoyed an excellent working relationship. Al considered Jim his friend as well as his superior.

Al then took one of the tools to the machine shop and learned that it and the others were useless. They were the wrong size for the firm's milling machines. During the afternoon, as it turned out, Jim stopped by to ask Al if some new supplies had arrived.

"Well," Rose said attentively, "did you say anything to him about the tools?"

"Oh yes," replied Al, and he related how Jim's face turned red as he admitted his fear that his "dumb mistake" might put his pending promotion in jeopardy. He had told Al, "The folks upstairs want results, not mistakes, so I just saw to it that the tools got lost." Then he said, "Al, if you're my friend, you'll make sure that they *stay* lost. They could be a considerable embarrassment to me today."

FOR DISCUSSION

1. If Al decides to report the missing tools, how would you say his values probably differ from Jim's?
2. What should Al do? Why?
3. How would you justify your actions if you were in Jim's place?

REFERENCES   *Opening quotation*

Charles H. Kepner and Benjamin B. Tregoe, *The Rational Manager* (New York: McGraw-Hill, 1965), p. 21.

1. This definition is based in part on one found in: Kepner and Tregoe, *The Rational Manager*, p. 180.
2. Russell L. Ackoff, *The Art of Problem Solving* (New York: Wiley, 1978), p. 12.
3. For more extensive discussion, see: Rodney D. Johnson and Bernard R. Siskin, *Quantitative Techniques for Business Decisions* (Englewood Cliffs, N.J.: Prentice-Hall, 1976), p. 40.
4. For example, see: Herbert A. Simon, *The New Science of Management Decision*, rev. ed. (Englewood Cliffs, N.J.: Prentice-Hall, 1977), p. 40.
5. Ibid., p. 46.
6. Chester I. Barnard, *The Functions of the Executive* (Cambridge, Mass.: Harvard University Press, 1938), p. 190.
7. "A Computer Model to Upgrade Zinc Profits," *Business Week* #2243 (August 26, 1972): 76.
8. Johnson and Siskin, *Quantitative Techniques for Business Decisions*, p. 69.

9. Irwin Kabus, "You Can Bank on Uncertainty," *Harvard Business Review* 54 (May–June 1976): 97.

10. For an excellent treatment of values and related concepts, see: Milton Rokeach, *Beliefs, Attitudes, and Values* (San Francisco: Jossey-Bass, 1968), p. 124.

11. Ibid.

12. For an interesting and candid account of the conflict between ambition and honesty, see: John Dean, *Blind Ambition* (New York: Simon & Schuster, 1976).

13. Allan J. Mayer and Michael Ruby, "One Firm's Family," *Newsweek* 90 (November 21, 1977): 87.

14. Archie B. Carroll, "Managerial Ethics: A Post-Watergate View," *Business Horizons* 18 (April 1975): 80.

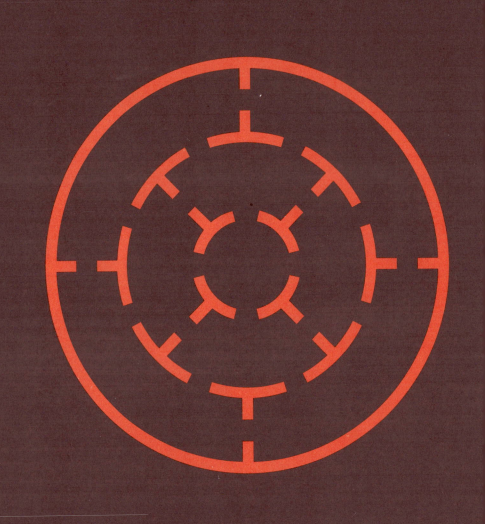

V

Managing People
at Work

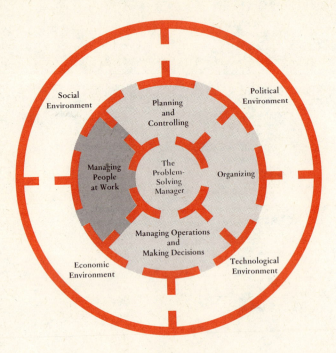

PART V IS ABOUT MANAGING PEOPLE AT WORK. MANY MANAGEMENT theorists and practitioners have said that people are our most important resource. Like any other valuable resource, people can be used appropriately and to full capacity or wastefully depleted. The overriding problem for management when dealing with people centers on getting employees to perform predictably and well in spite of subtle interpersonal differences and potentially disruptive group dynamics. To manage people more effectively, managers need to understand why people behave as they do, and they need to develop the necessary communication, leadership, and behavior management skills. Just as there is no one best way to design an organization, there is no one best way to manage those who contribute to organizational objectives. The health of our society and economy depends to a large extent on the problem-solving ability of our managers to induce individuals with differing backgrounds, perceptions, motives, values, and attitudes to commit themselves to the successful accomplishment of organizational objectives.

Chapter 11

Introduction to Organizational Behavior

Faulty assumptions about human nature are often self-fulfilling and may therefore lead to problems which are not easily diagnosed or corrected.

Walter R. Nord

LEARNING OBJECTIVES

When you finish reading this chapter, you should be able to

o Describe the difference between intuition and science.
o Highlight the nature of four intuitive models of organizational behavior.
o Identify the four main elements of the scientific method.
o Explain the roles of selectivity, organization, and interpretation in the process of perception.
o Contrast need and expectancy theories of motivation.
o Explain how an individual learns through shaping and modeling.

Managers in all types of organizations have said that *people* aré their greatest challenge. Human variety seems to account for a good deal of this challenge. For example, many of us complain that our work is too hard. We would gladly opt for a two-hour workday. But this is how a staff writer for a publishing house reacted to just such an opportunity:

> I have my own office. I have a secretary. If I want a book case, I get a book case. If I want a file, I get a file. If I want to stay home, I stay home. If I want to go shopping, I go shopping. This is the first comfortable job I've ever had in my life and it is absolutely despicable.[1]

Put yourself in the shoes of this individual's manager and ask yourself: "Does this make any sense?" At first glance, perhaps not, but it will after acquainting yourself with the field of organizational behavior in this and the next four chapters.

WHAT IS ORGANIZATIONAL BEHAVIOR?

Back in Chapter 2, organizational behavior was called a scientific extension of human relations. *Organizational behavior* was defined in that brief introduction as

> an academic discipline concerned with understanding and describing human behavior in an organizational environment. It seeks to shed light on the whole, complex human factor in organizations by identifying causes and effects of that behavior.[2]

This definition suggests that people behave in special ways when engaged in *organizational* activity. Consequently, in spite of the great variety of human behavior, organizational behaviorists attempt to study behavior in organizations systematically. According to Larry Cummings, a leader in the field of organizational behavior (OB), the task is not easy.

> OB's assertion that behavior within organizations is subject to systematic study is based on conceptualization of the object of study as non-random, systematic, and generally purposive. This way of thinking is significantly influencing our methodologies. The field is engaged in a sometimes painful search for cause and effect within our models.[3]

At the heart of this attempt to view a seemingly unpredictable phenomenon (human behavior) in systematic terms is the distinction between intuition and science.

INTUITION VERSUS SCIENCE

If we feel ill, we see a doctor. If we have legal problems, we consult an attorney. Doctors and lawyers are formally recognized experts in their fields. They qualify as experts because of extensive study and rigorous testing. But what kind of expert does the practicing manager consult when plagued by a behavioral problem at work? Occasionally, the manager will retain the services of a professional management consultant, one who specializes in problems of human performance. Far more often, however, the manager will rely on his or her intuition.

It is a curious fact that those who readily seek expert help with medical and legal problems tend to rely on home remedies when it comes to people problems. Part of the answer lies in the assumption that everyone is an expert on human behavior. Because of their daily interaction with others, many students of management and practicing managers are self-proclaimed experts about people. But just as home remedies tend to fall short of curing serious medical problems, behavioral home remedies also are frequently unsuccessful.

THE INTUITIVE APPROACH

The self-proclaimed expert on human behavior relies primarily on interpretations of his or her personal experience, or *intuition*. The intuitive approach to dealing with people can lead to problems. For instance, the president of a manufacturing company in a small midwestern community was shocked by the reaction of his employees to the Christmas gift he gave them. A couple of years earlier he had started the tradition of treating all his employees to a beautiful Christmas dinner at the local country club. Shortly before the most recent Christmas dinner an employee spokesman nervously approached him with a petition signed by the other employees requesting a cash bonus rather than the usual dinner at the country club. The president was surprised and dismayed, because he felt he was doing something really special and nice for his people. As it turned out, he discovered that his employees felt extremely uncomfortable getting all dressed up for what they considered an overly fancy dinner at the country club, a place they seldom went. Once he recognized his mistake, he discontinued the Christmas dinner tradition.

Although the manager in this example cannot be faulted for his good intentions, he can be faulted for relying too much on intuition. Without analyzing the situation, he assumed that his employees liked the same things he liked. He himself felt comfortable at the local country club. But his employees, who saw themselves occupying a lower social level, did not share his enthusiasm for dining at the high-status country club.

Is the intuitive approach to organizational behavior all bad? No. It simply has some limitations, and the problem-solving manager needs to be aware of those limitations. The two principal drawbacks to the intuitive approach are *bias* and *generalization.*

Bias Taking a slanted view of something or someone is called *bias.* Biased opinions often stem from preconceived notions or prejudices. A manager who is convinced that women and minorities do not make good employees will probably be biased in making decisions on hiring and promotion. A second source of bias stems from vested interests. For example, when job assignment, pay, and promotion hinge on the success of a particular program, of course the responsible manager's report will have a favorable bias. In general, top management should expect lower-level managers to report results slightly more favorable than is actually the case.

Generalization The manager who felt his employees would enjoy a Christmas dinner at the country club as much as he did was the victim of unwarranted generalization. On the basis of limited observation (himself), he thought he knew something about the likes and dislikes of others, a process called *generalization.* To a certain extent, each individual and each situation encountered by a manager is unique. It is unwise to generalize from one unique person to all people, or from an isolated instance to all situations.

THE SCIENTIFIC APPROACH Behavioral scientists attempt to rely on the scientific method rather than intuition when studying people at work. The scientific method is designed to systematically eliminate the effects of bias and unwarranted generalization. "The scientist's perceptions, beliefs, and attitudes are not taken as truisms, but are carefully checked against objective reality."[4] Sometimes, objective reality directly contradicts firmly established intuitive beliefs.

An outstanding example of reality contradicting an intuitive belief involves the relationship between job satisfaction and job performance. For many years, it was generally assumed that job satisfaction and job performance were positively related. In other words, according to intuitive belief, the greater the satisfaction, the better the performance. However, after reviewing twenty studies that tested this particular notion, one researcher concluded that the relationship, while positive, was too weak to have any theoretical or practical significance.[5] In a sense, scientific research keeps us honest.

The scientific method has four main elements. They are (1) hypothesis testing, (2) representative sampling, (3) objective measurement, and (4) control. To illustrate how each element of the scientific method operates, let us assume that we are considering an on-the-job research project to determine the effect of a four-day workweek on output.

Hypothesis testing   A *hypothesis* is a theoretical statement that may be verified or disproved by actual fact. In a sense, scientists use hypotheses as road maps in their search for actual facts. Hypotheses also lend discipline to scientific research because they force researchers to specify their purpose and expected results *before* collecting and interpreting their data. For our research project on the four-day workweek, a workable hypothesis would be: The subject employees will produce as much output in four ten-hour workdays as they did in five eight-hour workdays.

Representative sampling   If the results of a research project are to be generalized to another situation or a larger population of individuals, the situations or individuals under study must possess representative qualities. For example, one should not use only female subjects in a study of the effect on output of a four-day workweek and then claim that the results apply to men as well as women. In this case, there is a distinct possibility that women and men would react differently to a shorter workweek. Women are not necessarily representative of the general male-female population.

Objective measurement   The objective and precise measurement of variables under study is the hallmark of science. For those unfamiliar with the term, a variable is a factor that changes or fluctuates as time passes. This element alone accounts for much of the difference between the intuitive and scientific approaches. According to the authors of a behavioral science research guide:

> Usually the data are quantified in some way so that they can be systematically analyzed. Systematic and specifiable data collection and analysis is absolutely essential to the scientific method and is one of its major virtues.[6]

Once again referring to our study of the four-day workweek, the key variable that must be objectively measured is output. It is not sufficient for the researcher to determine who is performing well and who is not on the basis of personal judgment alone. Objective output data in the form of units produced or some other equally specific measure need to be collected.

Control The study of human behavior is difficult because people and their surroundings are so complex. Hence, behavioral scientists attempt to neutralize or *control* the impact of any variables they are not studying. For example, if the effect of different light levels on output is being measured, then the temperature should not be allowed to vary in the room where the study is taking place.

It is the need for control that makes laboratory studies popular among scientists. Unfortunately, although contrived laboratory settings permit careful control, much of the realism of the original situation is lost, along with the desirability of using the results in a practical setting. Practicing managers are reluctant to apply the findings of laboratory studies, which often use students as subjects, to the workaday world.

Another way to gain control in a study is to use a control group for comparison. For example, in our study of the four-day work-week, we could allow the employees in one branch of the company to go on a four-day week while those in another branch remain on a five-day week. Assuming that in other ways the situations in the two branches are equivalent, a comparison of the output from the two branches would help us measure the effect on productivity of the four-day workweek.

A MANAGERIAL PERSPECTIVE OF INTUITION AND SCIENCE

There is no doubt that the intuitive approach is a fact of life among managers.

> Some [managers] may argue that they never have enough time on their jobs to apply any systematic method to problems. They say they are forced by urgency to make snap decisions, to rely on intuition. They regard a systematic approach as slow and laborious, not suited to the demands of modern business.[7]

All things considered, intuition and science both can contribute to the understanding and effective management of people. Each approach has its own set of strengths and weaknesses (see Table 11.1). A balance needs to be struck between the two approaches. In spite of the fact that intuition is commonly used in the management of job behavior, there are at least two ways in which managers can make greater use of the scientific approach.

First, although managers are not scientists, they can rely at least in part on the scientific method. Greater use of objective measurement and control techniques is nearly always possible and desirable. Moreover, managers can develop and test hypotheses. For example, the hypothesis that salespeople will sell more if they have fewer

TABLE 11.1 Intuition versus scientific approach to management	**INTUITION** Reliance on Personal Feelings		**SCIENCE** Reliance on the Scientific Method	
	Strengths	Easy, fast, and convenient	Strengths	Precise and objective
	Weaknesses	Imprecise and subjective	Weaknesses	Time-consuming and viewed as inconvenient by busy managers

forms to complete could be tested with a representative sample of a company's sales force. The quality of decisions is greatly improved by this type of on-the-job research.

Second, managers are well advised to review research reports in the magazines and journals that focus on behavioral science. Two scholarly journals are the *Academy of Management Journal* and the *Journal of Applied Psychology*. Less technical reports of behavioral research appear from time to time in the *Harvard Business Review*, *Psychology Today*, and the *Personnel Journal*. Managers can learn a great deal about themselves and those around them by occasionally taking time to examine the studies in these journals. They are available in most libraries.

The problem-solving manager needs to bring intuition and science together in a productive combination. Research indicates that, although managers express confidence in the results of behavioral science research, they have been slow to adopt new ways of managing people.[8] Greater reliance on both the scientific method and the results of relevant behavioral science research will help promote greater understanding among managers, both of themselves and of those they manage. The net result should be more effective use of our most valuable resource, people.

INTUITIVE MODELS OF ORGANIZATIONAL BEHAVIOR

All of us rely on certain fundamental assumptions about people. Managers are no exception. Those with favorable assumptions will tend to see people as the key to organizational success. Managers with unfavorable assumptions will view people as a barrier to success. What are your assumptions about people? Do you see them as lazy, indifferent, and uninspired? Or do you see them as energetic, caring, and creative? Perhaps you see them as a combination of both. At this point, it is helpful to review some established models of organizational behavior. Each model is based on a set of intuitive assumptions about the nature of people.

A model is a simplified version of reality that shows the relationships among important variables. The four models of organizational behavior we will analyze and discuss here are the rational-economic, organization-man, Theory Y, and complex models.

**THE
RATIONAL-ECONOMIC
MODEL**

Adam Smith, author of the eighteenth-century economic treatise *Wealth of Nations*, proposed that economic self-interest was the key to orderly and efficient markets. The pursuit of economic gain

"YOUR WORK IS FINE, AND YOUR ATTITUDE SEEMS SATISFACTORY, BUT I UNDERSTAND THAT AFTER FIFTEEN YEARS WITH US, YOU STILL HAVEN'T LEARNED THE COMPANY SONG."

was to be expected because people were viewed as rational beings. This rational-economic view of people was reinforced by the father of scientific management, Frederick W. Taylor. In Taylor's own words, "What the workmen want from their employers beyond anything else is high wages."[9] This "economic man" assumption largely explains Taylor's devotion to piece rates. Under the piece-rate system a fixed amount of money is paid per unit of output; the more one produces, the more one earns. The surprisingly large number of contemporary advocates of the *rational-economic model* are convinced that all that people want from their jobs is more money.

THE ORGANIZATION-MAN MODEL

In 1956 William H. Whyte wrote *The Organization Man*. This book has become a classic among those who study human behavior. Although Whyte wrote in a slightly tongue-in-cheek manner, his message about modern organizational behavior was no joke. Whyte felt that people had gone from creating and developing organizations to worshiping them. He saw this transition as a dangerous step that could eventually turn employees into mindless, uncreative cogs in massive bureaucratic wheels.

According to Whyte's thesis, the organization man assumes that individual and organizational goals are identical. The organization man puts the company first. "Be loyal to the company and the company will be loyal to you."[10] Accordingly, the organization man believes that the organization is the ultimate source of power, social status, and creativity. Taken to an extreme, the organization-man model assumes that the organization gives the individual a reason for being. The organization man wants to work hard, but not too hard, and to be successful, but not too successful. Conformity is the byword of the organization man. The last thing he wants to do is rock the boat.

THE THEORY Y MODEL

A third model of organizational behavior was proposed by Douglas McGregor in 1960. McGregor saw employees as energetic and creative individuals who could achieve great things if only they were given the opportunity. He called the assumptions underlying this optimistic view *Theory Y*.[11]

McGregor's Theory Y assumptions are listed in Table 11.2 along with what he called his *Theory X* assumptions. The purpose of developing two sets of assumptions about people was to allow McGregor to contrast the modern or enlightened view he proposed (Theory Y) with the prevailing traditional view (Theory X), which he criticized.

TABLE 11.2
McGregor's Theories
X and Y

THEORY X Some Traditional Assumptions About People	THEORY Y Some Modern Assumptions About People
1. Most people dislike work and they will avoid it when they can.	1. Work is a natural activity, like play or rest.
2. Most people must be coerced and threatened with punishment before they will work. They require close direction.	2. People are capable of self-direction and self-control if they are committed to objectives.
3. Most people prefer to be directed. They avoid responsibility and have little ambition. They are interested only in security.	3. People will become committed to organizational objectives if they are rewarded for doing so.
	4. The average person can learn to both accept and seek responsibility.
	5. Many people in the general population have imagination, ingenuity, and creativity.

THE COMPLEX
MODEL

Proponents of the complex model of organizational behavior feel that the rational-economic, organization-man, and Theory Y models share one shortcoming; all are oversimplifications. They feel it is unrealistic to assume that all people act in the same way and that each individual's behavior remains the same all the time. People react differently to similar situations. For example, one individual eagerly seeks added responsibility, but another avoids it like the plague. Or a person may seek responsibility at one time and avoid it at another because of changed personal or work-related circumstances. The Theory Y model, used by itself, does not adequately explain these inconsistencies. Furthermore, the same person may behave differently at different times. For example, an employee may comply with company policy on dress and personal appearance when first hired but later challenge that policy by refusing to comply. The organization-man model does not allow for this kind of turnabout.

In a sense, the complex model is a compromise model. It does not throw out the more traditional models of organizational behavior; it simply refines and combines them into a realistic picture. One writer has warned against the danger of oversimplifying the individual-organization relationship: "Motives, perceptions, degrees of effort, and organizational experience all interact in a complex way to produce a given level of performance and a degree of involvement in the organization."[12] The complex model of organizational behavior is consistent with the open-system model of organizations. It is considered an intuitive model because it is based more on broad subjective assumptions than on objective research.

AN OVERVIEW

Looking back over these four models of organizational behavior, one begins to appreciate that the behavior of people at work cannot be tied up in a neat little intuitive package. As the complex model realistically suggests, the traditional models are sometimes true and sometimes false. True, money can motivate people to work; true, we have a tendency to worship the organizations we create; and true, the average employee has great potential. On the other hand, money is not the only thing that will motivate employees, people do not like to lose their identity in organizations, and some people show little interest in realizing their potential. Managers who carefully observe people and draw from the work of behavioral scientists soon realize that universal intuitive assumptions about people are unproductive. In this regard, it is helpful to remember that "when all people look alike, you are not looking close enough."

In sharp contrast to the intuitive models are three processes—perception, motivation, and learning—that behavioral scientists believe are fundamental in any attempt to explain why people behave as they do. Before discussing these behavioral processes in detail, we will first explore their role as intervening variables.

BEHAVIORAL PROCESSES AS INTERVENING VARIABLES

Behavioral scientists agree that some type of complex behavioral process is triggered when an individual interacts with the environment. Although they disagree as to its exact nature, some sort of process is obviously at work, because people do not bounce uncontrollably through life like pinballs bouncing here and there in a pinball machine. People are capable of interpreting and adjusting to their surroundings. Most behavior appears to have meaningful direction and purpose. People seem to be able to learn from experience. What, then, is the key to explaining why people behave as they do? Experts on perception, motivation, and learning have all come up with answers to this fundamental question.

It is useful to view perception, motivation, and learning as intervening variables. An *intervening variable* is a kind of bridge that connects and moderates the relationship between two other variables. The two other variables in this case are the environmental setting and a person's behavior.

A simple example helps demonstrate the role of an intervening variable. Many people are concerned about their weight today. They realize that they can lose weight by eating less. But how much less?

**FIGURE 11.1
Behavioral processes**

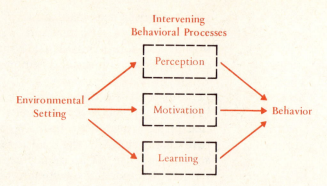

The relationship between one's intake of food and one's weight is moderated by an important intervening variable—metabolism. Those with high metabolism burn up lots of energy on a day-to-day basis. People with low metabolism burn energy slowly and thus require small amounts of food to keep their bodies healthy and active. Assuming that two individuals with the same diet and exercise habits are identical in all ways except for their metabolism, which one will tend to get fat? The one with low metabolism, of course.

Just as metabolism is an important intervening variable in the relationship between food consumption and weight, perception, motivation, and learning are important intervening variables in the relationship between one's environment and one's behavior. As illustrated in Figure 11.1, each of these intervening behavioral variables helps to explain why people behave as they do. But each does so in a significantly different way.

PERCEPTION *Perception* has been defined as "the process by which an individual gives meaning to his environment."[13] Although perception often is regarded as "seeing" things, we perceive with all our senses. The interesting thing about perception is that it causes objective reality to be interpreted in countless ways. There are times when disparity in perception can be amusing. The French think of *escargots* (stuffed snails) as a great delicacy. To most Americans, snails are a garden pest somewhat akin to worms. Many a French diner has inwardly laughed at the sight of tourists trying to eat snails with aplomb. The Americans' squeamishness results from the perception of a snail as a pest rather than food. Other times, perceptual problems can be disastrous. For example, in 1977, the worst air disaster in history occurred in the Canary Islands when a jet airliner that was landing collided with one that was taking off. Evidently, according to the investigation, the pilot of the plane on the ground perceived the tower's command to "stand by for takeoff" as the go-ahead to "take off." Twenty seconds later 583 people lost their lives.[14] Although perception may not be a life and death matter for the typical manager, a basic understanding of perception is important when it comes to managing people.

An expanded model of the perceptual process is displayed in Figure 11.2. Three subprocesses of perception are selectivity, organization, and interpretation. Each, in its own way, helps people interact meaningfully with the environment.

SELECTIVITY   *Selectivity* is a sensory screening process that allows us to sort out and notice only specific details of our environment. Each of us is bombarded constantly by environmental stimuli, all competing for our attention. These stimuli may be noises, lights, symbols, signs, or people. We would literally go mad if we did not have some mental process for sorting out and screening these competing stimuli. Fortunately, we have the ability to selectively pay attention to various environmental inputs. This selectivity occurs in two ways, through perceptual defense and through perceptual set.

Perceptual defense   How many times have you seen someone study with the radio or television going full blast? Those who can retain what they read in spite of competing stimuli have highly developed perceptual defenses. *Perceptual defense* is the screening *out* of environmental stimuli. The training director of a company may develop perceptual defense to criticisms of the training department's work. When other managers make critical comments to the training director, they may find that their remarks go in one ear and out the other.

One can readily see that perceptual defense has both a good side and a bad side. On the good side, busy managers cannot hope to be effective if they pay attention to every fact, detail, problem, bit of information, criticism, and question they encounter in a typical day. Managers must be selective to keep from being swamped by endless details. It is this need for selectivity that makes the establishment of priorities so important. Priorities represent a ranking of a manager's concerns in order of their importance. Important matters receive attention first, and matters of less importance are put off until later.

FIGURE 11.2
The perceptual process

As for the negative side of perceptual defense, blinders may help horses but they do little to promote managerial effectiveness. In other words, a manager may become too restricted when it comes to screening out competing stimuli. For example, buggy whip manufacturers who ignored the effect of automobiles on their market and did not switch to other products ended up in bankruptcy.

Perceptual set   Just as perceptual defense is a screening-out process, one might consider *perceptual set* a screening-*in* process. Perceptual set typically occurs when someone bases a conclusion on a hastily gathered first impression. For example, research has demonstrated that when people have been told to expect a new acquaintance to be "warm," they in fact perceive the person as warm, intelligent, and generally likable.[15] The reverse holds true for a negative set. Just as the term implies, we often become *set* in our perception of people and things in our surroundings.

One writer has offered the following excellent example of productive perceptual set in the work place:

> To see Juan Fernandez take a couple of quick steps from his turret lathe to deposit a finished part in a tote pan and then move briskly back to start work on the next piece appears to be efficient performance, to most people. But the fellows in industrial engineering immediately identify the action as evidence of an inefficient job layout. The way they see it, *no* steps should be taken, and better yet, the part should come out of the chuck and drop immediately into a tote pan untouched by Juan. The industrial engineers have a set to perceive wasted motion, which most of us miss. We are set to perceive what we value, what we're interested in, what we are trained to see, and what we've seen before.[16]

Perceptual set, like perceptual defense, has its advantages and disadvantages. A certain degree of perceptual set allows one to have an eye for detail and to be appropriately selective. However, too much perceptual set paves the way for prejudice and inflexibility.

ORGANIZATION   Selectivity is only the first step in the perception process. Once something has been selectively noticed, the subprocess of organization takes over. Through *perceptual organization* one arranges otherwise meaningless or disorganized stimuli into meaningful patterns. Organization takes place in three ways: grouping, figure-ground, and closure. Many entertaining optical illusions like the ones in Figure 11.3 play havoc with perceptual organization.

FIGURE 11.3
"What you see isn't always what you get!"

Image 1

Read this sentence out loud.

A BIRD IN THE
THE HAND IS WORTHLESS.

Image 2

Image 3

Images 1 and 2 reproduced by permission of the publisher from *Optricks*, by Melinda Wentzell and D. K. Holland, © 1973, Troubador Press, 385 Fremont Street, San Francisco 94105.

Grouping   Look at image 1 in Figure 11.3 and follow the instructions. If you look very closely, the sentence contains the word *the* twice. But because we normally group words line by line, a duplication in wording from one line to the next is easily overlooked. So too, managers may overlook subtle individual differences by grouping people. On the positive side, grouping helps us quickly and efficiently sort out unusual stimuli, such as defective products when testing for quality.

Figure-ground   Take a quick look at image 2 in Figure 11.3. What do you see? Was the first thing you saw a black vase against a white background, or did you see two white faces looking at each other against a black background? What you saw depended on what you perceived as the figure and what you perceived as the background. In the same fashion people often reverse the figure-ground relationships in their surroundings. In an organizational setting, one may initially perceive the recruiting officer as a principal figure and others in the organization as the background. Eventually, however, the recruiting officer fades into the background as supervisors, new friends, and others emerge as personally important figures. Similarly, important problems often get lost in a background of trivial problems.

Closure   Now take a fast glance at image 3 in Figure 11.3. If you see a jet airliner flying toward you from left to right you have relied on the perceptual process of closure. In effect, closure means filling in the blanks. Since you are accustomed to seeing complete pictures of airplanes, you perceptually complete an incomplete representation. We are all familiar with the tendency of people to conveniently fill in the blanks when they hear only part of a story. Rumors are often started this way. But closure can be extremely helpful when one is trying to identify and solve a complex problem.

INTERPRETATION   Sometimes two people perceptually select and organize a situation in the same manner, but they come away with very different views. The difference is in their interpretation of the situation. One person interprets the information one way, while the other interprets it another way.

Managers often interpret situations differently because of highly specialized and thus restricted perspectives. For instance, an engineer and a salesperson employed by a computer manufacturer may come out of a meeting with a customer with very different interpretations of what lies ahead. Suppose the customer wants to add remote-site terminals to an already complex computer installation. To the salesperson this means more sales revenue; to the engineer it means working out significant technical difficulties. The salesperson interprets the situation as an opportunity, but the engineer interprets it as a problem. They can be expected to react quite differently.

A MANAGERIAL PERSPECTIVE OF PERCEPTION   The obvious lesson about perception for managers is that people "see" things differently and, therefore, tend to behave differently. Although this is a simple lesson, the consequences of forgetting it can be serious when it comes to communication and effective interpersonal interaction.

Research on perception has provided managers with useful insights. For example, two behavioral scientists suggested the following conclusions:

1. Knowing oneself makes it easier to see others accurately.
2. One's own characteristics affect the characteristics he is likely to see in others.
3. The person who accepts himself is more likely to be able to see favorable aspects of other people.[17]

Thus it might be said that clear perception begins with a look in the mirror. Managers who see themselves clearly and favorably are more apt to see their superiors, peers, subordinates, and work setting clearly and favorably.

MOTIVATION

Managers have always been intrigued by the fact that some employees consistently work harder than other workers who are just as qualified. What motivates these individuals to work harder?

Managers need to know why people perform their jobs as they do. The study of motivation helps us to discover why people do things; it is one of the important intervening variables in the behavioral process. But what does the study of motivation involve?

The term *motivation* comes from the Latin word *movere*, meaning "to move." No one can simply examine a group of people out of context and decide which of its members are more highly motivated than others. Their behavior must be examined in context, in relation to their efforts to accomplish something. Put another way, if one is "to move," then one must have something to move *toward*. Consequently, the term *motivation* can be defined as the process that gives behavior purpose and direction.[18]

As one might expect, a number of theoretical explanations of the motivational process have been suggested. The diagram of motivation in Figure 11.4 combines two of the more popular theories. One of these suggests that we are motivated to do things that fulfill our *needs.* The other theory, in contrast, suggests that our *expectations*

FIGURE 11.4
The motivational process

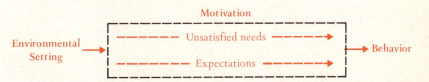

of the payoffs for doing something determine our level of motivation. Our object here is to examine and draw useful insights from both of these theories.

MASLOW'S THEORY OF MOTIVATION   In 1943 a psychologist by the name of Abraham Maslow proposed that people are motivated by a five-step hierarchy of needs.[19] Little did he realize at the time that his rather modest proposal, which was based on extremely limited clinical research, would become one of the most influential concepts in the field of management.[20] Perhaps it is because Maslow's theory is so straightforward and intuitively appealing that it has so strongly influenced those interested in work behavior. Maslow's message was simply this: people are constantly in need; when one need is relatively fulfilled, another emerges to take its place. He identified physiological needs, safety needs, love needs, esteem needs, and self-actualization needs and arranged them in a fixed *hierarchy of needs* (as shown in Figure 11.5). According to Maslow, most individuals are not consciously aware of these needs. Nevertheless, we all proceed up the hierarchy of needs, one level at a time.

Physiological needs   At the very base of the need hierarchy are physical drives. These include the need for food, water, sleep, and sex. Fulfillment of these lowest-level needs enables individuals to survive. Nothing else is important when these bodily needs cry out for fulfillment. However, the average, fairly well-adjusted individual experiences little serious deprivation of physiological needs. As Maslow has observed, "It is quite true that man lives by bread alone—when there is no bread."[21] But when we have plenty of bread to eat, the prospect of eating more bread is no longer a source of motivation. Other things become important.

**FIGURE 11.5
Maslow's hierarchy of needs**

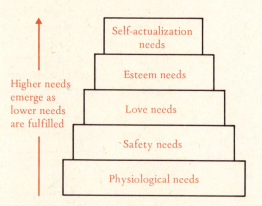

Higher needs emerge as lower needs are fulfilled

Self-actualization needs

Esteem needs

Love needs

Safety needs

Physiological needs

Safety needs   The next step in Maslow's need hierarchy is the area of safety needs. Once the basic physiological needs are satisfied, we want to assure our safety from the elements, enemies, and other threats. The average employee achieves a high degree of fulfillment in this area by earning a living and paying taxes. According to Maslow, prolonged deprivation of physiological and safety needs will create a seriously maladjusted individual.

Love needs   A physiologically satisfied and secure person focuses next on satisfying needs for love and affection. This category of needs is a powerful motivator of human behavior. People work hard to achieve a sense of belonging with others. As with the first two levels of needs, however, relative satisfaction of love needs paves the way for the emergence of the next higher level.

Esteem needs   People who view themselves as worthwhile individuals are said to possess high self-esteem. Self-respect is the key to esteem needs. Much of our self-respect and hence esteem comes from being accepted and respected by others. It is important for those who are expected to help achieve organizational objectives to have their esteem needs relatively well fulfilled. But, according to Maslow's theory, esteem needs cannot emerge if lower-level needs go unattended.

Self-actualization needs   At the top of Maslow's hierarchy resides an open-ended category that he labeled self-actualization needs. It is open-ended because it relates to the need "to become more and more what one is, to become everything that one is capable of becoming."[22] One may self-actualize by striving to become the best homemaker, the best plumber, the best rock singer, or the best manager. According to one source, the self-actualizing manager possesses the following characteristics:

1. Has warmth, closeness, and sympathy.
2. Recognizes and shares negative information and feelings.
3. Exhibits trust, openness, and candor.
4. Does not achieve goals by power, deception, or manipulation.
5. Does not project own feelings, motivations, or blame onto others.
6. Does not limit horizons; uses and develops body, mind, and senses.
7. Is not rationalistic; can think in unconventional ways.
8. Is not conforming; regulates behavior from within.[23]

This is a pretty tall order, even for the best of managers. It has been pointed out appropriately that "a truly self-actualized individual is more of an exception than the rule in the organizational context."[24] Whether or not productive organizations need more self-actualized individuals is subject to debate. On the positive side, self-actualizing employees might help break down the barriers to creativity and guide the organization in exciting new directions. On the negative side, too many unconventional nonconformists could wreak havoc with the typical administrative setup.

RELEVANCE OF MASLOW'S THEORY FOR MANAGERS

Behavioral scientists who have attempted to test Maslow's theory in real life claim that it has some deficiencies.[25] Even Maslow's hierarchical arrangement has been challenged. Practical evidence points toward a two-level rather than a five-level hierarchy. In this competing view, the physiological and safety needs are arranged in hierarchical fashion as Maslow contends. But beyond that point, any one of a number of needs may emerge as the single most important one, depending on the particular individual. Edward Lawler, a leading motivation researcher, has observed, "Which higher-order needs come into play after the lower ones are satisfied and in which order they will come into play cannot be predicted. If anything, it seems that most people are simultaneously motivated by several of the same-level needs."[26]

Although Maslow's theory has not stood up well under actual testing, it teaches managers one important lesson: a fulfilled need does not motivate an individual. For example, the promise of unemployment benefits may partially serve to fulfill an employees's need for economic security (safety need). But chances are that the added security of unemployment benefits will not motivate fully employed individuals to work any harder. Managers must anticipate each subordinate's unique need profile and present opportunities to fulfill *emerging* needs.

The esteem level presents managers with perhaps the greatest opportunity to motivate better performance. Challenging and worthwhile jobs and meaningful recognition offer people an opportunity to satisfy their esteem needs. Employees want to see themselves as capable, self-confident, useful, and worthwhile. Overspecialized, dead-end jobs stifle rather than fulfill emergent esteem needs.

EXPECTANCY THEORY OF MOTIVATION

Many of today's organizational behaviorists feel that there is more to motivation than needs. They note that a need will not motivate an individual if he or she sees little chance of fulfilling that need. Consequently, there is growing popularity for the notion that one's expectations play an important role in motivation. Expectancy theory holds that a person will work toward something (such as organizational objectives) when he or she expects the consequences of doing so to be both favorable and probable.

One early proponent of expectancy theory defined *expectancy* as "a momentary belief concerning the likelihood that a particular act will be followed by a particular outcome."[27] Each of us calculates our own subjective probabilities of success if we do something in a certain way. If we feel that our efforts will lead to successful performance and that our successful performance in turn will lead to a reward we value, then we will be motivated.

This expectancy approach not only appeals strongly to common sense; it has also received some encouraging empirical support from researchers.[28] We can look forward to revealing and exciting motivational insights from expectancy theorists in coming years.

RELEVANCE OF EXPECTANCY THEORY FOR MANAGERS

Assuming that employee contributions are dictated by their expectations, managers would do well to foster favorable expectations among employees. People will work long and hard when they feel that their efforts will pay off. These payoffs come in the form of successful task completion and rewards such as pay, promotion, recognition, and a feeling of achievement. Unfortunately, managers often overlook the need to develop favorable expectations. They program people for failure by thrusting them into unfamiliar situations. Failure then occurs because people tend to form inaccurate and negative expectations when faced with a new situation that is perceived to be threatening.

One way to encourage favorable expectations in the employee's mind is to expose the employee gradually to progressively more difficult tasks. In this manner the employee's skills, confidence, and expectations will all expand at the same time. Experience is an excellent teacher and developer of expectations.

LEARNING

What do driving a car, advocating free enterprise, acting out a racial prejudice, and being able to read a computer program have in common? At first glance, very little, but as a complex behavior each is the result of learning. As the term is used here, learning involves much more than acquiring information. Learning involves the process of adapting to and mastering one's environment. It is important to our discussion because "there is little organizational behavior that is not either directly or indirectly affected by learning."[29]

Learning can be defined as the translation of personal experience into new and different ways of behaving. This definition appears relatively simple, but a closer look reveals important fine points. Specifically, "new and different" means new and different behavior for the individual, not necessarily new and different behavior for people in general. A common skill like riding a bicycle is new and different for the child who has just completed his or her first ride. Furthermore, "new and different" does not mean better. Bad habits are learned, as well as good habits. Regardless of what is learned or how it is learned, a phenomenon called Thorndike's law of effect is at the heart of the process.

THORNDIKE'S LAW OF EFFECT

Shortly after 1900, a research psychologist named Edward L. Thorndike discovered that the consequences of present behavior greatly affect the nature of future behavior. Much of Thorndike's laboratory research was carried out with cats in puzzle boxes. Although people don't especially like to be compared to animals, they tend to interact with their environment in much the same way. Thorndike observed that his cats reacted wildly and unpredictably when first placed in an unfamiliar puzzle box. Soon, however, they settled down to attempt various methods of escape. Eventually they would discover the trick to the puzzle box and free themselves. Having once figured out how to escape, Thorndike's cats would immediately escape when placed back in the same puzzle box. In effect, Thorndike's cats had learned to adapt to and master the strange environment of the puzzle box. Through experience they learned how to escape and did so expertly whenever they were faced with the same situation.

As a result of his research, Thorndike formulated what he called his law of effect: behavior tends to be repeated when it is followed by a favorable consequence and tends not to be repeated when followed by an unfavorable consequence.[30] The term *favorable consequence*, as used here, refers to any personally rewarding experience. Of course, people find different things rewarding. Nonetheless, consequences are a powerful determinant of behavior. Thorndike's deceptively simple law of effect has been validated time and again through research and has important implications for the management of all types of behavior.

Thorndike's law of effect plays a role in two widely recognized theories of learning, called shaping and modeling. Figure 11.6 shows

**FIGURE 11.6
The learning process**

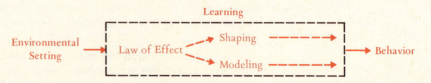

the role of shaping and modeling as people learn to adapt to and master their environment.

SHAPING   Many of the complex behaviors that we are capable of performing as adults are the product of a subtle but powerful learning process called shaping. *Shaping* amounts to learning complex tasks one step at a time. For example, it is virtually impossible for a person to slip behind the wheel of a standard-shift car for the first time and drive off smoothly. A series of gear-grinding trials is necessary before the task is mastered. But the jerking and grinding diminish as the novice driver moves closer and closer to mastering the skill. At the heart of this shaping process is the law of effect. Novice drivers are rewarded with smoother driving as they come closer to mastering the skill. Relapses are punished with increased jerking and gear grinding. Much of our behavior is shaped by environmental consequences.

Sometimes shaping simply happens, as in learning to shift gears, because the consequences stem naturally from the process taking place. Other times, however, shaping is systematically managed to produce a desired result. On-the-job shaping takes place when an individual is rewarded for improvement in the performance of a specific behavior. For example, a committee chairperson may "shape" a noncontributing committee member into a regular contributor with conditional praise. The term *conditional* means that the individual must behave in a given manner before being rewarded. At first, praise is given for any contribution at all. Later, as the contributions become more frequent, the chairperson praises only valuable contributions. In this manner, contributions are shaped to become both more frequent and more sophisticated. As I wrote elsewhere, "Shaping is an extremely practical way to facilitate individual performance improvement and get results for the organization."[31]

The shaping process is so common in our lives that we seldom stop to consider its significance. It has been suggested that shaping is at the very heart of the socialization process, through which individuals learn socially acceptable ways of behaving.[32] Parents, teachers, friends, bosses, and community leaders all have a hand in shaping the behavior of an individual. It is no wonder then that people behave in many different ways; each one of us has experienced different shaping influences.

MODELING   Although much of an individual's behavior is the product of shaping, some is acquired directly by observing others. The process of acquiring behavior by observing others is called *modeling*.[33]

Modeling differs from shaping in one major way. Relatively complex and sophisticated behavior appears quite suddenly through modeling. Shaping, on the other hand, takes time because simple behavior evolves into complex behavior one step at a time. For example, it would take a good deal of time to shape an unskilled individual into successfully programming a keypunch machine. The shaping process would include a sequence of steps for teaching the trainee to remove the drum, punch the drum card, insert the drum card, and replace the drum. Success with each step would have to be conditionally rewarded before proceeding to the next step.

This entire process could be carried out in much less time through modeling, by having the trainee watch a training film of the operation and then practice the operation on an actual keypunch machine. On the job, both live models and symbolic ones such as video tapes and instruction manuals can be used to demonstrate appropriate job behaviors.

Modeling has two basic dimensions. First, an individual may imitate someone else. Subordinates often imitate managerial behavior. "Imitation helps explain how a significant amount of complex organizational behavior, both desirable and undesirable, is learned."[34] Successful imitation itself can be a very potent reward. The second dimension of modeling is a bit more complex. Specifically, one is influenced by the rewards and punishments received by a model. Research has demonstrated that people learn at an early age to behave like models who are rewarded rather than like models who are not rewarded.[35] If we see a model being rewarded for doing something, we tend to believe that we will be rewarded for behaving in a similar manner. In other words, people tend to imitate behavior that appears to promise a reward.

A MANAGERIAL PERSPECTIVE OF LEARNING   Learning takes place whether managers are aware of it or not. The question is, Should managers get actively involved in the learning process, or just let it happen? At the very least, problem-solving managers should recognize that they shape subordinate behavior through their actions. Moreover, managers are highly visible behavior models. Managers who break rules cannot expect their subordinates to follow those same rules. "Do as I say, not as I do" policies are unrealistic.

SUMMARY   The study of organizational behavior helps present and future managers realize that people are not quite as unpredictable as they appear at first glance. Much of our knowledge about people is intuitive in nature. Unfortunately, bias and generalization often distort intuitive impressions of reality. The scientific approach, in contrast, is designed to eliminate the effects of bias and unwarranted generalization. Four identifying characteristics of the scientific approach are hypothesis testing, representative sampling, objective measurement, and control. Although managers are not behavioral scientists they can benefit from their own use of the scientific method and from a general knowledge of behavioral science research. Managers are challenged to balance intuitive and scientific knowledge about people at work.

At least four intuitive models of organizational behavior can be identified. The rational-economic model views people as rational beings interested primarily in high wages. The organization-man model assumes that individual and organizational goals are identical. Theory Y assumes that people enjoy work and are naturally energetic and creative. The complex model, which represents a combination of the first three, recognizes that human behavior is highly variable.

Behavioral scientists have uncovered three intervening variables that help explain the interaction between people and their environment. They are perception, motivation, and learning. All three act as moderating bridges between the environment and individual behavior.

Perception is the process by which individuals give meaning to their environment. Through the subprocesses of selectivity, organization, and interpretation, people try to make sense out of an otherwise confusing world. Managers need to realize that they perceive things differently than their subordinates do. Because people perceive things differently, they tend to behave differently.

Through the study of motivation, we discover the factors that give purpose and direction to behavior. There are two popular theories of motivation. The first is based on the assumption that people are motivated by unfulfilled needs. Need theory relies heavily on the concept of a hierarchy of needs, as developed by Abraham Maslow. A second approach to motivation is called the expectancy theory. In expectancy theory, the expected outcomes of performance determine the degree of an individual's motivation.

Learning is the behavioral process that translates personal experience into new ways of behaving. At the very core of the learning process is Thorndike's law of effect, which states that behavior with favorable consequences tends to be repeated and behavior with unfavorable consequences tends to disappear. Shaping and modeling are two of the primary processes by which behavior is learned.

TERMS TO UNDERSTAND

Organizational behavior
Intuition
Bias
Generalization
Hypothesis
Rational-economic model
Organization man
Theory Y
Intervening variable
Perception

Selectivity
Perceptual defense
Perceptual set
Perceptual organization
Motivation
Hierarchy of needs
Expectancy
Learning
Law of effect
Shaping
Modeling

QUESTIONS FOR DISCUSSION

1. When must a manager rely strictly on intuition in dealing with people?
2. How can the typical manager who is not a behavioral scientist benefit from the scientific method?
3. What do the rational-economic model, the organization-man model, and McGregor's Theory X model have in common?
4. In what way is the complex model of organizational behavior a compromise?
5. Why are perception, motivation, and learning called intervening variables?
6. How do grouping, figure-ground, and closure affect the way we perceive things?
7. Why might a self-actualizing individual have a difficult time in a mechanistic organization?
8. How can a manager use expectancy theory in attempting to motivate subordinates?
9. What role does Thorndike's law of effect play in learning?
10. From a practical management standpoint, what advantage does modeling have over shaping?

CASE 11.1 TROUBLE AT ELITE PEN

Last year was the best year in Elite Pen Company's seventy-eight-year history. Located in a small Iowa community on the Missouri River, Elite Pen has maintained a position enjoyed by virtually no other American pen manufacturer in recent years. It has avoided the vigorous pressure of foreign competition.

Although foreign pen makers are thinning out the competition in the ball-point and felt-tip markets, Elite continues to do what it does best. Namely, it makes one of the highest quality, hand-crafted fountain pens in the world. Fountain pens have staged a slow but steady comeback in recent years. Today, Elite Pen enjoys a near-monopoly position in this relatively small, prestige market. Profits have been so good that the treasurer has been investing surplus funds in land and assorted ventures.

Elite's management, although liberally sprinkled with old-timers, sees itself as fairly progressive. Elite Pen employees are paid more than any others in the region. Management attributes the firm's nonunion status and reputation for quality work to its generous pay plan. Recently, nearly everyone has been working overtime because of a rash of unusually large orders. Many employees are taking home nearly 50 percent more pay than usual. As the president recently told a group of community leaders, "Our people have motivation coming out their ears because they take home the fattest pay envelopes in the region." The pay situation promises to get even better when the new "productivity improvement plan" bonuses go out. Under the new plan, selected employees will receive sizable annual bonuses based on a complicated productivity formula worked out by the treasurer.

In view of how well things have been going lately, the president was shocked to receive a list of grievances mailed by an anonymous employee claiming to represent "a lot" of Elite Pen employees. Included on the long list of grievances were the following items:

- All the overtime is getting to be a pain in the neck. You guys in management may like to stay around here all night, but we enjoy being with our families and doing other things.
- The treasurer's new bonus plan is a joke. Nobody can figure out how the bonuses will be determined. As usual, management's pets will probably be the only ones to benefit. You're not fooling anybody. We're not going to work any harder for something we don't have any chance of getting.
- Why didn't you tell us you're going to close this plant? That's what everybody's saying. We know you bought some land back in Indiana. Why should we care about Elite Pen if you're going to run out on us?

FOR DISCUSSION
1. From the standpoint of perception, what is happening here?
2. Judging by what you know about the need theory of motivation, why is this employee unhappy?
3. What role does the expectancy theory of motivation play in this case?

CASE 11.2
NOW WAIT A
MINUTE!

Metropolitan Electric, a public utility, has a set procedure for hiring managers. First, the personnel department generates a list of applicants who meet all the technical requirements. Next, someone from personnel discusses each candidate on the list with the department head who has the vacant position. Finally, the department head makes the final selection after interviewing the top four candidates.

Recently, Clyde Williams, the field repair department head, was going over a list of candidates for a field repair supervisor position. After hearing the qualifications of each of a dozen candidates, Clyde and the personnel specialist agreed that Pat Thatcher was the most qualified. Pat seemed to have the right combination of technical and administrative experience. "Right," Clyde concluded, "it looks like Pat Thatcher is our man. He's head and shoulders above the others. I sure hope we can land him."

"True," answered the personnel specialist, "But I forgot to mention that it's *Patricia* Thatcher. He is a *she.*"

"Now wait a minute!" exclaimed Clyde. "We've got nothing but men out there in field repair. That's no place for a lady. It's a rough job. There's no way a woman could qualify for a situation like that."

FOR DISCUSSION

1. How do bias and perceptual set enter into this case?
2. If you were the personnel specialist, what would you say to Clyde?
3. It is against the law to refuse employment on the basis of an applicant's sex. Does this fact complicate the situation?

REFERENCES

Opening quotation

Walter R. Nord, *Concepts and Controversy in Organizational Behavior*, 2nd ed. (Santa Monica: Goodyear, 1976), p. 2.

1. Studs Terkel, *Working* (New York: Pantheon, 1974), p. 522.
2. Keith Davis, *Human Behavior at Work: Human Relations and Organizational Behavior*, 4th ed. (New York: McGraw-Hill, 1972), p. 5.
3. L. L. Cummings, "Toward Organizational Behavior," *Academy of Management Review* 3 (January 1978): 94.
4. Kenneth N. Wexley and Gary Yukl, *Organizational Behavior and Personnel Psychology* (Homewood, Ill.: Irwin, 1971), p. 2.
5. For details, see: Victor H. Vroom, *Work and Motivation* (New York: Wiley, 1964), p. 186.
6. Sheldon Zedeck and Milton R. Blood, *Foundations of Behavioral Science Research in Organizations* (Monterey, Cal.: Brooks/Cole, 1974), p. 7.
7. Charles H. Kepner and Benjamin B. Tregoe, *The Rational Manager* (New York: McGraw-Hill, 1965), p. 24.

8. See: James S. Bowman, "The Behavioral Sciences: Fact and Fantasy in Organizations," *Personnel Journal* 55 (August 1976): 395–397.

9. Frederick W. Taylor, *Shop Management* (New York: Harper & Brothers, 1911), p. 22.

10. William H. Whyte, Jr., *The Organization Man* (New York: Simon & Schuster, 1956), p. 129.

11. Douglas McGregor, *The Human Side of Enterprise* (New York: McGraw-Hill, 1960), chap. 4.

12. Edgar H. Schein, *Organizational Psychology*, 2nd ed. (Englewood Cliffs, N.J.: Prentice-Hall, 1970), p. 76.

13. Nord, *Concepts and Controversy in Organizational Behavior*, p. 22.

14. For an interesting report of this accident and its behavioral aspects, see: "Spaniards Analyze Tenerife Accident," *Aviation Week & Space Technology* 109 (November 20, 1978): 113–121.

15. For a typical example of this research, see: H. H. Kelley, "The Warm-Cold Variable in First Impressions of Persons," *Journal of Personality* 18 (1950): 431–439.

16. John Senger, "Seeing Eye to Eye: Practical Problems of Perception," *Personnel Journal* 53 (October 1974): 749.

17. Sheldon S. Zalkind and Timothy W. Costello, "Perception: Some Recent Research and Implications for Administration," *Administrative Science Quarterly* 7 (September 1962): 227–228.

18. For an excellent historical and conceptual treatment of basic motivation theory, see: Richard M. Steers and Lyman W. Porter, *Motivation and Work Behavior* (New York: McGraw-Hill, 1975), chap. 1.

19. See: A. H. Maslow, "A Theory of Human Motivation," *Psychological Review* 50 (July 1943): 370–396.

20. For a revealing study of what managers think about management theory, see: M. T. Matteson, "Some Reported Thoughts on Significant Management Literature," *Academy of Management Journal* 17 (1974): 386–389.

21. Maslow, "A Theory of Human Motivation," p. 375.

22. Ibid., p. 382.

23. George W. Cherry, "The Serendipity of the Fully Functioning Manager," *Sloan Management Review* 17 (Spring 1976): 73.

24. Vance F. Mitchell and Pravin Moudgill, "Measurement of Maslow's Need Hierarchy," *Organizational Behavior and Human Performance* 16 (August 1976): 348.

25. For example, see: Douglas T. Hall and Khalil E. Nougaim, "An

Examination of Maslow's Need Hierarchy in an Organizational Setting," *Organizational Behavior and Human Performance* 3 (February 1968): 12–35.

26. Edward E. Lawler, *Motivation in Work Organizations* (Monterey, Cal.: Brooks/Cole, 1973), p. 34.

27. Vroom, *Work and Motivation*, p. 17.

28. For example, see: J. Richard Hackman and Lyman W. Porter, "Expectancy Theory Predictions of Work Effectiveness," *Organizational Behavior and Human Performance* 3 (November 1968): 417–426.

29. Fred Luthans, *Organizational Behavior*, 2nd ed. (New York: McGraw-Hill, 1977), p. 280.

30. See: Edward L. Thorndike, *Educational Psychology: The Psychology of Learning*, Vol. II (New York: Columbia University, 1913), p. 4.

31. Robert Kreitner, "PM—A New Method of Behavior Change," *Business Horizons* 18 (December 1975): 86.

32. Consult the following source for additional information: Elliot McGinnies, *Social Behavior: A Functional Analysis* (Boston: Houghton Mifflin, 1970), p. 97.

33. For an instructive discussion of modeling, see: Albert Bandura, *Principles of Behavior Modification* (New York: Holt, Rinehart & Winston, 1969): chap. 3.

34. Fred Luthans and Robert Kreitner, *Organizational Behavior Modification* (Glenview, Ill.: Scott, Foresman, 1975), p. 139.

35. For example, see: Albert Bandura and F. J. McDonald, "The Influence of Social Reinforcement and the Behavior of Models in Shaping Children's Moral Judgments," *Journal of Abnormal and Social Psychology* 67 (1963): 274–281.

Chapter 12

Staffing

As organizations evolve, the complexity of the environments within which they operate will cause increased dependence upon the very people making up the organization.

Edgar H. Schein

LEARNING OBJECTIVES

When you finish reading this chapter, you should be able to

- Explain why people join work organizations.
- Discuss the individual-organization relationship in terms of exchange, involvement, and mismatch.
- Explain what human resource planning involves.
- Outline what occurs during the selection process.
- Explain how training relates to the staffing function.

When individual and organization interact, dramatically different things can happen. Both can prosper because of a mutually beneficial relationship, or, alternatively, they may discover a fundamental disharmony. Because the most important ingredient of modern work organizations is the individual, managers need to understand the basics of individual-organization interaction. Furthermore, they need to know how individuals are brought into the organization and how they are trained, or developed. The purpose of this chapter is to discuss several dimensions of staffing, the systematic matching of individual and organization.

THE STAFFING FUNCTION

One management theorist has defined *staffing* as

> the proper and effective planning of manpower requirements and the acquisition and development of personnel to perform the duties and responsibilities specified by the organization structure.[1]

This general definition embraces three distinct staffing activities. They are (1) human resource planning, (2) selection, and (3) training. Each activity is typically carried out by trained specialists operating out of a centralized personnel department. However, in highly decentralized organizations, managers all the way down to the first-line supervisors may share the responsibility for these staffing activities. Regardless of who carries them out, they must be given careful attention to make sure that each job is filled by a capable individual. Only when jobs are properly filled can the organization fulfill its intended purpose.

Before we examine these specific staffing activities, we need to establish a sound theoretical foundation. In the first portion of this discussion, we explore the reasons for joining organizations in the first place. The second, more comprehensive portion analyzes what happens when the individual and the organization are brought together and interact. Staffing activities can be ineffective if managers do not have this theoretical foundation.

WHY INDIVIDUALS JOIN ORGANIZATIONS

The practice of joining organizations begins at an early age in our highly organized society. Youngsters are encouraged by parents, friends, and teachers to join clubs, athletic teams, scout troops, and so on. To the maturing adolescent it becomes clear that taking part in organized activity is more rewarding than relying strictly on one's own resources. Sometimes, as in the case of schools, one is forced to join an organization. But membership in most organizations is voluntary. Because the joining-up process is so commonplace, few people stop to consider why individuals join organizations. Nonetheless, it is very important for managers to know the answer to this question. More specifically, managers need to know why *work* organizations attract individuals. Work organizations deserve special attention because they are the backbone of our productive society. It is within work organizations that individuals exchange their time and talents for a livelihood and a whole host of other payoffs.

We can identify three general reasons why individuals go to work for organizations. Those reasons are economic security, social support, and opportunity for growth. Table 12.1 contrasts individual effort with organized effort. Work organizations, in many ways, offer the individual more than he or she could get by acting alone.

One element that organizations offer to individuals is economic security. An individual who goes to work for General Motors has a great deal more economic security than someone who attempts to make and sell automobiles alone. (Of course, the union further assures economic security.) The company has an advantage over individual effort because it achieves economies of scale when it purchases large quantities of raw materials, uses mass production techniques, and relies on mass marketing strategies. A second element offered by the organization is social support. Many people simply wish to "belong." As social institutions, work organizations give individuals a social setting in which to operate. A third element that organizations offer is opportunity for personal growth. Because organizations gather together many human and material resources, they are able to provide special growth opportunities to their employees. An expanded analysis of the reasons that people join work organizations follows.

ECONOMIC SECURITY People have always had strong needs for security. Traditionally, security means protection from the elements and having enough food to eat. In prehistoric times, security needs were satisfied by a warm cave and a sturdy club. Later, in agrarian societies, security meant that "when the market was bad or cash crops failed, the

TABLE 12.1
Why individuals join organizations

DRAWBACKS OF INDIVIDUAL EFFORT	ORGANIZATIONAL STRENGTHS	WHAT ORGANIZATIONS CAN OFFER INDIVIDUALS
Economic insecurity	Economies of scale	Economic security
Isolation	Social setting	Social support
Limited opportunity	Larger resource base	Greater opportunity

farmer, if frugal and wise, could at least eat from his own garden."[2] Today, in modern industrialized society, security has come to mean a dependable flow of money to pay the mortgage or rent, provide groceries, and meet taxes and other financial obligations.

Both prehistoric man and the early farmer could fall back on their own resources for security, whereas modern individuals must turn primarily to paid employment for economic security. But it is no longer a matter of "work or starve" as it once was. Government-sponsored social security and welfare payments constitute an economic floor under everyone, including the unemployed. Nevertheless, work organizations still provide the greatest amount of economic security. As long as people can achieve more economic security through gainful employment than through government economic assistance programs, there will be a strong incentive to join work organizations.

SOCIAL SUPPORT   Closely related to the need for economic security is the need for social support. Except for the occasional loner, people are social animals. Not only do they want to be with others, but they want to be accepted by others. The need for social support has been called the need for affiliation by behavioral scientists. As one of them has pointed out, "The need for affiliation is truly a social motive; it reflects the desire for social acceptance."[3]

The social support that people gain from a work organization is quite evident in everyday conversation. For instance, the next time you are at a social gathering keep track of the number of times you hear people refer to the places where they work. Individuals are much more confident of their social status when they can speak as a member of an established organization. Moreover, coffee breaks, lunches, and bull sessions during the workday are a vital source of social support.

OPPORTUNITY FOR   Society is a dynamic balance between the forces of cooperation and
GROWTH   the forces of competition. A similar balance is found within organizations. Initially, people cooperate by going to work for an organization. Later, they compete in trying to climb the organizational ladder. Provided the competition for advancement does not become destructive, the organization stands to gain from interpersonal competition for growth opportunities.

Promotions are only one form of growth within work organizations. Individuals also may grow in skill, confidence, intellect, and mastery of difficult techniques. Organizations with vast resources provide excellent opportunities for this kind of personal growth. It would be virtually impossible for a research chemist at a modern pharmaceutical company to construct a comparable laboratory at home. Only a well-financed organization can afford to bring the appropriate laboratory equipment and a highly paid and properly trained group of chemists together. We might say that organizations, rather than necessity, appear to be the mother of invention.

We have just shown that individuals go to work for organizations to improve their chances for economic security, social support, and personal growth. But these needs are not always satisfied. Some employees get a barely adequate pay check and even that is threatened. On the other hand, only organizations that satisfy employees' needs for economic security, social support, and personal growth can expect to have a work force that is interested, involved, and committed.

AN ANALYSIS OF INDIVIDUAL-ORGANIZATION INTERACTION

Managers need to understand both people and organizations if they are to get anything accomplished. Even more important, they need to understand the interaction between people and the organizations in which they work. Borrowing an open-system term used in Chapter 6, the relationship between the formal organization and the individual is synergistic. By this it is meant that organizational behavior, the result of individuals interacting with the organization, is greater than the sum of its parts. The organization and its members add up to more than one plus one. The missing quantity in this equation is the interaction between people and organizations.

In the following pages we analyze individual-organization interaction from three different perspectives. First, we examine the exchange relationship between the two. Second, we discuss four types of individual involvement with the organization. Finally, we look at the problem of individual-organization mismatch.

AN EXCHANGE RELATIONSHIP

At one time, when sailing ships ruled the high seas, crew members would stop at a port and shanghai a few local drunks whenever they needed new personnel. The relationship between the individual and work organization in that situation was coercive. The poor soul who woke up aboard an Orient-bound sailing ship was faced with the choice of work or walk the plank. Fortunately, that is not the usual arrangement today.

We live in an economy in which goods and services are exchanged for money. This exchange relationship is an essential part of the labor market as well. The relationship between employer and employee is voluntary rather than coercive. In broadest terms, when individuals go to work for a company, government agency, or nonprofit organization, they agree to exchange their time and talents for money. However, as outlined in Figure 12.1, there is much more to this exchange than time and money.

Psychological contracts An employment contract is created when someone goes to work for an organization. Although employment contracts vary in amount of detail and are usually unwritten, they serve to establish an individual's desire to work and an organization's willingness to pay for that work. They are exchange agreements. But no matter how specific the terms of an employment contract may be, both the individual and the organization must do some reading between the lines. As indicated in Figure 12.1, many factors enter the exchange between employee and employer. Behavioral scientists have applied the term *psychological contract* to the combination of expectations that employees and employers have of one another.[4] While some of these expectations may be discussed during the hiring process, when the employment contract is developed, most of them are only implied. The result is a gray area of understanding between the individual and the organization. A great deal of individual-organization conflict occurs because of misunderstandings about the nature of this gray area.

There is concern today that psychological contracts are too vague, that too much is left to chance. For example, an employee may expect the company to provide frequent promotions. Although nothing in the employment contract specifically supports this

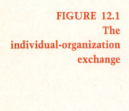

FIGURE 12.1
The individual-organization exchange

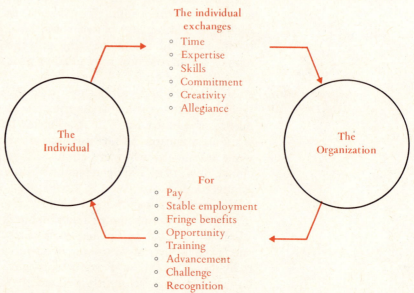

The individual exchanges
○ Time
○ Expertise
○ Skills
○ Commitment
○ Creativity
○ Allegiance

The Individual

The Organization

For
○ Pay
○ Stable employment
○ Fringe benefits
○ Opportunity
○ Training
○ Advancement
○ Challenge
○ Recognition

expectation, the individual works very hard to earn a promotion. When an expected promotion does not come about, dissatisfaction sets in and performance drops off. Eventually, the situation may get so bad that the individual will quit or be terminated.

Employing organizations can take steps to clarify the psychological contracts between themselves and their employees. At the time of hire, for example, the supervisor and the new employee can sit down and discuss the expectations each has of the other. For example, the supervisor could paint a realistic picture right from the beginning about the lack of promotion opportunities. Employees are much more receptive to bad news at the time of hire than they are after working hard to achieve what turns out to be a false hope. A whole range of topics including duties, privileges, obligations, and rights come under the umbrella of psychological contracts.

If psychological contracts are more carefully spelled out, there will be greater reciprocation, or mutual exchange, between the individual and the employing organization.[5] The coin of mutual exchange is expectations. Research comparing the expectations of recruiters and graduating college students showed that they were remarkably close.[6] Consequently, both parties stand to gain by bringing these mutual expectations out in the open as early as possible to expose any remaining areas of disagreement or misunderstanding.

An organizational perspective   Members of management can take steps to improve the individual-organization exchange. Procedures can be set up to give supervisors and potential employees the opportunity to sit down and discuss their relative expectations. Areas of agreement can be summarized, and areas of disagreement can be discussed. The organization may not be able to meet all of an individual's expectations, but at least the new employee will begin his or her employment with a realistic idea of what the organization expects in the way of work, commitment, and so forth. Similarly, the individual will have a more realistic idea of the opportunities for recognition, promotion, and other aspects of employment.

An individual perspective   The organization cannot bear all the responsibility for a mutually satisfying exchange between employee and employer. The individual needs to take some constructive steps as well. The obvious first step for someone seeking a job is to draw up a list of personal objectives for the next one to five years. These objectives should relate to pay level, status, promotions, responsibility, location, and other important factors. Next, the probability of attaining these objectives should be kept in mind while the job seeker talks with as many different organizations as possible. If an offer is received, he or she should open up the psychological contract process as much as possible. This procedure should lead to employment in which there will be ample opportunity to achieve personal objectives.

INVOLVEMENT The first important decision an individual makes about an organization is whether to join it or not. Once employed, attention turns to two other matters. Namely, the individual must decide how hard to work and whether or not to stay with the organization. Both of these decisions are affected by many factors. One very important factor is the degree to which one's psychological contract is fulfilled. Too many unrealized expectations will lead to second thoughts about working hard and staying with the organization. The crucial dimension here is involvement.

Involvement is defined as the degree to which the individual personally identifies with the objectives of the organization. Figure 12.2 shows that involvement has two dimensions. First, one's involvement may be positive or negative, for or against the organization. Second, the intensity of involvement may be low or high.[7] A combination of these two dimensions yields four basic types of involvement.

High negative involvement This type of involvement is the most undesirable of the four. High negative involvement paves the way for ending the individual-organization relationship. Termina-

FIGURE 12.2 Types of individual involvement in the organization

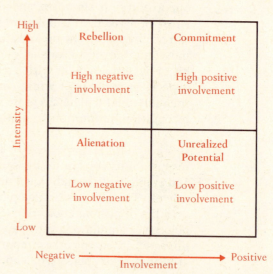

tion is inevitable, because the individual not only stops identifying with the organization's purpose but resorts to open rebellion against the organization. Open rebellion may take the form of rule breaking, sabotage, rumor spreading, and other kinds of disruptive or destructive behavior.

Low negative involvement   A common term for this type of involvement is *alienation*. Apathy runs high among alienated employees. They feel powerless and view their work as meaningless.[8] In short, alienated individuals feel out of tune with the organization.[9] They see little use in working hard because they do not identify with what the organization is trying to accomplish.

Low positive involvement   This type of involvement is a marked improvement over the two just discussed. When there is low positive involvement, the individual at least identifies with the employing organization's mission. The only problem is that the individual's involvement is not intense enough. As indicated in Figure 12.2, this is the zone of unrealized potential. The possibility of increased productivity hinges on management's ability to stimulate greater involvement and personal commitment to the organization's objectives. Chapter 15 introduces a number of promising approaches.

High positive involvement   This type of involvement is the key to organizational success. Those who become truly committed to the overall direction of the organization fall into the high positive zone, which is characterized by initiative and a willingness to identify and solve problems. Management relies on individuals with high positive involvement to put forth the extra effort so often needed when things are not going well. Moreover, employees who display high positive involvement serve as excellent behavior models for their coworkers.

All four types of involvement may be evident in a single work group. If there are more "positives" than "negatives," then the organization has a good chance of meeting its objectives. Without positive involvement there can be no commitment; without commitment there can be little if any organizational success.

INDIVIDUAL-ORGANIZATION MISMATCH   We are all familiar with situations in which square-peg individuals simply do not fit into round-hole organizations. Considering the wide variety of personalities in the labor force and the many different types of organizations in today's society, it is no wonder that individual-organization mismatches occasionally occur. A certain number of mismatches are unavoidable. However, a prevailing *trend* toward individual-organization mismatches is cause for concern. Such a trend has been identified by Chris Argyris, a respected scholar in the field of organizational behavior.

The incongruency thesis   Something is said to be incongruent with something else when the two don't match, when they are incompatible and not harmonious. Chris Argyris, with his so-called incongruency thesis, not only proposed a new perspective but tried to stimulate corrective action as well. In brief, the *incongruency thesis* states that the demands of the typical organization are incongruent with the psychological needs of the individual. Argyris believes that individuals naturally strive to be mature, but the organizations that employ them often encourage immature behavior. It is important to note here that Argyris uses the term *maturity* in a special way. He draws a distinction between chronological maturity (one's age) and psychological maturity. Since psychological maturity relates to personality development, a young person may be psychologically mature and an older person may be psychologically immature. In other words, these two types of maturity may vary independently.

In the following statement, Argyris points out that the typical organization limits rather than enhances psychological maturity:

> If the principles of formal organization [division of labor, hierarchy, and close supervision] are used as ideally defined, employees will tend to work in an environment where (1) they are provided minimal control over their workaday world, (2) they are expected to be passive, dependent, and subordinate, (3) they are expected to have a short time perspective, (4) they are induced to perfect and value the frequent use of a few skin-surface shallow abilities, and (5) they are expected to produce under conditions leading to psychological failure.[10]

The heart of Argyris's incongruency thesis is shown in Table 12.2. Notice how each pair of characteristics represents polar extremes. Since individuals may fall somewhere in between on each of the seven pairs of extremes, there are countless possible combinations of characteristics. Conceivably, every individual possesses a unique profile. Nonetheless, as Argyris claims, organizational life tends to pull us toward psychological immaturity.

	THE TYPICAL ORGANIZATION FORCES THE INDIVIDUAL TO BE PSYCHOLOGICALLY IMMATURE	THE AVERAGE INDIVIDUAL NATURALLY STRIVES TO BE PSYCHOLOGICALLY MATURE
TABLE 12.2 Argyris's incongruency thesis	Passive	Active
	Dependent	Independent
	Limited range of behavior	Broad range of behavior
	Shallow interests	Deep interests
	Here-and-now orientation	Future orientation
	Satisfied with subordinate status	Need for equal or superior status
	Limited self-awareness	Developed self-awareness

Striving for congruency   Can managers do anything to improve the match between individual employees and the organization? At least one group of researchers suggests that steps can be taken in this direction.[11] After discovering that the job satisfaction and performance of a sample of ninety-two industrial managers were dependent not only on their personalities but on the organizational climate as well, the researchers recommended altering the climate in case of incongruency or mismatch. For example, an organization with a cold, restrictive climate could become warm, open, and appropriately structured for the needs of the employees. Of course, if altering the organization's climate is either undesirable or impossible, favorable individual-organization matches can be achieved only by hiring those who are likely to thrive in the prevailing climate.

The threat of Argyris's incongruency thesis is convincingly real. Fortunately, problem-solving managers can minimize individual-organization mismatches by adjusting either the human side of the equation, the organizational side of the equation, or both. Specific alternatives are discussed in Chapter 15. Much remains to be learned about the matching process.

Now we will turn to the specific staffing activities of human resource planning, selection, and training.

HUMAN RESOURCE PLANNING

As discussed in Chapter 4, planning is fundamental to good management. Planning enables managers to better cope with an uncertain environment and more efficiently allocate scarce resources. In recent years, management scholars have begun to emphasize the need to plan the human side of organized endeavor.

There continues to be in organizations a failure, particularly on the part of line managers and functional managers in areas other than personnel, to recognize the true importance of planning for and managing human resources.[12]

Comprehensive human resource planning, referred to as manpower planning by some, ensures that the right people are in the right jobs at the right time.

HUMAN RESOURCE PLANNING DEFINED

Generally defined, *human resource planning* is the development of a staffing strategy for meeting the organization's future human resource needs. In more operational terms:

> This subprocess includes an analysis of the levels of skill in the organization; an analysis of current and expected vacancies due to retirement, discharges, transfers, promotions, sick leaves, leaves of absence, or other reasons; and analysis of current and expected expansions or curtailments in departments. Plans are then made for internal shifts or cutbacks in manpower, for training and development of present employees, for advertising job openings, or for recruiting and hiring new people, or for all of these approaches. Manpower planning must also be responsive to rapidly changing forces in society, including technological innovations, manpower availability and skill levels, and governmental rulings and court decisions growing out of Federal and state civil rights legislation.[13]

This degree of planning sophistication necessarily calls for a comprehensive systems perspective.

A SYSTEMS PERSPECTIVE

Human resource planning involves a systematic approach to staffing activities. Traditionally, staffing has suffered from a lack of continuity. People have been hired and trained on an "as needed" basis, which is hindsighted and therefore inadequate for today's rapidly changing conditions. What is needed is a foresighted, systematic approach that provides specific answers to the following questions:

1. Are the right numbers and kinds of people doing the things we need to have done?
2. Are we properly utilizing our people?
3. Do we have the people we need to satisfy our future needs?[14]

Answers to these questions can be obtained through a systematic approach like the one in Figure 12.3. First, present staffing needs are

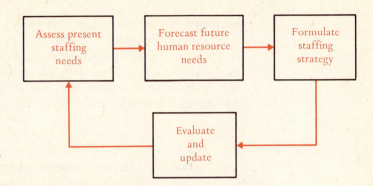

FIGURE 12.3
A basic model for human resource planning systems

assessed. Next, future needs of human resources are forecast. Third, a comprehensive staffing strategy is formulated. Finally, recycling permits evaluation and updating of the system.

Assessing present needs   Before any meaningful forecasting or strategy formulation can take place, management must assess the organization's present staffing picture. A time-consuming procedure called job analysis comes into play here. *Job analysis* is "the process of gathering pertinent information and determining the component elements of a job by observation and study."[15] Typically, a team of trained specialists zeros in on specific jobs by analyzing work flows, tracking the procedures for accomplishing departmental or subunit objectives, and interviewing individuals about the nature of their jobs. If job descriptions exist, they are updated. If not, they are created. A *job description* is a clear and concise summary of the duties of a specific job and the qualifications for holding it. Job descriptions are important and useful staffing tools because they help answer three questions: (1) Is the job necessary? (2) Does the job contribute to a coordinated effort? and (3) What qualifications does an individual need to fill the job?

By comparing updated job descriptions with the qualifications and duties of individuals presently holding those jobs, management can determine whether the organization is appropriately staffed. Overstaffing can be wastefully expensive, but understaffing can hamper the achievement of organizational goals. An appropriately staffed organization has the right number of people working in the jobs best suited to their talents.

A growing number of organizations are finding computerized personnel inventories useful. This type of data bank can be compiled most conveniently during the initial assessment of human resources. By keying each present employee's name and biographical summary into the computer along with such pertinent data as seniority, pay status, promotion record, and training experience, a time-saving personnel decision tool is created. For example, in a matter of seconds, a personnel manager can obtain a printout of the age distribution among upper-level managers. Using this data summary as an objective base, the personnel manager can predict where replacements will be needed as older managers retire.

Forecasting future needs   Chapter 4 discussed how planning forecasts are typically based on informed judgment, surveys, or trend analyses. Human resource planning is no exception. This second phase of the planning cycle, forecasting, calls for a comparison of projected demand and supply. Several factors need to be considered; forecasting requires a good deal of lateral thinking (see Table 12.3).[16] In considering demand, managers need to envision human resources as flowing into, through, and out of the organization. Like any other resource, human resources are subject to subtle erosion; that is, employees tend to leave the organization for a variety of reasons, and the organization must replace them. As for supply, both internal and external sources should be explored. One important element is prevailing trends in education. For example, if record numbers of people are studying computer programming in

TABLE 12.3
Factors to consider in forecasting the demand for and supply of human resources

Forecast Demand	○ Anticipated growth of the organization
	○ Budget constraints
	○ Turnover due to quits, terminations, transfers, retirement, and death
	○ Introduction of new technology
	○ Minority hiring goals
Forecast Supply	○ Number of employees willing and able to be trained
	○ Promotable employees
	○ Availability of required talent in local, regional, and national labor markets
	○ Competition for talent within the industry and in general
	○ Population trends (such as movement of families in the United States from the Northeast to the Southwest)
	○ Enrollment trends in government training programs, trade schools, and colleges and universities

schools and colleges, data processing firms may not need to rely so heavily on training their own personnel in the future.

The net result of human resource demand and supply forecasting should be a detailed list of future staffing needs. This list should tell how many people, of what kind, are needed when.

Formulating a staffing strategy In satisfying future staffing needs, management basically has two sets of options. The first set involves relying on present employees or hiring new ones. The second set of options centers on training programs to upgrade employee skills. These two sets of options can be combined. When they are, four strategic alternatives emerge: (1) do not train present employees; (2) train present employees; (3) hire but do not train outsiders; and (4) hire and train outsiders. Any one of these alternatives may be appropriate depending on the need forecast. Actually, in organizations that are changing and growing rapidly, all four alternatives may be used, depending on specific areas of need.

Evaluation and update Like many other systems, human resource planning needs a control loop, or means of monitoring the system. By comparing actual performance of the system with previously formulated plans, necessary corrections can be made. Unanticipated shortages or excesses of qualified people signal a defect in the planning system. Sometimes, management discovers that it has overlooked important demand or supply considerations. Whatever the problem, if corrective action is taken, the planning cycle should work more smoothly and effectively each time it is repeated.[17]

SELECTION To say that an organization is only as good as its people is a gross understatement. Even the best-intentioned organization, with the best-designed organizational structure, will falter if it is not staffed by appropriately skilled and motivated individuals. Through a *selection process*, management finds qualified people to fill specific jobs. As the organization's gatekeeper, the selection process is largely responsible for the quality of its human resources.

The first thing to consider, for all job openings except those at the lowest entry level, is whether to promote an insider or to hire an outsider.

PROMOTE OR HIRE? Management naturally hires outsiders for bottom-rung positions in the organizational hierarchy. But what about the many positions above the lowest entry level, whether newly created or recently

"First thing we do is cut down on our executive training program."

vacated? There may be promotable employees already working for the organization, and there is always the outside labor market. Each source has advantages.

Advantages of promoting an insider   There are at least three advantages to promoting from within: (1) promotion is less expensive than outside hiring; (2) promotable insiders are proven performers; and (3) promotion from within has motivational impact.

The cost of hiring someone from outside has skyrocketed in recent years. Both inflationary pressure and more complicated hiring practices are responsible. According to one compensation specialist, the hiring costs of employment agency fees, advertising, testing, interviewing, checking references, medical exams, relocation, and orientation pile up quickly. For example, in 1975 the cost of hiring a $7,800-a-year secretary averaged $1,520. That same year, a staggering $18,300 typically had to be spent hiring a $30,000-a-year middle manager.[18] Avoiding these hiring costs is a strong incentive to find and promote a qualified insider.

Whenever an outsider is hired, management runs the risk that someone who looks good on paper may not be able to handle a new and different job in an unfamiliar organization. In contrast, someone who is promoted from within is familiar with the organization, even if the particular job and coworkers are new. To a certain extent, promotable insiders have proven themselves. Evidence of an insider's worth comes from direct observation, whereas management can use only secondhand impressions in evaluating an outsider.

Experience has shown that people tend to work harder when they believe they have a good chance of being promoted. Moreover, a modeling effect occurs when employees see their deserving coworkers being promoted to better-paying, higher-status jobs. At the other end of the scale, dead-end jobs tend to dampen motivation and stifle commitment. Promotions, when regularly and fairly used, can be a powerful motivational factor.

Advantages of hiring an outsider   Countering the benefits of promoting a present employee are three advantages associated with hiring someone new: (1) bringing in outsiders helps prevent social inbreeding; (2) training costs are reduced when a qualified outsider is hired; (3) new people tend to introduce new perspectives.

Undesirable social inbreeding occurs when people are promoted on the basis of who they know rather than *what* they know. Hiring someone new can break any automatic cycle of favoritism that may exist.

Resorting to outside hiring also tends to keep training costs down. An insider who lacks the skills necessary for a higher position must be trained before promotion is possible. Consequently, there is a strong argument for hiring someone who already possesses the necessary skills.

New people often represent an infusion of new blood into the organization. They bring new perspectives, new ideas, and probing questions that can stimulate thinking among present employees. Also, the presence of talented newcomers can challenge employees to develop their own abilities.

If, after balancing the foregoing considerations, management decides to hire someone from outside, then outsiders must be systematically recruited and screened.

RECRUITMENT   *Recruitment* is the process of identifying those who are interested in being hired for a particular job. Recruiting is a boundary-spanning role that bridges human resource supply and demand. Methods of contacting new job applicants include the following:

o Want ads in newspapers and trade publications.
o Private employment agencies.
o Public employment services.

○ Placement services (such as colleges and professional meetings).
○ Walk-ins.
○ Referrals from present employees.

Among these various recruitment alternatives, no single method is best. Often the approach used is influenced by the position to be filled. For example, if a firm is looking for a president who will make $200,000 per year, it certainly would not place a want ad in the local pennysaver. An ad in the *Wall Street Journal* or the *New York Times* would be more appropriate. More likely, the firm will hire a private employment agency to conduct an executive search for a list of prospects. This approach, referred to as head hunting in the trade, is very expensive. If the organization is looking to hire specialists such as engineers or chemists, it is less costly to send an interviewer to selected professional meetings than to use a head hunter. Management trainees can be located conveniently through campus placement services. Applicants for nonmanagerial jobs may be found rather inexpensively through local want ads, public employment services, walk-ins, or employee referrals.

SCREENING   Just because someone is interested in a job does not mean that person is qualified. Thus a *screening process* is needed to separate qualified job applicants from those who are unqualified. In theory, a qualified individual can either do the job successfully or learn to do it successfully. In recent years, due to federal Equal Employment Opportunity legislation, managers in the United States have had to put more weight on learning potential than was traditionally the practice. This is true because members of minorities may not possess necessary job skills. Equal Employment Opportunity has almost revolutionized screening procedures in recent years. For that reason, we will discuss it in some detail in the next section.

Management writers commonly compare the screening process to a hurdle race. Among the common hurdles a job applicant must successfully clear are tests, reference checks, interviews, and physical examinations. The screening process varies, depending on the nature of the opening. An applicant for a commercial airline pilot's job has to pass a battery of psychological tests, an assessment of cockpit skills, numerous interviews, and a rigorous physical exam. In contrast, someone applying for an industrial stock-handling job may only have to demonstrate an ability to lift fifty pounds and carry it twenty-five feet.

At the heart of the screening process are the selection criteria, or standards. Since Equal Employment Opportunity has come on the scene, *selection criteria* are narrowly defined as personal character- istics that *demonstrably* predict job success. Statistically proving that a certain personal characteristic is tied to job success is a difficult and time-consuming task. The subject of selection criteria is very much up in the air today as the process of eliminating discriminatory hiring practices continues.

Although it is impossible at the present time to list generally acceptable selection criteria, it is possible to discuss how the criteria an organization selects can best be used when interviewing appli- cants. Interviewing deserves special attention because, as one personnel management authority has observed,

> The interview is probably the most widely used personnel technique, particularly in the selection procedure. Surveys show that almost all personnel managers use this method at some stage in the selection procedure.[19]

Although interviewing is widely used, research on it has been spotty. After reviewing the recent research on interview techniques and shortcomings, one writer made the following recommenda- tions:

1. The information gathered in an interview can be made more relevant if a structured interview guide is followed.
2. The interviewer should be familiar with the requirements of the open position.
3. Interviewer training helps reduce bias.
4. Interviews are useful for evaluating interpersonal skills and motivation.
5. First impressions can have less impact if the applicant is given time to talk.
6. The purpose of the interview should be evaluated.[20]

Following these recommendations can improve the chances of discovering whether an applicant and the organization are likely to be a good match.

EQUAL EMPLOYMENT OPPORTUNITY

As mentioned earlier, recent Equal Employment Opportunity (EEO) legislation has radically altered the selection process. The landmark legislation in this area was Title VII of the Civil Rights Act of 1964. Since that time, several amendments and related laws have been passed. EEO legislation now provides a broad umbrella of employ- ment protection for traditionally disadvantaged minorities.

The result of this legislation has been that in virtually all aspects of employment, it is unlawful to discriminate on the basis of race, color, sex, religion, age, national origin, handicapped status, being a disabled veteran, or being a veteran of the Vietnam Era.[21]

What all this means is that managers cannot refuse to hire, promote, train, or transfer employees simply on the basis of the characteristics listed above. Nor can they lay off or discharge employees on these grounds. All personnel decisions must be made only on the basis of ability to perform the job.

A more rigorous refinement of EEO legislation is affirmative action. By presidential order, public and private organizations that annually sell more than $50,000 worth of goods and services to the federal government and that have fifty or more employees are required to develop an affirmative action program. In effect, an *affirmative action program* is a plan for actively seeking out, employing, and developing the talents of those traditionally discriminated against in employment. Affirmative action is an attempt to make up for past discrimination. EEO, in contrast, is aimed at preventing future discrimination. Typically, affirmative action plans call for

1. Making concerted efforts to recruit minorities and women, including recruiting through the State Employment Service
2. Placing limitations on questions which may be asked in employment applications
3. Establishing goals and timetables, including determining available percentages of minorities and women in the local labor force
4. Avoiding testing, unless it meets established guidelines[22]

For the nearly 12,000 companies in the private business sector that must comply with EEO legislation and develop affirmative action programs, it has been a long and winding road.[23] Many of the requirements are contradictory. A step forward in one area may mean a step backward in another.

For example, American Telephone & Telegraph (AT&T) signed a consent decree with the federal government in 1973 to correct racial and sex imbalances allegedly caused by discriminatory hiring and promotion policies. The case was intended to convince other companies that the government was committed to enforcing EEO laws. The settlement included the immediate payment of $18 million in back wages to women who had been receiving unequal pay for equal work. Since that time, AT&T's 750-person EEO staff has changed the face of the nation's largest private employer. The number of women in middle- and upper-level management ranks rose from 9 percent in 1972 to 17 percent in 1978. During the same period, the company's employment of minority females rose from 79,000 to 96,000 and minority males from 31,000 to 43,000. Females are now working in traditionally male crafts, and males are now working as operators and clerks, traditionally female jobs. However, as noted in *Fortune*, these changes have had their price.

> The favoring of women and minorities that is required by the decree has necessarily also required some lowering of employment standards, and this combination has produced bruising side effects. The rules have embittered many of A.T.&T.'s white male employees, spawned procedures that have infuriated its unions, and arguably hurt operating efficiency.[24]

It is easy to see why EEO and affirmative action are emotional topics. But, as someone said, "Equal employment opportunity isn't just a good idea, it's the *law*."

TRAINING There is often a gap between what employees do know and what they should know. This gap may relate to either present or future job performance. Billions of dollars are spent annually in the United States to fill this knowledge gap through some sort of training. In spite of all this activity, however, there is general disagreement over the purpose of training. Some see it as the teaching of specific technical skills and contrast it with education, which is said to be the development of thought processes and more generalized knowledge. But training is more than this; it is a wide-ranging process that involves thought processes as well as technical skills. As the term is used here, *training* refers to the process of changing employee behavior, attitudes, or opinions through some type of guided experience. There are two basic kinds of training, on-the-job and off-the-job.

ON-THE-JOB TRAINING On-the-job training takes place in the actual work setting. In its most unsophisticated form, on-the-job training is left up to the coworkers of a new employee. Some call this the sink-or-swim method. The more experienced individuals act as models and are readily available to answer any questions the novice may have. This approach is considerably less expensive than formal training, but one of its weaknesses is that newcomers often learn how *not* to perform the job. For example, in a shop situation a newcomer may be advised by coworkers to leave the safety guard off a dangerous machine because it slows down the work flow. Although this may be true, the chances of a costly accident are greatly increased.

A more comprehensive form of on-the-job training is to assign a skilled instructor or coach to a novice. While learning by actually doing is still the basic idea, a source of accurate and reliable information and encouragement is readily available. This approach, although it takes less time than classroom training, may disrupt the normal flow of work or put expensive machinery in jeopardy. If the risk of the novice doing any real harm is relatively low, then on-the-job training can be a fast and inexpensive way of filling the new employee's knowledge gap.

OFF-THE-JOB TRAINING This second category of training is much broader than the first. It may involve lectures and discussion, films, workshops, role playing, or simulations. Each is different from the others and has its advantages and disadvantages.

Lectures and discussions are the traditional form of classroom teaching. A single instructor can dispense a great deal of information to a large group through lectures and discussion. Unfortunately, because the flow of information is largely one way, attention and hence actual learning may be minimal. Like lectures and discussions, films are a convenient way to reach large audiences. But learning may be minimal because the viewer is passive, rather than being an active participant.

In workshops, small teams of individuals probe job-related topics by sharing personal opinions. Although interest is usually high in workshops, discussion often bogs down in irrelevant details or goes off on a tangent. Besides, personal opinions often do not offer enough accurate information for efficient job training.

Role playing is an increasingly popular way of getting individuals actively involved in the learning process. Typically, the role player acts out his or her impression of how a person would handle a particular situation. When combined with video tape replays, role playing can be an intense learning experience. Trainers have mixed feelings about the value of role playing. Some say it is the best way to make sure that people actually know how to behave in desired ways, but others are concerned about the possible embarrassment and humilitaion of less articulate people.

Simulations attempt to put the trainee in a realistic situation without actually being on the job. This approach is appropriate when expensive equipment is involved. For instance, it would be foolhardy to allow half-trained novices to fly jet aircraft, tamper with computers, or operate turret lathes. Although this approach provides realistic experience, often with realistic mockups, it still is not the real thing. Simulations are one of the most costly forms of training.

The principal advantage and disadvantage of off-the-job training are two sides of the same coin. On the positive side, learning can be enhanced by getting the trainee away from the distractions of the job. On the negative side, work piles up when people are pulled from their jobs to participate in training. A workable compromise can be achieved by limiting off-the-job training to regularly scheduled sessions of fairly short duration. This arrangement permits trainees to schedule their work around planned training sessions.

Off-the-job training has become big business today. Therefore, it deserves management's close attention to make sure that training dollars are spent wisely. Payments to outside training specialists can grow to the point where the organization is better off creating its own training department staffed by full-time trainers. Some organizations have even built their own schools. For example, Holiday Inn University, located in northern Mississippi, provides off-the-job training to 5,000 Holiday Inn employees each year. The trainees enjoy the finest facilities and the newest in video tape capabilities during initiation training and, thereafter, in yearly refresher seminars.[25]

THE BASICS OF A GOOD TRAINING PROGRAM

Although training needs and techniques vary widely, managers can get the most out of their training budgets by following a few simple rules. According to training experts Bernard Bass and James Vaughan, an adequate training program should

1. Provide for the learner's active participation.
2. Provide the trainee with the knowledge of results about his attempts to improve.
3. Promote by means of good organization a meaningful integration of learning experiences that the trainee can transfer from training to the job.
4. Provide some means for the trainee to be reinforced for appropriate behavior.
5. Provide for practice and repetition when needed.
6. Motivate the trainee to improve his own performance.
7. Assist the trainee in his willingness to change.[26]

This list reminds us that the object of training is *learning*. Learning requires thoughtful preparation, carefully guided experience, and motivational support.

SUMMARY

Staffing is the process of planning to meet the need for, obtaining, and training organization members. The staffing function may be centralized in a personnel department or decentralized throughout the management hierarchy. Organizations cannot accomplish their intended purposes if they are not staffed by appropriately talented and motivated individuals.

Individuals join organizations for economic security, social support, and an opportunity for growth. Work organizations that satisfy these basic needs are likely to have active, involved, and committed employees. The relationship between today's employee and the modern work organization amounts to a comprehensive exchange involving much more than the trading of work for money. Unwritten psychological contracts are based on the expectations that individuals and organizations have of one another. Unrealized expectations can hamper job performance. A person's involvement with the organization may be either positive or negative, and of either high or low intensity. High positive involvement is the most desirable. According to Argyris's incongruency thesis, individual-organization mismatches occur when organizations stifle an employee's natural tendency toward psychological maturity.

Human resource planning is a systematic approach to assessing present staffing needs, forecasting future needs, and formulating a staffing strategy. Periodic evaluation is also needed, to keep the strategy up to date. The net result should be the right person in the right job at the right time.

Through selection, management finds qualified people to fill specific jobs. If the decision is to hire someone from the outside rather than promote a present employee, attention turns to recruitment and screening. Recruitment is the process of identifying those who are interested in being hired for a particular job. Screening separates qualified applicants from unqualified ones through the use of tests, reference checks, physicals, and interviews. Selection criteria based on factors that accurately predict job success help identify those who are qualified. Equal Employment Opportunity legislation has had a major impact on the selection process in recent years as society attempts to improve employment opportunities for women and minorities.

Training fills the knowledge gap between what someone does know and what that person should know. On-the-job training and off-the-job training are two major ways to change employee behavior, attitudes, and opinions. A sound training program is made up of elements that encourage the basic learning process.

TERMS TO UNDERSTAND

Staffing
Psychological contract
Involvement
Incongruency thesis
Human resource planning
Job analysis
Job description

Selection process
Recruitment
Screening process
Selection criteria
Affirmative action program
Training

QUESTIONS FOR DISCUSSION

1. Why must managers be concerned with the staffing function?
2. Why do individuals join organizations?
3. How does a psychological contract differ from an employment contract?
4. Why is low positive employee involvement a significant management challenge?
5. Argyris believes that there is an incongruency between individuals and organizations. How does he see this incongruency displayed?
6. How are present staffing needs assessed in human resource planning?
7. Why would a manager want to promote from within the organization rather than hire from outside?
8. How has Equal Employment Opportunity affected the selection process?
9. Are you covered by Equal Employment Opportunity legislation? What are the implications of your status?
10. How can a training program be designed to encourage learning?

**CASE 12.1
THE NEW ACCOUNTS DRIVE**

Susan Atwood is an operations officer at a commercial bank located in a large, midwestern city. She has been with the bank for seven and a half years, working her way up the career ladder from bookkeeper to officer. Susan has performed well in all phases of her employment. She has even gone out of her way to get her friends and relatives to open new accounts at the bank.

Recently, however, the bank initiated a new policy for all operations officers, who are now supposed to obtain new accounts by going out into the community to solicit business from local stores. Since the policy went into effect, Susan's performance has been slipping, and she has been heard expressing feelings of inadequacy and self-doubt. This morning she requested a transfer to another area of the bank.

FOR DISCUSSION

1. What is the meaning of this case from the standpoint of the psychological contract between Susan and her employer?
2. Why has an excellent organization-individual match apparently turned into a mismatch?
3. If you were the bank's training director, what type of training program could you develop to help Susan and any others who might be reluctant to approach strangers about opening new accounts?

CASE 12.2
YOUR WORK IS
UNACCEPTABLE—YOU'RE
PROMOTED!

Born and raised in a New York City ghetto, Rod Jackson is now twenty-two years old with a B.A. in English. Because of his excellent academic record in high school and some financial aid from state and federal agencies, Rod was able to attend a prestigious private university. He graduated in the top half of his class.

Three months ago Rod applied for a job with a medium-sized data processing firm. Members of the personnel department knew that top management would be happy to see Rod join the company, because federal agencies had been pressuring the firm about its discriminatory hiring practices. Nevertheless he was told that, if hired, he would have to start where everyone else did—at the bottom.

Rod noted on his application form that he had eye-hand coordination problems, and subsequent aptitude tests proved this to be true. In spite of this, Rod's first assignment was data input operator, a job requiring skillful eye-hand coordination.

Rod experienced a great deal of difficulty with his new job. He wasn't interested in the job, and because of his poor coordination, he was unable to attain the standard item count. After complaining to his superiors about the unfairness of this situation, he was surprised to find himself promoted to a supervisory position. However, he hasn't performed effectively as a supervisor either. He feels that his subordinates do not respect him, and they say that he was promoted because of his race and not because of his ability.

FOR DISCUSSION

1. How has Rod become the victim of circumstances intended to help him?
2. Critically analyze the company's position in this case.

REFERENCES

Opening quotation

Edgar H. Schein, "Increasing Organizational Effectiveness Through Better Human Resource Planning and Development," *Sloan Management Review* 19 (Fall 1977): 1–20.

1. E. Frank Harrison, *Management and Organizations* (Boston: Houghton Mifflin, 1978), p. 154.
2. C. Wright Mills, *White Collar* (New York: Oxford University Press, 1951), p. 8.
3. Theodore T. Herbert, *Dimensions of Organizational Behavior* (New York: Macmillan, 1976), p. 159.
4. Edgar H. Schein, *Organizational Psychology*, 2nd ed. (Englewood Cliffs, N.J.: Prentice-Hall, 1970), pp. 12–15.
5. Harry Levinson, "Reciprocation: The Relationship Between Man and Organization," *Administrative Science Quarterly* 9 (March 1965): 370–390.
6. Emanuel C. Salemi and John B. Monahan, "The Psychological Contract of Employment: Do Recruiters and Students Agree?" *Personnel Journal* 49 (December 1970): 986–993.
7. This breakdown is based on the following work: Amitai Etzioni, *A Comparative Analysis of Complex Organizations* (New York: Free Press, 1975), pp. 8–11.
8. See: Robert Blauner, *Alienation and Freedom: The Factory Worker and His Industry* (Chicago: University of Chicago Press, 1964).
9. For an interesting discussion of worker alienation in the United States, see: Report of a Special Task Force to the Secretary of Health, Education and Welfare, *Work in America* (Cambridge: MIT Press, 1973).
10. Chris Argyris, *Personality and Organization* (New York: Harper & Row, 1957), p. 66.
11. H. Kirk Downey, Don Hellriegel, and John W. Slocum, Jr., "Congruence Between Individual Needs, Organizational Climate, Job Satisfaction and Performance," *Academy of Management Journal* 18 (March 1975): 149–155.
12. Schein, "Increasing Organizational Effectiveness Through Better Human Resource Planning and Development," *p. 1.*
13. Wendell French, *The Personnel Management Process: Human Resources Administration*, 3rd ed. (Boston: Houghton Mifflin, 1974), p. 241.
14. James W. Walker, "Human Resource Planning: Managerial Concerns and Practices," *Business Horizons* 19 (June 1976): 56.
15. Leon C. Megginson, *Personnel and Human Resources Administration*, 3rd ed. (Homewood, Ill.: Irwin, 1977), p. 151.
16. For an excellent discussion of human resource forecasting, see: James W. Walker, "Forecasting Manpower Needs," *Harvard Business Review* 47 (March-April 1969): 152–164.
17. A helpful collection of readings dealing with all phases of

human resource planning may be found in: Elmer H. Burack and James W. Walker, eds., *Manpower Planning and Programming* (Boston: Allyn and Bacon, 1972).

18. Data drawn from: Robert E. Sibson, "The High Cost of Hiring," *Nation's Business* 63 (February 1975): 85–88.

19. Megginson, *Personnel and Human Resources Administration*, p. 232.

20. This list has been abstracted from a more extensive one in Neal Schmitt, "Social and Situational Determinants of Interview Decisions: Implications for the Employment Interview," *Personnel Psychology* 29 (Spring 1976): 97–98.

21. David A. Brookmire and Amy A. Burton, "A Format for Packaging Your Affirmative Action Program," *Personnel Journal* 57 (June 1978): 294.

22. Megginson, *Personnel and Human Resources Administration*, p. 160.

23. For typical problems in this area, see: "A Legal Cloud over Affirmative Action," *Business Week* #2515 (December 26, 1977): 40, 42.

24. Carol J. Loomis, "A.T.&T. In the Throes of 'Equal Employment,'" *Fortune* 99 (January 15, 1979): 45.

25. For more, see: "Holiday Inn University: More than a Training Facility," *Training and Development Journal* 32 (October 1978): 36–37.

26. Bernard M. Bass and James A. Vaughan, *Training in Industry: The Management of Learning* (Belmont, Cal.: Brooks/Cole, 1966), p. 86.

Chapter 13

Group Dynamics

Organizations are composed of [many] small groups that have a similar influence on behavior. They inculcate majority values in their members; they reward compliance and punish those who resist their demands.

Robert Presthus

LEARNING OBJECTIVES

When you finish reading this chapter, you should be able to

- Explain the difference between a friendship group and a work group.
- Discuss the factors that enhance group attractiveness and cohesiveness.
- Explain the significance of roles, norms, and interaction in group dynamics.
- Summarize the relationship between group dynamics and productivity.
- Explain why trust is an important variable in effective work group interaction.
- Analyze the role of conformity in organizations.
- Discuss conflict triggers and conflict resolution techniques.

People are both individuals and social beings. This sometimes frustrating combination was thoughtfully explored by Henry David Thoreau, the nineteenth-century American philosopher. Thoreau's two-year experiment with solitary living in the woods near Walden Pond is chronicled in his classic book *Walden.* Only by removing himself from the distractions of life in town could Thoreau reevaluate his relationship with society. He found that he was never alone, even if no one else was around, because he was the product of society. Everything Thoreau thought and did was social in origin. He was first and foremost a social being.

Although most of us will never have the opportunity to explore our relationship with society by living alone in the woods for a couple of years, each of us must resolve the inherent conflict between the demands of individuality and society. We need to understand the social forces that constantly shape and redirect our lives.

The best place to begin is with an analysis of group dynamics. Groups are the fundamental building blocks of society. Because the practice of management is essentially social in nature, managers must have a full appreciation of group dynamics.

THE WHAT AND WHY OF GROUPS

According to one organization theorist, "All groups may be collections of individuals, but all collections of individuals are not groups."[1] This statement is much more than a tricky play on words. It is important to understand that mere togetherness does not create a group. Consider, for example, the following situation. A half dozen people who worked for different companies in the same building often shared the same elevator in the morning. As time passed, they introduced themselves and exchanged pleasantries. Eventually, four of the elevator riders discovered that they all lived in the same suburb. Arrangements for a car pool were made and they began to take turns picking up and delivering one another. According to commonly accepted definitions of the term *group,* a group did not come into existence until the car pool was formed. The collection of unacquainted individuals who shared the same elevator was not a group. What factors had to be present before this collection of individuals could be called a group? The answer to this question is found in the sociological definition of *group.*

WHAT IS A GROUP?

A *group* may be defined as two or more freely interacting individuals who share a common identity and purpose.[2] Careful analysis of this definition reveals four important dimensions. First, a group must be made up of two or more people if it is to be considered a social unit. A single individual is not a social unit. Second, the individuals must freely interact in some manner. This is another way of saying that they must communicate regularly with one another. Third, the interacting individuals must share a common identity. Each must recognize himself or herself as a member of the group. Fourth, interacting individuals who have a common identity must also have a common purpose. That is, they must all be attempting to fulfill a similar need through association with the group.

It may appear from this definition that a group is the same as an organization. Although it is true that both groups and organizations consist of two or more people with a common purpose, we can identify a subtle but important difference. In order to be a group, a collection of people must freely interact; everyone must know and regularly communicate with everyone else. Sociologists generally agree that this type of close, personal interaction restricts the ultimate size of groups. Twenty people is commonly considered the upper limit for group-type interaction. A relatively small formal organization with only a handful of members may qualify as a group if they all freely interact. But organizations tend to be more impersonal than groups. The sheer size of many of today's organizations precludes free interaction among all of the organization's members. For example, two General Motors employees might meet on the street as complete strangers, only to discover later that they work for the same organization. However, each belongs to one or more different groups *within* General Motors. Thus the terms *group* and *organization* are not totally different concepts; they overlap to some extent.

What happens when individuals form groups? Before answering this question, we need to look at four assumptions about groups that underlie all the following discussion.

1. Groups are an ever-present feature of modern life. They are both necessary and inevitable.
2. People belong to a number of different groups at any given time and to a wide variety of groups throughout their lives.
3. Groups bring out both the best and worst in people.
4. An understanding of group dynamics allows one to be a better contributor to (and manager of) group activity.

TYPES OF GROUPS Human beings join together in groups for many different reasons. Some people join a group as an end in itself. For example, an accountant may enjoy the socializing and friendly chatter that go along with joining a group of friends for lunch every day. On the other hand, many join groups because they are a means to an end. A store manager who joins a bowling league in order to meet potential customers is using group membership as a steppingstone. Both the lunch group and the bowling group may be viewed as social in nature, but they provide very different opportunities.

The task of classifying groups is not easy. Should they be identified by primary purpose or in terms of member characteristics? A two-way classification by purpose is appropriate at this point. We will discuss friendship groups and work groups.

Friendship groups   As pointed out by Maslow and others, a feeling of belonging is a powerful motivator. People have a great need to fit in, to be liked, to be one of the gang. Whether the group is formed at work or during leisure time, it is still a *friendship group* if the principal reason for belonging to it is friendship. Friendship groups also satisfy esteem needs, because one develops a better self-image when accepted, recognized, and liked by others. Interestingly, friendship groups may have some unexpected payoffs. The experience of William Hewitt is a good example. A very active social life paved the way for young Hewitt to meet and later marry the great-great-granddaughter of John Deere. Eventually Hewitt became the chief executive officer of Deere & Company.[3] Belonging to a friendship group will not necessarily help one become the head of a $3 billion-per-year corporation, but a little friendship goes a long way.

Work groups   *Work groups* are social units created for the purpose of accomplishing a task. They may be called teams, committees, departments, or simply work gangs. Whatever their name, work groups usually are formed for the purpose of contributing to the success of a more encompassing organization. Work groups are much more formal and structured than friendship groups. Rather than joining work groups, people are usually assigned to them. One person is given formal leadership responsibility in a work group. Friendship groups, in contrast, ordinarily do not have a formally appointed leader, although an informal leader may emerge. For the individual, the work group and a friendship group at the place of employment may or may not overlap. In other words, one may or may not be friends with one's coworkers.

ATTRACTION TO GROUPS   Why are people attracted to groups? Managers who know the answer to this question can take steps to make the work group more attractive. The extent of an individual's relationship to either a friendship or a work group depends on two factors. The first is attractiveness, the outside-looking-in view. A nonmember will want to join a group if it is attractive and will not want to join if it is unattractive. The second factor is *cohesiveness*, which may be defined as the tendency of group members to resist outside influences. This is the inside-looking-out view. In a highly cohesive group the individual members tend to see themselves as "we" rather than "I." One might say that cohesive groups are internally attractive to their members. Highly cohesive group members quite literally stick together.

Factors that either enhance or destroy group attractiveness and cohesiveness are listed in Table 13.1. It is important to note that each factor is a matter of degree. For example, a group may offer the individual little, moderate, or great opportunity for prestige and status. Similarly, group demands on the individual may range from somewhat disagreeable to highly disagreeable. What all this boils down to is the fact that the decision to join a group and the decision to continue being a member of that group depend on all the factors in Table 13.1. Each individual weighs all the factors for and against group membership, and each individual perceives things differently. If the favorable factors outweigh the unfavorable ones, then the individual will join and remain in the group. If the balance should tip the other way, the incentive to be a member of the group will evaporate.

	FACTORS THAT ENHANCE ATTRACTIVENESS AND COHESIVENESS	FACTORS THAT DESTROY ATTRACTIVENESS AND COHESIVENESS
TABLE 13.1 Factors that enhance or destroy group attractiveness and cohesiveness	1. Prestige and status. 2. Cooperative relationship. 3. High degree of interaction. 4. Relatively small size. 5. Similarity of members. 6. Superior public image of group. 7. A common threat in the environment.	1. Unreasonable or disagreeable demands upon the individual. 2. Disagreement over procedures, activities, rules, etc. 3. Unpleasant experience with the group. 4. Competition between the group's demands and preferred outside activities. 5. Unfavorable public image of group. 6. Competition for membership by other groups.

Adapted from Dorwin Cartwright and Alvin Zander, eds., *Group Dynamics: Research and Theory*, 2nd ed. (Evanston, Ill.: Row, Peterson, 1960), pp. 78–86.

GROUP DYNAMICS   The term *group dynamics* implies that something happens within groups. In fact, the dictionary relates the word *dynamics* to activity and change. Groups are often highly dynamic. Scholars have studied groups for many years in the field and in the laboratory. Although it is difficult to capture the essence of group dynamics on paper, being aware of certain variables helps us understand what goes on when people form groups. In this section we explore three of these variables: (1) roles, (2) norms, and (3) interaction.

ROLES   According to Shakespeare, "All the world's a stage, And all the men and women merely players. . . ." We can very readily view the world as a stage. In fact, Shakespeare's analogy between life and play-acting can be carried one step further—to organizations and their component work groups. Although employees do not have script books, they do have formal positions in the organizational hierarchy, and they are expected to adhere to company policies and rules. Furthermore, job descriptions and procedure manuals spell out how jobs are to be done. In short, every employee has an organizational role to play. If the organization is properly structured and if everyone plays his or her role properly, then there is a greater chance for organizational success.

A social psychologist has offered the following description of a role:

> The term role is used to refer to (1) a set of expectations concerning what a person in a given position must, must not, or may do, and (2) the actual behavior of the person who occupies the position. A central idea is that any person occupying a position and filling a role behaves similarly to anyone else who could be in that position.[4]

A *role,* then, is a socially determined prescription for behavior in a specific position. Roles evolve out of social activity and they are socially enforced. Society rewards those who play their roles properly and punishes those who deviate from prescribed modes of behavior. The experience of former President Nixon attests to society's swift punishment of those who don't play their roles according to general expectations.

An important aspect of roles is multiple-role playing. Today's citizens, particularly those responsible for managing institutions, play multiple roles. Personal reputations and career ascent depend on the individual's ability to play several roles properly. At any given time, a number of very different roles may have to be played in

CONVERSATION WITH . . .

Arthur B. Reeves
Director of Labor Affairs
Phoenix Urban League
Phoenix, Arizona

Updike Studios.

PERSONAL BACKGROUND

Art Reeves is from Flagstaff, Arizona. After completing a tour of duty in the U.S. Marine Corps, he attended Northern Arizona University, graduating in 1966 with a B.S. in business administration. During his twelve years in management, Art has served as a senior accountant with Motorola, as a commercial real estate property manager, and as the executive director of a nonprofit economic development firm. Art's present employer, the Phoenix Urban League, is a nonprofit service organization that contracts with federal, state, and local agencies to provide improved housing, education, and employment opportunities for socially and economically disadvantaged persons. As the director of labor affairs for the Phoenix Urban League, Art Reeves is responsible for planning, coordinating, and directing programs designed to assist minorities and disadvantaged individuals to gain employment in skilled trades apprenticeship programs.

QUOTABLE QUOTES

What is your most significant achievement as a manager?

Mr. Reeves: Managing the formation of the first black-owned shopping center in the state of Arizona.

What do you think it takes to be a successful manager today?

Mr. Reeves: It takes a basic understanding of management principles, a good understanding of what motivates people, and the ability to coordinate the two elements to accomplish individual and organizational goals. Of course, all this must be done within environmental constraints.

What advice would you give an aspiring manager?

Mr. Reeves: Get to know the people you work with, both their strengths and weaknesses, so as to enhance personal and organizational growth. Force yourself to plan ahead and formulate alternatives for probable situations that might occur. Also, try to keep up to date on current information in your area of responsibility.

rapid succession. Moreover, a person's career may consist of a chain of differing roles, each with a unique pattern of demands.

Dixy Lee Ray, the first woman governor of Washington state, is a prime example of someone who had to face the challenge of vastly different career roles. Before she became governor, Ray had been a university professor, chairperson of the Atomic Energy Commission, and assistant U.S. secretary of state for scientific affairs. This dramatic shift in roles was made all the more difficult by the fact that each of her roles was stereotyped as being a male sex-role. Society sometimes prescribes who should play a particular role as well as how they should play it.

NORMS   Norms are said to define "degrees of acceptability and unacceptability."[5] In other words, *norms* are standards that serve a quality control function for behavior in society by helping individuals determine what is right or wrong, good or bad. Both norms and roles are socially developed, but norms are standards for general conduct rather than for performance in a specific position. Norms are usually unwritten, but they are still powerful.

Every mature group, whether friendship or work, generates its own pattern of norms that limit the behavior of its members. For example, a friendship group of employees who meet for lunch in the company cafeteria may enforce a norm against discussing work-related subjects. How is this norm enforced? Compliance is met with social reinforcement in the form of praise and recognition. Those who fail to comply with the norm may be criticized, ridiculed, or even ostracized. *Ostracism*, or rejection from the group, is the worst possible punishment in group dynamics. Groups derive much of their power over individuals through the ever-present threat of ostracism.

Norms have an important relationship to cohesiveness. In a highly cohesive group there is agreement over what the relevant norms are. Disagreement over group norms tends to erode cohesiveness. For example, a management advisory committee made up of department heads may establish and enforce a norm that requires each department head to carry a fair share of the work load. Deviations from this norm will diminish group cohesiveness.

INTERACTION In an earlier analysis of organizations as open systems, the term *synergy* was introduced. Synergy means that a system of parts working together adds up to more than just the sum of its parts. Groups, like organizations, are synergistic social systems. Simply understanding each member of a particular group is not enough. The true, dynamic nature of the group does not become apparent until person-to-person interaction is studied. *Interaction*, what goes on between and among group members, is what really counts.

The role of interaction in group formation Group formation is more evolutionary than revolutionary. This is especially true for friendship groups, but it is also true for cohesive work groups. It takes time for people to get to know one another. However, even though it takes time, group formation is not a haphazard process; it follows a definite cycle. According to one theory, individuals first share activities, then they interact, and eventually they come to share common sentiments.[6] The resulting self-feeding cycle is illustrated in Figure 13.1.

Suppose that four strangers from the business community are brought together to form a steering committee for the local United Fund. Since they have been asked to pursue a common goal (a successful fund-raising campaign), they are involved in a common activity. In order to plan and organize their activity properly, they must interact. Their interaction will consist of getting to know one another and sharing ideas about their task and how they should proceed. After several weeks of interaction they will tend to develop similar sentiments, or beliefs and attitudes, about what they are

FIGURE 13.1
Steps in the group formation process

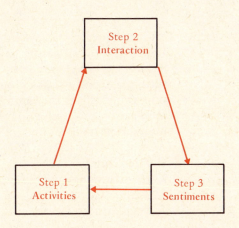

doing. In other words, interaction helps iron out interpersonal differences.

Although this group formation process is very subtle, because it occurs little by little over an extended period of time, it is a powerful force that binds vastly different individuals into a group whose members think and act similarly. Research has demonstrated time and again that group interaction is a potent shaper of sentiments, attitudes, and beliefs. People with similar sentiments eagerly pursue similar activities, and so the activities-interaction-sentiments cycle perpetuates itself.

The development of interactive skills   Some people are more effective in social interaction than others; they possess more highly developed interactive skills. Everyone begins to learn interactive skills shortly after birth. The close attachment between mother and child is, after all, a social phenomenon. Gradually, other family members and family friends enter the infant's social circle. Playmates and schoolmates later enlarge the growing youngster's social context. Table 13.2 traces the development of interactive skills from immaturity to maturity.

Although social maturity follows an orderly developmental sequence, the rate of development varies widely among people. An individual with inadequately developed or bypassed skills may be socially handicapped. By the time someone enters the work force, he or she should be at or very near the top of the three interactive skill ladders. The closer one is to the top, the more effective one is likely to be when interacting with others. Regrettably, some adults have not yet reached the top, and managers must help the developmental process along a bit. The behavior modification techniques discussed in Chapter 15 are helpful in this area.

Analyzing the interaction process   About thirty years ago Robert Bales developed a useful classification scheme for social interaction.[7] His classification is particularly relevant to work groups because he developed it to help study task groups in a laboratory setting. Laboratory task groups and on-the-job work groups have one important thing in common; both are formed for the express purpose of accomplishing something. According to Bales,[8] group interaction involves the following social transactions:

1. Friendliness
2. Humorous tension release
3. Agreement
4. Suggestions

TABLE 13.2
The development of interactive skills

	DEVELOPMENT OF SOCIAL SKILLS	DEVELOPMENT OF LANGUAGE SKILLS	DEVELOPMENT OF PROBLEM-SOLVING SKILLS
Social Maturity ↑	5. Close one-to-one friendships ↑	5. Use of language to solve problems ↑	5. Ability to introspect (objective self-analysis) ↑
	4. Participation in the peer group ↑	4. Censorship of speech ↑	4. Ability to conceptualize ideal relationship ↑
	3. Empathy (appreciation of others' feelings) ↑	3. Use of abstract concepts ↑	3. Ability to generate multiple solutions to problems ↑
	2. Parental identification ↑	2. Vocabulary and grammar development ↑	2. Comprehension of rules and norms ↑
Social Immaturity	1. Social attachment	1. Evoking a social response	1. Declining egocentrism (less selfish)

This figure drawn from "The Development of Social Interaction from Infancy through Adolescence," by Barbara M. Newman, is reprinted from *Small Group Behavior*, Vol. 7, No. 1 (February 1976), pp. 19–32 by permission of the Publisher, Sage Publications, Inc.

5. Opinions
6. Information (factual)

Each of these transactions can be viewed along a continuum ranging from "a great deal" to "very little." When individuals gather in a group to get something done, their interaction may be characterized by a great deal of friendliness or very little friendliness, by a great deal of humorous tension release or very little, by a great deal of agreement or very little agreement, and so on down the line. Of course, each continuum has degrees in between the extremes. For example, although members of a particular group may display relatively little friendliness, they may exchange a relatively great amount of factual information. There are many possible combinations.

The greatest single value of Bales's analysis of group interaction is that it helps make the point that either too little or too much of a good thing can hamper effective interaction within a work group.

TABLE 13.3
Striking a balance in work group interaction

	TOO LITTLE	AN APPROPRIATE AMOUNT	TOO MUCH
Friendliness	Distrust, guardedness	Climate of mutual acceptance	Displacement of task activity by informal chatter
Humorous Tension Release	Tension, stuffiness	Free and easy exchange	Displacement of task activity by humor
Agreement	Lack of conclusive action	Thoughtful evaluation and discussion	Rubber stamp consensus
Suggestion	Rigidity, blind conformity	Corrective action when necessary	Lack of conclusive action
Opinion	Limited personal involvement	Appreciation for others personal feelings	Subjective and pointless bull session
Factual Information	Lack of content or substance	Objective basis for learning	Dull, mechanical proceedings

For example, a little humor at the beginning of a committee meeting serves to loosen things up a bit. But too much can turn the meeting into an unproductive, backslapping joke session, and too little may lead to a tense and stuffy meeting. Similarly, effective group interaction depends on the appropriate balance of friendliness, agreement, suggestions, opinions, and factual information. Too little or too much of any one of these may detract from the task at hand (see Table 13.3). Managers need to balance these social transactions in order to promote greater work group effectiveness.

GROUP DYNAMICS AND PRODUCTIVITY

Productivity in the form of the effective and efficient accomplishment of organizational goals is the chief responsibility of all managers. Business organizations, for example, justify their existence by satisfying society's needs for goods and services. The reward for high productivity in the private business sector is survival, and the penalty for low productivity is instability and eventual decline. Considering how high the stakes are, it is no wonder that productivity is felt to be so important. Since productive organizations are essentially collections of work groups, the relationship between group dynamics and productivity is necessarily a major concern of managers. Do group dynamics help or hinder productivity? Is the manager's life made easier or more difficult by the dynamics of the work group? In this section we address these important questions by reviewing some of the classic studies on group dynamics.

OUTPUT RESTRICTION AT HAWTHORNE

A very important and disturbing dimension of group dynamics was uncovered during a later phase of the famous Hawthorne studies.[9] Prompted by hints of output restriction heard during the mass interviewing phase of the studies, the Hawthorne researchers decided to create a setting in which they could carefully observe how output restriction occurred. The result was the bank wiring observation room. A bank was a complex maze of terminals, wires, and connections. Wire had to be cut, stripped of its insulation in appropriate places, and connected to terminals. The connections were then soldered by a second worker and inspected by a third. An entire bank wiring work group (nine wirers, three solderers, and two inspectors) was selected to work under normal conditions in a special observation room. The idea was to simply observe an existing work group without manipulating any experimental variables.

The observers were intrigued as they watched the group's output level off at a point slightly below the company standard. Further observation indicated that the substandard performance was not accidental. The work group established its own norm regarding what constituted a fair day's work. That norm was strictly and systematically enforced. Anyone who worked hard to earn extra money by exceeding the company standard was called a rate buster and punished by the work group through ridicule and "binging" (a painful punch on the arm). "Chiselers" (those who produced below the work group's norm) and "squealers" received similar rough treatment. This system of output restriction was encouraged by the silent approval of lower-level management.[10]

Managers stand to learn an important lesson about work group dynamics from the Hawthorne bank wiring room study. Namely, the work group is a potentially counterproductive force. Although the manager's actions, work procedures, and rules and regulations may all point in the direction of higher productivity, the work group is likely to follow the path toward lower productivity. One of the never-ending challenges of management is to align work group norms with organizational goals.

COHESIVENESS IS A DOUBLE-EDGED SWORD

Just as a double-edged sword can cut in either direction, group cohesiveness can serve as either a productive or counterproductive influence. In a laboratory study of cohesiveness and productivity, Leonard Berkowitz exposed four groups of subjects to four different conditions.[11] In the first condition, the members of a highly cohesive group with high production and quality standards encouraged each other to complete a three-step assembly-line job as quickly as possible. This group was labeled the high standard/high cohesive group. The three other conditions were simply variations of the first. There was a high standard/low cohesive group, a group that was low standard/high cohesive, and a low standard/low cohesive group. Those in the highly cohesive group with low standards encouraged each other to take it easy and keep their output low. The study sought to determine which group would be the most productive.

As Figure 13.2 indicates, the high standard/high cohesive group outproduced the other three groups. This was exactly what the researcher expected; it confirmed his main hypothesis. When the work group members had a strong "we" feeling and encouraged each other to work hard, they got a great deal accomplished. However, things were quite different with the low standard/high cohesive group. It was the least productive of the four groups, in spite of its strong "we" feeling. Thus the Berkowitz study demonstrated that cohesiveness may bring out either the best or the worst in a work group. A high degree of cohesiveness among work group members is

FIGURE 13.2
The output of a cohesive group depends on its production and quality standards

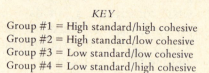

KEY
Group #1 = High standard/high cohesive
Group #2 = High standard/low cohesive
Group #3 = Low standard/low cohesive
Group #4 = Low standard/high cohesive

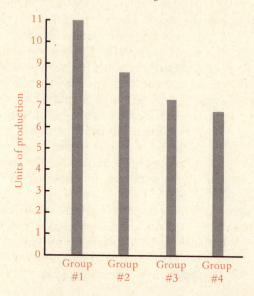

no guarantee of success. It may work either for or against organizational objectives, depending on the group's commitment to those objectives.

THE BUDDY SYSTEM Work groups are usually based on related skills, administrative convenience, or simply chance. What would happen if work groups were formed on the basis of friendship? This was precisely the question that intrigued Raymond Van Zelst nearly thirty years ago.[12] To see what would happen to productivity when employees had the opportunity to choose their own coworkers, the researcher asked over seventy carpenters and bricklayers for their top three coworker preferences. With minor adjustments to ensure a proper match of skills, two-man work teams were formed on a buddy-system basis.

The experiment was a marked success. Labor costs, material costs, and turnover dropped while job satisfaction increased. Overall, a 5 percent savings in total production costs was realized because of the buddy system. According to one of the participants in the study,

> Seems as though everything flows a lot smoother. It makes you feel more comfortable working—and I don't waste any time bickering about who's going to do what and how. We just seem to go ahead and do it. The work's a lot more interesting too when you've got your buddy working with you. You certainly like it a lot better anyway.[13]

In spite of the success of this experiment with group dynamics, a caution is in order. Skilled construction employees can be moved around much more readily than those who are tied to a routine job (such as an assembly-line worker). However, even with this limitation, there is great potential for taking advantage of coworker friendships when assigning work groups. This is particularly true for white-collar jobs or any jobs involving something other than assembly-line technology.

GROUP DYNAMICS AND PRODUCTIVITY IN PERSPECTIVE Research evidence on group dynamics and productivity is a mixed bag. Group norms, cohesiveness, and personal relationships present managers with both opportunities and obstacles. It seems that work group dynamics can make or break a productive effort. As documented at Hawthorne, managers may be plagued by counterproductive norms. But many of us have heard managers praise the way their people pull together or give something extra when things get a little rough. Group cohesiveness displays the same two-sidedness. A cohesive work group that identifies with the task at hand can achieve great things. A cohesive work group that does not identify with the job presents management with a united front of opposition. One of the bright spots in work group research is experimentation with buddy systems. By allowing people to select their own coworkers, many of the negative aspects of group dynamics can be avoided. Managers need to be creative in finding ways to make the best use of work group dynamics.

A MODEL OF EFFECTIVE GROUP INTERACTION

Managers are in an excellent position to help create a friendly and productive climate within the work group. Group members tend to look to the manager for direction and purpose. If the manager satisfies those needs for direction and purpose, then group productivity will be high. However, if the manager fails to meet the group's expectations, productivity will be hampered. Direction and purpose are not the only variables that managers control.

To a greater extent than they may realize, managers determine the level of trust within the work group. *Trust*, a belief in the integrity, character, or ability of others, is essential if people with differing attitudes, needs, perceptions, and backgrounds are to pool their efforts to achieve a common goal. This section clarifies the role of trust in work group dynamics.

Trust is not a free-floating group variable. It affects and is in turn affected by other processes in the group. Dale Zand's model of work group interaction does an excellent job of putting trust into perspective (see Figure 13.3). Zand sees the creation of trust as the first important step in establishing healthy member-to-member relationships.[14] Each phase of his model deserves to be examined more closely.

CREATING A CLIMATE OF TRUST

Primary responsibility for creating a climate of trust falls on the manager. Because of superior position in the organizational hierarchy and greater access to relevant information, the manager is expected to set the stage for what lies ahead. Failure to fulfill member expectations encourages cohesive counterproductiveness. Therefore, trust must be developed right from the beginning, when group members are still receptive to managerial influence. Trust is initially encouraged by being open and honest. Trusting managers talk *with* their people rather than *at* them. A trusting manager demonstrates a willingness to change if the facts show that a change is appropriate. Furthermore, mutual trust between managers and group members makes possible self-control as opposed to supervisor-control. Those who trust each other avoid taking advantage of others' weak points. Managers find that trust begets trust; in

FIGURE 13.3
Trust and effective group
interaction

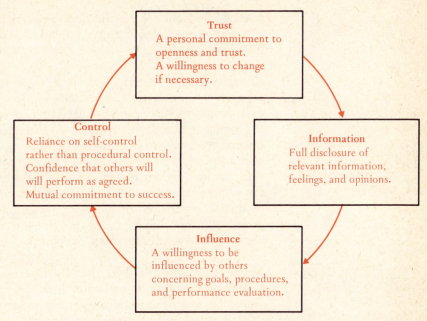

Trust
A personal commitment to
openness and trust.
A willingness to change
if necessary.

Information
Full disclosure of
relevant information,
feelings, and opinions.

Influence
A willingness to be
influenced by others
concerning goals, procedures,
and performance evaluation.

Control
Reliance on self-control
rather than procedural control.
Confidence that others will
will perform as agreed.
Mutual commitment to success.

Adapted from Dale E. Zand, "Trust and Managerial Problem Solving," *Administrative Science Quarterly* 17, No. 2 (June 1972): 231 by permission of *The Administrative Science Quarterly.* © 1972 by Cornell University.

other words, those who feel they are trusted tend to trust others in return.

TRUST LEADS TO MORE INFORMATION

Assuming that each member of a work group is a potential source of valuable information, it is desirable to get members to share their information. Sometimes workers fail to contribute fully to a group effort for fear of ridicule and criticism. A climate of mutual trust, however, serves to draw information out of people. With a free and open exchange of information the quality of group discussion and decisions increases sharply.

GREATER INFORMATION LEADS TO GREATER INFLUENCE

According to Zand's model, the free exchange of information causes each group member to be more open to influence. Groups are often ineffective because of members who fear embarrassment to such an extent that they build barriers around their beliefs and work practices and refuse to yield to the wishes or opinions of others. The situation is much different in a climate of trust; group members are willing to be influenced by others. Highly interactive and trusting group members judge facts by their merit rather than by the contributor's personality. This objective treatment of facts gives individuals feedback on the quality of their ideas. They can then self-adjust, instead of sticking stubbornly to a weak position for fear of embarrassment.

INFLUENCE LEADS TO CONTROL

Contrary to what one might suspect, the manager of a work group in which members trust each other exercises a great deal of control over the group. As the term is used here, *control* does not mean that the manager dictates every move for each group contributor. Rather, mutual trust allows the manager to provide the necessary information and resources so that the group can formulate and pursue its own challenging, yet realistic, goals. This type of control is based on the self-control exercised by each group member. Self-control is the product of a personal commitment to group success. Managers can actually expand their control by allowing committed group members to enjoy greater freedom in their pursuit of formal goals.

THE ISSUE OF CONFORMITY

Much is accomplished in this world because people conform to accepted standards of behavior. Imagine what a chaotic scene it would be if most automobile drivers suddenly stopped conforming to traffic laws. Your chances of arriving safely at your destination would be slim. The same holds true for norms, rules, and regulations at work. A certain degree of conformity is necessary to ensure the efficient accomplishment of organizational goals.

As the term is used here, *conformity* means complying with the perceived role expectations in a given situation. Conformity enhances predictability, and predictability is a foundation stone of the planning process. For example, planning would be useless if people could not be counted on to show up at work and perform their specified duties.

Group pressures encourage individuals to conform and act predictably. At this point we may be tempted to conclude that conformity is always a good thing, but this is not so. Those who conform may or may not be working toward organizational objectives. Is it always best to go along with the group?

RESEARCH ON CONFORMITY

Social psychologists have taught us a great deal about ourselves by studying the behavior of individuals and groups in controlled laboratory settings. One classic laboratory study was carried out by Solomon Asch.[15] Asch's study was intended to answer the following question: How will an individual behave when opposed by a unanimous majority. The results of his study were intriguing, but somewhat disturbing.

The Asch study began by assembling groups of seven to nine

college students, supposedly to work on a perceptual problem. Actually Asch was studying conformity. All but one of the group were confederates. They were told how to behave and what to say by Asch. The experiment was really concerned with the reactions of the one student—called the *naive subject*—who didn't know what was going on.

All the students were shown cards with lines similar to those in Figure 13.4. They were instructed to match the line on the left with the one on the right that was closest to it in length. The differences in length among the lines on the right were quite obvious. Each group went through twelve rounds of the matching process. The experimenter asked one group member at a time to present out loud his or her choice to the group. Things proceeded normally for the first two rounds as each group member voiced an opinion. Agreement was unanimous. Suddenly, on the third round only one individual—the naive subject—chose the correct pair of lines. All the other students chose a different pair. During the rounds in which there was disagreement, all but one of the group members conspired to select an incorrect pair of lines.

It was the individual versus the group. Asch has described what happened to the lone dissenter.

After the first one or two disagreements he [the experimenter] would note certain changes in the manner and posture of this person. He would see a look of perplexity and bewilderment come over the subject's face at the contradicting judgments of the entire group. Often he becomes more active; he fidgets in his seat and changes the position of his head to look at the lines from different angles. He may turn around and whisper to his neighbor seriously or smile sheepishly. He may suddenly stand up to look more closely at the card. At other times he may become especially quiet and immobile.[16]

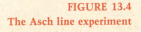

FIGURE 13.4
The Asch line experiment

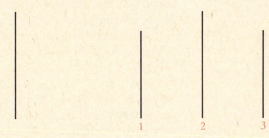

Standard line   Comparison lines

The naive subject was faced by a personal dilemma. Should he or she fight the group or give in to the obviously incorrect choice of the majority? Among thirty-one naive subjects who made a total of 217 estimates, two-thirds of the estimates were correct. The other third were incorrect; that is, they were consistent with the majority opinion. Individual differences were great. Only 20 percent of the naive subjects remained entirely independent. All the rest turned their backs on their own perceptions and went along with the group at one time or another. In other words, 80 percent of the subjects knuckled under to group pressure at least once in spite of the obvious fact that the majority was wrong.

MANAGERIAL IMPLICATIONS   Like other group dynamics, conformity has both a good side and a bad side. When the work group identifies with the overall direction of the organization and that direction is a good and decent one, great things can be accomplished. Conformity, in this context, is a positive force. However, as one authority has pointed out, "The group has a potential to produce blind loyalty, abject submission, and total obedience, and such conditions have invariably been dehumanizing in the end."[17] Conformity becomes a negative force when it encourages group members to deny their personal convictions and values for fear of group reprisal. Groups are a major source of the social support that most of us need. No wonder there is a strong tendency among organization members to compromise their own convictions in order to be one of the gang.

The case of Edward Gregory, a quality control inspector for General Motors, is an excellent example of the tug-of-war between supporting the status quo by following orders and sticking to one's personal convictions.[18] In 1966 Gregory discovered that improper welds in the rear quarter panels of late model Chevrolets could allow deadly carbon monoxide to seep into the passenger compartment. He submitted a suggestion to have the problem corrected. But since his suggestion would cost, rather than save, the company money, it was ignored. Gregory did not give up. He kept complaining to management about the problem, with the result that he was ridiculed and downgraded by company officials. Eventually he was moved out of his inspection job, and at one point he was threatened with being fired. When he had exhausted all routine channels, Gregory turned to outside help by contacting consumer advocate Ralph Nader. While Nader's group was working on the problem, tragedy struck. Four people reportedly were asphyxiated in Chevrolets with the faulty weld.

On February 26, 1969, three years after Gregory had discovered the problem, General Motors announced its recall of 2.4 million

Chevrolets manufactured between 1965 and 1969 to correct the faulty welds. The recall was the largest in automobile history and ended up costing General Motors over $100 million. Although no one will ever know how many lives were saved by this action, the general public can thank a persistent employee who did not give in to group pressures to conform. As an interesting postscript, Gregory is again inspecting cars for General Motors and has submitted no less than fifteen important suggestions for structural and safety improvements. Gregory's nonconformity might have cost General Motors a lot of money in the short run, but in the long run he helped make General Motors a more responsive and effective organization.

Clearly, one of the challenges facing problem-solving managers is to tell the difference between productive conformity and blind, ultimately destructive conformity.

MANAGING CONFLICT   Conflict is an inevitable by-product of group interaction. This is especially true in a work group, because it is typically a convenient collection of individuals with differing backgrounds, perceptions, attitudes, and values. *Conflict*, as defined by an expert in the field, "refers to all kinds of opposition or antagonistic interaction. It is based on scarcity of power, resources or social position, and differing value structures."[19] However, managers should not fall into the trap of assuming that all conflict is bad. Conflict has two faces, one constructive and the other destructive. An illustrative case of these two faces of conflict follows.

TWO FACES OF CONFLICT   Mary and Fred are second-level managers employed by a public utility in the Midwest. Each has a degree in business administration and roughly seven years with the organization. Their records indicate that both are capable of going places. Unfortunately, the next logical career step for both Mary and Fred is the division manager's spot. Only one of them can assume that position when the division manager retires next year. Depending on how management handles the situation, the organization can take advantage of constructive conflict or fall victim to destructive conflict. The constructive route would involve stimulating friendly competition between Mary and Fred for the division manager's position, spelling out the growth opportunities for each in advance. On the division manager's retirement, the better suited could assume that position and the other could be moved to a high-level spot elsewhere in the organization. Alternatively, management could passively stand by and let Mary and Fred slug it out, with the survivor stepping up to the division manager's spot and the loser probably leaving the organization or slipping into apathy.

The point of conflict in this case is a single superior position (a scarce resource) wanted by two people. By following the constructive route of encouraging friendly competition, the organization and the two parties involved would come out ahead. In a sense, everyone would win. But if Mary and Fred are permitted to resort to destructive competition involving false rumors and other administrative dirty tricks, management would be abdicating its responsibility to manage conflict. As one observer stated, "Constructive conflict is both valuable and necessary. Without conflict, there would be few new challenges; there would be no stimulation to think through ideas; organizations would be only apathetic and stagnant."[20]

The overriding challenge for today's manager is to tell the difference between constructive and destructive conflict and act accordingly. The signs of constructive conflict are greater effort and creativity, personal development and growth, and a zest for organizational life. In contrast, the symptoms of destructive conflict include indecision, resistance to change, emotional outbursts, apathy, and organizational goal displacement. By monitoring these various signs and symptoms, management can decide when it is appropriate to encourage conflict and when it is time to step in and attempt to resolve, or neutralize, it. There are two sets of tools available for managing conflict. The first, called conflict triggers, tend to stimulate conflict. Conflict resolution techniques make up the second set of conflict management tools. Resolution is necessary when conflict becomes destructive.

CONFLICT TRIGGERS

A *conflict trigger* is a circumstance that increases the chances of interdepartmental or interpersonal conflict. It can stimulate either constructive or destructive conflict. As long as a conflict trigger appears to be stimulating constructive conflict, it can be allowed to persist. But as soon as the symptoms of destructive conflict appear, steps need to be taken to remove or correct the offending conflict trigger. Among the important conflict triggers are:

○ *Ambiguous or overlapping jurisdictions* Unclear job boundaries tend to create competition for resources and control. Reorganization can clarify job boundaries if destructive conflict becomes a problem. The organization design alternatives in Chapter 7 can be helpful in this regard.

○ *Competition for scarce resources* As the term is used here, resources refer to funds, personnel, authority, power, and valuable information. In other words, anything of value in an organizational setting can become a scarce resource. Sometimes, as in the case of money and people, destructive competition for scarce resources can be avoided or ended by enlarging the resource base (such as increasing competing managers' budgets or hiring additional personnel).

○ *Communication breakdowns*   As discussed in the next chapter, communication is a complex process beset by many barriers. These barriers often provoke conflict. It is easy to misunderstand another person or group of people if two-way communication is hampered in some way. The battle for clear communications is never-ending.

○ *Time pressure*   Deadlines and other forms of time pressure can either stimulate prompt performance or trigger destructive emotional reactions. Daily working experience lets the manager know which individuals respond favorably to time pressure and which cannot handle it. Deadlines and work schedules are then set accordingly.

○ *Unreasonable standards, rules, policies, or procedures*   These conflict triggers often lead to destructive conflict. The best remedy is for the manager to be sensitive to subordinates' perceptions of fair play, so that extremely unpopular situations can be corrected before they trigger destructive conflict.

○ *Personality clashes*   Psychologists tell us that it is very difficult to significantly change one's personality on the job. Therefore the most constructive remedy for personality clashes involves separating the conflicting parties by reassigning one or both to new jobs.

○ *Status differentials*   To the extent that productive organizations continue to be arranged hierarchically, this conflict trigger is unavoidable. However, those who find themselves in a position superior to others can reduce destructive conflict by showing a genuine concern for the ideas, feelings, and values of subordinates.

○ *Unrealized expectations*   As pointed out in our discussion of psychological contracts in the preceding chapter, dissatisfaction grows when one's expectations are not met. Conflict is another by-product of unrealized expectations. Destructive conflict can be avoided in this area by taking time to discover and frankly discuss subordinates' expectations. Unrealistic expectations can be countered before they become a trigger for destructive conflict.[21]

Managers who anticipate these conflict triggers are in a much better position to manage conflict in a systematic and rational manner than those who wait for things to explode before reacting.

RESOLVING CONFLICT   Managers often find themselves in the middle of destructive conflict, whether it is due to inattention or to circumstances beyond their control. In these situations, one or more conflict resolution techniques need to be brought into play. Five of the more popular conflict resolution techniques are:

○ *Problem solving*   When conflicting parties take the time to identify and correct the source of their conflict they are engaging in problem solving. This approach is based squarely on the assumption that two or more heads are better than one. It involves all four steps of our problem-solving process as introduced in Chapter 3. Problem solvers focus their attention on causes, factual information, and promising alternative solutions rather than on personalities or scapegoats. The major shortcoming of the problem-solving approach is that it takes time, but the investment of extra time can pay off handsomely when the problem is corrected instead of being swept under the rug.

○ *Superordinate goals*   "Superordinate goals are highly valued, unattainable by any one group [or individual] alone, and commonly sought."[22] When a manager relies on superordinate goals to resolve destructive conflict, he or she brings the conflicting parties together and, in effect, says "Look, we're all in this together. How about if we forget our differences so we can get the job done?" The president of a manufacturing company might tell the production and marketing department heads who have been arguing about the desirable size of the finished goods inventory that the competition will beat them out if they don't start working together. While this technique often works in the short run, the underlying problem typically returns to haunt management in the long run.

○ *Compromise*   This technique tends to appeal to those living in a democracy. Proponents of this approach claim that everybody wins because it is based on negotiation, or give and take. But everyone also loses in a compromise, because each party must give up something of value. Like problem solving, compromise takes time that management may or may not be able to afford. However, unlike problem solving, the problem is worked around rather than solved.

○ *Forcing*   Sometimes, especially when time is a factor, management must simply step into a conflict and order the conflicting parties to handle the situation in a certain manner. Reliance on formal authority and power is at the heart of this approach to conflict resolution. As one might expect, forcing does not solve the problem and, in fact, may serve to compound it with hurt feelings and damaged egos.

o *Smoothing*   A manager who relies on smoothing says to the conflicting parties "Settle down. Don't rock the boat. Everything will be all right. Things will work out by themselves, you wait and see." This approach may win friends in the short run, but it does not solve the underlying problem. The problem will probably crop up again in magnified form. However, as with each of the other conflict resolution techniques, smoothing has its proper place. It can be useful when management is attempting to hold things together until an especially important project is completed and there is no time for problem solving or compromise and forcing is inappropriate.

Putting things in perspective, problem solving is the only approach that removes the source of conflict. It is the only approach that helps improve things in the long run. All the other approaches amount to short-run, stop-gap measures. However, as mentioned, problem solving takes time, time that management may not be willing or able to spend. When this is the case, one or more of the other approaches may be appropriate.

SUMMARY   A group is more than a collection of people. Two or more people must freely interact and share a common identity and purpose before they can be called a group. Because groups are an ever-present feature of modern life and because they bring out both the best and the worst in people, managers cannot afford to ignore group dynamics in the work setting. Both friendship groups and work groups are found in organizations. People join friendship groups to satisfy their needs to belong and to see themselves as worthwhile individuals. Work group members, in contrast, join together to accomplish some specific purpose. After someone has been attracted to a group, cohesiveness—a "we" feeling—ensures continued membership. The individual must balance a number of positive and negative factors when deciding to join a group and remain as a member; these factors can enhance or destroy group attractiveness and cohesiveness.

The term *group dynamics* refers to the constant activity and change within groups. Three basic dimensions of group dynamics are roles, norms, and interaction. A role is a socially determined prescription for behavior in a specific position. People play many different roles during a given period of time and a variety of roles throughout their lifetimes. Norms tell us what is right or wrong, good or bad about our general behavior. Compliance with norms is rewarded with social reinforcement; noncompliance is met with criticism, ridicule, and ostracism. Roles and norms are powerful determinants of behavior. Interaction plays a key role in group formation and development. Those who come together and share common activities must interact. This interaction contributes to common sentiments or beliefs and eventually to a decrease in interpersonal differences. Interactive skills are vitally important today. Usually they are developed early in life in a step-by-step sequence. Managers must sometimes deal with inadequately developed interactive skills among subordinates. Bales has developed a list of social transactions that managers should try to balance in order to promote the effectiveness of a work group.

Group dynamics may either help or hinder productivity. During the famous Hawthorne studies, researchers observed employees systematically restricting output by establishing their own output norm. Group cohesiveness has proven to be a two-edged sword. When the members of a cohesive work group want to accomplish something, they are likely to be very productive because they pull together. On the othere hand, productivity will be very low when a cohesive group decides to take it easy. One researcher has suggested that managers can take full advantage of group dynamics by using the buddy system in assigning work groups. Productivity can be improved by allowing employees to choose their own co-workers.

A climate of trust in which there is an open and honest exchange of information and opinions helps create an effective work group. When work group members trust one another there will be greater exchange of information, more interpersonal influence, and hence greater self-control, as opposed to control by a supervisor. The manager's job is more advisory than supervisory when group members are committed to doing a good job.

Like cohesiveness, conformity is a two-edged sword. A certain amount of conformity is necessary if plans are to be made and carried out, but unthinking conformity can compromise personal convictions and threaten organizational effectiveness. Conformity needs to be in balance.

Conflict is inevitable in organized settings. Therefore, conflict needs to be managed like any other organizational process. Realizing that conflict can be either constructive or destructive, managers can permit the various conflict triggers to persist until the symptoms of destructive conflict appear. Problem solving heads the list of conflict resolution techniques that can be used to neutralize destructive conflict.

TERMS TO UNDERSTAND	Group	Ostracism
	Friendship group	Interaction
	Work group	Trust
	Cohesiveness	Conformity
	Role	Conflict
	Norms	Conflict trigger

QUESTIONS FOR DISCUSSION

1. What are the advantages and disadvantages of a work group evolving into a friendship group?
2. How are attractiveness and cohesiveness related?
3. Think of a manager you know. What different roles does he or she play? Is there any potential for conflict among these roles? Explain.
4. How can group interaction suffer from "too much of a good thing?"
5. What group dynamics were observed in the bank wiring portion of the Hawthorne studies?
6. In what way is cohesiveness a two-edged sword?
7. What role does trust play in effective group interaction?
8. What are the risks of refusing to give in to blind conformity?
9. Can you think of a personal experience that illustrates the two faces of conflict?
10. Why should managers be aware of the various conflict triggers in addition to conflict resolution techniques?

CASE 13.1 THE FEARSOME FOURSOME

Clint Wilkenson had to hurry to catch his former friend Phil Akers as they headed out of the annual companywide production managers' meeting. As Phil turned to see who had grabbed his elbow, Clint said, "Hey, Phil, old buddy, how's it going? Long time no see."

"It sure has been a long time," replied Phil with a smile, "I'm fine. Boy, you really look great. How are things back at the old plant?"

True to form, Clint launched into a long-winded explanation of the latest happenings at work as the two headed out to the parking lot. Hearing Clint's voice brought back a lot of old memories for Phil.

Two years ago he, Clint, and two other Eastside plant supervisors named Stan and Bill were inseparable. Not only did the four men work together in the Eastside production operation, but they spent much of their free time together. Their families got into the act, too, with picnics and outings that the four thought up at work. They even had a bowling team named "The Fearsome Foursome," and bowled once a week all year long. They had shared a lot of good times together.

Two years ago Phil, and certainly the others, would have sworn that the Fearsome Foursome would go on forever. Little did they realize that a breakup was right around the corner. First, Phil's promotion and transfer came along. Shortly after that he and his family moved across town to cut his commuting distance to the Westside facility. Using the excuse that the drive back to Eastside was too much, Phil quit the bowling team. Actually, he had grown tired of being called a "big shot" second-level manager by the others.

A few months later, as Phil got the story secondhand, the team split up altogether. According to one report, Stan had angrily accused Bill of not picking up his fair share of the bowling tab. The two did not speak to each other for a month, and to this day they don't do anything together outside of work. Besides, as Phil reflected, even before his transfer each of the men had been getting pressure from his wife about not spending enough time at home.

As the two shook hands next to Phil's car, Clint remarked, "It's a shame the Fearsome Foursome had to split up."

"It sure is," answered Phil as he slipped behind the steering wheel of his car.

FOR DISCUSSION

1. What has happened here in terms of group cohesiveness?
2. Did the fact that this group was both a friendship group and a work group create conflicts?
3. Do you think it is possible for any group to remain cohesive for a long time today? Explain.

CASE 13.2
KEEP THEM
GUESSING

Jean King, the personnel director at Tasty Baking Company, has been unhappy with the performance of Lyle Joplin for some time. As the firm's compensation specialist, Joplin reports directly to Jean. As far as Jean can tell, all four of Joplin's subordinates are dissatisfied with the way he treats them. One was recently overheard complaining about being "spoonfed" information.

When Jean confronted him with the problem during a recent performance review, Joplin dismissed it as "just a personality clash." When Jean pressed the matter, Joplin asserted that he was the manager and he wanted to keep it that way. According to him, he gave his people only the information they needed to do the job at hand.

"If I tell them too much, they'll just get things all mixed up. Then I have to straighten them out," he told her. "Furthermore," he added, "the best way to keep people on their toes is to keep them guessing."

FOR DISCUSSION

1. How has Lyle Joplin hindered effective group interaction?
2. If you were the personnel director, how would you respond to Joplin?
3. Do you think that Lyle Joplin could change his managerial style? What might prevent him from doing so?

REFERENCES

Opening quotation

Robert Presthus, *The Organizational Society*, rev. ed. (New York: St. Martin's Press, 1978), p. 113.

1. Joseph A. Litterer, *The Analysis of Organizations*, 2nd ed. (New York: Wiley, 1973), p. 231.
2. For an excellent elaboration of this definition, see: David Horton Smith, "A Parsimonious Definition of 'Group:' Toward Conceptual Clarity and Scientific Utility," *Sociological Inquiry* 37 (Spring 1967): 141–167.
3. See Charles G. Burck, "For William Hewitt It Was an Easy Ascent," *Fortune* 94 (August 1976): 166–170+.
4. Albert A. Harrison, *Individuals and Groups: Understanding Social Behavior* (Monterey, Calif.: Brooks/Cole, 1976), p. 16.
5. Ibid., p. 401.
6. George C. Homans, *The Human Group* (New York: Harcourt, Brace & World, 1950).
7. See Robert F. Bales, "A Set of Categories for the Analysis of Small Group Interaction," *American Sociological Review* 15 (1950): 257–263.
8. Adapted from Robert F. Bales, *Personality and Interpersonal Behavior* (New York: Holt, Rinehart & Winston, 1970), p. 92.
9. For a complete account of the Hawthorne studies, see: F. J. Roethlisberger and William J. Dickson, *Management and the Worker* (Cambridge, Mass.: Harvard University Press, 1939).
10. For a discussion of management's silent approval, see Henry A. Landsberger, *Hawthorne Revisited* (Ithaca, N.Y.: Cornell University, 1958), p. 25.
11. See Leonard Berkowitz, "Group Standards, Cohesiveness, and Productivity," *Human Relations* 7 (1954): 509–519.
12. See Raymond H. Van Zelst, "Sociometrically Selected Work Teams Increase Production," *Personnel Psychology* 5 (Autumn 1952): 175–185.
13. Ibid., p. 183.
14. See Dale E. Zand, "Trust and Managerial Problem Solving," *Administrative Science Quarterly* 17 (June 1972): 229–239.
15. See Solomon E. Asch, *Social Psychology* (Englewood Cliffs, N.J.: Prentice-Hall, 1952), Chap. 16.

16. Ibid., p. 454.
17. Andrew Malcolm, *The Tyranny of the Group* (Toronto: Clarke, Irwin, 1973), p. 4.
18. Adapted from Ralph Nader, Peter Petkas, and Kate Blackwell, eds., *Whistle Blowing* (New York: Bantam, 1972), pp. 75–89.
19. Stephen P. Robbins, *Managing Organizational Conflict: A Nontraditional Approach* (Englewood Cliffs, N.J.: Prentice-Hall, 1974), p. 23.
20. Ibid., p. 15.
21. For an alternative list of conditions that tend to precipitate conflict, see Alan C. Filley, *Interpersonal Conflict Resolution* (Glenview, Ill.: Scott, Foresman, 1975), pp. 9–12.
22. Robbins, *Managing Organizational Conflict*, p. 62.

Chapter 14

Communicating and Leading

Without communication leadership cannot occur.

Jerry C. Wofford, et al.

LEARNING OBJECTIVES

When you finish reading this chapter, you should be able to

○ Identify the various steps in the basic communication process.
○ Explain the importance of informal communication and of nonverbal communication.
○ Outline how management can promote upward communication.
○ Discuss physical, semantic, and psychosocial barriers to communication and some ways to overcome them.
○ Briefly trace the evolution of leadership theory.
○ Discuss several factors that contribute to effective leadership.
○ Highlight the role of women as leaders.

One of the most challenging aspects of management is to get subordinates to understand and voluntarily pursue organizational objectives. Two very important interpersonal skills, communication and leadership, enable managers to meet this challenge. As the opening quotation for this chapter suggests, communication and leadership complement one another. They go hand in hand.

COMMUNICATING   Managerial communication takes in a great deal of territory. Virtually every management function and activity can be considered communication in one way or another. Planning and controlling typically involve a good deal of communicating, as do problem solving, organization design and development, decision making, and staffing. In fact, research has demonstrated that the average manager spends more time communicating than anything else. A unique work-sampling study was carried out among 136 managers at three different levels in a large research and development organization. The researcher found that the managers spent between 74 and 87 percent of their workday communicating (see Figure 14.1). Each successively higher level of management spent proportionately more time communicating. Interestingly, for all three levels of management, the predominant forms of communication were

FIGURE 14.1
Managers spend a majority of their time communicating

Data source: John R. Hinrichs, "Communications Activity of Industrial Research Personnel," *Personnel Psychology* 17 (Summer 1964): 199.

listening and speaking. Since the managers averaged only 8 percent of their day on the telephone, it was clear that most of their listening and speaking was done face to face. In fact, most of their *total* communication time was spent in face-to-face listening and speaking.[1]

Just because managers spend the bulk of their time communicating does not necessarily mean that they are effective communicators. One indication that managers feel a need for improvement in this area is the popularity of communication seminars in management development programs. One management writer summed up the state of managerial communication with this somewhat harsh appraisal: "Talk is cheap, so we spend it recklessly, overloading our message systems and thereby depreciating their contents. With so much garbage in the system, much of it will inevitably be sent out."[2] Before managers, or anyone else for that matter, can become effective communicators they need to appreciate that communication is a complex process commonly plagued by serious problems. This is especially true for the apparently simple activity of communicating face to face.

THE COMMUNICATION PROCESS   The well-known organizational behaviorist Keith Davis has defined *communication* as "the process of passing information and understanding from one person to another."[3] Communication is a social process. Whether one communicates face to face with a single person or with a group of people via television, it is still a social activity involving two or more people. If we analyze the communication process, we discover that it is a chain made up of identifiable links (see Figure 14.2). The essential purpose of this chainlike process is to send an idea from one person to another in such a way that it is understood by the receiver. Like any other chain, the communication chain is only as strong as its weakest link.

Encoding   Thinking is an exclusively personal process. It takes place within the human brain. But when we want to pass a thought along to someone else, an entirely different process comes into play. This second process, communication, requires the sender to package the idea in an understandable manner. Encoding enters the picture at this point. The purpose of encoding is to translate internal thought patterns into a language that the intended receiver of the message will understand.

Typically, managers rely on words, gestures, or other symbols for encoding. Their choice of symbols depends on several factors. One of these is the nature of the message itself. Is it technical or nontechnical, emotional or factual? Perhaps it could be expressed

FIGURE 14.2
The basic communication
process

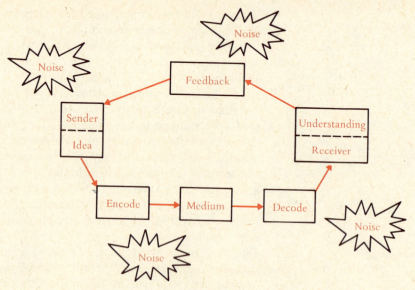

better with numbers than with words; this would be the case with a budget. To express skepticism, a shrug might be the appropriate choice.

The purpose of the message also needs to be considered. Is it intended to provide specific information needed for doing a job? Or is it intended to persuade, to change attitudes, to provide direction? There are as many purposes as there are situations, and it is important to consider what the message is supposed to accomplish. If a manager wants to propose a bold new program to his or her superiors, for example, then a dry technical report would probably not be persuasive. It would be inappropriate. Broad generalizations with a certain emotional appeal might be a better approach; technical details could come later.

Another important factor is deciding how to encode a message—that is deciding what physical form it will take. A manager would certainly use different language for a phone call than for a computer printout. The number of people to be addressed is also important. Usually, the greater the number of receivers, the more formal the language chosen. In talking face to face with one person, a manager can be more informal than when speaking to a hundred. The perceived characteristics of the receiver also enter into the encoding decision. A manager would speak to a secretary familiar with all the department's activities in a much different way than to an angry superior or a prospective customer.

Selecting a Medium Managers can choose among a number of media. They should consider the same factors that influenced the encoding decision. The nature of the message, its intended purpose, the number of receivers, and their characteristics all enter into the selection of a medium. Possible media include face-to-face conversation, telephone calls, memos, letters, computers, photographs, bulletin boards, meetings, and organizational publications. Communicating with those outside the organization opens up further possibilities such as news releases, press conferences, and advertising on television and radio or in magazines and newspapers.

Each medium has its own advantages and disadvantages. The telephone, for example, is a quick and easy way to give someone a message, but it doesn't allow for the valuable nonverbal feedback that is so much a part of face-to-face communication. The computer can handle a vast amount of detailed information, but it cannot transmit a manager's enthusiasm for a project. Letters and memos, although relatively time-consuming to prepare, have the advantage of providing the communicating parties with a permanent record of the exchange.

Decoding Even the most expertly fashioned message will not accomplish its purpose unless it is understood. After physically receiving the message, the receiver needs to comprehend the symbols and detect shades of meaning. If the message has been properly encoded, there will be no problem about the decoding. But perfect encoding is nearly impossible to achieve in an imperfect world. A positive willingness to receive the message is the first essential in decoding. The receiver also needs to know the language and terminology used in the message—and it helps to understand the sender's purpose and the background situation. Later in this chapter we discuss effective listening in greater detail.

Feedback Some sort of feedback, verbal or nonverbal, must be sent back to the original sender before the communication process is complete. The form of feedback is determined by the same factors that governed the encoding decision. In the absence of feedback, senders have no way of knowing whether their ideas have been understood. Knowing whether others understand us or not significantly affects both the form and content of our follow-up communication.

Noise Noise is not part of the chainlike communication process, but it may influence the process at any point. As the term is used here, *noise* is any interference with the normal flow of understanding from one person to another. This is a relatively broad definition. A speech impairment, garbled technical transmission, negative attitudes, illegible print or pictures, telephone static, partial loss of hearing, and poor eyesight all qualify as noise. Understanding diminishes as noise increases. In general, there are two ways to improve the effectiveness of organizational communication. The first is to maximize the understandability of verbal and written messages. The second is to minimize noise by anticipating and neutralizing potential sources of interference.

FORMAL VERSUS INFORMAL COMMUNICATION

In every organization, large and small, there are actually two communication systems: formal communications, and informal communications. Sometimes they complement and reinforce one another; at other times they come into direct conflict. Although, theorists have found it convenient to separate the two, distinguishing one from the other in real life can be difficult. Information required to accomplish official objectives is channeled throughout the organization via the formal system. Official or formal communication, by definition, flows in accordance with established lines of authority and structural boundaries. Media for official communication include everything from memos and letters to the telephone, bulletin boards, and in-house publications. But superimposed on this formal network is the infamous *grapevine*, the unofficial communication system.

An authority on grapevine communication has offered the following vivid description:

> The grapevine operates fast and furiously in almost any work organization. It moves with impunity across departmental lines and easily bypasses superiors in chains of command. It flows around water coolers, down hallways, through lunch rooms, and wherever people get together in groups. It performs best in informal social contacts, but it can operate almost as effectively as a sideline to official meetings. Wherever people congregate, there is no getting rid of the grapevine. No matter how management feels about it, it is here to stay.[4]

One survey of 341 participants in a management development seminar uncovered predominantly negative feelings among managers toward the grapevine. Moreover, first-line supervisors perceived the grapevine to be more influential than did middle managers. This second finding led the researchers to conclude, "Apparently the grapevine is more prevalent, or at least more visible at lower levels of the managerial hierarchy where supervisors can readily feel its impact."[5] Finally, it was discovered that employees of relatively small organizations (less than fifty people) viewed the grapevine as less influential than did those from larger organizations (over one hundred people). A logical explanation for this last finding is that smaller organizations tend to be more informal to begin with.

Despite the negative attitude of many managers, the grapevine has its good aspects as well as bad. It is true that the grapevine may spread inaccurate information, unfounded rumors, and discontent throughout the organization. On the other hand, it may serve as an emotional outlet for employee fears and apprehensions, help satisfy a natural desire to know what is "really" going on in the organization, and give employees a sense of belonging to its informal social structure. The grapevine can carry information through the organization with amazing speed. And it can offer managers the opportunity to learn what employees are thinking and feeling.

Considering that the grapevine can be an influential and sometimes negative force, what can management do about it? First and foremost, the grapevine cannot be extinguished. In fact, attempts to stifle grapevine communication may serve instead to stimulate it. A policy of monitoring the grapevine in a low-key manner and officially correcting or countering any potentially damaging misinformation is about all any management team can do. Some organizations have found rumor-control hot lines useful for neutralizing disruptive grapevine communication.

NONVERBAL COMMUNICATION

Sometimes, as we all know, communication is a "damned if you do and damned if you don't" proposition. If we speak our mind, we offend. If we keep our mouth shut, we are accused of holding out. To complicate this dilemma, the facial expressions and body movements that accompany our words can also cause problems. This nonverbal communication, sometimes referred to as body language, is an important part of the total communication process. In fact, one expert contends that only 7 percent of the impact of our face-to-face communication comes from the words we utter; the other 93 percent comes from our vocal intonations and facial expressions.[6] As the old romantic line goes, "Your voice may say no, but your eyes say yes, yes, yes."

There are three basic kinds of body language: facial, gestural, and postural.[7] Without speaker or listener consciously thinking about it, seemingly insignificant changes in facial expression, gestures, and posture send various messages. For example, a speaker can tell that a listener is interested through a combination of nonverbal cues including an attentive gaze, an upright posture, and confirming or agreeing gestures. Negative nonverbal cues let speakers know that they are off course with the listener. Unfortunately, many people in positions of responsibility such as parents, teachers, and managers ignore nonverbal feedback. When they do, they become ineffective communicators.

Like any other interpersonal skill, sensitivity to nonverbal cues can be learned. Listeners need to be especially aware of subtle nuances. There is a fine line of distinction between an attentive gaze and a glaring stare, between an upright posture and a stiff one. Knowing how to interpret a nod, a grimace, or a grin can be invaluable to managers. If at any time the response seems inappropriate to what one is saying, it is time to back off and reassess one's approach. It may be necessary to explain things more clearly, adopt a more patient manner, or make other adjustments. After all, the purpose of communication is to transfer ideas from one mind to another, and if a manager is not getting through, changes are in order.

But what about the nonverbal feedback that managers give rather than receive? A research study carried out in Great Britain suggests that nonverbal feedback from authority figures significantly affects subordinate behavior. Of the people interviewed, those who received nonverbal approval in the form of smiles, positive head nods, and eye contact from interviewers behaved quite differently from those who received nonverbal disapproval through frowns, head shaking, and avoidance of eye contact. Those receiving positive nonverbal feedback were judged by neutral observers to be significantly more relaxed, more friendly, more talkative, and more successful in creating a good impression.[8] So positive nonverbal feedback from managers is a basic building block of good interpersonal relations. In addition, as discussed in the next chapter under the heading of behavior modification, one way to make sure that good job performance continues is to provide positive feedback. A well-timed wink, nod of the head, or pat on the back tells the individual that he or she is on the right track and to keep up the good work.

In summary, it seems that managerial communication involves much more than mere words. Giving and receiving nonverbal feedback are also vital to successful interpersonal communication.

UPWARD COMMUNICATION

The monitoring of job-performance information from all corners of the organization permits management to make appropriate adjustments. This function was discussed in Chapter 5, "Controlling." But the need for information from below goes far beyond strictly objective task-related data. Subordinates' feelings, grievances, suggestions, and ideas also contain potentially valuable information. As it is used here, the term *upward communication* refers to a process by which subordinates are systematically encouraged to share their feelings and ideas with management.

Upward communication has become increasingly important in recent years as employees have demanded—and received—a greater say in their work lives. After making a survey of upper-level managers in 188 U.S. corporations, two communication researchers concluded in 1978 that:

> The flow of upward communication in organizations has seemed to improve markedly during the last five years. Organizations more actively seek new ideas from employees, they listen more closely to employees on matters of company concern, and there appears to be a dramatically increased willingness among employees to speak their minds.[9]

The general climate appears to favor the development of upward communication today.

Upward communication programs vary from situation to situation. Where unions represent rank-and-file employees, provisions for upward communication are spelled out in the labor agreement. Typically, unionized employees have a formal grievance procedure for contesting managerial actions and oversights. Grievance procedures usually consist of a number of progressively more rigorous steps. For example, union members who have been fired may talk with their supervisor in the presence of the union steward. If the issue is not resolved at that level, the next step may be a meeting with the department head. Sometimes the formal grievance process includes as many as five or six steps, with a third-party arbitrator acting as a last resort. Depending on the agreement between management and the union, the arbitrator's decision is usually binding and final. Formal grievance procedures also may be found in nonunion situations.

Besides formal grievance procedures, a number of other upward communication options are open to management. The following list is representative:

1. *Employee attitude and opinion surveys* Both in-house and commercially prepared surveys can bring employee attitudes and feelings to the surface inexpensively. However, statistical analysis and interpretation by hired consultants drives up costs dramatically. Employees are usually cooperative about completing surveys if they are convinced that meaningful changes will

result. Surveys with no follow-up action tend to alienate employees; they feel that management hasn't delivered what it promised and that they have wasted their time.

2. *Suggestion boxes*   Provided that those who submit suggestions receive prompt feedback and appropriate monetary incentives for good ideas, suggestion boxes can be a valuable tool.

3. *Open door policy*   This approach to upward communication has been both praised and criticized. Proponents say that when managers keep their doors open and subordinates feel free to walk in anytime and talk with them, problems are nipped in the bud. But critics contend that an open door policy encourages subordinates to leapfrog the formal chain of command. Furthermore, they argue that it is an open invitation to annoying interruptions when managers can least afford them.

4. *Informal gripe sessions*   Employees may feel free to air their feelings if they are confident that management will not criticize or penalize them for being frank. However, the term *gripe session* seems to encourage only negative communication—using a more positive name is helpful. One firm with which the author is familiar holds regular, informal "coffee talks" to stimulate upward communication.

5. *Task forces*   In spite of limited use, this approach to upward communication has excellent potential. A task force is a team of management and nonmanagement personnel assigned to a specific problem or issue. Typically, task forces are fact-finding and advisory panels. Multilevel participation in a task force encourages close contact between managers and subordinates, enhances creativity, and develops interpersonal skills.

6. *Exit interviews*   An employee leaving the organization, for whatever reason, no longer has a fear of recrimination from superiors. Unusually frank and honest feedback can be obtained in a brief interview with departing employees. However, exit interviews have been criticized for eliciting artificially negative feedback, because the employee may have a sour-grapes attitude toward the organization.

In general, attempts to promote upward communication will be successful only if subordinates truly believe that their contributions will have a favorable impact on their employment. Halfhearted or insincere attempts to get subordinates to open up and to become involved will do more harm than good.

BARRIERS TO COMMUNICATION   Earlier in this chapter we discussed noise, or interference, which commonly affects the communication process. Barriers to communication differ from noise in that they completely block the transfer of understanding, rather than merely interfere with it. In this section and the next we discuss barriers to communication and some ways of overcoming them.

Every step in the communication process is necessary to effective communication. If a step is blocked by a barrier, then it is impossible to complete the communication process. Consider the following situations:

- *Sender barrier* A management trainee with an unusual new idea fails to speak up at a meeting for fear of criticism.
- *Encoding barrier* A Spanish-speaking field worker cannot get an English-speaking farmer to understand a grievance about working conditions.
- *Medium barrier* After getting no answer three times and a busy signal twice, a customer concludes that a store's consumer hot line is a waste of time.
- *Decoding barrier* An older manager is not sure what a young supervisor means when she refers to an employee as "spaced out."
- *Receiver barrier* A manager who is preoccupied with the preparation of a budget asks a subordinate to repeat a previous statement.
- *Feedback barrier* During on-the-job training, the failure of the trainee to ask any questions makes a manager wonder if there is any real understanding.

The complexity of the communication process itself is a formidable barrier to communication. At any step, a barrier may block further communication.

Physical barriers Sometimes a physical object blocks effective communication. For example, a riveter who wears ear protectors probably cannot hear someone yell fire. Distance is another form of physical barrier. The three thousand miles between New York and Los Angeles and the time zone differences can wreak havoc with coast-to-coast communication in a national organization. People often learn to live with physical barriers, but sometimes they can be removed. For example, an inconveniently positioned wall can be torn out. An appropriate choice of media is especially important in overcoming physical barriers. A manager can reach 200 people instead of 25, despite having a soft voice, by simply using a microphone.

Semantic barriers   *Semantics* is the study of meaning in words. Words are an indispensable feature of everyday life. Unfortunately, words sometimes cause a great deal of trouble. In a well-worn army story, an angry drill sergeant once ordered a frightened recruit to go out and paint his "entire jeep." Later, the sergeant was shocked to find that the private had painted his *entire* jeep, including the headlights, windshield, seats, and dashboard gauges. Obviously, the word *entire* meant something different to the recruit than it did to the sergeant.

Words are abstract symbols to which we have attached socially recognizable meanings. In effective communication it is not the word that counts but the meanings that the sender and receiver attach to the word. Misunderstanding the meaning of words constitutes a significant barrier to effective communication.

Sometimes people literally speak different languages; the increase in the Spanish-speaking population in the United States accounts for the many public notices that appear in both English and Spanish. Regional differences in vocabulary may also cause difficulties; *tonic* in New England is a far different product from *tonic* in Arizona. Experts in a field, such as computer science or psychology, may become so accustomed to their own special terminology that they forget that other people may not understand them. In fact, almost every occupation has its special shop talk or lingo; those who don't understand the lingo don't know what is going on.

In recent years many people have criticized the English language for being sexist.[10] The words *he*, *chairman*, *brotherhood*, *mankind*, and so on are commonly used to refer to both men and women. The traditional argument is that everyone understands that these words refer to both sexes, and it is simpler to use the masculine form. Critics of this usage maintain that it subtly denies to women a place and an image worthy of their importance in society. In most cases the criticism is based on psychological and sociological considerations. Calling the human race *mankind* is seldom a real barrier to understanding. However, a Stanford University researcher found that "males appear to use 'he' in response to male-related imagery, rather than in response to abstract or generic notions of humanity."[11] In other words, *he* is commonly interpreted to literally mean *he* (just men), not *they* (men and women). If management wants to attract applicants for a new job opening, then it should avoid directives like this one: "If anyone is interested, he should contact the personnel director."

Unexpected reactions or behavior often result from semantic barriers. If a manager becomes aware that a receiver is experiencing difficulty in decoding the message, then one of the first questions to ask is whether there might be semantic problems. If so, it is essential to re-encode the message using different words that the receiver is more likely to understand. Sometimes, if the kind of communication is likely to continue and there is enough time, the receiver can learn the sender's special language. For example, hospital administrators often take a special course in medical terminology so they can better understand the medical staff.

Psychosocial barriers Psychological and social barriers are probably responsible for more blocked communication than any other barriers. People have such a variety of backgrounds, perceptions, values, biases, and expectations that it would be impossible for a manager to tailor a message that would overcome all possible barriers. However, awareness of general types of psychosocial barriers—as well as an understanding of people's basic needs—can help.

Psychosocial barriers can come from many different sources. Childhood experiences may result in negative feelings toward authority figures (such as bosses), racial prejudice, distrust of the opposite sex, or lack of self-confidence. Family and personal difficulties such as poor health, alcoholism, and emotional problems may be so upsetting that an employee is unable to concentrate on work. Experience on this or other jobs may have created anger, distrust, and resentment that speak more loudly in the employee's mind than any present communication. All of these raise formidable barriers to communication.

Sometimes the person sending the message knows the receiver well enough to recognize certain barriers and find a way around them. But usually the sender can only sense, through inappropriate or missing feedback, that the message is not being understood. If there are no obvious physical or semantic problems, then the problem may be psychosocial. Asking about the inappropriate feedback may help: "Is something on your mind today?" Or, "You don't seem too happy about doing this." Then the employee may be willing to bring the matter out in the open where it can be dealt with. But the employee may not know what the matter is or may not be willing to share it. In that case, the manager can only remember that everyone has needs for security, belonging, self-esteem, and self-actualization. A message that suggests fulfillment of one of these needs has a better chance of getting through.

BECOMING A BETTER COMMUNICATOR

It would be impossible in one short section to do justice to all the concepts and techniques that have been developed to improve communication. Entire libraries have been devoted to the subject. Therefore, we will briefly consider three communication skills that are especially important in today's organizational setting. These three skills are listening, writing, and running meetings. Often they are the key to managerial success.

EFFECTIVE LISTENING

Practically all training in oral communication in high school, college, and management development programs is in effective speaking. But what about listening, the other half of the conversational equation? Listening skills are the stepchild of training in communication skills. This is too bad, because the most glowing oration in the world is a waste of time if the listeners don't understand it. Listening takes place at two steps in the communication process. First, the receiver needs to listen in order to decode and understand the original message. Then the sender must listen in order to decode and understand the feedback. The same skills are needed for both steps.

We can hear and process information at a much faster pace than the normal speaker can talk. Consequently, listeners have some slack time, even though it is only microseconds, during which they can daydream, analyze the information they are receiving, or plan what to say in response. The key to effective listening is to manage that slack time properly.

Although it takes practice to become an effective listener, and reading a list of pointers is only a first step, here are several tips for more effective listening.

o Ask yourself where the speaker is coming from in terms of his or her usual attitudes, apparent frame of mind, health, and personal or job-related problems.
o Determine the overall purpose of the communication. Is it to inform, order, discuss, consult, or what?
o Ask yourself about the speaker's expertise in the topic being discussed. Is the speaker in a position to contribute to your knowledge?
o The language used should be clear to you. If it is not, try questions to find out what the speaker means. In the long run, studying the new or different language can help.

o Separate fact from opinion. How much of what is being said is based on objective fact and how much on subjective opinion?

o Isolate the speaker's main point. What is the speaker getting at?

o Periodically summarize in your mind what has been said. How much ground has the speaker covered?

o Never assume that you already know what the speaker is going to say. You may tune out something new and useful.

o Notice the speaker's nonverbal signals. Do they support the verbal message, or are they in conflict with it?

o Avoid becoming so preoccupied with your position, counterargument, or agreement that you stop listening. Is a verbal response necessary or will nonverbal feedback do?

Naturally, these tips are easier to follow when listening to a formal speech or to radio or television than when engaged in a vigorous face-to-face conversation. But in all situations effective listening helps overcome semantic and psychosocial barriers and permits more intelligent conversation.

EFFECTIVE WRITING   One of management's main complaints about today's college graduates is that they are poor writers. For example, a survey of personnel executives revealed that recent graduates experience considerable difficulty in four areas of writing.[12] Those areas are (1) being concise, (2) making meaning clear, (3) making the message accomplish its purpose, and (4) spelling (see Figure 14.3). These deficiencies in writing stem from an educational system that requires college students to do less and less writing. Essay tests have given way in many classes to the multiple-choice variety, and formal term papers are being pushed aside by team activities and projects. As a learned skill, effective writing is the product of regular practice. Students who do not get the necessary writing practice in school are handicapped when they step onto the managerial firing line.

Good writing is clearly part of the encoding step in the communication process. If it is done skillfully, it can help avoid semantic and psychosocial barriers.

Again, as in the case of effective listening, a few quick-and-easy steps will not erase a chronic writing problem. But to get the process started, Robert DeGise, the publications editor for Caterpillar Tractor Company, offers four helpful reminders.

1. *Keep words simple.* Simplifying the words you use will help reduce your thoughts to essentials, keep your readers from

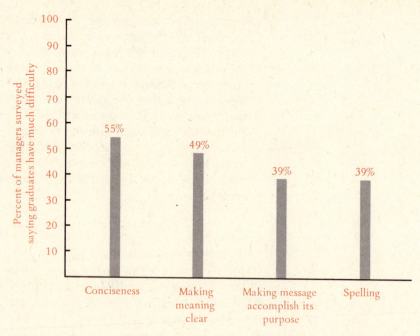

Data source: Hilda F. Allred and Joseph F. Clark, "Written Communication Problems and Priorities," *The Journal of Business Communication* 15 (Winter 1978): 32.

being "turned off" by the complexity of your letter, memo, or report, and make it more understandable.

2. *Don't sacrifice communication for rules of composition. . . .* Most of us who were sensitized to the rules of grammer and composition in our schools never quite recovered from the process. As proof, we keep trying to make our writing conform to rigid rules and custom without regard to style or the ultimate purpose of the communication.

3. *Write concisely.* This means express your thoughts, opinions, and ideas in the fewest number of words consistent with composition and smoothness. But don't confuse conciseness with brevity; you may write briefly without being clear or complete.

4. *Be specific.* Vagueness is one of the most serious flaws in written communication because it destroys accuracy and clarity, leaving the reader to wonder about your meaning or intent.[13]

Forewarned is forearmed, as the saying goes. The time to start a writing-improvement program is while you are still in school, not your first day on the job. One staunch supporter of good writing offers the following advice to college students: "Be sure that every course you take requires written assignments and that grades will penalize bad writing."[14]

RUNNING A MEETING   Meetings are an ever-present feature of organizational life. Whether they are convened to find facts, develop alternatives, or pass along information, meetings typically occupy a good deal of a manager's time. They are the principal format for committee action. Whatever the reason for a meeting, managers who chair meetings owe it to themselves and the organization to use everyone's time and talent efficiently. This can be done by following a few simple guidelines before, during, and after a meeting.

Before the meeting, the chairperson should distribute an agenda to participants stating

○ The date, time, and place of the meeting.
○ The members expected to be present.
○ The purpose of the meeting and the major points to be discussed.
○ Any necessary background data or information.
○ What materials or information, if any, should be brought to the meeting.
○ The anticipated duration of the meeting.
○ The person to contact if there are any questions about the meeting.

During the meeting, the chairperson should

○ Make sure that everyone in attendance has a copy of the agenda.
○ Reaffirm the purpose of the meeting, introduce new members, and answer questions about what is supposed to take place.
○ Encourage creative inputs early in the meeting while the energy level is high.
○ Stick to the agenda and time limit.
○ Close out lengthy discussion of seemingly urgent, but actually trivial, items.
○ Encourage rather than dominate discussion.
○ Keep things moving by cutting off repetitive discussion.
○ Briefly summarize and recap at the end of the meeting.

After the meeting, the chairperson should

○ Distribute minutes and attendance roster (if taken).
○ If formal minutes are not taken, distribute a brief summary or

status sheet to members to record agreement on actions taken and plans made.[15]

With practice, these guidelines become second nature. Running a meeting brings to a focus all the components of the communication process. The net result of running a meeting well is greater personal and group effectiveness.

The basic purpose of communication is to transfer understanding. But when it comes to getting subordinates to pursue organizational objectives, a special approach to communication is needed. Influence is at the heart of this approach. Managers exercise influence through leadership.

LEADING The subject of leadership has fascinated people in all walks of life since the dawn of history. Many references to both good and bad leadership can be found in the holy books of the world's major religions. A relentless search for good leaders has been one of the common denominators of human civilization. The search continues today.

LEADERSHIP DEFINED A great deal of research has been done on leadership, and, as might be expected, many definitions have been proposed for the concept of leadership. Much of the variance among these definitions is semantic; the definition offered here represents a workable compromise. *Leadership* is "a social influence process in which the leader seeks the voluntary participation of subordinates in an effort to reach organizational objectives."[16] The two key words in this particular definition are *influence* and *voluntary*. They help distinguish leadership from authority and power.

Authority, the right to ask someone to do something, involves domination rather than influence. Power, the actual ability to get people to do things, also involves domination rather than influence. Significantly, authority and power do not always go hand in hand. For example, when American soldiers refused to go on missions in Vietnam, their officers had authority but not power. Reversing the situation, an armed bank robber has the power but not the authority to acquire bank funds. Voluntary compliance does not enter the picture in these two situations. To encourage voluntary participation, leaders supplement any authority and power they may possess with their personal attributes and social skills.

The definition given here requires one refinement. Experts on the subject have drawn a distinction between formal and informal leadership. *Formal leadership* is the exercise of influence over others while in an official position of authority. In contrast, *informal leadership* is the unofficial exercise of influence over others. Informal leaders are a force to be reckoned with because they represent the "peoples' choice." They enjoy power based on trust and friendship. The output restriction observed during the Hawthorne studies, discussed in the last chapter, was the product of informal leadership. Although these informal leaders were not officially recognized by the company, their influence over their coworkers was greater than that of the supervisors. Compared to informal leaders, formal leaders are at a disadvantage because they are assigned to the group rather than selected from among group members by popular choice.

THE EVOLUTION OF LEADERSHIP THEORY Like the study of management, the study of leadership has been an evolutionary process. Leadership theories have been developed and refined by successive generations of researchers. Something useful has been learned at each stage of development. The purpose of this section is to identify and discuss the major steppingstones in the evolution of leadership theory.

Trait theory During most of recorded history the prevailing assumption was that leaders are born and not made. Famous

"Harry's really shaping up!"

Reprinted, by permission of the publisher, cartoon by Henry Martin, from *Research Spotlight, Management Review*, October 1977, p. 66, © 1977 AMACOM, a division of American Management Association. All rights reserved.

leaders such as Alexander the Great, Napoleon Bonaparte, and George Washington were said to have been blessed with the inborn ability to lead others. This so-called great-man approach to leadership eventually gave way to trait theory. According to one observer,

> Under the influence of the behavioristic school of psychological thought, acceptance was given to the fact that leadership traits are not completely inborn but can be acquired through learning and experience. Attention turned to the search for universal traits possessed by leaders.[17]

As the trait approach mushroomed during the early twentieth century, literally hundreds of physical, mental, and behavioral traits were linked to successful leadership. Trait theory eventually fell into disrepute because of lack of agreement over the most important traits of a good leader. Trait theory was criticized for being a chicken-and-egg proposition: Was George Washington a leader because he was brave, or was he brave because he was thrust into leadership positions at a young age?

It was not until 1948 that a comprehensive review of trait theory was carried out. After comparing over one hundred studies of leader traits and characteristics, the reviewer uncovered moderate agreement on only five traits. In the reviewer's words,

> The average person who occupies a position of leadership exceeds the average member of his group in the following respects: (1) intelligence, (2) scholarship, (3) dependability in exercising responsibilities, (4) activity and social participation, and (5) socio-economic status.[18]

This was a rather modest list, considering the hundreds of leader traits suggested. In the final analysis, traits amount to little more than convenient devices for informally classifying and stereotyping leaders.

Behavioral theory   During the era of World War II and continuing on through today, the study of leadership took on a whole new twist. Rather than concentrating on the traits of successful leaders, researchers turned to patterns of leader behavior or leadership styles. In other words, attention turned from who the leader was to what the leader actually did. One early laboratory study of leader behavior demonstrated that followers overwhelmingly preferred managers who practiced a democratic style over those with an authoritarian or laissez-faire (hands off) style.[19] Details of these classic leadership styles are listed in Table 14.1.

For years, theorists and managers hailed democratic leadership as the key to productive and happy employees. Eventually, however, their enthusiasm was dampened when critics pointed out that the original study relied on children as subjects and virtually ignored productivity. Although there is general agreement that these basic styles exist, debate has been vigorous over their relative strengths and weaknesses. Practical experience has shown, for example, that the democratic style does not always stimulate better performance. Some employees prefer to be told what to do rather than participate in decision making.

Meanwhile, a slightly different behavioral approach to leadership emerged. This second approach can be traced back to a team of Ohio State University researchers who defined two independent dimensions of leadership behavior in the late 1940s. One dimension related to the degree of trust, friendship, respect, and warmth the leader extended to subordinates—it was labeled consideration. The

TABLE 14.1
The three classic styles of leadership

	AUTHORITARIAN	DEMOCRATIC	LAISSEZ-FAIRE
Nature	Leader retains all authority and responsibility.	Leader delegates a great deal of authority while retaining ultimate responsibility.	Leader denies responsibility and abdicates authority to group.
	Leader assigns people to clearly defined tasks.	Work is divided and assigned on the basis of participatory decision making.	Group members are simply told to work things out themselves and do the best they can.
	Primarily a downward flow of communication.	Active two-way flow of upward and downard communication.	Primarily a horizontal communication among peers.
Primary Strength	Stresses prompt, orderly, and predictable performance.	Enhances personal commitment through participation.	Permits self-starters to do things as they see fit without leader interference.
Primary Weakness	Approach tends to stifle individual initiative.	Democratic process is time consuming.	Group may drift aimlessly in the absence of direction from leader.

second dimension involved the leader's efforts to get things organized and get the job done—it was called initiating structure.[20] Because these two dimensions of leader behavior could vary independently of one another, a map of possible leadership styles could be constructed. Figure 14.4 illustrates the relationship between consideration and initiating structure. Each of the four quadrants represents a different leadership style.

This particular scheme proved to be fertile ground for leadership theorists. Many variations of the original Ohio State approach soon appeared.[21] Leadership theorists began jumping on the bandwagon in search of the "one best style" of leadership. Perhaps because of its popular appeal, the high-consideration, high-structure style was hailed by many as the best all-around style of leadership. But research evidence in this area has been mixed. Although a positive relationship has been found between leader consideration and subordinate satisfaction, a review of relevant leadership studies led one researcher to conclude:

Despite the fact that "consideration" and "initiating structure" have become almost bywords in American industrial psychology,

FIGURE 14.4
Basic leadership styles

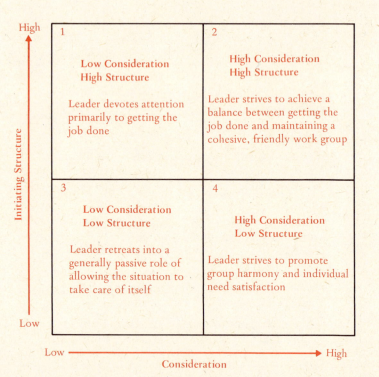

it seems apparent that very little is known as to how these variables may predict work group performance.[22]

Situational theory   Failure to identify the one best way of leading has enhanced the popularity of the situational approach to leadership. Although a number of situational-leadership theories have been developed, they all share one fundamental assumption: successful leadership occurs when the leader's basic style is appropriate to the situation. The situational approach implies that any of the four basic leadership styles in Figure 14.4 might be effective if the situation supports such a style. For example:

○ *Quadrant 1*   A low-consideration, high-structure style is appropriate if the work consists of individuals who are socially mature and highly cohesive but who do not understand or identify with the task at hand.

○ *Quadrant 2*   A high-consideration, high-structure style is appropriate if the work group consists of individuals who require social support from superiors, are not cohesive, and lack a strong identity with the task at hand.

○ *Quadrant 3*   A low-consideration, low-structure style is appropriate if the work group consists of highly motivated individuals who are socially mature and dedicated to the task at hand.

○ *Quadrant 4*   A high-consideration, low-structure style is appropriate if the work group consists of highly motivated individuals who are dedicated to the task at hand but require social support from superiors.

The "one best style" simply does not exist, according to situational thinking. As the elements of a situation change and interact, leadership needs to be flexible.

Among the many theories of leadership proposed to date, one stands out as the most thoroughly tested. Called the *contingency theory*, it is the product of nearly thirty years of research by Fred E. Fiedler and his associates. Fiedler's contingency theory of leadership gets its name from the following assumption:

The performance of a leader depends on two interrelated factors: (1) the degree to which the situation gives the leader control and influence—that is, the likelihood that he can successfully accomplish the job; and (2) the leader's basic motivation—that is, whether his self-esteem depends primarily on accomplishing the task or on having close supportive relations with others.[23]

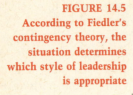

FIGURE 14.5
According to Fiedler's contingency theory, the situation determines which style of leadership is appropriate

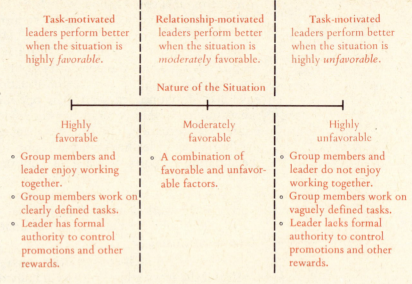

Task-motivated leaders perform better when the situation is highly *favorable*.

Relationship-motivated leaders perform better when the situation is *moderately* favorable.

Task-motivated leaders perform better when the situation is highly *unfavorable*.

Nature of the Situation

Highly favorable

Moderately favorable

Highly unfavorable

- Group members and leader enjoy working together.
- Group members work on clearly defined tasks.
- Leader has formal authority to control promotions and other rewards.

- A combination of favorable and unfavorable factors.

- Group members and leader do not enjoy working together.
- Group members work on vaguely defined tasks.
- Leader lacks formal authority to control promotions and other rewards.

Regarding the second factor, the leader's basic motivation, Fiedler believes that leaders are either task motivated or relationship motivated. These two motivational profiles are roughly the same as initiating structure and consideration.

A consistent pattern has emerged from the many studies of effective leaders carried out by Fiedler and others. As illustrated in Figure 14.5, task-motivated leaders seem to be effective in extreme situations when they have either very little control or a great deal of control over situational variables. However, in the moderately favorable situation, the relationship-motivated leader tends to be more effective. Consequently, Fiedler and one of his colleagues have summed up their work by noting that "everything points to the conclusion that there is no such thing as an ideal leader."[24] There are leaders, and there are situations. The challenge, according to Fiedler, is to match leaders and situations to form productive combinations.

BECOMING AN EFFECTIVE LEADER

What if you were not born a Rockefeller or a Kennedy, but you still want to become a leader? Although it may sound a bit unscientific, a strong and durable *desire* to become a leader is an important step in the right direction. That desire will fuel the effort needed to acquire various leadership skills.

We still know relatively little about how to develop leaders in spite of mountains of research on the subject. Much remains to be learned. In the meantime, it is possible to list a number of variables (see Table 14.2) that appear to set the stage for effective leadership.

TABLE 14.2
Some keys to effective leadership

IT HELPS FOR THE LEADER TO HAVE	IT HELPS FOR THE FOLLOWERS TO BE
o Appropriate technical expertise supported by a strong foundation of general knowledge. o A mastery of the language. o A desire to get things accomplished through people rather than in spite of them. o A willingness to be flexible when dealing with unique individuals. o A mentor who can urge, direct, and coach in addition to providing necessary feedback. o An ability to step back from a disorderly array of details and see things in perspective. o A knack for being in the right place at the right time.	o A cohesive group of individuals who identify with the job to be done. o Knowledgeable people who are still eager to learn. o People who view a difficult task as a challenge rather than a threat. o People who accept and learn through feedback.

IT HELPS FOR THE TASK TO BE	IT HELPS FOR THE ADMINISTRATIVE SETTING TO HAVE
o Meaningful work demanding responsibility. o Work that provides continuing challenge.	o Clear, challenging, yet attainable objectives. o Policies and rules that support rather than undermine effective leadership. o Clear lines of formal authority that support rather than undermine effective leadership.

Those who aspire to positions of leadership in management should be aware of these variables. Effective leadership does not occur in a vacuum.

The leader, follower, task, and administrative variables listed in Table 14.2 bring out one important point. There is much more to effective leadership than a willing and able individual. An unsupportive situation can stifle leaders with the greatest potential. To make matters worse, situations don't stand still. According to one expert, "Leadership must be conceived in terms of the interaction of variables which are in constant flux and change."[25]

Because of the many pitfalls and barriers that block the way to successful leadership, it is easy to appreciate why there is no simple cookbook formula for developing leaders. Abraham Zaleznik, a widely recognized sociologist, insists that leaders must be developed under the wise tutelage of a mentor. A *mentor* is an individual who systematically develops a subordinate's abilities through intensive tutoring, coaching, and guidance. Zaleznik explains the nature of this special relationship.

> Psychological biographies of gifted people repeatedly demonstrate the important part a mentor plays in developing an individual. Andrew Carnegie owed much to his senior, Thomas A. Scott. As head of the Western Division of the Pennsylvania Railroad, Scott recognized talent and the desire to learn in the young telegrapher assigned to him. By giving Carnegie increasing responsibility and by providing him with the opportunity to learn through close personal observation, Scott added to Carnegie's self-confidence and sense of achievement. Because of his own personal strengths and achievement, Scott did not fear Carnegie's aggressiveness. Rather, he gave it full play in encouraging Carnegie's initiative.
>
> Mentors take risks with people. They bet initially on talent they perceive in younger people. Mentors also risk emotional involvement in working closely with their juniors. The risks do not always pay off, but the willingness to take them appears crucial in developing leaders.[26]

It is interesting to note how mentors rely on shaping and modeling when developing the abilities of their understudies.

Finding ways to practice leadership off the job can also help managers develop their abilities. Serving in community organizations, for example, gives a manager the opportunity to experiment with different leadership styles in a variety of situations.

WOMEN AS LEADERS Year after year, the U.S. Department of Labor's Bureau of Labor Statistics reports the serious underrepresentation of women and minorities in managerial and administrative occupations (see Table 14.3). For example, as recently as 1976, 15 percent of all employed

TABLE 14.3
Percentage of workers in managerial and administrative positions

Year	WHITE		BLACK AND OTHER	
	Males (%)	Females (%)	Males (%)	Females (%)
1968	14.7	4.9	3.6	1.6
1972	14.0	4.8	4.8	2.3
1976	15.0	5.9	5.8	2.8

Data Source: U.S. Department of Labor, Bureau of Labor Statistics, *Handbook of Labor Statistics 1977*, Bulletin #1966, Table 18, pp. 58–61.

white males occupied managerial and administrative positions, while the figure for white females and nonwhite males was below 6 percent. In the same year fewer than 3 percent of all employed nonwhite females were able to obtain managerial or administrative jobs. Clearly, the formal leadership positions are going largely to white males rather than women and minorities. Since the plight of women in this area is representative of that of minorities as well, the special case of women as leaders is discussed here.

Research has indicated that stereotypes play an important part in the selection of people for leadership positions. *Stereotypes* are prejudicial categories into which we tend to shove people whether they fit or not; they may be positive or negative. Unfortunately, the stereotypes normally associated with women and minorities are exactly the opposite of the characteristics we would like to see in our leaders. One team of researchers discovered that both male and female college students associated leadership traits with males but not females. Men were viewed as aggressive, independent, unemotional, objective, dominant, and competitive. Women were viewed as talkative, tactful, gentle, neat, and security conscious.[27] According to another researcher, who found that successful male middle managers associate "male" characteristics with the managerial role, "This association between sex role stereotypes and perceptions of requisite management characteristics seems to account, in part, for the limited number of women in management positions."[28]

Are sex-role stereotypes valid? Do women lack the essential characteristics of successful leaders? The answer to both of these important questions appears to be no. One study of male and female managers uncovered no significant difference in leadership styles. Female managers were not more relationship-oriented and less task-oriented than their male counterparts, as the feminine stereotype suggests.[29] More research is needed in this area. Meanwhile, the imbalance in the leadership ranks will decline because of civil rights and Equal Employment Opportunity legislation and judicial decisions. In summary, women and minorities are headed for a greater share of managerial and administrative leadership opportunities in spite of long-standing negative stereotypes.

SUMMARY   Communication and leadership are complementary interpersonal skills. Managers who cannot communicate effectively stand little chance of being successful leaders.

Research indicates that managers spend more time communicating than anything else. The majority of their communication involves verbal face-to-face exchanges. An understanding of the basic communication process and barriers to communication is an important step toward becoming a more effective communicator. Communication basically involves passing understanding from one person to another by means of encoding the message, sending it via a medium, decoding the message, and sending feedback. Noise can interfere with communication at any of these steps.

Experts have distinguished between formal and informal communication. Formal communication is official, whereas the informal grapevine is the unofficial organizational communication system. Although managers tend to view the grapevine negatively, it has positive aspects and is here to stay. Nonverbal communication is another significant aspect of the basic communication process. Body language, including meaningful facial expressions, gestures, and body postures, helps people to communicate. A sensitivity to the nonverbal messages being given and received enhances effective face-to-face communication.

When managers encourage subordinates to share their feelings and ideas, they are promoting upward communication. Today's employees seem to desire more participation through upward communication. In addition to formal grievance procedures, there are a number of ways to get employees to share their feelings and ideas.

Managers can learn to become effective communicators in spite of noise and in spite of physical, semantic, and psychosocial barriers that can prevent the transmission of understanding. Three important communicative skills are listening, writing, and running meetings. Each can be accomplished more effectively by keeping a few basic pointers in mind.

Leadership is a process of influencing others to voluntarily participate in efforts to achieve organizational objectives. Formal leadership and informal leadership have different sources of power. Formal leaders possess formal authority, whereas informal leaders depend entirely on the trust and respect of followers.

Leadership theory has undergone an evolutionary development including trait, behavioral, and situational approaches. Trait theorists tried to identify the universal characteristics of successful leaders. In contrast, behavioral theorists searched for the one best style of leadership behavior. Situational theorists have compromised by attempting to find the appropriate styles of leadership for differing situations.

With the proper desire and an awareness of various situational variables, a person may become an effective leader. The developmental process is enhanced by the personal coaching and feedback of a mentor. Statistics indicate that women and minorities have not gotten their fair share of managerial and administrative positions.

Prejudicial stereotypes are largely to blame. Research has shown that men and women do not differ significantly in leadership styles.

TERMS TO UNDERSTAND

Communication
Noise
Grapevine
Upward communication
Semantics
Leadership

Authority
Power
Formal leadership
Informal leadership
Mentor
Stereotypes

QUESTIONS FOR DISCUSSION

1. Why is a knowledge of the basic communication process so important to managers?
2. Why is the grapevine here to stay?
3. What is the key to making upward communication programs work?
4. How can semantics become a barrier to effective communication? Can you think of your own example?
5. What approaches can a manager use to overcome psychosocial barriers?
6. How does leadership differ from authority and power?
7. What are the relative strengths and weaknesses of the classic authoritarian, democratic, and laissez-faire styles of leadership?
8. Do you agree with the claim of some experts that there is no "one best" leadership style?
9. How can a mentor help a person become an effective leader?
10. Do you think women and minorities are victimized by unfair stereotyping? Explain your position.

**CASE 14.1
BLOW OFF A
LITTLE STEAM**

Although the hourly employees at St. John's Hospital are not represented by a union, pressure has been growing in recent months to call for an election. Management feels that the interests of the community and the hospital would best be served by avoiding unionization. Union organizers point to the hospital's antiquated and terribly overloaded grievance process as evidence of management's insensitivity to employee needs. Margaret Silvers, an assistant administrator, admits off the record that the organizers have a valid point. Ever since joining St. John's three years ago, she has been concerned about what she thinks is a serious lack of upward communication. Most of the comments at today's management meeting confirmed her worst suspicions.

Comments from the food service manager represent the prevailing attitude at St. John's toward upward communication. Responding to Margaret's call for creative ideas, the manager suggested, "Why don't we just set up a weekly gripe session in each department. You know, give the troops a chance to blow off a little steam. Most of the complaints we hear day in and day out don't amount to anything anyway, just petty stuff. Once they get their pet peeves off their chests, they'll go back to work and not give it a second thought. They just want us to appreciate that they're working hard, that's all."

FOR DISCUSSION

1. Putting yourself in Margaret's place, how would you respond to the food service manager?
2. What particular type of upward communication program would you recommend to management? Why?

CASE 14.2
WILL THE REAL
LEADER PLEASE
STAND UP

Professor Lynn Schreiber was pleased with the way her leadership seminar had gone as she watched the last person leave the Center for Executive Development. In fact, it ranked as one of the best management development seminars she had conducted during her many years at Southwestern University. What had made the evening so outstanding was that the three classic leadership styles had been illustrated in unusually pure form by three different individuals. All three appeared to be in command of their job situations, yet they differed dramatically. Professor Schreiber reviewed the contrasting remarks of the three managers in her mind as she drove home.

A technical manager from a West Coast aircraft manufacturing firm had said, "I manage computer programmers, mathematicians, and other high-powered specialists. Half the time I don't even understand what they're talking about. My main concern is making sure that they have enough elbow room to apply their creative talents. They want freedom of action, not someone snooping over their shoulders. My people are professionals, and they expect to be treated like professionals. Their skills are in great demand today; one wrong move on my part and they're out the door. Generally, I just let them know what our budget and time constraints are and get out of their way. They take it from there. They know that as long as they produce, I can be counted on to make sure that they won't be bothered by anyone."

A bottling line supervisor at a local brewery had said, "My people come in, they do their jobs on the line, they collect their pay, and that's it. That's all they want. To be honest about it, I don't think any of them really likes the job. Only one ever graduated from high school. They work at the plant because they need to survive. Kids to feed, bills to pay, you know. A couple of times I tried to get them involved in dreaming up new ways of running the line, but they really resented it. They said they would be damned if they would do my job for me. So I just tell them what to do and that's that. I'm the first one to go to bat for them when they're doing a good job, but when one of them gets out of line I chew his butt out good. There's *my* way and the wrong way. When they do things my way, we get the product out right and fast."

Finally, a nursing supervisor at a local hospital had said: "We've got a real team. We all enjoy each other's company and depend on one another to do the job. It is not easy being a nurse these days. Every time we turn around there is a new piece of equipment to be mastered. And the patients are much more demanding than they used to be. I'm responsible for seeing that our patients get the proper care during my shift, but I couldn't meet that responsibility if I didn't rely heavily on my nurses for their commitment, dedication, ideas, and ability to take charge in difficult situations. I depend on them as much as they depend on me.

FOR DISCUSSION
1. Which of these managers has an autocratic style, which a democratic style, and which a laissez-faire style? How do you know?
2. How do you think these particular managers would fare if they switched places?

REFERENCES

Opening quotation

Jerry C. Wofford, Edwin A. Gerloff, and Robert C. Cummins, *Organizational Communication: The Keystone to Managerial Effectiveness* (New York: McGraw-Hill, 1977), p. 327.

1. For more details on this study, see John R. Hinrichs, "Communications Activity of Industrial Research Personnel," *Personnel Psychology* 17 (Summer 1964): 193–204.
2. David S. Brown, "Barriers to Successful Communication: Part I. Macrobarriers," *Management Review* 64 (December 1975): 28.
3. Keith Davis, *Human Behavior at Work: Organizational Behavior*, 5th ed. (New York: McGraw-Hill, 1977), p. 372.
4. Keith Davis, "Grapevine Communication Among Lower and Middle Managers," *Personnel Journal* 48 (April 1969): 269.
5. John W. Newstrom, Robert E. Monczka, and William E. Reif, "Perceptions of the Grapevine: Its Value and Influence," *The Journal of Business Communication* 11 (Spring 1974): 12–20.
6. See Albert Mehrabian, "Communication Without Words," *Psychology Today* 2 (September 1968): 53–55.

7. This three-way breakdown comes from Dale G. Leathers, *Nonverbal Communication Systems* (Boston: Allyn and Bacon, 1976), chap. 2.

8. See A. Keenan, "Effects of the Non-verbal Behaviour of Interviewers on Candidates' Performance," *Journal of Occupational Psychology* 49, No. 3 (1976): 171–175.

9. James M. Lahiff and John D. Hatfield, "The Winds of Change and Managerial Communication Practices," *The Journal of Business Communication* 15 (Summer 1978): 27.

10. For example, see Bobbye Persing, "Sticks and Stones *and* Words: Women in the Language," *The Journal of Business Communication* 14 (Winter 1977): 11–19.

11. Wendy Martyna, "What Does 'He' Mean? Use of the Generic Masculine," *Journal of Communication* 28 (Winter 1978): 138.

12. See Hilda F. Allred and Joseph F. Clark, "Written Communication Problems and Priorities," *The Journal of Business Communication* 15 (Winter 1978): 31–35.

13. Robert F. DeGise, "Writing: Don't Let the Mechanics Obscure the Message," *Supervisory Management* 21 (April 1976): 26–28.

14. Richard Mitchell, "Let's Hear it For Good English," *Across the Board* 15 (May 1978): 4.

15. This list of pointers was inspired by Antony Jay, "How to Run a Meeting," *Harvard Business Review* 54 (March–April 1976): 43–57.

16. Chester A. Schriesheim, James M. Tolliver, and Orlando C. Behling, "Leadership Theory: Some Implications for Managers," *MSU Business Topics* 26 (Summer 1978): 35.

17. Fred Luthans, *Organizational Behavior*, 2nd ed. (New York: McGraw-Hill, 1977), p. 439.

18. Ralph M. Stogdill, "Personal Factors Associated with Leadership: A Survey of the Literature," *The Journal of Psychology* 25 (1948): 63.

19. For details, see Kurt Lewin, Ronald Lippitt, and Ralph K. White, "Patterns of Aggressive Behavior in Experimentally Created 'Social Climates,'" *The Journal of Social Psychology* 10 (May 1939): 271–299.

20. For a useful summary of this research, see Edwin A. Fleishman, "Twenty Years of Consideration and Structure," in Edwin A. Fleishman and James G. Hunt, eds., *Current Developments in the Study of Leadership* (Carbondale: Southern Illinois University Press, 1973), pp. 1–40.

21. The two most popular extensions of the Ohio State Leadership studies may be found in: Robert R. Blake and Jane S. Mouton, *The Managerial Grid* (Houston, Tex.: Gulf Publishing, 1964);

and William J. Reddin, *Managerial Effectiveness* (New York: McGraw-Hill, 1970).

22. Abraham K. Korman, "'Consideration,' 'Initiating Structure,' and Organizational Criteria—A Review," *Personnel Psychology* 19 (Winter 1966): 349–361.

23. Fred E. Fiedler, "Job Engineering for Effective Leadership: A New Approach," *Management Review* 66 (September 1977): 29.

24. Fred E. Fiedler and Martin M. Chemers, *Leadership and Effective Management* (Glenview, Ill.: Scott, Foresman, 1974), p. 91.

25. Stogdill, "Personal Factors Associated with Leadership," p. 64.

26. Abraham Zaleznik, "Managers and Leaders: Are They Different?" *Harvard Business Review* 55 (May–June 1977): 76.

27. See Paul Rosenkrantz, Susan Vogel, Helen Bee, Inge Broverman, and Donald Broverman, "Sex-Role Stereotypes and Self-Concepts in College Students," *Journal of Consulting and Clinical Psychology* 32 (June 1968): 287–295.

28. Virginia E. Schein, "The Relationship Between Sex Role Stereotypes and Requisite Management Characteristics," *Journal of Applied Psychology* 57 (April 1973): 99.

29. For details, see J. Brad Chapman, "Comparison of Male and Female Leadership Styles," *Academy of Management Journal* 18 (September 1975): 645–650.

Chapter 15

Improving Job Performance

The creation of a stimulating, productive, and satisfying work environment can be beneficial for both management and workers if honest concern is shown for all parties involved.

Richard M. Steers and
Lyman W. Porter

There are no simple, cookbook formulas for working with people.

Keith Davis

LEARNING OBJECTIVES

When you finish reading this chapter, you should be able to

○ Distinguish between extrinsic and intrinsic rewards.
○ List and discuss four ways of improving job performance with rewards.
○ Explain what the A $\longrightarrow$ B $\longrightarrow$ C relationship means in behavior modification.
○ Discuss what occurs during each step in the three-step behavior modification process.
○ Explain how job enrichment counteracts boredom and alienation by introducing the ingredients of a decent job.
○ Explain what management can do about stress, cardiovascular disease, and alcohol abuse, three major threats to employee health.

No matter how one chooses to look at organized effort, people stand out as the key variable. Without people there would be no organizations, although more than one disgusted manager has remarked, "This would be a great operation if it weren't for the people in it." Organizational success hinges largely on the people involved. Uninterested, uncaring, apathetic, or alienated people constitute a major roadblock to organizational success. In contrast, enthusiastic, involved, and committed people are a valuable resource and a prime determinant of organizational survival and success. Since situations can bring out either the best or worst in people, it is up to management to create work environments that enhance rather than stifle human potential. In this chapter we review techniques for bringing out the best in people and improving their job performance.

MOTIVATION THROUGH REWARDS

All workers, including volunteers who donate their time to worthy causes, expect to be rewarded for their contributions. *Rewards* may be defined broadly as the material and psychological payoffs for doing something. These payoffs can have an immense impact on how long and hard someone works. A person who is pleased with the consequences of work is likely to put forth more effort than someone who feels shortchanged or cheated in some way. Managers have found that job performance and satisfaction can be enhanced by proper administration of rewards.

EXTRINSIC VERSUS INTRINSIC REWARDS

There are two different categories of rewards. *Extrinsic rewards* are payoffs granted to the individual by other people. Examples include money, fringe benefits, promotions, recognition, status symbols, and praise. The second category is called *intrinsic rewards*, which are self-granted and internally experienced payoffs. Among intrinsic rewards are a sense of accomplishment and feelings of achievement, self-esteem, and self-actualization. Typically, these two types of reward are not mutually exclusive. For example, employees often experience a psychological lift when they complete a big project, in addition to reaping material benefits.

Although behavioral scientists generally agree about the distinction between extrinsic and intrinsic rewards, they vigorously disagree over which kind of reward is more effective in motivating people to work harder. Maslow and other motivation theorists have stressed the importance of intrinsic rewards because they fulfill higher-level ego and psychological-growth needs (self-esteem and self-actualization). According to this view, high motivation comes from working at a challenging job that triggers feelings of self-worth. More recently, learning theorists impressed with the power of Thorndike's law of effect have pointed to the practical value of shaping performance improvement with extrinsic rewards. This second group feels that by tying rewards such as pay, promotion, status symbols, and praise directly to performance, a motivational effect is created.

Recent research evidence has further confused the issue. Laboratory studies have shown that the quickest way to kill the intrinsic reward a person derives from doing a task is to start paying the person for doing it.[1] In other words, material rewards seem to take the enjoyment out of doing something for the fun of it. For example, many amateur painters find that painting is not as much fun once they go professional and depend on it for a living. The debate over extrinsic versus intrinsic rewards goes on, but most managers have no choice but to rely heavily on extrinsic rewards, because many of today's jobs are short on properties that are intrinsically motivating.

IMPROVING JOB PERFORMANCE WITH REWARDS   Although it will not resolve the theoretical debate over extrinsic and intrinsic rewards, a practical compromise is possible. Basic to this compromise is the realization that both types of rewards are necessary and desirable; both types need to be administered appropriately. The basic motivation and learning theories discussed in Chapter 11 provide at least four tips for administering extrinsic rewards in a way that makes intrinsic rewards possible.

Rewards must satisfy individual needs   Whether it is a pay raise or a pat on the back, there is no motivational impact unless the reward satisfies an existing need. Not all people need the same things, and one individual may need different things at different times. Money is a powerful motivator for those who seek security through material wealth. But the promise of more money may mean very little to someone who seeks the ego stimulation associated with challenging work. An innovative and extremely promising way of improving the match between individual needs and extrinsic rewards is cafeteria compensation.

Cafeteria compensation is a plan for allowing each employee to determine the makeup of his or her fringe benefit package. Since fringe benefits can range as high as 50 percent of total compensation, the motivating potential of such a privilege can be sizable. According to *Business Week*:

> Under these plans, employers provide minimal "core" coverage in life and health insurance, vacations, and pensions. The employee buys additional benefits to suit his own needs, using credits based on salary, service, and age.

The elderly bachelor, for instance, may pass up the maternity coverage he would receive, willy-nilly, under conventional plans and "buy" additional pension contributions instead. The mother whose children are covered by her husband's employee health insurance policy may choose legal and dental care insurance instead.[2]

Of course, this type of fine tuning of rewards is restricted mostly to larger organizations that can afford the extra bookkeeping. Nonetheless, cafeteria compensation is an encouraging step toward fitting rewards to people, rather than vice versa.

One must believe that effort will lead to reward   According to the expectancy theory of motivation, an employee will not try for an attractive award unless it is perceived as attainable. For example, the promise of an expense-paid trip to Hawaii for being the leading salesperson will prompt only those who feel they have a decent chance of winning to go out and sell more. Those who see no chance of winning will not be motivated to put forth the extra effort.

Rewards must be equitable   Something is equitable if people perceive it to be fair and just. Each of us carries a pair of equity scales in our heads with which we weigh equity balances and imbalances. Figure 15.1 shows one scale for personal equity, and another for social equity. The personal equity scale tests the relationship between effort expended and rewards received. The social equity scale compares our own effort/reward ratio with that of someone else in the same situation. Interestingly, research has demonstrated that inequity is perceived by those who are overpaid as well as by those who are underpaid.[3] Since perceived inequity is associated with feelings of dissatisfaction and anger, jealousy, or guilt, inequitable reward schemes tend to be counterproductive.

Rewards must be linked with performance   Ideally, an if-then relationship should exist between work and rewards. If the work is accomplished satisfactorily, then the reward should be granted. This relationship is especially important for pay, because it is the universal extrinsic reward for work.[4] In recent years, however, there has been a trend away from pay based on work accomplished in favor of pay based on the passage of time. Time-based pay includes hourly wages, annual salaries, and pay raises tied to seniority (time with the organization). In contrast, performance-based pay includes piece rates, merit pay, and commissions.

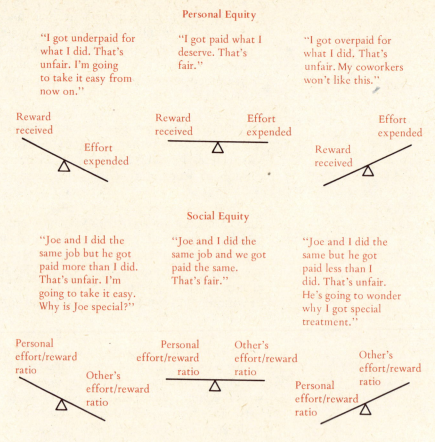

FIGURE 15.1
The calculation of
personal and social equity

The trend toward time-based pay has stirred the concern of some behavioral scientists. They feel that when an employee's pay is tied to the passage of time, there is little incentive to work harder. Is the answer a return to piece rates, in which a fixed amount of pay is given for a specific unit of output? Not really. In our modern, service-oriented economy many people work at jobs lacking readily identifiable units of output. Imagine the difficulty of paying a bank president or teacher on a piece rate basis. However, as two experts on job performance have observed:

It does not make much sense to pay wages and salaries without obtaining some sort of motivational return. Where incentive systems are appropriate, the organization would be well advised to allocate and utilize at least a portion of its wage-increase money for merit compensation.[5]

In short, managers need to make sure that those who give a little extra get a little extra.

<table>
<tr><td>**BEHAVIOR**
MODIFICATION</td><td>

Frustrated by years of searching for the elusive internal causes of job performance, a growing number of theorists and managers have turned to applied learning theory. The roots of this perspective can be traced to a pair of pioneering psychologists, John B. Watson and Edward L. Thorndike, who did their work during the early twentieth century. From Watson came the advice to concentrate on observable behavior rather than on internal states. Those who prefer to deal strictly in terms of observable behavior instead of hypothetical inner states such as needs, motives, purposes, or expectations are called *behaviorists*. From Thorndike, as we discussed in an earlier chapter, came an appreciation of the way in which consequences control behavior. In accordance with Thorndike's law of effect, favorable consequences encourage behavior and unfavorable consequences discourage behavior. However, it remained for B. F. Skinner, the noted Harvard psychologist, to integrate Watson's and Thorndike's contributions into a precise technology of behavior change.

</td></tr>
</table>

Skinner is the father of operant conditioning.[6] *Operant conditioning* is the study of how behavior is controlled by the surrounding environment. While some find Skinner's replacement of self-control with environmental control repulsive and dehumanizing, there is little argument about the fact that operant conditioning does occur. Much of our behavior is the product of environmental shaping. But can operant conditioning techniques be systematically managed to change everyday behavior? Advocates of behavior modification say yes.

Behavior modification (B. Mod.) is the practical application of Skinnerian operant conditioning techniques to everyday behavior problems. The basic purpose of behavior modification is to systematically manage the controlling environment to get people to do the right things more often and the wrong things less often. This is accomplished by managing the antecedents (prior events) and consequences of observable behavior. The special relationship between environmental antecedents and consequences and observable behavior is at the heart of B. Mod.

<table>
<tr><td>**THE ABCs OF**
BEHAVIOR
MODIFICATION</td><td>

If we see a coworker come in late every time the boss is out of town on business, we might conclude that this individual has a bad attitude or is dissatisfied because of unfulfilled needs. Or we might label the individual inherently lazy, sneaky, or unethical. But from a

</td></tr>
</table>

behavior modification perspective, each of these explanations is a waste of time because each involves a hypothesis about what is going on inside the person, and that can be hard to measure or change. Instead, B. Mod. calls for an analysis of the interaction between the individual's observable behavior and the surrounding environment. More precisely, it calls for identification of the *Antecedent* (A) ⟶ *Behavior* (B) ⟶ *Consequence* (C) relationship.

An *antecedent* is an environmental cue that prompts an individual to behave in a certain manner. Antecedents do not force an individual to behave in a prescribed manner, as a hot stove forces you to withdraw your hand when you touch it. Rather, through experience we learn to read antecedents as signals telling us it is time to behave in a certain way to get what we want or avoid what we don't want. In our example of the tardy coworker, the antecedent for coming in late is the absence of the boss. If the boss is scheduled to be at work, the employee comes in on time. But if the boss is scheduled to be out of town, the employee reports in late. Hence the antecedent may be said to control the behavior.

The B portion of the A ⟶ B ⟶ C relationship stands for behavior. Instead of focusing on the individual's personality, a B. Mod. practitioner pinpoints a specific observable behavior. In this case, the behavior of coming in late is the key. There is little room for subjective interpretations of objective behavior in this approach. The person is either on time or late, period. Many managers who are accustomed to using terms such as *need* and *purpose* or various unflattering labels have a difficult time simply looking at behavior. But, according to one behaviorist writer: "No matter how we look at it, management is getting other people to do things that have to be done. It is clearly a practice that implies we are going to have to manage other people's *behavior*."[7] (Emphasis added)

Again, in line with Thorndike's law of effect, *consequences* encourage or discourage behavior. Completing our A ⟶ B ⟶ C analysis of the tardy employee, the consequence is favorable because the employee gets away with coming in late. This obviously favorable consequence simply encourages the employee to come in late the next time the boss is scheduled to be out of town (antecedent). Now if the boss returns from a scheduled trip early and yells at the employee who shows up late, this orderly A ⟶ B ⟶ C relationship would be upset. The employee would think twice about coming in late next time the boss is scheduled to be out of town.

By viewing job performance in A ⟶ B ⟶ C terms, managers are in a position to begin to improve performance through behavior modification.

MODIFYING BEHAVIOR

B. Mod. proponents claim that managers might as well learn how to modify behavior systematically because they do it in one way or another already. As an expert in the area has pointed out:

> Managers who deliberately set out to change employee behavior and admit this are much farther ahead of their colleagues who motivate employees to "change their attitudes" or "affect their personalities." . . . Managers who use behavioral technology to get their staff to do the job are merely doing with foresight and in a carefully planned fashion what they formerly did haphazardly—changing employee behavior.[8]

For example, a manager who attempts to criticize and threaten a subordinate into working harder is swinging a crude caveman's club at a behavior problem that requires skillful management of the A ⟶ B ⟶ C relationship. The three-step behavior problem-solving process illustrated in Figure 15.2 points the way to more effective management of behavior problems.

Step 1: Pinpoint the behavior problem   If employees don't know how to do their job, a training problem exists. In contrast, when employees know how to do their job but don't do it, a behavior problem exists. A training program is needed in the first instance, but B. Mod. is appropriate in the second. Since behavior modification is designed to make desirable behavior occur more often and undesirable less often, two questions need to be asked when pinpointing behavior problems.

FIGURE 15.2
The basic behavior modification process

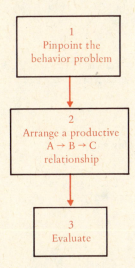

1. Is the individual engaging in the *right* behavior too seldom?
2. Is the individual engaging in the *wrong* behavior too often?

An example of the first situation would be the employee who comes up with an excellent suggestion only infrequently. An example of the second would be a committee member who disrupts meetings with too many humorous comments. Many job performance situations can be perceived in terms of precisely opposite behavior. Is a person with a tardiness problem late too often or on time too seldom? As we will see a little later, this can be a significant distinction when it comes to modifying behavior.

Step 2: Arrange a productive A $\longrightarrow$ B $\longrightarrow$ C relationship Unproductive A $\longrightarrow$ B $\longrightarrow$ C relationships develop because antecedents and consequences support rather than discourage undesirable behavior. For example, in the first sequence in Figure 15.3, the combination of a sarcastic antecedent and a positive consequence encourages poor performance. In the second sequence, the antecedent is fine, but the consequence is negative. Thus good performance is unintentionally discouraged. By stepping back from the situation and adopting an A $\longrightarrow$ B $\longrightarrow$ C perspective, the manager can arrange the antecedents and consequences to support good performance. The third sequence in Figure 15.3 illustrates a productive A $\longrightarrow$ B $\longrightarrow$ C relationship.

FIGURE 15.3
Antecedents and consequences determine the nature of future behavior

ANTECEDENT $\longrightarrow$	BEHAVIOR $\longrightarrow$	CONSEQUENCE	BEHAVIORAL OUTCOME
"I suppose you don't have the Jones report completed yet."	"No way, I'm swamped with work."	"That's OK, don't worry about it."	Employee continues to make excuses rather than getting the job done on time.
"How are you coming on the Jones report?"	"Here it is, a whole day early."	"I see; now you can finish Mary's project."	Employee stops handing work in early because it does not pay.
"How are you coming on the Jones report?"	"Here it is, a whole day early."	"Good work! I know you enjoy working on the new accounts. Why don't you spend the rest of the day doing that."	Employee continues to complete work early because it leads to praise and preferred assignments.

Although often overlooked, the management of antecedents is a practical and relatively simple way of encouraging good performance. As Table 15.1 indicates, there are two ways to go about managing antecedents. Barriers can be removed; helpful aids can be provided. These steps simply ensure that the path to good performance is clearly marked and free of obstacles.

Managing the consequences of job performance is more complex than dealing strictly with antecedents. This is true because there are four different kinds of consequence. Two encourage behavior while two others discourage behavior.

The two types of consequence that encourage behavior are called positive reinforcement and negative reinforcement. *Positive reinforcement* is the process of encouraging a specific behavior by presenting a consequence the individual finds pleasing. For example, a machine operator who maintains a clean work area because he is praised for doing so has experienced positive reinforcement. As the term implies, positive reinforcement reinforces or builds behavior in a positive manner.

Negative reinforcement is the process of encouraging a specific behavior by withdrawing or terminating something the individual finds displeasing. For example, children learn the power of negative

	BARRIERS Remove Barriers That Prevent or Hinder the Completion of a Good Job.	AIDS Provide Helpful Aids That Enhance the Opportunity to Do a Good Job
TABLE 15.1 **Managing antecedents by** **removing barriers and** **providing helpful aids**	○ Unrealistic objectives, plans, schedules, or deadlines. ○ Uncooperative or distracting coworkers. ○ Training deficiencies. ○ Contradictory or confusing rules. ○ Inadequate or inappropriate tools. ○ Conflicting orders from two or more superiors.	○ Challenging, yet obtainable objectives. ○ Clear and realistic plans. ○ Understandable instructions. ○ Constructive suggestions, hints, or tips. ○ Clear and generally acceptable work rules. ○ Realistic schedules and deadlines. ○ Friendly reminders. ○ Posters or signs with helpful tips. ○ Easy-to-use forms. ○ Nonthreatening questions about progress.

reinforcement early in life when they discover that the quickest way to get something from their parents is to cry and scream until they get it. In effect, the parents are *negatively* reinforced for complying with their child's demands because the child then terminates the crying and screaming. In a social context, negative reinforcement amounts to blackmail. "Do what I want or I will continue to make your life miserable" is the byword of the person who relies on negative reinforcement to encourage behavior.

The two types of consequence for discouraging behavior are called extinction and punishment. *Extinction* is the process of discouraging a specific behavior by ignoring it. For example, managers sometimes find that the best way to keep subordinates from asking redundant questions is simply not to answer them. *Punishment* is the process of discouraging a specific behavior, either by presenting an undesirable consequence or by withdrawing something desirable. For example, a manager may punish a tardy employee by assigning the individual to a dirty job or docking the individual's pay.

It is important to remember that positive and negative reinforcement, extinction, and punishment are all direct consequences of behavior. If they come *before* the behavior, control becomes impossible. For example, if a manager gives a subordinate a cash bonus before a difficult task is completed, the probability of the task ever being completed drops significantly. The incentive has been lost. Behavior modification works only when there is a clear connection between a specific way of behaving and a given consequence.

Step 3: Evaluate   Evaluation of a behavior modification program is relatively straightforward and simple. If the intent is to get someone to engage in a particular behavior more often, simple observation will reveal whether this has happened. Conversely, a behavior that has been purposely discouraged will occur less often if the program has been successful. In the event that either a desirable behavior does not occur more often or that an undesirable behavior does not occur less often, the manager must go back to step 2 and try another A ⟶ B ⟶ C arrangement.

GUIDELINES FOR SUCCESSFUL BEHAVIOR MODIFICATION

For two very good reasons, there are no guarantees of success with B. Mod. programs. First, human behavior is highly variable, and workable A ⟶ B ⟶ C relationships vary from person to person. We are not all under the control of the same antecedents and consequences. Second, managers simply do not control all antecedents and consequences that may affect job behavior. For example, attention and laughter from coworkers reinforces counterproductive clowning. As indicated in the previous chapter, informal communication is largely beyond the direct control of management. The trick is to link desired consequences to working, so that the employee learns that working pays off more than clowning. In effect, the manager attempts to win a reinforcement tug-of-war with the employee's coworkers. In spite of these limitations, managers can enhance the effectiveness of their B. Mod. programs by following three basic guidelines. They are (1) focus on what is *right* with job performance, (2) use positive reinforcement whenever possible, and (3) schedule positive reinforcement appropriately.

Focus on what is right with job performance   Behavior modification proponents prefer to build up desirable behaviors rather than tear down undesirable ones. Since productive behaviors need to be encouraged, managers should focus on the positive aspects of job performance when arranging productive A $\longrightarrow$ B $\longrightarrow$ C relationships. This stance is preferred because it creates a healthy, positive work climate rather than an unhealthy "Aha, I caught you!" climate.

> In an arbitrarily punitive supervisory climate, subordinates are forced into an immature posture of constantly looking over their shoulders for signs of the boss. Subordinates in a positive supervisory climate, in marked contrast, actively pursue stated objectives in a mature manner.[9]

A positive supervisory climate is created by making it clear what behaviors are required to get the job done and supporting those productive behaviors with helpful antecedents and positive reinforcement.

The Emery Air Freight experience shows the power of a supportive supervisory climate. By following a relatively simple, four-step, B. Mod. program, Emery Air Freight was able to save $3 million in three years in its warehouse operations.

1. *Pinpoint key performance-related behaviors*   A performance audit at Emery found that the air freight container utilization rate was only 45 percent. This rate came as quite a surprise to the managers, who had believed the rate to be around 90 percent. Clearly, there was plenty of room for improvement in the behavior of loading containers before putting them on board the planes.

CONVERSATION WITH . . .

Sharon K. Agatep
General Operator Services Director
General Telephone Company of
   California
Santa Monica, California

Photo by Barnaba-Rolf

PERSONAL BACKGROUND

Sharon Agatep joined General Telephone Company while working toward her B.A. in psychology/sociology at Whittier College. During the last five years, she has taken postgraduate courses in business administration at Claremont College and the University of Southern California. Sharon has spent fourteen years in management, having held a number of positions in personnel and other operating departments. In her present capacity, she is responsible for directing and administering the personnel and activities concerned with providing toll, directory assistance, and other operator services companywide. Sharon Agatep is in charge of thirty-seven toll and directory assistance offices throughout the state of California encompassing 4,000 employees and an annual budget of $50 million. Since her department is highly labor intensive, Sharon has had to develop her expertise in labor relations, Equal Employment Opportunity, and other personnel functions.

QUOTABLE QUOTES

Can you describe how you went about solving a particularly difficult managerial problem recently?

Ms. Agatep: An employee who was placed in my organization reporting directly to me was extremely unhappy because she felt she should have been promoted to a higher position. She was emotionally disturbed and brought to the department a very negative attitude, which had an impact on her immediate staff as well as the rest of the department. With a great deal of counseling in a straightforward approach, I was able to show her how counterproductive her behavior was and that ultimately it could destroy her existing position and future career opportunities. She has greatly improved her attitude and has become a very effective manager.

What do you think it takes to be a successful manager today?

Ms. Agatep: It is imperative that we as managers identify the employees' skills as well as their desires to ensure proper placement of our greatest assets.

2. *Establish a realistic output objective* After careful studies of the container loading operation, managers at Emery established an overall utilization-rate objective of 95 percent. More modest objectives were formulated for those with very poor performance records.

3. *Provide for self-feedback* Emery dockworkers were given a specially prepared feedback form for keeping track of their container utilization rates. When their daily rate rose above 45 percent, they were the first ones to know that they were on the right track. This feedback form permitted self-reinforcement and self-management.

4. *Positively reinforce improvement* Emery managers monitored the dockworkers' feedback sheets and positively reinforced any improvement with praise and other desired consequences. As a result, the 95 percent utilization objective was achieved in a matter of days with considerable savings to the company.[10]

A brief A $\longrightarrow$ B $\longrightarrow$ C analysis helps highlight the significant elements of Emery Air Freight's very successful behavior modification program. Both the realistic objectives and the feedback forms were antecedents pointing the way to better performance. Loading the air freight containers more fully was the specific behavior. Finally, performance improvement documented on the feedback forms and supervisory praise and recognition were the positive consequences. This particular arrangement proved to be a productive one indeed for Emery Air Freight.

Use positive reinforcement whenever possible Behaviorists claim that in the long run positive reinforcement is the most effective way of modifying behavior. Extinction is thought to work too slowly. Negative reinforcement and punishment, although they may produce rapid behavior change, tend to be plagued by undesirable side effects. Among those side effects are:

1. *Inadvertent permanent damage to behavior*   For example, a manager who thoughtlessly laughs at a new employee's bright idea in front of others may accidentally stifle future contributions.

2. *Temporary suppression of undesirable behavior*   As the old saying goes, when the cat's away, the mice will play. This problem plagues managers who insist on using punishment and negative reinforcement to get things done. Since the manager's presence becomes an antecedent signaling the threat of negative consequences, employees only work when the manager rides herd on them. Things tend to fall apart when punitive managers turn their backs.

3. *Emotional outbursts*   People tend to resent the coercive nature of negative reinforcement and punishment. Consequently, negative managers must cope with unproductive fear, resentment, and retaliation.[11]

When positive reinforcement is tied to productive behavior, employees work hard to complete the job in order to enjoy desirable consequences. Table 15.2 suggests many positive consequences. Since positive consequences can lose their incentive effect after prolonged use, managers need to use imagination when arranging A $\longrightarrow$ B $\longrightarrow$ C relationships.

Schedule positive reinforcement appropriately   Both the type and the timing of consequences are important in B. Mod. When a productive behavior is first being tried out by an employee, a continuous schedule of reinforcement is appropriate. Under *continuous reinforcement* every instance of the desired behavior is reinforced. For example, a bank manager who is training a new loan officer to handle a difficult type of account praises the loan officer for every successful transaction until the behavior is firmly established. Once the loan officer seems able to handle the transaction, the bank manager can switch to an intermittent schedule of reinforcement. As the term implies, *intermittent reinforcement* calls for reinforcing some, rather than all, of the desired responses. One way to appreciate the power of intermittent reinforcement is to think of the enthusiasm with which people play slot machines; these gambling devices pay off on an unpredictable intermittent schedule. In the same way, occasional reinforcement of established productive behaviors with meaningful positive consequences is an extremely effective management technique.

CRITICISM OF BEHAVIOR MODIFICATION

Although B. Mod. is a relative newcomer to the management scene, it has stirred more than its fair share of controversy. Pointing to successful applications with attendance, job performance, and job safety problems,[12] proponents claim that a working knowledge of B. Mod. is a must for managers who are responsible for getting things done through others. They praise B. Mod. for being simple, logical, and theoretically uncluttered. Most of all, they claim it works.

Interestingly, most critics of B. Mod. do not argue with the claim that it works. What offends them are the apparently mechanical assumptions it makes about the relationship between the individual and the environment. The critics dislike the manner in which behavior modification advocates conveniently disregard what goes on inside the person. The following comment by a severe critic of B. Mod. sums up this perspective:

> I am unalterably opposed to behaviorism, not because I am biased, but because it flies in the face of the most elementary and self-evident facts about human beings: that they possess consciousness and that their minds are their guides to action, or more fundamentally: their means of survival. I am not against the judicious use of contingent rewards and punishments; it is the behaviorist philosophy of man that I oppose.[13]

In the final analysis, it is for managers themselves to decide whether B. Mod. techniques are appropriate or inappropriate.

To a large extent, behavior modification involves improving job performance by changing the individual to fit the job. But a second course of action is open to management. Sometimes it is possible and desirable to change the job to fit the individual. This alternative approach is called work reform.

WORK REFORM

The average adult spends approximately two thousand hours a year on the job, half of his or her waking life. A *job*, as the term is used here, is the specific task or set of tasks an individual performs while earning a living. Challenging and interesting jobs can be a stimulating addition to one's life. Boring and tedious jobs, however, can become a serious threat to the general quality of one's life, not to mention one's physical and mental health. Unfortunately, social observers claim to have detected a downward trend in the quality of

MONETARY	SOCIAL	
A pay raise	Praise	Compliment
A cash bonus	Friendly greeting	Feedback on performance
Company stock	Recognition	
Fringe benefits	Request for suggestions	Invitation to coffee or lunch
Paid vacations		
Paid personal holiday (e.g., birthday)	Pat on the back	Coaching
	Smiles and other nonverbal recognition	Recognition in company publication
Profit sharing		
Trading stamps (green stamps, etc.)	"Bull sessions" about family, hobbies, etc.	Discussion of satisfactory work progress
Coupons redeemable at local stores	Discussion of favorite topics (sports, etc.)	Request for advice
Movie or dinner theater passes		
Sporting event tickets or season passes	Expression of appreciation in front of superiors, peers	Request for informal recommendations
	Discussion of anticipated problems	Explanation of company or unit mission
		Notes of thanks

Part of this table is adapted by permission from *Organizational Behavior Modification*, p. 101, by Fred Luthans and Robert Kreitner. Copyright © 1975 by Scott, Foresman and Company.

work life. This trend prompted Studs Terkel to introduce his book *Working*, a collection of perceptive interviews with workers from all walks of life, with the following stinging appraisal:

> This book, being about work, is, by its very nature, about violence—to the spirit as well as to the body. It is about ulcers as well as accidents, about shouting matches as well as fistfights, about nervous breakdowns as well as kicking the dog around. It is, above all (or beneath all), about daily humiliations. To survive the day is triumph enough for the walking wounded among the great many of us.[14]

The big question is, How valid is this pessimistic appraisal? Is it a lopsided view of reality, or is it representative of the general attitude toward work?

TABLE 15.2 (*cont.*)

STATUS SYMBOLS	OPPORTUNITY
Formal recognition as employee of the year, month, or week	Job with more responsibility
	Job rotation
Special commendation	Opportunity to explain "great" ideas
Promotion	Early time off with pay
Wall plaque	Extended breaks
Desk accessories	Extended lunch period
Private parking space	Opportunity to participate in important discussions, decisions
Special training	
Private office or improved work area	Opportunity to work on personal project on company time
Rings, trophy, watch	Opportunity to use company tools or facilities for personal project
	Use of company recreation facilities
	Time off with pay to work on community projects
	Time for job-related creative expression
	Time off for physical fitness programs

A special study commissioned by the federal government reported in 1973 that it detected a strong undercurrent of dissatisfaction among American workers. According to the report:

> Over the last two decades, one of the most reliable single indicators of job dissatisfaction has been the response to the question: "What type of work would you try to get into if you could start all over again?" Most significantly, of a cross section of white-collar workers (including professionals), only 43% would voluntarily choose the same work that they were doing, and only 24% of a cross section of blue-collar workers would choose the same kind of work if given another chance. . . . [15]

Citing widespread dissatisfaction with work, a growing number of management theorists are calling for *work reform*, which is a systematic attempt to improve the quality of work life by enhancing the challenge of the work. The purpose of this section is to examine the dilemma of specialized labor, identify the ingredients of a decent job, and introduce a specific work reform technique called job enrichment.

SPECIALIZATION OF LABOR: A DILEMMA

Frederick W. Taylor's scientific management movement created an undying faith in the notion that the key to greater productivity was increased specialization of labor. This notion proved valid for many years. Work was divided and subdivided so that work forces of unskilled laborers could achieve high levels of productivity. Until 1950, at least, the net results were less waste, more predictable performance, and greater output.

In recent years, however, the trend toward greater specialization of labor has been challenged. The basis for this challenge is the "human factor." Costly tardiness, absenteeism, more grievances, higher turnover, strikes, and even sabotage have begun to offset the traditional economies of specialization. These behavioral problems are emotional reactions to tedious, boring, and monotonous work. The relationship between unit cost and specialization is illustrated in Figure 15.4. The *boredom and alienation barrier* is the point at which behavioral problems such as absenteeism and turnover caused by overspecialized jobs drive up the cost of producing each unit of output.

It is difficult to tell what proportion of our labor force is alienated by overspecialized jobs. Highly publicized cases of revolt against assembly-line boredom have created a feeling of impending crisis. One well-known situation developed at General Motors' Lordstown, Ohio, assembly plant in early 1972. When operating at full

FIGURE 15.4
The relationship between specialization of labor and unit cost

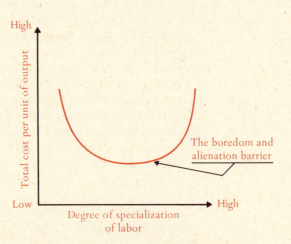

capacity, the newly completed GM plant could turn out 100 Vega automobiles per hour. It was a brilliant example of production engineering, by traditional standards. Work along the assembly line was so highly specialized that the average job took only 36 seconds to complete. *Business Week* summed up what it called the Lordstown syndrome in the following manner:

> Workers now complain that the latest automation technology has made much speedier production possible. But the work is less creative and just as physically arduous. Better educated workers find the adjustment hard to make. The result is more absenteeism, a higher work turnover, and less quality in the work turned out.[16]

GM management saw things differently. According to the chief executive officer of GM, the mass media blew the whole matter out of proportion. He insisted that GM's assembly-line employees are highly paid (more than the average teacher), receive generous benefits of over $3,000 per year, are twenty-three times safer at work than anywhere else, and are generally satisfied.[17]

Although the Lordstown syndrome has shown up elsewhere, the problem appears to call for caution and problem solving rather than panic. After all, only a small fraction of today's employees work on assembly lines. Most people work in jobs providing services. But the trend toward greater specialization is slowly creeping into service and higher-level jobs as well. All managers need to be aware of the specialization of labor dilemma, and they should try to create a realistic balance between productivity and employee welfare when designing jobs.

THE INGREDIENTS OF A DECENT JOB

As we saw in Chapter 12, people join work organizations for economic security, social support, and opportunity for growth. Therefore, a *decent job* may be defined as one that satisfies these basic needs. A decent job fosters the development of a healthy personality. Many of us have firsthand experience with jobs that dehumanize the individual through tedious repetition and insulting lack of challenge. Realizing that individuals tend to work longer and harder at interesting and challenging jobs, managers should try to provide every employee with a decent job. The ingredients of a decent job are meaningfulness, responsibility, and knowledge of results.[18] Each deserves close examination.

Meaningfulness   A job is considered meaningful if the answer to each of the following three questions is yes. (1) Does the individual perform a number of different challenging activities? (2) Does the individual work on a whole piece of work rather than on an insignificant portion of a larger job? (3) Does the individual's job have an important impact on the success of the organization or the welfare of society in general?

Let's apply these three tests to two very different jobs. One involves the operation of a punch press in which silver-dollar-sized disks are punched out of a large piece of 3/16-inch sheet steel. The punch is triggered by a foot pedal. The second job is that of a project manager for a public utility that serves the electrical, gas, and water needs for a major Western city. This project manager is in charge of the $28 million conversion of a power plant from oil to coal.

In terms of meaningfulness, how does the punch press job measure up? Test #1: It took the operator less than five minutes to master the job; it has been the same repetitious, boring, ear-shattering routine ever since. Test #2: The punch press operator, after seven months on the job, still isn't sure what is done with the metal disks. Test #3: Since the operator doesn't know why the job is being performed, there is little feeling of importance about the job. The operator likes to joke around with coworkers about who has the dumbest job. The job is a source of money and nothing else. It's just a matter of waiting for something better to come along.

What about the meaningfulness of the project manager's job? Test #1: Each day is like a hurdle race, and each hurdle is different. The project manager has a hand in virtually every aspect of the conversion project, including planning, engineering, cost accounting, construction, and personnel administration. According to the project manager, the job keeps one too busy to complain; it's an endless challenge just to keep on top of everything. Test #2: The project manager is in charge of the whole project. It is up to the project manager to put all the pieces together. Test #3: Because the conversion will enable the utility to continue producing a reliable source of economical electricity, the project manager firmly believes it is one of the most important jobs in town. Reflecting on the position, the project manager does not even see it as a job; it is a way of life. Each day on the job adds excitement and meaning to life.

It is obvious which of these jobs has the potential to get the individual involved, excited, and committed to doing the best job possible. Virtually all jobs can be analyzed for meaningfulness in this manner.

Responsibility   A feeling of personal responsibility is the direct product of autonomy. According to a team of organizational behaviorists, *autonomy* is . . .

the degree to which the job gives the worker freedom, independence, and discretion in scheduling work and determining how he will carry it out. People in highly autonomous jobs know that they are personally responsible for successes and failures.[19]

In short, employees who actively *control* their work situation, rather than passively follow orders, are autonomous and hence feel personally responsible for their work. The project manager's job, just discussed, represents a high degree of responsibility.

Knowledge of results   Knowledge of results depends on feedback to the person doing the job. Some jobs, such as sales, have a high degree of feedback built into the job. A successful sale tells the salesperson how to sell, and lost sales make it clear how not to sell. Other jobs lack self-contained feedback. Teachers, for example, often complain about a lack of feedback. After all, many years must pass before grade school children can demonstrate their ability to cope with adult life.

In addition to getting feedback from the work itself, an employee may also receive feedback from superiors. Verbal criticism and praise are very powerful forms of supervisory feedback. Everyone learns through feedback, but all too often people are forced to work in a feedback vacuum. "A feedback vacuum exists when employees do not know where they stand on a day-to-day basis relative to organizational goal attainment."[20] The feedback vacuum must be filled if full human potential is to be realized.

The ingredients of a decent job are not an either/or proposition; each is a matter of degree. One may have a somewhat meaningful job with limited responsibility and receive occasional feedback. For greater job satisfaction and job performance, the more of each ingredient the better.

MAKING THE BEST OF HIGHLY SPECIALIZED JOBS   For technological and other reasons managers sometimes must improve job performance in spite of highly specialized jobs. The work itself cannot be made intrinsically rewarding, but the worker's expectations can be made more realistic, and the circumstances of the job can sometimes be improved. There are at least four options available. They are realistic job previews, job rotation, job enlargement, and limited exposure.

Realistic job previews   Dissatisfaction with the job often results from unrealized expectations. If the new employee expects an interesting and challenging job, then dissatisfaction will probably set in when actual job experience proves dull and boring. Management often creates unrealistic expectations in recruits in order to entice them to accept the job. This practice is likely to result in costly turnover. Replacements are hired and the cycle repeats itself.

A workable alternative is the *realistic job preview*, which is an honest assessment of what a new job entails. On-the-job research has demonstrated the usefulness of giving recruits a realistic preview of both the good and bad aspects of the job. Telephone operators who saw a realistic job preview film before being hired had fewer thoughts of quitting and accounted for fewer quits than a similar group of operators who viewed a traditional "good news only" recruiting film.[21] Although realistic job previews show promise, they don't solve the problem of overspecialized jobs. They merely help create a better match between the individual and the particular job.

Job rotation   As the term implies, *job rotation* is the practice of moving people from one job to another. The idea is to keep employees from becoming stagnant. If highly specialized jobs are a must, then job rotation can serve to neutralize the boredom and alienation barrier discussed earlier. Job rotation introduces a degree of novelty. The trick is to rotate people often enough to prevent boredom but not so often that they feel they are being bounced about.

Job enlargement   *Job enlargement* involves combining two or more specialized tasks. For example, an automobile assembly-line worker could mount all four wheels instead of just one. This strategy is limited by the claim of organized labor that it is simply a devious ploy for getting more work out of people. The claim is valid if the job is enlarged while pay remains the same. If pay and performance are kept in balance, job enlargement can be used to reduce overspecialization by introducing a modest degree of novelty and complexity.

Limited exposure   Still another way of coping with a highly fragmented and tedious job is to limit the individual's exposure to it. A number of organizations have promoted high performance on routine jobs by allowing individuals to earn their way off the job. This is done by establishing a challenging but fair performance standard and allowing the worker to go home when it is reached.[22] Some employees find the prospect of earning eight hours' pay for five to six hours of steady work extremely motivating.

JOB ENRICHMENT   Can anything be done to increase the motivational potential of monotonous and repetitive jobs? According to a number of behavioral researchers, the answer is yes. They contend that jobs can be enriched. Very simply, *job enrichment* occurs when a job is redesigned to include the ingredients of a decent job— meaningfulness, responsibility, and knowledge of results. In job enrichment challenge is borrowed from higher-level jobs and injected into jobs that lack challenge. Job enrichment involves a downward shift of planning, decision-making, and control responsibility. The net result is a job that means more to both the individual and to the success of the organization. The theory behind job enrichment deserves attention because it reveals why job enrichment works.

Herzberg's two-factor theory of motivation   Over twenty years ago Frederick Herzberg proposed a theory of employee motivation based on satisfaction.[23] The theory implied that a satisfied employee is motivated from within to work harder, but a dissatisfied employee is not self-motivated at all. Herzberg's research uncovered two kinds of factors associated with employee satisfaction and dissatisfaction (see Table 15.3), and so his theory has come to be called the two-factor theory.

Herzberg derived his list of dissatisfiers by asking a sample of

TABLE 15.3
Herzberg's two-factor theory of motivation

DISSATISFIERS Factors Mentioned Most Often by Dissatisfied Employees	SATISFIERS Factors Mentioned Most Often by Satisfied Employees
1. Company policy and administration	1. Achievement
2. Supervision	2. Recognition
3. Relationship with supervisor	3. Work itself
4. Work conditions	4. Responsibility
5. Salary	5. Advancement
6. Relationship with peers	6. Growth
7. Personal life	
8. Relationship with subordinates	
9. Status	
10. Security	

Adapted from: Frederick Herzberg, "One More Time: How Do You Motivate Employees?" *Harvard Business Review* 46 (January-February 1968): 57.

about two hundred accountants and engineers to describe job situations in which they had felt exceptionally bad about their jobs. An analysis of their responses revealed a consistent pattern. Dissatisfaction tended to be associated with complaints about the job context or immediate work environment.

Herzberg then derived his list of satisfiers, which supposedly motivate performance. He did so by asking the same accountants and engineers to describe job situations in which they had felt exceptionally good about their jobs. Again, a consistent pattern of response was noted. But this time different situations were described. Now the opportunity to experience achievement, receive recognition, work on an interesting job, take responsibility, and experience advancement and growth were mentioned. Herzberg observed that these satisfiers centered around the nature of the task itself. In other words, employees appeared to be motivated by job content, what they actually did all day long.

Herzberg concluded that enriched jobs would stimulate self-motivation. In other words the work itself rather than pay, supervision, or other environmental factors was the key to motivation.

Three steps toward job enrichment   If conditions are appropriate, job enrichment may be helpful in improving job performance. Among the conditions necessary for the success of a job enrichment program are top management's firm commitment to the concept of enrichment, technological feasibility, and a desire on the part of affected employees to work on more challenging jobs. When these conditions are present, the following three steps toward job enrichment can counter the boredom and alienation that stem from overspecialization.[24] Notice that these three steps are based on the ingredients of a decent job.

○ *Step 1   Meaningfulness:* Develop jobs around natural modules of work. Complete handling of a customer's situation or the completion of an entire product or unit of output by a single individual are examples of natural work modules. Indiana Bell Telephone Company enriched the highly fragmented job of compiling directories by giving each clerk the responsibility for compiling the entire directory for a given geographic area. Soon clerks came to view the directories as their own, and the efficiency of their work improved dramatically.[25]

○ *Step 2   Responsibility:* Increase the individual's control over the work module as much as the situation permits. One side effect of shifting increased responsibility to lower levels is that managers have less busy work. Managerial attention can then be directed toward planning and organizing, where it belongs. Self-control is the objective of step 2.

○ *Step 3   Knowledge of results:* Provide for frequent and accurate feedback to those who are doing the work. For example, at Volvo's Kalmar plant, automobile assemblers who work on enriched jobs are responsible for their own quality control inspection.[26] They are the first to know when corrective action is needed. According to a leading job enrichment expert, "People have a great capacity for mid-flight correction when they know where they stand."[27]

A critical appraisal of job enrichment   When job enrichment was first proposed by Frederick Herzberg as a way of providing the achievement, recognition, and responsibility necessary for motivation, it was hailed as a major breakthrough in the management of people. It acquired a reputation as a cure-all for a wide assortment of job performance ills. As time went by, however, reports surfaced of both successful and unsuccessful attempts at job enrichment. Once praised by all, job enrichment fell victim to severe criticism; the notion of job enrichment had been oversold. Still, in spite of limitations, job enrichment remains a useful work reform technique.

Researchers have reported that fear of failure and lack of confidence can stand in the way of effective job enrichment.[28] But job enrichment will work when it is carefully thought out, when management is committed to its success, and when employees desire the additional challenge.

MANAGING THE WHOLE PERSON   Managers have concentrated for so long on what goes on in an employee's mind that the employee's physical well-being has been all but forgotten. Now that stress-related disorders such as high blood pressure and ulcers, heart attack and stroke, and alcoholism have reached what experts are calling epidemic proportions, managerial concern for employee health is growing. In this section, we look at three serious threats to employee health: (1) stress, (2) cardiovascular disease, and (3) alcohol abuse. Beyond being a health threat, each is a barrier to satisfactory job performance.

STRESS   When our prehistoric ancestors were faced with a charging beast, they had two choices. They could stand and fight the beast, or they could run away from it. Their bodies were mobilized for this fight-or-flight response by a complex change in body chemistry that we have come to call *stress*. Stress helped our prehistoric ancestors survive by enabling them to fight harder or run faster than normal. Times have changed, however, and stress has become less a survival mechanism and more a health hazard. Today's employees do not face charging beasts; instead they have to deal with work overload, unreasonable deadlines, angry superiors, financial worries, and domestic difficulties. Those who respond to these modern problems as if each were a charging beast tend to suffer from the undesirable side effects of stress, such as headaches, lower back pain, indigestion, loss of sleep, ulcers, nervous tension, heart attack, and stroke. Managers need to learn how to deal with stress, both in themselves and in their subordinates.

According to Hans Selye, a leading authority on stress, "Complete freedom from stress is death."[29] Stress is inevitable. In fact, a certain amount of stress is actually desirable, because it activates and energizes people. Thus we should direct our attention to managing stress rather than to eliminating it.

Stress can be handled in one of two ways, destructively or constructively. Employees who try to escape from their uptightness with alcohol and barbiturates ("downers") walk a self-destructive path. Alcohol and drugs only serve to compound the damage of severe stress. A more constructive alternative is to follow some simple but effective self-help guidelines that spell out the word *cope*.

> Control the situation.
> Open up to others.
> Pace yourself.
> Exercise and relax.[30]

An expanded version of these coping guidelines is presented in Table 15.4. Those who learn to manage stress are healthier, happier, and more productive.

CARDIOVASCULAR DISEASE The human heart has a big job cut out for it. Day and night, during the entire life of the individual, the heart must pump approximately 100,000 times per day to keep roughly eight pints of blood recirculating through 60,000 miles of blood vessels.[31] Like any other complex system, the human circulatory system weakens and eventually breaks down. The most common circulatory failure is *cardiovascular disease*, or hardening of the arteries that supply the heart and brain with oxygen-rich blood. When heart tissue no longer receives blood because of clogged arteries, it dies; if enough of the heart dies, the individual dies of a heart attack. A person suffers a stroke when the arteries to the brain become clogged. Heart attack

TABLE 15.4
Coping with stress

Control the Situation	○ Avoid unrealistic deadlines.
	○ Do your best, but know your limits. You cannot be everything to everyone.
	○ Learn to identify and limit your exposure to stressful situations and people.
Open Up to Others	○ Freely discuss your problems, frustrations, and sources of uptightness with those who care about you.
	○ When in doubt, smile! A sincere smile often can defuse emotion and build a bridge of goodwill.
Pace Yourself	○ Plan your day on a flexible basis.
	○ Don't try to do two or more things at the same time.
	○ Counter unproductive haste by forcing yourself to slow down.
	○ Think before reacting.
	○ Live on a day-to-day basis rather than on a minute-by-minute basis.
Exercise and Relax	○ Engage in regular noncompetitive physical activity (e.g., take a ten- to twenty-minute walk each day). Those who are in good physical condition can stay in shape by jogging, swimming, riding a bike, or playing tennis, handball, or racquet ball on a regular basis (three or four times a week). See your doctor when in doubt about your physical condition.
	○ When feeling uptight, relax for ten to twenty minutes once or twice a day by following these simple steps:
	1. Sit comfortably with eyes closed in a quiet location.
	2. Slowly repeat a peaceful word or phrase over and over to yourself in your mind.
	3. Avoid distracting thoughts by keeping a passive mental attitude.

and stroke have reached epidemic proportions in industrialized countries. Today, cardiovascular disease kills more Americans, Canadians, and Western Europeans than all other causes combined. To make matters worse, heart attack and stroke are not exclusively associated with old age. Each year in the United States over 175,000 members of the labor force—people under the age of sixty-five—die of cardiovascular disease. And for every fatality, two nonfatal but disabling attacks occur. The cost to business and industry has been estimated at over $50 billion annually.[32]

A "that's too bad" attitude toward cardiovascular disease is clearly inappropriate; individuals and their employers need to join forces in the fight against cardiovascular disease.[33] Much of the battle must be fought on an educational front. More people need to realize that heart attacks and strokes are preventable. Factors such as cigarette smoking, high blood cholesterol, high blood pressure, and stress all significantly increase the risk of cardiovascular disease. But they can all be identified and corrected. Company-sponsored screening programs have proven effective at identifying employees who are potential victims of cardiovascular disease.[34] Furthermore, company-sponsored diet and quit-smoking clinics and exercise and fitness programs have helped individuals beat back the threat of cardiovascular disease.[35] The alternative—an overfed, underexercised, and less than fully productive labor force—is unacceptable from both economic and humanitarian standpoints.

ALCOHOL ABUSE   Alcoholism affects approximately 8 percent of the labor force in the United States.[36] Although it was long thought to be a character disorder, *alcoholism* is now considered a disease in which the individual's social and economic roles are disrupted by the abuse of alcohol. Very few alcoholics are actually the skid-row-bum type; the vast majority are average citizens. Alcoholism cuts across all age brackets, both sexes, and all racial and subcultural categories. It is costing public and private employers billions of dollars annually in absenteeism, accidents, and impaired productivity. As with cardio-vascular disease, management can either do nothing and absorb the added expense or get actively involved and do something to enhance human potential and job performance.

The manager's primary concern should be job performance. Typically, alcoholism reveals itself to the manager in the form of increased absenteeism, tardiness, sloppy work, and complaints from coworkers. As soon as a steady decline in performance is observed, the manager should confront the employee with his or her poor performance record. The manager should never make any reference to possible alcohol abuse; it is up to the employee to admit to such a problem. Once the employee has admitted that alcohol is a problem, then it is up to the manager to refer the person to appropriate sources of help. Managers must not play doctor when it comes to handling the alcoholic employee. Most large work organizations have in-house doctors and/or employee counselors. Managers in small organizations without sophisticated employee services should refer the alcoholic employee to community resources such as Alcoholics Anonymous.

Employee alcoholism is a large and growing problem. There are no easy answers. Progress will come only from carefully developed company policy and rigorous follow-up by individual managers. The following policy of "constructive coercion" is a step in the right direction:

1. Management must define alcoholism among its employees as a health problem requiring therapy.
2. Management must adopt a treatment attitude toward this health problem, offering assistance in securing therapy.
3. It [should] be understood that after a reasonable opportunity for progress, the employee will be dismissed unless there is noticeable improvement in work.
4. The policy [should] be communicated widely by corporate officers with their full approval.[37]

Employees, their families, the organization, and society in general all stand to gain from the fight against stress, cardiovascular disease, and employee alcohol abuse. All three are serious threats to both personal health and effective job performance.

SUMMARY   Since people are the key to organizational success, managers need to take specific steps to improve individual job performance. One alternative is to motivate employees with properly administered extrinsic and intrinsic rewards. Employees will be motivated to perform better if they believe that their effort will lead to rewards that will satisfy their needs. Furthermore, motivation is increased when equitable rewards are clearly linked to performance.

Behavior modification, the practical application of Skinnerian operant conditioning, concentrates on environmental control of actual job behavior rather than on internal states of mind, such as needs. In behavior modification, person-environment interaction is viewed in Antecedent $\longrightarrow$ Behavior $\longrightarrow$ Consequence terms. Managers can encourage a specific behavior by systematically managing its antecedents and consequences. The basic behavior modification process has three steps: (1) pinpoint the behavior problem, (2) arrange a productive A $\longrightarrow$ B $\longrightarrow$ C relationship, and (3) evaluate. In step 2, desirable behavior can be encouraged by replacing antecedent barriers with helpful aids. Moreover, desirable behavior can best be encouraged through positive reinforcement that is appropriately timed. Behavior modification programs tend to be more effective when managers positively reinforce what is right with job performance rather than work to stamp out undesirable behavior. New behaviors require continuous reinforcement, but intermittent reinforcement is best for established behaviors.

Evidence of increased dissatisfaction among today's employees has led a growing number of experts to call for work reform. At the heart of the problem lie overspecialized jobs, which workers find boring and alienating. The three ingredients of a decent job are meaningfulness, responsibility, and knowledge of results. Sometimes managers are forced by the situation to do the best they can with highly specialized jobs. If this is the case, they can turn to realistic job previews, job rotation, job enlargement, and limited exposure to help employees adjust to the boredom and monotony. A more constructive alternative is job enrichment. Inspired by Frederick Herzberg's two-factor theory of motivation, which identifies job satisfiers and dissatisfiers, job enrichment calls for redesigning jobs to include the ingredients of a decent job.

Too often managers forget that they are responsible for managing the whole person. Physical health is as important as mental health. Three serious threats to the physical health of today's employees are stress, cardiovascular disease, and alcohol abuse. By facing up to these problems in themselves and in their subordinates, managers can make a significant contribution to better job performance and the general quality of life.

TERMS TO UNDERSTAND

Rewards	Intermittent reinforcement
Extrinsic rewards	Job
Intrinsic rewards	Work reform
Cafeteria compensation	Boredom and alienation barrier
Behaviorist	Decent job
Operant conditioning	Autonomy
Behavior modification	Realistic job preview
Antecedent	Job rotation
Positive reinforcement	Job enlargement
Negative reinforcement	Job enrichment
Extinction	Stress
Punishment	Cardiovascular disease
Continuous reinforcement	Alcoholism

QUESTIONS FOR DISCUSSION

1. Comparing extrinsic and intrinsic rewards, which do you feel is more effective at motivating people? Why?
2. Why is equitability of rewards important?
3. What evidence of Watson's and Thorndike's classic work can be found in modern behavior modification?
4. Why is the A $\longrightarrow$ B $\longrightarrow$ C relationship helpful for both understanding and controlling organizational behavior?
5. Think of a behavior you would like to modify in yourself. What antecedents and consequences would you work with?
6. Why should managers concentrate on positive reinforcement?
7. Do you feel there is a need for work reform? Why?
8. Think of the best job you ever had. Did it possess the ingredients of a decent job? Explain.

9. How does job enrichment differ from job enlargement?
10. What is the difference between dealing with stress destructively and dealing with it constructively? Give examples.

CASE 15.1
BUSY BEAVERS

Carol Wilson is the manager of a Nichol's Discount Department Store. Carol's determined effort has paid off handsomely for the Nichol's chain, which includes over four hundred stores nationwide. For three years running, her store has ranked among the top ten in profitability. Carol is quick to credit the dedication and commitment of her people for this outstanding record. According to a companywide job-satisfaction survey conducted six months ago, Carol's employees turned out to be tops among all the Nichol's stores in job satisfaction. Naturally, Carol had some doubts about the new program dreamed up at the company's home office last month.

Citing the need to improve companywide job satisfaction and performance, the home office is directing each store manager to implement a Busy Beaver Program. After studying the detailed instructions, Carol has reluctantly launched the program at her store.

According to the program's guidelines, the store supervisors are supposed to hand out Busy Beaver pins to employees who are observed doing an exceptional job. If someone is observed doing a substandard job, the supervisor is supposed to take a pin back from the individual. If that person has no pins at the time, a notation is made on a special record that the individual "owes" the store a Busy Beaver pin. The program also calls for giving any employee who earns twenty-five pins a half day off with pay. Throughout the day, special tape recorded messages periodically announce that the store's employees are busy as beavers trying to please the customers. For the most part, the employees seemed enthusiastic about the Busy Beaver program when it was announced two weeks ago. However, the program appears to be in serious trouble today.

Using comments from both the supervisors and the employees, Carol has compiled the following list of problems associated with the Busy Beaver Program:

o The supervisors are complaining that they are wasting valuable time handing out pins.
o A number of employees have been overheard complaining that the tape-recorded messages are childish.
o According to one supervisor, a number of employees believe that the Busy Beaver program is nonsense. They see no way they can earn twenty-five pins before the program ends in two weeks.

- One employee complained directly to Carol that one of the supervisors has taken away more Busy Beaver pins than he has given out.
- So far, only one employee has earned the half day off. However, she refused to exercise the privilege. When asked why by her supervisor, she said she was afraid of being kidded by her coworkers about being the supervisor's pet.
- A note has been placed in the suggestion box recommending that the company grant a general pay raise rather than waste its money on half-baked incentive schemes.

FOR DISCUSSION

1. What is wrong with this particular reward scheme?
2. What could Carol do to make the Busy Beaver Program work?
3. Does Carol's store even need such a program? Explain.

CASE 15.2
FRITZ IS OFF THE WAGON

Joe Washington could detect a nervous tone in Mrs. Tomkins's voice as she acknowledged who was calling. Joe, a supervisor at Toronto Manufacturing Company, had called to find out why her husband, Fritz, had not come to work for the last two days. After some evasive hedging, Mrs. Tomkins finally broke down and tearfully admitted that she hadn't seen Fritz for two days. She was afraid he was out on a drinking binge. It wasn't the first time, she said; he'd be home when he ran out of money. Mrs. Tomkins told Joe that Fritz had a history of alcohol problems. What made it so bad this time was that Fritz had been on the wagon for six months. He had been doing so well, she sighed.

None of this came as a surprise to Joe. He had long suspected that Fritz had drinking problems, but he had never actually discussed it with him. Lately, however, Joe's job performance had been sliding. He was often tardy, or absent altogether, and the quality of his work had been slipping badly. Furthermore, a couple of Fritz's coworkers had hinted vaguely to Joe that "something had to be done about Fritz."

FOR DISCUSSION

1. Assuming that Fritz shows up at work in the next couple of days, what should Joe do?
2. In your opinion, is Fritz's drinking problem any of Joe's business? Explain your position.

REFERENCES

Opening quotations

Richard M. Steers and Lyman W. Porter, *Motivation and Work Behavior* (New York: McGraw-Hill, 1975), p. 558; Keith Davis,

Human Behavior at Work: Organizational Behavior, 5th ed. (New York: McGraw-Hill, 1977), p. 3.

1. For example, see E. L. Deci, "Paying People Doesn't Always Work the Way You Expect It To," *Human Resource Management* 12 (Summer 1973): 290–298.
2. "Companies Offer Benefits Cafeteria-style," *Business Week* #2560 (November 13, 1978): 116. For a review of the theory behind flexible compensation, see: William B. Werther, Jr., "Flexible Compensation Evaluated," *California Management Review* 19 (Fall 1976): 40–46.
3. See J. Stacy Adams and Patricia R. Jacobsen, "Effects of Wage Inequities on Work Quality," *Journal of Abnormal and Social Psychology* 69 (1964): 19–25.
4. For an excellent review of compensation practices, see: Allan N. Nash and Stephen J. Carroll, Jr., *The Management of Compensation* (Monterey, Calif.: Brooks/Cole, 1975).
5. L. L. Cummings and Donald P. Schwab, *Performance in Organizations* (Glenview, Ill.: Scott, Foresman, 1973), p. 53.
6. For an interesting account of operant conditioning applied to human behavior, see: B. F. Skinner, *Science and Human Behavior* (New York: Free Press, 1953), pp. 62–66.
7. Thomas K. Connellan, *How to Improve Human Performance: Behaviorism in Business and Industry* (New York: Harper & Row, 1978), p. 30.
8. Ibid., p. 32.
9. Robert Kreitner, "PM—A New Method of Behavior Change," *Business Horizons* 18 (December 1975): 84–85.
10. For more detailed accounts of the Emery Air Freight program, see: "At Emery Air Freight: Positive Reinforcement Boosts Performance," *Organizational Dynamics* 1 (Winter 1973): 41–50; and W. Clay Hamner and Ellen P. Hamner, "Behavior Modification on the Bottom Line," *Organizational Dynamics* 4 (Spring 1976): 3–21.
11. Adapted from: Fred Luthans and Robert Kreitner, *Organizational Behavior Modification* (Glenview, Ill.: Scott, Foresman, 1975), pp. 117–123.
12. For illustrative research reports, see selected issues of the *Journal of Applied Behavior Analysis* and the *Journal of Organizational Behavior Management*.
13. Edwin A. Locke, "Myths in 'The Myths of the Myths About Behavior Mod in Organizations,'" *Academy of Management Review* 4 (January 1979): 135.

14. Studs Terkel, *Working* (New York: Pantheon, 1974), p. xi.
15. Report of a Special Task Force to the Secretary of Health, Education, and Welfare, *Work in America* (Cambridge: MIT Press, 1973), p. 15.
16. "The Spreading Lordstown Syndrome," *Business Week* #2218 (March 4, 1972): 69.
17. See Richard C. Gerstenberg, "Danger in Public Misconception," *U.S. News & World Report* 73 (December 25, 1972): 55–58. For a broader perspective in this area, see Ross Reck, "Can the Production Line Be Humanized?" *MSU Business Topics* 22 (Autumn 1974): 27–36.
18. Adapted from J. Richard Hackman, Greg Oldham, Robert Janson, and Kenneth Purdy, "A New Strategy for Job Enrichment," *California Management Review* 17 (Summer 1975): 57–71.
19. Ibid., p. 59.
20. Robert Kreitner, "People are Systems, Too: Filling the Feedback Vacuum," *Business Horizons* 20 (December 1977): 54.
21. For more details, see John P. Wanous, "Effects of a Realistic Job Preview on Job Acceptance, Job Attitudes, and Job Survival," *Journal of Applied Psychology* 58 (December 1973): 327–332.
22. See M. A. Howell, "Time Off as a Reward for Productivity," *Personnel Administration* 34 (November–December 1971): 48–51.
23. See Frederick Herzberg, Bernard Mausner, and Barbara Bloch Snyderman, *The Motivation to Work*, 2nd ed. (New York: Wiley, 1959).
24. Adapted from Robert N. Ford, "Job Enrichment Lessons from A.T.&T.," *Harvard Business Review* 51 (January–February 1973): 96–106.
25. This example comes from the preceding source.
26. For a full explanation, see Pehr G Gyllenhammar, "How Volvo Adapts Work to People," *Harvard Business Review* 55 (July–August 1977): 102–113.
27. Ford, "Job Enrichment Lessons from A.T.&T.," p. 99.
28. For example, see William E. Reif and Fred Luthans, "Does Job Enrichment Really Pay Off?" *California Management Review* 15 (Fall 1972): 30–37.
29. Hans Selye, *Stress Without Distress* (Philadelphia: Lippincott, 1974), p. 32.
30. These guidelines have been adapted from: Meyer Friedman and Ray H. Rosenman, *Type A Behavior and Your Heart* (Greenwich, Conn.: Fawcett, 1974); Herbert Benson, *The Relaxation*

Response (New York: William Morrow, 1975); and "Executive's Guide to Living with Stress," *Business Week* #2446 (August 23, 1976): 75–80.

31. These figures are from American Heart Association, *Heart Facts 1976*, 44 East 23rd St., New York, N.Y. 10010, p. 1.

32. See J. Stamler, "Primary Prevention in Mass Community Efforts to Control the Major Coronary Risk Factors," *Journal of Occupational Medicine* 15 (January 1973): 54–59.

33. For more on this, see Robert Kreitner, "Employee Physical Fitness: Protecting an Investment in Human Resources," *Personnel Journal* 55 (July 1976): 340–344.

34. For example, see Robert Kreitner, Steven D. Wood, and Glenn M. Friedman, "Just How Fit Are Your Employees?" *Business Horizons* 22 (August 1979): 39–45.

35. For a review of corporate fitness programs, see Richard L. Pyle, "Corporate Fitness Programs—How Do They Shape Up?" *Personnel* 56 (January–February 1979), 58–67.

36. For an excellent account of this problem, see Kevin W. Kane, "The Corporate Responsibility in the Area of Alcoholism," *Personnel Journal* 54 (July 1975): 380–384.

37. Ibid., p. 384.

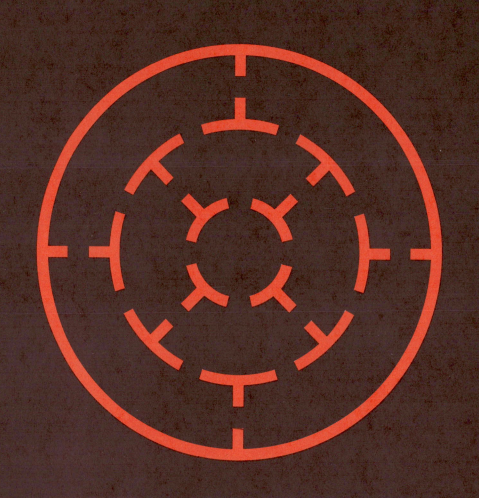

VI

The Environment of Management

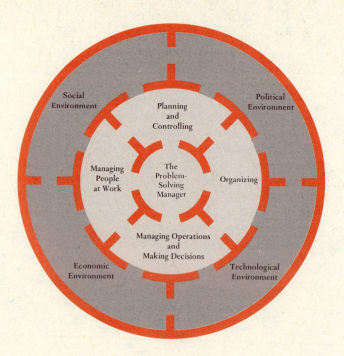

PART VI EXPLORES THE SOURCES OF CHANGE IN THE ENVIRONMENT OF management. Management is not practiced in a vacuum. To a very great extent, managers do what the environment outside their organizations allows them to do. Balances are achieved between what the organization is capable of doing and what society will permit it to do. Today, and for the foreseeable future, the word *change* best sums up the environment of management. But an awareness of constant change is not enough. The problem-solving manager also needs to be aware of the major sources of change on the management horizon. For example, multinationalism, population shifts, changing attitudes toward work, public distrust of government and business leaders, the energy crisis, persistent inflation, and the public's demand for greater corporate social responsibility all pose significant new problems for management.

Chapter 16

The Social and Political Environment

Our time, all of us would agree, is a time of momentous changes.

Peter F. Drucker

LEARNING OBJECTIVES

When you finish reading this chapter, you should be able to

- Explain why we are said to be living in the age of transience.
- Explain how the changing age distribution of Americans will impact management during the 1980s.
- Highlight the nature of the new work ethic.
- Discuss the significance of egalitarianism for managers.
- Identify and discuss two circumstances that shape today's political climate.
- Discuss the significance of four political and legal pressure points for managers.

Management is not an isolated activity in a safe and secure vacuum. Instead, it is a dynamic process that constantly interacts with a changing environment. To a large extent, management does what the environment surrounding the organization allows it to do, or makes it do. As an illustration of the influence that environmental forces have on the practice of management, consider the situation in which Ford Motor Company found itself in 1978.

○ Ford's cherished reputation as an innovator was starting to slip in light of significant innovations by General Motors.
○ Twelve hundred Ford dealers had organized to protest the parent company's treatment of them.
○ Ford recalled 1.5 million Pintos and Bobcats to correct an alleged fuel tank safety hazard after a California jury awarded a Pinto accident fire victim a record $127.8 million in damages.
○ The firm's financial outlook was beginning to prompt sour appraisals from Wall Street investment analysts.
○ Ford was looking ahead to an expenditure of $30 billion by 1985 to meet Federal safety and pollution control standards.
○ Out-of-court settlements of product safety and warranty lawsuits were costing Ford hundreds of millions of dollars.
○ Claiming that Henry Ford II, the chairman, had misused company funds, a group of dissident shareholders filed a $50 million suit against the firm.[1]

These problems add up to a nearly incredible set of circumstances. However, Ford Motor Company has not been the only large organization to experience this type of environmental pressure in recent years. Today, business as usual often means an ongoing program of adapting to competing external forces. Even nonprofit organizations such as universities, hospitals, and governmental agencies at all levels are feeling tremendous environmental pressures. A framework is needed for better understanding them.

Ignoring the impact of the general environment on management is like ignoring the effect of weather and road conditions on high-speed driving. As illustrated in Figure 16.1, the general environment of management includes social, political, economic, and technological dimensions. Each presents managers with unique opportunities and obstacles that will shape strategic planning, as discussed in Chapter 4. Managers cannot formulate and pursue organizational objectives until they have considered public sentiment, government regulations, economic conditions, and techno-

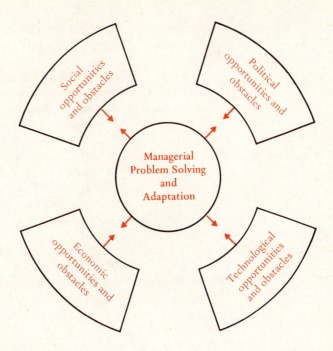

FIGURE 16.1
Management in a complex and changing world

logical advances. They need to be aware of what is going on outside their organizations and to respond accordingly.

In this and the next chapter we take a problem-solving approach to the environment of management. First, problem situations and major trends in each environmental area are introduced and discussed. Then we explore their implications for management, with emphasis on problem-solving responses to environmental forces.

THE AGE OF TRANSIENCE

This chapter and the next have a single dominant theme: managers are faced with a constantly changing general environment. As an old saying about people and change remarks: 20 percent of the people don't know that anything's happening, 70 percent of the people don't understand what's happening, and the remaining 10 percent of the people *make* things happen. Problem-solving managers, by definition, must put themselves in the third category if they are to succeed, and a long step toward success consists of simply recognizing that change is inevitable.

Alvin Toffler's widely read book, *Future Shock*, discusses the impact of change on modern society. Toffler is convinced that we are experiencing an unusual form of change today, one that he calls *transience*. By this he means an accelerating rate of change. According to Toffler:

> We can, by analogy, think of transience as the rate of turnover of the different kinds of relationships in an individual's life. Moreover, each of us can be characterized in terms of this rate. For some, life is marked by a much slower rate of turnover than for others. The people of the past and present lead lives of relatively "low transience"—their relationships tend to be long lasting. But the people of the future live in a condition of "high transience"—a condition in which the duration of relationships is cut short, the through-put of relationships extremely rapid. In their lives, things, places, people, ideas, and organizational structures all get "used up" more quickly.
>
> This affects immensely the way they experience reality, their sense of commitment, and their ability—or inability—to cope. It is this fast through-put, combined with increasing newness and complexity in the environment, that strains the capacity to adapt and creates the danger of future shock.[2]

Managers tend to be people of the future, in Toffler's language. Consequently, they experience a great deal of transience and are potential victims of future shock. The question that remains is: How can managers prepare for the future? How can they avoid future shock?

In the first place, managers need to *anticipate* significant environmental patterns and trends and prepare accordingly. They must keep an ear to the ground, so to speak. Social, political, economic, and technological changes can overwhelm organizations that fail to collect and interpret reliable information on what is going on in the world.

Anticipation of and preparation for change is much different from mere reaction to change. The term *reaction* implies that change is already in full swing before anything is done about it; by then it is too late. For example, petroleum-dependent businesses that were caught off guard by the Arab oil embargo of 1973 could only react; they were not prepared. They failed to anticipate the explosive combination of Mideast politics and U.S. dependence on foreign oil. The cost of mere reaction, in that case, included unmet commitments to customers, costly inventory replacement, and lower profits.

Reaction to change is past-oriented; it stems from blind faith in the status quo. *Anticipation* of change is future-oriented and helps the problem-solving manager avoid future shock.

THE SOCIAL ENVIRONMENT   Imagine yourself in the position of having to explain the nature of contemporary society to a visitor from a distant land. How would you begin? If you talked only of concerts, Labor Day picnics, quiet strolls in the park, and good times with friends, your listener would walk away with an unrealistically placid picture of our society. On the other hand, your visitor would get a gloomy and depressing impression if all you mentioned was the rising cost of oil and gasoline, Vietnam refugees, abject poverty, and the rising crime rate. It is not easy to accurately describe modern society in all its positive and negative aspects.

This situation helps us understand some of the changes in sociological theory over the years. Some theorists have focused only on the cooperative aspects of society, while others became preoccupied with conflict and competition. Realizing that neither extreme view describes all of our complex, contemporary society, modern sociologists have formulated a compromise view, the synthesis perspective. This *synthesis perspective* sees society as the product of a constant tug-of-war between stability and change. The synthesis perspective of society is based on the following assumptions:

1. The processes of stability and change are properties of all societies.
2. Societies are organized but the process of organization produces conflict.
3. Societies are dynamic social *systems*.
4. Complementary interests, consensus on cultural values, and coercion hold societies together.
5. Social change may be gradual or abrupt, but all societies experience constant social change.[3]

The synthesis perspective is realistic because it takes into consideration both cooperation and competition. It is neither unrealistically optimistic nor overly pessimistic. The forces of cooperation draw society together, while the forces of competition and conflict pull it apart. The net result is a dynamic balance characterized by constant change. Our discussion of the social environment of management is based on this perspective.

A comprehensive treatment of today's social milieu would fill volumes. All we can do here is identify some of the more important social trends. Three trends that affect the practice of management today are demographic shifts, changing attitudes toward work, and egalitarianism. Each of these trends promises to shape the future direction of management.

DEMOGRAPHIC SHIFTS

Demography is the statistical study of human populations. Demographic statistics reflecting population growth, in particular, have received a great deal of attention in recent years. At the present rate of growth, the world's population will double in approximately thirty-five years. Assuming that the world does, in fact, have a population of roughly nine billion people in the year 2015, it will be a very different world from the one we know. This worldwide population explosion will place severe demands on food production, scarce resources, waste disposal systems, and governing institutions. However, if we focus only on the United States, a very different picture emerges. Today's record low birthrate in the United States suggests that this country's population growth will slow considerably and perhaps even cease after the year 2000.

In addition to studying population growth rates, demographers also study the distribution of specific characteristics in the population. For example, the age distribution in the United States, as illustrated in Figure 16.2, has intriguing implications for management.

The Pepsi generation grows up   The most significant aspect of America's shifting age distribution is the fact that the record number of babies born between 1947 and 1957 has now grown up. This postwar baby boom has placed severe strains on all dimensions of society as it has moved from one age bracket to another. According to *Newsweek*:

> About 43 million children were born then—a fifth of the present population. They crowded the schools in the 1950s and 1960s, then flooded the job market in the 1970s. By the 1980s and 1990s they will be a middle-aged bulge in the population, swelling the 35- to 44-year-old age group by 80 per cent—from 23 million people today [1977] to 41 million by 2000. And early in the next century they will reach retirement, still the dominant segment of the total population.[4]

As the generation of the postwar baby boom grows older, the average age of Americans will climb. In 1970, the median age in the United States was below 28. It will pass 30 in the early 1980s and eventually reach 35 by the year 2000. One consequence will be a shift away from a preoccupation with youth to a growing concern for older citizens.

Managerial implications   Managers, along with the rest of society, will feel the impact of the maturing postwar baby-boom

FIGURE 16.2
Age distribution tells an
important story

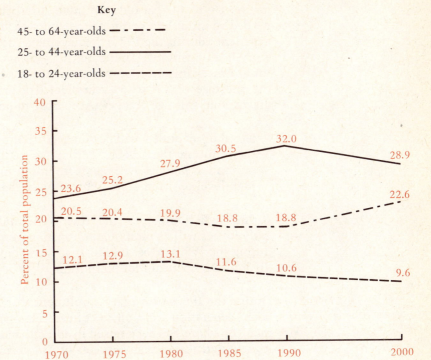

Key

45- to 64-year-olds — · — · —

25- to 44-year-olds ————

18- to 24-year-olds — — — —

Data source: U. S. Department of Commerce, *Statistical Abstract of the United States: 1977*, pp. 6–7.

generation. This population bubble will significantly affect the makeup of the labor force and the nature of the goods and services it produces. "The soft drinks, blue jeans, and records that symbolized the youth market are not likely to be in such great demand in a predominantly middle-aged society."[5] Special strains will be placed on human resource planning.

The 1980s will see a dramatic rise in the 25–44 age bracket and a relative tapering of both the 18–24 and 45–64 age brackets. This situation will create keen competition among those from 25 to 44 for jobs and promotion opportunities. However, people entering the labor force after high school or college will find more opportunities and less competition than their counterparts found during the 1970s. A decline in the percentage of people aged 45–64 could create a talent shortage at the top-management level during the 1980s.

For each of these circumstances, management will need to plan and use human resources appropriately. As promotion opportunities for the 25- to 44-year-olds diminish, alternative incentives will be needed to stimulate performance and satisfaction. Contrary to its experience during the 1970s, management may find it difficult to fill entry-level positions. Therefore, it is reasonable to expect a push toward mechanization of routine, entry-level jobs. But what about the shortage of 45- to 64-year-olds? Top managers are normally drawn from this age bracket. According to one expert:

> Headhunter outfits will be doing a thriving business—even bigger than during the 1960s. Perhaps a rethinking of traditional promotion policies will result in promoting younger people into high-level positions even more rapidly than in the past.[6]

If this prediction comes true, then some middle managers in their early forties will be promoted to top management ahead of schedule during the 1980s. Most middle managers, however, will experience vigorous competition for promotion.

CHANGING ATTITUDES TOWARD WORK

During the 1960s university enrollment soared as the postwar baby boom generation went off to college. This large group of students, many of whom had been raised in affluent and permissive surroundings, felt critical of many aspects of American culture. As they saw it, material wealth did little to solve society's problems. Parents, teachers, and political leaders who said one thing and did another appeared hypocritical. Frustration and disillusionment created an explosive situation. The war in Vietnam, which was involving more and more young men each year, became a key issue. To students of draft age, the war in Vietnam was a clear and present threat; college campuses around the country erupted with violent demonstrations. The so-called youth movement was under way.

The youth movement matured during the early 1970s as it questioned all established aspects of our society. One observer characterized the aims of the youth movement as follows:

> Advocates express desire for "a better quality of life," defined as a cleaner environment, consumerism, rights of minority groups including women, egalitarianism with emphasis on redressing all economic and social inequities, and more participatory decision making.[7]

Work was one of the features of modern life that was critically explored by the youth movement. A significant new attitude toward work emerged.

The new work ethic Pointing to increased absenteeism and turnover among younger workers in recent years, a number of social observers have proclaimed the death of the work ethic. But closer analysis has showed this judgment to be unwarranted.

A recent survey of over three thousand individuals employed by a variety of companies across the United States explored the attitudes of today's young workers.[8] In general (see Table 16.1), attitudes toward work differed between younger (aged 17–26) and older (aged 40–65) workers. Although younger workers do not value the work ethic as strongly as older workers do, it is still very much alive among the younger group. However, younger workers do not seem as willing as older workers to become deeply involved in company and community affairs. They tend to be more committed to friendship ties than are older workers.

Although younger workers are considerably less committed to a single organization, they still believe in work, in what might be termed a new work ethic. For instance, after surveying over 23,000 *Psychology Today* readers, most of them young, researchers concluded:

> People seem to believe again in the value of hard work and in developing themselves at the workplace. On the other hand, they are not likely to be easy to satisfy or retain as employees. They are likely to demand a great deal, and, if they don't receive it, will look elsewhere.[9]

TABLE 16.1
What younger workers think is important

- Younger workers do not believe hard work and pride in craftsmanship are as important as older workers believe them to be.
- Younger workers have more negative attitudes toward their specific jobs, the company, and top management than do older workers; these differences cannot be attributed to the kinds of jobs they are assigned.
- Younger workers are much less committed than older workers to their company, and they report more negative attitudes about its role in the local community and economy.
- Younger workers regard government or church welfare and help from family and friends as more acceptable than older workers do.
- Younger workers are more concerned than older workers are about having their fellow workers like them; they say that it is more important to get along with friends than it is to work hard on a job.

Source: David Cherrington, "The Values of Younger Workers," *Business Horizons* 20 (December 1977): 29. Copyright, 1977, by the Foundation for the School of Business at Indiana University. Reprinted by permission.

But what exactly are today's young employees looking for? According to the editors of *Intellect*, "Young workers look for the same things as executive-level employees—interesting work, a chance to use their minds, a chance to develop skills and abilities, and participation in decisions regarding their jobs."[10] Today's employees want to be recognized as individuals rather than mindless cogs in giant productive wheels. They want to feel good about themselves and what they do all day.

The orientation toward leisure is another feature of the new work ethic. For many, leisure has replaced work as the primary focal point of life. This does not mean that younger people do not want to work; they simply derive *more* meaning from leisure-time activities. It is a matter of balance. Today the balance weighs more heavily in favor of leisure. Work is still an important part of the picture, but it is no longer viewed as life's primary activity.

Although some insist that the current attitudes of younger employees toward work are signs of moral decay, many others are encouraged because the young are beginning to think for themselves. They no longer permit boring and unchallenging work to dominate their lives. Work, however satisfying, is just one aspect of a full and meaningful life.

Managerial response   Organizational success during the 1980s will depend to a large extent on how well managers read and adjust to the new work ethic. "The goal for management is to be aware of and prepared for new and surfacing employee needs, before it is forced to take reactive, ignorant, and resistive postures."[11]

The old carrot-and-stick approach of trying to motivate employees by dangling more money in front of their faces and threatening them from behind with the loss of their jobs will no longer work. There are two reasons. First, money has limited motivational potential. Research has demonstrated that

> people have in mind a level of compensation that they consider adequate for them. If their pay falls below this level, then money becomes more important than interesting work. If wages or salary are above this level, then whether they consider their job interesting assumes more importance.[12]

As far as the threat of unemployment goes, it is effectively neutralized by widespread willingness to accept public assistance and by the erosion of organizational loyalty. Losing a job today is not the "economic capital punishment" it once was, except, of course, during severe and prolonged economic recessions.

FIGURE 16.3
Flextime in action

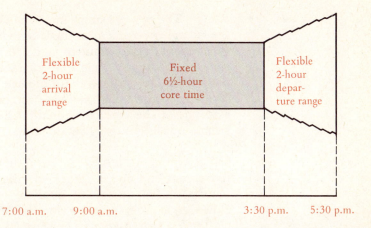

7:00 a.m.   9:00 a.m.   3:30 p.m.   5:30 p.m.

Workers' desire for more meaningful jobs will put pressure on managers to adopt various forms of work reform such as job enrichment. More participatory decision making also meshes well with the new work ethic. Innovative ways of putting meaning and challenge into daily work are a top priority for the 1980s.

The increased importance of leisure promises to further test management's ability to be creative and flexible in managing people. Already we have seen the standard 8 to 5, forty-hour workweek come under fire. Taking its place is *flextime*, which allows employees to determine their own arrival and departure times within specified limits.[13] However, as Figure 16.3 illustrates, all employees must be present during a fixed core time. If an eight-hour day is required, as in Figure 16.3, an early bird can put in the required eight hours by arriving at 7:00 A.M., taking a half hour for lunch, and departing at 3:30 P.M. In contrast, someone who is running late can come in at 9:00 A.M. and leave at 5:30 P.M. Flextime has been praised as a way of fitting the work day to individual needs, but it has been criticized for adding to overhead administrative expenses. Time and experience will help managers decide how to deal with this cost-benefit relationship. The new work ethic may eventually reshape most aspects of human resource management.

EGALITARIANISM   Although the term *egalitarianism* may be unfamiliar to many, the concept it stands for is not. *Egalitarianism* is a social philosophy advocating social, political, and economic equality. The drive for equality is strong throughout the world today, particularly in the United States. According to one leading business publication: "A push for equality that cuts across the nation's entire social and economic fabric is becoming perhaps the most commanding fact of life in the U.S. today."[14] This belief has been echoed by *Business*

Week: "The greatest single force changing and expanding the role of the federal government in the U.S. today is the push for equality."[15] What makes egalitarianism so important is the fact that, despite constitutional and legislated guarantees of equality, significant portions of U.S. society claim to have been shortchanged. Both the civil rights movement and the women's liberation movement are evidence of the drive for equality. Both will continue to have a sizable impact on the practice of management in coming years.

The civil rights movement   It is difficult to define the civil rights movement and put it into a specific time frame because it is a multifaceted response to evolving conditions in U.S. society. However, in order to have a working definition, we will consider the *civil rights movement* as a concerted effort among American blacks and other racial and ethnic minorities to protest social, political, and economic inequality. Many observers trace the movement back to 1955, when a black woman named Rosa Parks refused to sit in the back of a bus in Montgomery, Alabama. Since that time, civil rights activists have marched, protested, picketed, and boycotted in the name of greater equality. The violent ghetto riots of the 1960s are generally considered by sociologists to have been related only indirectly to the civil rights movement, not actually part of it. Martin Luther King and other civil rights leaders were committed to nonviolent protest.

This social upheaval has had a number of consequences. Most important is federal and state legislation that attempts to eliminate discrimination in education, housing, and employment. As each piece of the civil rights legislation was signed into law in the 1960s and 1970s, blacks and other minorities took one step closer to equality—at least that's what everyone assumed. Now that these laws have been on the books for a reasonable length of time, a reappraisal of the situation is in order.

A relatively accurate way to gauge equality is to compare selected groups on the basis of annual income. Economic well-being is a central factor in modern life. A good income indicates a decent-paying job and access to quality education and housing. Unfortunately, as shown in Figure 16.4, the trend in recent years has not been encouraging. American blacks still lag far behind whites in annual income. It has been pointed out that

> despite considerable efforts the racial imbalance of poverty is not improving. Blacks are still earning about three-fifths of whites. Blacks are still unemployed at twice the rate of whites, and are still in poverty three times the rate of whites.

FIGURE 16.4
Statistics of inequality:
family income distribution
for white and black
families in 1976

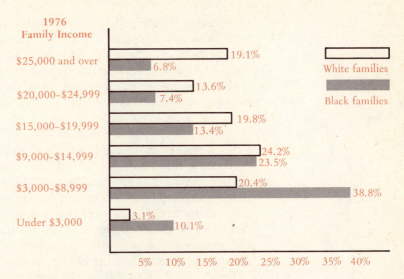

Data source: U. S. Department of Commerce, *Statistical Abstract of the United States: 1977*, p. 441.

The most discouraging statistics of all show that education is not paying off for blacks. Blacks now almost equal whites in years of educational attainment. Yet white high-school graduates still earn more than black *college* graduates.[16]

Blacks, Hispanics, American Indians, handicapped individuals, and other minorities are getting tired of being told that things are getting better, when they are not. It is little consolation to Americans living in poverty that they are better off than the poor in other nations. Poverty is measured by comparison with reference groups in one's own culture.

What happens now? Will the civil rights movement continue to carry the banner of equality for minorities? One observer believes that it "has virtually collapsed as a significant force in present-day American society."[17] This conclusion was prompted by two major factors. First, the civil rights movement became associated with the anti–Vietnam War movement. Consequently, when the war ended and people hurriedly dismissed it from their minds, the civil rights movement faded from the limelight as well. Second, public weariness with protest after the turbulent 1960s and early 1970s has tended to stifle civil rights activism. By the late 1970s, organized civil rights protests were few and far between.

The 1980s will be a time of reckoning for the civil rights

movement. Whether it is dead or still a living force remains to be seen. Whatever happens, it can take credit for prompting the passage of today's equal education, housing, and employment opportunity laws. The question now is: Can these laws be made to work? As far as the equal employment opportunity laws are concerned, managers hold the key to effective execution of the law.

The women's liberation movement   The contemporary *women's liberation movement*, which is rooted in a broader feminist movement that reaches back into the nineteenth century, may be defined generally as an organized social force aimed at extending the range of choices open to women. A recognized authority in this area has outlined the goals of the women's liberation movement: "Equality of education, equality of opportunity, equality of income, and status on a par with men are about the most basic and immediate demands of the new feminists."[18]

Figure 16.5 shows how far women still have to go in one important area, namely management. Although they make up more than 50 percent of the U.S. white-collar labor force, women occupy less than one-quarter of the managerial and administrative positions. Those who do make it into the ranks of management find it a slow climb. For example, *Business Week* polled forty-three major U.S. corporations in 1978 to determine the impact of equal employment opportunity laws on the status of women in management. Only seven of the firms had any women *at all* in top-management positions.

Not only are women generally restricted to lower-level jobs, but they tend to be paid less as well. According to a U.S. Department of Labor study, "Women who worked at year-round full-time jobs in

FIGURE 16.5
Statistics of inequality: male and female managers

White-Collar Employees in 1977

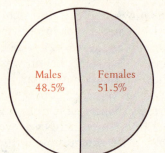

Managers and Administrators in 1977

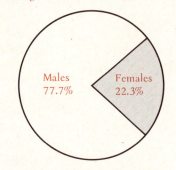

Data source: U. S. Department of Commerce, *Statistical Abstract of the United States: 1977*, p. 406.

1974 earned only 57 cents for every dollar earned by men. . . . In 1974, women with 4 years of college had lower incomes than men who had only completed the 8th grade, and only 59 percent of the income of men with 4 years of college."[19] The overall conclusion of the study was that the gap between male and female earnings had actually widened between the years 1955 to 1974, the very period during which the majority of our equal employment opportunity laws were passed.

Like racial and ethnic minorities, women are not soothed with assurances that they have "come a long way." They still have a very long way to go before being full partners with men in the world of work.

Egalitarianism and management The trend toward greater social, political, and economic equality affects the practice of management in three areas. Those areas are hiring, promotion, and compensation.

As discussed in Chapter 12, federal civil rights legislation makes it mandatory for businesses to hire on the basis of ability rather than race, sex, religion, or national origin. Managers who ignore this legislation are saddled with costly fines (or the loss of government contracts if they do business with the government). The government's ultimate objective is to ensure that everyone who is qualified for a particular job has an equal opportunity to be hired. However, the government does not force organizations to hire unneeded individuals or, except by special court order, impose quotas for the hiring of minorities.

Managerial decisions concerning promotion are also being affected by egalitarian legislation. This legislation was passed because women and minorities were not occupying their fair share of higher-level (and higher-paying) jobs. As in the case of hiring, the government has had to both encourage and force compliance with legislated egalitarian standards.

For years, women and nonwhites received less pay than white men even though they were doing the same work. Federal equal pay legislation now makes it illegal to pay two people who are doing the same job different amounts on the basis of their sex or race. Once again, an egalitarian ideal has become law.

The civil rights legislation of the past two decades shows that the federal government is aggressively pursuing an egalitarian policy. Equality of opportunity is a high national priority. Whether one agrees with the spirit of egalitarianism or not, the new legislation will have an immense impact on the way managers pursue their organizational objectives. Managers who merely react to egalitarian pressures will have more problems than those who keep informed and anticipate its many effects.

We turn now to the political environment of management.

**THE POLITICAL
ENVIRONMENT**

The political arena, perhaps more than any other, is characterized by constant change. Often it seems confusing, but if we stop to examine the fundamental processes of democracy, apparent confusion can yield to a sense of order and purpose.

As depicted in Figure 16.6 the American political system is a continuous cycle of actions and reactions. For example, expressions of public discontent are actions that prompt reaction in the form of revised political party platforms and promises by office seekers. The platforms and promises, in turn, determine how voters will react at the polls. Once elected, public officials must live up to their promises if they want to be reelected. Otherwise they will probably be replaced by other candidates who promise improvements. Although political campaigning may appear noisy and disorderly, in theory it is part of an orderly political process designed to put the most qualified citizens in positions of public responsibility.

Unfortunately, as we all know, theory and practice are not always the same. When variables such as hollow campaign promises,

**FIGURE 16.6
Politics as a circle of
actions and reactions**

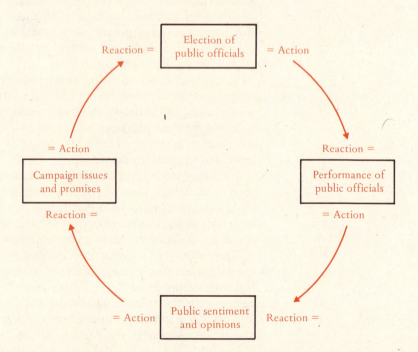

lobbying by special interests, and voter apathy are introduced, the political horizon gets a bit cloudy. Because managers are citizens as well as members of socially, economically, and politically powerful organizations, they need to know how America's political system does work. In this section we will define the term *politics*, analyze two contemporary political realities, and explore four political and legal pressure points for managers.

POLITICS DEFINED

In broadest terms, *politics* is the art (or science) of public influence and control. Society is made up of many individuals and groups with conflicting interests and objectives. There are probusiness and antibusiness groups, prounion and antiunion groups, integrationists and segregationists, liberals and conservatives. The list of special interest groups today is extremely long and still growing. It is the job of the political system to balance special interests in a generally acceptable manner.

In effect, the political process determines who gets what, when and how. Smooth operation of the process depends on the following two conditions:

1. All conflicting interests and differing viewpoints must be permitted legitimate expression.
2. Proponents of conflicting interests and differing viewpoints must be confident that they will be given a fair chance to realize their objectives by working within the system.[20]

The First Amendment to the U.S. Constitution, which guarantees all citizens freedom of speech, helps to ensure that all conflicting viewpoints are expressed. The first condition is generally satisfied in our society, but special interest groups sometimes run into trouble on the second condition. Groups such as the Mafia and the Ku Klux Klan try to realize their objectives by working outside the system. In doing so, they represent a serious threat to an orderly society. A society is unhealthy when large numbers of interest groups pursue their objectives through violence and other illegal means rather than through the political and economic system. On the other hand, a society in which all interest groups work within the system to achieve a degree of public influence and control is comparatively healthy.

Managers are members of an extremely powerful interest group that has traditionally worked within the political system. Consequently, they have a big stake in the system, and any discussion of the practice of management needs to consider its political setting.

"OF COURSE WE'RE AN EQUAL OPPORTUNITY EMPLOYER. OUR MR. FRISCH IS CATHOLIC, MR. STAMOS IS GREEK, MR. MENDEZ IS CHICANO, MR. GREEN IS JEWISH, MR. ARDWAY IS PROTESTANT, MR. DAVIS IS BLACK, MR. KWAN IS CHINESE…"

MODERN POLITICAL REALITIES

According to one authority, political turbulence and uncertainty is one of six major challenges facing future managers.[21] Two factors are of special concern: (1) unrealized expectations, and (2) breach of public trust. One cannot fully appreciate the political realities facing modern managers without first understanding these two factors which contribute to political turbulence and uncertainty.

Unrealized expectations When the troops came home from World War II, they dedicated themselves to building a safe and comfortable society for their loved ones. They worked hard so that their children would not have to suffer depressions and wars as they had suffered. Confidence in their ability to build a better world manifested itself in an unprecedented birthrate. The result was the postwar baby boom generation, which could afford to think about the more philosophical aspects of life because it didn't have to worry about where people would get their next meal. Born into an era of unprecedented affluence, the post–World War II generation developed a grand set of expectations about economic security and about such virtues as honesty. Unfortunately, the war in Vietnam, economic recessions in the 1960s and 1970s, and revelations of corruption among public officials soon tumbled their lofty expectations. Psychologists tell us that unrealized expectations lead to dissatisfaction and frustration. Beginning in the late 1960s, public dissatisfaction and frustration became important political issues.

Charles A. Reich, in his best-selling book *The Greening of America*, identifies three evolutionary states of consciousness. He calls them Consciousness I, II, and III. Although Consciousness I prevailed during the nineteenth century, Consciousness II during the first half of the twentieth century, and Consciousness III only recently, Reich feels that all three states of mind can be found in today's population. Consciousness I people are individuals in the pioneer tradition. As rugged individualists, they believe they can accomplish what needs to be done by themselves. Consciousness II people feel comfortable in a social and highly organized world. They believe it is only through organizations that they can gain access to the good things of life. Consciousness III people, according to Reich, have weighed the costs and benefits of the "good things of life" and have come away with a greater preference for individuality and aesthetics than for money and material well-being. This third group also, in Reich's words, "sees a society that is deeply untruthful and hypocritical."[22]

As one might expect, Consciousness IIIs suffer from a great many unrealized expectations. They tend to embrace the new work ethic. However, contrary to what one might think, Consciousness IIs, who steadfastly believe in the work ethic and cherish their organizational identification, also have fallen victim to unrealized expectations. The good life has proven to be somewhat elusive. Rebellious offspring, persistent inflation, and cynicism have taken their toll among members of the older generation. Consequently, dissatisfaction and frustration are widespread today, and highly visible elected officials have become the scapegoats. In other words, general dissatisfaction has spilled over into the political arena.

Breach of public trust   Until June 17, 1972, the name *Watergate* simply identified an apartment and office complex overlooking the Potomac River in Washington, D.C. But an attempted burglary there on that date, in the Democratic party's national headquarters, and a host of related events turned Watergate into a household word.[23] Today, Watergate identifies a tragic period in American history when a president was forced to resign and a number of high-ranking government officials, including a former U.S. attorney general, were sent to jail.[24] Watergate has become a synonym for abuse of power, corruption, and breach of public trust.

Social critics and political observers have had a journalistic field day with Watergate. Some believe that Watergate confirmed the accusation that America is ethically and morally bankrupt. They feel that Watergate is a symptom of more serious, underlying social ills. Other observers, however, proudly claim that in the Watergate crisis the U.S. Constitution passed its severest test with flying colors. Whether one views Watergate pessimistically or optimistically, a disturbing political reality remains. Namely, Watergate contributed to a dramatic decline of public confidence in government during the 1970s. For example, in 1964, 76 percent of the American public expressed confidence in the ability of government officials to do the right thing. By 1972, when the Watergate break-in occurred and the Vietnam War was drawing to a close, that figure had fallen to 52 percent. By the time the Watergate era had run its course in 1976, public confidence in government had plunged to 33 percent, an all-time low.[25]

What does this lack of confidence in government mean for the future? According to one authority:

> Some students of government see this mood producing significant changes in the U.S. political system: emergence of a new third party, a more authoritarian leadership, or a continued fall-off in voting and virtual abandonment of the electoral process to special interest groups.[26]

No one can accurately foresee all the long-term changes likely to take place in the American political system. One can only speculate on the basis of information at hand. It is clear that declining public confidence in government has led to widespread voter apathy. In a democracy voter apathy is a serious problem. "Turned off" citizens do not go to the polls to elect leaders who can correct the sources of their dissatisfaction and reestablish voter confidence. A democracy is a self-cleansing political system, but that mechanism breaks down unless large numbers of well-informed voters go to the polls.

Overall, the American political scene is characterized by uncertainty. Will the democratic form of government as we know it die because of public cynicism and apathy? Can our political system select leaders who will moderate public dissatisfaction and restore public trust in government? As with all else in the management environment, the only certainty on the political horizon is change.

POLITICAL AND LEGAL PRESSURE POINTS FOR MANAGERS

Politics and law go hand in hand. It is impossible to mention one without including the other, and this alliance pervades the political setting of management. Therefore we discuss here four political and legal pressure points for managers: big government, partisan politics, ethics, and personal accountability.

Big government   Astute political observers have noted a fundamental change in legislation since the early 1960s. The greatest impact of this change has fallen on managers of profit-making businesses. Traditionally, congressional legislation affecting business was economic in nature. Laws such as the Sherman Anti-Trust Act and the Federal Trade Commission Act were passed to break up monopoly power and ensure fair pricing and trade practices. "Today the focus and emphasis of regulation is directed toward other goals. Pollution, consumerism, minority employment, employment of women, safety, and job satisfaction are the issues of the day."[27] In effect, Congress has begun to legislate a better quality of life. Such legislation is social in nature, rather than economic.

This trend has two major implications for business managers. First, the more than fifty important acts affecting business passed since 1960 have created a huge government bureaucracy of commissions and regulatory agencies. (This accounts, in large part, for the fact that the federal government is the nation's largest single employer.) Second, business managers are spending significantly greater amounts of their time reporting to government agencies. For example, one large U.S. company, Champion Spark Plug, annually sends more than 500 reports to fifteen federal bureaus and agencies and 2,500 reports to state and local agencies across the country.[28] All of this takes time, money, and effort that could otherwise be channeled into the pursuit of organizational objectives, business managers argue. A special task force at Dow Chemical discovered that the firm spent $147 million to comply with domestic regulations in 1975. Furthermore, after dividing regulatory expenses into three categories—appropriate, questionable, and excessive—the Dow task force concluded that $50 million, or 34 percent of its 1975 regulatory expense, was excessive.[29]

Above all else, the trend toward big government is responsible for the deep involvement of business managers in politics. Managers have become politicians because they feel it is necessary.

Managers and partisan politics   Managers who stand to gain or lose when political power changes hands have learned that every vote counts. For example, John F. Kennedy won in 1960 by less than one vote per precinct, and Richard Nixon won in 1968 by less than three votes per precinct.[30] In spite of strict laws governing the role of corporations in partisan politics, many managers have tried to influence the outcome of important elections in various ways. As the following report by *Time* indicates, not all managers have a clean bill of health in this area.

> One scandal has surfaced after another with deplorable regularity, as major corporations have been found making illegal political contributions and pay-offs. The predictable results are a serious erosion of public confidence in, and a sharpening cynicism about, the motives of businessmen. To make matters worse, the penalties imposed on guilty companies have been almost ridiculous—fines so small that they do little to instill confidence in the whole process of law enforcement.[31]

Business managers counter with the claim that a few bad apples are making all of them look bad. In spite of limitations on political involvement, managers can legally do a number of things in politics.

What managers do in politics on their own time and with their own money is their own business. It is also acceptable for managers to use corporate resources to encourage, on a nonpartisan basis, activities such as registering and voting among employees, suppliers, and customers.[32] However, when the corporate name or corporate funds enter the picture, managers are severely restricted in regard to backing a single party or a particular candidate. One option is to exercise political influence through registered lobbyists. Lobbyists make sure that key legislators are aware of an organization's opinions, problems, and desires. It is estimated that approximately 80 percent of the nation's thousand largest companies have full-time representatives in Washington, D.C.[33]

Pressure for ethical conduct   Accompanying the recent decline in public trust in government has been an erosion of public confidence in managers. Although this may simply be a case of guilt by association, highly publicized cases of illegal campaign contributions have confirmed the public's worst suspicions about managerial conduct. One expert, who noted that recent polls have consistently shown that business is mistrusted by one-half to three-quarters of all Americans, concluded: "Americans mistrust corporate leaders, companies, industries and products with growing force and many observers feel that the peak of popular vituperation has not yet been reached."[34] The net result of this ill feeling is a political climate demanding more ethical conduct from politicians and managers. The time has come for managers to address the topic of ethics in a straightforward manner.

Ethics is the study of moral obligation involving the separation of right from wrong. So far in this book we have touched on two ethical issues. In Chapter 10 the erosion of personal values was examined in relation to the decision-making process, and the issue of conformity was explored under the heading of group dynamics in Chapter 13. The question here is: How can one adhere to ethical values in the face of pressure to conform and still get results? An organizational behaviorist has framed a workable solution: "The challenge in all this for a concerned management is to integrate a healthy pressure for performance and profitability with a healthy respect for individual consciences and differences of opinion."[35] In short, a "success at any cost" mentality can no longer be tolerated. A salesperson, for example, who finds a high-pressure sales strategy unethical should be allowed to voice a dissenting opinion, not pressured into an unwilling conformity.

What about formal codes of ethics? Are they the answer? Experience in recent years has shown codes of ethics to be a step in the right direction but not a cure-all. A simple piece of paper will not mystically steer people in an ethical direction. Formal codes of ethics for organization members must satisfy two requirements if they are to encourage ethical conduct. First, the codes must refer to specific practices such as kickbacks, payoffs, record falsification, and misleading advertising claims. General platitudes about good business practice or professional conduct are not effective. Vague language and generalities merely encourage employees to read between the lines. Second, organizational codes of ethics must be firmly supported by top management and equitably enforced through a system of rewards and punishments. Spotty enforcement is the quickest way to kill the effectiveness of an ethical code.

No simple cookbook approach can develop the right ethical code for a particular organization or subunit. Much of the burden falls on the problem-solving abilities of the managers involved. However, the following guidelines offer constructive direction:

○ You will face ethical dilemmas, created by value conflicts, for which there may be no totally satisfactory resolution. But don't use this condition to rationalize unethical behavior on your part.

○ Don't expect ethical codes to help solve all problems. Codes can create a false sense of security and lead to the encouragement of violations.
○ If you wish to avoid external enforcement of someone else's ethical code, make self-enforcement work.
○ Don't deceive yourself into thinking you can hide unethical actions.[36]

In the final analysis, ethical conduct, not words, will reverse the decline of public trust in management. To the extent that ethical codes encourage ethical conduct, they are an important and necessary management tool.

Personal accountability   Recent changes in the political and legal scene have made today's managers much more personally accountable for illegal activities than in the past. For example, a 1975 Supreme Court ruling upheld the conviction of the president of a multi-billion dollar food chain who was fined personally when his subordinates failed to comply with a law requiring the extermination of rats in a company warehouse.[37] A 1977 U.S. District Court decision went even further. In that case, two firms manufacturing paper were fined a record $2 million for price-fixing. Two vice presidents who were involved in the price-fixing were fined a total of $70,000 and sentenced to four-month jail terms.[38] In other words, the courts are now beginning to hold managers personally responsible for the actions of their companies.

This situation is sure to become more pronounced because of the recent passage of tough laws with stiff penalties for noncompliance. These laws cover equal employment opportunity, pollution control, product safety, and employee health and safety.

There are at least two important implications of the trend toward greater personal accountability. First, managers will find it increasingly difficult to hide in the bureaucratic shadows of their organizations when a law has been broken. Managers who make illegal decisions stand a good chance of facing the consequences of their actions in a court of law. Second, increased personal accountability will probably influence managers to make more conservative decisions. This could turn out to be a serious problem, because high success often goes hand in hand with high-risk decisions.

SUMMARY   Successful managers take into account the social, political, economic, and technological aspects of the environment in which they must operate. Those who ignore environmental realities may end up suffering from future shock. The best defense against future shock is anticipation and preparation for change, rather than mere reaction to it.

The social setting of management is a synthesis of the forces for stability and change. Society has both stable and changing characteristics; it is marked by cooperation as well as conflict. Managers who understand today's social trends are in a better position to manage successfully in the future. One important set of social trends is in the area of demographics. Now that the postwar baby boom generation has entered the work force and the birthrate is declining, the average age of the American population is rising. During the 1980s, the percentage of workers age 25–44 will increase dramatically, while the percentage of those 45–64 will decline. This situation could create a shortage of top managers along with limited promotion opportunities for 25- to 44-year-olds.

Attitudes toward work are changing. However, contrary to popular belief, younger employees have not entirely lost the will to work. But they expect their jobs to offer challenge and meaning. Even for young workers with interesting jobs, leisure has largely replaced work as life's focal point. Among the promising managerial responses to the new work ethic are work reform and flexible work scheduling. Managers also have to deal with egalitarian legislation that attempts to remove social, political, and economic barriers for women and minorities. In spite of egalitarian reform, minorities and women still lag far behind in economic and employment status.

In theory, the democratic process is a self-adjusting circle of actions and reactions. Factors such as voter apathy, however, have thrown the future of the democratic process into question. Today's political climate has been severely affected by public frustration due to unrealized expectations and the breach of public trust. Public confidence in government and business is at an all-time low.

The trend toward social, rather than strictly economic, legislation has created a huge governmental bureaucracy. Managers tend to resent the time and expense required to comply with government reporting procedures.

Managers are strictly prohibited from supporting individual candidates or political parties with the company name or funds. Evidence of illegal campaign contributions in recent years has tarnished the political reputation of management. By striving to promote more ethical conduct among all employees, management can help improve its public image. Because of strict laws on various aspects of managerial conduct and recent court decisions, managers stand a greater chance than ever of being held personally accountable for organizational activities.

TERMS TO UNDERSTAND

Transience
Synthesis perspective
Demography
Flextime
Egalitarianism

Civil rights movement
Women's liberation movement
Politics
Ethics

QUESTIONS FOR DISCUSSION

1. Why must today's managers know what is happening outside their organizations?
2. What evidence of transience can you detect today?
3. In your opinion, how will a doubling of the world's population in the next thirty-five years affect the quality of life in the United States?
4. What is your present attitude toward work? Does your attitude toward work differ significantly from that held by your parents? Explain.
5. What do you think of egalitarian legislation?
6. Do you think the women's liberation movement has any justification?
7. Why is voter apathy a serious threat to a democracy?
8. How did Watergate affect the political climate in the United States?
9. Do you think managers are generally ethical or unethical? Defend your position.
10. Are the courts justified in holding managers personally accountable for the actions of their organizations? Explain.

**CASE 16.1
WHAT MAKES THEM TICK?**

Bob Ridell has been with Century Pharmaceutical for twenty-eight years, ever since his discharge from the navy. He has been a production supervisor for the last nineteen of those years. At 49, Bob is the oldest first-line supervisor at Century. Privately, Bob admits that not having a college degree is probably the reason he hasn't made it to middle management. Nevertheless, Bob is highly respected among his fellow supervisors. He seems to have a special ability to understand and get along with the younger employees, who are a constant source of frustration to his peers.

Recently Ike, a swing-shift supervisor, stopped Bob as he was leaving the plant for the day. Ike asked him how things were going; and after a few moments, Bob knew he had something important on his mind. With a little prompting from Bob, Ike opened up and poured out his frustrations about the younger people.

Although Ike is ten years younger than Bob, he still is quite a bit older than the people who work under him. As Ike sees it, his young subordinates just aren't living up to their potential. He questions their loyalty as well. Ike is sure that they would take a job with another company in a minute if the opportunity arose. He just doesn't know what motivates them. Although they express a desire for more money, they seem reluctant to work harder to earn it. According to Ike, they often are content just to sit around and complain about the work being dull and boring. Ike claims that his younger employees shun the idea of moving up to a job with more responsibility because, they say, it would demand too much of their time.

"I just can't figure these kids out," Ike concluded, "they seem to want a say in everything, but then they resist getting intimately involved in their work. They don't appreciate all that the company does for them. You seem to get along well with your young people, Bob. Tell me, what makes them tick?"

FOR DISCUSSION
1. Put yourself in Bob's place and answer Ike's question.
2. What should Ike do to get in better touch with his younger subordinates?
3. What do you look for in a job?

CASE 16.2
SHADES OF GRAY

In response to a newspaper reporter's question about the ethical conduct of managers, a top-level manager who asked to remain unnamed said:

> Ethics involves the difference between right and wrong, the difference between black and white. In management we very seldom deal strictly in terms of clear-cut black and white distinctions. Most of our decisions are based on subtle shades of gray. We have no choice but to rely on the individual's sense of professionalism. Top management cannot dictate morality. Even if we wanted to, we couldn't. People are either moral or immoral. Morality is and always will be a personal concern. If the organization gets tangled up in the area of morality, our primary responsibility of getting the job done will be shortchanged. Today, the unethical competitor has the upper hand. Now don't misunderstand me, I'm not advocating unethical conduct. I'm just saying that it's a fact of life today. One organization can't do much to reverse a societal trend.

FOR DISCUSSION
1. How would you respond to this position?
2. What steps would you recommend to this manager for promoting ethical conduct within the organization?
3. Why be concerned with ethics at all?

REFERENCES   *Opening quotation*

Peter F. Drucker, *The Age of Discontinuity* (New York: Harper & Row, 1969), p. 3.

1. Adapted from: "What Clouds Ford's Future," *Business Week* #2545 (July 31, 1978): 72–73.
2. Alvin Toffler, *Future Shock* (New York: Bantam, 1970), p. 46.
3. D. Stanley Eitzen, *Social Structure and Social Problems in America* (Boston: Allyn and Bacon, 1974), pp. 12–14.
4. "The Graying of America," *Newsweek* 89 (February 28, 1977): 50.
5. Ibid., p. 58.
6. Leonard Nadler, "If You're Planning for Tomorrow, Remember . . . It's Not What It Used to Be," *Management Review* 67 (May 1978): 28.
7. Alfred L. Seelye, "Societal Change and Business-Government Relationships," *MSU Business Topics* 23 (Autumn 1975): 7.
8. See: David Cherrington, "The Values of Younger Workers," *Business Horizons* 20 (December 1977): 18–30.
9. Patricia A. Renwick, Edward E. Lawler, and the *Psychology Today* staff, "What You Really Want from Your Job," *Psychology Today* 11 (May 1978): 65.
10. "Youth Views Business and Society," *Intellect* 103 (November 1974): 80.
11. M. R. Cooper, B. S. Morgan, P. M. Foley, and L. B. Kaplan, "Changing Employee Values: Deepening Discontent?" *Harvard Business Review* 57 (January–February 1979): 124.
12. Renwick and Lawler, "What You Really Want from Your Job," p. 57.
13. For a brief and interesting discussion of flextime, see: Glenn J. Schnur, "Here Comes Flextime," *Management Accounting* 59 (June 1978): 50–52.
14. "Equality: American Dream—Or Nightmare?" *U.S. News & World Report* 79 (August 4, 1975): 26.
15. "Egalitarianism: Threat to a Free Market," *Business Week* #2409 (December 1, 1975): 62.
16. "The Bad News About Black Incomes," *Business and Society Review* #21 (Spring 1977): 4.
17. Paul E. Kraemer, *Awakening from the American Dream* (Chicago: Center for the Scientific Study of Religion, 1973), p. v.
18. Kirsten Amundsen, *A New Look at the Silenced Majority* (Englewood Cliffs, N.J.: Prentice-Hall, 1977), p. 144.

19. "Labor Month in Review," *Monthly Labor Review* 100 (January 1977): 2.

20. David R. Segal, *Society and Politics: Uniformity and Diversity in Modern Democracy* (Glenview, Ill.: Scott, Foresman, 1974), pp. 2–3.

21. See: Neil H. Jacoby, "Six Challenges to Business Management," *Business Horizons* 19 (August 1976): 29–37.

22. Charles A. Reich, *The Greening of America* (New York: Bantam, 1970), p. 246.

23. For a brief but revealing chronology of Watergate events, see: "The 'Third-rate Burglary' That Toppled a President," *U.S. News & World Report* 77 (August 19, 1974): 24–26, 29.

24. See: "Four Key Convictions in the Watergate Affair," *U.S. News & World Report* 78 (January 13, 1975): 15–17.

25. Data drawn from: David M. Alpern, "The Skeptical Voters," *Newsweek* 87 (April 12, 1976): 30–31, 33.

26. Ibid., p. 33.

27. Seelye, "Societal Change and Business-Government Relationships," p. 5.

28. "The Law Closes in on Managers," *Business Week* #2431 (May 10, 1976): 110–116.

29. Drawn from: "Dow Chemical's Catalog of Regulatory Horrors," *Business Week* #2477 (April 4, 1977): 50.

30. See, for example: "What Businesses Can Do in Politics," *Nation's Business* 60 (August 1972): 30–35.

31. "Gulf Leads Toward a Cleanup," *Time* 107 (January 26, 1976): 54.

32. "What You Can—and Can't Do in a Political Campaign," *Nation's Business* 62 (August 1974): 22–23.

33. For more on lobbying, see: "Why the Corporate Lobbyist Is Necessary," *Business Week* #2220 (March 18, 1972): 62–65.

34. John F. Steiner, "The Business Response to Public Distrust," *Business Horizons* 20 (April 1977): 74.

35. James A. Waters, "Catch 20.5: Corporate Morality as an Organizational Phenomenon," *Organizational Dynamics* 6 (Spring 1978): 14.

36. Steven N. Brenner and Earl A. Molander, "Is the Ethics of Business Changing?" *Harvard Business Review* 55 (January–February 1977): 71.

37. See: "The Law Closes in on Managers," p. 111.

38. "Paper Bag Price-fixing," *Business Week* #2555 (October 9, 1978): 56.

Chapter 17

The Economic and Technological Environment

The global engine of economic growth is clearly losing steam. This slowdown did not originate in some sudden human failure to manage the economic system. Rather, it is rooted in humanity's relationship to the carrying capacity of biological systems and to the dwindling reserves of several key nonrenewable resources such as oil.

Lester R. Brown

LEARNING OBJECTIVES

When you finish reading this chapter, you should be able to

○ Highlight the contributing factors of our present energy problem.
○ Explain how institutionalized inflation could affect the practice of management.
○ Outline the significance of the three dimensions of technology.
○ Explain what innovation lag is and why it is an important managerial concern today.
○ Explain how technology assessment can balance the two faces of technology.

By considering the general environment of management, divided into social, political, economic, and technological aspects, we can better understand the challenges facing management today. But this orderly breakdown is only a matter of theoretical convenience. Real life is never so neatly divided. The outside forces that exert pressure on management are tangled in a complex web that requires careful examination and sorting out.

For example, consider the situation faced by major oil companies in 1978. Up to that time they had invested heavily in U.S. western coal reserves, expecting long-term profits from converting coal to oil and gas. Optimism in the industry had soared in response to the Carter administration's 1977 goal of doubling U.S. coal production by 1985. But as the realities of the situation developed, this optimism faded.

> It had become clear that the strip-mining of Western coal was going to be more costly than expected because of a new law requiring reclamation of mined land. Then it became doubtful if the nation's railroads could haul the output of coal that was being projected. The economics of Western coal took another blow when the Environmental Protection Agency decreed that plants burning it must use stack scrubbers to reduce sulfur dioxide emissions despite the coals's low sulfur content compared to that of Eastern coal. Finally, the long strike by the United Mine Workers proved that the union had little control of its members, and the settlement promised nothing in the way of increased productivity from underground mines.[1]

This situation reveals a host of interrelated social, political, economic, and technological considerations. The point is that such situations demand keen analysis and a bit of managerial detective work in order to bring all the environmental forces into focus. The purpose of this chapter is to round out our discussion of the general environment of management by exploring its economic and technological aspects.

THE ECONOMIC ENVIRONMENT

In times of economic uncertainty we often turn to economists for insights about the future. Unfortunately, economic forecasts sometimes foster rather than dispel uncertainty. For instance, an inside joke among economists relates the story of the chap who was asked to forecast what the stock market would do in coming months. He replied, "I think it will go up. Then again, it could go down. Of course, if it does neither, it will stay the same."

Nevertheless, even though economic forecasts occasionally leave something to be desired, economics is important to management. *Economics* is the study of how scarce resources are used to create wealth and how that wealth is distributed. It is management's job to administer scarce resources on a daily basis. To discharge this responsibility properly, managers need to be familiar with prevailing economic forces. With that end in mind, let us examine two contemporary economic themes, energy and inflation. Each promises to shape the practice of management significantly in the future.

ENERGY
Energy plays a central role in economics and management for two reasons. First, things of economic value cannot be obtained or created without the use of energy. Second, misuse of energy resources in recent years is just one symptom of careless attitudes toward limited resources in general. By focusing on energy we can learn a great deal about managing the entire range of natural resources.

As used here, the term *energy* means resources that have the capacity to do work. There are both living and nonliving sources of energy. Human beings and their domesticated animals represent living energy; subsistence agricultural and preindustrial societies are sometimes called "sweat economies" because of their heavy reliance on living energy. Modern industrialized economies, in contrast, are powered primarily by nonliving energy resources. Experts estimate that only about 2 or 3 percent of the energy used annually in the United States comes from living sources.[2] The rest comes from nonliving sources such as wood, water, coal, oil, and uranium. Except for wood and water, these nonliving energy resources were created millions of years ago under extraordinary conditions that no longer exist. For the foreseeable future, the health of our economy will be closely tied to the availability of these exhaustible energy resources.

When future generations look back upon this present era, its most striking aspect is likely to be our naive relationship to energy. It is a curious relationship indeed. First, we in the United States have come to rely most heavily on oil, one of the country's least abundant energy resources (see Figure 17.1). Second, we have persisted in using a finite and exhaustible oil supply as if it would last forever; our appetite for energy is voracious. The net result is a problem (many call it a crisis) of enormous complexity that relatively few people fully comprehend. While we cannot hope to treat all aspects of the energy problem in the space of a few pages, we can frame a realistic perspective. Perhaps more than anyone else, managers of our energy-consuming, productive organizations need a clear perspective of the energy situation.

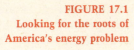

FIGURE 17.1
Looking for the roots of America's energy problem

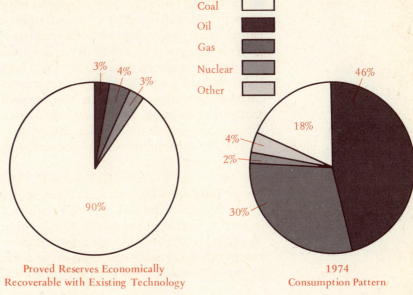

Proved Reserves Economically
Recoverable with Existing Technology

1974
Consumption Pattern

Source: Federal Energy Administration, *National Energy Outlook 1976*, p. xxii.

Putting the energy problem in perspective Prior to the 1973 Mideast oil embargo, America's energy demands grew dramatically. One team of experts has isolated five contributing factors that developed after World War II.

1. Steadily declining energy prices relative to the prices of other goods and services.
2. Expanding consumer population.
3. Introduction and rapid market penetration of energy-intensive consumer products that provide basic amenities (such as individualized transportation, comfortable habitat, and household conveniences).
4. Increasing cost of labor, which increased the substitution of capital and energy for labor.
5. Major increases in disposable income, enabling rapid expansion of consumer buying power.[3]

The direct result of this set of circumstances is our present economy, which is geared to a plentiful supply of cheap energy. Now that inexpensive energy is gone, however, the entire economic picture has changed.

Without realizing it, the United States had worked itself into an energy corner by 1973. The economy of the country and the lifestyle of its people were firmly committed to oil as the primary source of cheap energy. Because demand outstripped domestic supply, a growing share of that oil had to be imported. When the OPEC cartel interrupted shipments of oil to the United States and to other industrialized nations in 1973, Americans were shocked to find themselves waiting in line for more expensive gasoline. However, when the embargo ended and the lines at local gas stations disappeared, people turned their attention to other things. Unfortunately, the energy problem did not end when the embargo ended. It had only just begun.

After the 1973 OPEC oil embargo the United States continued to rely heavily on petroleum imports in spite of a fourfold increase in the world price for oil. In 1978, when the United States was importing nearly 50 percent of its oil, public opinion polls revealed that half the American population refused to believe there was an energy crisis.[4] A former chief scientist at the U.S. Bureau of Mines, on the other hand, offered the following assessment:

> We have sufficient energy resources to supply our basic needs for many decades, but the costs will rise continually. The country still does not understand the problem. The layman wants to believe in inexhaustible, cheap gasoline and in this has been supported by many unsubstantiated claims. The time has come to realize that no miracle is imminent and we must make do with what we have. We will never again have as much oil or gas as we have today, nor will it be as cheap. Nuclear energy has been a major disappointment. Solar energy will be slow in developing and, contrary to popular opinion, quite expensive. Coal is the only salvation for the next few decades.[5]

As indicated in Figure 17.2, the U.S. government expects our heavy dependence on fossil fuels (coal, gas, and oil) to continue during the 1980s. Although nuclear fission may play a greater role during the 1980s, it will continue to lag behind the fossil fuels.

Exotic energy technologies—converting coal to oil or gas, ocean thermal energy conversion, solar power, geothermal energy, or nuclear fusion—are a long way off because of developmental problems. A corporate planner for Exxon Corporation has cautioned: "The real concern today must not be on the far distant future but on getting from here to there. It is the transition period itself where our challenge is most direct."[6] Every transition alternative has its limitations. Conservation has been criticized because it merely stretches existing energy supplies rather than creating new ones.

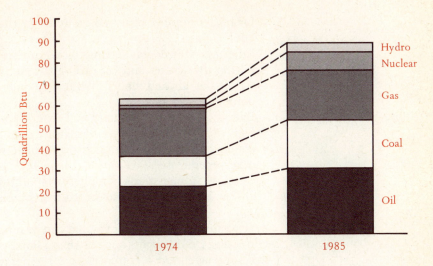

FIGURE 17.2
How the U.S. will meet its growing energy demands during the 1980s

Source: Federal Energy Administration, *National Energy Outlook 1976*, p. xxv.

Critics of nuclear fission claim that it is more expensive than anticipated due to inflated construction costs and limited fuel supplies. Issues of nuclear plant safety and untested methods of nuclear waste disposal disturb a growing number of people. Conversion from the use of oil and gas to coal by industrial firms and utilities has been criticized by environmentalists concerned about air pollution. There is no easy solution to the current energy problem; every opportunity has its drawbacks. The overall challenge during the 1980s is to seek an appropriate balance between energy opportunities and economic, social, and environmental costs. Management will play a central role in this effort.

Implications for management Now that cheap energy has become a thing of the past, managers need to update their orientation toward energy. Wasteful technologies cannot be tolerated. Conservation of scarce energy resources will be a top priority for managers while safe and effective energy technologies are being developed. A step in the right direction is to have a team of energy analysts carry out an energy audit of the organization's facilities.

An *energy audit* is a systematic assessment of an organization's actual-versus-desirable energy use.[7] Trouble spots found by energy auditors typically include:

○ Inadequately insulated buildings.
○ Unnecessary lighting (ornamental lights, for example).

○ Oversized and/or untuned vehicles in the organization's motor pool.
○ Improper thermostat settings (government regulations call for 65° during the winter and 78° during the summer).
○ Air leaks around doors, windows, and other building access points.
○ Energy-wasteful machinery and work habits.
○ Loss of recoverable waste heat (for example, waste heat from air conditioning units can be used to heat water for washing and other operations).
○ Careless storage of fuel supplies (evaporation, leakage, and weather damage are a threat to stored fossil fuels).

An enormous potential for savings can be realized by identifying and correcting trouble spots such as these. Furthermore, an energy audit gives management a factual base for generating measurable objectives aimed at more efficient energy use. Without specific documentation of wasteful practices and related costs, management will have a difficult time convincing employees that conservation is both possible and necessary. The challenge is to move organization members beyond mere talk to constructive action in conserving scarce energy resources.

Experts today are calling for comprehensive energy management programs. An *energy management program* is an organizationwide commitment to more efficient use of scarce energy resources. Industrial firms are pointing the way in the following manner:

As part of energy management, companies are changing the fundamental way they manufacture their products. They are changing the way they generate energy for manufacturing, the mix of fuels they use, and the degree of their dependence on whatever fuel they use. They are changing their relationships with their energy suppliers, and in some cases are moving to own and operate their own supply source.[8]

Energy use has become a key consideration in the decision-making process where energy management programs are in effect. Even fundamental decisions, such as the siting and architectural design of new buildings, are made with energy conservation and efficiency in mind.[9]

Individual commitment is essential to efficient energy use. One way to encourage energy awareness is to communicate the energy management program policies and objectives with a stimulating educational program. Employees who contribute energy-saving ideas and behavior should be rewarded with a systematic program of positive reinforcement. Gone are the cheap energy days when it was acceptable practice to cool overheated buildings by throwing open a few windows. Present energy economics are such that we can no longer afford to heat or cool the great outdoors.

INFLATION   Economist Paul Samuelson defines *inflation* as "a time of generally rising prices for goods and factors of production."[10] Although we hear a great deal about inflation today, it is nothing new. The U.S. economy has seen many inflationary periods come and go over the years. Typically, some sort of extraordinary situation such as World War II or the dramatic rise in the price of oil in 1973 triggered a period of inflation that was followed by a recession, which served to cool the economy. During the late 1970s, however, the cyclical nature of inflation was replaced by a persistent upward climb in prices even though there were no extraordinary circumstances.

Economic experts now say we are saddled with *institutionalized inflation*, which is a steady rise in prices prompted by the structure of the economy itself. In other words, economic institutions such as government, business, and organized labor are fueling inflation by attempting to achieve their respective objectives—low unemployment, greater profits, and higher wages. As an economic condition, institutionalized inflation affects what managers can and cannot do. Like other environmental variables, inflation presents managers with a unique set of opportunities and obstacles.

Inflation is a subtle but powerful economic force that eats away at a healthy economy like a cancer. The most visible evidence of inflation is that tomorrow's dollar buys less than today's dollar. For example, as indicated in Figure 17.3, a dollar worth 100 cents in 1967 was only worth 50 cents in 1978. Stated differently, in 1978 it took two dollars to buy what one dollar bought back in 1967. Today, a 6 to 10 percent annual inflation rate has become commonplace. Observers contend that this institutionalized inflation can be traced largely to a reluctance on the part of the federal government to raise taxes, cut government spending, and restrict the supply of money, the three traditional weapons against inflation.[11] The net result is that we may simply have to learn to live with nagging inflation. If so, then managers will have to accept greater governmental control of the economy. They will also need to learn the psychology of inflation.

Toward a highly controlled economy   In a relatively free economy inflation is controlled by the marketplace. When prices get too

FIGURE 17.3
Inflation shrinks the
purchasing power of the
dollar

1967 $1

1973 $.75

1978 $.50

10   20   30   40   50   60   70   80   90   100

Cents

Data source: U. S. Department of Commerce, *Survey of Current Business.*

high, consumers stop buying. When consumers stop buying, management is forced to cut its prices, and in turn, its payroll expense by laying off employees or reducing wages. But as our economy has grown in size and complexity, this traditional, self-correcting mechanism has been compromised. Today, we are said to be locked into a wage-price spiral in which businesses are forced to charge higher prices because employees (particularly those in unions) demand higher wages. Completing the spiral, both private and public sector employees say they must demand higher wages to cope with higher prices. In this chicken-and-egg situation it is difficult to distinguish cause from effect. The ultimate government weapon for this spiraling inflation is mandatory wage and price controls. Typically, managers in the private business sector resent wage and price controls as an infringement on their decision-making prerogatives. Nonetheless, mandatory wage and price controls have been used before, and our present dilemma with institutionalized inflation suggests that they may be used again. A brief review of the recent track record of wage and price controls in the United States may be helpful at this point.

On August 15, 1971, President Nixon instituted America's first peacetime wage and price controls. The wage and price freeze dismayed many Americans but left them hopeful that inflation would be curbed. The freeze of Phase I gave way to selective controls in Phases II, III, and IV. With each new phase public confusion and business-sector resentment grew. Finally, on April 30, 1974, the entire plan was scrapped.

A writer for *Fortune* observed, "This adventure began with exhilaration. . . . But the euphoria soon drained away. The elaborate structure of controls collapsed in confusion and defeat [1974], when controls were mercifully ended."[12] Proponents of wage and price controls claim that this experiment with peacetime controls failed only because it was full of loopholes and was improperly administered. They believe mandatory controls can stem inflation if wisely and equitably administered.

Has the United States seen the last of wage and price controls? In 1974 *Business Week* said no.

In an age of relentless worldwide inflation, it would be both premature and politically naive to assume that America's experimentation with incomes policies in general and controls in particular is ended. . . . An important precedent has been set, and the example of Western Europe suggests that once a country resorts to an incomes policy, it is very likely to pursue the same path again and again.[13]

Today, in spite of their opposition, top-level business managers seem resigned to the fact that wage and price controls are around the corner. A nationwide survey of chief executive officers in 1978 showed that 44 percent of them foresaw wage and price controls in the near future.[14] The issue today is not whether wage and price controls will be implemented, but *when* they will be implemented. But how will the implementation of wage and price controls affect the practice of management?

In the private business sector, especially among large firms, the planning process involves establishing revenue objectives that will allow the firm to recover expenses and achieve a desired level of profit. Prices of products and services are adjusted to accommodate revenue objectives. If the government tells management what price

CONVERSATION WITH . . .

Luke G. Williams
President and Chief Executive
 Officer
American Sign & Indicator
 Corporation
Spokane, Washington

Dorian Studio.

PERSONAL BACKGROUND

After serving in the Pacific with the U.S. Navy during World War II, Luke Williams returned to Spokane, his hometown, to open up a commercial sign business with his brother, Chuck. With the threat of bankruptcy frequently knocking at the door, their business slowly began to take shape between 1947 and 1953. The big breakthrough occurred in 1951, when Chuck suggested the idea of a sign with alternating time and temperature on a single lampbank. On December 24, 1951, the first of these displays was installed on a Spokane bank. After years of innovative work in the areas of leasing and service contracting, Luke Williams's firm has become the largest specialized sign leasing company in America. Today, over 90 percent of the familiar time and temperature displays seen throughout the United States, Mexico, Canada, and Puerto Rico are owned by American Sign & Indicator. Moreover, the firm's scoreboards serve numerous professional and college sports arenas including the Rose Bowl and Cincinnati's Riverfront Stadium. In addition to his administrative duties, Luke is very active in public affairs and civic activities.

QUOTABLE QUOTES

What advice would you give an aspiring manager?

Mr. Williams: Take care of the company and the company will take care of you. Be results oriented and understand that money is a by-product of accomplishment. You accomplish results and the money will be there.

Do you have any personal observations about the practice of management today?

Mr. Williams: Some very talented people do not develop their full potential because of their refusal to participate in management above their own comfort level.

What do you think it takes to be a successful manager today?

Mr. Williams: Judgment, tenacity, industriousness, and leadership.

---

it can charge for a given product or service, the entire planning process will be affected.

A price ceiling will prevent management from passing higher costs along to customers. Creative problem solving will be required to protect desired profit margins in the face of pricing restrictions. Cost control and efficiency will become more important than ever. Production efficiencies will have to be realized by using raw materials and resources conservatively, redesigning products and services to reduce production and materials costs, and influencing employees to work harder in spite of government wage restrictions. This challenge will demand the best that managers have to offer. Price controls, if imposed, will eliminate price increases as a way of compensating for production and administrative inefficiencies. Controls will force management to hunt down and correct wasteful inefficiencies that might ordinarily be tolerated.

Dealing with psychology of inflation   Persistent inflation can be expected to have a number of behavioral side effects that make human resource management more difficult. *Real income*, the purchasing power of one's income, is the key here. Although inflation creates the illusion of a fatter paycheck, real income may actually drop. For example, an employee who gets a 5 percent annual raise when inflation is riding at 10 percent ends up with a 5 percent pay cut. This unhealthy situation, especially when it threatens to be chronic, is a serious obstacle to productivity.

The situation will call for management's best problem-solving approach. Incentive schemes undreamed of today will have to be tried and tested if the inflation-riddled dollar continues to lose its value as a motivating force. Nonmonetary fringe benefits such as day care facilities for the children of female employees could become commonplace. Also, as the material rewards for working are eroded by inflation, workers will put more pressure on management to provide jobs that are intrinsically motivating. Job enrichment and other creative work reforms may become the rule rather than the exception, because a dull, monotonous job is insufferable when real income is being eaten up by inflation.

Barring governmental wage controls, another behavioral consequence of persistent inflation could be an increase in militant unionism. This situation prevails in England today. Unionized employees regularly paralyze the country by striking when their wage demands are not met. This tactic drives a wedge of mutual distrust between management and labor, thus making efforts to motivate better job performance much more difficult. Considering the dramatic growth in white-collar and public-employee unions in recent years, this problem could affect the entire economy.

In summary, one economic reality stands out clearly. Resource scarcity and a shrinking dollar will require managers to devise new ways to do *more* with *less*. As we turn now to the technological environment of management, we will see that it, too, presents a unique set of opportunities and obstacles.

THE TECHNOLOGICAL ENVIRONMENT

The term *technology* usually conjures up exotic visions of moon walks, off-shore oil rigs, test-tube babies, and other dramatic innovations. But technology has its ordinary side as well, and it pervades our world today. Consider Daniel J. Boorstin's droll observation:

> Each forward step in modern technology tends to reduce the difference between the older categories of experience. Take, for example, the once elementary distinction between transportation and communication: between moving the person and moving the message. While communication once *was* an inferior substitute for transportation (you had to read the account because you couldn't get there), it is now often the preferred alternative. The television screen (by traditional categories a mode of communication) brings together people who still remain in their separate living rooms. With the increasing congestion of city traffic, with the parking problem and the lengthened holding patterns over airports, our television screen becomes a superior way of getting there. So when it comes to public events, now you are often more there when you are here than when you are there![15]

If managers are to adapt to a changing environment, they must understand the role technology plays in change.

WHAT IS TECHNOLOGY?

For our present purpose, *technology* is defined as the process of broadening our control of the surrounding environment through the use of tools and ideas. Technology has three important dimensions.

It is (1) an extension of science, (2) an evolutionary process, and (3) more than just machines.

Technology as an extension of science   As an extension of science, technology helps put scientific principles and facts to practical use. Physical, biological, and social scientists study literally everything under the sun (and beyond it, too). The twentieth century has been labeled appropriately the "scientific age." And many if not most of the scientific advances have been applied in our everyday lives. It is no wonder that people typically use the words *science* and *technology* interchangeably.

Actually, science and technology involve two related but different processes. As an authority on technology has pointed out, "Science is the quest for more or less abstract knowledge, whereas technology is the application of organized knowledge to help solve problems in our society."[16] For management the key aspect of technology is its problem-solving application.

Technology as an evolutionary process   Technology translates scientific principles and facts into reality in an evolutionary manner. That is, each idea stands on the shoulders of others that came before. Like the popular childhood game of leapfrog, technological advances are more often than not extensions and refinements of earlier advances. A single technological advance may inspire dozens of others.

The synthetic fiber nylon is an excellent example of technological evolution. It took a long time to synthesize nylon. But once nylon was developed, nylon products such as stockings, rope, and fishing poles multiplied rapidly. The same evolutionary process occurred after the development of transistors and integrated circuits.

Technology as more than just machines   The word *technology* makes most people think of machines. As used here, however, the term means much more than mechanical gadgetry. Technology also involves knowledge—the knowledge to build, operate, and maintain machines.

Suppose, for example, that the time barrier could be bridged and a modern computer were suddenly to materialize in the cave of a prehistoric Neanderthal family. Although the cave dwellers might attack the intruder or superstitiously bow and pray to it, they would lack the knowledge to operate it. Thus the computer, a miracle of modern technology, would be utterly useless because there would be no electricity to run it, no programmer to feed it data, and no technician to repair it. Computer technology involves not only the computer itself but the knowledge to operate and maintain it as well.

TECHNOLOGY AND THE INNOVATION PROCESS

The full meaning of technology emerges in the *innovation process*, which is the systematic development and practical application of a new idea. A great deal of time-consuming work is necessary to develop a new idea into a marketable product or service, and many never do become technically feasible, let alone marketable.

The innovation process consists of three steps. The first is conceptualization, when the new idea originally occurs to someone. Development of a working prototype is the second step. This step is sometimes called *product technology*, because it involves designing a product that will actually work as intended. The third step is to develop practical production processes that will make the new idea marketable. This step is called *production technology*. The innovation process requires both product technology and production technology. It is management's job to identify product technologies as soon as possible and develop production technologies to take advantage of the new knowledge. Without management's contribution, the generation of new ideas can be a waste of knowledge, time, and money.

The computer as an innovation   The modern electronic computer is an excellent example of the three-step innovation process at work. The original idea for an automatic calculating machine has been traced back to the work of an English mathematician named Charles Babbage. In 1833, Babbage proposed an "analytic engine" that was supposed to calculate, store data, and print out answers (precisely the same functions carried out by modern computers). Unfortunately, Babbage's ideas were so advanced and required such sophisticated technology that he never saw his dreams materialize. Over one hundred years passed before an operational computer was built. As one historical review of the modern computer notes: "Conceived as a giant steam powered assemblage of brass gears, cams, and wheels, Babbage's machine was never built. In fact, its total concept was not realized until 1946, with Bell Laboratories Model V."[17] The Bell Laboratories prototype was a breakthrough in product technology.

Production technology was later brought into play by IBM and other companies to complete the innovation process. Another twenty years passed before efficient production technologies created a marketable balance between product quality and price. Today, nearly a century and a half after Babbage's new idea, computers find widespread application. Innovation takes time.

Innovation lag   The time it takes for a new idea to become a widely used product or service is called the *innovation lag*. The longer the innovation lag, the longer society must wait to benefit from a new idea. Over the years, the trend has been toward shorter innovation lags, but the process can still be painfully slow.

One expert has found that the innovation lags for ten major twentieth-century innovations averaged nineteen years. For example, the heart pacemaker was conceived in 1928 but not put into general use until 1960—a thirty-two year innovation lag. The innovation lags for hybrid corn and the video tape recorder were twenty-five years and six years respectively.[18] Although an innovation lag of six years seems short by comparison, six years is still a long time for society to wait to enjoy the benefits of a new idea.

Reducing the innovation lag is one of the great challenges facing today's problem-solving manager. A step in the right direction is to create an organizational climate in which bright ideas are given an opportunity to blossom into marketable products. Too often management unconsciously sets up artificial barriers to creativity. An exciting example of what can be done to encourage creativity is Texas Instruments' IDEA program. Each year the firm hands out $1 million worth of $25,000 grants to employees with bright ideas for a new product or process. This program allows the creative employee to concentrate solely on his or her special project. Many of the IDEA-sponsored projects have paid off for Texas Instruments. "The $19.95 digital watch that tore apart the market in 1976 got its start as an IDEA program in the Semiconductor Group."[19] It is possible to shorten innovation lag considerably if a positive approach is taken.

MANAGEMENT AND THE INNOVATION PROCESS

Managers must be constantly alert for new ideas in the general environment. In order to survive, organizations must take in and absorb new ideas and new ways of doing things. However, new ideas will be productive only if the innovation process is completed by the organization. Actually, innovation may take place within the organization on four different fronts: (1) product or service innovations, (2) production innovations, (3) organizational innovations, and (4) people innovations.[20]

Product or service innovations   This form of innovation relates to an organization's products, whether tangible or intangible. Product technology is applied here. Both individuals and organizations can use new goods and services as well as new variations of existing goods and services. Semiconductor technology within the electronics industry shows the impact of significant product innovation. According to *Business Week*:

It has reduced the retail price of an electronic calculator to less than $10 from $1,600 in a single decade, and it transformed the 3-ton, $200,000 computer of 23 years ago into a 12-oz. hand-held unit priced at $300 today.[21]

Other useful product innovations include a variety of products ranging from electric typewriters and miracle drugs to disposable diapers. Among service innovations, society has eagerly adopted fast-food restaurants, direct long-distance dialing, and credit cards.

Production innovations   This second form of innovation relates to the way in which organizations produce goods and services. Again, Texas Instruments has been one of the leaders. The firm automatically assembles nearly 75 percent of its hand-held calculators in the following manner:

At one work station, for example, a television camera locates the calculator on the conveyor for a robot, which picks it up and loads it into a carousel that applies foot pads and the date code. A second robot off-loads the calculator. Farther down the line, a similar setup loads a completed calculator into a test system that pushes the keys with bursts of air while a camera-equipped minicomputer "reads" the calculator display in a check for errors.[22]

This process, which sounds like a scenario from science fiction, has helped Texas Instruments cut the price of a hand-held calculator from $45 to $10 in just four years.

Organizational innovations   Although most people think only of physical products when innovation is mentioned, *organizations* also can be improved through innovation. For example, the matrix organization design discussed in Chapter 7 is an innovative way to make organizations more flexible. By giving project managers the authority to pick and choose teams of technical specialists for the job at hand, large and complex projects can be completed effectively and efficiently. A need for organizational innovation still remains in task design, upward communication, organization development strategies, and feedback systems.

People innovations   Since human beings are an organization's most valuable resource, management cannot afford to overlook innovations in managing people. New and improved methods of recruiting, hiring, training, paying, and motivating people are always needed. The video-taped training session is a recent innovation that has proven fruitful. Its success derives from the fact that trainees receive immediate feedback on their practice sessions. Self-analysis and self-criticism have proven to be excellent learning aids. Flextime, as discussed in the last chapter, is another promising people innovation.

Considering these different areas for innovation, it becomes clear that managers are limited only by their imaginations and their desire to improve upon the past.

EVALUATING PRODUCT TECHNOLOGIES   Because new products are so important to productive organizations, let us take a brief look at nine criteria that help managers judge the economic value of a proposed product.[23] These standards are most effectively applied during the planning process. The idea is to screen proposed products prior to full-scale production so that time and money will not be thrown away on unmarketable products.

○ *Functional need*   Does the product have the capacity to fill an existing need in the marketplace? For example, will people purchase electric tooth brushes in preference to ordinary tooth brushes?

○ *Competing products*   Can the product compete effectively with other products? For example, can a new brand of tennis racket compete against established brands? Is there room in the market for a new racket with, perhaps, new features? Or are consumers now buying running shoes instead of tennis rackets?

○ *Price*   How much will the final product cost the customer? Is it a reasonable and competitive price? Leasing or credit arrangements may enter the picture here.

○ *Ease of use*   Will the product do what it is supposed to do in an easy and trouble-free manner? Is it well designed? Will the user find special features of the product useful as time goes by?

○ *Operating cost*   Will the typical user find the operating costs reasonable? This includes the costs of energy resources such as oil, gas, or electricity as well as normal maintenance.

○ *Reliability*   Can the user expect to get faithful service from the product during its expected lifetime? In short, can the user count on the product?

○ *Service*   If a product breaks down, how much time and expense will the user have to invest to get it repaired? How convenient are service centers for customers? For example, Caterpillar has enjoyed active sales for years because of its reputation for fast and convenient service. Good service means a great deal to construction firms that lose money when unrepaired heavy equipment stands idle.

○ *Compatibility*   If the product will be used as part of a larger system, will it fit other components? For example, in recent years small computer manufacturers such as Amdahl have successfully entered the highly competitive computer market by making and selling IBM-compatible hardware.

○ *Appropriateness*   Is the product idea appropriate for organizational objectives and resources?

A positive aspect of these planning criteria is that they are general enough to apply to most products, simple or complex, tangible or intangible. Screening products in this way is an important part of managing the overall innovation process.

THE TWO FACES OF TECHNOLOGY   Almost everyone agrees that we live in an age of accelerating technological change, but vigorous disagreement has arisen over the value of technology itself. Is technology the key to a more productive, safer, and happier world, or is it drawing the blueprint for our untimely destruction? The two faces of technology can be seen everywhere today. Nuclear technology can either illuminate or incinerate a city, depending on how it is applied. Labor-saving devices are said to be major contributors to an unhealthy, sedentary lifestyle. Pesticides and insecticides that help put food on our tables can poison us as well. Managers have to consider both the constructive and destructive aspects of technology because they are the ones who make important decisions during the innovation process concerning what and how particular technologies will be applied. They need to know what is at stake in discharging this important responsibility.

The positive face of technology   For years technology has been viewed by many as the grease that allows the wheels of social and economic progress to turn.

Innovation creates jobs, boosts productivity, and contributes to exports and a strong, healthy balance of trade. Above all, innovation generates economic momentum and helps guarantee American preeminence in a world where power and progress are often measured in terms of technological achievement.[24]

Technology is seen as the key to solving society's more difficult problems as well. For example, according to a leading industrial scientist:

> If fully employed, science and technology could improve the value of our natural and human resources and lead to additional economically and socially advantageous products whose production would create more jobs. Further research could lead us to lower costs as a counter to inflation, substitutes for materials in short supply, and ways of acquiring what we need with less harm to the environment.[25]

These statements leave one feeling quite optimistic about what technology is doing and can do.

The negative face of technology   On the other hand, technology has come under fire in recent years for causing, rather than curing, society's problems. Detractors do not criticize innovations for not working; instead they blame them for doing *more* than intended. In the words of an English economist:

> Sometimes a single innovation, like the automobile, does a great deal more than its inventors ever claimed for it. Among other things, it creates clamor, dust, fumes, congestion, and visual distraction in all built-up areas: it helps to make all the great cities of the world more alike in the ensuing frenzy and frustrations. It enables Americans to kill each other off at the rate of some fifty thousand a year. And it has played a predominant part in transforming America from a nation of settled communities to a nation of transients.[26]

What the critics of technology are saying is that innovations tend to have unanticipated, long-run side effects, many of them undesirable.

Implications for managers   Futurist Alvin Toffler has coined a new term for critics of technology: *technophobes*. They are said to suffer from an unreasonable fear of technological change. Toffler believes that "reckless attempts to halt technology will produce results quite as destructive as reckless attempts to advance it."[27] Another writer has reinforced Toffler's position: "The heightened prominence of technology in our society faces us with the interrelated tasks of profiting from its opportunities and containing its dangers."[28] The question is, how is this balance to be achieved? The answer appears to lie in technology assessment.

Technology assessment is an attempt "to systematically study the widest sweep of impacts or consequences for society of the introduction, expansion, or modification of a technological development or project."[29] At the present time, relatively few organizations in the private sector are engaging in full-fledged technology assessment. However, as society continues to demand socially and environmentally harmonious goods and services, more business firms can be expected to make these assessments.

Any program of technology assessment necessarily has to be an ongoing affair because technology itself is an evolutionary process. The most challenging part of a technology assessment program is identifying long-term consequences. For example, imagine the difficulty, back when Henry Ford was tinkering with his horseless carriage, of anticipating the air pollution, energy waste, and suburban sprawl attributed to the automobile today. Some have suggested that managers hire science fiction writers and futurists as consultants when assessing technological impact. Imaginative lateral thinking certainly is needed to ask questions beyond the traditional "Will it sell?"

There are a number of places in existing management systems where a comprehensive program of technology assessment can enter the picture. First, and most important, assessment of long-term technological impact is needed when top management is formulating strategic plans. Beyond that, specific products and the processes used to produce them can be assessed when they are being considered during the intermediate planning stage. It is important to realize, however, that the success of a technology assessment program depends on the degree of open-systems thinking among all managers, not just a few. Perhaps the day will come when managers at all levels will give serious thought to the social and ecological impacts of specific problem and decision alternatives prior to suggesting them. That way we can have goods and services to fill our present needs *and* a relatively unspoiled world for our grandchildren's grandchildren.

SUMMARY

Managers need to do some detective work to sort out the various aspects of the environment in which they operate. Among those aspects are economic and technological factors. Managers are responsible for administering scarce resources, both living and nonliving. Their chances of success are greater if they understand the roles of energy and inflation in today's economy.

Our economy is highly dependent on nonliving energy resources, especially imported oil. Realizing that oil and other fossil fuels are exhaustible resources, we need to search for renewable energy sources that are socially and environmentally acceptable. Every alternative has its limitations, so managers and others need to use existing energy supplies conservatively. Energy audits and comprehensive energy management programs can help in this regard.

Persistent inflation has become institutionalized in recent years. Regardless of what is done about it, the practice of management will be affected. Mandatory wage and price controls are the government's ultimate weapon against stubborn inflation. However, peacetime controls do not have a good track record in the United States. If wage and price controls are implemented, as many top managers feel they will be, management will have to achieve additional efficiencies of operation, because it will be impossible to pass along cost increases to consumers. As the psychology of inflation turns negative due to the erosion of real income, new and creative ways of motivating employees will have to be developed. Persistent inflation may increase militant unionism, thus driving a wedge between management and labor. The theme for management in tomorrow's economic environment is to do more with less.

Technology has three dimensions. It is an extension of science, an evolutionary process, and more than just machines. Technology is applied through the innovation process. This innovation process consists of the translation of a new idea into a working prototype and ultimately into an economically marketable product or service. Innovation lag is the time it takes to complete the innovation process. Problem-solving managers can shorten innovation lag by creating a supportive climate for innovation. There is a need for product or service, production, organizational, and people innovations today.

A number of criteria should be considered when screening proposals for new products. They include functional need, competing products, price, ease of use, operating cost, reliability, service, compatibility, and appropriateness. Beyond these, experts are pointing to the need for comprehensive technology assessment. This means that managers should consider long-term social and environmental consequences before adopting specific product and production technologies. In this manner, the organization can benefit from the positive face of technology while neutralizing its negative face.

TERMS TO UNDERSTAND

Economics
Energy
Energy audit
Energy management program
Institutionalized inflation
Real income

Technology
Innovation process
Product technology
Production technology
Innovation lag
Technology assessment

QUESTIONS FOR DISCUSSION

1. Why should managers be concerned with the economic and technological environment?
2. What are the implications of our heavy reliance on oil to satisfy our energy needs?
3. In what ways can you improve the energy efficiency of your present lifestyle?
4. In your opinion, is there an energy crisis today? Defend your position.
5. How has inflation affected you in recent years? Do you feel anything can be done about inflation? Explain.
6. Do you think mandatory wage and price controls will work in the United States? Explain your position.
7. What is the difference between product technology and production technology?
8. How can the innovation process be more effectively managed?
9. Can you think of two people innovations that would be useful in managing tomorrow's employees? Explain how they would work.
10. Why is there a need for technology assessment today?

CASE 17.1 NO SAVINGS FROM THE SAVE PROGRAM?

The executive board of Central University Hospital has become increasingly concerned about the hospital's utility bills in recent years. Today the hospital pays three and a half times what it did just two years ago for natural gas and electricity. Public pressure to stem the rapid rise in hospital costs has created a troublesome cost-price squeeze. Three months ago when the board officially kicked off its energy conservation program, optimism ran high among the board members that cutbacks in energy use would provide significant relief from rising utility bills. They called the program SAVE, an acronym for "Stretch America's Valuable Energy," and hoped the catchy name would help the program stick in people's minds.

Since the SAVE program was intended to be primarily educational in nature, it featured the following:

○ Eye-catching stickers on any doors and windows that were typically left open. They read:

Keep me closed
and SAVE

○ Similar stickers above light and machine switches.

Turn me off when
not in use
and SAVE

○ A third variety of sticker above thermostats.

Thermostats to be adjusted
by custodians only—SAVE

○ Colorful posters, with novel phrases recommending energy conservation, strategically located throughout the hospital.
○ A list of energy-saving tips in each employee's pay envelope one
payday.

The first monthly utility bill after the SAVE program had gone
into effect encouraged the board. Although the 2 percent savings
over the previous month was not as large as expected, the board was
confident that greater savings would be forthcoming. Naturally,
they were dismayed to find virtually no change in the next month's
utility bill. The third month's bill, received last week, prompted the
director to call for a complete reappraisal of the SAVE program.
Although there hadn't been a utility rate increase during the month,
the hospital's utility bill went up by 8 percent. This jump could not
be attributed to severe weather or other extraordinary conditions.

FOR DISCUSSION

1. Why has the SAVE program apparently failed?
2. What recommendations would you make to the executive board
   for revamping the SAVE program? Why do you think your
   recommendations will get results?
3. In your view, what is the key to getting people to conserve
   energy? What are the societal implications of your particular
   approach?

**CASE 17.2
SO MUCH FOR
GOOD IDEAS!**

Hannah Simmons is a lab technician who designs testing devices for
computer hardware. A highly creative individual, she is constantly
reading the trade journals and attempting to use the new ideas in
them. Almost a year ago Hannah completed the design of a
revolutionary new all-aluminum testing device. She submitted the
drawings to the R&D review committee with great enthusiasm, but
nearly a year has passed without any word about the fate of her new
design.

Today Hannah asked the head of the review committee about the
delay. As far as Hannah can determine from the reply, the production manager feels that the device looks good on paper but a working
model cannot be built because of the incompatibility of the required
welds with the shop's present welding setup. As a result, Hannah's
design has been shelved indefinitely.

FOR DISCUSSION

1. How does this situation relate to the problem of innovation lag?
2. What recommendations would you make to the company for avoiding this type of situation in the future?
3. If you were Hannah, what would you do at this point?

REFERENCES

Opening quotation

Lester R. Brown, "Global Economic Ills: The Worst May Be Yet to Come," *The Futurist* 12 (June 1978): 168.

1. "The New Diversification Oil Game," *Business Week* #2531 (April 24, 1978): 79.
2. J. Edwin Becht and L. D. Belzung, *World Resource Management* (Englewood Cliffs, N.J.: Prentice-Hall, 1975), p. 69.
3. Demand and Conservation Panel of the Committee on Nuclear and Alternative Energy Systems, "U.S. Energy Demand: Some Low Energy Futures," *Science* 200 (April 14, 1978): 151–152.
4. Grover Heiman, "Energy: Searching for Substitutes," *Nation's Business* 66 (September 1978): 80.
5. Earl T. Hayes, "Energy Resources Available to the United States, 1985 to 2000," *Science* 203 (January 19, 1979): 239.
6. Norton Belknap, "Energy—The Long Term Prognosis," *Managerial Planning* 26 (January-February 1978): 38.
7. For useful information in this area, see: "An Energy Casebook for Management," *Administrative Management* 38 (August 1977): 24–27; and David Clutterbuck, "Energy Management Becomes a Burning Issue," *International Management* 32 (August 1977): 34–38.
8. Michael L. Millenson, "Industry's Own Search for Energy," *Across the Board* 15 (May 1978): 16.
9. For an interesting discussion, see: William R. White, "Energy Efficient Industrial Design," *Industrial Development* 146 (July-August 1977): 7–11.
10. Paul A. Samuelson, *Economics*, 10th ed. (New York: McGraw-Hill, 1976), p. 270.
11. For more on this, see: "The U.S. Structures Itself to Live with Inflation," *Business Week* #2570 (January 29, 1979): 78.
12. Walter Guzzardi, Jr., "What We Should Have Learned About Controls," *Fortune* 91 (March 1975): 103.
13. "Did Controls Flunk Their First Peacetime Test?" *Business Week* #2328 (April 27, 1974): 106.
14. "Chief Executives Fear Wage-Price Controls," *Nation's Business* 66 (April 1978): 36.

15. Daniel J. Boorstin, "Tomorrow: The Republic of Technology," *Time* 109 (January 17, 1977): 37.

16. Jerome B. Wiesner, "Technology and Innovation," in *Technological Innovation and Society*, eds. Dean Morse and Aaron W. Warner (New York: Columbia University Press, 1966), p. 11.

17. The Office of Charles & Ray Eames, *A Computer Perspective* (Cambridge, Mass.: Harvard University Press, 1973), p. 140.

18. See: Robert C. Dean, Jr., "The Temporal Mismatch—Innovation's Pace vs Management's Time Horizon," *Research Management* 17 (May 1974): 12–15.

19. "Texas Instruments Shows U.S. Business How to Survive in the 1980s," *Business Week* #2552 (September 18, 1978): 84.

20. This breakdown has been drawn from: Kenneth E. Knight, "A Descriptive Model of the Intra-firm Innovation Process," *The Journal of Business* 40 (October 1967): 478–496.

21. "Texas Instruments Shows U.S. Business How to Survive in the 1980s," p. 69.

22. Ibid., p. 89.

23. These criteria have been adapted from: Alan R. Fusfeld, "How to Put Technology into Corporate Planning," *Technology Review* 80 (May 1978): 53.

24. "The Breakdown of U.S. Innovation," *Business Week* #2419 (February 16, 1976): 56.

25. Simon Ramo, "Using Technology to Advance Human Progress," *Nation's Business* 64 (December 1976): 20.

26. E. J. Mishan, "What Monsters Technology Hath Wrought!" *Business and Society Review* #26 (Summer 1978): 6.

27. Alvin Toffler, *Future Shock* (New York: Bantam, 1970), p. 431.

28. Emmanuel G. Mesthene, *Technological Change* (New York: New American Library, 1970), p. 34.

29. "Technology Assessment Seeks Role in Business," *Chemical & Engineering News* 55 (March 28, 1977): 12.

Chapter 18

Social Responsibility and International Management

While most observers concur that businesses have social responsibilities, considerably fewer are in agreement as to the nature of these responsibilities.

Sandra L. Holmes

The only reasonable defense of the multinational corporation is now the truth. That it has power must be conceded. The only durable defense is to hold that such exercise of power is inevitable and, if subject to proper guidance and restraint, socially useful.

John Kenneth Galbraith

LEARNING OBJECTIVES

When you finish reading this chapter, you should be able to

o Define social responsibility.
o Explain how the enlightened self-interest model of social responsibility differs from the classical economic model and the managerial model.
o Define a social audit and discuss its role in a social responsibility program.
o Explain what a multinational is.
o Discuss the controversy surrounding multinational corporations.
o Put into perspective the political and cultural aspects of international management.

As the social, political, economic, and technological environment of management has changed, the practice of management itself has changed. This is especially true for managers in the private business sector. It is far less popular today than it was in the past for business managers to stand before the public and declare that their only job is to make a profit. In an era in which the public is wary of abuse of power and the betrayal of trust, business managers are expected to make social as well as economic contributions. The internationalization of business has simply magnified the pressure for broader managerial responsibility. Consequently, in this chapter we examine the social responsibilities of management as they are carried out both here and abroad.

SOCIAL RESPONSIBILITY

Social responsibility has meant many things to many people through the years. When John D. Rockefeller was at the zenith of his power as the founder of Standard Oil Company, for example, he handed out dimes to rows of eager children who lined the streets. Rockefeller did this on the advice of a public relationist who believed the dime campaign would counteract his widespread reputation as a monopolist who had ruthlessly eliminated his competitors in the oil industry. That the dime campaign was not a complete success, however, was indicated by the forced breaking up of Standard Oil under the Sherman Antitrust Act of 1890.

No doubt, Rockefeller believed he was fulfilling some sort of social responsibility by passing out dimes to hungry children. Since Rockefeller's time, however, the concept of social responsibility has grown and matured to the point where many of today's companies are intimately involved in social programs. These social programs include community development and urban renewal, ecology, and consumer satisfaction. Social responsibility now ranks as one of the basic management functions and presents management with many challenging problems.

The purpose of this section is to define social responsibility, to examine three contrasting models of business behavior, to look at some actual expressions of social responsibility, and to introduce and discuss the social audit.

WHAT DOES SOCIAL RESPONSIBILITY INVOLVE?

Social responsibility is a relatively new concern of the business community. For the most part, social responsibility is a product of the 1960s. The following account describes the historical backdrop for social responsibility of business organizations:

The Eisenhower era of the 1950's was, by and large, an era of good feeling between business and the American public.

But beginning in the 1960's, an adverse tide of public opinion began to rise against business. A more affluent, better-educated, more critical public began to question the value of ever-increasing production, the resulting pollution and environmental decay, and the defective products and services being produced; and they began to protest the public's seeming inability to influence the behavior of the business system. Frustration over the Vietnam War added fuel to the fires of discontent. Suddenly, consumerism, stockholderism, racial equalitarianism, antimilitarism, environmentalism, and feminism became forces to be reckoned with by corporate managements.[1]

Events during the 1970s, such as Watergate and corporate bribery scandals, only reinforced the public's demand for greater social responsibility in the business sector. The notion of social responsibility appears to be here to stay. Unfortunately, there is little agreement as to exactly what the responsibility consists of.

The first step toward pinpointing social responsibility is to define the term. Keith Davis, a leading expert in the field, has offered the following definition: *Social responsibility* "implies that business decision makers recognize some obligations to protect and improve the welfare of society as a whole along with their own interests."[2] According to this viewpoint, the corporate citizen, like any other citizen, derives rights from society in return for the responsibilities it carries out. In a democratic society rights and responsibilities necessarily go hand in hand.

Our general definition of social responsibility needs to be refined a bit. This can be accomplished by outlining what does and does not qualify as socially responsible behavior. A company is being socially responsible when it anticipates and actively strives to satisfy an emerging societal need. For example, in the late 1970s when research was still underway to determine if the fluorocarbon propellants in aerosol spray products were a threat to the delicate ozone layer in the earth's atmosphere, S. C. Johnson & Son voluntarily stopped using fluorocarbons in packaging its wax products. Eventually, fluorocarbon propellants were outlawed. But Johnson's action was socially responsible because it was anticipatory and was carried out voluntarily without coercion from the government.

In contrast, when laws must be passed or court orders issued before a company will respond to societal needs, the company is not being socially responsible. A prime example of this type of behavior was the American automobile industry's response to the growing desire for cars that were more energy efficient and less polluting.

Endless court battles and reluctant compliance with special legislation fall outside the realm of social responsibility.

THREE MODELS OF BUSINESS BEHAVIOR

Social responsibility encompasses two major variables. One is society's expectations and the other is business's behavior. In this section we examine three contrasting models of business behavior. They are the classical economic model, the managerial model, and enlightened self-interest model. Each approaches social responsibility differently. And although each is a product of historical evolution, all three models of business behavior have active supporters today.

The classical economic model   This model can be traced back to the eighteenth century, when businesses were owned largely by entrepreneurs or owner-managers. Competition was vigorous among small-scale operators. Short-run profits were the overriding concern of the early entrepreneurs. Of course, the key to attaining short-run profits was to provide society with needed goods and services. According to Adam Smith, the father of the classical economic model, an "invisible hand" promoted the public welfare. Smith believed that the efforts of competing entrepreneurs had a natural tendency to promote the public interest when each tried to maximize short-run profits. In other words, Smith believed that the public interest was served by individuals pursuing their own interests.

This classical economic model has survived to modern times. For example, the well-known economist Milton Friedman has no doubts about the role of business in society. According to Friedman, "Few trends could so thoroughly undermine the very foundations of our free society as the acceptance by corporate officials of a social responsibility other than to make as much money for their stockholders as possible."[3] Thus, according to the classical economic model, short-run profitability and social responsibility are one and the same thing.

The managerial model   This second model of business is a product of the mid-twentieth century. It recognizes the separation of owners and managers in the modern corporation. According to the managerial model, hired managers should be concerned with more than simply maximizing shareholder return on investment. They should strive to balance the claims of many groups including suppliers, customers, employees, owners, and the community. Within the managerial model there is room for actively promoting the public good. Proponents of the managerial model see business managers as profit *optimizers* rather than profit maximizers. Competing demands for the organization's resources effectively prevent profit maximization, according to the managerial model.

The enlightened self-interest model   The managerial model has been severely criticized in recent years for distracting business managers from their pursuit of profits. After all, it is pointed out, profits are the key to survival, and survival is the ultimate organizational objective. Consequently, the enlightened self-interest model has been proposed as a refinement of the managerial model. *Enlightened self-interest* is a refocusing of management's attention on profit maximization while still recognizing the need to address societal demands. According to this model, it is in management's self-interest to help improve the general environment in which it operates. As one authority has put it, "There is no conflict between profit maximization and corporate social activity," because, he adds "the contemporary corporation must become socially involved in order to maximize its profits."[4] In short, the enlightened self-interest model of business says it's the long-run that counts. This is in direct contrast to Adam Smith's short-run view of self-interest. Businesses that do not help solve society's problems today will be out of business in the long-run.

A matter of personal preference   Each of the foregoing models of business behavior is supported by a convincing rationale. It is up to the managers in each organization to decide which model best applies. If profit maximization is important, then a choice must be made between the classical economic model and the enlightened self-interest model. The former contends that short-run profit maximization is necessary for survival, whereas the latter stresses that survival is necessary for long-run profit maximization. For those who do not accept the concept of profit maximization, the managerial model suggests balanced concern for a number of competing demands. Except for those who adhere to the classical economic model, there is general agreement that business managers must become socially involved. We now turn to some of the major forms this social involvement can take.

SOCIAL RESPONSIBILITY IN ACTION   There are countless ways in which a business might become socially involved. However, businesses have been especially active in four major areas of social responsibility. Those four areas are philanthropy, urban renewal, ecology, and consumer satisfaction. In these areas it is evident that business managers can do much to improve the general quality of life. Consistent with our earlier distinction between active participation and mere compliance, we focus here on *voluntary* social commitments in these four areas.

Philanthropy   Efforts to promote human welfare by means of gifts to others are called philanthropy. Gifts may take the form of money, goods, or services. Corporate philanthropy typically brings to mind sizable cash contributions to schools, hospitals, and community fund drives. Highly publicized corporate contributions from time to time have fostered a general image of corporate generosity. But records of the last twenty years indicate that U.S. corporate giving has averaged less than 1 percent of pretax income. This is somewhat surprising considering that U.S. tax law clearly encourages corporate giving. Charitable contributions of up to 5 percent of pretax income are allowable tax deductions for corporations.

Research has uncovered another surprising fact about corporate giving. Contrary to popular opinion, there is no positive relationship between philanthropy and corporate size.[5] In short, the biggest do not give proportionately the most. A reasonable explanation is that smaller corporations tend to be one-plant operations. Consequently, their philanthropy has greater local impact, with direct benefits for both the community and the company. Philanthropy apparently is less appealing to corporate giants because the benefits, like their operations, tend to be widely dispersed.

In recent years, the imagination of the business community has been stirred by unique and trend-setting expressions of philanthropy. For example, in the mid-1970s J. M. Huber, Union Camp, and Weyerhaeuser showed the forestry industry a unique way of enhancing the public welfare. The three companies collectively donated 19,395 acres of forest land valued at $7,215,000 to public agencies, with instructions that the land be preserved in its natural state.[6] Generations of individuals will be able to enjoy large areas of unspoiled nature because of this exercise of corporate philanthropy.

Another exciting alternative to simply giving cash grants was inaugurated in 1972 by Xerox Corporation. That year Xerox continued to pay the salaries of twenty-one employees who were given from six months to one year's leave of absence to work on community development programs of their choice. (Applications were screened by an employee board.) Xerox's Social Service Leave program is still going strong. Participants have contributed to a wide variety of programs for the inner city, prisons, and the handicapped. Although much of the success of this program is due to the enthusiastic support of its participants, it has also been firmly supported by top management, which assures candidates that they can go on leave if their application is accepted. Moreover, top management guarantees that the same or at least an equivalent job will be waiting when the employee returns. Xerox feels that by lending its employees to worthwhile community programs, it is donating its most valuable asset, its people.[7]

Other major employers have been slow to follow Xerox's lead in this particular form of philanthropy. However, it is common practice in business and industry today to lend managerial talent for short-term service to the United Way and other charitable organizations.

Urban renewal   Urban renewal is an offshoot of the National Housing Act of 1949, which placed primary responsibility for urban renewal in the hands of the federal government. It was hoped at the time that urban renewal would halt the decay of America's major cities by upgrading housing, providing convenient mass transportation, and creating needed jobs. Despite the investment of billions of dollars over a thirty-year period, however, publicly funded urban renewal has been labeled a failure. One observer has noted why:

> Urban renewal had a negative effect on housing, especially for those with low incomes. More housing units were demolished than were constructed. Furthermore, most of the units were designed, and priced, for occupancy by middle and upper income groups. The poor, original residents were forced to move and compete for a reduced supply of low-cost housing. The net effect was frequently an increase in housing costs for the poor and the transfer of the slums from the renewal areas to other locations in the community.[8]

It is against this dismal backdrop that a number of companies have made their move toward greater social responsibility by contributing to urban renewal.

One outstanding example is the Brooklyn Union Gas Company. Rather than fleeing to the suburbs along with many of its customers, Brooklyn Union Gas decided to remain in the center city and strive to make it a good place to do business. Its approach was fairly simple. Old, dilapidated, and abandoned brownstone houses were purchased and fixed up. A few were reserved as models to interest others in this form of grass-roots urban renewal. But most of the refurbished houses were sold. Soon other businesses as well as individuals caught on and a wave of restoration hit surrounding decaying neighborhoods. Portions of Brooklyn that had been given up as a lost cause got a new lease on life. Over a ten-year period

Brooklyn Union Gas spent $400,000 on their urban renewal program.[9] Conceivably, if enough businesses in other parts of the country follow in the footsteps of Brooklyn Union Gas, private industry may succeed where publicly financed programs have failed.

Ecology   In its scientific meaning, *ecology* involves the study of all organism-environment interactions. But most of us simply think of the natural environment and pollution control when we hear the term *ecology*. In recent years ecology has received a great deal of attention in the popular press as ecologists point out our carelessness in interacting with the natural environment. Although the self-cleansing ability of our air, land, and water resources has permitted centuries of abuse, our free ride at the environment's expense appears to be at an end. Signs of environmental strain are found everywhere in the form of polluted lakes and streams, smog-filled skies, and vegetation-stripped land.

One response to environmental degradation has been the formation of the U.S. Environmental Protection Agency (EPA). This agency is charged with developing environmental standards and enforcing environmental protection laws. Predictably, the young agency has had its difficulties. A Harvard researcher points to the crux of the problem:

> The incredible array of environmental protection laws passed in the last few years has created its own by-product of confusion that seems every bit as murky as our skies or rivers ever were. My examination of the laws and their effects on several major industries—paper, oil, aluminum, lead, metal finishing and electroplating among them—suggests that even the most diligent managers don't understand the complex and pervasive ways in which environmental controls have affected vast segments of our economy.[10]

As always, managers must strive continuously to stay abreast of new legal constraints placed on their activities. But, as an EPA official has written, merely following the law is not enough. This official stressed the need for voluntary compliance and a spirit of affirmative cooperation between government and business: "The law alone will never make our air and water clean."[11] In other words, environmental protection is one of the social responsibilities of management.

A number of companies have done a great deal in the area of ecology and environmental protection. Unfortunately, these socially responsible programs do not get front-page treatment in the popular media. The public generally gets only the bad news concerning business and the natural environment. One notable exception is 3M Company's "Pollution Prevention Pays" (3P) program. This innovative ecological program prompted the EPA to give the company a special commendation. The overall goal of the 3P program is "to get personnel to stop thinking about pollution removal and instead stress product reformulation, equipment changes, process modification, and materials recovery."[12] Emphasis in 3M's program is clearly on prevention rather than cure. An appealing bonus plan for contributors in addition to top-management support has helped make the 3P program a success. The first nineteen projects in the 3P program saved 3M approximately $10 million. These preventive projects enabled 3M Company to cut its annual pollution by 73,000 tons of air pollutants, 500 million gallons of waste water, and 2,800 tons of sludge.[13] The cost of cleaning up such a mess once it had escaped into the environment would have been staggering. 3M's *problem-solving* approach to pollution prevention is encouraging evidence that, with a little imagination, business can be ecologically responsible and show a profit.

Consumer satisfaction   According to the so-called marketing concept, the primary purpose of everyone employed by a business is to satisfy customer needs. It is a well-known fact that the road to bankruptcy is lined with dissatisfied customers. There are three reasons for widespread consumer dissatisfaction today.

First, increased consumer mobility has disrupted postsale contact between buyers and sellers. Anyone engaged in personal selling knows that sellers must work to promote customer satisfaction after the sale. This is done by answering questions and handling complaints. This kind of follow-up has become difficult because people move around so much today. About one-fifth of the population moves every year. It is not uncommon, for example, for an individual to buy a car in New Jersey and have it repaired in Kansas while moving to California. Meaningful seller follow-up is impossible when the buyer is here today and gone tomorrow.

Second, increased use of self-service marketing techniques has impersonalized the buyer-seller relationship. Mom and Pop, who used to own the corner grocery store, could provide a personal touch not to be found in the supermarket now serving several neighborhoods. Frequent one-to-one contact between buyer and seller enhances customer satisfaction. Self-service has separated buyers and sellers.

Third, goods and services have increased in complexity in recent years. The automobile is probably the best example of this trend. With all its safety and pollution control equipment, the modern automobile is more likely to need expert service than its simpler predecessor.

Considering the collective impact of consumer mobility, self-service, and product complexity, it is easy to see why there is a vigorous consumer movement today. When things go wrong, consumers get angry; and when consumers get angry, they tend to organize and speak out against business. Business response to the consumer movement has followed two different routes. The first route is reluctant submission to organized public pressure and resulting consumer welfare legislation. Consumer advocate Ralph Nader has been a driving force in this area. The second route is social responsibility, whereby businesses take the initiative in promoting consumer satisfaction or voluntarily cooperate with consumer demands. A promising development in this area is the creation of consumer-affairs departments in a growing number of businesses. Polaroid is one example of this kind of concern for consumers.

> Polaroid Corp., in Cambridge, Mass., maintains a 300-person consumer services department to perform such chores as rewriting ads that might mislead buyers and dropping in on Polaroid camera repair centers to check on quality. And—because small stores sometimes duck customer complaints—the department makes sure that Polaroid's free service phone number is printed in big type on every product.[14]

Consumer satisfaction is being enhanced in other, more fundamental, ways as well. For example, concern for product safety is playing a greater role during the product design stage.

In the final analysis, social responsibility in the area of consumer satisfaction is good for business, because satisfied customers tend to come back.

KEEPING SCORE WITH THE SOCIAL AUDIT

Profit and loss statements and balance sheets are records of a company's financial status. It would be virtually impossible to determine the relative success or failure of a profit-making organization without the use of standard financial reports. To ensure that investors and the general public get an accurate picture of the company's financial status, the law requires periodic audits. An audit is a systematic review of financial reports to make sure that everything is in order. This general concept of the financial audit has inspired social responsibility experts to suggest the development and use of social audits.

Formally defined, a *social audit* is "a commitment to systematic assessment of and reporting on some meaningful, definable domain of a company's activities that have social impact."[15] In short, proponents of social audits feel that the time has come for accountability in the area of social responsibility. Investors and the public are demanding to know what is being done in the name of social responsibility.

Developing a social audit   Because the direct costs and benefits of social programs are not readily apparent, social audits are much more primitive than traditional financial reports. For example, imagine the difficulty of assessing the long-run economic benefits of an industrial pollution control program intended to reduce the risk of cancer in a large metropolitan area. Measuring this kind of payoff is much more difficult than assessing the direct economic benefits of a new drill press, for example, because cancer might not show up for twenty years. In view of this measurability problem, social auditors must begin in very general terms and move toward more specific terms. They can do this by following five basic steps:

1. List all programs with social impact. See Table 18.1 for a representative listing.
2. Explain the rationale behind each program. This portion of the social audit should answer the question, "Why is the organization involved in this area?"
3. State the objective(s) of each program.
4. Outline the progress of each program to date. The measurability problem can be avoided during this step by offering a descriptive account, in nonquantitative terms, of what has been accomplished.
5. As much as possible, quantify and match the direct costs and benefits of each program.[16]

The future of social audits   Some observers contend that social audits will become a relic of the early 1970s. Research indicates that significant new approaches to social auditing are not being developed and that existing approaches are not being widely adopted.[17] However, in spite of a lack of significant progress in social auditing, social responsibility appears to be alive and well. For example, a 1977 survey of the annual reports of the 500 largest companies in the United States uncovered social responsibility disclosures in 91.2 percent of them.[18] It appears that social auditing is still in the early stages of development. But a lack of significant new breakthroughs

TABLE 18.1
Social responsibility takes many forms

Environment	○ Pollution control.
	○ Restoration or protection of environment.
	○ Conservation of natural resources.
	○ Recycling efforts.
Energy	○ Conservation of energy in production and marketing operations.
	○ Efforts to increase energy efficiency of products.
	○ Other energy-saving programs (e.g., company-sponsored car pools).
Fair Business Practices	○ Employment and advancement of women and minorities.
	○ Employment and advancement of disadvantaged individuals (e.g., handicapped, Vietnam veterans, exoffenders, former drug addicts, mentally retarded, and hard-core unemployed).
	○ Support for minority-owned businesses.
Human Resources	○ Promotion of employee health and safety.
	○ Employee training and development.
	○ Remedial education programs for disadvantaged employees.
	○ Alcohol and drug counseling programs.
	○ Career counseling.
	○ Employee physical fitness and stress management programs.
Community Involvement	○ Donations of cash, products, services, or employee time.
	○ Sponsorship of public health projects.
	○ Support of education and the arts.
	○ Support of community recreation programs.
	○ Cooperation in community projects (e.g., recycling centers, disaster assistance, and urban renewal).
Products	○ Enhancement of product safety.
	○ Sponsorship of product safety education programs.
	○ Reduction of polluting potential of products.
	○ Improvement in nutritional value of products.
	○ Improvements in packaging and labeling.

Adapted with permission from: *Social Responsibility Disclosure: 1977 Survey of Fortune 500 Annual Reports*, Ernst & Ernst, 1300 Union Commerce Building, Cleveland, Ohio 44115, pp. 27–33.

in social auditing does not necessarily signal the death of the concept. Like many other radically new concepts, social auditing is developing sporadically. Vigorous activity in the overall area of social responsibility assures that social audits will continue their development and that they will be around for a long time. In the final analysis, the public's demand for greater accountability among managers will prevail.

INTERNATIONAL MANAGEMENT

Air travel and modern telecommunications are turning the world into a global community. As people and information move from place to place with amazing speed and frequency, the world seems to be growing smaller and its inhabitants more similar to each other. But while these technological factors have been widely publicized, a third globe-shrinking force has been quietly at work. In many respects, this third force has contributed the most to a smaller world in which similarities prevail. This third force is corporate multinationalism.

Because of the dramatic growth in multinational corporations since World War II, people, technology, capital, goods, and services are crossing international borders as never before. Like any other type of productive enterprise, the multinational corporation needs to be effectively and efficiently managed. Consequently, *international management*, the pursuit of organizational objectives in an international setting, has emerged as an important discipline in recent years.

The purpose of this section is to put international management into focus by defining the multinational corporation, examining the controversy surrounding it, and taking a look at the challenges of managing in an international realm. Our focus is on broad social responsibility rather than specific how-to techniques. The problem-solving management process discussed in earlier chapters is equally applicable in an international context.

WHAT IS A MULTINATIONAL?

The multinational label has been attached to a growing number of privately owned corporations over the last twenty years. These multinational corporations (MNCs) have many characteristics in common. They tend to be quite large in terms of the assets they directly or indirectly control; they tend to wield a great deal of social, political, and economic power on a worldwide scale; and they tend to be the subject of controversy and criticism. By way of formal definition, one authority has defined the *multinational enterprise* as

> A number of affiliated business establishments that function as productive enterprises in different countries simultaneously. To have such capacity the firm must possess host-country-based production units such as factories, mines, retail stores, insurance offices, banking houses, or whatever operating facility is characteristic to its business.[19]

Thus true multinationalism involves more than the movement of investment capital across international borders. It involves more than the export of goods from a producer country to a consumer country. In a mature MNC, capital, technology, goods and services, information, and managerial talent flow freely from one country to another as required to meet business conditions. Profit potential rather than national boundaries dictates the multinational manager's strategies. For example, the gasoline you buy the next time you fill up could very well come from the floor of the North Sea via an intricate global network of Dutch capital, Norwegian leasing, German engineering, British facilities and management, and American shipping and marketing. The rationale for such a multinational conglomeration is profit. This kind of multinational interdependence literally explodes with managerial opportunities and obstacles.

THE SCALE OF MULTINATIONALISM

To appreciate the growing importance of international management, it is necessary to grasp the huge scale of multinationalism. One indicator of multinational activity is the extent of U.S. direct investment abroad. As shown in Figure 18.1, U.S. direct investment in other countries increased more than two and one-half times

FIGURE 18.1
U.S. direct investment abroad, 1966–1976

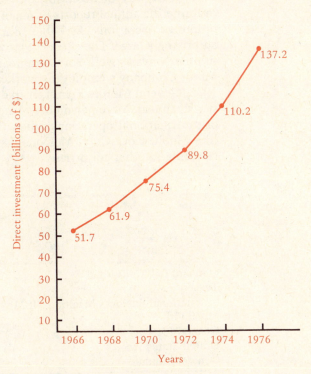

Data derived from Obie G. Whichard, "U.S. Direct Investment Abroad in 1976," *Survey of Current Business* 57 (August 1977): 42.

between 1966 and 1976. Although some critics see this dramatic rise as evidence of neocolonialism designed to exploit cheap foreign labor and strip less developed countries of their natural resources, others see it as a positive sign. For example, with regard to oil-producing nations, one observer has pointed out that:

> The host country profits from the public income generation by royalties and taxes, from the private income derived from wage payments and other expenses in the local economy, and, above all, by the acquisition of modern technology and management skills.[20]

Of course, the United States is not the only nation to make direct investments abroad. Scores of nations have direct investments in the United States. For example, Sanyo Electric Company, a Japanese firm, owns and operates a television manufacturing plant in Arkansas, and Volkswagen manufactures automobiles in Pennsylvania.

Another way of detecting the scale of multinationalism is to examine the annual reports of major U.S. corporations for evidence of foreign operations. As Table 18.2 indicates, the figures are often surprisingly large. The effects of growing multinationalism are seen in other ways as well. For example, in 1976 fewer than half of Ford Motor Company's employees worked in the United States. Also in 1976, General Motors manufactured over 27 percent of its cars and trucks abroad. More personally, Americans are struck by the extent of multinational operations when they encounter familiar names like Mobil, Coca-Cola, McDonald's, Burger King, and Ford when traveling in other countries.

TABLE 18.2
A look at selected multinationals

COMPANY	NET INCOME Percentage Attributed to Operations Outside U.S. in 1976
Standard Oil (California)	48%
Texaco	45%
International Business Machines (IBM)	44%
Mobil Oil	38%
General Electric	32%
United States Steel	18%
General Motors	18%

Source: Derived from consolidated financial statements found in the firms' respective annual reports.

THE CONTROVERSY SURROUNDING MULTINATIONALS

As mentioned earlier, MNCs are controversial. Proponents cheer multinationals as the first step toward a peaceful and prosperous global community in which national identification and boundaries will play a secondary role. Critics, however, attribute to MNCs such diverse problems as the growing gap between rich and poor nations, worldwide inflation, political corruption, uncontrolled urbanization, and military hardware overkill. Obviously, since thousands of firms qualify as multinationals, MNCs cannot all be tied up neatly in a single "good guy" or "bad guy" package. MNCs, taken as a group, have engaged in a wide variety of honorable and disgraceful practices. The purpose here is to identify and discuss three major questions concerning MNCs, so that the reader is able to draw some personal conclusions. The three questions deal with the exporting of jobs, national sovereignty, and bribery.

Do MNCs export jobs?   The AFL-CIO and other voices of the American labor movement are convinced that MNCs which transfer their production processes from a location inside the United States to a foreign subsidiary are, in effect, exporting jobs. Consider the huge proportion of electronic and photographic equipment, for example, that is produced overseas for U.S. companies. At one time most of the electronic and photographic equipment purchased by Americans was made by Americans. There is no question that production-level jobs have been exported when one finds, for example, a "made in Japan" label on the back of a Sears TV.

MNCs see things differently. They take a long-run view. In the long run, they say, more jobs are created than are lost, and employment statistics support their argument. For example, between 1966 and 1970 the number of American employees of a sample of 298 MNCs grew at an annual rate of 2.7 percent, compared with 1.8 percent for all U.S. firms.[21]

How can we reconcile these two seemingly valid positions, one for and one against MNCs? The key is short run versus long run. When Zenith reluctantly decided to follow its competitors by moving its television production facilities overseas to take advantage of cheaper labor rates, it was criticized for exporting jobs. In the short run, it did exactly that. But in the long run, industrywide, the firm created more jobs than it exported. Lower labor costs translate to competitive prices that stimulate sales and enable the company to grow. As it grows, it creates additional administrative and sales positions for U.S. employees. So, in the long run, the net employment picture works out favorably. Unfortunately, relatively well-paid but semiskilled workers get lost in the shuffle between the short and long run as the MNCs employ more educated specialists.

Both business and government are left with the costly and time-consuming task of retraining displaced individuals for employment in upgraded positions. But MNCs are forced into the role of scapegoat.

Do MNCs threaten national sovereignty?   National sovereignty means that a nation, within its own borders, is the supreme power and final authority. This principle is the key to our present world order. Wars have been fought and countless lives lost because the principle of national sovereignty has been challenged by aggressive nations. Today, MNCs are seen by some as a serious threat to national sovereignty because, in the pursuit of profit, a firm may disrupt a host nation's economy or politics. This becomes particularly easy, critics argue, when the economic power of multinationals exceeds that of smaller host countries.

The most damaging evidence presented by MNC critics is the infamous International Telephone and Telegraph (ITT) case. As revealed by ITT management during testimony before a Senate Foreign Relations subcommittee in early 1973, the giant multinational tampered with the internal affairs of Chile for its own purposes. In 1970 ITT, according to a *Business Week* commentary, "tried to enlist the Central Intelligence Agency and other government agencies in schemes to prevent the election of Marxist Salvador Allende as Chile's president, and to disrupt the country's economy. Their goal: To avert the expropriation of ITT's Chilean subsidiary."[22] Exactly how much damage ITT's action did to Chile will probably never be known. But the ITT case left one haunting question: Just how extensive is the MNC threat to national sovereignty?

When it comes to MNC behavior in host countries, is ITT's escapade the rule or the exception? According to a study carried out by The Conference Board* of U.S.–controlled MNCs operating in Canada and Italy, the ITT case seems to be an exception.

> In general, when it comes to such matters as industrial relations, information disclosure, and general adherence to the laws of the host country, American companies are described as exemplars. These companies are recognized as having introduced higher wages, advanced developments in industrial safety, a wide range of amenities in the work place, and as operating with scrupulous adherence to fiscal, financial, commercial and industrial laws.[23]

---

*An independent, nonprofit business research organization.

Although the study touched on only two host countries, the evidence is encouraging. Nevertheless, MNCs need to take special steps to ensure that they do not erode the national sovereignty of host countries, particularly in small, poor countries with relatively unstable governments.

What about those bribes and payoffs?   In 1974, when the Securities and Exchange Commission (SEC) was looking into illegal corporate contributions to Richard Nixon's 1972 reelection campaign, a curious discovery was made. Little by little, the SEC investigators learned that a number of well-known U.S. multinational corporations had relied on bribery and payoffs when doing business overseas. These initial revelations turned out to be only the tip of an iceberg of corruption. By 1978, in response to SEC promises of leniency for firms disclosing information voluntarily, over four hundred U.S. corporations had admitted to making $800 million in questionable payments abroad. Public reaction to these "confessions" has been indignant, to say the least. According to one observer: "To the increasingly vociferous critics of the multinational corporation, payoffs to foreign officials or political parties strengthens the demand for stringent regulations."[24] MNC supporters, on the other hand, have defended payoffs as a necessary aspect of

"To close on an upbeat note, I'm happy to report we received twenty-two per cent more in kickbacks than we paid out in bribes."

Drawing by Dana Fradon; © 1976 The New Yorker Magazine, Inc.

doing business in countries where such behavior is not only tolerated, but an unavoidable fact of life.

Payoffs and bribes are commonplace in many countries around the globe. Two kinds of payoffs and bribes have been defined, lubrication bribes and whitemail bribes.[25] *Lubrication bribes* involve relatively small amounts of money that grease the wheels of bureaucratic progress. A firm doing business in Italy, for example, may find that a *bustarella* (an envelope stuffed with lire notes) gets a particular license clerk to do his job. In contrast, *mordida* ("the bite") passed along to a Mexican building inspector may help ensure that he does *not* do his job. Although the name may vary from country to country, the purpose of lubrication bribes is always the same, to make sure that things move along smoothly. Lubrication bribery is so deeply entrenched in parts of Asia, Africa, the Middle East, and Latin America that even the critics of MNC behavior admit that it is very difficult to avoid.

Whitemail bribery is an entirely different matter. Rather than going to the little guy, as in the case of lubrication bribes, *whitemail bribes* are large sums of money used to buy influence in high places. Because large amounts of money are involved, whitemail bribery funds must be "laundered" by keeping them in secret accounts and passing them through unofficial channels. For example, in 1975 Lockheed, the aerospace giant, admitted that it had paid out at least $22 million to officials and politicians in a number of foreign countries during the previous five years.

> During the same period, it [Lockheed] had obligated itself to pay consultants—legitimately or illegitimately retained to expand foreign sales—a mindboggling $202 million. Moreover, Lockheed conceded, it had maintained a secret fund of some $750,000 from which it had paid $290,000 in commissions and "other payments."[26]

Because of the huge amounts of money involved, whitemail bribes have been criticized by the SEC because public investors are not informed about them, by the Internal Revenue Service because they are illegal tax deductions, and by others who claim they are immoral and unethical. Meanwhile, the supporting argument remains the same: payoffs and bribes are a necessary part of doing business overseas.

A study of sixty-five major U.S. corporations, forty of which admitted to making questionable payments abroad, has put the foreign bribery issue into clearer perspective.

Where questionable payments were effective, they often seem to have transferred orders from one American company to another. If both companies had followed the same ethical standards that govern competition in the home market, no payments would have been necessary.[27]

This finding neutralizes the argument that payments must be made in order to compete successfully overseas. The researcher came to the following conclusion:

Improper payments, it therefore appears, are literally a losing game. They may bring short-term benefits, but they involve enormous risks in the form of scandal and even prosecution. To protect itself and its managers, a corporation operating overseas should have a comprehensive, integrated system for preventing questionable payments.[28]

In short, a firm needs a clearly defined set of ethical standards for overseas conduct and a top management team that will make sure that employees at all levels comply with it.

MULTINATIONAL CHALLENGES   Multinational managers, like all other types of managers, need to be problem solvers when it comes to the basic functions of planning, control, organizing, and decision making. However, unlike the typical manager, multinational managers encounter significant new challenges when they leave the United States. The two greatest challenges involve political instability and cultural diversity. Each deserves a closer look.

Political instability   Citizens of established democracies such as the United States and Canada take political stability for granted. They do so because the transfer of power from one political party to another occurs in an orderly way without bloodshed or political upheaval. Unfortunately, for the majority of nations, political instability is a constant fact of life. MNCs doing business in politically unstable countries need to keep a cautious eye on the struggles for power. This can be a difficult task when several political parties are bidding for control of the government.

Political winds can shift quickly with dramatic impact in an unstable situation. For example, in 1966 the Christian Democratic government in Chile invited Dow Chemical Company to build a plastics plant in Concepción, Chile. Construction began, and Dow's partnership agreement with the Chilean government was hailed as a model throughout South America. Four years later, in 1970, just three months before production began at the new plant, the Socialist-Communist candidate, Salvador Allende, won an upset victory and became president despite ITT interference in the election process. In the new political climate, Dow fared poorly. The government asked for a majority share of the plastics plant in 1971, and in 1972, Allende's government seized the entire Dow operation outright and ordered its foreign managers to leave the country. The political tide turned once again in 1973 when a military coup toppled the Allende government. By 1974, Dow was back in Chile by invitation of the new government.[29]

The most amazing aspect of Dow's experience in Chile is that similar scenes have been repeated over and over again with other firms in other host countries. Technically, a takeover is referred to as *nationalization* or *expropriation*. The most sweeping expropriation of U.S. business property occurred in 1960, when Fidel Castro overthrew the Batista dictatorship in Cuba. To date, the United States has not received one penny of compensation for this $1.5 billion takeover of hundreds of private American business interests. According to one expert, expropriations have increased in both frequency and geographic dispersion since 1960.[30] It is easy to see how political turmoil can overshadow all other facets of management for multinational corporations.

Since MNCs cannot legally dictate what the political climate in a particular host country will be, the best thing is to learn to live with those in power. One author has highlighted the philosophy behind such peaceful coexistence.

> Most host governments accept the need for foreign investment. Many realize that they need the resources, technology, management skills, capital, and foreign exchange that foreign investment can bring. But governments increasingly want foreign investment on terms that maximize the contribution to national goals and minimize the threat to national sovereignty.[31]

In other words, *multinational reciprocity*, a mutual exchange of benefits between a foreign-owned organization and a host country, is replacing the lopsided colonial exploitation of the past. Host governments are beginning to screen investments by foreigners more carefully and are insisting on a greater degree of local participation in capital investment, employment, and profit distribution.

Cultural diversity   Culture is the unique system of perceptions, beliefs, and language symbols that influences the behavior of a certain population. It is difficult to distinguish the individual from his or her cultural context. In a manner of speaking, you are your culture and your culture is you. Consequently, people tend to be very protective of their cultural identity. Careless defiance of cultural traditions by outsiders often has the impact of personal insult. Multinational managers who want to profit from favorable relationships with people of differing cultures cannot afford to run roughshod over cultural diversity. They need to be sensitive to the fact that others see and do things differently—not better, not worse—just differently.

Cultural sensitivity, a sincere attempt to recognize and honor someone else's cultural values, can be learned. Recall our discussion in Chapter 3 of overcoming cultural barriers to creativity. Unfortunately, in the past, American business firms and the U.S. government have not adequately prepared managers and officials for exposure to foreign cultures. The "ugly American" image was the product of a sink-or-swim method of cultural familiarization. More recently, however, both private industry and the federal government have learned the social and economic value of formal cultural education for individuals (and their families) who are scheduled to work overseas.

Language skills top the list of assets for those who want to be culturally sensitive. Although estimates vary widely, there are some 3,000 different languages spoken around the globe, each with its own unique subtleties of meaning. For instance, a clock "runs" in English while it (literally translated) "walks" in Spanish. Consequently, English-speaking people appear to be in a hurry to Spanish-speaking people. Thus language affects behavior. Multinational managers can be much more confident that they are conveying the right meaning when they are familiar with the local language. Common language paves the way for trust and respect. MNCs have an obligation to prepare their managers with appropriate language skills before sending them abroad.

Formal language training also has a secondary benefit. It imparts the perceptual and behavioral aspects of a culture while introducing a new language. As indicated in Table 18.3, multinational managers may encounter huge differences in perception, behavior, and symbolism. Their effectiveness depends partly on their sensitivity to these cultural differences.

SUMMARY The areas of social responsibility and international management are presenting business managers with many significant new social challenges.

Social responsibility involves the voluntary anticipation and

TABLE 18.3
Cultural sensitivity: a comparison of organizational behavior between Japanese and U.S. personnel

CHARACTERISTIC	UNITED STATES	JAPAN
Personal Emphasis	Individualism (I, me) "Lone wolf" personality	Groupism (part of we) "Band wagon" personality
Interpersonal Relationships	Independence encouraged	Mutual dependence encouraged
Worker Participation	Less Competition Elitism	More Collaboration Egalitarianism
Competence	Ability (talent) Specialist preferred	Total personality Generalist preferred
Decision Making	Top-down Quick Individualistic	Bottom- or middle-up Slow Consensual
Conflict	To be confronted and surfaced Emphasis on conflict management	To be avoided or "melted" through nemawashi * Emphasis on agreement management
Communication	Verbal and written	Nonverbal and implied
Sense of Belonging (Loyalty)	Low	High
Nature of Change	Abrupt Complete Surgical	Evolutionary Renew or repair Massage not surgery
Basis of Employment and Promotion	On merit	Life-long employment Seniority

*There does not appear to be an English word that is equivalent to nemawashi. Literally, this Japanese term means "going around the roots." In other words, when transplanting a tree one must be careful to dig deeply so that the roots will not be severed or unduly damaged. Regarding organization behavior, the Japanese individual who wishes to sell an idea and/or make a change will work behind the scenes ("around the roots") to sound or feel out, test with, and gently persuade those he needs to convince for the idea to be adopted or the change to be made. He will not allow conflict to occur. He may have to compromise his plan somewhat, but he patiently and steadfastly sticks with his effort of convincing the other persons. Later when the idea or change is proposed officially, the consideration and adoption of the proposal is largely ceremonial.

Reprinted with permission from: Maurie K. Kobayashi and W. Warner Burke, "Organization Development in Japan," *Columbia Journal of World Business* 11 (Summer 1976): 113–123.

satisfaction of society's needs by business managers. A firm is not considered socially responsible when it passively waits for a law to be passed or reluctantly complies with a court order. There are three models of business behavior. Social responsibility plays a different role in each. In the classical economic model, the only social responsibility of business is to make as much profit as possible. According to the managerial model, business managers should be profit optimizers, rather than profit maximizers, in order to balance competing social demands. Finally, proponents of the enlightened self-interest model feel that social involvement is the key to profit maximization and, ultimately, survival. Contemporary social responsibility is being expressed in the areas of philanthropy, urban renewal, ecology, and consumer satisfaction. Social audits are recommended to keep track of the costs and benefits in social responsibility programs.

The discipline of international management has emerged in recent years because of the growing influence of multinational corporations (MNCs). Profit potential rather than international boundaries dictate where and how an MNC does business. MNCs are controversial today. Supporters point to growing peaceful prosperity stemming from the vigorous movement of people, capital, technology, and goods and services across international boundaries. Among a number of criticisms, MNCs have been accused of exporting jobs, threatening the national sovereignty of host countries, and operating in a corrupt atmosphere of bribery and payoffs. Evidence suggests that these accusations, while having some merit, do not characterize the typical MNC. Two major challenges facing managers working abroad are political instability and cultural diversity.

TERMS TO UNDERSTAND		
	Social responsibility	Multinational enterprise
	Enlightened self-interest	Lubrication bribe
	Ecology	Whitemail bribe
	Social audit	Multinational reciprocity
	International management	Cultural sensitivity

QUESTIONS FOR DISCUSSION

1. What does social responsibility involve? Can you describe a socially responsible business with which you are familiar?
2. How does the enlightened self-interest model compare and contrast with the classical economic model?
3. What was the nature of Xerox's unique approach to philanthropy?
4. What was special about 3M Company's "Pollution Prevention Pays" program?

5. What are social audits and why are they needed today?
6. In what way are multinationals different from domestic organizations? What are the managerial implications of this difference?
7. Why is a long-run view helpful in refuting the claim that U.S. MNCs export jobs?
8. Do you think multinationals are a threat to national sovereignty? Explain your position.
9. What is the case against foreign bribery and payoffs?
10. Why is cultural sensitivity important?

CASE 18.1
YOU'RE ALL WET!

John Whittaker reviewed the day's events in his mind as he watched the company jet taxi up to the airport ramp. As chief executive officer of the seventh largest chemical firm in the world, Consolidated Chemical Company, he shoulders enormous responsibilities. Increasing public pressure in recent years concerning minority hiring, pollution control, and overseas payoffs hasn't made his job any easier. In fact, it was public pressure that prompted him to develop his "outreach" program. The purpose of this program is to rebut, in public forums around the country, what he feels is unfair criticism of the company.

Today's forum was the first to be held on a major university campus. Everything had gone smoothly until half way through the question-and-answer session. At that point a student stood up and challenged Whittaker's remarks by saying:

I think you're all wet when you talk about how socially responsible your company is. You mentioned that you had hired 25 percent more minorities this year than last. But isn't it true that your firm is being forced to hire more minorities for fear the government will stop purchasing chemicals from you? I don't call that social responsibility, I call it following the law. I call it social *obligation!*

FOR DISCUSSION

1. Does the student have a valid point? Explain.
2. Putting yourself in Whittaker's place, how would you respond to this criticism?

CASE 18.2
THEY ALL DO IT

An overseas salesperson for a multinational firm was overheard recently making the following statement:

Bribery is a way of life in many countries. Everyone does it and everyone expects it. Americans who are quick to condemn payoffs don't really understand the facts of the situation. An underpaid foreign customs official who has a family to feed and bills to pay doesn't demand a small bribe because he's dishonest or immoral. He does it to survive. His superiors justify his low pay because they expect him to make a little money on the side. You know, like they do with waiters and waitresses in the United States who are expected to make most of their money through tips. It just isn't fair for Americans to force their beliefs and moral judgments on people from other countries.

FOR DISCUSSION

1. Do you think this position is justified? Explain.
2. If you were managing a U.S.-owned multinational firm, what do you think could be done to discourage overseas bribery?
3. Is there justification for the philosophy of "when in Rome, do as the Romans do"?

REFERENCES   *Opening quotations*

Sandra L. Holmes, "Executive Perceptions of Corporate Social Responsibility," *Business Horizons* 19 (June 1976): 34.
John Kenneth Galbraith, "The Defense of the Multinational Company," *Harvard Business Review* 56 (March-April 1978): 87–88.

1. Neil H. Jacoby, *Corporate Power and Social Responsibility* (New York: Macmillan, 1973), p. 6.
2. Keith Davis, "Social Responsibility Is Inevitable," *California Management Review* 19 (Fall 1976): 14.
3. Milton Friedman, *Capitalism and Freedom* (Chicago: University of Chicago Press, 1962), p. 133.
4. Jacoby, *Corporate Power and Social Responsibility*, pp. 196–197.
5. Drawn from: Gerald D. Keim, "Managerial Behavior and the Social Responsibility Debate: Goals Versus Constraints," *Academy of Management Journal* 21 (March 1978): 57–68.
6. See: "Giving Land to Save It," *Business Week* #2449 (September 13, 1976): 53–54.
7. For an interesting summary, see: "Social Service Leave: Five Years Old and Looking Good," *Xerox World* #24 (April 1976).
8. Bruce L. Jaffee, "What Happened to Urban Renewal?" *Business Horizons* 20 (February 1977): 87.
9. See: Vernon Louviere, "How a Business Fights Housing Blight," *Nation's Business* 65 (June 1977): 59.
10. Robert Leone, "Heavy Hands on the Pollution Controls," *The Wharton Magazine* 1 (Fall 1976): 26.
11. John R. Quarles, Jr., "Pollution Control—Not by Law Alone," *The Conference Board Record* 13 (April 1976): 51.

12. "3M Gains by Averting Pollution," *Business Week* #2459 (November 22, 1976): 72.
13. Ibid.
14. "Corporate Clout for Consumers," *Business Week* #2500 (September 12, 1977): 144.
15. Raymond A. Bauer and Dan H. Fenn, Jr., "What *Is* a Corporate Social Audit?" *Harvard Business Review* 51 (January-February 1973): 38.
16. These steps are based in part on recommendations found in the following sources: David F. Fetyko, "The Company Social Audit," *Management Accounting* 56 (April 1975): 31–34; and Raymond A. Bauer, L. Terry Cauthorn, and Ranne P. Warner, "Auditing the Management Process for Social Performance," *Business and Society Review* #15 (Fall 1975): 39–45.
17. For additional discussion, see: "Social Accounting: A Puff of Smoke?" *Management Review* 66 (November 1977): 4.
18. Drawn from: *Social Responsibility Disclosure: 1977 Survey of Fortune 500 Annual Reports*, Ernst & Ernst, 1300 Union Commerce Building, Cleveland, Ohio 44115.
19. E. J. Kolde, *The Multinational Company* (Lexington, Mass.: D.C. Heath, 1974), p. 5.
20. Neil H. Jacoby, "The Multinational Corporation," *The Center Magazine* III (May 1970) as reprinted in: A. Kapoor and Phillip D. Grub, eds., *The Multinational Enterprise in Transition* (Princeton, N.J.: The Darwin Press, 1972), p. 39.
21. See: Dominic Sorrentino, "Employment and Payroll Costs of U.S. Multinational Companies," *Monthly Labor Review* 97 (January 1974): 66–67.
22. "The Questions the ITT Case Raises," *Business Week* #2273 (March 31, 1973): 42. For an interesting follow-up report, see: Michael H. Crosby, "ITT's Chile Confession: A Definite 'Maybe,'" *Business and Society Review* #18 (Summer 1976): 66–67.
23. Joseph LaPalombara, "Myths of the Multinationals," *Across the Board* 13 (October 1976): 41.
24. Peter Nehemkis, "Business Payoffs Abroad: Rhetoric and Reality," *California Management Review* 18 (Winter 1975): 6.
25. Ibid., p. 7.
26. Morton Mintz and Jerry S. Cohen, *Power, Inc.* (New York: Bantam, 1976), p. 169.
27. Barry Richman, "Stopping Payments Under the Table," *Business Week* #2535 (May 22, 1978): 18.
28. Ibid.

29. Drawn from: Herbert E. Meyer, "Dow Picks up the Pieces in Chile," *Fortune* 89 (April 1974): 140–152.
30. See: James K. Weekly, "Expropriation of U.S. Multinational Investments," *MSU Business Topics* 25 (Winter 1977): 27–36.
31. Vern Terpstra, *The Cultural Environment of International Business* (Cincinnati, Ohio: South-Western, 1978), pp. 240–241.

Chapter 19

Metamanagement

The successful managers of the eighties will be those who can manage a slower rate of growth and react very quickly to changing opportunities.

William M. Agee

If you have built castles in the air, your work need not be lost; that is where they should be. Now put the foundations under them.

Henry David Thoreau

LEARNING OBJECTIVES

When you finish reading this chapter, you should be able to

o Identify and briefly describe four different perspectives of the world in general.
o Explain the meaning and significance of the term *metamanagement*.
o Discuss quality of life as a metamanagement challenge.
o Explain why scarcity deserves to rank as a metamanagement challenge.
o List and discuss the four laws of ecology.

According to John Gardner, a respected political observer, "We can't talk of America's future apart from that of the planet."[1] Thinking back to the spaceship earth perspective introduced in Chapter 1, it logically follows that management's future also is tied to that of the planet. Today's world is too small and too crowded to ignore the impact of our actions on the world around us.

Realizing that individuals view the world in vastly different ways (see Table 19.1), a metamanagement perspective is introduced in this final chapter. *Metamanagement* is an orientation that recognizes that managerial behavior is affected by and, in turn, affects an open system of global proportions. Because the prefix *meta-* means "to go beyond," metamanagement involves thinking in terms that go beyond the day-to-day practice of management. A broad perspective of this type is necessary, because days add up to years, which in turn add up to eras. The performance of today's managers will determine in large part whether our present era will be viewed positively or negatively by future generations.

Three specific metamanagement challenges deserve exploration. They are quality of life, scarcity, and ecology.

QUALITY OF LIFE Definition is the most difficult problem in discussing quality of life because personal preferences vary so widely. The quality of a motorcycle enthusiast's life is enhanced by speeding down a country road on a noisy bike. But pity the poor individual who moved to the country for peace and quiet. These two persons have very different definitions of a high-quality life. From a broader perspective, the "average" quality of life is a matter of social concern. Today, we are faced with the challenge of deciding what the average quality of life should be for future generations. Of course, deciding *what* the future quality of life should be is only half of the problem. We must also decide *how* changes in the average quality of life should be brought about.

Managers, particularly those in the private business sector, cannot avoid being involved in the quality-of-life issue. If society decides that material well-being is the standard for a high-quality life, then management needs to develop new product and production technologies for increased consumer demand. This could be difficult, however, as *Business Week* has pointed out:

A grim mood prevails today among industrial research managers. America's vaunted technological superiority of the 1950s and 1960s is vanishing, they fear, the victim of wrongheaded federal policy, neglect, uncertain business conditions, and shortsighted corporate management.[2]

TABLE 19.1
Varying perspectives of the future

A. CONVINCED NEO-MALTHUSIAN*	B. GUARDED PESSIMIST
Finite pie. Most global non-renewable resources can be estimated accurately enough (within a factor of 5) to demonstrate the reality of the running-out phenomenon. Whatever amounts of these resources are consumed will forever be denied to others. Current estimates show we will be running out of many critical resources in the next 50 years. The existing remainder of the pie must be shared more fairly among the nations of the world and between this generation and those to follow. Because the pie shrinks over time, any economic growth that makes the rich richer can only make the poor poorer.	*Uncertain pie.* The future supply and value of both old and new materials are necessarily uncertain. Past projections of the availability of materials usually have been gross underestimates. One can concede this could happen again, but current estimates seem relatively reliable. Current exponential growth clearly risks an early exhaustion of some critical materials. Prudence requires immediate conservation of remaining resources. Excessive conservation poses small risks while excessive consumption would be tragic.

*Thomas Malthus, a nineteenth-century English economist, predicted that the world's population eventually would outgrow the supply of food thus leading to widespread starvation.
Source: Table 1. A, B, C, and D of "Four Views of the Earth-Centered Perspective (page 10) in *The Next 200 Years*, by Herman Kahn et al. Copyright © 1976 by Hudson Institute. By permission of William Morrow & Company.

Pointing to this collision course between increased demand and diminishing innovative potential, along with persistent poverty, resource depletion, and pollution, proponents of "voluntary simplicity" claim that one's quality of life is not determined by material possessions. Two writers have defined *voluntary simplicity* in the following manner:

The essence of voluntary simplicity is living in a way that is outwardly simple and inwardly rich. This way of life embraces frugality of consumption, a strong sense of environmental urgency, a desire to return to living and working environments which are of a more human scale, and an intention to realize our higher human potential—both psychological and spiritual—in community with others.[3]

TABLE 19.1 (*cont.*)	C. GUARDED OPTIMIST	D. TECHNOLOGY-AND-GROWTH ENTHUSIAST

Growing Pie. Past technological and economic progress suggests that increasing current production is likely to increase further the potential for greater production and that progress in one region encourages similar developments everywhere. Thus as the rich get richer, the poor also benefit. Higher consumption in the developed world tends to benefit all countries. Excessive caution tends to maintain excessive poverty. Some caution is necessary in selected areas, but both the "least risk" and the "best bet" paths require continued and rapid technological and economic development.

Unlimited pie. The important resources are capital, technology and educated people. The greater these resources, the greater the potential for even more. There is no persuasive evidence that any meaningful limits to growth are in sight—or are desirable —except for population growth in some LDC's.† If any very long-term limits set by a "finite earth" really exist, they can be offset by the vast extraterrestrial resources and areas that will become available soon. Man has always risen to the occasion and will do so in the future despite dire predictions from the perennial doomsayers who have always been scandalously wrong.

†LDC stands for less-developed country.

If a significant number of people choose to fashion their lifestyles around some sort of voluntary simplicity, the consequences could be enormous for management. The impact could be felt in production as well as consumption. People who would rather "make" than "buy" would require tools and techniques rather than finished products. Those who prefer to work for themselves will not be eager to work for large, impersonal organizations. And those who believe work can be a pleasurable pastime will be unwilling to put up with dull, monotonous, and routine jobs.

To be adequately prepared, the problem-solving manager needs to interpret shifts in society's quality-of-life orientation very carefully. One thing is certain, shifts *will* occur. Even traditionally conservative voices predict significant shifts in the average lifestyle. According to *U.S. News & World Report*, people in the future will be

CONVERSATION WITH . . .

Joseph A. Castillo
President
Astro Blueprint Company, Inc.
Tucson, Arizona

Photo courtesy of Mr. J. Castillo.

PERSONAL BACKGROUND

Joe Castillo has come a long way since his family moved to Tucson from his native Los Angeles in 1942. In 1950, while still a junior in high school, Joe started in the blueprint business as a part-time delivery boy. Within four years he occupied a managerial position. In 1958, at the age of twenty-six, Joe opened his own blueprint business with only $600. During the growth years, he became actively involved in local and state politics. Among the political offices he has held are city councilman, state senator, and county supervisor. Today, Astro Blueprint, with branch offices in Tucson and Phoenix, records gross sales of a half million dollars annually. As a sixth-generation Mexican-American who is fluent in Spanish as well as English, Joe Castillo is an active supporter of minority business ownership.

QUOTABLE QUOTES

How did you go about solving a particularly difficult managerial problem in the last year?

Mr. Castillo: Problem: should we open an office in Phoenix? (a) We made inquiries of potential customers to see if they would give us the opportunity to bid for their business. (b) We surveyed the number of potential customers within a five-mile radius such as architects, contractors, engineers, and so on. (c) We located our competitors on a map and looked for a business location for our office. (d) We checked economic forecasts from a local bank and Chamber of Commerce statistics. The situation looked right, so we opened our Phoenix branch.

Do you have any personal feelings about the practice of management today?

Mr. Castillo: Many managers feel that because they have a degree in management they will automatically be advanced. Not so—promotions and raises are based on results. Results come about through hard work, perseverance, good internal politics, and being consistent. Management is a greater challenge today and every year requires even greater skills.

"more dependent on their inner resources than on credit cards and status symbols."[4]

SCARCITY   As we discussed in Chapter 4, managers need to plan because of an uncertain environment and scarce resources. It is this second dimension of the future that concerns many today. Pessimistic critics are not only concerned about ultimately running out of all our valuable nonrenewable resources, but they are also disturbed by the uneven distribution of those resources. The United States, for example, with one-sixteenth of the world's population, is consuming approximately one-third of the world's nonrenewable resources.[5] Although experts and nonexperts alike may quibble over exactly how long it will take to exhaust our various nonrenewable resources, the fact remains that we are faced with a rapidly growing population and a finite planet. On Connecticut Avenue in Washington, D.C., a ten-digit "population clock" keeps track of the world's growing population like an automobile odometer. The total presently is increasing at a rate of 172 people a minute, 10,300 an hour, 250,000 a day, 1.7 million per week, 7.5 million per month, and 90 million per year.[6] Despite this tremendous growth in population, our resources are limited.

Rather than getting caught up in the self-defeating argument of exactly which nonrenewable resources (such as oil, gas, coal, uranium, and metal ores) will run out precisely when, we focus here on the ways that managers can make the most of what remains. If we are to maximize our benefits from the remaining nonrenewable resources on this planet, there must be:

o *Increased capitalization for exploration and production*   Massive amounts of capital will be required to exploit remote sources (such as off-shore drilling) and marginally productive resources (such as oil shale) in an environmentally responsible manner.

○ *Increased emphasis on conservation through more efficient technologies* For example, in colder climates, the waste heat from electric generating stations can be used to maintain adjacent greenhouses.

○ *Increased emphasis on recycling* It is estimated that it takes less than 10 percent as much energy to recycle aluminum as it does to mine and produce it in the first place. Solid waste deserves to be viewed as a valuable resource, not trash to be discarded.

○ *Increased use of alternative sources of energy and materials* Solar, geothermal, and hydrogen energy can supplement and eventually replace fossil and nuclear energy. Laser beams channeled through glass strands may eventually replace cumbersome and costly telecommunication cables.

It is significant to note that these suggestions involve not only specific techniques but a way of thinking as well. Efficiency needs to be foremost in the minds of both today's and tomorrow's managers. Waste should be hunted down relentlessly. As mentioned in Chapter 17, future managers will be called upon to do more with less.

ECOLOGY   Only recently have we begun to fully appreciate the staggering complexity of ecological networks. Many of our ecological lessons have been learned the hard way. This is evidenced by unsightly and unhealthy air, land, and water pollution and prematurely extinct plant and animal species. Ecological behavior requires sophisticated problem solving.

A useful departure point for a problem-solving approach to ecology is the following set of "laws of ecology" formulated by Barry Commoner, a leading ecologist:

1. *Everything is connected to everything else* The global ecosphere is an integrated system with countless interdependent subsystems. Adjustments or changes in one subsystem send ripples of change, often with unpredictable consequences, throughout the ecosphere. For example, the insecticide DDT, once liberally sprayed on elm trees to kill the beetle that spreads Dutch elm disease, accidentally disrupted an entire food chain. With the coming of autumn, DDT-coated elm leaves fell to the ground and rotted into the soil. Earthworms that ate remnants of the sprayed leaves became contaminated. Finally, the following spring, unsuspecting robins ate the contaminated worms and died of DDT poisoning.[7] Although birds may not seem as

important as humans, the fate of lower animals foreshadows the fate of humans.

2. *Everything must go somewhere* In an integrated system nothing is thrown away. For example, solid waste buried in a landfill may be temporarily out of sight and unavailable, but it is still with us. Similarly, the plastic drink container thrown carelessly by the roadside could lie there for a thousand years without significantly changing form. The challenge is to keep our valuable natural resources in convenient forms suitable for recycling.

3. *Nature knows best* This is the law most people trust the least, because nature either moves too slowly (as in growing food crops to maturity) or with devastating and fickle speed (tornadoes and flash floods). Unanticipated long-run ecological consequences have come back to haunt many projects originally heralded as significant improvements on nature. For example, recent biological evidence suggests that the highly successful "Smoky Bear" forest-fire-prevention campaign has stimulated an overabundance of some forest-dwelling animals normally held in check by forest fires. When dealing with natural cycles, ecologists suggest that it is better to do nothing and leave things to the ultimate wisdom of nature than to press ahead with some ill-conceived cure-all. In the natural environment, no management is better than bad management.

4. *There is no such thing as a free lunch* This law should have a familiar ring to those who have taken a course in economics. It simply means that all material goods, even those produced in abundance by nature, ultimately have a price that someone must pay. Air and water, long viewed as free goods, now have a price tag attached in the form of pollution prevention and clean up devices. In effect, the present generation is picking up the tab for free lunches enjoyed by countless generations. What kind of unpaid ecological tab will the present generation pass along to its offspring? It will certainly include millions of acres of strip-mined land, thousands of tons of deadly nuclear waste, and badly depleted water tables.[8]

At first glance, these laws of ecology appear too general to be useful. However, anything less than very general statements would fail to do justice to the immense scope and complexity of our ecosystem. Once again, at this point we are not dealing as much with specific techniques as we are with *a way of thinking*. In the future, ecological thinking will involve doing a lot of homework during the problem-solving process in order to anticipate the ecological consequences of various courses of action. It is naive to expect humans to have absolutely no negative impact on the natural environment, but it is reasonable to expect them to do more good than harm to the only planet we have.

A FINAL WORD   The three metamanagement challenges just discussed are not mutually exclusive. They overlap to a great extent. Success or failure in one area inevitably will spread to the other two areas. Therefore, managers should always keep in mind that the quality of their problem solving today will determine the quality of life on spaceship earth in the years to come. The challenge is immense.

TERMS TO UNDERSTAND   Metamanagement   Voluntary simplicity

QUESTIONS FOR DISCUSSION
1. Why is it important for managers to look beyond the day-to-day practice of management?
2. How has a metamanagement perspective affected your thinking about the practice of management?
3. Why is it important for middle- and lower- as well as top-level managers to adopt a metamanagement perspective?
4. After carefully reviewing the alternative world models in Table 19.1, which one do you believe most closely parallels your own view? What will the future hold if most managers adopt your particular view?
5. How would you sum up the quality of your life at present? Would better management of our public and private organizations improve the quality of your life? Explain.
6. What evidence of voluntary simplicity do you see today?
7. How will less emphasis on material wealth affect the role of work in one's life? What will this mean for management?
8. Why do managers have a particularly large stake in the wise use of our nonrenewable resources?
9. What do you think about Commoner's four laws of ecology?
10. Can you think of any other areas besides quality of life, scarcity, and ecology that should be considered metamanagement challenges? What about civil rights, poverty, hunger, and morality?

REFERENCES   *Opening quotations*

William M. Agee, "Futurism: A Lesson from the Private Sector," *Business Horizons* 21 (June 1978): 16.
Henry David Thoreau, *Walden* (New York: Holt, Rinehart and Winston, 1965), p. 270.

1. John Gardner, "What America Must Do in the Next 10 Years," *The Christian Science Monitor* (May 7, 1976): 35; reprinted in *Current* #186 (October 1976): 34.
2. "Vanishing Innovation," *Business Week* #2541 (July 3, 1978): 46.
3. Duane S. Elgin and Arnold Mitchell, "Voluntary Simplicity: Life-style of the Future? *The Futurist* 11 (August 1977): 200–201.
4. "America's Third Century: A Look Ahead," *U.S. News & World Report* 81 (July 5, 1976): special supplement.
5. Herman Kahn, William Brown, and Leon Martel, *The Next 200 Years* (New York: William Morrow, 1976), p. 19.
6. See: TRB, "Tick, Tick, Tick," *The New Republic* 177 (December 3, 1977): 3, 38.
7. See: Rachel Carson, *Silent Spring* (New York: Fawcett, 1962), pp. 98–102.
8. Adapted from: Barry Commoner, *The Closing Circle* (New York: Bantam, 1971), chap. 2.

Name Index

Subject Index

MANABEMENT
A Problem-Solving Process

KREITNER

You can help me respond to the interests and needs of future readers of *Management: A Problem-Solving Process* by completing the following questionnaire and returning it to:

College Marketing
Houghton Mifflin Company
One Beacon Street
Boston, MA 02107

1. Name of institution _____

2. Number of students in your class _____   3. Your age _____

4. Your probable major _____

What was your overall impression of the text?

	Excellent	Very Good	Good	Fair	Poor
5. Writing style	☐	☐	☐	☐	☐
6. Usefulness of information	☐	☐	☐	☐	☐
7. Definitions of new terms and concepts	☐	☐	☐	☐	☐
8. Illustrations	☐	☐	☐	☐	☐
9. Relation of illustrations to text discussion	☐	☐	☐	☐	☐
10. Effectiveness of the following learning aids:					
a. Learning objectives	☐	☐	☐	☐	☐
b. Manager profiles ("Conversation with . . .")	☐	☐	☐	☐	☐
c. Chapter summaries	☐	☐	☐	☐	☐
d. Terms to understand	☐	☐	☐	☐	☐
e. Questions for discussion	☐	☐	☐	☐	☐
f. Cases	☐	☐	☐	☐	☐
11. Usefulness of examples in clarifying the text discussion	☐	☐	☐	☐	☐

Please cite specific examples to illustrate the above ratings. _____

_____

_____

_____

_____

_____

12. Which chapters were not required reading for your class? _____

13. Were there any features of the text you particularly liked or disliked? Which ones, and why? _____

_____

_____

_____

_____

_____

14. Were there any topics not covered that you believe should have been covered? _____

_____

_____

_____

_____

15. Did you use *Understanding Management*, the study guide accompanying the text?
    ☐ Yes   ☐ No

16. Did you instructor require its use?   ☐ Yes   ☐ No
    Did your instructor recommend its use?   ☐ Yes   ☐ No

17. Was the study guide an effective aid in using the textbook?   ☐ Yes   ☐ No

Do you have any other suggestions that might help make this a better textbook? _____

_____

_____

_____

_____

_____